Saturday Morning

"*Saturday Morning TV* is a must for everyone who grew up with television. Both Howdy and I are delighted that we are a part of this most fascinating account."

—BUFFALO BOB SMITH,
creator and star of *Howdy Doody*

"At last here's a behind-the-scenes look at thirty years of Saturday morning TV with appearances from all my old friends and probably yours. The revealing recollections of the people responsible for the programs bring back many fond memories for me, and I'm sure they'll do the same for you."

—DON HERBERT, TV's Mr. Wizard

"Required reading for all the Kuklapolitan Players! Gary's account is accurate and affectionate."

—BURR TILLSTROM, creator and
guiding force behind *Kukla, Fran and Ollie*

"It was the good luck of the *Superman* TV show to attract as entertaining . . . a writer as Gary Grossman as its chronicler. Now all Saturday morning TV has the same luck. What a good book this is!"

—JACK LARSON, producer, writer, actor, and TV's
Jimmy Olsen, cub reporter for *The Daily Planet*

"*Saturday Morning TV* is the most stimulating and exhaustive work. . . . Coupled with the fact that it reads like a novel, *Saturday Morning TV* is also a personal review of many of the so-well-remembered top Superheroes. Gary not only did his homework, he grew up with these characters. He knows us. Top this if you can! This is Captain Midnight signing off with the code of the Secret Squadron: Justice, through strength and courage. Out!"

—RICHARD WEBB, author, lecturer, actor,
and TV's Captain Midnight

"Reading *Saturday Morning TV* is like eating popcorn—you just can't stop. It provided me with a tantalizing time-trip back to my TV-dominated childhood, and I'm sure thousands of other readers will be as mesmerized as I was."

—LEONARD MALTIN, author of
Of Mice and Magic: A History of Animation

Contents

To my loving and concerned parents,
Evelyn and Stanley Grossman—

Thank goodness I never listened to them
when they told me to turn off the TV set!

Acknowledgments

To my colleague Tim Rupp, for his thoroughly professional and tireless effort researching data. confirming facts, and providing constant support.

To Bob Rubin, for working long hours under hot lights to expertly rephotograph, retouch, and restore many of the valuable photographs contained on the following pages.

To Helene Seifer, who doesn't remember many of the early shows mentioned in this book but shares my belief that children's TV could be far better, and is working in the medium to make it so.

And to the staff of the Boston Public Library Microtext Department, The *Boston Herald American* research library and its director, John Cronin, the Action for Children's Television Library, Burt Dubrow, Leonard and Alice Maltin, Ken Meyer, Sam Donato, Alex McNeil, Don Phelps, Jim Thompson, Nat Segaloff, Mildred Blowen, Eric Hoffman, and Jane and David Otte.

Also, WGBH-TV, Boston; *Popular Science* magazine; *Popular Mechanics* magazine; *Variety;* ABC; CBS; NBC; PBS, The Children's Television Workshop; and my editors and mentors at Delta Books, Christopher Kuppig and Gareth Esersky.

And Lew Anderson, Paul Ashley, Barbara Anderson, Joseph Barbera, Jack Barry, James Brown, Buster Crabbe, Walter Cronkite, Jerry Fairbanks, Sandford Fisher, Sonny Fox, Christopher Glenn, Kirby Grant, Peter Graves, Alan Hale, Jr., Jon Hall, Bill Hanna, Joel Heller, Don Herbert, Dick Jones, Bob Keeshan, Ed Kemmer, Claude Kirchner, Jack Larson, Pinky Lee, Shari Lewis, Jack Lord, Guy Madison, Jock Mahoney, Brad Marks, Lee Mendleson, Clayton Moore, Ed McMahon, Jimmy Nelson, David DePatie, Norm Prescott, Gene Rayburn, Cliff Robertson, Arthur Rush, Soupy Sales, Bob Smith, Bill Scott, Martin Stone, Burr Tillstrom, Frank Thomas, Rex Trailer, Richard Webb, and Paul Winchell.

Introduction

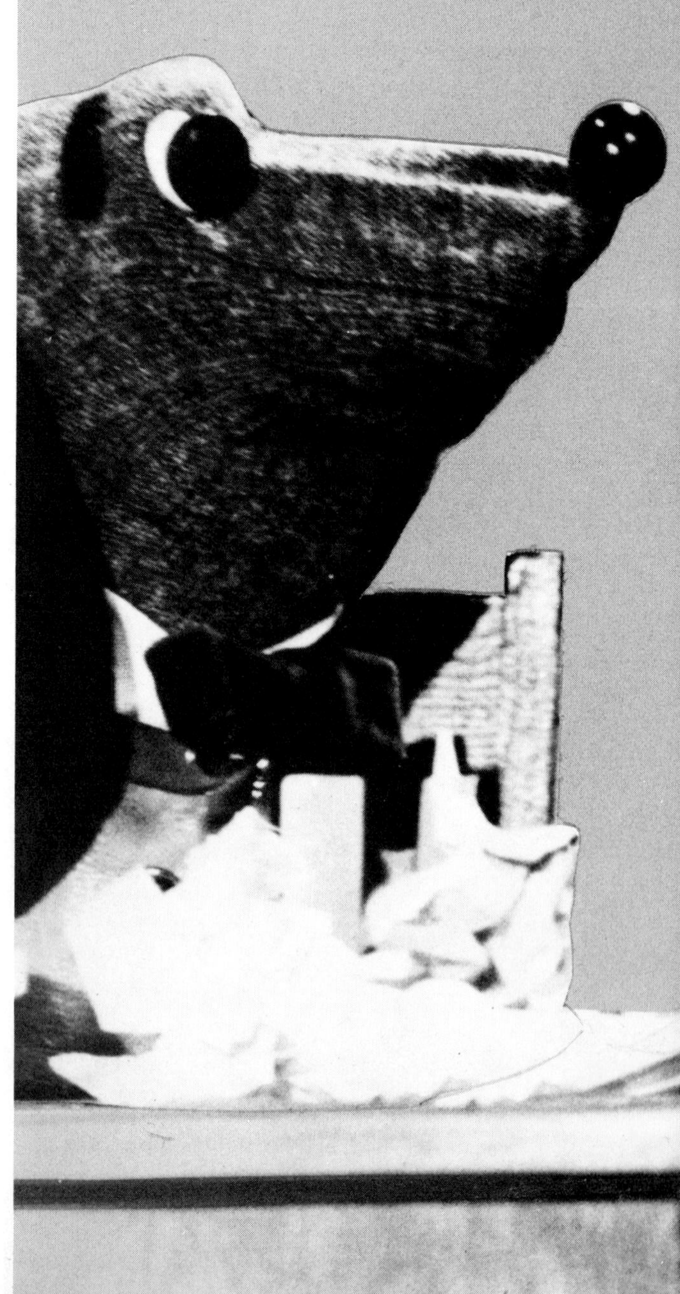

Much of Saturday morning television is "ghastly," says Shari Lewis. Presumably Hush Puppy agrees.

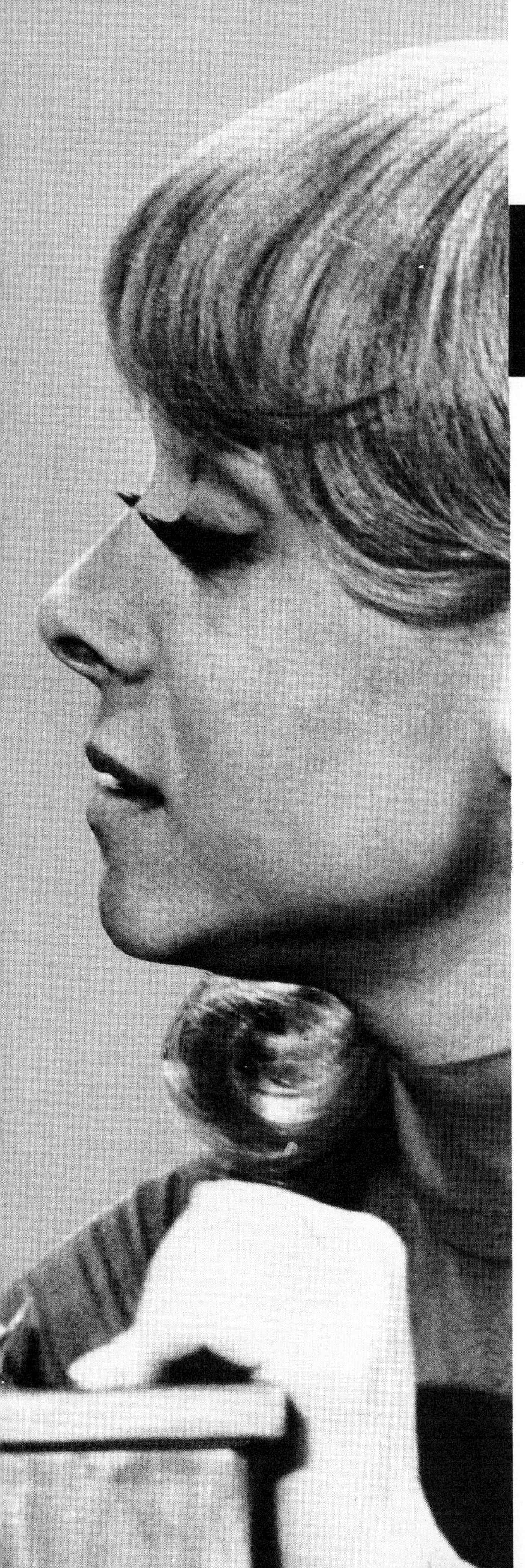

In this age of Count Chocula and Frankenberry cereals, when children eat the creatures for breakfast instead of the other way around, Saturday morning television is a monstrous mess.

Today, many of the people who design the deplorable network schedule consider themselves bold and innovative. Yet these children's TV executives who play with Saturday morning blocks of time usually offer pap when the kids deserve more nourishing programs.

Their lineups make money, but in a juvenile, follow-the-leader fashion each network has paved over the major creative inroads of early television and surrendered the dramatic licenses to supermen, spider women, talking magpies, jabbering dogs, and singing mice.

In their favor the networks do present news, sports, and health inserts—though often disguised as hectic cartoons to minimize viewer turnoff. And they have aired laudable dramatic and informational programs—but usually in the lower-viewed, early-afternoon time slots. However, the damage has already been done. Live characters, resident teachers, puppets and their puppeteers, and adult hosts are out of work. Network officials explain these outdated programming forms can't beat the cartoons that are televised Saturdays between 8:00 A.M. and noon. Apparently no network is deliberately willing to telecast shows that will receive top honors but last-place ratings. And no two groups of people are more upset about it than today's disgruntled producers and yesterday's Saturday morning stars.

"Saturday morning is a national tragedy," states Lee Mendelson, producer of the prime time *Peanuts* specials and a 1970 critically acclaimed show called *Hot Dog*. "I'm the last one for censorship, but if the damned networks don't do anything about it somebody should."

"Ideally, I would like commercial programming more controlled with the government making certain standards mandatory," says Shari Lewis. "I normally don't believe in government control, but our children deserve protection that they're not getting from the networks."

Lewis grew up in and with TV in the 1950s and now argues, "The quality of children's television is quite ghastly. The networks are totally irresponsible where children's programs are concerned. The only exception seems to be in the area of daytime dramas. But the networks produce very few of these each year."

"About the only thing kids have now are cartoons," complains actor James Brown, Lieutenant Rip Masters on *The Adventures of Rin Tin Tin*. "I can't see anything I'd really suggest for kids."

"I think children's TV is dreadful," believes *Winky Dink and You* host, Jack Barry. "As it is now, children's TV is absolutely commercial and if I had my way, it's nothing I would have a child of mine see. But they don't care. They watch it anyway."

"I cannot watch the shows," Soupy Sales says. "They're all cartoons, and to my mind, cartoons are not television because the figures can't really be humorous like live show characters. The kids have really become accustomed to animation, but they need live people."

"Kids can't identify with cartoon characters. Who wants to be a mouse?" asks Kirby Grant. The star of *Sky King* is angry that his show and the work of colleagues have no place on TV anymore. "I guess we're like the dinosaurs. Maybe we've lived too long."

The man who played Tom Corbett, Space Cadet, views Saturday morning with the same frustration. "Today, I don't think there's any character who could inspire youngsters."

Frank Thomas emphasizes his argument. "We've demolished our inspirational heroes. Nobody's perfect, we know, but it's nice to look up to somebody even if it's a Saturday morning creation of fact or fiction that embodies what we would like to be. I still get a good feeling when I hear that somebody went into space and aeronautics careers just because of Tom Corbett."

"There just aren't any role models for kids today," adds *Fury* star, Peter Graves. "I think it's a shame. I don't watch an awful lot of Saturday morning television, but what I've seen

"I don't see anything [on Saturday morning] I'd suggest for kids," offers Rin Tin Tin *star James Brown. (note from 1976 repackaging of 1950s series)*

comes right off the drawing boards and I don't like it."

"They've lost the actors and given Saturday morning to the special effects and animation departments. No one will remember characters today as we were in the 1950s," reinforces Richard Webb, TV's Captain Midnight.

"All the pioneers are out of work," Frank Thomas says. "Now the networks are just running around doing carbon copies. It's become a very frightened medium. They're so busy trying to do *Sagebrush Jones, Frontier M.D.*, and touch all the bases."

"It's a junkyard," *Bullwinkle* cartoon producer Bill Scott asserts without hesitation. "By and large, much of the material that's going on Saturday now is in its fifth, sixth, seventh, and seventeenth reruns. For a long time, the material that's especially made for Saturday morning has been produced strictly on a cost basis. And I think part of the great outcry against children's television is because anybody who watches what kids are getting exposed to can get ill over the level of production."

"The programs are purely entertainment today. Generally, they're exploitive," says Bob Keeshan, Captain Kangaroo to kids. "I don't think that today's children's programming is something the industry can point to with great pride."

"It's junk," maintains Richard Webb.

"Is Saturday morning really a junkyard?" Norm Prescott, co-owner of Filmation Studios, responds. "Well, to the networks, it's a gold mine. The money made on Saturday morning is probably the biggest single profit center that the networks have. But to the point of view of parents, teachers, and educators—those who are concerned and interested—I'm sure they feel that many shows do not provide meaningful social or educational values."

"I think Saturday morning has had some fine shows and some awful ones, and certainly I've contributed to both," admits DePatie-Freleng animation company co-owner, David DePatie.

"It isn't a gold mine or a junkyard," observes Joseph Barbera, partner of Hanna-Barbera Productions. "We're supplying a certain kind of entertainment based on a certain time period and innumerable rules which are laid down on Saturday morning. It may be a terrible waste of creativity, but I don't think it's any more of a junkyard than the nighttime lineup."

TV Programs Recommended for Children by *National Parent-Teacher* Magazine June 1950

ABC

Ireene Wicker's *The Singing Lady*
America's Town Meeting
Twenty Questions
Paul Whiteman's TV Teen Club

CBS

Candid Camera
The Goldbergs
Lucky Pup
Ford Theater

NBC

Howdy Doody
Kukla, Fran and Ollie
Quiz Kids
We, the People
The Voice of Firestone
The Aldrich Family

Saturday morning television is taken for granted by children and debated by adults who easily remember when Saturday was still a day for children to play outside.

The first children's shows to air in 1947—DuMont's *Oky Doky Ranch* and *Small Fry Club;* NBC's *Junior Jamboree* with Kukla, Fran, and Ollie; and *Puppet Playhouse* starring Howdy Doody—were telecast in the early evening hours. Most stations didn't even sign on until noon or later.

So few sets, let alone shows, existed in mid-1948 that a Detroit appliance-store owner dispatched his employees to the neighborhoods to drum up TV receiver sales at houses that didn't have an antenna. It was a simple enough assignment to locate TV-less homes. Fewer than 325,000 TV sets were in operation nationwide, compared to the 65 million American-owned radio receivers.

A year later, 3 million TVs were plugged in and thirty-one American communities publicized in their Chamber of Commerce guides the fact that they were served by a TV station. There was still no children's television on Saturday morning, but in July 1949, NBC viewers could see one-hour Naval Air Reserve training films at 9:30 A.M. on the network's *Sands Point Navy Training Program.* Viewers could tune into the show at neighborhood bars, the Baltimore and Ohio Railroad's Washington run, or the Allentown, Pennsylvania, public library. The same year, jukebox operators reported a loss in revenue at taverns containing TVs, and an RCA serviceman repairing sets in the New York area expressed surprise at the drab homes with $500 sets.

In 1950, ABC made the first attempt to catch children's attention on Saturday morning. On August 19 the network premiered the zoo show *Animal Clinic* at 11:00 A.M. and *Acrobat Ranch,* a circus production, at 11:30. The schedule changed on September 23 when *Saturday at the Zoo* aired at 11:00 A.M., followed by *Animal Clinic* at noon. On October 7 there was another shift as the puppet program *Chester the Pup* won the noon slot. And on December 30, 1950, Jay Stewart hosted *Funfair* at 11:00 A.M.

NBC broke into the Saturday children's market in late 1950, airing various films, *The Magic Clown,* and *Rootie Tootie,* the forerunner of *Rootie Kazootie.*

CBS countered with its first Saturday kids' entry on October 14, an 11:00 A.M. to 12:15 P.M. program called *Us Kids.*

It was a slow start to what became a fast-paced medium.

"I don't recall anything special about Saturday morning at that point except that the networks had some vague idea that they wanted programs for kids. That's why we developed *Crusader Rabbit* and sold our *Speaking of Animals* films to television," says movie producer Jerry Fairbanks.

"We didn't know there'd be a future in television," offered Jon Hall, TV's *Ramar of the Jungle.* "It was really a risk."

"Television was a new thing," says actor Ed Kemmer of *Space Patrol.* "People watched programs then they wouldn't watch now. But nobody had any idea what would last."

"When we went into production on *Wild Bill Hickok* in 1950, no one knew what the impact of TV was going to be," Guy Madison says. "The one thing it took was guts, because the studios usually wouldn't let their contract players appear on TV."

from Television Guide *(1950)*

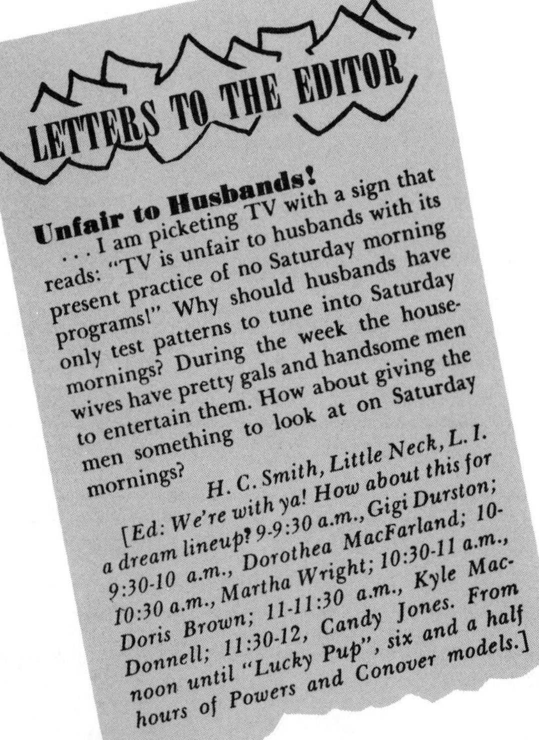

LETTERS TO THE EDITOR

Unfair to Husbands!

. . . I am picketing TV with a sign that reads: "TV is unfair to husbands with its present practice of no Saturday morning programs!" Why should husbands have only test patterns to tune into Saturday mornings? During the week the housewives have pretty gals and handsome men to entertain them. How about giving the men something to look at on Saturday mornings?

H. C. Smith, Little Neck, L. I.

[Ed: We're with ya! How about this for a dream lineup? 9-9:30 a.m., Gigi Durston; 9:30-10 a.m., Dorothea MacFarland; 10-10:30 a.m., Martha Wright; 10:30-11 a.m., Doris Brown; 11-11:30 a.m., Kyle MacDonnell; 11:30-12, Candy Jones. From noon until "Lucky Pup", six and a half hours of Powers and Conover models.]

October 1947 Four Network Saturday Morning Schedule

NO NETWORK SERVICE

October 1957 Three Network Saturday Morning Schedule

	ABC	CBS	NBC
8:00			
8:30			
9:00			
9:30		Captain Kangaroo	
10:00			Howdy Doody
10:30		The Mighty Mouse Playhouse (C*)	The Gumby Show (C)
11:00		Susan's Show	Fury
11:30		Saturday Playhouse	Captain Gallant
12:00		The Jimmy Dean Show	True Story
12:30			Detective's Diary
1:00		The Lone Ranger	
1:30			

*(C) denotes cartoons

October 1967 Three Network Saturday Morning Schedule

	ABC	CBS	NBC
8:00			
8:30			
9:00	Casper, The Friendly Ghost (C)	Frankenstein Jr. and the Impossibles (C)	The Super Six (C)
9:30	The Fantastic Four (C)	The Herculoids (C)	Super President (C)
10:00	Spider-Man (C)	Shazzan! (C)	The Flintstones (C)
10:30	Journey to the Center of the Earth (C)	Space Ghost (C)	Samson and Goliath (C)
11:00	King Kong (C)	Moby Dick and the Mighty Mightor (C)	Birdman (C)
11:30	George of the Jungle (C)	The Superman-Aquaman Hour of Adventure (C)	The Atom Ant/ Secret Squirrel Show (C)
12:00	The Beatles (C)		Cool McCool (C)
12:30	American Bandstand '68	Jonny Quest (C)	
1:00		The Lone Ranger (C)	
1:30			

*(C) denotes cartoons

October 1977 Three Network Saturday Morning Schedule

	ABC	CBS	NBC
8:00	The All New Superfriends Hour (C)	The Bugs Bunny/ Road Runner Hour (C)	The C.B. Bears (C)
8:30			
9:00	Scooby's All-Star Laff-A-Lympics (C)	What's New, Mr. Magoo? (C)	The Young Sentinels (C)
9:30		The Skatebirds	The New Archies/Sabrina Hour (C)
10:00			
10:30		Space Academy	I Am the Greatest: The Adventures of Muhammad Ali (C)
11:00	The Krofft Supershow '77	The Batman/ Tarzan Adventure Hour (C)	Thunder
11:30			Search and Rescue: The Alpha Team
12:00	The ABC Weekend Specials	Wacko	Baggy Pants and the Nitwits (C)
12:30		Fat Albert and the Cosby Kids (C)	The Red Hand Gang
1:00	American Bandstand	The Secrets of Isis	
1:30		The CBS Children's Film Festival	

*(C) denotes cartoons

"The motion picture companies were laying people off, but they still wanted to knock TV down," Buster Crabbe explains. "They did everything they possibly could: arguing it was a fad; it's going to wash out; it won't work. But once television got going—well, you know what happened."

The expanding daily schedule was pulled in by more receivers in 1950. An estimated 7,463,000 sets were in service. Models were built into the walls of some Levitt and Sons houses in Levittown, Pennsylvania, and New York and sets were available on the Short Line bus route between Los Angeles and San Francisco.

In 1951 children's shows were still not an eye-opener on Saturday morning, but kids watched an average nineteen and a half hours a week. It was the first year that the TV industry crossed into the profit column with $4,600,000 in earnings compared to a $9,200,000 loss in 1950. A 1948 to 1952 Federal Communications Commission (FCC) freeze limiting the existing television outlets to 108 in 63 cities continued. However, the facilities were already doing half the business of the radio broadcast industry with its 1,200 markets covered by 2,000 stations.

Meanwhile, children had more late-morning network viewing alternatives including *Grand Chance Roundup*, *Smilin' Ed's Gang*, *TV Digest*, *Dick Tracy*, *Junior Hi-Jinx*, *Jon Gnagy*, *Foodini the Great*, *Kids and Company*, and *The Betty Crocker Star Matinee*. Primarily, however, the Saturday schedule was comprised of local, not network, shows and handout films from encyclopedia companies, private business, and the United States government.

In late 1951 and 1952 the children's schedule was showing signs of tinkering and testing. NBC trimmed, then moved *Kukla, Fran and Ollie* and gave serious thought to transferring *Lucky Pup*, *Tom Corbett*, *Ranger Joe*, and *Magic Cottage* to Saturday morning, thus making room for adult shows in the valuable evening time periods.

In July 1953, CBS announced an ambitious late morning–early afternoon Saturday lineup with *Rod Brown of the Rocket Rangers*, *Big Top*, and *The Lone Ranger*. *Sky King* also flew onto the scene and *Quiz Kids* proved that children's shows could be the answer for Saturday morning.

Placement of the bulky TV set often disrupted living room floor plans. Manufacturers had salable solutions.

The networks also programmed *Terry and the Pirates*, *Youth Wants to Know*, *Tootsie Hippodrome*, *Winky Dink and You*, and *Captain Midnight*.

In February 1954, NBC promoted a schedule code named "Operation Saturday." The initial card to premiere in the fall would have started at 8:00 A.M. with a junior edition of *The Today Show*. For the 9:00 A.M. broadcast Eddy Arnold was to host *Down on the Farm*. Zookeeper Marlin Perkins, Mr. Wizard (Don Herbert), and botanical expert John Ott were designated as contributors.

A half-hour college-credit program was planned for 10:00 A.M. News with Frank Blair was scheduled next, and a Saturday version of the weekday *Home Show* was blocked for 11:00 A.M.

The effort was scrapped when executives realized the package would not be attractive to youngsters. After due consideration, the network revised its proposal, keeping two objectives in mind: program in half-hour segments and appeal to youngsters with adult hosts.

On November 20, 1954, NBC unveiled the new assault on children: *Happy Felton's Spotlight Gang* started the day at 10:00 A.M. with films, games, and acts. *Winchell and Mahoney* appeared at 10:30. Next came Jimmy Weldon's *Funny Boners* and *Tom Corbett, Space Cadet*.

"It suddenly became a very creative medium with shows like those on the air," says comedian Soupy Sales. "Some of the programs showed old movies, others presented cartoons, but they all had hosts, puppets, and bits. They didn't have a big budget, but they were live and it was a great time."

"Everybody was learning then," says ventriloquist Jimmy Nelson. "There was no right way or wrong way. You just faced the cameras and did your best."

The networks sold advertisers on the argument that Saturday programs were the number one means to communicate with children. Kidvid advertising, they said, could influence human behavior. They denied that violent programming would have the same effect on children.

Network sales departments quickly became interested in the growth trends of the audience. But it was not the physical height children might reach that concerned network officials. As the 1960s approached, they measured demographics and viewer attention-span and determined that low-budget cartoons were a better buy than live studio shows.

"The tide turned to cartoons in 1962 or 1963," Soupy Sales remembers. "That's when the salesmen became the heads of programming and management. They're charming guys. They could sell the Brooklyn Bridge. What they do is great, but they really don't know a trombone player from a tap dancer, because it's not their line. And almost overnight they said, 'We're paying thousands of dollars a week to a host whose show we can't repeat. Let's put on new cartoons or cartoon reruns.' "

Guided by such reasoning, live shows were killed off, uncle hosts became lost relatives, Western heroes rode off for good, and science fiction couldn't keep up with economic reality. The networks entered the cartoon era, turned Saturday morning into a programming ghetto, and milked the property for maximum efforts like any negligent absentee landlord.

Today, Saturday morning programming is a game for computer programmers who attempt to match target audiences with cartoon shows. The trade calls it "routining," or delivering the *right* program to the *right* group of youngsters at the *right* time.

The early morning hours go to the two-to-five-year-olds, who broadcasters say are content with any image as long as it moves. They mostly get reruns. The new production dollar goes to the six-to-eleven-year-olds after 9:00 A.M. and the twelve-year-olds, who usually begin their viewing at 10 A.M.

Midmorning has been Saturday's most valuable time slot. In the early years live shows settled into the 10 A.M. block, some for an extended period. However, as broadcasters dropped the studio shows from the schedule and primarily aired cartoons, they began to shift the lineup almost seasonally. Young viewers have been confused by all the movement, and observers have become aware that Saturday morning television has dissolved into a haphazardly programmed cartoon carnival with few winning acts. The trend can be seen by isolating NBC's 10 A.M. to 10:30 A.M. (ET) offerings from the date that the network's children's service began at that hour in 1954, into 1980.*

Happy Felton's Spotlight Gang	11/20/54—2/26/55
The Pinky Lee Show	3/5/55—12/17/55
The Children's Corner	12/24/55—4/7/56
The Pinky Lee Show	4/14/56—6/9/56
Howdy Doody	6/16/56—9/24/60
The Shari Lewis Show	10/1/60—9/28/63
The Hector Heathcote Show (c)†	10/5/63—9/26/64
Underdog (c)	10/3/64—9/25/65
Secret Squirrel (c)	10/2/65—12/31/66
The Flintstones (c)	1/7/67—8/30/69
H. R. Pufnstuf	9/6/69—9/5/70
Doctor Dolittle (c)	9/12/70—9/4/71
Barrier Reef	9/11/71—12/25/71
The Jetsons (c)	1/8/72—9/2/72
Roman Holidays (c)	9/9/72—12/16/72
Underdog (c)	12/23/72—9/1/73
Butch Cassidy and the Sundance Kids (c)	9/8/73—12/29/73
Sigmund and the Sea Monsters	1/5/74—8/31/74
Land of the Lost	9/7/74—9/4/76
McDuff, the Talking Dog	9/11/76—11/20/76
Speed Buggy (c)	11/27/76—9/3/77
The New Archies/Sabrina Hour (c)	9/10/77—11/5/77
The Bang-Shang Lalapalooza Show (c)	11/12/77—1/28/78
Go Go Globetrotters (c)	2/4/78—9/2/78
The Godzilla Power Hour (c)	9/9/78—10/28/78
Godzilla Super 90 (c)	11/4/78—9/1/79
The Harlem Globetrotters and Dynomutt (c)	9/8/79—9/15/79
The Super Globetrotters (c)	9/22/79—12/1/79
Fred and Barney Meet the Shmoo (c)	12/8/79—

*Many shows moved from or to other time slots. Their on-air dates here are not intended to be a record of their total TV life. (All material researched by Timothy C. Rupp)

†(c) denotes cartoon show

Parceling to 35 million viewers is not an easy job, Filmation Studios' executive Norm Prescott says. "We know that preschool kids love to watch visual images. If the characters are broad, wild-looking, if they move fast and the gags are there, they don't have to understand all the dialogue. They're mesmerized by the pictures. With the older groups, however, we have to concentrate on dialogue because the kids are listening for the meaning and content of the story and the character relationships.

"Most shows are purchased on the basis of thirteen to sixteen half hours," Prescott continues. "They're played over two years, repeated about 6.7 times. That's how they make their money. Hanna-Barbera's *Scooby-Doo* and our *Fat Albert* have run for years and years with new episodes made all the time. But those are the flukes. The average show will only run for two years now."

"It's almost like wagering on a horse race," Hanna-Barbera co-founder Joseph Barbera explains. "We keep betting and finally we make a big killing like *Scooby* that keeps us going for another season. And if over the years we gather enough episodes, we can sell them in syndication."

It's a far cry from the time when the Lone Ranger defended Saturday morning for decades, *Watch Mr. Wizard* lasted for more than ten years, and *Howdy Doody* held onto its Saturday slot through much of the 1950s.

And according to media insiders and outsiders, it's a far cry from what Saturday morning television might evolve into.

"I'm optimistic," says Jimmy Nelson. "We may possibly see a ventriloquist with his own show again or a magician. I'm not saying Mark Wilson or me, because he and I have had our shots, but people like us are still coming along. I'd like to say that we'll see a return to the 1950s, with much better production values."

Nelson's vision may be more wishful thinking than realistic foresight. Nearly everyone else is seeing wall-to-wall cartoons.

"I imagine that cartoons will be playing forever," says *Rootie Kazootie* puppeteer Paul Ashley.

"In the short run, we'll have cartoons," adds Joel Heller, CBS's executive producer of *30 Minutes*. "Cartoons don't get old.

"As far as the networks are concerned, there may be a long-range problem," Heller states. "The question is how long will the networks remain in business as far as children's programming is concerned. Discs, satellite-relayed shows, and cassettes may break open the Saturday morning schedule."

Charles D. Ferris, chairman of the Federal Communications Commission during the Carter administration, predicted that the new delivery-systems would vastly alter the old precepts. "You should no longer accept all the traditional ground rules of the three-network over-the-air broadcasting system," Ferris said in 1979, the year his FCC Task Force on Children's Television called for a complete overhaul of the Saturday morning TV schedule. "For the first time in memory, the technology, the society, the creative community, and the regulators seem to be moving in the same direction."

"If cable becomes strong there may be places for people to learn again," Soupy Sales states. "If not, then Saturday probably won't exist in any creative way. It just might be an accumulation of reruns where broadcasters play the cartoons and kids take it or leave it."

The future of commercial TV's Saturday involvement becomes even more hazy when obscured by the debate over advertisements. Today, the schedule offers direct access to kids' spending power. Commercials are manipulative and effective. They keep the network ledger-sheets balanced and the children's shows budgeted. Take them off the air, broadcasters warn, and the program pipeline may be cut off.

"I'm afraid that ten years down the pike, Saturday morning could very easily evaporate as we now know it, if indeed those who are against commercials win," cartoon creator David DePatie prophesies. "We're all very concerned about the Federal Trade Commission inquiries in respect to commercials. The pressure is off us as programmers now. We've cleaned up our act considerably. It's turned to commercials. If they're taken off, I really don't know what would happen."

"I don't have a very bright outlook about network television," Joseph Barbera declares. "I just think they're being ruled out of business. But we have to gear for the future. The other areas are slowly coming up, and we'll produce for them."

"I gotta confess, I couldn't care less what

"The future of children's TV is now for others to decide," says Buffalo Bob Smith.

WANTED
$100 REWARD
One Hundred Dollar reward for information leading to identification and location of the 8 children who were on original Howdy Doody Show December 27, 1947.
In case of ties or duplicate information, I will be the sole judge to determine the sharing of this reward.
SIGNED
Howdy Doody
NBC-TV
NEW YORK

happens," says Bob Smith, who like other former TV hosts really wonders why there's no room for him in TV today.

For a long time, the *Howdy Doody* star and his 1950s colleagues have been disgusted with what they've seen happen to the commercial, yet personal medium they loved. They're held in high esteem by yesterday's children and held in no regard by today's broadcasters. Their role models shaped lives. Most of today's characters could not ever hope to do the same.

"I think children who watch Saturday morning today are missing a lot of good clean, wholesome fun," says Buffalo Bob.

Cliff Robertson, star of the 1953 CBS series *Rod Brown of the Rocket Rangers*, seconds Smith's notion. "My daughter gets fed the canned, overused, ready-made, capsulized shows on Saturday today. I get the feeling that they're stamping them out. It's the same thing as in the franchise food marts. Now, the difference between her generation and mine is that when I was a kid, we went to a hamburger place and it was a hamburger place, run by someone

Who said What???

Match the phrases in Column I with their character in Column II.

	I		II
A	"Spaceman's Luck!"	**1**	Sergeant Preston of the Yukon
B	"Yo, Rinty!"	**2**	Jingles
C	"Pluck your Magic Twanger, Froggy"	**3**	Cisco Kid
D	"Gosh-A-Rootie!"	**4**	Commander Scott
E	"I'm comin', Beany"	**5**	Jinks the Cat
F	"I'll do the thinnin' around here"	**6**	Froggie the Gremlin
G	"I hate meeces to peeces!"	**7**	Cadet Happy
H	"Ea-Yauk-Ee"	**8**	Chief Thunderthud
I	"10-4, 21-50, Bye"	**9**	Tonto
J	"Well, King, this case is closed"	**10**	Tom Corbett
K	"Kowa Bunga"	**11**	John J. Fadoozle
L	"Crabby Appleton—he's rotten to the core"	**12**	Cecil the Seasick Sea Serpent
M	"Heh, Wild Bill, wait for me!"	**13**	Quick Draw McGraw
N	"Gosh! Don't know m'own strength"	**14**	Popeye
O	"He don't know me very well, do he?"	**15**	Farfel
P	"Okay, Chief, I'll get on it right away"	**16**	Bullwinkle J. Moose
Q	"NI-I-ICE"	**17**	Rootie Kazootie
R	"Git 'em up, Scout!"	**18**	Tweetie Pie
S	"America's Number One 'Boing' Private Eye"	**19**	Tom Terrific
T	"Ahhh, Pancho"	**20**	Corporal Rusty
U	"That's all I can stands cause I can't stands no more"	**21**	Dick Tracy
V	"Hiya kids, hiya, hiya"	**22**	Chief Dan Mathews
W	"Now here's something we hope you'll really like"	**23**	Midnight the Cat
X	"Smokin' rockets!"	**24**	Rocket J. Squirrel
Y	"The engines!"	**25**	Andy Devine
Z	"Chocolate!"	**26**	Jeff and Porky

answers:
A10 B20 C25 D17 E12 F13 G5 H26 I22 J1 K8
L19 M2 N16 O18 P21 Q23 R9 S11 T3 U14
V6 W24 X7 Y4 Z15

who was proud of their hamburgers. They weren't selling billions. They just had a little place. We benefited from those. And they were good. Well, I think in a way, my kids could do with a little more nutritious television, just as they could do with a little more nutritious hamburger."

Children are indeed missing something. And consumer groups, parents, and the government are not to blame. They're only television's scapegoats. Networks make more money now than ever before and put less concern into creative program options.

Some aspects of children's television needed drastic improvement, and over the years the broadcasters responded. But the majority of changes have unfortunately ended up favoring the TV pocketbooks over the viewers' minds. The medium was cheapened rather than given the necessary investment of time, money, and consideration. It's no wonder people recall early Saturday TV as having been better.

"If you remember the shows we did with fond memories," concludes Jimmy Nelson, "then I guess we did our jobs. At least that's what I like to think."

Who will be able to say that in ten years? Scooby-Doo?

Hanna-Barbera's Big Dog, Scooby-Doo.

1 Saturday Morning

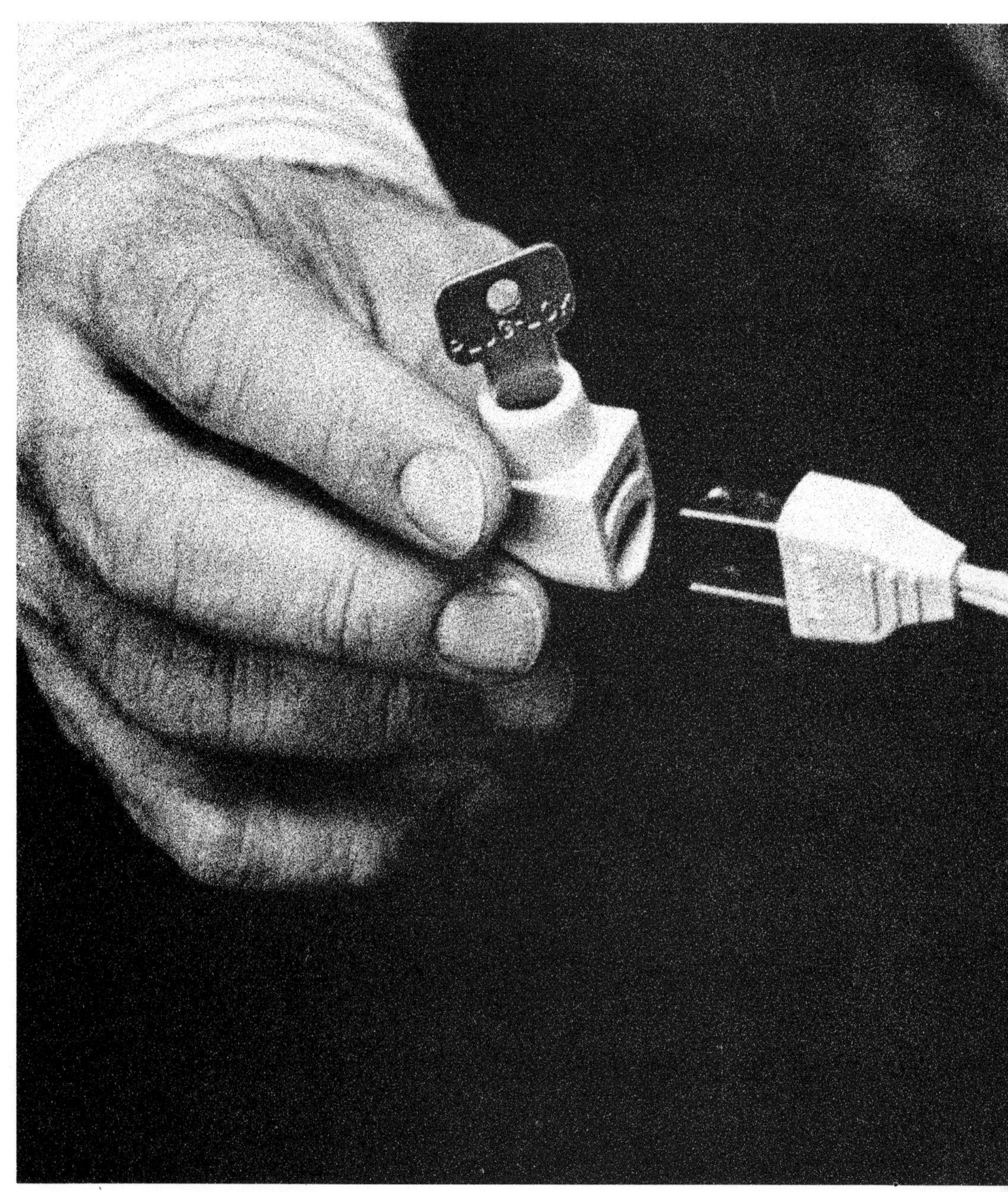

The Plug-Lok, a 1979 antiviewing device for parents developed by the Kenny Company of St. Louis.

Fever

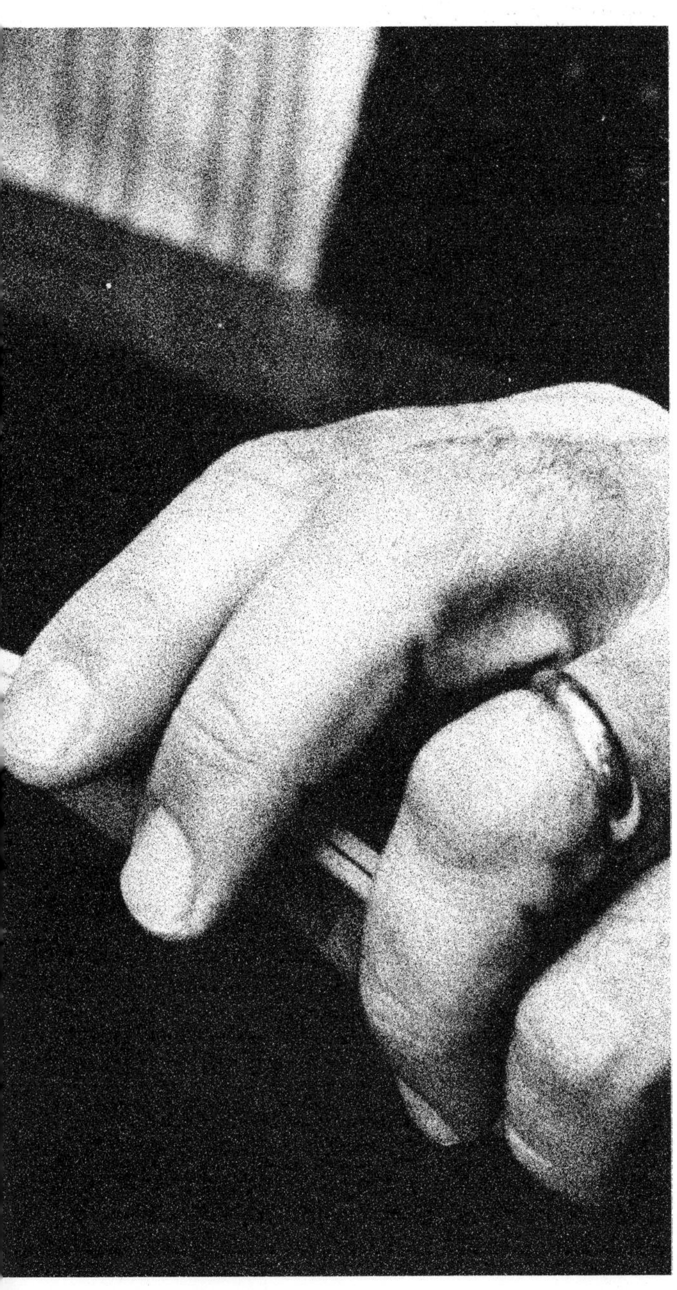

Before Mrs. Allison Palmer resigned from her Bergenfield, New Jersey, teaching position in 1950, there was something she insisted on telling her principal. Of the twenty-two children in her first- and second-grade classes, twenty-one had TV sets at home, and the results had been disastrous.

She claimed that as children's parents acquired television sets the students became restless and rambunctious, because they spent more time indoors and forgot about exercising and fresh air. During class, she said, they fidgeted, waiting for the end of the school day when they could return home and stare at the set.

"You know what they talk about?" she asked rhetorically. "Hopalong Cassidy. Over and over. Just cowboys and Indians and Hopalong Cassidy. It's no wonder they are bored by school. How can I compete with Hopalong Cassidy?"

Mrs. Palmer learned quicker than many others that TV had a marked effect on viewers, particularly children. The set was more than a technological baby-sitter. She believed it intruded, interrupted, even altered behavior.

Mrs. Palmer happily left her Bergenfield job, moving to Nevada where mountains blocked TV reception. The escape was temporary, however. In a few short years, TV's ubiquitous eye would reach everywhere.

Back in the cities the impact of the tube was being gauged, measured, and analyzed by educators, legislators, and doctors of varying degrees. Was TV having a pronounced effect on children? If so, was it physical or psychological? Was television a blessing? Or was it, as TV pioneer Lee De Forest charged in 1948, a "benign Frankenstein?"

The earliest answers to these questions were as fuzzy as the first television pictures. TV's

William Boyd on TV's Positive Postwar Influence (1954):

"Instead of running around in all directions vainly seeking amusement—mother, father, sister and brother found it in the last place they'd expect—right in their own living rooms. Our kids have fathers and mothers again; our fathers and mothers have their kids back with them. That I think is the real miracle of television."

critics worried that the new invention held Mephistophelean powers ranging from provoking a child's simple stomachache to hastening the destruction of civilization.

In 1952, for example, the Archbishop of Canterbury, the Most Reverend Geoffrey F. Fisher, stated that TV threatened great danger. "The world would have been a happier place if television had never been discovered," he said.

During an early 1950s Boston University commencement address, school president Dr. Daniel L. Marsh prophesied that the nation might eventually be filled with morons unless TV viewing was curbed. Similarly, Chancellor Robert Hutchins of the University of Chicago warned that "under the impact of television, I can contemplate a time in America when people can neither read nor write, but will be no better than the lower forms of plant life." And Harvard anthropologist Dr. Earnest A. Hooton maintained in 1951 that our ability to read had deteriorated because television offered, for the most part, "foolish, harmful material which stultifies audiences." He feared that viewers would eventually regress "to the status of a well-controlled domestic."

Poet and critic John Ciardi added, "Children's programs are an offense to civilization . . . the cartoon shows are a disgrace. The emcees of kids' shows are sickening oafs. The tone of the shows is barbaric. I hold TV to border on moral corruption and civic disloyalty."

Louis Kronenberger, professor of theater arts at Brandeis University, warned in 1958 that TV is "the greatest cultural calamity in this country's history." And actress Helen Hayes said in 1949 that "TV will mean the end of all art in the theater. . . . It's awful, reducing everything to that little bread box . . . all that rehearsal for just *one* performance."

Choruses proclaiming cultural doom were heard wherever a TV station was signing on.

Yet, in the background, barely audible through the decibels of emotional anti-TV rhetoric, were the quietly spoken words of the concerned, somewhat philosophical few, who simply said, "Life should be lived, not watched."

Originally, most TV researchers had difficulty finding their subjects watching at home. Though the medium's influence was swelling, the sheer expense of a new set prohibited most people from making a purchase. Through the late 1940s, TV sets, averaging $350 to $400 (one-third to one-fourth the price of an average 1948 DeSoto, Plymouth, or Oldsmobile), remained a luxury more desired than owned. Consequently, until the cost was lowered substantially, people hungry for a TV fix had to go out before they could tune in.

The one place where TV sets were initially turned on for adults and youngsters alike were the nation's bars. Parkey Radigan was typical of many community-minded tavern-owners in 1948. At 5:30 each evening he capped his beer taps, kicked out the adults, and gave kids the run of his Hoboken, New Jersey establishment to watch Buffalo Bob Smith's *Howdy Doody Show* and Bob Emery's *Small Fry Club.*

"I realized that the kids ought to have a chance to see what was going on too," barkeep Radigan told a reporter for *Variety.* "Most of them came from poor families and can't afford to see a big ball game or for that matter, too much of any kind of entertainment. And besides, it seemed like a good way to keep them off the streets."

But there was a predictable backlash. Children in bars? Unconscionable, said those worried that barside viewing would lead to a wave of adolescent alcoholism. Two months after Radigan started his "children's hour," the New Jersey Liquor Board shut off his set. The board sternly reminded the bartender that his was an adult business off limits to kids, no matter how he defined his civic duty.

The boom fell on other bars as well. In Minnesota, the Women's Christian Temperance Union (WCTU) launched a fund-raising campaign to buy sets for community centers and recreation halls "so that young people will not have to go to taverns to watch the broadcasts."

The Detroit American Legion initiated a comparable program. The post opened its club doors and set up folding chairs from 4:00 P.M. to 6:00 P.M. each Sunday to give youngsters a place other than a bar to watch television.

In many homes TV began dictating when dinner would be served, baths run, or bedtime established. An early study of New England viewers found that in households with recently installed TV sets, children were allowed to stay awake twenty-five minutes later than in homes that did not have a TV yet. And in 1951 some Syracuse, New York, doctors reported incidences of parents sending their children to bed at 8:00 P.M., only to wake them two hours later for their favorite programs.

Fearful that TV had the power to do more than simply delay the inevitable evening ritual, some people suggested that the contraption should be banned altogether. In 1949, for example, the wife of the famed newspaper columnist Leonard Lyons condemned TV in general and children's shows in particular. She said she saw nothing on the schedule to warrant transmission.

A few years later the International Catholic Association for Radio and Television took a slightly modified view and recommended that children should not be left alone in front of the television set. The organization proposed the establishment of a minimum-age requirement for viewing.

The Pilot Radio Corporation had the next best solution. In 1950 the firm announced the marketing of a newly designed set for parents who couldn't control their children's TV habit. Pilot developed a sixteen-inch tube equipped with doors and a heavy bronze lock.

In the 1970s and 1980s there were still those claiming that the TV lock was the answer to the Saturday morning viewing problem. Ted Pylant, salesman for an Arkansas TV station and author of *Television We Protest,* marketed a lock for $8.95. And Morton T. Werner from Clayton, Missouri, designed what he called Plug-Lok and sold it through the mail for $4.95.

Others had more drastic remedies. In 1968, FCC Commissioner Nicholas Johnson encouraged viewers to sue the networks if they believed their children had been harmed by programming, and three years later Action for Children's Television (ACT) campaigned that families should "turn off television, Saturday."

No stopgap measure was ever more dramatic than Archbishop John O'Hara's suggestion to Roman Catholics within his diocese. People should give up TV for Lent, he wrote in his pastoral letter. Apparently for the sake of fairness he threw in radio, too.[1]

Physicians across the country joined in the growing criticism. Those distrustful of the new living room intruder blamed TV for causing varied health problems from toe to head.

In 1952, Dr. E. G. Burke, president of the Wisconsin Society of Chiropodists, warned that children who spent too much time watching TV could be stricken with bad feet as a result of inactivity.

One year later Dr. J. I. Kendrick, a Cleveland specialist, voiced concern about a new children's ailment he called frog knees or "frogitis." The doctor explained that the malady could develop when children viewed TV with their legs folded back to their sides like a frog. Such a squat position, he alleged, placed undue strain on the inner-leg ligaments, inhibiting growth trends and possibly leading to deformity.

Chicago doctor Wilford L. Cooper diagnosed still another TV-related affliction—"TV bottom." At a 1959 medical convention Dr. Cooper explained that the disorder was similar to coccygodynia, a temporary ache in the tailbone often induced by long auto rides. But the physician observed that the TV-induced version had particular characteristics. "TV bottom" lasted longer than the old ailment, he said. "Why?" asked his colleagues. For many people, he responded, televiewing goes on night after night, and "there sits the difference."

In 1952, Syracuse doctors had isolated "TV tummy," an illness that affected children who became too excited during action-packed viewing. The difficulty was presumably accompanied by cramps, stomach spasms, and pains. The doctors advised parents of the major early-warning sign: children fleeing the TV room "until the bad man isn't on the screen anymore."

1. Radio also came under attack in Australia. *The New York Times* reported in 1950 that Dr. G. E. Philpots, a Melbourne dentist, argued that radio contributed to bad teeth. Philpots believed that crime programs upset children's nervous systems, and that the lack of steady nerves retarded proper growth of teeth.

A 1951 advertisement for a color filter

Magnifying Television Importance

By John Cronin

For centuries, man had lived in comparative darkness; people had only the candle and the hearth to give light. Finally, at the end of the 19th and the beginning of this century, Edison and his cohorts perfected the electric light. Mankind had finally been brought out of the darkness.

During the '20s, '30s, and the '40s, American homes were marked by the glow of the light which emanated from livingroom windows. Families sat in their sofas and chairs, read and/or listened to the radio and survived the Depression, faced war and enjoyed prosperity. And then, America returned to darkness! Lights darkened again, windows only showed a gray/white luminescence. Television had returned us to the "Dark Ages." Families crouched around this "radio with a picture tube" and watched the little characters move on the screen.

And little they were. The experimental screens ranged anywhere from two inches to five inches, diagonally.

To ease eye strain, many companies began to market magnifying screens which purported to so enlarge the TV image that one's li-

Nonprescription viewing from the early 1950s

vingroom became an "in-house movie theatre." For prices ranging from $4.95 up to $19.95, Dad could buy this marvel of engineering genius, take it home, attach it to the television, and in a matter of hours, the family could sit back and watch their "giant screen" TV.

For people who had a five-inch screen, the magnifier usually resembled the glasses that Marvin Kaplan wore when he played Alfred Prinzmetal on *Meet Millie.* In fact, most people who had these small screens weren't aware of the amplitude of Millie's figure until they got the magnifying glass!

For owners of the seven-inch screen, the magnifier was more sensibly designed, because it didn't distort the image nearly as much. Yet, the great weakness of the lens was that it did distort. For example, John Cameron Swayze, the first national newscaster, either had a seriously paunchy stomach or a broad chin, depending on where the glass was mounted.

Salvation was on the way, however. Those people, who during the latter part of the 1940s had spent hundreds of dollars to have the first TV in their neighborhood and had squinted at their small screens, were to be finally rewarded with the introduction in 1950 of a truly giant TV screen—the twelve-inch model.

The development was only surpassed by color filters or the "color wheel." With the advent of commercial TV, its insatiable audience immediately wanted to see their favorite shows in color—any color. American entrepreneurship was not to be frustrated by this new challenge. Color wheels, much like the rotating wheels used to illuminate Christmas trees, were quickly offered on the market to satisfy this new lust for only $5 or $6. How much "richness of color" viewers got depended on how fast or slow the wheel rotated, and how blind the audience was from either looking at a tiny screen or the distorted magnified images.

No one said TV-watching would ever be easy.

Air Force pediatrician Richard M. Narkewicz contributed to the reams of research with his study of thirty youngsters who watched television to the point of excess. He noted chronic fatigue, loss of appetite, headaches, and vomiting in their behavior and labeled the illness "tired child syndrome."

"Kids are living right inside that little box," Dr. Narkewicz said upon releasing his study in the early 1960s. Reporting to the American Academy of Pediatricians, he stated that he had prescribed a sedative to ease youngster's TV anxiety.

In 1953, Atlanta, Georgia, dental specialist Dr. S. R. Atkinson drilled a sharply honed criticism against TV. Constant viewing, he said, could result in "TV jaw" or "television malocclusion," a condition possibly provoked when children repeatedly lie on the floor and push their eyeteeth inward with their knuckles.

A voice expert anticipated worse. In 1957, *Newsweek* reported the concern of a British speech therapist who said the TV-addicted family that "sits in trance before the idiot's lantern" runs the risk of losing its ability to converse.

Of all the physicians who criticized TV, however, optometrists claimed to see the harmful effects most clearly. As early as 1947 doctors and nurses tending to students in the Los Angeles school system warned children not to look at the receivers their parents might have at home.

Should youngsters succumb to temptation and view the hypnotic eye, the Pioneer Scientific Corporation had a suggestion. In a 1948 ad placed in *The New York Times*, Pioneer stated, "Children's young eyes especially need the protection of a Polaroid Television Filter." They offered varying models from $6.50 to $25.00, each promising to end eyestrain.

The following year the New York State Optometric Association endorsed the use of such filters to neutralize the "snow." The group also cautioned viewers never to watch TV in total darkness.

Philadelphia doctor John C. Neill recommended in 1950 that after an evening concentrating on the picture tube, people should sit for twenty minutes in a darkened room before driving. The physician theorized that unless people took more care of their viewing, eye troubles would multiply. He had already concluded that 10 percent of all vision problems in the United States were television-related.

The Better Vision Institute came up with a solution to visual discomfort caused by TV. In 1952 the institute developed new precision-ground and polished eyeglasses with faintly yellow lenses. The coloration was said to facilitate viewing.

In time the weight of credible scientific proof overshadowed most discussions of TV bottom, TV tummy, TV jaw, or TV squint. Yet while talk of such obtuse and dubious physical ailments gradually diminished, criticism of TV's influence on children did not abate. It simply shifted to the question of what, if any, psychological effect television might have on young minds. And although the debate involved a long, often convoluted list of concerns, one argument attained prominence: Violent shows were viewed as dangerous to children. Many parents, educators, and critics were angry enough about the issue to fight.

Anti-violence critics used TV studies as their ammunition. One of the earliest surveys was aimed at disarming cowboys, handcuffing villains, imposing speed limits on car chases, and straitjacketing Saturday morning ruffians. Frank Orme, an independent TV watchdog, made a study of Los Angeles television in 1952 and noted, in one week, 167 murders, 112 justifiable homicides, and 356 attempted murders. Two-thirds of all the violence he found occurred in children's shows. In 1954, Orme said violence on kids' shows had increased 400 percent since he made his first report. He maintained that television had become a brutal school for violence with neatly packaged lessons of brutality, thievery, and mayhem.

Westerns were the target of most people who campaigned against violence. Typical of the reaction was a letter sent to *The New York Times* in July 1950 by a Brooklyn resident. "It has gotten so that I never turn on the TV unless I know what I'll see because it will be a killing Western." Meanwhile, wrote the irate viewer, "the children where I board won't look at anything else."

In 1954 a Senate subcommittee on juvenile delinquency heard testimony that grammar school children spent twenty-two to twenty-seven hours a week facing the set. The senators also saw clips of Western and adventure shows that had regular weekend play. The scenes depicted victims who were shot, knifed, drowned, electrocuted, burned, and buried alive.

Mrs. Clara S. Logan, president of the National Association for Better Radio and Television, told the committee members that "crime and violence are dominating factors in approximately 40 percent of all children's TV programs." Among those shows she singled out as "objectional" were *Captain Midnight, Dick Tracy, The Bowery Boys* movies, and the weeknight series *Captain Video and His Video Rangers.*

Al Hodge, famous for his Captain Video portrayal, appeared at the hearings wearing his civvies and blasted off a volley aimed at short-circuiting Logan and other foes.

Surprisingly, an indication of the real impact TV was having on society could be measured not by the distinguished senatorial session but by the awe the congressmen bestowed on the country's most revered pre-Sputnik astronaut.

Captain Midnight, *testified the National Association for Better Radio and Television at the 1954 Senate juvenile delinquency hearings, was one of TV's most "objectionable" programs. Children made the adventure show a hit.*

The senators consistently addressed the star by his television title, Captain Video.

"Captain," asked Senator Robert C. Hendrickson, chairman of the subcommittee, "in your show would you stomp on somebody's hand?"

"No," testified the DuMont network star.[2] Furthermore, he said, Video Rangers always kept their stun guns holstered unless they needed to get the drop on a dangerous alien. And villains once captured, he added, were then brainwashed of their evil and nefarious ways at "rehabilitation centers."

Hendrickson was respectful but unmoved. Following testimony from Hodge and network officials the chairman proposed that the government appoint a "TV czar" who would be charged with dictating appropriate viewing habits and arresting crime, science fiction, or Western programs that might tend to foster juvenile delinquency.

Senator Estes Kefauver made a similar recommendation in August 1955 at the conclusion of the Senate's crime investigations. He admitted he had "been unable to gather proof of a direct causal relationship between the viewing of acts of crime and violence and the actual performance of criminal deeds." However, he nonetheless proposed the creation of local "Citizens Councils" comprised of "sober, unbiased adults" who would maintain a "steady watch over the programs offered to children and properly report offensive material to responsible sources."

Such autocratic TV generals or video vigilantes never took command. But in 1955 a research group, the Children's Program Review Committee formed by NBC, suggested that the TV industry itself clean house. Dr. Frances Horwich, host of *Ding Dong School*, Mildred MacAfee Horton, former head of Wellesley College, and Dr. Robert M. Goldenson, a family-relations expert, spent four months viewing Saturday

2. DuMont was a television network administered from New York flagship station WABD (now WNEW-TV). Network service began in 1946, although WABD signed on two years earlier. The East Coast hookup initially included Washington, D.C.–owned and operated station WTTG and part-time affiliation with outlets in Schenectady, New York, and Philadelphia. Founder of the system was engineer Dr. Allen B. DuMont, who developed and manufactured the first all-electronic TV sets at his New Jersey laboratory. DuMont marketed fourteen-inch home TV sets as early as 1938.

Since DuMont did not own the maximum number of stations allowed by the FCC (five VHF stations), the network was at a competitive disadvantage. NBC, CBS, and ABC began controlling audiences, and in 1955 the DuMont Network folded. For a time a few old DuMont shows, such as *Captain Video*, continued on WABD, but television's fourth network never really had either the resources or the national saturation to survive.

Congressmen viewed DuMont's Captain Video *as violent. In 1954 actor Al Hodge countered that his low-budget science fiction series was less interested in star wars than in teaching international cooperation.*

morning shows. At the end of the study period the committee issued a critical report that deplored TV for depicting action that would be forbidden at home. The committee members flagged property destruction and seltzer-water squirting. They also complained that the medium offered airtime to TV characters who used bad grammar and regularly telecast programs that overemphasized money and crudeness.

Over the years other studies have claimed that TV has contributed more directly to creating a violent nation. For example, the marked increase in handgun sales, particularly Colt's Buntline Special Single Action .45, were linked to the popularity of Westerns.

Dr. Frances Horwich, host of NBC's Ding Dong School, *also headed a 1955 network committee that determined TV could teach children bad lessons not otherwise permitted in the home.*

"Those guns were first made in the 1870s," Colt's director of development, L. R. Knaver, told *Variety* in 1958. "But there's a tremendous resurgence of interest in the weapons today created largely by the TV series depicting life in the old West."

Similarly, Lee Kuluvar, a Minnesota conservation department firearms and safety coordinator, noted a 700 percent rise in the state's handgun accidents in the five-year period between 1953 and 1958. The cause, he stated: America's affair with the TV Western and its "quick draw" practices.

"Westerns have had a decided effect on firearms production," added Fred A. Roff, Jr., vice-president of Colt's Patent Firearms, during a 1958 Washington radio interview. He indicated that the demand for Western-type guns had stepped up manufacturing to a modern record of ten thousand per month. Roff estimated that by the time the average male youngster reached his teens, he had played with fifteen to twenty replica guns. However, the Colt executive insisted that "Western TV shows, as Western movies, should be judged not on the fact that guns are employed, but on whether the basic plot is one that brings the Golden Rule out convincingly to youngsters who are watching it."

In 1959 the private activist group the National Association for Better Radio and Television took a different stand. Gunplay does adversely affect young viewers, they argued. "Seeing constant brutality results in hardness, intense selfishness, even in mercilessness," the association charged in a complaint entitled "Fifteen Reasons Why Crime-Westerns Are Not Acceptable TV Fare for Children."

Law enforcement officials had long agreed. Police chiefs of Boston, New Haven, and other cities told Senate investigators in 1955 that many young offenders in custody claimed that TV had taught them how to fight, steal, and even kill.

Newspaper headlines supported the assertion. In 1958 two Oklahoma brothers aged ten and twelve robbed and murdered a local grocer and his helper. Once apprehended, they gave television credit for their expertise.

In the mid-1950s, *Newsweek* reported that two Maryland sixteen-year-olds translated a television extortion plan to real life and attempted to steal $30,000 from a businessman. In California a twelve-year-old was found hanging from

TV Competitions

Sports helped put television in the win column, and television helped keep many sports in the black.

The profitable relationship between the medium and the athlete began on May 17, 1939, when NBC focused a single camera on Bakers Field and televised a Columbia-Princeton baseball game. Seven years later NBC added a few cameras to its remote truck and telecast the Joe Louis–Billy Conn heavyweight championship fight. *The Washington Post* seemed more impressed with the video coverage than the match and observed, "Television looks good for a 1,000 year run."

As technology improved, years progressed, and the TV day expanded, sports shows competed during most time slots. Local stations kept kids off the streets and put them into the alleys with weekend-afternoon bowling programs. Networks heard the ring of silver and gold from nightly prime time boxing sales.

Yet, if adults got the best sports programming available—the World Series, the Kentucky Derby, and prizefights—then television gave children the leftovers—rinky-dink roller derbies and wrestling matches with ringers.

Saturday morning became a dumping ground for both these "sports." The contests, carried live, on film, and, later, on videotape, pitted athletic gladiators against each other, while Roman-like children watched with glee.

The roller derbies, a dizzy blur of violence on a track 142 feet by 74 feet was a hit by 1949. Skaters who had half their teeth missing and a good many broken bones were turned into national figures. Likewise wrestlers, with mushy gray-matter where their brains had once been, were heroes to millions of youngsters.

The shows were fast-paced, action-packed, and often preplanned. The Saturday wrestling bouts and roller contests were TV shows, not sporting events. And like other kidvid, they had good guys and bad guys, heroes and villains.

The wrestlers had more steps than Nureyev, more theatrical expressions than Lon Chaney. The roller skaters, meanwhile, often preplanned the games. Such "strategy" was calculated to make viewers as anxious about these shows as they were when a nefarious gunman got the drop on Roy Rogers. Surprisingly, the programs even outdrew the King of the Cowboys, lasting in syndication through the present.

a motel shower, apparently trying to reenact the gruesome details of a TV horror program. In 1977 *The New York Times* printed an interview with a Chicago physician who reported he had treated two children who had jumped off a roof playing Batman. Another counselor said he was seeing a youngster who set his house on fire after viewing an arson incident on TV.

Perhaps the most notorious cases of TV's alleged deadly potential came to light with news of a brutal rape of a San Francisco girl in 1974 after broadcast of the NBC TV-movie, *Born Innocent*, and the murder of a Miami woman by a Florida youth who claimed he was a victim of "involuntary television intoxication."

In both recent court cases television was placed on trial as much as the criminal defendants. Even though the medium was cleared of any direct responsibility, some broadcasters acknowledged the "possiblity" that TV programs could adversely affect youngsters.

Traditionally, however, it's been educators, not attorneys, who have raised the loudest, most effective voices against TV. Long before college-board scores began their plunge in 1964, teachers and administrators, alarmed that turned-on households might be turning off students, fiercely fought the encroachment of TV. Protest began marshaling as early as 1949, when Clifton, New Jersey, elementary school principal Charles M. Sheehan observed what he termed "television profile." He said the malady was easy to detect. Pupils who eyed too much TV couldn't hold their heads up.

The school official stated that on one hand the despised invention caused a decline in school grades; on the other hand it offered a welcomed elixir for teachers with problem students. "Last year at this time," Sheehan told *Newsweek*, "there were but two failures in one class. This year, in the same class there are 30." He further determined that almost all of the failures had TV sets in their homes. Notably, however, none of the below-average students offered the discipline problems they had in the past, he added. They were too tired to be rambunctious.

In 1958 a suburban Buffalo, New York, school administrator had determined that children were devoting equal time to school and television—twenty-seven and a half hours a week. What's more, of the elementary-age students surveyed in the Synder, New York, school system, 51 percent stated they would choose a parental spanking to a TV blackout of their favorite program. "Television," said the educator, "is changing American children from irresistible forces into immovable objects."

Twenty years later the same point was argued by Edward R. Stone, headmaster of Kimberton Farms School near Phoenixville, Pennsylvania. Stone said that students appeared more interested in programs than syllabuses and were more likely to memorize commercials than multiplication tables. "He is tired," Stone said of the young TV-viewer. "His eyes have a staring quality, not lively; he is either apathetic or hyperactive, each in the extreme."

As television antennas replaced weather vanes as the most prominent object above the nations's houses, concern about TV's effects on children intensified. In time the spurious accusations gradually gave way to credible arguments, and the sycophants lost ground to the sociologists.

Now in this third generation of TV viewing it is the extent of harmful influence, not the question of TV's existence, that is at issue. Today, the critical view is primarily narrowed to three subjects: gratuitous violence, sexual stereotyping, and Saturday morning commercials.

Research in these areas, however, can no longer be conducted effectively by lone but committed citizens, such as the disgruntled Bergenfield, New Jersey, teacher and her contemporaries who scribbled their notes onto 3 by 5 cards. The fight of the 1980s is waged by national special-interest groups that must now feed their complicated data into computer memory circuits. Yet most parents and children today are unconcerned about TV's influence on their lives. They simply enjoy watching it and leave the worrying to others. The apathy is not particularly new. In 1949, *Parents' Magazine* predicted that "TV would be a real asset in every home . . . parents will wonder how they got along without television."

And in 1950, Dr. Elizabeth Hurlock argued in the American Medical Association's magazine, *Today's Health*, that all the bother about the new medium was unnecessary. Fear not, she said. TV is merely "a new toy, and its novelty will wear off."

Tested Patterns

Television was a hungry young monster, devouring material as it grew, ever expanding to earlier time-periods as it became fatter.

The Saturday lineup initially began midday or later. However, as more families connected their sets in the late 1940s and early 1950s, stations reached for whatever programming they could quickly beg, borrow, barter, or buy.

Quite reasonably, programmers stocked up on old movie serials, "B" Westerns, and parlor comedies, some of which cost as little as $5 or $10 per showing. Saturday TV listings across the country read like a catalog of Republic, Monogram, and Columbia pictures. Quality mattered little in those days. Broadcasters, rarely discriminating between good and bad, scrounged for shows to fill the available space. Old movie serials made a natural choice.

While DuMont telecast Gene Autry's fifteen-year-old science-fiction Western *The Phantom*

Our Gang—TV's Little Rascals—from left: *Carl (Alfalfa) Switzer, Billy (Buckwheat) Thomas, George (Spanky) McFarland, Darla Hood, Eugene (Porky) Lee, and Baby Patsy May.*

from the collection of Alice and Leonard Maltin

Charley Chase and Muriel Evans in the 1933 comedy short Nature in the Wrong. *Charley discovers he's a descendant of Tarzan.*

Empire in the fall of 1950, local stations scheduled tales of crime-buster Dick Tracy perilously clinging to life on a parachute; rocket ace Flash Gordon defending Earth from the ravages of Ming; secret agent Blackhawk fighting the mob; and aerial adventurer Tailspin Tommy swooping out of the clouds to defeat sinister foreign spies. It was all reprocessed action; all previously shown in movie theaters; and all sold to this airborne medium for bargain-basement prices.

King Features wisely realized that if they owned the serials that were most in demand, they could control the syndication market. In a complicated $250,000 deal involving two other syndicators, Flamingo Films and Filmcraft, Inc., King released four old serials to more than twenty-five TV stations in November 1949. Included in the package were *Don Winslow of the Coast Guard*, *Don Winslow of the Navy*, *Red Barry*, and *Ace Drummond*.

When stations inevitably started exhausting the serial supply and the audience predictably tired of reruns, there were still other ingenious entrepreneurs like Art Gross from New York's Guild Films, ready with viable alternatives. Gross bought cheap feature films and forgotten serials, recut them into twelve or fifteen segments and shot new openings and cliff-hanger endings that he edited to the episodes. He then released these reconstructed stories to local TV stations.

Guild Films reworked the Western adventure *Sign of the Wolf* with King the Wonder Dog, *Trail of the Royal Mounted* featuring Chief

Lash LaRue usually fought his way through ambushes and range wars. But there were friendlier times for this cowboy in The Daltons' Women, *one of many Westerns repeated on TV Saturday mornings. Fuzzy St. John and Pamela Blake costarred.*

from the collection of Alice and Leonard Maltin

The 1940 Three Stooges comedy, You Natzy Spy*—a Hitler spoof set in Moronica—an early TV repeat.*

The films of Oliver Hardy and Stan Laurel were released to TV without the comedians receiving any residuals or having control over cuts. Their humor here is not over TV but over a 1935 publicity photo for Sunday newspaper comics.

White-Cloud, and *King of the Bull Whip* starring Western hero Lash LaRue.

Comedy shorts were also a natural for TV. For years children had laughed at the antics of Charley Chase and Leon Errol during their Saturday afternoon jaunts to the Bijou. Why not provide the same opportunity for a new generation on Saturday morning?

One of the first acts to benefit from this economic rebirth was the Three Stooges. In October 1949, ABC bought exclusive rights to thirty of the Stooges' early Columbia releases. Ten years later, 85 stations carried the 194 Stooges comedies produced between 1933 and 1958. The trio, at various times was comprised of Moe Howard, Larry Fine, Joe DeRita, Joe Besser, Curly Howard, and Shemp Howard, began a second career in feature films and the nightclub circuit.

In contrast to the Three Stooges TV sales, Charlie Chaplin's shorts were never the moneymakers on television that they had been in the theaters. First of all, the subtleties of Chaplin's humor and the grace of his movements were lost on TV. Second, Chaplin's silent comedy seemed uncomfortably out of place in a medium that was screaming with sound. And third, Chaplin's liberal politics in an increasingly conservative country made him a bad financial risk for black and white TV stations operating close to the red. New York TV station WPIX was one of the first outlets to cancel a Chaplin film contract under pressure. It acted with dispatch in 1950 after receiving a letter from the Hudson

County, New Jersey, branch of the Catholic War Veterans. The organization's commander urged WPIX executives to "withdraw the series." He said the comedian had "definite Communist leanings," and he shouldn't be held in esteem as "an idol to the American public."

"It makes no difference if the pictures were made five, ten or twenty or more years ago," the Catholic War Veterans' regional leader stated. "Entertainment for art's sake just does not exist when you talk about Communism."

Although the allegations against Chaplin were untrue and merely a testament to the blacklisting rage that was spreading across the country, WPIX program manager Warren Wade reportedly canceled the Chaplin pictures hours after receiving the protest letter. The series aired only one week and was replaced by a show featuring baseball slugger Jackie Robinson.

Similar action followed across the country, and it wasn't until 1955 that *Variety* declared that Chaplin was again becoming a safe purchase for Saturday mornings. The trade magazine acknowledged that Chaplin's "political question lingers," but considering the number of requests for his early one- and two-reel comedies, it hoped stations would "distinguish between pre-political Chaplin and the later reputation, particularly since Chaplin received no money from TV sales of the shorts."

Certainly less controversial than Chaplin and consequently more profitable than his early pictures were the Our Gang comedies, which began appearing on television in 1954. First syndicator for the Hal Roach comedies was Interstate TV. The company acquired the television rights to ninety-two of the popular shorts. Ten were early silents, the balance of the one-reelers in the package had sound. Another fifty-two Our Gang episodes were purchased the following year by Onyx Pictures.

In what can best be termed a furious selling-war, Interstate and Onyx battled for the upper hand in the market. But both companies quickly discovered that stations, impressed with the high ratings (upward of 40 and 50 percent of the TV audience in some areas), gladly bought from both distributors, thus preventing a competing station from broadcasting Our Gang in the same city.

By mid-1955 the shorts were seen in sixty-one cities. WPIX telecast them every day in New York. In St. Louis the old juvenile comedies outrated all three competing programs combined. And according to a report in *Time*, Our Gang was number one in Detroit, Cleveland, and Los Angeles and a favorite of adults as much as kids.

Time attributed Our Gang's success to the films' lighthearted, whimsical, stars. "They are good kids without being goody-goody," *Time* stated. "They have a genius for getting into jams, but are ingenious for getting out. They may build a gang-sized hook and ladder, charge downhill in it and fling sky-high all pedestrians along the way. They may start a war, but nobody really gets hurt. The custard pies fly in a multitude of directions, but at the end, the warriors are apt to be licking meringue rather than their wounds."

Spanky and his gang were reported to never have received a dollar's worth of residual pay from the hundreds of thousands flowing between the TV stations and distributors. The youngsters had earned their day's pay decades earlier with no mind toward a medium that had yet to be fully developed. Even the older comedians, who enjoyed TV-renewed popularity, usually shared little or none of the take.

Stan Laurel complained about the situation to a *TV Guide* reporter in 1954. He argued that the rules regarding television sales were patently unfair to the performers. "We made all the films on salary," he recalled, "and everybody figured the life of a movie then was five years. It's a little disturbing to see ourselves on TV now. We're being used to sell products we never even heard of, and someone else is making all the money."

John McCabe, author of *Mr. Laurel and Mr. Hardy* (New American Library, Inc. 1968) also gave space to Stan Laurel's rage. "Look at that!" Laurel told McCabe when a commercial interrupted a broadcast of a Laurel and Hardy short. "That's why I hardly watch our pictures anymore. It upsets me so damned much to see how they turn the plot of our pictures into a hash. We worked so carefully to get the sequences of action just right in the editing process, and then some idiotic fool comes along and cuts the film up in big chunks just to squeeze in a mess of advertising.

"Continuity, establishing shots—most of them gone," he continued. "The pictures just don't

Another Situation

Saturday morning has traditionally been a last resort for sitcom reruns, not a home for original comedy. Occasionally new situation comedies have debuted in the children's ghetto. However, broadcasters have long realized that since youngsters will laugh at anything reasonably funny, the cheapest laugh remains the repeat or the cartoon.

There was a dramatic exception to this comedy rule. ABC found fa-

Above: In 1976, The Monster Squad—*Bruce Wolfman (Buck Kartalian), Dracula (Henry Polic II), and Frankenstein (Michael Lane)—scared up viewers for the NBC sitcom.*

Right: The Kids from C.A.P.E.R. (left to right: *Biff Warren, John Lansing, Cosie Costa, and Steve Bonimo) fought crime while Bob Lussier and Robert Emhardt* (rear, left and right) *played a TV reporter and a police chief in the 1976 NBC production.*

vor with the radio sitcom *A Date With Judy* when it premiered on Saturday morning, June 2, 1951. The series moved to prime time on July 10, 1952. Pat Crowley first starred as teen-ager Judy Foster. When the show reappeared on Thursday nights, Mary Linn Beller portrayed the bouncy bobby-soxer.

Judy was not the only Saturday date attracting young audiences in 1951. *Two Girls Named Smith,* the story of small-town sisters trying to make out in New York, aired on ABC from January 20 to October 31 and actually starred two girls named Peggy—Peggy Ann Garner and Peggy French.

Reruns began crowding out new sitcoms in 1954.

The Campbell Soup Company was so convinced, in fact, that *The Abbott and Costello Show* would have a renewed life during kidvid hours that it proposed a contract with the comedians that specified that local stations had to air the syndicated version before 6:00 P.M. on Saturdays to prevent it from competing with the nighttime broadcast. Outlets were obliging, for in 1954 the show was a cross-country favorite, virtually attracting all the young viewers when it aired in such cities as Minneapolis, at 9:30 A.M., Davenport, Iowa, at 10:30 A.M., and Syracuse, New York, at 11:30 A.M.

Other stations had no difficulty winning fans in 1954 and 1955 with repeats of *Colonel Humphrey Flack,* a series starring Alan Mowbray as an amiable conman and Frank Jenks as his trusted aide.

December Bride and *I Married Joan* had many happy returns in Saturday syndication in the mid-1950s. *Amos 'n' Andy* had a discriminating following among children, while *Blondie* had fun in 1958 repeats and *The Life of Riley* thrived.

The Aldrich Family was often visited, and *Tugboat Annie*

A comedy of errors—the oddball 1977 CBS series Wacko *that failed to make viewers laugh and CBS executives happy. Charles Fleischer, Bo Kaprall, and Julie McWhirter starred in the slapstick production.*

Left: Pat Crowley and Jimmy Sommers on the 1951 Saturday morning sitcom A Date with Judy.

chugged along each Saturday in dozens of markets.

Phyllis Coates, Superman's first TV Lois Lane, turned in her typewriter for the dishwasher and played the mother of a nine-year-old on *This Is Alice.* The 1958 syndicated series costarred Patty Ann Gerrity as Alice Holliday.

TV executives invited *Dennis the Menace* to tear into the Saturday schedule in 1963 and decided that whenever cartoons couldn't succeed, they'd leave *Leave It to Beaver* reruns to do the job.

In the 1960s, UHF stations reran *I Love Lucy* until children hated her and made *My Little Margie* a big star.

Responding to pressure in the next decade to drop violent cartoons, the three networks tried again to build a schedule on original situation comedies. *Far Out Space Nuts* cracked the CBS lineup in 1975 with Chuck McCann and Bob Denver playing two food-loaders who are catapulted into space when they push a button marked "launch," thinking it said "lunch."

Lancelot Link, Secret Chimp, an undercover agent who operated in a furry world populated by talking chimps, monkeyed around in 1970. Eighteen real chimps appeared in the show. In 1976, one man in a gorilla costume teamed up with *F Troop* veterans Larry Storch and Forrest Tucker to form the trio of Spenser, Tracy, and Kong, better known as *The Ghost Busters.*

The spook-hunters merely needed to tune to NBC the same year and catch *McDuff,* a hundred-year-old sheepdog ghost, visible to the veterinarian whose office he haunted.

Since *The Man From U.N.C.L.E.* had been a relative success, NBC believed *The Kids from C.A.P.E.R.* would inherit the following. The 1976 Saturday morning comedy, coproduced by Alan Landsburg and Don Kirshner, featured four young boys who formed the "Civilian Authority for the Protection of Everyone—Regardless." The police unit started more trouble than it finished, however.

Dracula was battier than ever when NBC aired the 1976 comedy *The Monster Squad.* Frankenstein and Bruce Wolfman joined the vampire to fight crime from their wax-museum headquarters.

Another network character had a personality problem. Forty-five-year-old schoolteacher John Martin (Herb Edelman) drank from the fabled Fountain of Youth and thereafter kept reverting back and forth between his own age and that of a twelve-year-old (Robbie Rist) in NBC's *Big John, Little John* (1976).

Meanwhile, Kaptain Kool and the Kongs were kings of *The Krofft Supershow,* a 1976 live-action comedy-adventure series that also aired comic episodes of "Wonderbug," "Big Foot and Wild Boy," and "Magic Mongo."

Two years later CBS revitalized slapstick with *Wacko.* The energetic series was paced so fast, however, that it zoomed past its hyper audience and right off the network by the year's end.

More recently broadcasters have turned back the clocks and returned to reruns and cartoons. Since today's advertisers on *Happy Days, Mork and Mindy,* and *Diff'rent Strokes* count youngsters as greedily as they do teens and middle-aged women, it is unlikely that television will again make the creative choice—but the economic mistake—of 1951 and 1976, and enthusiastically produce sure-fail sitcoms specifically for Saturday morning.

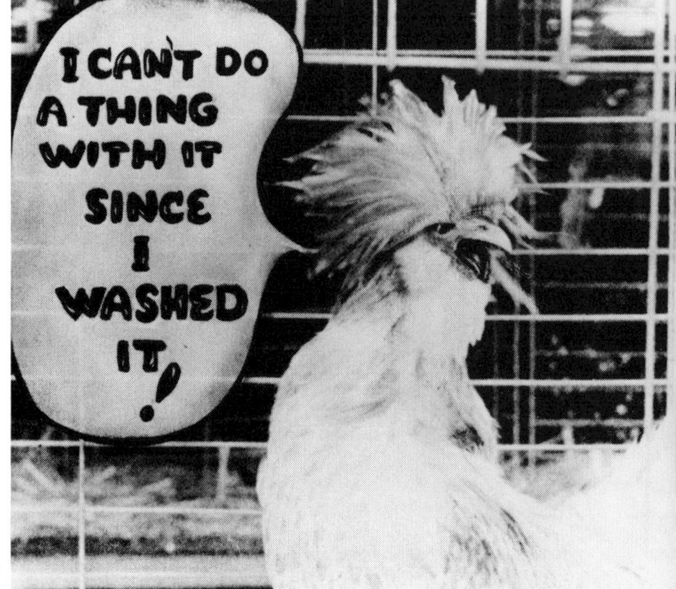

Jerry Fairbanks's Speaking of Animals *film shorts were a regular Saturday morning filler for TV stations in the 1950s. The ballooned sayings have been drawn in by Fairbanks's production company to indicate what the animals said on film.*

make sense on television. I'd rather they'd show them entirely or not at all. That's why I don't look at us much. Why see a lot of good work turned into a jigsaw puzzle? I'd even be willing to edit them for nothing, but I know they don't care."

Nearly all of the Laurel and Hardy films were sold to TV. Besides the legitimate films, ten- to fifteen-minute sequences were cut from larger films and released under bogus titles.

To recoup some of the money available from the medium, the pair talked of producing their own TV series. "We're definitely planning a TV show," Laurel stated in the *TV Guide* interview. "But it won't be live. We made a hit in the movies because our pace made slapstick funny. Instead of just hitting someone in the face with a pie, we slowed down and showed our reactions. Reactions make slapstick funny. For that you need film."

In 1955, Laurel and Hardy began negotiating with Hal Roach, Jr., son of the famed movie mogul, and NBC for two ninety-minute color specials. John McCabe wrote that the shows were to be done in the best tradition of the team's old comedies. The programs never materialized, however. Ten days before shooting was to commence, Stan Laurel suffered a stroke.

In time Oliver Hardy also took ill. He dropped from 300 to 185 pounds, then had a crippling stroke that left him without speech and movement. Hardy died in 1957.

In the early 1960s, cartoon producer Larry

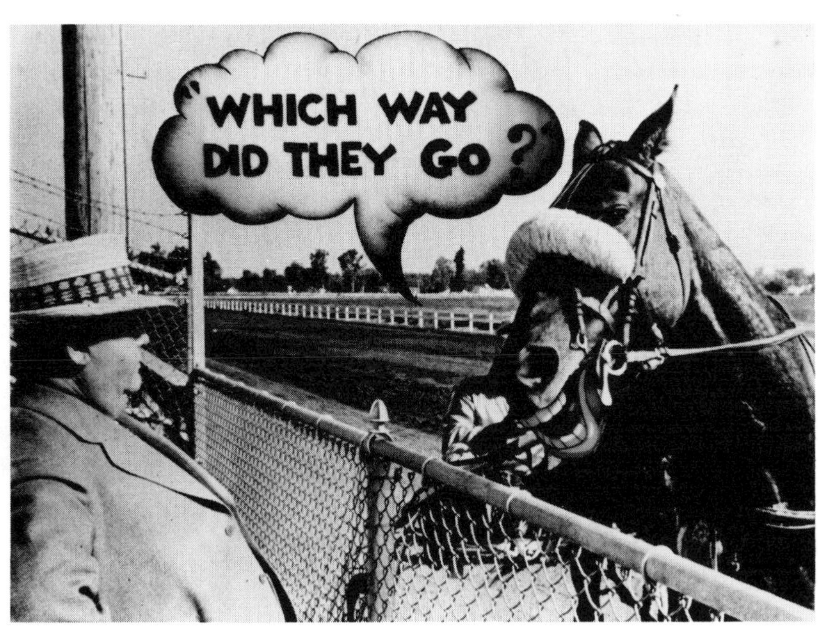

Harmon secured permission from both Hardy's widow and Stan Laurel to create a Laurel and Hardy cartoon series for Saturday morning television. The series finally aired in 1966, one year after Stan Laurel's death.

Thanks to movie producer Jerry Fairbanks, many TV stations filled their film libraries with live stock—to be more precise, Fairbanks's Academy Award–winning comedy series, *Speaking of Animals*. The fifty ten-minute-long shorts, shot at Paramount Studios from 1941 to 1950, pictured jabbering animals commenting on life.

The comedies were as much a hit on TV as they were in the movies. The reason? "Animals aren't dated," Fairbanks argues a full forty years after his first series was made. "They wear the same costumes."

Fairbanks, who took an Oscar in the early 1940s for his short, *Cow Cow Boogie*, says that the process of combining the live action of the animals on film with their animated mouths was a staggering technical challenge. To accomplish the impossible mission, Fairbanks used a modified rear-screen projection process in tandem with a rotoscope system. "Rotoscoping," Fairbanks explains, "is a method by which the mouths of the animals were replaced by semi-animated human mouths. We would film live actors such as Mel Blanc and Sterling Holloway in black face with their lips painted white. That way we could have just their lip movements visible on film. The images were then traced frame by frame, reshot as animation that in turn was matted into the actual animal footage.

"It was a rather tedious and long operation," Fairbanks remembers. "We wanted it to look realistic, not just like some of the talking animal shorts where a voice is simply dubbed in while the animal is chewing his cud. We had a credo. When the rotoscope was finished, we had to be able to lip read the words without sound."

Fairbanks, known for other film productions at Paramount including *The Popular Science Series*, *Unusual Occupations*, and *Strange As It Seems*, contributed more to TV than just his old shorts. Fairbanks designed the three-camera film camera shooting technique, the backbone of situation comedy production from *I Love Lucy* to *Mork and Mindy*, and contributed to the development of the medium's first zoom lens, which he patented as "*Zoomar*™." Fairbanks also produced three of TV's earliest film shows, *Public Prosecutor*, *Front Page Detective*, and *Hollywood Theater Time*.

In the late 1940s he edited his *Unusual Occupations* films into the TV-filler, *Television Close-up*, and recut a dated Paramount travelogue into twenty-six ten-minute films called *Going Places with Uncle George*, both of which were released to stations. Perhaps his most famous TV production, however, was the medium's first made-for-TV cartoon, *Crusader Rabbit*.

In addition to all his network chores, Fairbanks used his *Speaking of Animals* process in TV commercials, most notably ads for Clark Bar candies. He had similarly been hired to animate a talking animal sequence in the Hope-Crosby feature film, *Road to Morocco*.

Local TV stations went to the bank with Fairbanks's barnyard. They also built audiences, ratings, and commercial sales on George Pal's Puppetoons. The fanciful puppet-cartoons, produced at Paramount from 1941 to 1947, like *Speaking of Animals*, were handcrafted films.

Rather than animating characters on motion picture stock, however, Pal used a stop-motion technique, moving puppets ever so slightly for each frame of film shot. The animation procedure took up to four and a half months to complete each eight-minute fable.

The most famous and most misunderstood Puppetoon starred Jasper, a wide-eyed black character whom Pal intended as a tribute to black culture and ethnic folk tales. Charges of racism cut into TV sales, however, and the fourteen Jasper stories met with mixed video reception. Pal, producer of *When Worlds Collide* and *The Time Machine*, returned to his first love in 1971 to shoot a special Puppetoon—*Tool Box*, featuring woodworking tools choreographed as a ballet—for Chuck Jones's Saturday morning ABC series, *Curiosity Shop*.

During the early days of TV, Hollywood ignored the small-town medium and only tolerated the New York–based networks. Yet, as theater attendance began to dwindle, film companies realized that business deals with the enemy might temporarily help their cash-flow problems.

Columbia Pictures was one of the first studios to turn on to TV profits. In 1954 the studio sold Hygo Corporation the rights to about twenty "B" Westerns and 50 single-reelers, including a number of once popular "Wild Bill" Elliott features. Columbia executives maintained that the films had long since outlived their theatrical value. The TV sales were pure gravy.

Within a year nearly all the other movie studios took a serious look at the films they, too, had considered outdated. Republic consequently released a block of 27 films, called The Diamond Group, comprised of the low-budget facility's most expensive projects. Another 20 titles followed shortly thereafter. Meanwhile, Universal assembled a package of 97 Tom Mix, Rod Cameron, and Buck Jones Westerns. And Warner Brothers added another 600 films to the growing rental list. RKO unloaded its library of 470 features to C&C Super Corporation for $15,200,000.

Sensing that perhaps there could be even more money made in direct rentals to stations than sales to distributors, Columbia decided to release all remaining films through its subsidiary Screen Gems. Republic followed Columbia's example. Through its subsidiary, Hollywood Television Service, the studio offered 76 additional John Wayne, Susan Hayward, Claire Trevor, and Vera Hruba Ralston pictures. The total library was valued at $40,000,000 in potential rentals.

Variety reported that Republic had been holding back these "better" films until Columbia and RKO announced their marketing strategies. The films, often cut down to allow for commercial time, helped fill NBC's 1956–57 Saturday and Sunday series *Cowboy Theatre*, hosted by Monty Hall.

Not all viewers were going "great guns" over the Westerns, however. Senator Robert C. Hendrickson complained in 1954 that when the old cowboy films were trimmed, the tamer scenes were eliminated and the violent, objectionable material was emphasized. He demanded that villainous characters be corralled, but the Congressman couldn't overtake the hard-riding Western characters. They had already laid claim to the children's market.

While the country was stockpiling nuclear arms in preparation for a potential atomic battle, television was primarily concerned with range wars in the old West. Twentieth-century bombers

Children's Radio Shows Transferred to Saturday Morning Television (and Vice Versa)

The Abbott and Costello Show
The Adventures of Rin Tin Tin
The Adventures of Superman
Amos 'n' Andy
The Archie Show
Boston Blackie
Buck Rogers in the 25th Century
Captain Midnight
The Cisco Kid
A Date with Judy
Death Valley Days
Dick Tracy
Doctor Dolittle
Don Winslow of the Navy
Dragnet
Fantastic Four
Father Knows Best
Flash Gordon
The Gene Autry Show
The Green Hornet
Hopalong Cassidy
The Joe Palooka Story
Jump, Jump
Juvenile Jury
Land of the Lost
Lassie
The Lone Ranger
Mandrake the Magician
My Little Margie
Our Miss Brooks
Paul Winchell and Jerry Mahoney
Popeye the Sailor
Red Ryder
Renfrew of the Royal Mounted
Rootie Kazootie
The Roy Rogers Show
Sergeant Preston of the Yukon
Sky King
Smilin' Ed's Gang
Space Patrol
Tales of the Texas Rangers
Tarzan
Terry and the Pirates
Tom Corbett, Space Cadet
Wild Bill Hickok

flew overhead, but Saturday morning audiences turned to stories of nineteenth-century sodbusters and gun-toting, guitar-strumming cowpokes.

Good guys like "Wild Bill" Elliott, Red Ryder, Sunset Carson, Bob Livingston, John Wayne, Hoot Gibson, and Ken Maynard never fired first, yet they always won. They rarely killed sneering, leering opponents; they merely incapacitated them by expertly shooting the pistols out of their hands, thus leaving formal punishment to the law. *TV Guide* noted in a mid-1950s article that such Westerns, "never big money makers in movie houses, became the sensation of television."[1]

Bill German, a sales representative for Republic's Hollywood TV Service, told the magazine that all cowboy films had a tremendous "residual value" because of the constant audience turnover.

Perhaps no one realized that fact better than former silent star-turned-soft-spoken Western hero, William Boyd—more formally known around TV parts as Hopalong Cassidy.

In mid-1948, Boyd began shooting his theatrical movies with television in focus. The nineteenth-century character was thinking for the future. Producer Cassidy asked his writers to build cliff-hanging climaxes into the features every twelve and a half minutes so commercials could be conveniently inserted once the pictures appeared on TV.

Simultaneously, Boyd initiated negotiations with United Artists to buy back his movies, many of them fourteen years old, in order to control their television release.

After an agreement was reached the Hoppy Westerns began appearing on TV in late 1948. The movies captivated new audiences every week

1. Westerns were eventually a top market attraction, but considering the abbreviated broadcast schedule in TV's infancy, cowboys were not always a winning draw. In June 1949 executives at New York's ABC station, WJZ (now WABC), feared that it was more likely children would be outside playing between 5:00 and 7:00 P.M. during the summer than watching TV. Westerns were dropped June 13, and "film shorts" geared for older viewers were programmed in their place.

Below: Hopalong Cassidy rounded up giant audiences in 1948 and turned the East Coast–based medium into his personal Western empire.

Opposite: Roy Rogers was lassoed by wife Dale Evans and a Republic Studios contract that for years prevented him from riding onto TV for a weekly series and competing against his own film reruns. A series called Queen of the West *was also planned for Evans in 1950 by Union Television Corporation, though never produced.*

BILL BOYD
HOPALONG CASSIDY

and freed Boyd from ever worrying about money again. Los Angeles station, KTTV, for example, rented one for $250. Twelve months later KTTV repeated the film for the fifth time and paid a rental of $1,000. Not only did Boyd make a bundle from syndication, he signed a 5 percent royalty deal on Hopalong Cassidy children's outfits and toys, and cashed in on hundreds of personal appearances at stores, rodeos, and fairs. Furthermore, Boyd starred in a Mutual Broadcasting network radio show, sold rights to a comic strip, and signed a hefty recording contract. Despite his sudden resurgence in popularity, Boyd initially refused to shoot any Westerns expressly for TV. In June 1949 he argued that a "telepix" series averaging $10,000 per episode wouldn't hold up against his more expensively produced pictures. However, within a few months he drew a pen as fast as he unholstered a six-shooter and signed a fifty-two-show TV deal with NBC.

If William Boyd had a relatively smooth ride to TV success, then Roy Rogers's trip was bumpier than an angry steer. To fans, Rogers might have been the undisputed King of the Cowboys, but as far as Republic Pictures was concerned, he was just another actor they had lassoed with a binding contract.

Rogers wanted to follow Hoppy's happy trails to commercial TV. However, his studio boss, Herbert Yates, shot down his plans, wishing instead to release the Rogers features to television himself. Yates claimed exclusive rights to the movies, adding he could sell the films to television and not even pay the star. Rogers disagreed. Six-guns were never drawn in the fight that ensued, but lawyers carried the battle all the way to the U.S. Supreme Court.

"By 1951, we saw that Hopalong Cassidy was doing big business on TV," remembers Art Rush, Rogers's manager of nearly forty years. "Well, Roy wanted to jump to TV, too. He had been doing radio for Quaker Oats for five years, and the sponsor was pressing us to switch to TV."

But Rush explains that Republic cut Rogers off at the pass. They wouldn't let him out of his contract. He was signed to appear in up to seven films a year, and the studio didn't want a Rogers TV show to compete against their movies at the theater or in any subsequent sales to TV.

Yates had reason to be concerned about Roy Rogers turning from a studio employee to a lone ranger. TV Westerns were eating away at what *Variety* called the "oaters." Columbia had produced fourteen Westerns in 1950. The following year the studio cut down to six. Republic went from nineteen to twelve over the same period, while Monogram cut back from twelve to eight.

"Previously 'B' westerns were considered insurance for studios and always sure to recoup its investments," wrote *Variety* in 1952. But television quickly changed that economic fact of life, and Republic fought for its life, for a time keeping Roy Rogers's name in the newspapers and his face off the TV screen. "When I couldn't deliver Roy to Quaker Oats for TV," Rush states, "they canceled our radio show." Believing that the Republic chief was thoroughly unreasonable, Rush hopped a cross-country train to New York to sell an advertising agency on Rogers's proposed TV series.

"The very morning I arrived, I discovered that Yates had sent telegrams to all the ad companies stating that 57 Roy Rogers films were ready for TV release." Rush was certain that all chances for a TV series were dashed by Republic's surprise maneuver, but one agency became interested in the prospect and signed General Foods as a sponsor for the controversial character. The key to the deal was an escape clause that allowed the contract to be nullified if Rogers's old movies were indeed ever syndicated. The show premiered on NBC in October 1951.

To ensure his deal with General Foods, Rogers sought an injunction against Republic to prevent telecasting of his films. Rogers was convinced he would win a court battle against the studio. His last contract with Republic had, according to manager Art Rush, guaranteed "100 percent rights" to his voice and likeness. Hence he thought his permission was needed for any TV release of his films or commercial tie-ups. The clause was included, Rush states, "because Roy, the number one box office attraction, could build up a TV station just with the use of his name. To my knowledge, no other star had the clause in his contract.[2] Consequently, we won that round hands down. Republic was told by the court that they could not sell Roy's films to TV without his approval."

The Roy Rogers saga might have ended there had it not been for a similar injunction against Republic filed by Western star Gene Autry in November 1951. He lost the case and control of his films, but appealed to the Ninth United States Court of Appeals, the same judicial body that was hearing Republic's appeal on Rogers's lower-court ruling.

Though many circumstances of the Rogers and Autry cases differed, the court decided to hear them together—a maneuver Rush says Rogers never wanted, since the fine print on his contract made his case significantly different from Autry's.

On June 9, 1954, the court rendered a split decision, effectively reversing the previous results and thereby making Republic Pictures the winner in both. One ruling overturned Los Angeles Federal Court Judge Pierson M. Hall's decision that allowed Republic to deal Autry's movies to TV. Wall Street sources told *Variety* that Republic stood to make over $5 million from the decision in immediate TV rentals.

Soon after the ruling was announced, TV stations stampeded for the Rogers and Autry films that Republic had in its stable. The studio prepared eighty-one Rogerses and fifty-seven Autrys for distribution. Thirty-one of the Roy Rogers Westerns were filmed in color, but Republic decided to delay their release for two years, until it was known whether color TV would be available on a large scale.

Understandably, Rogers feared that TV release, color or not, would force General Foods to exercise its escape clause. Autry, in a somewhat parallel situation because his weekly TV show might also compete with his movies, was buoyed by a memo from Leslie Harris of CBS-TV. Harris believed that the court decision wouldn't materially affect either cowboy star. He pointed out that the court decree specified that the films' running times couldn't be cut below fifty-three minutes, nor could the story value be trimmed to the extent where an edit "lessened Autry's stature as an actor." Additionally, stations couldn't edit the films to give the impression that the cowboys endorsed any commercial products during the frequent advertising breaks.

The stipulations prevented Republic from sell-

2. Rogers's contract clause was not the first instance of an individual trying to protect against an unauthorized TV sale. In July 1935, Edna Ferber reportedly refused to sell her novel *Come and Get It* to Samuel Goldwyn unless her contract specified that radio and TV rights were reserved to her.

ing half-hour Autry or Rogers films to compete with the thirty-minute TV shows. Harris thus argued that no competitive threat existed. Noting that distribution of Hopalong Cassidy movies hadn't eroded sales of Hoppy's half-hour TV show, he said, "If anything, release of the features will help sales of the half hour versions."

Autry was still unsure and Rogers feared General Foods' cancellation. The Western stars, convinced that they could win in yet a higher appeal, rode the case to the Supreme Court.

Republic, meanwhile, swamped with requests for the films, kept the movies under lock and key until the final decision was handed down.

Rogers and Autry, anxious for a definitive ruling, filed their brief a week before the August 31, 1954, deadline. Their appeal marked the first instance a TV-related suit reached the country's highest court.

Rebroadcast, Retitled

by Timothy C. Rupp

Old television programs never die, they just fade away . . . or they return in the guise of network and syndicated reruns, revisions, and revivals. An oft-used prescription for these resurrected shows is "Change the title!"

When networks decide to rebroadcast earlier episodes of one of their current prime time programs, they usually seek to limit viewer confusion by changing the title for rebroadcasts at an alternate time. Over the years there have been numerous examples. Young horse-opera fans, for instance, discovered that after the *Gunsmoke* had cleared in Dodge City a rerun *Marshal Dillon* came into view on their television screens, and that farther to the southwest in TV-land the Cartwright family had struck a *Bonanza* and changed their show's rerun brand to that of their ranch, *Ponderosa.* After *Wagon Train* had been pulled into yet another circle around the campfires, it required the brave leadership of *Major Adams, Trailmaster* to move 'em out westward for rerun screening. In an effort to deceive the seemingly ever-present Indians, if not the viewers, about the Major's eventual successor, the show also reran as just plain *Trailmaster.*

Similarly, when earlier episodes of a program went off the network into syndication while later episodes continued to run on the network schedule, a title switch was utilized not only to encourage viewership of both programs, but to avoid, in some instances, possible legal complications. Notable among children's shows was an ingenious and well-trained *Lassie* that gave birth to syndicated *Jeff's Collie, Timmy and Lassie,* and, probably for reasons of equal time, *Lassie and Timmy.* Meanwhile back at the ranch, *Fury* could be found romping in the syndication corral as *Brave Stallion.*

Some programs flickered off the screen seemingly for the last time, only to be resurrected under a new title and with a revised format. In television's early years the fortunes of *Lucky Pup* finally ran out, but the old Bunin hand puppets came to life again in the villainous magic of *Foodini the Great.* The *DuMont Kindergarten* provided mothers with *The TV Babysitter,* who subsequently took her cartoon "Wilmer the Pigeon" along over into *Magic Cottage.* Even the cosmic adventures of Captain Video and his Video Rangers were issued another ID late in their run, but those young viewers who saw through that format change gained access to *The Secret Files of Captain Video.* More than a decade after some brief network play in *The Children's Corner,* one of the most sensitive and enduring reincarnations took place in *Mister Rogers' Neighborhood.*

A move from one network to another might necessitate a format and title change, as was the case when *Harbourmaster* sank at CBS only to float to the surface again on ABC as *Adventures at Scott Island.*

Yet another evolutionary process could be discerned in the metamorphosis of *Time for Beany* and *Matty's Funday Funnies* into *Matty's Funnies with Beany and Cecil,* and at last into simply *Beany and Cecil.*

Sometimes video heroes were linked too closely with certain sponsors, thus necessitating title changes. When *Captain Midnight* was unable to share his Ovaltine with his syndicated clone, it was left to *Jet Jackson, Flying Commando,* his redubbed name on the sound track, to chase down the enemies of America and a new sponsor. Or consider the dilemma of the *Rootie Tootie Club* when the maker of a brown, cylindrical candy rolled out the threat of legal action against that show's title, but some sleight-of-hand puppetry came up with *Rootie Kazootie* as a way out of that sticky mess.

Two significant children's programs underwent title switches in early 1948. The first, which may have been the most popular kids' show ever, came out of New York's variously titled *Puppet Television Theatre* and *Puppet Playhouse.* But soon the program's marionette star had some strings pulled and the title changed to *Howdy Doody.*

Meanwhile, in Chicago an irrepressible troupe of Kuklapolitans demanded more time and attention than they were getting on the multifaceted *Junior Jamboree;* the result of that title transformation was three delightful decades of *Kukla, Fran and Ollie*'s bright and witty entertainment.

Even children's shows had to face the harsh realities of life—and death—as demonstrated with the passing of the beloved leader of *Smilin' Ed's Gang.* But Devine intervention permitted the old Buster Brown show to carry on Saturday mornings as *Andy's Gang.*

Through it all, however, the syndication route has proved to be the means of salvation for those many shows that appeared time and again on America's video screens—with or without title changes. Along the way *King Leonardo and His Short Subjects* were reduced to *The King and Odie,* and *Private Secretary* became familiar enough to young viewers to be introduced as *Susie.* In old England *The Adventures of Robin Hood* took refuge in *Sherwood Forest,* while over in North Africa *Captain Gallant of the Foreign Legion* sought relief from the heat of the Sahara in the relative anonymity of *Foreign Legionnaire.* But two great and enduring heroes, *The Lone Ranger* and *Superman,* still fight on to save the West and Metropolis with titles intact—not to mention the black mask and, occasionally at least, a business suit and a pair of glasses.

On October 18 the United States Supreme Court informed both stars that they were not going to become hog-tied by the legal entanglement. Rogers and Autry were denied a review, thereby leaving the Ninth United States Circuit Court decision standing. Republic was free to syndicate the movies.

The studio surprised many industry observers at this point, leasing the films for three years to MCA-TV instead of its own syndication subsidiary, Hollywood TV Service.

After the decision, Gene Autry gradually pulled out of acting and spent more time directing his Flying A Productions, the company that supplied TV with many popular Saturday shows including *The Range Rider*, *Buffalo Bill, Jr.*, *Annie Oakley*, and *The Adventures of Champion.*

General Foods, meanwhile, did not abandon Rogers. In fact, his 107-episode series continued to be a ratings success for many years. Nonetheless, Rogers was hurt by the ruling. He never appeared in a Hollywood-produced motion picture again. The surefire box-office sensation of the 1940s was unsalable in the 1950s.

"We can't figure it out," recalls Art Rush. "From the minute Roy finished with Republic and went into television, not one studio would take him." Rush was politely told that Westerns were on the decline, and therefore Roy Rogers's old tracks were impossible to follow. However, Rush remains convinced that Rogers's reputation was poisoned by the suit. He's certain that studio conservatism made producers wary that if Rogers took one company to court, he'd do the same with another.

Rogers told an Associated Press reporter in 1959 that the studios were afraid to touch him. "Oh, we've had deals come up and we'd talk to people, but as soon as the negotiations got to the top men, the deals were suddenly dropped. I believe the producers blackballed me because I had the nerve to fight Yates."

"It was one of the cruelest deals any star has ever been dealt," Rush adds. "Roy didn't deserve it."

A Republic lawsuit also kept studio cowboy Gene Autry at bay in the early 1950s.

By the early 1960s the Western boom was in serious decline. Networks were programming more and more cartoons, and independent stations were finding that full-length Westerns were victimized by time. There were individual holdouts, certainly, but overall the second generation of TV viewers plugged into space-age fantasy and abandoned the celebrated cowboy heroes of old. Additionally, many stations replaced Saturday morning Western reruns with never-before telecast and heavily promoted Universal horror classics, including *Dracula*, *The Wolf Man*, and *The Invisible Man.*

And since network TV production was increasing, local stations no longer needed dated celluloid leftovers from the motion picture studio vaults. In time, most of the one-reel comedy shorts, simplistic cliff-hangers, and cowboy adventures disappeared. Saturday morning TV shed its first skin.

3 A World

Howdy, early 1950s

on and off a String

Puppeteers are no dummies. Since 1947 they've realized—just as Jim Henson does today—that children use TV as a looking glass into a more fanciful world than their own. For millions of viewers the thirty-five-year-old magical living room window has provided countless excursions into lands of make-believe where diminutive characters like Howdy Doody, Johnny Jupiter, Lucky Pup, Farfel, and Kermit the Frog have ruled.

In the late 1940s and early 1950s particularly, puppet shows were a children's TV standard. Until the mid-1950s, when broadcasters reasoned that airtime and studio space were becoming too valuable to waste on kids' shows, nearly every local station and each of the four

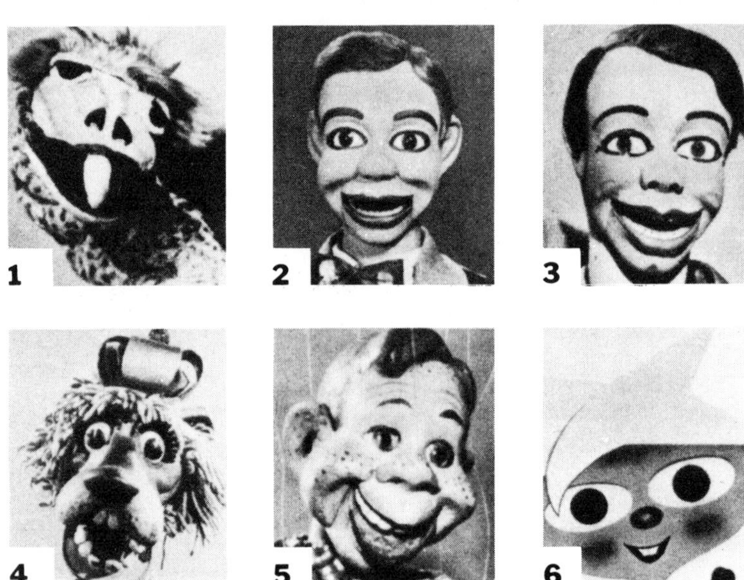

TV's family puppet tree includes five famous practitioners and five famous characters. Match the human with the humanoid. For extra credit, pair the lone cartoon figure with his television father.

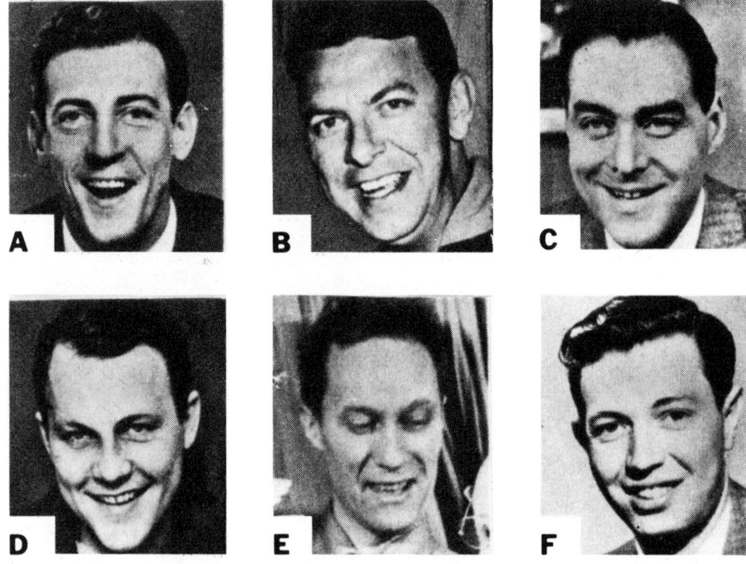

Ollie (1), Kukla's tame dragon, roamed with Burr Tillstrom (D). Jerry Mahoney (2) says words that Paul Winchell (A) puts in his mouth. Puppet-maker Frank Marshall carved Jerry and Danny O'Day (3), but Jimmy Nelson (F) pulls Danny's string. Charlemane the Lion (4) made TV his kingdom under the guidance of Bil Baird (E). Howdy Doody (5) and Buffalo Bob Smith (B) were the biggest stars of children's TV, and Winky Dink (6) called for help from youthful viewers and his TV cohost, Jack Barry (C).

networks tied young viewers to the screen with puppet strings.

As a consequence the most famous behind-the-scenes manipulators of early TV were not network presidents and bluenosed stockholders. They were the fraternity of successful puppeteers, skilled in ventriloquism, writing, comedy, and social commentary. Foremost among these early artists were Burr Tillstrom, Bil and Cora Baird, Hope and Morey Bunin, Paul Winchell, Jimmy Nelson, Paul Ashley, and Shirley Dinsdale. Their work was uniformly appealing without being childish and was almost always live, improvised, and unpredictable.

The shows were usually shot with nothing more than the bare essentials: one camera, one microphone, and a curtain stage tucked in a studio corner. Kukla and Ollie worked in such quarters. So did Buffalo Billy, Uncle Mistletoe, Rootie Kazootie, and scores of other characters.

Youngsters marveled at these puppets, shrunken versions of themselves, thriving in a world of fantasy expanded by the television signal. The characters lived every imaginative adventure a child could conjure. Pint-sized viewers saw pint-sized versions of themselves or the heroes they wanted to be. Children didn't mind if puppeteers chose hand puppets, marionettes, or hardwood dummies. They all had their hour on TV, and most were on Saturday morning.

The first-known TV puppet show aired November 6, 1931, over experimental station W3XK in Wheaton, Maryland. Bernard H. Paul, later a puppeteer on Baltimore station WBAH-TV, brought the marionettes to life on the test broadcast.

Sixteen years later, when puppet shows became the rage, it was time for *Howdy Doody*. From December 27, 1947, to September 24, 1960, the audience revered the show, making it TV's most talked about and loved production. NBC, meanwhile, traded on the audience's early affection, turning the knee-high figure and his real-life sidekick into the industry's best salesmen.

"General Sarnoff, the president of RCA, once said that with the exception of Milton Berle, we were responsible for selling television to the public," says Buffalo Bob Smith.

Howdy Doody contained nothing more exotic than an audience, a puppet stage, and a virtuous tale. Howdy's strings were in full view, his feet clumped awkwardly, his mouth was often out of sync with his voice. The imagery still wasn't destroyed by the ungraceful look. Kids riveted themselves to the set, day after day, growing older, wiser, and more in love with the urban cowboy.

Howdy Doody experienced a quick gestation period and an easy birth. Bob Smith, a Buffalo disc jockey making a name for himself in New York, developed the program after just one meeting with NBC.

"Before we started, the kids had Bob Emery's *Small Fry Club* on DuMont," Smith says. "Emery's show was strictly a limited operation. He used drawings and read letters. There was very little if any real production involved, but it still gave NBC the impetus to come up with something for kids," Smith explains. At the time, Smith was hosting a local Saturday morning NBC radio show called *Triple B Ranch,* the three *b*'s representing Big Brother Bob. Primarily the program featured quizzes with public school teams. "My manager thought we should talk to the TV people," Smith adds. "We felt the time was right to switch to television so we went to Warren Wade, then head of TV, who explained that NBC wanted to introduce a puppet show. We asked him if he'd come to the studio the following Saturday and watch our radio show. He gladly agreed."

By the end of the broadcast, Wade and his NBC colleagues seemed convinced they had the man to host their puppet shows. With the two-word directive "Do it," Smith moved into television as the emcee of a show that contained silent movies, an audience of twelve to fourteen kids and a smiling marionette named Howdy Doody.

Reviewers were ecstatic about the new show called *The Puppet Playhouse.* Their enthusiasm, translated to print, soon brought viewers: first thousands and then, as the number of NBC stations increased, millions. "The reviews were sensational," Smith offers. "Our first show was reviewed by *Variety,* and I'd consider it one of the greatest I've ever had in my whole life. It did a lot to get us started."

Variety maintained that *Howdy Doody* was the answer to a parent's prayer; a surprise video present, a perfect invention to calm a noisy household. "In the middle class home, there is perhaps nothing as welcome to the mother as

from the collection of Burt Dubrow

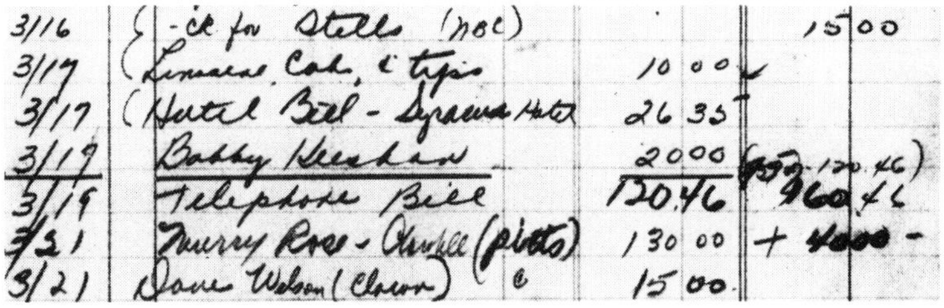

3/16	-ck for Stella (NBC)		15 00
3/17	Limousine, Cab, & tips	10 00	
3/17	Hotel Bill - Syracuse Hotel	26 35	
3/19	Bobby Keeshan	20 00	
3/19	Telephone Bill	130.46	
3/21	Murry Ross - Clarabell (photo)	130 00	
3/21	Dave Wilson (Clown)	15 00	

Vic Smith, Buffalo Bob's brother, oversaw many Howdy Doody personal appearances in the 1950s. He appeared as Buffalo Vic and occasionally hired a free-lance actor to portray Clarabell. Here, however, Bob Keeshan is indicated in Smith's ledger as having gone on the road. Note that the future Captain Kangaroo was paid $20.

something that will keep the small fry intently absorbed and out of possible mischief. This program can almost be guaranteed to pin down the squirmiest of the brood."

"John Crosby was absolutely marvelous with us too in his *New York Herald Tribune* review," Smith recalls. "And Billy Rose gave us nothing but accolades. *The New York Times* also put it atop their 1948 TV honor roll, citing the program for its 'imagination, variety and wholesomeness.' "

There were, however, a few people who snubbed the show. "Some called *Howdy Doody* 'loud, noisy and silly.' . . . Well," continues Smith, "anyone who's ever seen a four-year-old play with a chair and a table and call them a tree and a telephone pole knows that kids live in a land of fantasy. *Howdy* was never aimed at college professors. It was basically fantasy, slapstick and broad humor."

The program found the balance between mirth and mayhem. Physical contact stopped short of punches. Pratfalls appeared accidental rather than intentional. A plot ran through each show, sometimes carrying over for a day or more. And with a fast-moving mixture of live action, cartoons, films, and commercial pitches for Colgate toothpaste, Mars candy, Ovaltine, Poll-Parrot shoes, or Wonder Bread, *Howdy Doody* was a hit on every local street and a smash on Madison Avenue.

Through the first three months the network tried out a number of time slots for the production. In early January 1948, *Puppet Playhouse* was scheduled for Saturday airing. In February, NBC tested Thursday and Saturday, and by early March the network ran *Howdy Doody* first on Wednesday, Thursday, and Saturday, then on Tuesday, Thursday, and Saturday. A month later it had settled into its now-famous weeknight routine.

Initially, *Howdy Doody* was set in a circus, not the Western land later known as Doodyville. Because the kids were rambunctious, sometimes to the detriment of the telecast, Smith added an off-camera clown to quiet anxious ones. Clarabell was silent himself, and his example encouraged good behavior. Since he also made youngsters in the Peanut Gallery laugh he was quickly upgraded to an on-air character.

The first actor to don Clarabell's greasepaint and zebra-striped outfit was Bob Keeshan, a young NBC page who later stepped from anonymity to visibility as Captain Kangaroo. Bobby Nicholson assumed the role when Keeshan left in 1951. Three years later, Lew Anderson took the role. It was Anderson who also appeared as Clarabell in the 1976 *Howdy Doody* syndicated TV revival.

"Clarabell really related to children," Anderson explains. "He was mischievous, and always so happy to be around kids."

Clarabell could steal the show with just a squirt from his seltzer bottle or a toot of his "yes-no" bicycle horn box. His antics made him a favorite of kids and an enemy of many career clowns.

"There was great resistance to Clarabell," Anderson remembers. "More people would see him on one day than the total audience that might

Double Doody

see a real clown over his entire lifetime. A lot of circus people resented that, and I can understand why."

Howdy was not without his own controversy. In 1948 puppeteer Frank Paris walked off with the original freckle-faced marionette in a dispute involving merchandising rights. The entire incident was successfully covered up with an ingenious scenario that incorporated Howdy's announced candidacy for the 1948 presidential election. While the controversy was in litigation and a new puppet was being constructed, Howdy was said to be campaigning.

Time showed interest in the Doody candidacy by publishing his platform promises: "Cut rate banana splits, two Christmas holidays and one school day each year, double sodas for a dime, plenty of movies, more pictures in history books,

1st cov - 5:45.25 - 5:46.40
2nd comm 5:57.30 - 5:58.15

NBC TELEVISION
TELECAST REPORT JAN 2

SUST. [ ]
TITLE OF PROGRAM Puppet Playhouse COM. [X]
ORIGIN NYC DAY MON DATE 1/2 1950 STATION WNBT NET Yes
SCHEDULED ON 5:30 OFF 5:59.15 ACTUAL TIME ON ____ OFF ____
STATION IDENTIFICATION AT 5.59.25 NAME OF SPONSOR MARS ANNOUNCED AT 5:45.25

ORIG. OF TOT. PRGM: (Breakdown time) STUDIO 22.15 FILM 7:00 MOBILE UNIT ____
ORIG. OF COM: (Breakdown time) STUDIO 2:00 FILM ____ MOBILE UNIT ____
*FORM OF PROGRAM: DRAM [ ] DRAM-MUS [ ] MUSIC [ ] VARIETY [X] TALK [ ] SPORTS [ ] NEWS [ ]
DEMONSTRATION [ ] DISCUSSION [ ] TRAVEL [ ]
*CHARACTER OF PROGRAM: ENTERTAIN [ ] GENL AFFAIRS [ ] EDUCAT'L [ ] RELIG [ ] JUV [X] POLITICAL [ ]

REHEARSALS: DRY HRS ____ DAYS ____ CAMERA REH HRS 2:45 DAYS 1

M P ACKNOWLEDGMENT: VISUAL ____ TIME ____
AUDIO ✓ TIME 5:59.15

TRANSCRIBED MUSIC ✓ NO. OF RECORDS 1
ORCHESTRA REH. HRS 1 NO. IN ORCHESTRA 1 CONDUCTOR Whipple

NO. OF PERFORMERS OR OTHER PARTICIPANTS ____ ANNOUNCERS ____

Remarks and Comments: Bob Smith Good Show
Bob Keeshan
Dayton Allen
Rhoda Mann
Bill LeCornec

MASTER SCRIPT ATTACHED REPRESENTS AS ACCURATELY AS POSSIBLE THE VERBAL, MUSICAL AND VISUAL CONTENT OF THIS PROGRAM AS ACTUALLY BROADCAST.

Mildred C. Norman + — Prod. Asst. or ~~Script Girl~~
Roger Muir - Robert Rippen — Producer-Director

* CHECK ONLY ONE REPRESENTING MAJOR PORTION OF PROGRAM.

A cover sheet to a 1950 Howdy Doody *script*

from the collection of Burt Dubrow

Howdy Doody was two-faced.

The original figure, described by *Time* as a "lop-legged, mop-wigged puppet with a Snerdish grin" walked off the program in May 1948 with his puppeteer, Frank Paris. A replacement was quickly carved in California and made his debut in early June.

The substitution occurred after Paris left over a salary/merchandising dispute. "Originally NBC paid him a fee for making Howdy Doody and several other puppets we used," recalls Buffalo Bob Smith. "And when Macy's came in to talk about licensing, Frank got the idea that he should be in on it. We felt we owned the figure, and the upshot was that he left with Howdy just three hours before a show.

"At airtime, we had no puppet," Smith continues, "so our writer Eddie Kean and I came up with the idea that Howdy was out in Portland, Oregon, campaigning for the president of the kids—an idea we had already begun. We picked the farthest place we could and explained that he met his handsome rival Mr. X and realized he wouldn't get any votes from the girls unless he had plastic surgery."

Smith told the viewers not to worry. A better-looking Howdy would soon return. The excuse bought time for Thelma Thomas, a West Coast Walt Disney artist, to create a new face.

"We called the Disney office that evening and I did Howdy's voice on the telephone. The show had not been seen out there yet, so all I could do right away was give her an indication of what he sounded like," Smith says.

As the weeks passed, NBC and the studio exchanged drawings and Paris passed legal papers.

"We stalled until we had the head from California and the body made here by Scott Brinker," Smith states. "When they were together, boy did he look gorgeous. He looked like the all-American boy." The figure cost a reported $2,000.

Puppeteer Rhoda Mann took over Howdy's strings and within a year Rufus Rose joined the show, designing and operating other characters.

Paris unsuccessfully sued NBC for $200,000 in July 1949, requesting that the court issue an injunction against the network for using the name Howdy Doody. Meanwhile, he aired a rival 5:00 P.M. to 6:00 P.M. puppet show on New York station WPIX in 1948 called *Peter Pixie.* Paris intended to use the original Howdy Doody figure for his show, but he was unable to do so by court order.

"The old Howdy," Paris told reporters in 1949, was "only good for kindling now."

from the collection of Burt Dubrow

Howdy Doody and look-alike contest winner Billy Oltmann (1950)

Opposite: A Howdy Doody *scrapbook* (top to bottom): *Bob Smith, Howdy and Bobby Nicholson as Clarabell; Phineas T. Bluster, Bill L'Cornick as Chief Thunderthud and Flubadub; Dilly Dally, Bill L'Cornick as Oilwell Willy and Inspector John J. Fadoozle (America's Number One "Boing" Private Eye); Captain Wendy Scuttlebutt, Bill L'Cornick as Dr. Singasong, Hop, Skip and Jump.*

plus free circus and rodeo admissions." The Doody campaign was replete with buttons. Smith expected a manageable reaction to the on-air offer, but two days after the announcement was made, the first order of five thousand had been exhausted, and requests were still arriving by the sackful.

Howdy, according to his own literature, "the only candidate *completely* made of wood," won. Specifically, he was elected president of the kids via ballots collected on Wonder Bread labels.

The president-elect's running mates were his costars. With the exception of *Sesame Street,* TV has never assembled a better winning team. Besides Clarabell and Buffalo Bob, there was Tim Tremble, Chief Thunderthud (founder of Doodyville), and Phineas T. Bluster (Howdy's arch nemesis). Also on the ticket were Flubadub (a bizarre creature that gave Buffalo Bob endless headaches); police inspector John; fidgety Dilly Dally; and his sister, Heidi Doody. The good-natured character also strung along with Eustas, Mr. Huff, and Princess Summer-Fall-Winter-Spring. When the beautiful Indian maiden pitched camp on the show, *Billboard,* an industry trade paper welcomed her. "The effect was like a breath of fresh air. The harshness and crudeness which so many parents objected to in *Howdy Doody* now appears to have been largely a case of too much masculinity."

Helping to round out the wiry cast was Lanky Lew; Phineas's friendly brothers, Dr. Jose Bluster and Hector Hamhock; Seabee Captain Scuttlebut; Sandra Witch; the Bloop. Alene Dalton and Lowell Thomas, Jr., joined the show as the Story Princess and the Traveling Lecturer when NBC turned on the color cameras September 12, 1955.[1]

Howdy's commercial success made fortunes for those who held the puppets' purse-strings. Toys, lunch boxes, shirts, and figurines with Howdy's

1. Howdy had tested color earlier. On June 26, 1953 *Howdy Doody* became NBC's first program to televise in color during regular broadcast hours. The experimental telecast occurred only one day. However, in February 1954 the show aired for a full week in color.

face couldn't be manufactured quickly enough. Howdy Doody cereal-box-top premiums sold cereals that kids might not have otherwise eaten (see Chapter VIII, "Batteries Not Included"). And when NBC ran a contest to locate a legitimate double of Howdy Doody, the network perused 17,231 snapshots before settling on five-year-old entrant Billy Oltmann, from East Patchogue, New York. Oltmann, an uncanny look-alike in his bandana and Western shirt, appeared on the five hundredth performance of the show and was showered with five hundred gifts.

For the youngster who wasn't a Howdy Doody look-alike, it was next to impossible to get a seat. "We'd get requests from women as soon as they got pregnant," says Smith. "They'd write in and say they wanted seats in four years. But hardly anyone who ever wrote got a ticket. Most were doled out internally. We only had forty seats a day. I got four, each cast member received two or four a week, every sponsor got another ten a day, and network personnel also received some."

Fire department rules barred more than forty kids from sitting in the Peanut Gallery. Smith says the city even positioned a guard at the studio door to maintain the municipal order. "We had to live by the ironclad law. Kids either had a ticket or they just plain didn't get in."

Only the highest-placed influence could bend the rules, and even then with great difficulty. "One day our producer, Roger Muir, called me from a rehearsal," Smith recalled. "When I walked into the control room I was met by Niles Trammel, president of NBC, who asked me what kind of show I was running. He had promised a kid that he'd have a seat in the Peanut Gallery and then he found out that he couldn't get in without a ticket. 'Why, I've never needed a ticket to get any place in my life,' he angrily told me."

Trammel's appearance was only overshadowed by the identity of the eager child. The youngster, says Smith, was Andrew Hoover, and his grandfather, the former President of the United States, intended to watch the show in Washington that night. Smith knew there was only one way to squeeze Andrew in. He'd use him on a commercial. "Tonight we have an ad for Welch's grape juice," he explained to his boss. "If you can guarantee that when I ask the boy if he likes the drink, he'll say 'oh, yeah,' then he

from the collection of Burt Dubrow

can sit next to me. I'll tell the fireman that this is the kid the sponsor sent over to use in the commercial." Smith says the story ended happily. The president's grandson gulped down the drink with great satisfaction and responded on cue.

Howdy Doody, like NBC, was growing rapidly. The program premiered on the network's six stations in New York, Boston, Philadelphia, Washington, Baltimore, and Schenectady. As NBC signed on new outlets, Howdy won more favor.

The national press made certain that everyone knew about *Howdy Doody*. Still, to help promote the show, the network, and the local carrier, and to encourage the millions of non-TV families to commit their savings to the purchase of a television set, NBC regularly sent the cowboy puppet on the public-appearance trail.

Immediately after Bob Smith's 1954 heart attack, Gabby Hayes hosted Howdy Doody. *He was visited by Paul Winchell and Jerry Mahoney in an October 12 broadcast from New York's Century Theatre.*

Howdy Duty

The best, the brightest or the funniest moment of *Howdy Doody* becomes harder to recall as time passes the puppet show by. But both Buffalo Bob and Lew (Clarabell) Anderson tell one story with great affection. It involved a youngster with a bladder too full to wait until the program's end. The child, frantically motioning to a page for assistance, was pointed to the direction of the bathroom. Unfortunately, a hollowed-out pumpkin, in place for an upcoming Halloween segment, was strategically positioned midway between the Peanut Gallery and the boys' room. The obvious happened—the youngsters all watched; Bob Smith watched; and though the cameras did not point at the scene, the cameramen, doubled over with laughter, had a difficult time steadying the shot of the puppet stage.

Howdy's influence extended to Canada on November 15, 1954, when the Canadian Broadcasting Corporation (CBC) presented their own five-day-per week version of the show. Buffalo Bob's counterpart was Timber Tom, a forest ranger played by Robert Goulet, years before he left Doodyville for Broadway. Joining Timber Tom and Howdy in the 5:00 P.M. show were Mr. Bluster and Mr. X. A new personality, Princess Haida, possessed mysterious powers inherited from her Indian medicine men ancestors.

A June 23, 1949, Chicago trip also provided an opportunity to test the technology as well as hype the show. With Howdy and Clarabell in the Windy City and Buffalo Bob remaining in New York, NBC technicians set up a split screen, reportedly the first instance of a two-way, cross-country broadcast.

Smith recorded Howdy's voice before airtime. Puppeteer Rhoda Mann, stationed in Chicago, heard the actual audio transmission over a television receiver and worked Howdy's mouth and movements to fit the words. Chicago youngsters participating in the studio believed they were talking directly to Howdy. In actuality, they were answered by the prerecorded voice in New York.

The routine was repeated on February 12, 1952, during the telecast of the thousandth program. Mann performed in Los Angeles, and the full studio show, with Howdy's voice, originated in Manhattan. Kukla, Fran, and Ollie also made a live guest-appearance on the same show via a remote hookup in Chicago. The celebration marked the first time any network TV show had reached one thousand broadcasts.

In 1951, Howdy telecast another first: a partial eclipse of the sun. Dr. Roy K. Marshall, host of his own NBC show, *The Nature of Things*, stood atop the RCA building in New York while a camera pointed skyward. The event was carried over *Howdy Doody* at 5:45 P.M., March 4.

Publicly, Howdy took the honors for chalking up many other broadcasting achievements. Privately, Buffalo Bob Smith stood prouder than the young NBC peacock. Smith never pulled the strings on the show, but he guided Howdy Doody every step of the way. He not only provided the voice for the character, but he gave him his conscience, his philosophy, and his character.

"Bob's always been very professional," says Lew Anderson. "It's corny, but I'd say that the image he exudes on the air is exactly the way he is. Bob's a perfectionist and a hard worker. He's a part of history. I suppose he's a legend."

Smith, twenty-nine when *Howdy* signed on, might have also been an accomplished musician, a popular TV-radio host, and an able adult role model; but he was no ventriloquist. Before Howdy's words were prerecorded, Smith had to rely on the director to cut to Howdy's close-up so he could read the lines off 2½-by-4-foot cue cards. "My dialogue is printed in black letters," he explained in a 1940s interview. "Howdy's are in red; Mr. Bluster's in orange; the Flubadub in blue; Dilly Dally in green; and the Inspector in yellow." He described the collage of colors as something out of "a drunken Van Gogh nightmare."

"If I looked right past Howdy's face, I'd see a TV monitor," Smith recalled. "When I saw the director take the shot of Howdy alone, I'd speak for him. To help, I used to give obvious word cues like, 'What do you think, Howdy?' Believe it or not, throughout the time we used this system we never tripped up."

Smith switched to prerecorded conversation for his characters by the time he left for a two-week Caribbean vacation in February 1949. The vacation, Smith's first absence, was explained to audiences as a hunting expedition to locate the Flubadub, a gangling, fuzzy-headed animal that wore a flowerpot hat, had a duck's head, a cocker spaniel's ears, a giraffe's neck, a dachshund's body, a seal's flippers, a pig's tail, and a cat's whiskers. "She shouldn't be too hard to spot," Smith told the kids.

Smith chronicled the search in a letter to an early publication, *Television Guide*.

> *Gosh, kids, I know what you're saying to yourself as you look at this week's "Kids Korner" in* Television Guide. *Where is the picture of the Flubadub we were promised? Well, we just couldn't get a picture. And here's the reason why. When I captured the Flubadub for Clarabell, I put "it" on the boat all right, and everything was just fine. Now one morning we were going past the island of Bermuda. The Flubadub smelled all the beautiful flowers on the island. And before I knew it, he jumped right off the boat into the ocean. I yelled, "Flubadub Overboard!" Everyone looked and looked, but no luck. Now, as soon as we find the Flubadub, we'll take its picture.*

Lew Anderson in and out of uniform

For a year after his heart attack Bob Smith appeared on Howdy Doody *from this makeshift basement studio in his New Rochelle, New York, home.*

from the collection of Burt Dubrow

There was actually little time for the busy Smith, a New Yorker only since 1946, to take any vacations. NBC saw dollar signs in the spelling of $mith. They figured that if he could rate with the kids, why not the same with the parents? Hence, on September 2, 1948, NBC brought *The Bob Smith Show* to TV. *Variety* extended some of its daytime applause to this nighttime venture, personally calling Smith, "indubitably one of tele's brightest male personalities . . . many-sided . . . pleasantly peppy." The review was less flattering when it came to the show. The publication observed that the Thursday-evening broadcast lacked cohesion.

Smith also hosted an early morning NBC radio program that originated from a makeshift studio in his New Rochelle home, and a Saturday morning radio version of *Howdy* that premiered in 1952. The radio program, says Smith, was "more inventive than the TV show"; and it featured guitarist Tony Mottola, organist Doc Whipple, and Howdy's washboard band.

In 1954, Smith added a 10:00 A.M. to 11:00 A.M. radio show to compete with Arthur Godfrey and a midday local TV program. According to *Time*, all of this on top of Howdy-duty earned him $350,000 a year and a physical warning that he was overextended. "I was literally killing myself," he volunteers. September 8, 1954, Smith awoke with crushing chest pains. Fans quickly learned it was a heart attack.

"NBC was marvelous about it," he continues. "They said, you have one job. Get better for *Howdy Doody*."

With Smith out of circulation, however, NBC searched for a suitable replacement. For a time Paul Tripp, host on *Mr. I. Magination* and *On the Carousel* was said to have the inside track. However, when the decision was made, it was Western star Gabby Hayes, and New York disc jockey Ted Brown who rode out the period for Buffalo Bob. Smith returned to the show on a part-time basis beginning January 17, 1955, via a live hookup in his home. Brown, better known as Bison Bill, stayed with the show through September.

"The sponsors wanted me on the show to do the commercials," Smith says. "The doctors didn't want me on the road fighting traffic five days a week, so they constructed a studio in my home."

"They built a rustic set, called it Pioneer Vil-

from the collection of Burt Dubrow

Buffalo Vic Smith (right), *Bob Smith's brother, on a public appearance. The Clarabell pictured did not appear in the TV show but was one of many actors hired for the weekend assignments.*

lage, and said I was on a secret mission here. I was on every day, talked to the studio and did commercials. Occasionally, Clarabell came out and brought me a present."

The heart attack brought other changes. Bobby Nicholson, Keeshan's replacement as Clarabell, moved into Smith's daytime radio show, and Lew Anderson, who had appeared on the same program with his vocal group, The Honey Dreamers, became the third actor to play the clown.

"Surprisingly," Anderson confesses, "I had never seen the show. I was just told to put on the makeup and nobody would know the difference."

Howdy Doody himself was ailing during the mid-1950s. TV's perennial youngster was being passed up by many of his earliest fans. Though others quickly tuned in as soon as they learned to reach for the dial, the network was beginning to turn off to the puppet. "I've got to confess," Smith says. "There was one point I thought

Howdy Doody Songs*

Never-ever-ever pick a fight,
Cause it never-ever proves who's right

Be kind to animals,
They think you're grand,
Be kind to animals, they'll lick your hand.
And take them for a regular walk
And if they could talk, they'd say,
Thanks for being kind to animals
We love to be treated that way

My face may not be handsome
I may be light or fair,
But here in America,
You're welcome, every body's welcome . . . everywhere.

Save your pennies, soon you'll have a nickel,
Save your nickels, soon you'll have a dime.
Save your dimes, and soon you'll have a quarter . . .
And a quarter oughta make you awfully glad you saved a dime.

*reprinted with permission from Bob Smith

'Howdy Doody' would go on forever and ever. But that suddenly changed."

The handwriting, faint on June 16, 1956, was nonetheless on the wall. The daytime *Howdy Doody* was dropped, and the program was relegated to 10:00 A.M. Saturday morning as a replacement for *The Pinky Lee Show.*

"We were perturbed," fumes Smith, "We knew the program was becoming prohibitively costly." It wasn't so much the actual expense of the show, he explains, but the value of the time slot. "Our daily airtime could bring more money with adult shows. Naturally, we wanted the daily slot because merchandising was stronger five days a week than just on Saturday. But we had no voice in the matter."

In an attempt to save even more money, *Howdy* was videotaped for its last few years—one of the first regular shows to be prerecorded on the new system. "They figured it was cheaper to tape our shows than to tie up the studio space every week. We'd do five at a time, then take four weeks off. Once through, they'd tear the set down and put something else up."

While adult programs could bring more money to the network on weekdays, cartoons were also becoming more profitable than large-staffed puppet shows on Saturdays. "*Howdy Doody* was being squeezed out," Smith says. "We could see the whole trend was changing. The end was in sight."

The end came September 24, 1960, 2,343 programs after it had all begun. NBC scheduled an hour-long color retrospective, issued tickets to employees' children, and rolled the tape machines. "It was pathetic," recalls Smith. "We had a big party and some people felt it was just a matter of weeks or months before we'd be back on television in some way, shape, or form." *Howdy Doody* would return, but not for sixteen years.

"I think nearly everybody in the country saw our last show," believes Lew Anderson. "People remember it so well today. All through the program Bob told viewers that Clarabell had a special surprise. The camera dollied in real close. We had been together for such a long time, and everybody was pretty broken up, so the only thing I could say was 'Good-bye, kids.' The audience was silent."

For one last time, the cast sang their way off camera: "It's time to say good-bye, good-bye until some other day when we may be with you again." The image faded to black, but not from memory.

"When Clarabell spoke, I looked at my son, Chris, watching at home with me," Smith explains. "He had a tear in his eye. I ran out of the house and quietly went to the golf course. I didn't play very well that day.

"We didn't make any effort to get back on until after our *Howdy Doody* revival started in 1971," Smith admits. "When I saw the reaction of college students, I again realized how important Howdy had been in their lives."

"The time seemed really right," concurs Anderson, who had likewise worn his Clarabell costume for the series of personal appearances. "People around the country asked us if they would ever again have a TV show that was as good as *Howdy Doody.*"

With interest peaking, and the syndication market ripe for Howdy, Doodyville rose once more in 1976. This time the series originated in a Miami studio, where Smith and Anderson joined producer Roger Muir. Much was as it had been. However, a great deal had changed; too much, in fact, for *Howdy Doody* to recapture the spirit of its halcyon days. "The show was good and slick," says Anderson, "but as I look back, we made a major mistake. In an attempt to adjust to the seventies, we tried to play to youngsters as well as court the older, nostalgic viewers. We had a mixture of four hundred kids and parents in the Peanut Gallery, and so many people made it less intimate."

The maneuver could have been successful had stations been obliging and scheduled the show in the early evening. However, in syndication *The New Howdy Doody Show* never received a single, nationwide airtime. Outlets telecast it in whatever time slot was available, most likely at 7:30 A.M. or 3:00 P.M. Such scheduling made adult viewing difficult.

"We geared it too much for the alumni when it should have been written as it originally had been," Anderson adds.

"Yes, we made a mistake," Smith concurs. "I think we did a good show, but it was too far off the original concept. We should have been a little more low-keyed."

Anderson believed it could have been better organized, too. "We did ten shows in six days," he states. "And we used the audience only for

Wednesday, September 10, 1958

The World on a String

By BOB SMITH

SCENE: Doodyville, U.S.A. (Studio 6-B, NBC, N.Y.)
(BUFFALO BOB SMITH BUSILY WRITING AT DESK. HOWDY DOODY ENTERS. HIS STRINGS GET FOULED IN A PROP TREE. HE RETREATS.)
(MUFFLED CURSES FROM PUPPET BRIDGE.)
(HOWDY RE-ENTERS.)

HOWDY: (SINGS) "It's Howdy Doody Time! It's Howdy Doody Time!
Bob Smith and Howdy too . . . say Howdy Do to you!
Let's give a rousing cheer—"

BOB: Oh, cut it out, Howdy! We're not on the air now.

HOWDY: But, Gosh, Buffalo Bob, I feel like singing.

BOB: Can't you sing something else?

HOWDY: But that's our theme song.

BOB: Yes, but I've heard it 2,240 times!

HOWDY: What are you writing, Buff?

BOB: (PROUDLY) Howdy, VARIETY has asked me to write an article about HOWDY DOODY's 10 years in television.

HOWDY: Great! What did you write?

BOB: All I've got so far is the title. Listen to this: "HD & BB STILL TOPS WITH MOPS."

HOWDY: Gosh, Buff—what does that mean?

BOB: That's VARIETY talk. "HD" stands for Howdy Doody. And, of course, you know who "BB" is.

HOWDY: (EXCITED) Brigitte Bardot? Boy oh boy, Buff—is she going to be on the show with me?

BOB: "BB" stands for Buffalo Bob!

HOWDY: (DISAPPOINTED) Oh!

BOB: Brigitte Bardot! Say, you are getting older. Let me take a closer look at you.

HOWDY: What's wrong, Buff?

BOB: I'm not sure whether those are freckles . . . or pimples!

HOWDY: What does the rest of the title mean?

BOB: "STILL TOPS WITH MOPS"? Mops stands for moppets—children. Now let's see. What will I write in this article? How's this for a beginning? "The first performance of the HOWDY DOODY SHOW took place on Dec. 27, 1947. Since the, the show has had 2,240 performances; it has merchandised over 600 Howdy Doody products; it has—

HOWDY: Excuse me, Buffalo Bob, but those figures are pretty dull. Why don't you write about the big election?

BOB: You mean for Miss Rheingold? Well, I voted for that pretty little blond . . .

HOWDY: Stop teasing me, Buff. You know I'm talking about the time the children of America elected me President of the Kids.

BOB: That's right, Howdy . . . and it hit all the newspapers and national magazines. But that's kid stuff. I think I'll tell them about the time the whole city of Buffalo turned out to see me.

HOWDY: What did you do? Go over Niagara Falls in a barrel?

BOB: Alright. We'll skip that too. Listen, Howdy—this article is going to be ready by everybody on Madison Ave. So put on your gray flannel Thinking Cap and see if you can come up with a good idea.

HOWDY: I've got it, Buffalo Bob! Tell them how I won the Peabody Award.

BOB: You won it? Howdy-buddy, don't you think somebody else deserves a little credit for that?

HOWDY: You mean our producer, Roger Muir?

BOB: Well . . . yes. And who else?

HOWDY: I know! Clarabell the clown . . . and Chief Thunderthud . . . and Mr. Cobb . . . and all the cameramen, and the technicians, and—

BOB: I know all that, Howdy. But aren't you forgetting one other person who had an important part in winning that Peabody Award?

HOWDY: (THINKS A MOMENT) Of course! How could I forget? It's Mr. Peabody! Without him, there wouldn't be any award.

BOB: I give up. Look Howdy, I think we ought to forget about our past accomplishments. Let's write about what we're going to do in the future. Do you have any good ideas for this coming season?

HOWDY: I have a great idea, Buff. How about getting a cute girl-puppet on the show as my girlfriend? I'd like to have some fun too. After all, Im not made of wood.

BOB: Forget it, Howdy. This is just a stage you're going through. It's called "puppet love."

HOWDY: Well, gosh, Buffalo Bob—what are we going to do on our show this year?

BOB: I know what we'll do, Howdy. (WRITES) "This year the HOWDY DOODY SHOW will do the same thing it has been doing for past 10-and-a-half years; it will provide wholesome entertainment for the children of America."

HOWDY: I'll buy that, Buff.

BOB: Okay, Howdy-buddy—let's get this off to VARIETY.
(BOB AND HOWDY GO OFF SINGING)

BOTH: "It's Howdy Doody Time. It's Howdy Doody Time.
Bob Smith and Howdy too . . . now say Good-bye to you . . .

Burt Dubrow (left) *and his TV idol*

Burt Dubrow, creator and executive producer of Warner Cable's award-winning program *America Goes-Bananaz!*, producer of ABC's *Kids Are People, Too* and a talent agent, owes his interest in television to a New Rochelle, New York, neighbor—Bob Smith. Dubrow recalls his first meeting and his relationship with Howdy Doody's alter ego:

It was in the mid-1950s that I first met Bob. I was seven or eight years old and someone told me at school that Buffalo Bob Smith owned a nearby liquor store. We all laughed, but a friend insisted it was true. He suggested that if I took the M-bus, I could go there right after school and my mother would never know.

On the chance that he was right, I went. That bus ride ultimately led to my career.

I got off the bus in the general vicinity of where Buffalo Bob's store was supposed to be. It was in a small part of town, the kind of place you've seen on Bonanza *reruns, so I couldn't get lost.*

Pretty soon I found the store. I walked in and a man behind the counter asked if he could help me. I said yes and asked him if this was "Buffalo Bob's." He told me it was, and I popped the important question, "Well then, is Buffalo Bob here?"

In an answer I wasn't prepared to hear from this man in dark glasses and street clothes, he said, "I'm Buffalo Bob." As he started to talk there was something about the inflection of his voice that sounded familiar, but the physical being in front of me didn't look like anyone I'd ever seen before. In time, however, his voice became familiar. He slowly began to appear a little bit like my TV hero and I honestly remember as a kid thinking, "Wait a minute, it's him!"

I finally said something bold like, "Can I have your autograph?" He said, "Sure, son," and pulled out pictures with him and Howdy.

A week later I thought I had to go back there. I figured if I pulled it off the first time, why couldn't I do it again. The show was on Saturday by then, so after school seemed like the best time to catch him. I must have returned sixteen or seventeen times, to the point where he sent me across the street to meet his brother, Vic, who owned a shoe store. They used to joke, "Bob was in booze, Vic was in shoes."

One thing led to another, and finally Bob gave me twenty-five tickets to the show for my class.

Years later I was still going to see Howdy Doody *but as emcee of the early 1970 college road shows. At the time I was twenty-one or twenty-two, and so were the people in Bob's audience. They considered me one of the luckiest people they'd met, since I traveled with Buffalo Bob. And they held Bob in the same reverence that they always had because the image he projected on the stage was as personable as his work on TV. He'd come out and his presence indicated, "Hi, kids. I'm back. I'm here. I haven't gone anywhere. I was your first friend and you can still count on me!"*

After the show it was amazing. Hundreds of people—fat, tall, skinny and long-haired—would throw their arms around him. I've never seen anything else like it. Personally I adore the Sesame Street *characters, but unfortunately I don't think kids will ever feel the way about them as they do Bob. He has a magic that won't be repeated.*

As a performer, I'd have to admit Bob Smith is the best I've seen in my life. He's a very talented man and if Bob were to walk out on stage tomorrow, he'd give 1,000 percent.

I used to introduce Bob to the folks as "the man that every little boy idolized and every little girl wanted to marry." He once asked me where I came up with that gem. I told him I didn't know, but it's true. And what's more, that's why I was working with him. That's why I wanted to meet him, and that's why I'm in TV.

He gave me his sincere smile, shrugged his shoulders and took it all in.

a few sequences. They never saw a complete show. It was easier to tape that way, but we missed the important spontaneity of the live audience."[2]

Even if Smith had been able to reclaim more of the original feeling, he admits that the new show might not have lasted. "The old days and the fun are gone," he says disappointedly. "When we started, it was such a different ball game. NBC merely called up sponsors like Colgate and said we have the greatest vehicle in the world for you. It's called *Howdy Doody*. After one conversation and one screening, they were with us. It's impossible to get a show or sponsor that easily today," Smith adds.

"*Howdy Doody* was a way of life for kids," says Anderson. "Before *Howdy Doody* there was little else but test patterns. Everyone over thirty grew up with him. Sure it was silly and loud, but it was never violent and never off-color.

"Somebody once likened *Howdy Doody* to Peter Pan—a character who never dies, never changes," he concludes. "I think that's how most people would like to remember him. I think that's why he's so appreciated today."

Sadly, however, the children of *Howdy Doody* are the very TV programmers who have no time for Buffalo Bob's homespun TV-style: no time for a hardwood puppet espousing American values; no time to eat a little humble apple pie. They remember the show fondly but love the money that accumulates from cheaper cartoons.

We may feel that it's still *Howdy Doody* time; that it always will be. But in reality Buffalo Bob Smith is right. Its time has passed. Digital clocks have replaced *Howdy Doody* watches, and as much as we want TV executives to consult Howdy's hands when they check the time, all they see is an electronic readout pulsating to the technology and life-style of the 1980s.

Predating *Howdy Doody* by two months was Burr Tillstrom's variety show *Junior Jamboree*, the forerunner of *Kukla, Fran and Ollie*. The one-hour program premiered on WBKB, Chicago, October 13, 1947. On November 29, 1948, it moved to NBC affiliate WNBQ for its daily 7:00 P.M. Midwest network debut, and on January 12, 1949, the show linked with the growing East Coast network.

Though Tillstrom's work is primarily associated with television's infancy and formative years, the puppeteer was heavily involved with the medium during its lengthy "prenatal state." Tillstrom, a self-taught artist, was just twenty-one years old when he made his first TV appearance in 1939. His introduction to the medium came when he fortuitously passed up a trip to Europe and visited a children's-theater exhibit at Chicago's Marshall Field department store. There, amid the radio display, was an assembly of huge, extraworldly equipment that held everyone's attention. The young puppeteer, with Kukla in hand, watched the technicians turn the lights on a makeshift set and focus a gigantic optical device. Moments later a science that defied explanation to most people produced a television picture of the scene.

"I said, 'I've got to be on this. This is what I want.' " Tillstrom recalls stating. "The engineers flipped over Kukla and the RCA people said, 'Sure kid, we'll give you a chance.' " Tillstrom stepped behind a makeshift stage while up front, Garry Moore, the host of a Chicago radio show called *Club Matinee*, toyed with the puppets. "He was the first guy ever to appear on TV with Kukla," Tillstrom says for notation in the history books. Kukla was three years old by the time he performed with Moore. The little bald-headed, bulb-nosed figure was, in fact, the first hand puppet Tillstrom ever made.

"I had never been acquainted with hand puppets before," Tillstrom says. "I was eighteen and I had just quit college to join the WPA Park Project [theater] in Chicago. The director of the group suggested we all try to make some hand puppets, and I decided that when I finished mine I would give it to a friend who had given me great advice." After stitching together loose fabric from a WPA ragbag, he fashioned the character now familiar throughout the world. Tillstrom looked at the completed puppet and was unwilling to give him up. "When I had him all ready to go, he looked so beautiful. I really loved him, so I asked my mother what I should do. She said keep him and make another for a gift."

2. Anderson has prepared a *Howdy Doody* spin-off that he says has profited from the mishaps incurred in the revival. *Clarabell and Krystal's Astro Circus* stars Anderson and Marilyn Patch. (Patch had played Happy Harmony, the female lead in the 1976 *Howdy Doody* series.) The non-network production, ready for syndication, is removed from Doodyville. The show is set on an alien planet called Mirth that Clarabell accidently rockets to while playing at a missile base.

Kukla was named in the fall of 1936 by Russian prima ballerina Tamara Toumanova, an idol of Tillstrom's. "I was a big fan of ballet and I went backstage right after I made Kukla. Tamara was putting on her makeup in the mirror. I placed the puppet over her shoulder and she exclaimed, 'Kukla!', a very affectionate Russian term for doll."

Oliver J. Dragon, a friendly beast with velvet lips, bedroom eyes, and a toothy smile, was born a year later. "I needed another character. Kukla was wonderful, but I thought he would never be complete until he had a partner," Tillstrom recalls with Geppetto-like concern. "Ollie is counterpart to the Alligator in Punch and Judy shows, but as you know, he doesn't care to be linked to that." Tillstrom compared Ollie more to Mickey Mouse's Pluto. He intended Ollie to stammer, snort, and huff, but never, never to puff flames. "Dragon," he says, "is the generic term and the family name. He's proud of it, and his ancestors had long ago stepped out of the bog of ignorance of fire-breathing historical time."

Kukla and Ollie performed two thousand shows at the RCA-TV exhibit at the 1939 New York World's Fair. In 1940, they appeared on a ship-to-shore telecast from midocean to Bermuda, and in 1941 they participated in the first broadcasts of Chicago station WBKB.

With Kukla and Ollie in tow, the only one yet to join the trio was Fran Allison. Allison, a Chicago radio star, first worked with Tillstrom seven years before the act was truly formed. Volunteering to spend a few minutes in front of the Wrigley Building pitching prewar Defense Bonds, she found herself feeding straight lines to Kukla, the Patriotic Puppet, and an unseen puppeteer. "She met Kukla and Ollie before I met her," Tillstrom muses.

Allison didn't work with the puppets again until well after the war, when Tillstrom began final preparation on his first regular TV series (a production he says that RCA believed would help "bring television out of the saloons and into the homes").

"We had talked about writers, but then there was the problem of turning the script's pages when both my hands were busy." That problem was conveniently solved when Tillstrom decided

The Kuklapolitan Players of Chicago: Kukla, Burr Tillstrom, Ollie, and Fran Allison

he would ad-lib the show rather than read from prepared pages. Yet to do that successfully, he needed a real-life foil. Only one person came to mind, the woman who was then playing Aunt Fanny on *The Breakfast Club*—Fran Allison. "I came in on the Monday of our first show. Fran and I shook hands and we went to work that night."

In time the rest of the Kuklapolitan players also made their debut: Buelah the witch (named for producer Beulah Zachary); Madame Ophelia Ooglepus, the grande dame of the opera and a Tillstrom favorite that dates back to the World's Fair; Fletcher Rabbit, a droopy-eared postman whose mother was a suffragette; Mercedes, an attractive ingenue; Captain Crackie, a proper Southern gentleman and escort of Madame Ooglepus; Ollie's cousin, Doloras Dragon; his mother, Olivia Dragon; Cecil Bill, a sailor turned stage manager; and Clara Coo Coo.

The Kuklapolitan players were driven strictly by whim and whimsy. Considering neither Tillstrom nor Allison worked with a script, there was often no preplanned notion of the show's subject until airtime. "Fran and I would respond to what was happening that day, that hour, that minute. It was an absolutely living show."

Tillstrom recalls one day when Fran was vacationing and he was particularly hard-pressed for a theme. The red camera-light flashed on, Ollie walked out looking unhappy, and Kukla asked, "Why are you so miserable?" "Fran's away, everyone's away and I don't have any ideas for a show," Ollie answered, "I think I'm going to retire." Without even thinking, Tillstrom had a story; an allegory about despair; a fable that was rich in humor.

Tillstrom's quick thinking was never more evident than the day Marlin Perkins, host of NBC's *Zoo Parade*, brought a nervous skunk onto the set for a Halloween show. Although thoroughly deodorized and relatively domesticated, the critter wasn't house- or, for that matter, stagebroken.

"Marlin put him on the stage and the skunk decided that was the place to do it, right in front of all those millions of people." Perkins embarrassedly carried the skunk off, and Fran doubled over in laughter. "Everyone broke up," Tillstrom continues. "Everyone except Kukla. He came back to the stage with a mop and cleaned it up saying. 'This happens in the best of regulated families.' "

The story made the national wire-services within an hour. The skunk never made a return engagement.

Allison, as much a key to the show's success as either Kukla or Ollie, has always maintained her off-stage distance from her cloth colleagues. "Fran only likes to see them in motion," Tillstrom surprisingly reports. "She doesn't come backstage. She feels ill at ease seeing Kukla and Ollie hanging lifelessly on their hooks."

Tillstrom, on the other hand, could never separate himself from the puppets and consequently could never take a break from the show except during prescheduled summer vacations.

"I never missed a day. Everyone else could leave. Fran could go off to California or Florida, and even when I couldn't stand the Chicago snow or slush another minute, I couldn't leave. If I didn't work, nobody worked."

Tillstrom had to appear on days when he had a cold, on days when he felt queasy, and on days when his head was in a fog. For some inexplicable reason the puppeteer's companions never sounded as if they, too, were ill. "I could be as sick as a dog, but the characters never had it. I remember times I'd almost have laryngitis, and they could be heard fine."

Every day the show went on, and every day *Kukla, Fran and Ollie* became more popular. Within a year of the premiere there was hardly a TV viewer whose ears didn't pick up when the show's bouncy theme hit the airwaves:

Here we are
Back with you again.
Yes, by gum and yes by golly,
Kukla, Fran and dear old Ollie.
Here we are again. Here we are again.[3]

Time pointed out that the show had "an odd narcotic pull." By the time Chicago joined the East Coast coaxial cable in January 1949—a communications link that Ollie was officially charged with protecting—the program had built up an audience rating of 72 percent of the nation's viewers. A "Kukla, Fran and Ollie" newsletter, the *Kuklapolitan Courier*, reached 6,000 viewers in 1948. When the June 1950 issue went to press, the circulation had increased to 200,000, and Tillstrom dropped all mention of the publication from the air because he was swamped with requests. The show also received more than 8,000 letters a week. And if the volume of mail wasn't already enough, Tillstrom offered a sixty-four-page offset *Kukla, Fran and Ollie* picture book for $1.

The show's pervasive influence was first measured the very week of the 1947 debut. Two hundred fifty fans sent handkerchiefs to Kukla after the character blew his round nose on the nearby curtain. "When the handkerchiefs came in I knew there were viewers out there who cared. And I realized the awesome truth that I was affecting people's minds, thoughts, and feelings."

NBC paid dearly for Tillstrom's ability. In January 1951 the network reportedly renegotiated his original $5,500-per-week pact and signed him to a new four-year contract that cost NBC $10,600 per week the first two years, $11,600 weekly the third year, and $12,600 each week the fourth year. Tillstrom, in turn, used the fees to produce the show and pay the production staff. The contract was expensive, but Tillstrom, whose handling of the puppets, according to *Variety*, "borders on the work of a genius," delivered a show that was instrumental in turning families on to television. "To a devoted few," wrote *Time*, *Kukla, Fran and Ollie* was "TV's only real reason for existence."

The show was also a working experiment as well as a proven success. The network pressed the Kuklapolitans into service to test its color equipment as early as 1949. When NBC was ready to formally celebrate the beginning of the color era—September 1953—it paid homage to the pioneers, aiming its cameras at Burr Tillstrom's special production of *St. George and the Dragon*.[4]

Unfortunately, NBC's initial affection for the puppetry troupe had already begun to wear off. On Monday, November 21, 1951, the network trimmed the show from its daily thirty minutes to a quarter-hour run and slotted comedians Bob and Ray in the remaining time period. NBC justified its move by arguing that two of *Kukla, Fran and Ollie*'s four sponsors, Proctor and Gam-

3. © Vera Nova Music, 1947.

4. Burr Tillstrom also helped NBC test color equipment early in 1952 when the network used 7:45 to 8:50 Saturday morning for color transmissions. The government had not yet lifted the ban on the production of color sets, but NBC telecast color test-patterns receivable in black and white until 8:30, and live shows for the remainder of the time. Among the live presentations were *Kukla, Fran and Ollie;* a short puppet program with *Howdy Doody* puppeteer Rhoda Mann; Jon Gnagy drawing sessions and flower-arrangement lessons.

ble and *Life* had withdrawn from the younger child-oriented program in favor of advertising on shows that would attract older viewers. The myopic but profit-seeking network executives saw this as an opportunity to cut, then cancel the beloved show.

Despite a wave of protest from millions of fans, an unrelenting crusade from the nation's TV critics, and fallout even from political circles, NBC did not countermand its program order. Instead, network president Sylvester (Pat) Weaver prepared a letter of explanation for irate viewers who had written in. The statement was published in *The New York Times,* December 9, 1951.

> *First we must tell you that this program is without doubt the favorite of our "NBC Gang," and that nothing would be done that was not considered the best for Burr and the show. There will be conflict of opinion on the move, but there cannot be on the purpose. NBC's purpose is to advance its interests in the show.*

Weaver maintained that the network was not killing the show, which, he said, faced prospects of affiliate cancellation if it continued in its half-hour format. He said his action would actually save it.

"As one of the brightest stars in the NBC diadem, our policy was simple: we had to preserve *Kukla, Fran and Ollie* for the largest possible network. The fifteen-minute version is our present solution."

Few among Kukla's fans accepted Weaver's logic. Critic Jack Gould wrote in his *New York Times* column that "The decision to limit Ollie, the most wonderful of all dragons, and Kukla to fifteen minutes is explained by the National Broadcasting Company on the grounds that sponsors could be found for shorter periods, but not for the larger stints. However, the network's story overlooked one point. The show that replaced Ollie and his friends was presented on a sustaining basis."[5]

Playwright Robert Sherwood, author of *The Petrified Forest,* wrote what he called "a letter of violent protest," complaining that NBC's excuse "fails to make any sense to me. If some of the wonderful quality of this show is lost in truncated form (and I am afraid this inevitably will be the case) then its value will be accordingly reduced for the sponsors as well as for everybody else. The loss of this rare and remarkable program would be a calamity."

Time took issue with NBC as well, criticizing the network for issuing "a complicated explanation for its hatchet-work" and arguing that until the cut *Kukla, Fran and Ollie* had flourished like an oasis of intelligent fantasy surrounded by a desert of mindless shows. "The oasis was still there," *Time* noted, "but it was growing smaller."

The Washington *Times-Herald* carried a letter asking "Who's responsible for this brainstorm—someone who's mad at the human race?" Even Lillian and Dorothy Gish took up the fight. While attending a formal NBC party the famed silent-screen actresses wore placards that demanded the network restore the show to its full thirty minutes.

And Burr Tillstrom, at his satirical best, did not let the ruling go without mention on the occasion of his first abbreviated telecast. Speaking through Ollie, he requested that everyone speed up their conversations, compressing a full-length program into the collapsed time slot. In one last barb the puppeteer shortened his name in the closing credits to "Burtlestrom."

Within a year NBC made the next fateful decision regarding *Kukla, Fran and Ollie.* The show was stripped from its weekday slot and, on August 25, 1952, shunted off to a four o'clock Sunday afternoon. (In some cities, kinescopes had already been airing on Saturdays.)

Two years later *Kukla, Fran and Ollie* was gone from NBC completely. The last show aired June 13, 1954, but the group would not be without a TV home for long. The Kuklapolitan Players revived the fifteen-minute weekday format on ABC beginning September 6, 1954.

Ollie the dragon opened the first return show with the intention of verbally slaying his former keepers. He immediately snorted that he was happy to work where he could call the television vice-presidents by their first names. The dragon then fired up Fran to telephone NBC and request that someone send them their coffeepot inadvertently left behind. Upon reaching the exchange, Fran told a befuddled secretary that the

5. Sustaining basis refers to a practice whereby networks underwrite program costs but commercial time is sold by local stations rather than the network.

coffeepot was nothing "spectacular," presumably an in-joke directed at NBC's byword for its heavily promoted color "spectaculars." Allison was then informed that a requisition was needed before the pot could be returned. Her call was then transferred to Pat Weaver's office. Once connected, all she could say before hanging up was, "So how are the folks?"

Tillstrom's honeymoon at ABC eventually soured, and the relationship ended within three years. On August 30, 1957, the production went dark once again when Tillstrom rejected the network's plan to syndicate the show rather than air it on affiliated stations. ABC replaced *Kukla, Fran and Ollie* with Howard Cosell's *Sports Focus* and was hit with protest just as NBC had been before. The most distinguished letter came from Adlai Stevenson, who wrote, "Surely such assassination . . . cannot be permitted in this enlightened land." Stevenson was mistaken, however. ABC did not reconsider, and Tillstrom refused the compromise bid for syndication.

"There's no place in TV for us anymore," the puppeteer said in a 1957 interview. "The industry has gotten too used to us. They've taken us for granted. People in TV would rather make money than provide entertainment." Publicly, he stated he was ready to leave "the world of ulcers" and declined an offer to return to a local Chicago program. Privately, Tillstrom hated to say goodbye to the medium he loved. From the moment he had first seen TV demonstrated, he had felt that television was invented for his characters. Too quickly had he learned differently.

"It was the same old story," he remembers. "Our time was going. We would have had to go on a syndication basis and some cities wouldn't have been available." Ten years of struggling with the networks was enough, he says. "It was time for a rest."

Tillstrom has reappeared periodically. In 1960 he provided election commentary on *The Today Show;* a few years later he took the Kuklapolitan Players out of their boxes for a five-minute syndicated series, and then again, in the early 1970s, for a PBS revival of the show that was eventually distributed to commercial stations. He's also been a commentator on a local Chicago station, worked on commercials for Parkay margarine, and reunited Kukla and Ollie with Fran for a ten-year run as hosts of *The CBS Children's Film Festival.*

Today, Tillstrom looks back on TV with the vision of an elder statesman who's wary of new battles and proud of old political victories. "Fran and I are still fairly agile, but I just don't see how we'd do a daily show again," he says. "There are other things in the world besides television; other things beyond fame.

"I don't feel driven to remain in the limelight," Tillstrom continues. "As always, I have to do something that's good, but I don't see TV as the end. At times it was an enormously happy, marvelous, hardworking part of my life. However, I'm really a professional peasant and I don't like fame to remove me from what's going on in the real world. I've never totally thought of myself as a puppeteer. I see myself as some-

The Kuklapolitans in their 1976 PBS edition of Kukla, Fran and Ollie

Paul Winchell and Jerry Mahoney
A family portrait, 1947

James

one who uses puppets. I'm really just a creator and a storyteller. And now, my ambition is to do nice things with them."

Above all else Burr Tillstrom is a matchmaker who has knowingly paired a generation or more of children with the world's most cherished commodity. "I hope it doesn't sound too holy, but we loved our audience and they loved us," he said in a 1957 interview that rings true today. "*Kukla, Fran and Ollie* was just a big love affair."

Paul Winchell not only threw every variation of his voice into television, he also bodily threw himself into the medium. Since 1948, Winchell has hosted nine shows and has been heard in hundreds of cartoons and hundreds more TV commercials.

Jerry Mahoney, his most famous puppet, sits in a chair in Winchell's San Fernando Valley, California, home while Winchell pursues two careers. He remains active at the unseen microphone creating new voices for Hanna-Barbera cartoon characters and is busy tinkering in his workshops throughout the greater Los Angeles area.

The performer, it seems, has turned part-time inventor, designing and patenting such objects as a motor-driven artificial heart that he and a partner have been testing.

Winchell's off-camera time has also led to the invention of a device that transfers gas from one car to another, a refrigerator defroster, a reversible Halloween mask for children, and a new rotoscope-type animation process.

Both his vocation and avocation—performing and inventing—are natural outgrowths of his years at the Manhattan School of Industrial Arts where, at age thirteen, he constructed his first version of Jerry Mahoney.

Initially, Jerry was a hand puppet. However, Winchell's natural inclination to build soon saw a hand-carved dummy replace the puppet. (Later, puppet-carver Frank Marshall prepared a professional version of Jerry.)

Winchell bought, then discarded, a twenty-five-cent instruction book on ventriloquism, choosing instead to teach himself the art. After six months of practice he debuted at school and won support of his principal, who made a special wig for Jerry out of a chenille rug and suggested that the youngster audition for *Major Bowes' Original Amateur Hour.* The suggestion soon paid off in a $100 prize and ultimately a lucrative, lifetime career.

Winchell's network TV premiere came in October 1947, when he and his alter ego appeared on a DuMont variety program, *Show Business, Incorporated,* telecast in New York and Philadelphia. During the next year he guested on Ed Sullivan's *Toast of the Town, The Bob Smith Show, We, the People* and *The Milton Berle Show.* However, in 1948, Winchell switched from guest to star when he cohosted *The Bigelow Show* on CBS with Joseph Dunninger, "The Master Mentalist."

Though puppeteer and puppet teamed on *The Paul Winchell-Jerry Mahoney Show* (1950–1954), it was Winchell's Mahoney, like Bergen's Charlie McCarthy, that was becoming the center of attention.

The twenty-five pounds of wood, metal, rubber, latches, springs, levers, glass eyes, and a broomstick spine were shaped into a figure that didn't really enjoy women, disliked living out of suitcases, and only tolerated Winchell. At peak fame he had thirty-two complete Brooks Brothers ensembles, probably making Jerry Mahoney the Beau Brummell of dummies. The combustible character was so hot, in fact, that Winchell was actually called Paul Mahoney. He hated it.

"I guess you'd call it a form of jealousy," Winchell said in a 1954 interview in *The Boston Record American.* "Don't get me wrong. I'm not off my trolley. I know that Jerry's a dummy and he doesn't exist, even if I have bought him nearly 300 changes of costume which is a lot of clothes for a guy who doesn't exist."

Author Ben Hecht wrote a short story called *The Rival Dummy* that, perhaps, could have come to fruition in Winchell's case had he not shown the professional wisdom to advance his personal career. In Hecht's story a jealous ventriloquist ax-murders his wooden dummy, changes his name to avoid detection, and fearfully awaits the day police will discover his crime. Winchell never chopped away at Mahoney, he just began to leave him home.

"Gradually, I found myself faced with the dilemma that comes to most ventriloquists," he added in the newspaper interview. "I was snowed under by the personality of the dummy. Mail began to pour in to 'Paul Mahoney' and 'Jerry Winchell.' I was Jerry's straight man. Everybody knew who Jerry was, but they were beginning to forget the name of the guy who operated him. To that extent it was jealousy."

As a means of severing the ventriloquist's string, but not the professional umbilical cord that tied him with his dummy, Winchell initiated skits on his Thursday-night NBC variety series in which he alone acted with Sir Cedric Hardwicke, Viveca Lindfors, Gene Lockhart, Bela Lugosi, Hedy Lamarr, and Robert Preston.

Outside his own show, he turned down many offers to guest star with Mahoney, a notable exception being a *Lights Out* installment which cast him as a ventriloquist who had no control over what his dummy said. In another assignment, he played a convincing murderer. After the performance he was flooded with letters that complained he had frightened children.

A family portrait, 1977

While he sought balance in his life, Winchell nonetheless acknowledged in a 1954 *TV Guide* article that, "I know which side my bread is buttered on. Jerry is emphatically not going to become less important." With his dummy comfortably on his knee, Winchell moved to Saturday morning, filling an important position in NBC's first big push to create a weekend morning children's programming block. *Winchell and Mahoney* debuted 10:30 A.M., November 20, 1954. The show was staged inside Jerry's clubhouse, where twenty youngsters competed for prizes and watched Winchell, his characters, and accordionist Milton DeLugg alternate between clowning and teaching.

"I'm really trying to prove a little point with this show," he told *Boston Record American* TV columnist, Anthony LaCamera, in 1955. "I honestly feel that a show like mine can be informative as well as entertaining.

"Formerly I was interested only in putting out a good comedy program, but working with kids gives one an added sense of responsibility. I find myself taking much more of a personal interest—trying to accomplish good for the sake of doing good," he explained to the media critic.

One segment on the show awarded a monthly Winchell-Mahoney Junior Achievement medal to a deserving boy or girl who had accomplished a laudable deed or an act of heroism. Songs also dealt with topics including how fish breathe, birds fly, volcanoes erupt, blood circulates, or

snow falls. Jerry Mahoney added tips on the need to brush teeth, respect parents, and act politely.

Winchell used Knucklehead Smiff and a scholarly mouse named Irving as his teaching devices. On a typical show, Knucklehead, stymied by a homework problem, would tap on a piece of cheese. Irving would then pop out, discuss the question, and with gags laced through the dialogue, come up with the answer.

"When you try to give the kids straight information they resent it," Winchell said. "They won't sit through a classroom lecture out of school. So you have to dress it up. You might compare it to giving them their milk, but throwing in a little chocolate syrup so that they'll drink it."

But Winchell admitted in another interview that even sugar-coated education was hard to swallow on Saturday morning.

"The first thing I learned is that kids aren't interested in learning. Give 'em the idea that you're going to teach them something and brother, you're dialed out."

As expected, he resisted long educational lessons and relied on short comedy bits. And for comedy's sake, Winchell didn't mind occasionally tossing a pie into the works.

In one show, for example, band leader Milton DeLugg had to undergo an initiation for Jerry's club. The test was to steer barefooted and blindfolded between rows of pumpkin pies. The camera shot provided the hint of what was to come—a close-up of DeLugg's feet. The youngsters were in hysterics, split between their natural inclination to warn the musician and their desire to see the inevitable. As the script would have it, however, DeLugg safely traversed the course. At that moment, Winchell walked onto the set to congratulate DeLugg and tripped into all six pies.

"Anyone who has had any contact with kids knows that they're terrific imitators," Winchell told a reporter after the fall. "So far as I'm concerned, it's a foregone conclusion that most, if not all, of these stunts we do will be imitated by the kids who watch them. So we have to examine them from every angle to make sure they'll be as harmless as possible."

Throughout the years, Winchell has been a faithful and constant visitor to children's hospitals. A polio victim himself, he took great care

Opposite: Ireene Wicker, TV's The Singing Lady *(1950)*

Below: Paul Winchell and Jerry Mahoney during a 1953 visit to the Roxbury, Massachusetts, Children's Hospital.

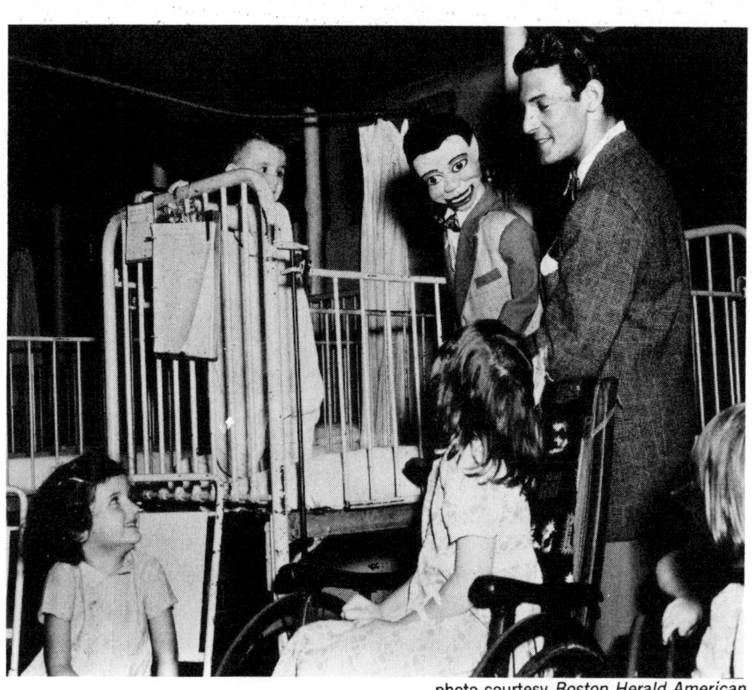

photo courtesy *Boston Herald American*

to visit similarly afflicted children in the 1950s and other bedridden kids in the post-polio years.

Typical of Winchell's devotion was an early visit he made to a New York Medical Center ward to see a young Greek girl who had been wounded by a hand grenade in guerrilla fighting. She had seen Winchell on TV and asked to meet him.

At the hospital he was disturbed when the youngster greeted his dummy with cries of "Kukla, Kukla." "I don't think she wants to see me. I think she wants to see Burr Tillstrom with his Kukla and Ollie," he told the nurse.

The nurse corrected him. "Kukla," she said, is "doll" in Greek just as it is in Russian. Winchell proceeded to put on a show for the girl and the other youngsters in the hospital ward.

In 1957 the performer returned to the variety format for a three-year hitch, which afforded him sole billing on *The Paul Winchell Show.* Milton DeLugg, Frank Fontaine, and Jerry Mahoney co-starred. The same year he guest hosted ABC's Saturday afternoon children's series *Popsicle Five Star Comedy.* By 1960 he was busier than ever, hosting an NBC special, *All-Star Circus* taped in Copenhagen, Denmark, and appearing as a regular panelist on *What's My Line* and *Keep Talking.* In 1963, he starred on ABC as host of *Cartoonies* (see Appendix A). Two years later he syndicated *Winchell and Mahoney* when the networks abandoned their experienced adult talent for wall-to-wall cartoons. It wasn't until 1972 that he rejoined his old home, NBC, for a year's stint on the Saturday morning game show *Run-around.*

By 1948 each of the four networks and nearly all of the nation's local stations courted kids with fuzzy, furry, and hardwood characters. Ireene Wicker and the Suzari Marionettes settled on ABC after trying out formats in New York, Philadelphia, and Schenectady. New York independent station WPIX telecast *Pixie Playhouse* the same year featuring Peter W. Pixie, a mermaid with a Mae West sashay, and a witch who tortured victims by subjecting them to old radio jokes. Frank Paris, Howdy Doody's original puppeteer, worked the strings.

In 1948, CBS gave *Lucky Pup,* a playboy pooch with a $5 million inheritance, a network run. The hand puppet and his pal, Jolo the

Behind the scenes, July 1949, with CBS's Lucky Pup. *Hope and Morey Bunin operate Foodini, the wicked magician* (right) *and Pinhead, his stooge. The Bunins used three floors of stages, hustling from one to another for segment changes.*

1950, Television Guide

KIDS KORNER

Dear Friends:

Puppets live in a world of their own. They cannot do all the things that people can do; but, on the other hand, neither can people do all the things that puppets can do. It's much more fun, we think, to bring our audience into a puppet world than it would be to have Jolo, Lucky Pup, Pinhead, and the Great Foodini (the characters who are now appearing on our new television program "Lucky Pup") try to adapt themselves to human behavior. (See cover)

There's no reason why politicians should have a monopoly on promises, so we want to make some to you, our television audience-to-be. Since television, like the comic-strip cartoon, is visual, we will try to tell our story more with pictures than with dialogue. And, because we never know whether our audience is age one or one hundred, we shall proceed on the premise that everyone is more or less adult rather than more or less childish.

We hope you'll find our program fun. And you can help us make it so. Like the lady in Robert Burns' poem, we cannot see ourselves as others see us. It's up to you who do see us to write and tell us about it. We really will appreciate your criticisms and suggestions.

Sincerely,
Hope and Morey Bunin
(for their puppets)

FOR THE CHILDREN

Comics on Parade: Mon. thru Fri. - 4:45; Sat. - 4:50; Sun. - 4:05 ⑪ **Small Fry:** Mon. thru Fri. - 6:00 ⑤ **Howdy Doody:** Mon. thru Fri. - 5:30 ④ **Junior Frolics:** Wed. thru Sun. - 5:00 ⑬ **Scrapbook, Jr. Edition:** Sun. - 6.00 ② **Pixie Playtime:** Sat. - 4:05 ⑪ **Cartoon Teletales:** Mon. ⑪ Wed. - 5:30 ⑦ **The Singing Lady:** Tues. & Thurs. - 5:30 ⑦ **Lucky Pup:** Mon. thru Fri.- 6.45 ② **Birthday Party:** Thurs. - 7:00 ⑤ **Movie Serial:** Wed.-Sun.-5:30 ⑬

ABC gave Foodini the Great his own show at 11:00 A.M. *Saturday mornings in 1951. Ellen Parker hosted.*

Twenty-year-old ventriloquist Shirley Dinsdale poses with Judy Splinters before taking over for the vacationing Kukla, Fran and Ollie *in 1949.*

Lucky Pup narrator Doris Brown, flanked by Hope and Morey Bunin. Lucky Pup nestles on Brown's left arm while Foodini looks over her shoulder (1949).

Clown, were creations of Hope and Morey Bunin. Lucky's archenemies were the evil but bumbling magician Foodini and his stooge Pinhead. The fifteen-minute series aired weeknights at 6:30 P.M., was recorded on kinescope, and reedited for Saturday broadcast. Doris Brown hosted the show, which was sponsored by Sun Dial shoes, Ipana toothpaste, and Good and Plenty candy. When CBS dropped the series in 1951, ABC bought the Bunins' production and elevated Foodini to starring status. The show was renamed *Foodini the Great.* Both Ellen Parker and Lou Prentis (Wilma Deering on TV's 1950 *Buck Rogers* science fiction series) hosted the show and kept tabs on Foodini's plans to turn hard workers into unwilling philanthropists and reap unearned riches for himself via his Soft-Touch-O-Scope ray. The show had a four-month run.[6]

Available in either quarter-hour or half-hour length in 1950 was NBC's *Cyclone Malone,* a puppetry version of *The Perils of Pauline.* Cyclone, a true cliff-hanger hero, was duty-bound to save his sweetheart, Cosy, from the clutches of such dastardly villains as the Lizard. *Cyclone Malone,* however, had more in common with Mighty Mouse than a traditional serial character. His rescues always culminated with heartfelt songs and promises of everlasting love. The show, created by Ann Davis and Dorothy Novis, originated as a local production on Los Angeles station, KNBH (KNBC) in 1949.

One already established puppet-free show latched onto the bandwagon rather than face the possibility of being passed up by puppet-hungry youngsters. DuMont's *Small Fry Club,* starring Bob Emery, added a filmed puppet segment with the intention of selling the inserts to schools after three telecasts.

Also in 1949, *Sleepy Joe,* an ABC radio program, stretched his arms into television and appeared for fifteen minutes Monday through Friday at 6:45 P.M. A syndicated color version of the show featuring announcer Jimmy Scribner and puppeteer Velma Dawson, went on the market in 1951.[7]

---

6. Morey Bunin has remained active in the trade through the 1970s. Most recently he patented a figure that combined animation and live puppet techniques. The puppets are used in industrial presentations.

7. New York's ABC station, WJZ, carried the show for less than a month (October 3 to October 28, 1949). At the end of October, the affiliate reduced its programming schedule and remained off the air during the time *Sleepy Joe* had appeared.

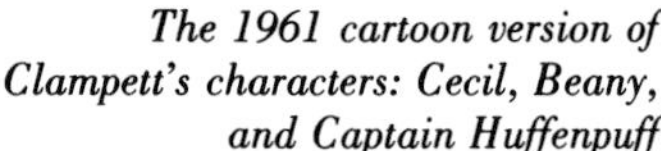

The 1961 cartoon version of Clampett's characters: Cecil, Beany, and Captain Huffenpuff

East Coast viewers, meanwhile, delighted to the Western setting of *Oky Doky Ranch.* The program, a DuMont TV production, premiered on network flagship station WABC (named for network president Allen B. DuMont), in 1947 as *Tots, Tweens and Teens.* Wendy Barrie and Rex Trailer were the show's hosts. On October 4, 1948, the title changed and, with the exception of a summer hiatus in 1949, ran until October 22, 1949. Dayton Allen was the voice of Oky Doky before he left for *Howdy Doody.* Trailer later became a host of shows in Philadelphia and Boston and starred in the 1972 nationally syndicated science series, *Earth Lab.*

While Oky Doky pictured the old West from a Manhattan studio, California youngsters were at least geographically closer to the real McCoy watching Judy Splinters, a western doll under the able control of Shirley Dinsdale. The KTLA Los Angeles show was a local favorite before picking up stakes and moving to Chicago to replace *Kukla, Fran and Ollie* for the summer of 1949. By October 1949, Splinters had become such a hit that she moved farther east to New York, where her broadcasts were carried live over the small NBC network and transferred to kinescope for her West Coast fans.

Dinsdale won the 1948 Emmy in the children's TV show category and was the first California TV personality to be launched on the network. She didn't win the favor of *The New York Times* critic Jack Gould, however. TV's toughest viewer said that neither she nor her dummy looked good in close-ups, and he recommended that half of the problem could be solved if Dinsdale used a prettier doll.

The biggest catch of 1949 was a seasick sea serpent named Cecil. The waterlogged creature who seemed happiest in waves of applause, teamed with a youngster with a frozen grin named Beany. Together they made *Time for Beany,* a puppet series that originated at KTLA, a national hit when it went into syndication the next year.

Time for Beany's credits read like a "Who's Who of Children's Television." The show was created by Bob Clampett, who had directed the Bugs Bunny cartoons. Stan Freberg mouthed the words of Cecil. Daws Butler, later known for his voices of Quick Draw McGraw, Huckleberry Hound, Yogi Bear, and hundreds of other characters, spoke for Beany. Bill Scott, partner with Jay Ward on *Rocky and His Friends,* was a chief writer, sharing space at the Paramount Studios office with Charlie Shos, who would also eventually work on Bullwinkle. Additional voices were dubbed by comedian Jerry Colonna.

What separated *Time for Beany* from most other early puppet programs was more than the three thousand miles between Los Angeles and New York. "Beany," explained Clampett in a 1954 *TV Guide* interview, "was television." He said that instead of simply presenting a puppet show with a head-on camera angle, *Time for Beany* utilized all that the medium had to offer. "It could be done only on TV," he said. "We use connected stages, not just one; painted backdrops whose illusion would be lost in a theater, and camera tricks."

TV Guide visited backstage and saw what looked like utter confusion. "Between the stage and backdrops is a four-by-six-foot space in which actors doing the voices must maneuver without breaking shins or jamming elbows into someone's mouth. Scripts are attached to a roller device, turned when a puppet manipulator gets a hand free."

Satirical scripts also served to widen the gulf between the sea-serpent series and competing shows. Rather than strictly creating a juvenile character, Clampett introduced such figures as Marilyn Mongrel, Tearalong the Dotted Lion, Louie the Lone Shark, and Dizzy Lou the kangaroo (named for Desilu).

"Stan and I ad-libbed those characters' lines like crazy," recalls Daws Butler, who besides doing the ever-smiling Beany provided the voice for Uncle Captain and Professor X. "We set each other up. We were marvelous foils for one another. And as I remember, we drove the cameramen and the director crazy because we were live."

Freberg, Butler says, "was like a bull in a China shop. His flamboyance, broadness and humor rubbed off on us. We had a great relationship, and a good friendship. I think it's been the only real collaboration I've had that was fruitful."

For five days a week over five years, Freberg and Butler stepped up to Clampett's microphone. Freberg's presence was reportedly so important to the ratings that when he was off the show with the flu for ten days in 1951, KTLA-TV officials denied his absence, not wishing viewers to tune away.

In 1961, *Time for Beany* evolved into a cartoon series called *Beany and Cecil.* The beany-

Bob Clampett's Beany puppet (1950)

capped boy and his amiable pet were back, as was actor Daws Butler. But the satire that had charmed the early series didn't survive in the transition to animation. Cecil, once a thriving creature, found these new waters stagnant. He washed ashore December 19, 1964.

At a time when Bob Clampett was still busy with *Beany and Cecil,* he introduced *The Buffalo Billy Show.* This 1950 CBS series (airing on Sunday afternoon in most locales) featured the tales of an adventure-seeking youngster who moved west in a covered wagon with his Aunt Ima Hag, an Indian fighter named Pop Gunn, his horse Blunderhead, and Dilly the Armadillo. According to an October 25, 1950, *Variety* review, however, Buffalo Billy seemed more interested in uncovering chocolate sweets than reaching sunny California. The publication said that Billy's Fanny Farmer candies commercials appeared out of place and "somewhat incongruous," particularly with "Aunty and Billy discoursing about their favorite chocs deep in injun territory." Clampett, Don Messick, and Joan Gardner were the voices of the show's characters.

Also to premiere in 1950 was *Alkali Ike,* a puppet series starring ventriloquist Al Robinson and his Western dummy; ABC's *Mr. Magic and J.J.,* featuring twenty-year-old magician Norman Jensen; Philadelphia's *Willie the Worm,* a show whose loyal following swamped the station switchboard with calls when the San Francisco United Nations telecast forced a delay of a daily broadcast; and ABC's *Paddy the Pelican,* a daily Chicago-based series starring youngster Mary Frances Desmond and offering viewers a weekly newspaper, *The Paddy Pelican Junior Journal,* for $4 a year.

Competing with *Paddy the Pelican* was CBS's *Life with Snarky Parker,* a Bil and Cora Baird and Frank Fazakas puppet production, produced and directed by then-TV executive, Yul Brynner.[8] Snarky, the lead character, was deputy sheriff of a Western town. With aid from his horse, Heathcliffe, he attempted to rid Hot Rock of a dangerous varmint named Ronald Rodent.

8. Even before *Life with Snarky Parker,* the Bairds had proven themselves to CBS brass. The husband and wife team appeared on the network's 1948 Christmas Eve musical telecast, *Surprise from Santa.*

Opposite: Rootie Kazootie, originally called Rootie Tootie until Tootsie Roll lodged a complaint

Rootie, emerging from the weekly deluge of letters in 1950

Kazootie puppeteer, Paul Ashley

Rootie Kazootie's arch enemy, Poison Zoomack

Far and away the most talked-about new puppet series of 1950 was *Rootie Kazootie.*

"Rootie, like Howdy Doody, was a little boy with a big heart, a typical four-year-old trying to make inroads to adulthood," says puppeteer Paul Ashley. "And he and his dog, Gala Poochie Pup, were protective of his girlfriend, Polka Dottie, because Poison Zoomack was always trying to steal her polka dots."[9]

Rootie aired weeknights at 6 P.M. and Saturdays for a time, and was occasionally directed by Dwight Hemion, who has since become a major television director. The fun-loving lad might have taken his cues from others, but he needed Ashley for guidance. The puppeteer held the strings, since he was first approached to do the show by producer Steve Carlin.

"Carlin, head of children's records for RCA, saw an ad I had placed in the New York Yellow Pages and said he'd like to see my puppets," Ashley offers. "After I visited his office he asked if he could take them to a meeting. I said I wasn't certain and told him that the puppets took a long time to make, and I didn't really know him." Carlin, already convinced he could create a popular puppet show if Ashley's steady hands were at work, left his watch with the puppeteer as collateral. Carlin then took Ashley's puppets to NBC and secured a contract.

Canadian Todd Russell was hired to host the show. The big man dwarfed the puppets and helped turn *Rootie Kazootie* into a giant hit.

So successful was the show that RCA, the program's first sponsor, reported that a Roy Rogers's Rodeo Album immediately netted a 400 percent sales increase after one plug by Rootie. Reaction that strong told officials that the local WNBT program—initially called *Rootie Tootie*—should be aired over the NBC network.

The belief was reinforced after a Saturday, March 31, 1951, broadcast. The program offered a membership to the Rootie Kazootie Club, a souvenir button, and a color picture of the character. The dime come-on triggered more than 18,000 responses in one week.

Ashley says he wasn't surprised by the public's reaction. "We knew how to hold everybody in suspense. There were a lot of little puddles in the chairs after our show," he explains. "Rootie used to get into some different jam every day. The action started with him breaking through a tissue in the beginning of the show while the theme song played: 'Who is the boy who is full of zip and joy? He's Rootie Kazootie.' Then Rootie or Polka Dottie would sing with Todd, and we'd cut to a commercial." On days when Coca-Cola paid the bills, Rootie would be shown sipping the drink through a straw, an effect achieved by having a stagehand pull the bottle's hidden cork from below the table.

Joining Russell, who also appeared as host on the Saturday morning giveaway show *Pud's Prize Party* and NBC's nighttime series *Wheel of Fortune*, was John Schoepperle as Mr. Deetle Dootle. Ashley often did voices on the show, but primary duty for the main characters went to Frank Milano and Naomi Lewis.

The series signed off in April 1953 when, according to Ashley, the producer announced he had to cut the budget. The staff had the option to continue with reduced salaries or leave. "They voted to leave, and it was a very sad day in my life," Ashley states.

Following *Rootie Kazootie*'s demise, Ashley and his puppets appeared on NBC's daily 9:00 A.M. program, *The Home Show,* and later co-

9. Gala-Poochie Pup was originally named Nipper for the RCA corporate symbol. When RCA withdrew sponsorship, the dog was retained; spots were painted and his name was changed.

starred with Chuck McCann on *Let's Have Fun* and *Laurel, Hardy and Chuck,* telecast in New York.

Ashley still works today, both performing with his marionettes and hand puppets and carving figures. Ashley created the new Howdy Doody puppet used in the 1976 syndicated series.

Songs, stories, comic chatter, and elfish pranks provided the ingredients for Mary and Harry Hickox's 1951 syndicated series *Jump Jump of Holiday House.* Also nosing into the syndication market that year and becoming the runaway star of *Barnyardville Varieties,* was a sexy blond pig named both Shirley Swine and Penny Pig. Sue Hastings' marionette character, like Jim Henson's Miss Piggy, stole the bacon. According to a *Billboard* article, after producers screened the color pilot film for kids, Shirley (Penny) was chosen by viewers as the plaything they most desired.

ABC preferred the zoo to the barnyard and aired a monkey character in 1951 named *Ozmoe.* This chimp wasn't kept on a string, however. Creator Henry Banks constructed Ozmoe and his associates, including Poe the crow, Sweet-Pie the mermaid, and Sam the Clam, out of a latex rubber compound and operated them via an electronic remote-control system. The setting was

ABC's nonexistent subbasement Studio Z, where the puppets mingled among the legs of TV engineers.

Quizmaster Johnny Olsen talked to a more traditional puppet named Red Goose for sponsor "Red Goose" shoes on DuMont's 1951 talent show *Kids and Company* and the Paul Ritts animal puppets conversed with Bill Sears, who leisurely sat on a park bench from December 9, 1951, to May 31, 1953, for CBS's Sunday show, *In the Park.*

Time gave CBS "high marks" for Bil and Cora Baird's "imaginative settings and marionettes on *The Whistling Wizard,* an ambitious 1951, 11:00 A.M. Saturday morning production. Children watched the show with great awe, while industry scientists tuned in with keen interest. For a short time, *The Whistling Wizard* was broadcast in "incompatible color"—a color system tested then rejected by the Federal Communications Commission. Unlike NBC's color, which could still be received on regular black and white monitors, CBS's venture was not visible on the standard set, and children could only hear the audio of the show whenever the network tested its color video.

When visible, *Whistling Wizard* was a delight. *Broadcasting* noted its "expert staging and lighting." *The New York Times* zeroed in on "its elaborate production, deft staging and fluid mobility." *Saturday Review* called the Bairds "the leading regisseurs in the country of the guignol or puppet world." And *Variety* appreciated the show's "sophisticated side, clever dialogue, fine illusions" and noticed more than a hint of literary characteristics in the string characters. "Judging from the construction of the dolls, the motion of their eyes and the voices of the puppeteers," the trade paper wrote, *The Whistling Wizard* figures had been borrowed from "such assorted sources as Dickens, comic strips, folklore, and fairy tales."

Many of the stories were indeed modern versions of classic tomes including the *Sorcerer's Apprentice,* the Perseus legend, and the myths of Davy Jones and medieval dragons.

And where literature didn't provide a story, setting, or character, the Bairds drew from life. The Dooley, for example, the show's Whistling Wizard who talked with a slight brogue, was the father figure and represented law and authority. Young J. P., the Wizard's ward, was an industrious lad with a bright future and was apparently modeled after J. P. Morgan.

The other characters rounding out the regular cast included Heathcliffe, a carryover from *Life with Snarky Parker*, Flannel the mouse, and Charlemane the lion. The villain of the show was Spider Lady, a nefarious woman who performed her black magic upon uttering the words "Elia Kazan."

In all, the Bairds worked more than forty puppets in their marionette madhouse. Miraculously, the strings hardly tangled while the lives of the characters joyously intertwined.

The Whistling Wizard's alluring charm was owed as much to production values as the inviting stories. Gone were the typical marionette trappings: the curtain and the arch—structures and obstructions that had limited camera moves

In the Park's Bill Sears is surrounded by Sir Geoffrey the Giraffe, Albert the Chipmunk, Calvin the Crow, and Magnolia the Ostrich. Cigarette smoking, such as Calvin's, was put out of children's television years after this December 1951 CBS show aired.

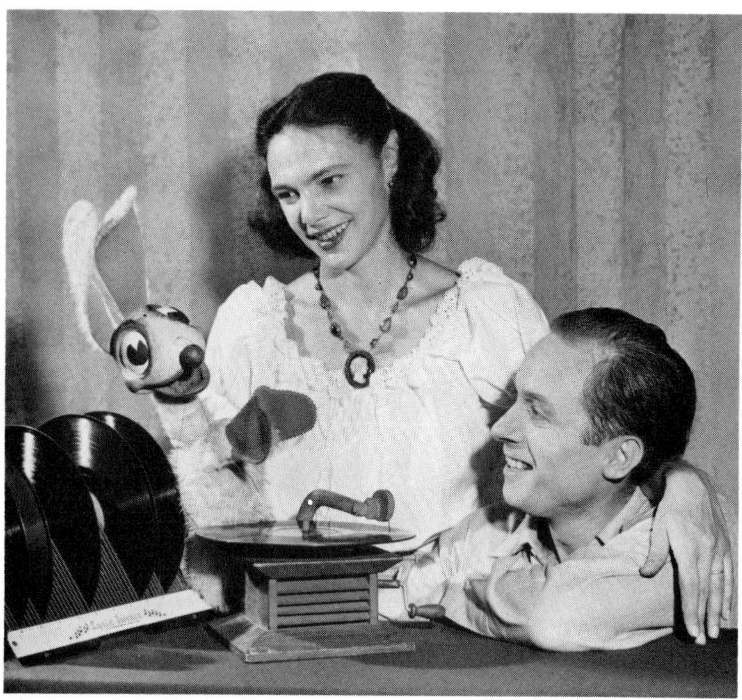

Bil and Cora Baird brought dozens of puppets to television. Here, they're seen working with Groovy, a screwball disc jockey rabbit, in The Bil Baird Show *(1953).*

to a static audience view. Liberating the performance expanded the story, as Bob Clampett had also discovered. *The Whistling Wizard* spoofed institutions and the norm. The purpose, explained Baird in a 1951 interview, was to take the conventional world and make it more recognizable through fantasy.

The Bairds also brought their wares to a biweekly music program in 1953, *The Bil Baird Show,* as well as to *Your Show of Shows,* CBS's *The Morning Show* with host Walter Cronkite, and Westinghouse's *Adventures in Numbers and Space.*

Returning in most of the productions to operate the marionettes were the Bairds and colleagues Frank Fazakas and Frank Sullivan.

When the FCC freeze on station construction thawed in 1952 and the rule limiting the number of American stations to 108 in 63 cities was discarded, syndicated series, particularly puppet shows, warmed viewers up to the new outlets. *The Adventures of Blinkey,* one such program, followed Blinkey, a Dorothy-like character, through an enchanted puppet world. The intriguing aspect of this show, created by Lucille Emerick, was its combination of live-action and puppetry. Blinky started out as a real-life boy (Michael Mann), but he was soon transformed into a puppet representation of himself once he crossed over to the make-believe land.

Uncle Mistletoe and His Adventures, originally intended as a local Chicago show in 1948 on WENR-TV, won enough favor by 1952 to warrant nationwide distribution. As a local production, *Uncle Mistletoe* featured Jennifer Holt, but the former Western actress left for NBC's *Panhandle Pete* in 1951. Doris Larson replaced Holt as the Lookout Lady. Throughout its broadcast life Johnny Coons, later a popular network host, provided the puppets' voices.

Uncle Mistletoe premiered strictly as a promotional device for Chicago's Marshall Field department stores. Mistletoe. a one-foot-high character, presumably Santa's business manager, was created for window displays. Besides Mistletoe the show's characters included Obadiah Pig and Tony Pony.

Bracken Productions released a 15-minute 1952 series called *Willie Wonderful,* employing hand puppets whose eyes and mouths could move. Stars of *Willie Wonderful* were the show's lead character, a young boy, Phineas Q. Throckmorton, his fairy godfather, who looked a great deal like W. C. Fields; Eleanor the elephant; and Girard the giraffe.

Philadelphia's Willie the Worm crawled onto CBS in 1952 for the midday Sunday series *Junior Hi-Jinx.* Willie, distinguished by his beanie and horn-rimmed glasses, lived under a college campus and came out to tell Aesop's fables, jokes, and science lessons.

Fearless Fosdick, Al Capp's Dick Tracy character, also aired in 1952, with the Mary Chase marionettes dressed up for the police duty and assigned to NBC.

From Chicago came *Hold 'er Newt* (1950), a daily puppet show set in a small town general store. The same year, CBS Syndication Sales, and Children's Television Films released *Betsy and the Magic Key.* The series starred the Sue Hastings Marionettes and was previewed during the Christmas holiday by patients at the children's ward of New York's Bellevue Hospital.

In 1953, Aladdin's classic tales figured into the syndicated marionette production, *Don Q., Dick and Aladdin.*

Across the dial, DuMont was rocketing forward with one of TV's most creative programs, *Johnny Jupiter.* The Saturday series had two separate landings. The first, a live puppet program lasting from March 21 to June 13, 1953, was set in a television studio where a janitor named Ernest P. Duckweather (Vaughn Taylor) could not resist playing with the dials. His fascination led to a startling discovery. By tinkering with the rows of levers, buttons, and switches, he could communicate with emissaries from the planet Jupiter—Johnny, his Oxford-accented sidekick, B-12, and a dutiful robot named Major Domo.

Through the puppet characters, DuMont producer Martin Stone and scriptwriter Jerry Coppersmith held a mirror to the foibles of contemporary Earth; a perspective visible to *The New York Times* critic Jack Gould.

"*Johnny Jupiter,*" Gould wrote, was a "delightfully wild item of video fantasy that has charm, intelligence and a wonderful satirical point of view. It is something not to be missed."

Johnny's and B-12's attacks on Earth were

Johnny Jupiter (1953)

strictly verbal. They criticized taxation and television. The planet Jupiter, they said, had television, but it is used for punishing children when they spend too much time reading books or playing with slide rules.

Johnny explained that he couldn't understand why Earth has any traffic problems. Vehicular congestion on Jupiter was solved simply by picking out the most crowded street and erecting signs that read "Parking Allowed." And the Jupiterian wondered why Earthlings made such a fuss for beautiful women, when it is the homely girl who needs the attention.

One week Duckweather auditioned for a TV News program on Jupiter and ended up satirizing American commentators and the pressure brought to bear by special-interest groups.

As Duckweather announced an item about a pair of moon dwellers apprehended by the satellite patrol, the Moon Dwellers Association telephoned to protest. The item was dropped. Next he began "a shocking exposé about underwater plant life" that was greeted by objections from the Underwater Vegetable League. He killed the story.

"And here's a juicy tidbit," continued Duckweather, only to be stopped in midsentence by a phone call from the Juicy Tidbit Society. Duckweather signed off with a song entitled, "The Program That Doesn't Offend."

The creative force behind this early show was writer Coppersmith, who took Martin Stone's cue and parodied American convention as successfully as Monty Python pokes fun at the British. "Writing the scripts is not easy, but it's a lot of fun," Coppersmith told *The New York Times*. "It gives me a lot of personal satisfaction. We know that both children and adults watch the show, but I didn't write for either group. I write for my own enjoyment. I assume that if the script satisfied me, it will satisfy others, too."

Variety felt that Coppersmith's work might be "above the heads of the audience," however. The review spoke an unfortunate truth, for even a decade later the satirical *That Was the Week That Was*, a prime time program, discovered that television was not an instrument for subtlety. Viewers favored slapstick to innuendo, action to verbalization.

Martin Stone, owner of Kagran, the merchandising arm of *Howdy Doody*, produced *Johnny Jupiter* and hoped that his space-age show would take off even better if syndicated on film. Stone consequently sold commercial time to M&M candies, found slots in eighty markets, and set Duckweather's adventures in the Frisbee General Store where the janitor, now Wright King, conversed with the Carl Harm puppets. Pat Peardon played Duckweather's girl friend. Cliff Hall joined the cast as Mr. Frisbee. This second version premiered in many cities September 5, 1953. This time *Variety* felt the show had hit its mark, commenting that *Johnny Jupiter* was "fused with all the elements that appeal to small fry—slapstick comedy, puppetry and sci fi."

The real spirit was gone, however.

Other TV personalities of 1953, such as Mary Hartline and Roxanne, may have been viewed as television's first sex goddesses, but Shari Lewis has earned a greater distinction in the decades since. She's become Saturday's only lasting love. From the first day she signed on the air, youngsters have seen her as the perky and sweet older sister, while adolescents have measured her against the girl next door. Colleagues, on the other hand, have looked beyond the beautiful blond locks and rosy cheeks and have been humbled strictly by the talent and ability.

Like her own puppets, Lewis describes herself as a handmade product. "My parents shaped me the way some people needlepoint," she explains. "They trained me and that training was exquisite. I studied ballet, drama, three instruments, and my father even made me take a week of juggling."

Indeed Lewis's father, Dr. Abraham Hurwitz, an accomplished magician and a professor of child guidance, probably exerted the greatest influence in her life. Years later the subject of her father came up, of all places, after a Command Performance at the London Palladium.

"Princess Anne asked me how I chose ventriloquism, a field she thought highly unusual for a girl. I told her my father was a magician and we always had magic and puppets around the house. I started ventriloquism when I was eleven. It seemed the natural thing to do."

Upon hearing her explanation, the Princess paused only one beat, then replied, "Yes, one does tend to become involved in one's family profession."

Lewis's initial plunge into radio and television, however, was far less successful than intended. In 1952 she won *Arthur Godfrey's Talent Scouts* and was subsequently awarded three appearances on his radio show. "Unfortunately," she remembers, "I had just one comedy routine, which I had already performed on *Talent Scouts.* With nothing else ready, I was canceled. My first victory brought me my first defeat."

Undaunted, she hit the typewriter, developed new material, and less than a year later tried again. At age eighteen, her first TV show, *Fun 'n' Facts,* debuted. Lewis seized the oppportunity with all the enthusiasm of a chorus line ballerina suddenly stepping out in solo. In a matter of weeks she beguiled her audiences and reveled in the spotlight. Today, she finds TV a completely different experience.

"The quality of children's television is quite ghastly now. Except for an occasional afternoon dramatic special," the four-time Emmy-winner says, "the shows are cranked out like sausage."

"Children are up for sale to the highest bidder," she continues. "The highest bidder wants the largest ratings, and the largest ratings usually produce the very worst shows."

The worst? Cartoons, she declares, adding that even her last NBC program was replaced by a cartoon. "They offer the best possibility to air a great deal of blood and guts and a tremendous amount of movement with no conscience or humanity."

As for advertisements on children's TV, Lewis believes "Commercials are less the danger than the miserable quality that is being fed the children."

Recollections of her own shows and the characters that starred in *Fun 'n' Facts* (1953), *Shari and Her Friends* (1954), *Shariland* (1957), *Hi Mom* (1958), and *The Shari Lewis Show* (1960) bring much happier conversation.

Her biggest break, she recalls, came in 1956 when CBS enlisted her for duty on *Captain Kangaroo.* Up until that time Lewis had generally worked the traditional hardwood dummies and appeared on local New York television. CBS, however, asked her to develop something more delicate, more childlike.

"The only thing I had then was a little lamb puppet that I had kept in the drawer. I took it out and not knowing what to do with him, I sat in front of a mirror and tried a basic improvisation. To this day, that's essentially what Lamb Chop and I do—improvise."[10]

There's always the feeling in those exchanges between Shari and Lamb Chop that the performer isn't playing the lines for a fast joke. Her routines appear to be thinly disguised encounter-sessions; her characters are obviously integral parts of her psyche and not mere fabrications.

"Any character that an actor does that isn't a portion of one's ego cannot live," Lewis argues. "If I have to think about what Lamb Chop is going to say, then I might as well not say it."

In 1975, Lewis returned to television with *The Shari Lewis Show*, a thirty-minute monthly series

10. Years before Lamb Chop began grazing on Saturday morning, Shari taught an outer-space dummy named Randy Rocket the ways of contemporary Earth and performed with Taffy Twinkle, a redecorated turn-of-the-century "Willie Talk" doll.

A Conversation with Shari Lewis and Lamb Chop

Shari: Get up, darling.

Lamb Chop: I don't want to get up.

Shari: Come on, honey, we're going to be interviewed.

Q. HELLO?

Lamb Chop: Hello.

Q. GOOD MORNING, LAMB CHOP. HOW ARE YOU?

Lamb Chop: I don't know.

Q. YOU'RE AS SHY AS I REMEMBER. DO YOU EVER GET MOMENTS OF BOLDNESS?

Lamb Chop: Only if you try to get fresh.

Q. DO ANY OF YOUR FRIENDS GET FRESH?

Lamb Chop: Only new ones. My bestest new friend is Grizzly. He's a bear. A big bear. He's from the ghetto.

Q. LIKE YOGI?

Lamb Chop: No. No. He's from the ghetto. And there's a big baby doll now and Mr. Bearly. He runs Bearly Broadcasting, the television station we worked at on our last show.

Q. WHAT ABOUT HUSH PUPPY?

Lamb Chop: He's not working a whole lot. I haven't spoken to him for a long while.

Q. HOW ABOUT SHARI? HOW DO YOU REALLY FEEL ABOUT HER?

Lamb Chop: Well, I'm very attached to her. I love her. I wouldn't go out on my own. I think I'd feel very sheepish if I did that. She sometimes goes out without me. But when she does she feels lonely. I know.

Q. YOU'VE MET SOME FAMOUS PEOPLE THROUGHOUT THE YEARS. IS THERE ANYONE WHO REALLY MADE YOU VERY NERVOUS, WHO MADE YOUR PAWS SWEAT?

Lamb Chop: Puppets don't sweat. I think everytime I've met Prince Phillip I get nervous. He shakes my foot, I like him a lot.

Q. WHEN SHARI DOESN'T FEEL WELL DO YOU CATCH HER COLD TOO?

Lamb Chop: Sometimes, but when she can't talk I can because I use a different part of her vocal chords.

Q. DO YOU HAVE ANY IDOLS?

Lamb Chop: I'm not idle. I work very hard.

Q. WHAT ABOUT SATURDAY MORNING TELEVISION TODAY. DO YOU LIKE IT?

Lamb Chop: I don't watch it because it's junk. If Saturday morning television came through the mail, I'd send it back as junk mail.

Q. DO YOU WANT TO BE ON TV AGAIN?

Lamb Chop: Well, I'm sort of on now. Shari and I are on nutritional spots for NBC about a dozen times every Saturday. I do things like trying to leave a cookie under the pillow and claim it's for the Tooth Fairy. And Shari says the Tooth Fairy doesn't want cookies and I say, "Well, I'm all out of teeth."

Q. BUT WHAT ABOUT ANOTHER REGULAR SHOW?

Lamb Chop: Maybe someday. Right now I like working with symphony orchestras. I've done Chopin with thirty or forty symphonies.

Q. THAT'S A GREAT DEAL OF WORK, YOU MUST HAVE A SOCIAL SECURITY CARD.

Lamb Chop: Nope, I don't even have an American Express Card and the Muppets do! Good night.

Shari Lewis before reaching voting age, but old enough to earn the respect of the nation's audience

that aired on NBC's owned and operated stations and was later syndicated. Lewis describes the production as a *Mary Tyler Moore Show* with puppets. Among the twenty-five animal characters working for the Bearly Broadcasting Studios (BBS) was a kangaroo named Captain Person. "I was the token human on the program," she offers.

Over the years, Shari Lewis has been a diligent and dedicated stage mother to such familiar foot-high TV offspring as Lamb Chop, Charlie Horse, and Hush Puppy, and has had her hand in writing as much as in puppetry.

For more than twenty-five years the effervescent ventriloquist has charmed youngsters on Saturday mornings and pounded the keys the remainder of the week. Lewis wrote her first book, *The Shari Lewis Puppet Book* (New York: Citadel Press), in 1958, penned six more by 1962, collaborated with her husband for a *Star Trek* episode in the late 1960s, and has churned out a daily syndicated newspaper column for the last few years. The column, she says, was an outgrowth of her parental concern. "I was really very distressed to find my daughter wasn't reading the newspaper. I proposed the idea of a children's column to a syndicate, and the concept was immediately bought."

In 1979, Holt, Rinehart, & Winston began publication of her newest book venture—the first of ten children's books—all part of a Kids-Only Club series designed by Lewis. Each of the thirty-six books contracted for delivery are designed by Lewis to teach youngsters assorted skills, from putting on a profit-making carnival to inventing a game or creating Halloween masks.

As for a renewed career in TV, Lewis is less willing than ever to compete with cartoons. She calls the existing Saturday morning schedule "truly terrible," and is relatively content to stay free of the medium. Instead, Lewis regularly appears as a guest conductor with many of the nation's top symphony orchestras and has been a successful attraction on the nightclub circuit since 1964.

Yet, as *Time* noted in the mid-1950s, Shari Lewis is here to stay. The magazine's description of her "as perky as one of the wind-up toys she frequently displays . . . and without a doubt the biggest package of energy and talent in TV" is as accurate today as ever. She'll return as long as there are TV critics like *The New York Times*'s John Crosby, who says, "She is altogether too good for your preschool children and should have a show aimed at older children, say me."

In 1954 ventriloquist Jimmy Weldon talked turkey with his duck dummy on NBC's *Webster Webfoot* and another gander thought he was king of the United States on ABC's *Garfield Goose and Friend.* A year later, Brett Morrison, The Shadow of radio, lent his voice to the fifteen-minute syndicated series *Bobo the Hobo and His Traveling Troupe.* The same year Eleanor Olha starred in WCBS's Saturday morning educational program, *Hickory Dickory Dock,* and Fred Rogers, who would eventually be known as the caretaker of *Mister Rogers' Neighborhood,* was heard teaching proper manners and foreign culture on NBC's short-lived puppet series, *The Children's Corner.*

One of the busiest, most familiar Saturday morning puppeteers of the 1950s didn't even have a regular TV show. Jimmy Nelson and his two irresistible dummies, Farfel and Danny O'Day, primarily appeared on Nestlé's commercials intercut throughout *The Lone Ranger, Sky King, The Mighty Mouse Playhouse,* and *The Roy Rogers Show.*

"My wife and I used to sit and see these commercials running one right after another on Saturday morning, and I remember her saying, 'What is this? The *Jimmy Nelson Spectacular?*' " he jokes.

"We did all our commercials in New York," he adds. The shows themselves were done in California and he rarely had the time or the opportunity to mix with his weekend costars. "I actually only saw Roy Rogers once," he says, "and that was in the lobby of the Ambassador Hotel in Los Angeles." Nelson was wearing a tuxedo and Rogers approached him mistaking the ventriloquist for a hotel employee. "He was lost and he came up to me and said, 'Excuse me, sir, which way is the main ballroom?' I said, 'I'll tell you where it is, but you should know I'm the fellow who does the commercials on your program.' "

Nelson received a handshake but no tip.

Nelson did host one production that was actually more of a commercial than a program.

Jimmy Nelson

I was doing a late-night show in Wichita, Kansas, for a half-dozen people. Someone had been playing with a little stuffed dog and left it on the piano and I was just ad-libbing. I picked up the dog and pulled out this timid, soft-spoken, apologetic voice and people started to laugh. I figured if I'm getting laughs on straight lines I have to develop this character. The next few nights I brought the little stuffed toy and he basically developed into Farfel. The name was what my piano player used to call me. Farfel is a little noodle-type thing used in cooking, so freely translated it meant "little noodle." It seemed to fit the dog.

The concept was born in that nightclub and I immediately contacted Frank Marshall, my figure-maker in Chicago, who had made Danny for me. We went through different designs before I settled on the one I liked. Farfel's been great, and of course there's the extra advantage of having a wooden dog as a pet. He doesn't have to be walked.

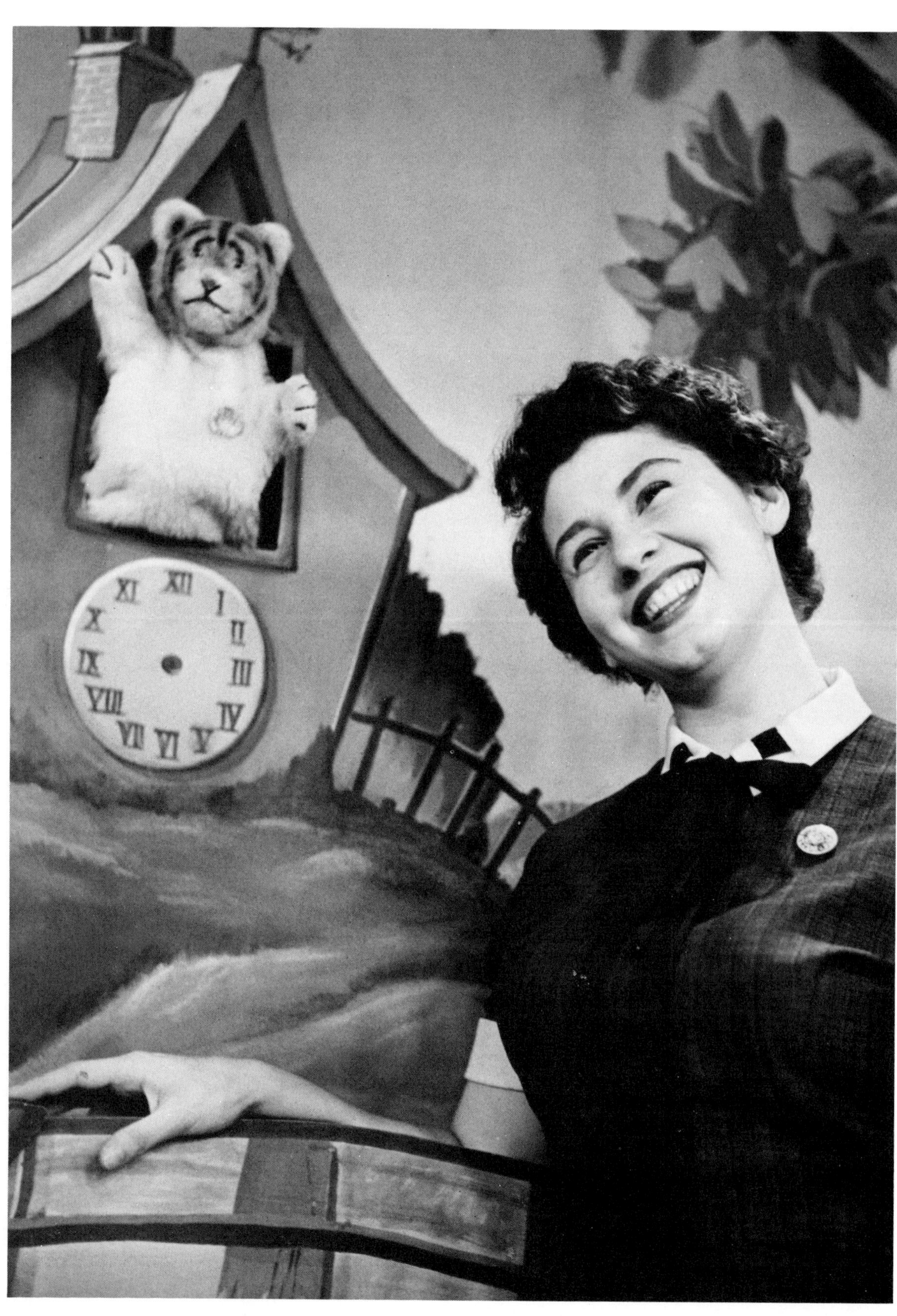

In 1956 he starred in *Toyland Express*, a Christmastime series that presented the latest in children's games, toys, and dolls (see Chapter VIII, "Batteries Not Included" and Appendix A).

"I never considered myself a kiddie entertainer," says Nelson. The ventriloquist was more widely known for his evening performances as a pitchman for Texaco commercials on *The Milton Berle Show* and regular appearances on *The Ed Sullivan Show*, Jackie Gleason's DuMont variety show, *Cavalcade of Stars*, and two quiz shows, *Bank on the Stars*, and *Come Closer*. But to any kid with a sweet tooth, it is Nelson's sixty-second performances that are best remembered.

"If you want to say I was a Saturday morning actor, it's strictly because of the ten years of Nestlé's commercials beginning in 1955," he explains. Nelson's favorite companion on the spots was Farfel, his droopy-eared pooch, who always spelled out the sponsor's name in a sleepy drone.

By the mid-1950s puppets were evident in every city during the children's hours. Even stations that had no network affiliation and couldn't afford syndicated fare still had their own local versions of popular shows.

To the uninitiated TV-viewer—the minority by 1956—the airwaves must have looked like a home for puppets. In Chicago, WBKB-TV aired Sir J. Worthington Wiggle. WLW-TV in Dayton, Ohio, presented Don Williams's assorted animal figures, while *Rugby the Rabbit* appeared on WABC-TV in New York. In Milwaukee, WISN-TV broadcast *The Magic House*. Dallas's KRLD-TV offered Gerry Johnson's puppets announcing birthdays and commercials, and Frank Webb's characters taught art on KEY-TV in Santa Barbara, California.

Bobby Nicholson traded in his Clarabell outfit when he hosted *The Gumby Show* in March 1957. Sharing the hosting chores on the first Saturday morning NBC show was Buffalo Bob Smith. The limelight, however, belonged to the tiny clay figure, Gumby, animated via a stop-motion technique similar to the system that propelled *Davey and Goliath*.

A Conversation with Danny O'Day

Q. DANNY, WHEN IS YOUR VOICE GOING TO CHANGE?

O'Day: Probably never. And anyway, the funny part about it is that it's Nelson's voice before it changed. Apparently he was able to hang onto it.

Q. THERE SEEMS TO BE A STRONG RESEMBLANCE BETWEEN YOU AND JERRY MAHONEY. DID YOU BOTH COME FROM THE SAME BLOCK OF WOOD?

O'Day: You might say the same family tree. We were carved by Frank Marshall. Frank worked on Jerry some years before me, however.

Q. DANNY, YOU'VE GIVEN US WONDERFUL MEMORIES, BUT WHY ARE YOU OUT OF WORK TODAY AND DO YOU THINK KIDS ARE MISSING ANYTHING?

O'Day: I think they're missing a great deal. With the exception of Kermit and the rest of the Muppets, we're unemployed. The Muppets have done a remarkable job of bringing puppets back to television, but we still have a long way to go. I'd like to see someone like Jerry or me on TV again: someone with a Pinocchio complex—a wooden kid. Kids can just sit back and enjoy the gags, jokes, one-liners, and little situations between the ventriloquist and his figures that they're missing now.

Q. DANNY, DO YOU LOOK THE SAME TODAY?

O'Day: I look adorable. Of course I do get repainted once a year. And I have a new hairpiece. I really look good.

Q. ARE YOU THINKING OF EVER GOING TO COLLEGE?

O'Day: I've been there—you might say I've been to the college of hard knocks all my life.

Q. THANK YOU, DANNY, I HOPE YOU'LL GET BACK ON TV; THE SAME GOES FOR YOUR DAD, JIMMY NELSON.

Nelson: *(interrupting)* Isn't it something, you talking to a dummy and me playing with dolls? But that's the way I've made my living ever since I was a teen-ager.

O'Day: That's all right, isn't it?

Nelson: You bet, 'sall right.

O'Day: 'Sall right.

Opposite: Josie Carey, the only "live" member of puppeteer Fred Rogers's The Children's Corner, *seen in the 10:00* A.M. *and 11:00* A.M. *slots Saturday in 1955 and 1956 on many NBC affiliates.*

Gumby (1957)

In 1958, ABC's *The Uncle Al Show* employed the Larry Smith hand puppets for an 11:00 A.M. telecast, and Black Tooth, Marilyn Monwolf, White Fang, Hippy, and Pookie shared *Lunch with Soupy Sales* an hour later.

In 1963 technology and old-fashioned marionettes were united by Sylvia and Gerry Anderson to form "Supermarionation." The process utilized a plastic marionette that moved by traditional means but was equipped with an electronic brain. In full operation, characters' eyes could slide sideways and blink, and lips, wired to solenoid cells, could move in synchronization to a prerecorded soundtrack. Thin control lines (.005 inches thick) were sprayed with anti-glare paint usually rendering them invisible on the screen. And as a final step the figures were made even more realistic by affixing photographs of real eyes to their faces.

Supermarionation appropriately appeared in futuristic adventures; a genre the English Andersons would dabble in through production of TV's *UFO* and *Space: 1999*.

The pilot project was *Fireball XL-5*, a thirty-minute twenty-first century story with Colonel Steve Zodiac and copilot Venus defending Space City from the Briggs Brothers and Mr. and Mrs. Superspy. The series had a two-year flight on NBC starting in 1963.

Stingray splashed into the syndication market in 1965 with Supermarionation hero Troy Tempest commanding the submarine *Stingray* under orders of the World Aquanaut Security Patrol.

Cut from the same mold were the characters in the Andersons' 1967 syndicated series, *Captain Scarlet and the Mysterons.* The plot, however, differed, as the friendly exploratory Earth forces of Spectrum inadvertently touched off an interstellar war when the inhabitants of Mars took them for the vanguard army of a planetary invasion. Ed Bishop, Commander Straker in *UFO*, recorded the voice of Captain Blue, a Spectrum agent.

The Thunderbirds took off in 1966, available in either one-hour or a pair of thirty-minute cliff-hangers. This Supermarionation adventure was set on a remote Pacific atoll that housed International Rescue, a career rescue-team headed by Jeff Tracy and his son, Scott.

In 1968 the Andersons produced *Joe 90*, a series about a nine-year-old boy who doubled

Above: The Thunderbirds, *Gerry and Sylvia Anderson's 1968 Supermarionation series*

Below: The Andersons' "Supermarionation" characters were a combination of traditional marionettes and electronic robots. Their eyes shifted and blinked and their lips moved.

as an unofficial operative for the World Intelligence Network. Joe was no ordinary youngster. He could run faster than a train, and reason with his genius IQ after being jolted by rays from Big Rat (Brain Impulse Galvanascope Record and Transfer).

A year later *Sesame Street* again proved that puppets were actually more fanciful unadorned than supercharged. The contribution of The Muppets to the success of the multiple-award-winning Public Broadcasting Service show is unarguable. Jim Henson's daily vision turns everyday inanimate objects into lively subjects. His magic is greater than Merlin's; his imagination, as evidenced by *The Muppet Show*, is as broad as Disney's.

After *Sesame Street* premiered, it appeared that puppets might be back in vogue, though not back in volume. A handful of network shows worked in make-believe characters with real-life kids. ABC's *Curiosity Shop*, for example, relied on puppets in 1971. *Lidsville*, another 1971 ABC

The Skatebirds are pursued by Scat Cat on CBS's 1977 Hanna-Barbera production.

Bigger Than Lifelike

In the late 1960s a wave of giant puppet-shows swept through Saturday morning as the networks reacted to pressure from lobbyists and activist groups. Sid and Marty Krofft's oversized characters, in particular, outgrew the confines of the small puppet theater and overran the entire TV studio with *H. R. Pufnstuf, The Bugaloos,* and other shows. However, the Kroffts' characters were not TV's first king-size puppet outfit.

In 1954 an ear-flapping cloth elephant appeared between shows on NBC Chicago station WNBQ-TV to advise youngsters to brush their teeth. Kids digested his message; two American Federation of Labor (AFL) unions battled over his insides. One union claimed that the man manipulating Elmer the Elephant's trunk with his arm was an actor. The other argued that the job should go to a stagehand. The National Labor Relations Board (NLRB) settled the dispute in July 1954 and ruled that Elmer's innards belonged to an actor.

Full-size peopled-puppets have appeared on *Captain Kangaroo* and many of Shari Lewis's shows, but it was Hanna-Barbera's *The Banana Splits Adventure Hour* (1968) that sent the wardrobe departments into overtime. The live-action series featured four characters: Drooper (lion), Bingo (gorilla), Fleegle (dog), and Snorky (baby elephant). "The show simply evolved when we decided to make some of the characters we were drawing larger and thereby give them more charm," says co-creator Joseph Barbera.

The series was successful for one year. Its second season was less well received. "We learned the hard way," Barbera explains. "We did all new segments but we didn't change the background. When a kid turned on to see, it seemed to be the same old show. They didn't even wait to hear the material. We should have changed the look, but it was still good. Later we made the *Skatebirds* and we've since put all of our large characters into our theme parks and touring shows."

In 1969, *H. R. Pufnstuf* also premiered on NBC. British actor Jack Wild, the Artful Dodger in the film *Oliver* (1968), starred as Jimmy, the owner of a talking golden production depicted a magical puppetland inhabited by hats. *The New Zoo Revue*, a syndicated series, used puppets stuffed with people and smaller versions that fit a hand.

In 1978, Jim Henson's *The Muppet Show* became the first syndicated program ever to win an Emmy in the variety category. Hanna-Barbera prepared a prime time puppet show, *B. B. Beagle* for the 1980s. Generally, however, television has cut its strings with puppeteers.

"My show is very much a one-man show," says Burr Tillstrom. "And TV is far too complicated a business for an individual effort to survive today. It's an industry now," he adds. "The average puppeteer can't work on that scale. A puppeteer is a very creative person. And today's TV is constructed more than created."

In the early years TV provided a place for the individual creator. But those naïve times, like the kinescopes that documented the work, haven't lasted forever. Adults have only fading memories of the Saturday morning puppet shows. Today's youngsters have little more than forgettable cartoons.

Jack Wild holds his talking flute as Mayor Pufnstuf acts as his guardian in the 1969 Sid and Marty Krofft oversized puppet series H. R Pufnstuf.

flute named Freddie. The two, adrift on a boat, eventually encountered Pufnstuf, the mayor of a magical land where castles and trees could talk.

The reception of the Sid and Marty Krofft series prompted the producers to air *The Bugaloos* in 1970. Martha Raye headlined the cast as Benita Bizarre immediately after she appeared in a movie version of *Pufnstuf.* As the wily witch, Bizarre, she attempted to destroy the peace of Tranquility Forest and its quartet of bee musicians, the Bugaloos.

The Kroffts produced *Lidsville* for ABC in 1971. Charles Nelson Reilly portrayed Hoo-Doo, the magician. Butch Patrick costarred as Mark, a youngster with an insatiable appetite for tricks. Also seen were dozens of hat characters including Nurse Hat, Cowboy Hat, Top Hat, and Raunchy Rabbit Hat.

Two years later, *Sigmund and the Sea Monsters* emerged on NBC. The Krofft series featured midget Billy Barty as Sigmund Ooz, a black sheep from a sea-monster clan, and his two human companions (Johnny Whitaker and Scott Kolden). Rip Taylor and Margaret Hamilton also had continuing roles. Sigmund was lost in the ocean of reruns in 1975.

The New Zoo Revue, a 1972 syndicated children's show, offered 195 half-hour adventures of a life-size frog named Freddie; Henrietta, a southern bell hippo; and Charlie, the wise owl. Producer Barbara Atlas geared the show for preschoolers—an audience she insists that network television ignores. "Preschool shows are the least desirable, but they should be the most wanted," Atlas says with frustration.

Also syndicated was Premore Productions' *Tony the Pony,* the story of Jonathan (played by Poindexter) and his magical horse. The animal was stuffed, but with actors Steve Richmond and Tony Barverio, who walked, talked, sang, and danced through Rulonia, where rules are made and tested; Innertubonia, where lost balloons go; and the Magic Cellar, where worn-out toys are repaired.

Many other life-size puppets have been visible throughout the years. However, the Muppets' gigantic success with small puppets contributed to the reduction of the oversized characters in the mid-1970s and put the characters back into perspective.

4

Uncle Hosts and Other Video Relations

Filmation spoofed kids'-show hosts in 1975 with a short-lived ABC sixty-minute, then thirty-minute comedy, Uncle Croc's Block. *Charles Nelson Reilly starred as a costumed host who hates what he's doing. As Uncle Croc he introduced cartoons ("M*U*S*H," "Wacky & Packy," "Fraid E. Cat," and "Super Friends").* Uncle Croc *was full of unusual characters. The show was set in a TV studio where director Basil Bitterbottom (Jonathan Harris) and Rabbit Ears visited him. The program signed off February 14, 1976.*

For more than thirty years children have looked at television and up to the adult hosts who populated their favorite shows. The medium has paraded an army of make-believe captains, sure-shooting cowboys, neighborly uncles, and cornball comedians, each holding youngsters' attention with a mixed bag of participatory games, moralistic lessons, and cheap films.

The fondest hope of any young viewer in the 1950s and 1960s was the chance to meet Buffalo Bob, Uncle Johnny Coons, or Pinky Lee. More tickets were demanded than available to their shows, so except for a quick glimpse of them at a crowded personal appearance, children's contact with these important adults, though often juvenile-acting role models, was usually through the living room TV set.

Few people were held in greater esteem than these live Saturday morning heroes. The TV hosts were the welcomed baby-sitters in the post-war years. A lecture to brush after every meal might be heeded when offered by Smilin' Ed, Bob Emery, or Soupy Sales. But their services were not cheap. For, no matter what else can be said, they were great salesmen. And when they suggested kids stock up on Popsicles, Three Musketeers, or Hostess cupcakes, it was difficult for any parent to countermand the order.

Product names would work their way into contests as well as straight advertisements. Before otherwise restricted, commercial logos were suspended over bleachers and kids were usually invited to participate in commercial demonstrations.

The constant sales-pitches, however, are not what linger in the minds of most who tuned to those early "uncle" shows. Adults today generally have fond recollections of the rarely met, but reliable, weekend visitors. What people recall are the lessons—from the useful to the mundane. Viewers learned how to blow bubbles and how to rope horses, why a policeman is a friend, and why alligators shouldn't become pets.

Everything was made to seem important. The live figures offered what cartoon characters never could: authority, believability, and love.

Whether they were wearing uniforms, civvies, six-guns, or open shirts; whether they spoke directly into the camera or to the studio audience; whether they were network stars or local facsimiles, they helped shape the early picture of TV.

Adult hosts peaked in the mid-1950s. After the FCC ended the freeze on stations in 1952, and new outlets beamed from hundreds of previously unserved TV cities, adult figures were hired to bring the magic of TV to children.

Locally, there were such shows as young David Eisenhower's 1954 favorite in Washington, D.C., *Hoppity Skippity*, or Cleveland's *Mr. Jupiter* with actor Joe Berg. In Fresno, California, children in 1953 tuned to *Miss Pat's Playroom*, while Syracuse, New York, viewers watched *Magic Toy Shop* and Charlotte, North Carolina, tots saw Fred Kirby, the singing cowboy. Philadelphia kids followed *Ridin' the Trail* and *Rex Trailer's Ranch House*, until their local cowboy hero rode to Boston in 1956 to shoot a sizable hole in the weekend ratings with *Boomtown*.

The Old Rebel and Pecos Pete Show aired in Salem, North Carolina; Gene Kinnery starred in *Easy Does It* in Phoenix; *Uncle Hugo and Popeye* was telecast in Milwaukee; and J. D. Beemer, son of radio's Lone Ranger, Brace Beemer, hosted a fifteen-minute show called *Cowboy Colt* on Detroit station WXYZ-TV.

Uncle Pete Boyle was another Philadelphia star, Brakeman Bill McClain rolled into Seattle-Tacoma, Sonny Fox developed a lifelong following starting in 1955 thanks to the four-hour show *Wonderama* on WNEW in New York. Artist Bob Cottle hosted the daily *Captain Bob* in Boston, and *Bronco Bill* spun Western yarns on Schenectady's *Tales of the West*

Salty Brine's Shack was a regular hangout in Providence, *Uncle Gus* made friends in Manchester, New Hampshire, and *Major Quinn* ruled the Albany airwaves.

Ranger Joe and *Chief Halftown* camped out in Philly; *Uncle Howdy's Junior Flint Jamboree* entertained Lansing, Michigan, kids; *The Captain Mal Show* aired in Mobile, Alabama; and *The Jingles Show* jangled onto Fort Wayne, Indiana, TV.

There were hosts with naturally gray hair and those who incessantly died their locks black. Some sported scruffy prospector beards and others were baby-faced and clean-shaven. Many kept puppets on a string, many more yet talked to kids in nearby bleachers and celebrated birthdays by giving lucky youngsters a sponsor's product.

Network TV productions had bigger budgets, more elaborate sets, and often better shows than any the local affiliates could air. *Howdy Doody* took top honors. Toss-up for second place was among *Uncle Johnny Coons*, *Pinky Lee*, *Captain Kangaroo*, Paul Winchell's many shows, and Happy Felton or *Andy's Gang*. And if TV uncles were successful, then Shari Lewis was probably the favorite young video aunt and Susan Heinkel the most popular niece on television.

The shows were a profit center, but more so for local stations than for networks. The networks gradually found they could make more money on cartoons than producing extravagant live productions. For hometown affiliates, it was another matter.

With sponsors clamoring for top hosts to announce commercials on their own shows and in other time slots, many characters grew rich off their visibility. The stations, in turn, discovered that a low-budget children's show made dollars and sense.

Children would usually snap to whenever their favorite hosts introduced the latest toy gun, soft drink, doll, or sugar-coated treat.

Selling-power was amazing. Children wanted what they saw, and the hosts told them what they wanted.

Twenty-five years of this unbroken commercial trance was enough, said parents in Newton, Massachusetts, who constituted Action for Children's Television (ACT). After renewed pressure on the National Association of Broadcasters, the NAB finally ruled in 1972 that hosts had to give up their lucrative sales pitches. The NAB Code, a nonbinding bible that most stations voluntarily abide by, was amended in January 1, 1973, to say:

> *Children's program hosts or primary cartoon characters shall not be utilized to deliver commercial messages within or adjacent to the programs which feature such hosts or cartoon characters. This provision shall also apply to lead-ins to commercials when such lead-ins contain sell copy or employ endorsement of the product by program host or primary cartoon characters.*

The directive didn't eliminate commercials from kids' shows, but it killed most sponsors'

In the 1950s there were few cartoon shows. Of those that aired, many had adult hosts. Captain Bob Cottle, pictured here, appeared on NBC's Ruff and Reddy. *He replaced Jimmy Blaine, who was the show's first host.*

from the collection of Alice and Leonard Maltin

Popular New York children's show host Officer Joe Bolton snaps at Moe Howard during a personal appearance by The Three Stooges *star.*

incentives to support hosts and erased TV stations' reasons for keeping their studios tied up with a daily or weekly children's production. As a result, stations coast to coast said "uncle" and abandoned most of their kids'-show hosts.

"It's like a plague that's going around the country," said Miami host, Skipper Chuck Zink, in a 1973 *TV Guide* article. "There are fewer and fewer local children's TV shows, and that's too bad, because there are more and more children now than ever."

Certainly broadcasters could have continued to keep the shows on the air, but with their profit-making apparatus disassembled and advertisers withdrawing, they discovered, as the networks had earlier, that cartoons were cheaper to buy and cheaper to air.

"Simultaneously, a lot of stations saw that if they rented out their studios to other people doing commercials, they could have a double leader going," explains Sonny Fox, former host of *Let's Take a Trip* and *Wonderama,* as well as a one-time NBC children's TV vice-president. "While their studios are taking in money by leasing to outside commercial companies, they're on the air with film and tape, making more."

Jack Valentine, CBS's singing cowboy, ambled through Action in the Afternoon. *The live weekday series was telecast from Philadelphia station WCAU in 1953.*

"A live program needs at least a half dozen members of the International Brotherhood of Electrical Workers, two cameramen, a floor director, maybe three engineers in the backroom and a director. At an average of $300 per week for each member that adds up to a lot of money," kids'-show host Mr. Patches (Jack Miller) told *TV Guide* in 1973. "It's easier and cheaper to punch up a piece of film."

Another factor influenced stations, particularly in regard to weekday kids' shows. "The key word here is 'demographics,' " continued Fox. "When local stations got more sophisticated about demographics, they found out that in the after-school slots, although they could sell kids' shows, the bucks they could get for the minute didn't begin to compare to the money they would earn if they sold to a women's audience. They discovered they could make more by not doing kids' shows."[1]

Further NAB sanctions in the 1970s took guns away from Saturday cowboy characters, quieted hyperactive studio games, and capped the seltzer bottles. Shows noticeably changed. And young viewers, more attracted to fast-paced action and slapstick humor than what they were suddenly getting, disowned most of the remaining TV uncles.

"Even today, *Captain Kangaroo*, and *Mister Rogers*, generally regarded as good programs, are not watched by as many children as cartoons are," complains Bob Keeshan, who has made a career as an uncle-host, most notably Captain Kangaroo.

Keeshan says that without the strong profit-motive, broadcasters just aren't going to turn airtime over to adult hosts.

But Sonny Fox, now a TV producer, argues, "I think it is incredible that many stations making millions don't have their own kids' programs." Fox would like to see Federal Communications Commission pressure brought to bear to improve the stations' response. "I think that the FCC should rule that stations wouldn't have their licenses renewed *unless* they did at least one locally produced show a week for children. There are over 700 local commercial sta-

1. *Variety* had predicted the end of the children's host as early as 1952. The trade magazine believed the weekday uncle programs would disappear. At the time there seemed to be an unlimited number of sponsors who wanted to reach kids and kids only, yet the weekday afternoon and early evening time periods were already becoming "too valuable for kids." Stations, the publication foresaw, would eventually switch to family or adult viewing.

tions in this country. Right away there'd be 700 new shows. Two hundred of them might have something worthwhile. And out of those there should be a few exceptional shows," Fox believes.

For now, TV's retired or semiretired children's hosts, who aren't quite sure why they're out of full-time work, hate what they see.

"I really cannot turn on television Saturday morning before 12:30 without throwing up," Soupy Sales says without a hint of joking. Though he's still active, but only through syndication, he speaks for those colleagues less fortunate. "There is nothing creative. It is strictly a money-making thing and they're very selfish, because considering that stations and networks have that much time, it's only right they should give live performers a chance again."

Pinky Lee is a bit more pensive about his unemployment: "I just feel sorry for kids today."

Since TV stations didn't beam any programs on Saturday morning in its earliest years, kids'-show hosts were initially found in late-afternoon and evening time slots. The "first small success in children's video," according to *Newsweek*, was Big Brother Bob Emery's *Movies for Small Fry*. The DuMont series signed on New York station WABD, Tuesday, March 11, 1947,

a full half-year before *Kukla, Fran and Ollie* and *Howdy Doody.* Emery narrated old movies off-camera, but by April, DuMont decided he should be seen—and seen much more frequently.

With success came a title change to *Small Fry Club,* and full network exposure. Emery spoke on a wavelength that kids, not parents, tuned to. His show was an outgrowth of a radio program he had originated in Medford, Massachusetts, in 1921. *Small Fry Club* taught politeness and respect. He recommended that youngsters drink milk, obey parental requests, and, of course, watch the show. On this last point authors Tim Brooks and Earle Marsh noted, he succeeded. In *The Complete Directory to Prime Time Network TV Shows* (Ballantine Books, 1979), they observed that Emery had received 1,200 requests for *Small Fry Club* membership in May 1947. By January 1948, the tally was up to 15,000 a month, and within two years the total active membership had reached 150,000.

Emery stayed with the show until 1951. He joined Boston-area radio station WBMS on October 11, 1952, for a midday version of the program, and soon thereafter returned to TV on the city's first TV station, WBZ.

Big Brother Bob Emery, DuMont's father figure to thousands of young viewers on the 1947 Small Fry Club

Uncle figures, or for that matter, kindly aunts, were relative to the success of many other network shows. Helen Parkhurst hosted a group of eight to fourteen-year-olds in unrehearsed discussions of their problems on ABC's *Child's World.* The show premiered November 1, 1948, at 8:00 P.M. and was based on her year-old radio show.

The same month, Pat Meikle and her husband, producer Hal Cooper, enrolled viewers of WABD in *DuMont Kindergarten.*[2] The 8:30 A.M. weekday series was eventually retitled, *The TV Baby Sitter,* with Meikle still using drawings to tell the adventures of pidgin-English-speaking Wilmer the Pigeon.

In June 1949, Meikle graduated from the spin-off of *DuMont Kindergarten* and moved into the network's *Magic Cottage.*[3] There, she again related children's fables through her pictures and was careful not to present any violent stories.

Brother Chuck Luchsinger and Brother Jack Luchsinger, a pair of cartoonists, also used the sketchpad to tell stories on ABC's *Cartoon Teletales.* The 1948 to 1950 show, with anecdotes of Pinto the Pony, Cletus the Caterpillar, and

2. As a child, Hal Cooper had appeared on Bob Emery's radio program.

3. Drawing on the format of *Magic Cottage,* ABC aired *Chester the Pup* for three months beginning Saturday, October 7, 1950. The fifteen-minute program dealt with the misadventures of Chester and his master, Drizzlepuss. The show was produced in Chicago, sponsored by Mason candy, and hosted by artist Sid Stone.

CBS brought cartoonist Carroll Colby to the easel, named him Cousin Kib, gave him Patti Milligan as a cohost, and signed on the program *Billy Boone and Cousin Kib,* July 23, 1950. Boone was a cartoon strip about two-thirds completed before airtime. Kib merely filled in the few lines at show time and created other pictures from such everyday objects as string and flypaper.

And *The Adventures of Danny Dee,* a 1954 series carried live on DuMont's New York station, WABD, and on film in Philadelphia, Chicago, and Boston, featured the doodles of Roy Doty.

Alice the Alligator, aired two weekdays at 5:30 P.M., then Sunday nights over the network's eight-station link. Some stations telecast the show on Saturdays via kinescope. As many as 3,700 viewers wrote in each week in hopes of winning drawing pencils.

With Saturday morning still unclaimed by children and broadcasters in 1949, New York station WCBS-TV scheduled Paul Tripp's imaginative *Mr. I. Magination* on Sunday at 6:30 P.M. beginning April 24. Within a month, the show moved to 7:00 P.M. and was relayed to Philadelphia, Baltimore, and Washington, D.C.

Tripp, author of *Tubby the Tuba* and other children's stories, created, wrote, and starred in the show owned by Norman and Irving Pincus. Programs opened with Tripp, dressed in brakeman's overalls, transporting viewers to Imaginationland on his magic locomotive. Assisting Tripp on camera and behind the scenes were Ruth Enders (his wife) and Ted Tiller.

During the show, Tripp's train stopped at various locales: Ambitionville, Inventorsville, Seaport City, and "I-Wish-I-Were" Town, where heroes of history and fiction appeared. Despite the popularity of *Mr. I. Magination* network planners said he wasn't worth his hour's time. The series went dark June 17, 1951. Viewers and parents protested, and the program was revived by CBS at 6:00 P.M., January 13, 1952. Its return was probably the first instance of public outrage reversing network cancellation plans. CBS took the credit, however, in a *New York Times* ad:

> *Returning today by popular demand!* Mr. I. Magination *. . . because it's like no other program in the world . . . because it's full of charm and humor and fantasy . . . because watching it is always a truly delightful experience . . . children of all ages have demanded the return of* Mr. I. Magination. *So Paul Tripp is back . . . conducting tours through space and time, fiction and history . . . turning young friends into their favorite heroes.*

On April 19, 1952, *Mr. I. Magination* switched to the then emerging Saturday schedule for 1:00 P.M. airing. But by June 28, 1952, Tripp's train left stations for the last time. The

Wilmer the Pigeon, a regular character on Pat Meikle's series The TV Baby Sitter *and* Magic Cottage

show that was "like no other program in the world" became like many others—canceled.

Also to sign on in 1949 was CBS's weeknight series *Chuck Wagon,* starring Sheriff Bob Dixon. The ad-libbed, one-hour program rolled on March 7, driven by a $200-a-week budget for films and $300 per week for guest actors. *Billboard* reported that each show had only thirty-minutes of rehearsal. Five minutes would have been ample, considering *Chuck Wagon* couldn't ward off the thundering ratings of *Howdy Doody,* telecast at the same time on NBC. The show moved to Sunday morning on December 24, 1950.

By 1950 most stations had pushed back their Saturday sign-on times to at least 11:00 A.M. Many broadcast shows even earlier. One of the first uncles to knock on the Saturday morning door was ABC's Jack Stillwill, host of *Acrobat Ranch.* Stillwill, dressed in cowboy garb, presented games, variety performers, and acts, beginning August 19.

On August 26, 1950, Smilin' Ed McConnell transferred his radio show, *Smilin' Ed's Gang,* to TV. The NBC series initially aired at 6:30 P.M. Saturdays but moved to the morning on August 11, 1951. (See Appendix A.)

The show had premiered on radio in 1942 and had made Buster Brown shoes a household word and the company a multimillion-dollar operation. At one time, the firm's entire advertising budget was allotted to Smilin' Ed, a rotund, easygoing, affable man with the savvy of a Madison Avenue advertising executive. McConnell sold himself, his personality, and his clients' product. Once youngsters bought his cornball approach, they acceded to his requests and asked their parents to buy his shoes.

When the program transferred to television, Buster Brown reportedly quadrupled its $8,000,000 business. Meanwhile, TV also enhanced the show. Where Ed had previously read stories from a book, the gang saw filmed adventures.

Variety called the series' tales "low budget." Buster Brown found them highly profitable, thanks to Frank Ferrin, a former ad man who had originally sold the sponsor on McConnell and then McConnell on using film for TV shows.

The programs, produced on an average weekly

A New York Times *review proclaimed of* Mr. I. Magination *in January 1950, "Mr. Tripp's show is not mistitled. He offers a wonderful excursion into the realms of fantasy . . .* Mr. I. Magination *is one of those shows which meets the supreme test: it fulfills a parent's fondest wishes yet it is absorbing for the young."*

Smilin' Ed McConnell with a gremlin named Froggy on his back (1951)

budget of $5,500, were never telecast live. Instead, film of Ed and cutaways of the perpetually laughing audience were intercut with stories of India starring University of Southern California student Nino Marcel. Marcel's portrayals of Gunga Ram (alternately spelled Ghanga) were shot on a junket to the Far East, then matched with existing studio jungle-footage to produce cheap, serial-like adventures.

McConnell, in his sixties during the height of his TV visibility, had been smiling since he discovered radio as a career in the early 1920s. Both he and his producer Frank Ferrin smiled even more, because the pair had had the foresight to shoot their Indian cliff-hangers in color, making the show more salable in years to come.

Wherever network cables reached, kids knew the Buster Brown jingle about the dog Tige who lived in a shoe. There was a certain amount of dial-twisting to locate the series, however. The show originated as *Smilin' Ed McConnell and his Buster Brown Gang* on NBC, Saturday at 6:30 P.M., August 26, 1950. It switched to CBS for 11:30 A.M. Saturday airing on August 11, 1951, then to ABC on August 22, 1953, and finally back to NBC two years later.

When McConnell died in 1954 the show went into reruns, and Buster Brown put on his walking shoes to search for a new host. Andy Devine, Jingles on *Wild Bill Hickok,* was subsequently hired on October 9. The program was retitled *Andy's Gang*. Devine was made for the role.

The oversized actor filled every inch of McConnell's seat when the show returned to NBC at 9:30 A.M. on Saturday, August 20, 1955.

Devine fielded Froggy the Gremlin's insults, listened to Midnight the Cat purr "NI-I-ICE" and played with a hamster named Squeaky Mouse.

Other segments included tales of Puddles, a faithful but often hapless pup; talks with storyteller Uncle Fishface; and fables about General Frijoles, a Mexican bandit. Andy infrequently sang, but always less than divinely.

Television's most popular artist was better known for his distinctive goatee than any everlasting works of art. Jon Gnagy's weekly sketches were instantaneously seen in 1950 by more Americans than those who had ever journeyed to the Louvre to view the "Mona Lisa."

The self-taught commercial artist had started in TV as early as 1946, teaching his viewers the fundamentals of drawing over experimental outlets. Greater visibility came on November 20, 1950, when CBS inked the video artist to a contract and set him to work on a series of fifteen-minute color films.

Gnagy was criticized by art connoisseurs just as surely as Clarabell inspired the wrath of career clowns. The Committee on Art Education, a national organization which boasted membership of 1,200 educators in the early 1950s, adopted a special resolution objecting to the program.

"Television programs of the Jon Gnagy type are destructive to the creative and mental growth of children," the committee argued. "Creative education is based on the development of each child's individuality, the opportunity to use his own experience and to explore new media and techniques. The use of superficial tricks and formulas, found in the Jon Gnagy type of program, destroys this objective."

The host stood firm, admitting to *The New York Times* in 1952 that his show didn't pretend to be a school for artists. "Let's not call my program art," he conceded. "It's a fence-straddling combination of entertainment and education. My purpose is to get as many people as possible to sketch on their own and to be observant of the things around them. I'm trying to encourage them to turn their doodles—ev-

Andy Devine left Wild Bill Hickok *and teamed up with Froggy and Midnight on* Andy's Gang, *the successor program to* Smilin' Ed and His Gang.

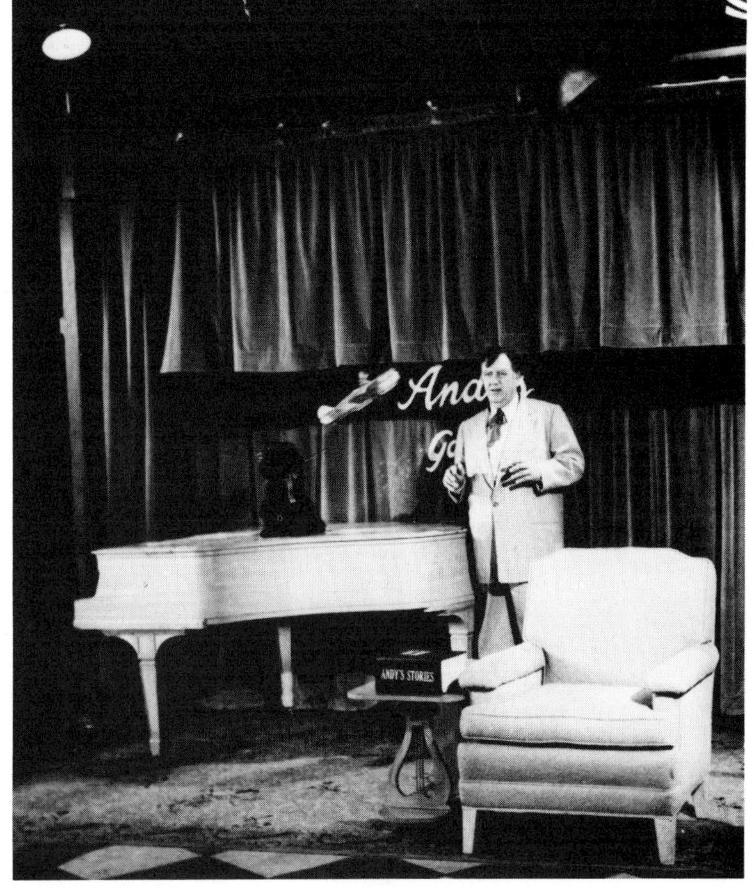

eryone is a doodler—into more intelligent objects. If people are observant, and learn a few principles of drawing, they can re-create from memory anything they want to draw."

The Committee on Art Education complained that Gnagy's procedure was dictatorial. "The drawing process is dictated to the child by the teacher, whereas the teacher should merely make suggestions along the line the child is developing."

"I'm in sympathy with the esoteric viewpoint," Gnagy responded, "but I can't do esoteric work and remain on the air. The average person is imitative, not creative. He won't do much drawing on his own unless shown how. I deny that I am destroying any creative talent with so-called dictatorial methods."

Gnagy maintained that his show, at various times called *Draw with Me, You Are an Artist,* and *Jon Gnagy Learn to Draw,* had balance. The program, he said, taught lessons and style and attempted to instill art appreciation by displaying paintings on loan from the Museum of Modern Art and New York's Metropolitan Museum of Art.

Gnagy, a transplanted Midwesterner from Pretty Prairie, Kansas, admitted that as a youngster he couldn't even draw a circle. After an illness, however, he began to paint. During World War II he taught camouflage techniques at Franklin Institute in Philadelphia. Later he became a sign painter, a lecturer, and then, with plaid shirt and vandyke, the identifiable TV host.

Gnagy told critics that his theory of instruction was actually based on the principles of Cézanne. Using the cube, the ball, and the cone as his tools, he took to the air, carefully scripting each 2,000-word show. The result, simplified though controversial, was step-by-step instruction on how to draw or, at the very least, how to copy Gnagy.

George "Gabby" Hayes, usually relegated to playing sidekicks, finally had top billing, though never on Saturdays. On Sunday, October 1, 1950, the scruffy actor strode up to the NBC cameras for the premiere edition of *The Gabby Hayes Show.* In his first major solo act, the former partner of Hopalong Cassidy, Gene Autry, Roy Rogers, and John Wayne introduced Western dramas, plugged commercial products, and narrated bits of folklore.

Guests included many of Hayes's old saddle pals, including Roy and Dale, Trigger and Bullet.

Hayes also appeared on a second production that premiered December 11, 1950, and aired Monday, Wednesday, and Friday until expanding to weeknights across the board in 1951. Quaker Oats and Peter Paul candy were Hayes's sponsors during its two-year span.

The decision to drop Hayes on December 23, 1951, was met with anger by *The New York Times:*

> *To the other casualties among superior children's programs on television, add one more. It is the Sunday afternoon dramatization of episodes from American history presented over NBC at 5 P.M. with Gabby Hayes as narrator.*

Though Hayes was down, the bewhiskered, toothless rascal was not yet out. The veritable old geezer, star of 174 horse operas, returned to the airwaves via Mutual Radio and, later, television.

Surprisingly, it was upon his rebound that his lifelong secret got out. Hayes told *Variety* that although he made an excellent living during his thirty-year ride in Westerns, he detested his performances and called their rebroadcast "for the birds."

"I hate 'em," he stated. "Simply can't stand 'em. They always are the same, you have so few plots—the stagecoach holdup, the rustler, the mortgage gag, the mine setting and the retired gunslinger. Why, I made all those movies and hardly knew I was acting in them."

As for made-for-TV Westerns, Hayes said they were even worse. "All they do on TV in the Westerns is talk, talk, talk. At least we had action in our pictures."

Gabby Hayes died, February 9, 1969, at age eighty-four.

In late 1951, Bob Keeshan left *Howdy Doody* after a dispute and became a consultant to a daily local New York show, *Uncle Lumpy's Cabin,* starring Hugh Brannum. The show would founder, but the Keeshan-Brannum combination endured. In time, Brannum would become Mister Greenjeans

In the early 1950s, Jon Gnagy's painting lessons encouraged children to draw and art critics to cringe. The show gained both friends and enemies.

on Keeshan's long-running CBS series, *Captain Kangaroo.*

The program, showing the seeds of *Kangaroo,* featured the affectionate Lumpy reading from *Li'l Orley* stories illustrated by a rear-screen projection system called the "picture cupboard," and talking to Sam the Postman, a regular visitor to the cabin. The show, "entertaining, yet clumsy and dull-witted," according to a *Billboard* review, may have tempted some youngsters to watch, but ABC claimed that few sponsors signed on. *Uncle Lumpy's Cabin* was dropped and replaced by *Saddle Pal Club* on November 19, 1951. As was the case when many live-host shows were dropped, the change prompted a New York mother to write a letter of protest to *The New York Times:*

> *May I suggest this perhaps opens up a question as to television's responsibilities regarding public service to children. Uncle Lumpy was presented as a composite or synthesis of the old-time values we all like our children to know. So now they have replaced Uncle Lumpy by a man who daily hands out guns to all the children in the studio audience. Not all parents these days think it is cute to teach children that guns are sources of amusement.*

The show was returned to the air by NBC for a 5:00 P.M. Saturday afternoon stint beginning December 6, 1952.

Also seen in 1952 were DuMont's *Happy's Party* with Ida Mae Maher and, in New York, *The Buster Crabbe Show,* with the star of the *Buck Rogers* and *Flash Gordon* serials. This time Crabbe appeared as a Westerner, answering letters, dispensing historical anecdotes, and introducing his own cowboy movies. The thirty-minute show aired weeknights at 5:30 P.M. on WOR-TV. In 1953 he signed with the local ABC affiliate to host Westerns on *Buster's Buddies.*

Crabbe, one of many movie Tarzans, was not to be outdone. Maureen O'Sullivan, Jane in a number of the jungle pictures with Johnny Weissmuller, hosted her own syndicated show in 1951, *The Children's Hour.* This sixty-minute film production aired Hal Roach studio stock films including *Stray Lamb,* Our Gang comedies, *Crummy the Clown,* and *The Little People.* O'Sullivan introduced each of the four segments.

Bozo the Clown guest-starred on ABC's 1951 series *Half-Pint Party,* a fifteen-minute weekday 4:45 P.M. show that was telecast live from New York beginning February 12 and syndicated elsewhere on Saturdays. Al Gannaway was host and pianist of the show through its Saturday afternoon 1:15 P.M. assignment in early 1952 on WCBS-TV (New York).

Since 1950, Jesse Rogers, a Philadelphia hillbilly singer, had been riding his horse Topaz into the studio and singing with his recording group, the Silver Saddle Ranch Boys. Apparently they hit the right note. ABC aired the program on nineteen stations in 1950, sixteen in 1951, and in March 1952, CBS heard the music and

There have been many local station hosts who have dressed as Bozo the Clown since the 1950s. However, Boston broadcaster Frank Avruch was the lucky actor who was chosen to portray Bozo in a 130-episode syndicated version, in national release since 1962. Avruch videotaped the shows at WHDH-TV, Boston, and headlined an international tour for UNICEF in the mid-1960s. He is seen here at the 1966 New York World's Fair making an appearance on behalf of the United Nations. Today, Avruch is resident host of many programs at WCVB-TV, Boston, including The Great Entertainment *and* Sunday Open House.

bought the series for its own network. The show was sponsored by Ranger Joe cereal.

DuMont invited youngsters to attend *Little Lady Party* from September 28, 1952, to January 11, 1953. Ireene Wicker hosted the series. Little Lady toiletries bought the airtime. After the show was canceled, Wicker moved onto *Story Time*, which first appeared Sunday, February 1, 1953, on ABC.

In 1953 stations could buy *Sing A Doodle*, a fifteen-minute syndicated effort with Lazy Bill Huggins singing and seventeen-year-old artist Joan Lee making sketches of his songs. Meanwhile, CBS introduced the cartoon film series, *Space Funnies*, piloted by Captain Jet (Joe Silver). The program aired Sunday, July 5, 1953 and won a Saturday slot on August 20, 1955.

Three years later, Silver was hosting a revised version of *Captain Jet*, for local New York telecast. Silver wore a space-age suit, spoke in quasi-scientific buzzwords like "Jumpin' Jetstreams" and warned members of his Space Hopper Club to beware of radiation monsters.

In 1953, NBC introduced an innovative programming notion—a block of two hours called *Saturday* hosted by Herb Sheldon.

The 7:00 A.M. to 9:00 A.M. entry was preempted in most cities, however. With the network still uncertain about the nature of children's television, they tried to pair kid shows with adult-oriented features. The first hour was designed for youngsters; the second contained special features, educational stories, weather reports, travel tips, and news. The grand ex-

Jack Barry, host of Winky Dink and You, *poses with his costar on his finger.*

periment actually lasted for nearly two years and before it lost its slot to Shari Lewis's *Shariland* on March 16, 1957, it was accordioned to an hour's length between 8:00 A.M. and 9:00 A.M.

Jack Barry, for years host of *Juvenile Jury* and *Life Begins at 80*, co-developed, with Dan Enright and Ed Friendly, one of the most intriguing TV concepts ever to air. The product of their 1953 collaboration was *Winky Dink and You*. Part cartoon, part live action, *Winky Dink and You* premiered on CBS, Saturday, October 10 at 11:00 A.M. The show itself was engaging; its claim, however, lay in a revenue-making gimmick: the Winky Dink Magic TV Kit. The fifty-cent premium provided a sheet of clear acetate that would attach to the TV screen.[4] Youngsters could then draw on the set and thus participate in the show's storytelling.

Winky Dink wasn't completely Barry's brainchild, admits the show host. "Two outside artists from an ad agency had a vague idea about some way of writing on a screen. They didn't know how, but they brought it to our company and the format evolved.

"Using simplified stop-motion animation—limited animation in its crudest form—we presented Winky Dink's cartoon story. At some point in the adventure, the kids would see something like Winky Dink and his pet dog Woofer come up to a river with no way to get across. So we'd say, 'Okay, boys and girls, quickly get your crayons and draw a little boat—a rowboat, a straight line, a tub, anything.' I'd show them right where to draw it, it would appear that Winky Dink would then get into it and go across the river," Barry says.

Winky stumbled into different predicaments every episode. Only the impromptu artistic talent of the nation's viewers seemed to save him. In one episode, kids drew a harp for him to play, another time a fire engine raced to a blaze and viewers sketched a ladder for Winky to climb.

"We sold millions of those kits," Barry states. "It was well thought out."

Many money-conscious mothers or ingenious kids, however, found that see-through plastic food-wrapping would adhere to the set just as well.

In addition to the *Winky Dink* segments, Barry toyed with other characters, some played by Dayton Allen. "But the basic thrust of the show were the little cartoons where the kids at home supplied part of the drawing on the screen," Barry states.

Winky Dink and You stands out in memory as a captivating production, but it fared less well on a week-to-week basis than did its competition. Says Barry, "It strictly didn't rate that well. It was on for almost four and a half years, but it never got the kind of audience that the straight cartoon shows started pulling."

Barry was a kingpin in TV production, having emceed many top-rated gameshows. Over the years he's either produced or hosted: *Twenty-One* (1956–58) as well as *Tic Tac Dough*, (1956–59, 1979), *The Big Surprise* (1955–57), *Concentration* (1958–61), *The Generation Gap* (1969), *High-Low* (1957), *Juvenile Jury* (1947–54), *Life Begins at 80* (1950–56), *The Reel Game* (1971), *Wisdom of the Ages* (1952–53), *Joker's Wild* (1978), and a syndicated children's game called *Joker! Joker! Joker!* (1979). Still, as one of TV's best-remembered uncles, he says that he's always felt a special kinship to his children's audience.

"To me, *Winky Dink* offered a great opportunity that never flourished. It was particularly a great opportunity for schools." Barry believes that the use of a "working screen," affixed to the actual monitor, could have had applications in teaching math or science. No longer, however. "I tried to reintroduce the program and the concept some time ago, but was discouraged on the basis that consumer groups were concerned about anybody getting too close to a TV set.[5] I would have had to devise some method, some mechanical apparatus, which viewers could use while sitting further back. It just got to be too complicated."

Despite the influx of cartoons, despite lower ratings, and despite ultimate cancellation, Barry reaffirms that *Winky Dink and You* was unique and apparently unforgettable.

"The participation was staggering," Barry adds. "It's nice that people recognize me for

4. In 1944, Lois Fisher aired an experimental program on Chicago TV in which she used a patented device whereby children could trace her drawings on their own screens. She later appeared in a 1950 Chicago-based children's show called *Lois and Looie*. Fisher still drew children's stories. Her sketches helped stimulate kids'-book sales.

5. *Winky Dink* reappeared shortly in 1969 as a five-minute syndicated cartoon.

Joker's Wild and *Joker, Joker, Joker,* which have been an enormous hit throughout the country. But there are always those who will say, 'Mr. Barry, I remember when I used to help draw Winky Dink on your show.' I look up and say without hesitation, 'Thank you, and I bet you're about thirty-two years old,' and I'm usually right within six months."

Pinky Lee owes his Saturday-morning TV career to one youngster.

Unknown to the vaudeville comedian, after he was laid off from production of *Those Two* with Vivian Blaine, Josh White, son of producer Larry White, hounded his father to hire Lee for a children's show.

The elder White did not know Pinky Lee but acted on his son's wishes. He combed the New York agencies to locate Lee and ultimately connected. "He got me, asked if I'd come to New York," Lee recalls. "The afternoon I arrived, NBC bought the show and we were on several weeks later as a daily fifteen-minute program.[6] After a while they said, 'We gotta put this on Saturday morning for a half hour, too.' It was all because of young Josh.

"I played the same little guy on TV that I did in the burlesque," Lee adds. "I was what you call a nebish, a pathetic little guy. I didn't try to copy Chaplin, but I realized through him that in order to be a great tragedian you had to be a great comedian."

Lee also says he owes his style to Laurel and Hardy, Larry Semon, and Lloyd Hamilton, a comic "who could make you cry."

"I remember one show I did when we had a character named Mr. Grumpy. He owned the whole town, the bank, the circus, the department store . . . everything. And I played a character who worked for him and supposedly made $6.23 per week. Well, stingy old Mr. Grumpy decided to give everyone a vacation. We were all going to go for a trip in his car, but when it came time to leave there was no room for me," Lee recounts.

Lee said he drew on the characteristics of his favorite silent comedians for the payoff. "We had a real automobile on the stage and as they rode off, Mr. Grumpy said, 'Next year, Pinky. Next year.' I tried to hop on the fender, the tail, and the trunk. No luck. I was left with my little bag containing a toothbrush and socks. I was all set with no place to go and the organ played *All Alone Am I.* Well, I'll tell you something," he continues, his voice quieting with recollection, "There wasn't a dry eye in the audience or in the crew because it was done so beautifully by everybody."

The sketch appealed to Lee's sense of comedy and tribute, but for the sake of his viewers' attention span, he usually moved to a double-time beat. The slow and deliberate execution of silent-comedy routines was generally lost in the pressure-cooker medium.

"It's a funny thing. I'm a rather fast-moving comedian, and yet, I used to do what we call a long take. I'd stand there close to a minute and look and look and look and the laugh would build and build and build. I was a very fast comedian who often worked very, very slowly."

Usually, however, Lee was known for his madman's pace. From the moment he would burst a balloon and sing the lyric, "Yoo Hoo, It's Me," he'd be on the move. First he'd dance, then he'd romp through the audience. He seemed to pause for a breath only when Molly Bee or Jymmey Shore sang a song or Barbara Luke or Jimmy Brown performed an act. Whether he was supervising "Game Time" or performing in a skit, Lee was in motion. He was loud and physical. His TV comedy was bombarded by parental complaint and squeals of delight from kids.

"I worked in a frenzied way because there were so many elements we had to get in the twenty-six minutes," he acknowledges. "When you figure the commercial time and everything else, I wanted to give kids an entertainment-packed show. There was just no time for diddle-daddle. We got through with one thing and boom, we went right into something else."

Time might have been against him, but Lee's archenemy was *New York Times* reviewer Jack Gould. In a scathing November 8, 1954, assessment, Gould charged that Lee's program was "a conspiracy against parents." Gould had never been a Lee fan. In 1951 he wrote that his work on *Those Two* "suffers from a dearth of both material and versatility." The early review was

6. In 1950, Lee hosted a live local show at NBC's Los Angeles station KNBH. The production aired on kinescope in the East. There was talk that the show would move to New York and air live cross-country once the coaxial cable was completed, but the program was canceled after its thirty-ninth performance when an RCA distributor could not afford to pay an extra $1,000 in production costs. The total budget was $2,000.

Pinky Lee, TV's most energetic children's host, ran out of steam on September 20, 1955, collapsing onstage during a live coast-to-coast telecast. Lee recovered, but his daily TV career did not. He continues to appear today, but primarily in burlesque shows and TV specials.

kind compared to his assault on Lee's children's show. Gould maintained that the program was "tasteless" and "witless" and was a "crude half-hour that calculatedly exploits behavior in children that sensible mothers and fathers do their best to curb. . . . Mr. Lee's show," he added, "is a veritable blueprint of what not to do during the children's hour."

Every sentence of Gould's review contained strongly worded criticism. "The screen lights up," he continued, "and there is hysterical bedlam—screaming and wild jumping up and down by Mr. Lee. He induces little children to do the same, and even worse, their mothers. The whole operation is a sort of organized frenzy designed to whip children into a high emotional pitch.

"Mr. Lee states on the air that he is reliving his childhood. This is not true," Gould concluded. "There was no television in Mr. Lee's childhood; he had a chance."

"The man broke my heart," Lee says remembering the publication. "He was the only guy who really had it in for me. I finally had a meeting with him and I said, 'Mr. Gould, I admire you, you're a brilliant critic, but you talk as if I'm doing a show for people way up here,' and I stretched my arms high. 'I'm doing a show for people down here. I'm doing it for the everyday kid. I talk on one level. I'm just a plain and simple little guy.' "

The meeting had no effect on Gould, however. "I couldn't have sold him a bill of goods, and that was that."

"I loved what I was doing," Lee says in retrospect. "And I'll tell you something," he says in his familiar lisp, "people can say what they want about me, but there were a lot of performers doing children's shows that actually hated kids. They did the show because they were making money, but they didn't like kids and they made no bones about it."

Lee, born Pincus Leff, adds that despite the damnation from critics, "I was the cleanest comedian in burlesque and I did the show the same way. I never sang love songs. I was never in love. There was no kissing on my show, no Jane Russell–type jokes, no violence. There were no gestures alluding to the derriere or other parts of the anatomy, and words like 'lousy' or 'stinker' were absolutely forbidden. It was a happy, wholesome show.

"I loved what I was doing," he says. "I loved working with kids and with mothers and fathers. And I did things no one else had the guts to do."

That brassy style disturbed critics and colleagues alike. Some industry insiders called Lee, "the comedian that comedians hate." For years, Milton Berle and Pinky Lee had a running feud over a snipe Berle made at a Waldorf-Astoria dinner. "Every comedian of any value was there," Lee says, rattling off the names of Sid Caesar, Jack E. Leonard, Joey Adams, Joe E. Lewis, Henny Youngman, Morey Amsterdam, and Herb Shriner. "And he said, 'Boy, if a bomb hit this joint, Pinky Lee would be a big hit!' Well, I took exception to that and I let it be known."

Years later, Lee was visited by Berle between performances at the Dunes Hotel in Las Vegas. "I didn't want to see him. In fact, I refused to see him, but he wouldn't leave until we talked. I told Milton, 'You're a rat and you treated me like a dog. I didn't deserve that.' He said he'd wait until the act was over, then he would take me out. 'You're going to nightclub with me, then dinner and then breakfast,' Berle demanded. And, by golly, he wouldn't let go of me and that's how we made up."

While some people might not have always found Lee's humor to their taste, viewers made the comedian the rage of the nation.

"I had people run home from their offices to watch the show," Lee proudly states. The greatest reaction, however, came during a Cleveland, Ohio, personal appearance.

"NBC was approached by a Cleveland department store owner who asked to have a network personality visit during the kids' school vacation. 'We can give you Pinky Lee,' " the comedian recalls them saying. "They asked, 'Who was Pinky Lee?' and not knowing, they reluctantly took me. They advertised that I would appear at the store, but I understand there were so many phone calls that they tried to get a theater. With nothing available, they moved me into the grand ballroom of the Statler Hilton, which accommodated about 2,500 people.

"Well, the result was that about 20,000 kids and parents lined up for blocks," Lee continues. "They broke store windows and stopped traffic for hours. I still did a show, but the hotel complained that fans were on every floor, up in the stairway, and in the lobby. Guests couldn't come in and they couldn't get out. So I had to talk to them. Some people hoisted me to the top of a bus and with a police bullhorn I pleaded with the people to go home."

After the Cleveland reception, NBC wanted Lee to barnstorm in other department stores, schools, and playgrounds. He objected. "Let's face it," he explains. "It's not the easiest thing to go out and entertain kids away from your element. I depended on a piano and a captive audience. I consequently turned down public appearances in grocery stores where they would have paid me $5,000 to walk in. I used to say, 'Please, I don't want your money, I'm no good to you like that. I need to perform like a performer, not in schools.' I said if I can't entertain the way Pinky Lee can entertain, then I will not go on. I only want them to see me at my best."

To be at his best, Lee needed his hat and his coat. They were as important to his character as the cane, derby, and baggy pants were to Chaplin.

The origins of Lee's wardrobe went back to his early vaudeville days and a 1930s play date at Pottstown, Pennsylvania. "The hat was the first item," he says. "I used to come on dressed in a beautiful silk gabardine suit. Those were the days when you could buy a suit like that for $45 or $50. I topped off the outfit with a little kid's felt hat. But just before one performance I couldn't find my hat. I remember worrying, 'My God, what am I going to do? I'm not going to be funny without my hat.' I ran to the stage and there was a lady with her little boy in her arms. The child was wearing a large black-and-white checkered hat. I said, 'Lady, can I please borrow it?' "

The woman agreed, Lee ran to the stage and immediately got a laugh. After the act he returned the hat to the woman, who told Lee, "Keep it, you look better in it than my kid."

Lee was fitted for his matching coat next. While working Earl Carroll's *Vanities* he wore a plaid zoot suit. After the show folded, he cut the coat down to add it to his regular wardrobe. In time, however, he wore it on stage with checkered slacks, a checkered shirt, and a red tie.

In the 1950s, Max Hess, owner of Hess's, a large department store in Allentown, Pennsylvania, offered Lee $10,000 for his hat. Lee politely turned down the offer, and though he says his hat is ready to fall apart, he still uses it when he performs today. "I handle it very, very, carefully."

Lee was less careful with his own health. In 1954, *Time* called him "one of the hardest working men in TV." The news magazine said he expended "more energy than anyone this side of Jerry Lewis." The six-show-per-week schedule was physical torture, quickly wearing him down. The natural result was an illness in 1955.

"I worked my rear end off," he says. "I had to do a new show six days a week and I saw my family very little and got only four hours of sleep each night. One day I collapsed in the middle of a show."

"People thought it was a heart condition, but it was my nose," Lee explains. "I was being poisoned from a nasal drip." The comedian believes that a combination of his grueling schedule and physical exhaustion contributed to the sudden illness.

After Lee's on-air collapse, he was told by doctors that if he wanted to live, he had to quit. Lee moved from Los Angeles, where his show had been airing since its earliest day in New York, and made a temporary home in Arizona until he fully recovered.

Within a year, Lee considered returning via a new format. He designed a weekly half-hour film series reminiscent of Saturday movie serials called *Perils of Pinky*. The project did not air. However, he did appear on NBC's *Gumby* for a few months as a replacement for Bobby Nicholson, the show's original host. It was, by his own admission, a step off the top rung of a successful ladder.

"My heart is crying," he told syndicated writer Dick Kleiner in a September 1957 interview. He pointed out that the show paid less money than he'd earned in fifteen years. By the time he deducted personal expenses, he claimed, his take-home was only $34 a week. Yet, for less money than he'd seen in years, he wanted to work on TV. "I have no pride. I just want to do the thing I love the best—entertain children."

"Let's face it," he added. "I'm not a very talented guy. I dance a little, I sing lousy. I don't even tell jokes any more on my programs. But I do have a knack for making friends with children."

In 1965, ABC invited him to return to the format he knew. Lee starred in a weekday show that was originally scheduled to air at 4:30 P.M. but ended up at 7:30 in the morning. Lee was certain the network was making a serious scheduling error. "I'm a visual comedian," he says. "And I was upset that I couldn't convince those guys that the time slot wasn't suitable."

"It was the *Pinky Lee Show* in title only. I did a lot of things they wanted me to do, and nothing I wanted. As a result, it wasn't the type of show I had done on NBC. I thought it might work out, but I was wrong."

Today, Lee takes his inimitable hat off the rack when he tours with a burlesque show or appears on a TV variety program. But like most of the 1950s hosts, Lee must be content with memories shared by middle-aged Americans, rather than entertaining contemporary youngsters.

"If I've done nothing else," he says, "I've at least left some love with children who have grown up. It's wonderful to know that I've gone through show business for many, many years and I've reached a very great height to say I've touched people's hearts and I've stayed there."

Bob Keeshan might more aptly be called Father Time than Captain Kangaroo. For more than a quarter century the New Yorker has successfully ridden the rough and unpredictable television airwaves, outlasting Buffalo Bob, Pinky Lee, Jon Gnagy, Paul Tripp, and every other national children's TV host, to become the country's most trusted surrogate parent.

Keeshan has been playing host to young viewers since 1947, when at the age of twenty he left the ranks of the network pages and dressed in the familiar Clarabell the Clown costume on NBC's *Howdy Doody*.

In all his years as Buffalo Bob's seltzer-toting fall guy, Keeshan never spoke a word—communicating only via Harpo Marx type honks from a pair of bicycle horns.

But Keeshan had something to say, particularly when it came to children's programming. Four years after he had first suited up, Keeshan

left *Howdy Doody* in a pay dispute with other actors and began to develop characters of his own. After advising Hugh Brannum's *Uncle Lumpy's Cabin*, his first non-Clarabell creation was on September 21, 1953 on *Time for Fun*, a WABC-TV show in which, as Corny the Clown, he narrated 1930s cartoons until he noticed the racial slurs.

"You know the ones," he explained in a 1950s Associated Press interview. "The dog and the cat go out dancing and end up in Harlem—it says Harlem right on the door. They go upstairs and you see cannibals dancing with each other. Awful stuff."

Still, the show served as an important turning point in Keeshan's life. "It was the transitional show for me," he adds. "Corny was very quiet and very different from Clarabell. I sat on a park bench and for $300 a week I was very gentle."

After Clarabell and Corny, Keeshan stepped out of the clown clothes altogether and moved into *Tinker's Workshop*, a 1954 local New York show also on WABC-TV.

The highly rated program caught the attention of CBS executives, who decided to transfer the low-keyed New York show to a daily nationwide time slot. They signed Keeshan, then twenty-eight years old, and his coproducer Jack Miller to a contract and built a show and a clubhouse around them.

Bob Keeshan, out of his Clarabell suit and with a new puppet friend, Mr. Bunny Rabbit. He left Howdy Doody *in 1951 and signed on as Captain Kangaroo four years later.*

At 8:00 A.M., October 3, 1955, Keeshan—looking like an elderly beanbag of a man in a motorman's uniform with oversized pockets—strolled out under the network lights. He has known little else other than the early morning ritual ever since.

The day before the premiere, CBS advertised that their new show was a must-see:

> *Good news for parents! (and for children) Starting tomorrow morning at 8, CBS Television presents the gentlest children's show on the air as the kindly Captain Kangaroo re-creates the private wonderland of childhood in his Treasure House. It is a "live" and enthralling hour-long program.*

CBS wags even predicted the show would outrate NBC's *Today* since a 1955 network survey determined that 30 to 40 percent of the viewers between 8:00 and 9:00 A.M. were kids. Three months later, *Captain Kangaroo* was indeed leaping ahead, and *Today* counteracted by trying to pitch more to children. As a result of the ratings, CBS commissioned the Captain to open his Treasure House on Saturday morning as well, in head-to-head competition against ABC and NBC's audience-grabbing cartoons.

Kangaroo pocketed rave reviews from nearly every critic, educator, and parent. *Variety* wrote, "In short it's smasheroo for Kangaroo." *Newsweek* was thankful that "There is, mercifully, no studio audience of hyper-stimulated youngsters."

From the beginning Keeshan has had a repertory of actors to help him find the key to successful children's TV if not to the door of the clubhouse. His chief aide has been Mr. Greenjeans (Hugh "Lumpy" Brannum) so named for his dress and outdoors interests. Cosmo "Gus" Allegretti, Kangaroo's other featured player, has acted as Dancing Bear and handled the show's lovable puppets: Bunny Rabbit, Miss Worm, Mr. Moose, and the venerable Grandfather Clock. Additionally, John Burstein has played Slim Goodbody, a newer character who inhabits Nutri-City and teaches proper health tips.

Before videotape tied Keeshan to an easier production schedule, the show was performed twice each day; once for East Coast viewers, then three hours later for West Coast youngsters.

Speaking as calmly out of uniform as he always does in his baggy pants, Keeshan today strikes the pose of a concerned parent rather than a profit-seeking producer. He earned nearly $100,000 a year by 1956, but he argues that his prime directive has always been quality, not money.

"I go to great lengths to maintain Kangaroo when I'm in character," he told *TV Guide* in 1961. "Of course, the whole success of the show depends on the relationship of the average six- or eight-year-old with Captain Kangaroo. So far as he's concerned, there is no Bob Keeshan."

Captain Kangaroo doesn't fall into any neat descriptive package, he proclaims. It isn't so much a show, he says. It's a philosophy, a state of mind, an approach, a style of TV programming he considers a grade above other kidvid options. "The sum total of everything I've ever done has come together on the show." He draws on his stint as a Marine, night school at Fordham, appearances with symphony orchestras, and even marksmanship with Clarabell's squirter. He knows what's tasteful and what's not. He chooses appropriate subjects and discards exploitive possibilities.

Early into his CBS career he vowed that he would never pitch for pill manufacturers, joke about food, or present magicians who locked themselves in closets or trunks. Even *Tom Terrific*, the show's cartoon feature, is conspicuously devoid of violence.

Keeshan believes that he discovered the secret for staying on the air a long time ago. "And it's not television violence," he states. "Violence is part of life and there is no getting away from it. But there is also gentleness in life and this is what we have tried to stress on our shows. I think it has been proven that you can entertain without resorting to violence. So I ruled there'll be no slapstick, no horror, and no violence no matter how innocently presented.

"Any abundance of excitement is not good," he says. "Children can't be at a high pitch all the time; it's just not healthy. There must be balance just as there is in life itself."

Keeshan keeps a close guard over material that fills the show, but he argues that parents should be the final judge of his program. "To me, television can never be a mother substitute. In these days when rules are breaking down all over," he told a *Boston Globe* reporter in 1972, "the importance of proper upbringing is greater than ever. TV can be a blessing to man-

Captain Kangaroo in the polyester decade

kind. But those who used it as a baby-sitter will pay in loss of communication with the child, loss of respect, and all the other ills that beset the young."

In his mid-fifties, the mustachioed Keeshan can now discard much of the makeup originally used to create his character. He finally looks the part of the aging, portly captain. His hair has grayed and his girth has filled out well past the Marine requirements. But today's youngsters see exactly what their parents had seen before them—an ageless, neighborly man. And despite the fact that the younger *Today* hosts and the co-anchors on *Good Morning America* now attract more viewers than the CBS veteran, Keeshan's home network devotedly keeps the Captain working the rooster shift. Call it dues, call it heritage, call it experience.

Ask Keeshan about his long-time relationship with the network and it's soon obvious that some of his furrowed lines are battle scars of worry that date back to 1958.

The production was costing CBS between $1.5 million and $2 million a year, and according to network accountants, the show wasn't worth the commercial revenue it brought in. CBS announced that economic pressures might muster the Captain off the airwaves. And indeed the show might have been canceled had ten thousand viewers not protested immediately. Sensing a mistake-in-the-making, CBS reconsidered on the grounds that *Captain Kangaroo* was "an excellent public service." One anonymous executive was more truthful, however, when he told *Time*, "We were terrified of the mothers."

CBS tried to kill the show again in 1965, but viewers again clamored, flooding the switchboard and mailroom. And when one-time Boston CBS affiliate WHDH-TV cut the show from an hour to a half hour, Action for Children's Television mounted a full-fledged campaign to have the program restored.

"The TV station made two huge tactical errors," Keeshan remembers. "The first was replacing the show with *Bozo the Clown.* The second was denying children and mothers on the picket line access to the station bathrooms. In a matter of ten days or so, ACT achieved the restoration of the Captain. They've since become even more influential nationally, helping to improve much of children's TV."

In the show's third decade, no one at CBS

dares talk aloud about dumping the Captain. The man and his program link media history with contemporary programming. Captain Kangaroo is both an institution and a viable character.

Today, the show is not a runaway ratings hit, but CBS contends that 3.5 to 4.5 million people, tiny by broadcast standards, is still a respectable daily membership for the Treasure House.

"I think people at CBS recognize that the program is different, that we're special and we serve a special audience," Keeshan volunteers. The show remains for yet another reason, he offers. "In this day of government and consumer involvement in programming, it's obvious to everyone why CBS is happy to be doing the show."

Captain Kangaroo may be a hero, a friend, an uncle, and the winner of three Peabodys, an Emmy, and a Sylvania Award, but to CBS he is more. He's a tradition, as prestigious as Walter Cronkite.

Keeshan's long-running show, a video perpetual-motion machine, ended its Saturday morning stint for one year in 1964 but was replaced by another 8:00 A.M. production starring Keeshan, *Mr. Mayor,* on September 26, 1964. The replacement series, a varation on the same theme, cast Keeshan as a middle-aged man who busied himself with all the town doings. Singer Bill McCutcheon, actress Jane Connell, and puppeteer Cosmo Allegretti played supporting roles. "Captain Kangaroo" returned to Saturday morning in 1965 and continued in the weekend slot until September 7, 1968.

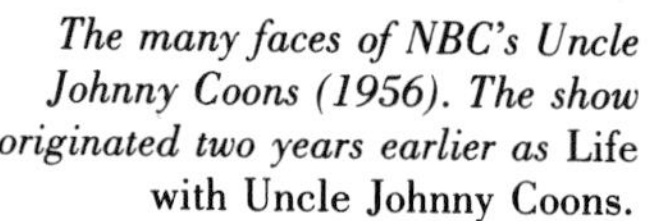

The many faces of NBC's Uncle Johnny Coons (1956). The show originated two years earlier as Life with Uncle Johnny Coons.

Keeshan is realistic enough to know that he may one day lose to the CBS sales department. Should the inevitable occur, he says, he'll remain on TV in whatever form possible. "I'll be there. I'm prepared to dance and sing in whatever method or medium is necessary."

Other children's performers have come and gone. Some, like Uncle Johnny Coons, have left a memorable mark before signing onto other roles.

Coons, a 190-pounder from Chicago, once described as the "Pied Piper of television" and as "a comic figure made out of a rubber balloon," hosted a Saturday series *Life With Uncle Johnny Coons*. The program premiered on CBS on September 4, 1954, then moved to NBC, March 3, 1956.[7]

Coons wore no funny clothes but still acted the clown. His perky, popping, and peppy series was geared for laughs. Coons talked to Blackie, an invisible dog, and Joe, an equally invisible giant. From week to week he pretended to be a milkman, a cowboy, or a Kentucky colonel. He introduced cartoons and narrated silent films, advocated cleanliness and proper diet, and invented Rube Goldberg–type contraptions that never worked. It was a solo performance, sustained by Coons' adept humor, Swift and Company's frankfurter commercials, and ads for various Lever Brothers products.

"I'm not a crusader," Coons stated in a 1955 interview. "All I try to do is give the kids something to laugh about, to sort of tickle their funny bones. Kids may not learn a lot watching me, but they have fun."

Typical of the reaction to him was an appearance at a press club father-son luncheon in Chicago. Other celebrities in attendance were introduced and politely received. When it came time for Coons to stand, Associated Press reporter Bernard Gavzer reported, "The house practically went up for grabs as the children went wild." Said one spectator, "I never heard of the guy, but my kids know him better than they do their real uncles."

7. In 1950, Coons was a weekday storyteller on NBC's 5:15 P.M. show *Panhandle Pete and Jennifer*. Coons, a "Pixiesh old gent with an implausible white handlebar mustache and manner to match," according to *Billboard*, told Western stories to Jennifer Holt, who portrayed a rancher housewife. Commercial time for the fifteen-minute network show sold for $1,350. The same airtime, if made available today, would cost sponsors hundreds of thousands of dollars.

One of the hottest TV hosts cooking in the pot in 1955 was a young comedian named Soupy. As his name suggested, Soupy Sales served a bouillabaisse of unexpected, irreverent, and outrageous behavior, and a delicious whipped-cream pie, to millions of viewers every week.

Sales (Milton Hines) was dubbed Soupbone to match his brothers' nicknames, Hambone and Chickenbone. His boundless energy was presumably derived from the same unknown powersource that fueled Mack Sennett's silent film troupe, the Marx Brothers, the Ritz Brothers, the Three Stooges, and, recently, Steve Martin and Robin Williams. Supercharged, Sales propelled his 1953 Cincinnati radio and TV show to Detroit and infected Midwest youngsters with a zaniness that defied sedation.

The Saturday afternoon Detroit program, *The Soupy Sales Show*, and his daily production, *Soupy's On*, seemed suited to ABC's program taste. The network delivered the WXYZ-TV star as a 1955 summer replacement for *Kukla, Fran and Ollie* and as a regular Saturday noon presentation in 1959. He's been a video treat, recording artist, and nightclub performer ever since.

Sales performed in the center ring of his crazy lunchtime circus. Supporting performers were usually stuffed: puppets, that is, such as White Fang, the country's biggest dog; Black Tooth, a pup with an incoherent growl; and Pookie, a happy-go-lucky pooch that often looked hapless and out of luck.

Sales cavorted with his cohorts wearing a polka-dot bow tie and disheveled top hat. He carried himself on a pair of legs that always appeared as if they would give out, particularly when he was carrying something breakable or eatable. Though he was every bit the clown that Clarabell was, or the character that Pinky Lee played, Sales rejected the notion of wearing any additional costume.

"Everyone was saying I had to have a costume or a mask. If you did a kids show then, you had to have a costume," he recalls. A conversation with a colleague who played a TV clown thoroughly convinced him otherwise, however. "I can get right out of my makeup and outfit," the clown told Sales. "And when I do, I can go out and nobody knows who I am. Nobody bothers me. You can't. Everyone knows who you are." Sales agreed but said without hesitation, "And when you want a raise, they can say, 'Don't mess with us, we can paint someone else up, so now get lost!' "

"Consequently, when I got to Detroit, I decided to play myself," he affirms. "I chose a top hat, a big bow tie, and a black sweater, and it was as simple as that."

After seven years in Detroit, ABC moved Sales' show to Los Angeles. There he found unlimited targets for his TV pies.

When Burt Lancaster appeared, he insisted on a pie. "I want a pie square in my face so I can be a hero to my children. They are avid fans of your show," he was quoted as saying.

Sales also accommodated Dean Martin and Bob Cummings, both of whom wanted to make good with their children. By the early 1960s there was a waiting line to get pied by Soupy that included Sammy Davis, Bob Hope, Tony Curtis, Jimmy Durante, and Frank Sinatra. In all, Sales figures that he's seen twenty thousand TV pies fly since Detroit, while hardly putting on a pound in his thirty-year broadcasting career.

"I've never done a pretentious show," Soupy explains. "It's always had a live feeling; the kind of thing that comes across when you don't know what's going to happen next. I've never done anything simply because I thought I could get away with it. I've just wanted to do the funniest show. Today, no one's doing my kind of TV. Physical humor is dying out."

That thoroughly unexpected quality, Sales' trademark, has not always rested well with everyone. After moving his show to New York station WNEW-TV in 1966, he was suspended precisely because management couldn't control him. Sales asked youngsters to search for their parents' pocketbooks and wallets, find the green paper within, and mail it to him.

"I had about a minute to fill on a show and I told the kids to send in the money. I had done the same joke in Detroit and in Los Angeles, but this time a woman from New Jersey wrote a letter to the FCC and sent a copy to the station. I think it was a terrific moment in television. They said it was the greatest rip-off since the Brink's robbery."

Sales was booted from the air. But instead of his being damaged by the incident, it worked in his favor. "I became more popular. The public went bananas. They jammed the switchboard."

Sales was reinstated. As for the money, he says he received $80,000 or $90,000, "all in Monopoly money or fake cash." Sales adds, "I did get one dollar from a girl, so I put it into some fund-raising canister outside the station. When they asked at a meeting how much I got, I said, $80,000. They went into catatonic shock."

Sales' money request is legendary. Stories about him using blue material on the show, however, are unfounded. "I've been credited with a lot of things I've never said or done. It's followed me everywhere," he says. Sales admitted that his show was corny, odd, and camp. But he toughens when he hears accusations about airing dirty jokes.

"Listen," he demands. "There are no dumb people in this business. There may be some who are dumb for one or two weeks, but they aren't going to stay in this if they're dumb."

Though he was never off-color on the air, his crew thoroughly miffed Sales during a live in-joke that has since become the classic television outtake.

"I heard a woman screaming at the door," recalls Sales, with laughter already invading the story. "As was planned, I was supposed to go to the door and there'd be a pair of women's shoes followed by a pair of men's shoes. Then the routine called for me to do a double take into the camera and introduce the commercial."

That's what Sales thought would happen. The real scene, not actually televised, played differently. "I heard the screaming," Sales continued, "and I said to myself, 'it's going fine.' The number-two camera swung around to my right and I thought, 'Oh, good, he's going to get a close-up.' Then I opened the door, and unknown to me, they replaced the shoes with a naked girl and then piped in David Rose's 'The Stripper!' It scared me to death. I looked to the monitor and saw the camera shot of the girl and I thought, there goes my career, there goes my life!

"The shot, however, was merely being fed to a videotape machine and was not telecast, but I didn't know that. All I could do was break up and try to keep going."

Unfortunately, with the exception of the famous outtake and the Frank Sinatra pie, few of Soupy Sales' early shows exist today. The

Soupy Sales as himself. Ed Sullivan is trying hard to follow his guest on a July 1965 broadcast.

265 editions WNEW-TV videotaped were reportedly erased. The WXYZ-TV shows have been destroyed, as were the ABC network productions.

"They didn't know what to do with the shows," he says. "The programs can't be compared to anything else on TV, and most of them are gone."

In 1979, Soupy Sales videotaped a new series of 90 shows or, according to his count, he had opportunity to either taste or toss another 280 pies. *The Soupy Sales Show*, syndicated by Viacom and aired weeknights on many stations, is kept a safe distance from the magnetic eraser. TV's most electric host wants something that he's done to last.

At eleven o'clock, Saturday morning, May 4, 1957, a pert twelve-year-old sat in her magic chair and soared from the Chicago studio into the nation's airwaves. She was Susan Heinkel, a natural actress fitted with an unusual format.

Susan's Show, carried over sixty-nine CBS stations, presented the weekly travels of the youngster to the mystical Wonderville, a land replete with a Cartoon-a-Machine operated by a troll, a tight-lipped character named Mr. Pegasus, and the Foolish Forest inhabited by an all-animal orchestra.

The program originated on local Chicago TV,

Twelve-year-old Susan Heinkel starred in Susan's Show, *a playful 1957 CBS production from Chicago. Each week the petite star and her terrier, Rusty, traveled to a wonderland to cavort with magical characters.*

but CBS scheduled the WBBM-TV production for a network slot, making the bright-eyed preteen the country's youngest on-air hostess and a local Emmy Award winner in 1958–1959.

Heinkel performed amid a stage full of oversized props designed to make her look smaller than her four-foot-nine-inch frame. Occasionally, the inanimate objects crowding into the studio would converse with her. There was the talking stove that offered her an opportunity to speak about fire safety and the Cartoon-a-Machine which churned out CBS-owned Terrytoon features. Joining her in the whimsical escapades was her terrier, Rusty, who once spoiled Susan's relation with one of her 13 sponsors by lifting a leg at an inappropriate moment and voting against a dog food dish.

Heinkel, discovered at age three in a St. Louis Christmas pageant, was out of work by fourteen. The show was canceled and she remained in Chicago to finish high school and free-lance.

In December 1960, Jack Spear marched onto ABC as Pip the Piper, a magical flutist. Pip was not the only one to pipe up on the show, however. Miss Merrynote (Phyllis Spear) chimed in with songs and Mr. Leader (Lucien Kaminsky) added a cantankerous comment whenever possible. The trio toured various haunts of the musical Pipertown, harmonized tunes, and demonstrated unknown games that children might enjoy. NBC took over the ABC show July 24, 1961, and broadcast it in color through September 1962.

Educators have said Fred Rogers hosts the best program for young children—a show that bores parents but quietly appeals to tots. *Mister Rogers' Neighborhood* premiered on Canadian television in 1964 as a series of daily fifteen-minute programs. The next year the show expanded to thirty minutes and aired on Pittsburgh's ABC affiliate. In 1966 the Eastern Education Network bought a hundred programs, and in 1968, NET took an option on *Mister Rogers' Neighborhood,* airing it on 120 stations. (See Appendix A.)

In 1979, Rogers began hosting a series of prime time talk-show specials designed to help parents cope with their children's expanding worlds. The two telecasts were *Mister Rogers*

King Friday XIII with TV's surviving adult host–puppeteer, Fred Rogers

Talks with Parents About School and *Mister Rogers Talks with Parents About Superheroes.*

From the start, Rogers has spent his scant $6,000-to-$10,000-per-show budget as if it were a million. He created a program that has relied more on content than packaging. It focuses on children's uniqueness, not cognitive skills as does PBS's fast-paced sister program, *Sesame Street.* And Fred Rogers' saccharin style, compatible with the three-year-old diet, offers a friendly voice, a well-mannered role model, and a dedicated teacher.[8]

According to *Psychology Today,* studies have shown that children exposed to *Mister Rogers' Neighborhood* over two weeks' time become more willing to share toys with their peers, more cooperative with adults, and more imaginative in play. Additionally, children tuned to *Sesame Street* tend to keep their eyes glued to the set, while youngsters watching Rogers allowed their eyes to wander without any apparent loss of recall.

8. Rogers says that he owes his easygoing style to Gabby Hayes, who once advised him to forget the huge audience beyond the camera and "concentrate on playing to one buckeroo."

The report is a testament to the dedication of Fred Rogers, who has combined a TV career with theological studies. He is an ordained minister of the United Presbyterian Church and had previously worked on NBC's *Voice of Firestone* and a 1955–1956 puppet show called *The Children's Corner.*

The fusing of a broadcaster's eye for the world with a minister's concern for humanity can be seen in every detail of *Mister Rogers' Neighborhood.* Segments are long, thoughtful, and personal. The puppet voices may sound alike, a fact not missed by kids as they get older, but all of his characterizations are reassuring and calm. He talks about a child's world and the lessons appropriate to three- and four-year-olds. There's no pressure to compete, to excel, or even to grow up. Fred Rogers simply says everyone makes his day special and everyone watching is unique.

Fred Rogers' neighborhood may not be the most visited stop along memory lane for the nostalgic TV-viewer, but the dedicated humanitarian made his address one of the most well known among the newest generation's youngsters.

Relative successes—TV's most durable "uncle host" figures, Fred Rogers (left) *and Bob Keeshan. The two dedicated performers paired for a 1979 Public Broadcasting Service TV special called* Springtime with Mister Rogers. *The telecast marked the first time the two veterans of children's television appeared together in a TV special.*

5

Star Treks and Time Travels

Picture real-life versions of *Star Wars* R2D2, C-Threepio and even old Ben Konobi crowding around a gigantic television screen thirty light-years away. As farfetched as it sounds, it's possible that America's TV ratings-race may not be confined to Earth.

For decades scientists have sent satellites hurtling through the solar system in search of life. Our farthest penetration, however, has been less calculated and far less thoughtful. The loudest messages that have announced there is a technological society on Earth are those emitted from television broadcasts. Thus, Howdy Doody, the Lone Ranger, and Captain Midnight may just be this planet's greatest intergalactic ambassadors, traveling into outer space on an electronic beam at the dazzling rate of 186,000 miles per second.

AM radio waves usually don't leave Earth. Often they can be received thousands of miles away when they bounce off a sixty- or seventy-mile-high layer of the ionosphere, but under normal circumstances, that's as far as they get.

Television waves, on the other hand, operate

Frank Thomas became the idol of youngsters and the role model for America's astronauts. Thomas starred in Tom Corbett, Space Cadet, *a live science fiction series advised by scientist Willy Ley.*

on higher frequencies and travel along a horizontal plane following the curvature of the Earth. The usual nature of these signals limit viewers to a sixty-mile radius from the transmitting tower. Yet because they beam out in a straight line to the point where the Earth curves, they can keep going and slice through the upper reaches of the atmosphere.

As expensive and sophisticated as the NASA space probes are, scientists have needed to equip them with transmitters that are less than 100 watts. The frequencies, relatively close to the wavelength that TV uses, can be received over tremendous distances in space. The TV signals we watch, particularly UHF, are broadcast with as much as 5 million watts. So powerful are these transmissions that their range is incalculable.

Carl Sagan, noted American astronomer and NASA advisor, says that with 250 billion stars in the Milky Way, it's likely that the galaxy is humming with life, and our closest intelligent neighbors may be only thirty light-years away.

Thirty light-years, at the rate TV signals travel, would equal thirty years on Earth. Any potential extraterrestrial video watchers would therefore have a dated view of us. To them, Johnny Carson would be a young comic who does an occasional guest shot on *The Ed Sullivan Show*, Richard Nixon is a vice-president of the United States, and the Dodgers still play baseball in Brooklyn.

Buster Crabbe—Flash Gordon and Buck Rogers in the 1930s movies—notes that if it takes thirty years for TV signals of his serials to reach another world, then it will take an equal amount of time to hear a reply from the tuned-in aliens. "If that all happens, and I'm saying 'if,' my grandchildren, grown up by then, will know that I really traveled to the stars."

At least one commentator is more than a little bit worried about the possibility, however. "We are a violent people; destructive and hell-bent," says Harry Essex, Hollywood screenwriter of films that included *It Came from Outer Space* and *The Creature from the Black Lagoon*. "Television violence has the potential for becoming the universal example of human beings to others. Whether accurate or not, violence is the greatest human projection."

Assuming that our broadcasts are seen in the depths of space and a benevolent audience de-

---

Match the spaceships in column I to the proper program in column II.

I	II
A The Galaxy	**1** *Rocky Jones, Space Ranger*
B The Enterprise	**2** *Rod Brown of the Rocket Rangers*
C The Terra V	**3** *Captain Video*
D The Orbit Jet	**4** *Tom Corbett, Space Cadet*
E The Beta	**5** *Star Trek*
F The Polaris	**6** *Space Patrol*

---

answers: A3 B5 C6 D1 E2 F4

cides to pay a friendly visit, Essex believes they would arrive with one simple message: "We must stop you from destroying yourself!" Essex adds that TV programmers, unaware or unconcerned about our image on Alpha Centuri, have often beamed a heartless, unsympathetic view of alien life to other worlds via early TV broadcasts. In Essex's mind it may be too late to correct "the lousy public relations of the last three decades."

There are, however, others who insist that the early TV depiction of life beyond our own planet does not speak that badly for Earthlings.

"In our simplistic way, we were depicting right overcomes might and do-unto-others," says Cliff Robertson, star of the 1953 Saturday series *Rod Brown of the Rocket Rangers*. "We were depicting simple virtues. Rod was always getting into a fight with somebody. But there was a Boy Scout thing about the show and its encounters with aliens."

"We had fights," explains Frankie Thomas in an interview regarding his series, *Tom Corbett, Space Cadet*. "And we used a ray to freeze people. But the blasters were more referred to than used."

Ed Kemmer, Buzz Corry on *Space Patrol*, similarly dismisses arguments that his show would ever give viewers "a bad case of the creeps"; and during a Senate subcommittee hearing on juvenile delinquency and violence in television back in 1954, Al Hodge told the Congressmen that *Captain Video* was "meticulous to the point of not even using the word 'kill.' "

Certainly science fiction show episodes dealt with war, but often they focused more on the terrible ravages of battle than the execution of alien warriors. Buzz Corry, for example, piloted the "Terra" to a planet whose inhabitants had been destroyed by hatred. The hero then raced back to Earth to prevent our planet from following the same course.

The hazards of nuclear contamination were worked into an episode of *Rod Brown of the Rocket Rangers* called "The Man Who Was Radioactive," and also into *Rocky Jones, Space Ranger* when the queen of Medina becomes a victim of radiation on "The Forbidden Moon." These episodes, like many others, carried strong antiwar sentiments and a camouflaged plea for disarmament during an era of atomic weapons buildups.

Captain Video (Al Hodge), pointing the way to the future. The Video Ranger (Don Hastings) assisted his mentor in this most famous of all DuMont network productions.

Certainly the outer space trappings provided settings for unusual creatures that potential alien viewers might find offensive. However, if in their own way they can excuse the obvious dramatic liberties taken by these shows and recognize the inherent concern most stories had toward intergalactic cooperation, then perhaps our future encounters will yet be close, warm, and friendly.

Captain Video was television's pioneer astronaut. The twenty-second-century adventurer, created and written by James Caddigan and Maurice C. Brock for the twentieth-century DuMont network, resembled Roy Rogers more than his space-age cousin Buck.

When the show premiered its weekday run on June 27, 1949, Richard Coogan was wearing the quasi-militaristic uniform of the cosmic cop.[1] Fifteen-year-old Don Hastings, meanwhile, filled out the modified scout outfit as the energetic Video Ranger.

With their Opticon Scillometer (a length of tubing), their Radio Scillograph (a palm-sized communicator), their Cosmic Ray Vibrator (a device that shook weapons out of the hands of opponents), and an arsenal of other devices constructed out of mop handles, household items, and whatever else the $25-per-week special-effects budget would afford, the daring duo thwarted the likes of the future's most nefarious villains. Heading their most wanted list were Dr. Pauli, Mook the Moon Man, Nargola, Hing Foo Seeng, Dr. Clysmok, and Tobor (robot spelled backward).

The Captain and his ward policed the solar system from their lofty mountain retreat. Between these live TV battles the Captain dialed in his other agents on his Remote Tele-Carrier. Properly adjusted, such cowboy heroes as Tim McCoy, Ken Maynard, Bob Steele, and Sunset Carson came into focus, all of whom supposedly fought on behalf of Video justice. The adventures, of course, were old Westerns and serials, cut into short segments to pad out the space show.

The series went six days a week in January 1950, with the same $25 special-effects budget, making it, as *The New York Times* once reported, "a triumph of carpentry and wiring rather than of writing."

Coogan agreed in a March 1950 interview. "We have to run through it to get the laughs out. The lines are so corny that we always break up in rehearsal. If it was all new when we got on camera we couldn't keep a straight face."

The pressure of live TV, Monday through Friday, could and did strain the nerves of actors. Coogan said that Bram Nossem had played Dr. Pauli, the hero's electronic adversary, until the pace exhausted him. When Hal Conklin took over the role, viewers were told that Dr. Pauli had undergone plastic surgery in order to trick the Captain.

Captain Video also went through his own transformation. In 1950, Al Hodge, radio's Green Hornet, replaced Coogan and boarded the rocket ship *Galaxy*. The Western adventurers were left on Earth as the Captain blasted off with Richard Wagner's *Flying Dutchman* playing in the background, Morse code spelling out "P . . . O . . . S . . . T" in the foreground, and the DuMont announcer proclaiming:

> *P . . . O . . . S . . . T. . . . P . . . O . . . S . . . T. . . . The cereals you like the most! The cereals made by Post . . . take you to the secret mountain retreat of Captain Video! Master of Space! Hero of Science! Captain of the Video Rangers! Operating from his secret mountain headquarters on the planet Earth, Captain Video rallies men of goodwill and leads them against the forces of evil everywhere! As he rockets from planet to planet, let us follow the champion of justice, truth, and freedom throughout the universe! Stand by for . . . Captain Video . . . and his Video Rangers!*

Captain Video matriculated to the motion pictures, the first TV program to be adopted for the parent medium. The 1951, Columbia Pictures' fifteen-chapter rocket-ship serial never really took off, however. Judd Holdren and Larry Stewart played the lead roles, but neither their acting nor the script were recognizable to the TV audience.

By 1953 even the TV version was hardly the hit it had once been. DuMont had aimed a reducer ray at its former ratings' giant, shrunk it to fit in a daily fifteen-minute time slot and grounded the Captain. Rather than fighting extraworldly villains, he was battling to stay on

1. Coogan nightly moved from hot jams to hot scenes. After *Captain Video* broadcasts he went to Broadway to play opposite Mae West in *Diamond Lil*.

the air, hosting old cartoons and serials on *The Secret Files of Captain Video*. The films appeared on a TV monitor contained in the domesticated *Tobor*'s midsection.

Captain Video, at one time the foremost hero of the airwaves, dissolved into a local New York show in 1956 on WABD, and faded to black August 16, 1957.

Tom Corbett, Space Cadet had a much more stable journey across the airwaves. The series star trekked on a five-year TV and radio mission, beginning 6:45 P.M., October 2, 1950.

While the competition would abandon reality for the sake of the plot, Tom Corbett always maintained an acceptable link with scientific accuracy even though the inventions and situations were beyond the scope of the average viewer.

German-born Willy Ley, an international authority on rockets since the 1920s, was retained as technical advisor. His supervision put Corbett's ship, the *Polaris*, on a reality-based course. Ley included references to gravity-less space that contained dangerous microscopic particles that could puncture the ship's outer skin and antimatter that could destroy life if it came in contact with positive matter.

In one episode a writer inserted a line reading, "In ten years, three men have met death while patrolling the Mars-Jupiter comet watch." Ley considered the mathematical possibilities, taking into consideration time for space travel. He made pages of calculations and requested that the line be changed to say that "three men died in fourteen years." Ley advised the cast and crew on weightlessness and helped technicians make a space walk look realistic. To provide the illusion, producers had a studio floor painted black. A mechanical dolly draped in black fabric then held Corbett or another cadet in what appeared to be the dark void. A special prism camera lens could flip the image from horizontal to vertical for varying angles. On screen it looked like the figures were floating in space.

While Ley scrutinized the technical side of the show, Frankie Thomas, son of Frank and Mona Thomas, both accomplished thespians, gave futuristic situations meaning for the 1950s. As the senior cadet training for service in the Solar Guards, Thomas made the world of 2350 through 2355 seem inviting. In Corbett's day, war no longer exists, diplomacy and deadly weapons are outlawed. Feuding countries had long since banded to form the peaceful Commonwealth of Earth, weapons such as the deadly "paraloray" are normally kept out of reach and are only used when the cadets or full-fledged Solar Guards explore uncharted space.

It was a world centuries away from the Cold War; a world that intrigued Thomas and captured the open-minded imagination of the young viewers. Like Clayton Moore's Lone Ranger and George Reeves's Superman, Corbett was one of the few conspicuous TV roles that provided both great satisfaction and no escape. Following the show's 1955 demise, Thomas accepted few acting assignments and changed careers on the theory, "After Tom, where could I go?"[2]

Thomas was one of four actors considered for the part by Rockhill Productions' producer, Mort Abrams. Most noteworthy among those who were

Jack Lord:

I appeared on Tom Corbett, Space Cadet *and I remember that Frankie Thomas was so far ahead of all of us. I was actually working as a Cadillac salesman at the corner of 57th Street and Broadway at the time and going to school at night at the Neighborhood Playhouse. I wasn't even a full-time actor. I was just scrounging around trying to get jobs, and I recall that everyone on the show looked up to Frankie as a very big star at the time because we were all struggling actors hoping to get a foothold in the business, and he was rather successful and was coming to television as a conquering hero.*

2. Today, Thomas is one of the country's leading recreational bridge experts, as well as a syndicated newspaper columnist, and an author of four books: *Sherlock Holmes Bridge Detective* (Pinnacle Books, 1976), *Sherlock Holmes Bridge Detective Returns* (Pinnacle Books, 1977), *Sherlock Holmes and the Golden Bird* (Pinnacle Books, 1979), and *Sherlock Holmes and the Sacred Sword* (Pinnacle Books, 1977). He is also writing a book on Tom Corbett, Space Cadet.

turned down was a young actor named Jack Lemmon.

"When they were casting the show, they wanted a pivotal character who could hang in there and carry the ball, learn the lines and be conscious of the overhead microphone," says Thomas. "I guess I was right for the time because I was one of the only actors my age then who had done a daily series. I had appeared on what I think was the first TV soap opera, *A Woman To Remember.* Thomas also had made a name for himself on Broadway and had a wealth of radio experience and motion picture credits. He was signed for Space Academy duty and given an unprecedented contract that prevented anyone else from ever playing the Corbett role. His co-stars were Jan Merlin (Cadet Manning, the school cutup), Al Markim (Cadet Astro, a Venusian), Frank Sutton (Cadet Rattison), Margaret Garland (Dr. Joan Dale), and Michael Harvey (Captain Larry Strong).

The *Polaris* first lifted off the CBS launching pad fifteen minutes before DuMont's *Captain Video.* Jackson Beck, also the announcer on the *Superman* radio show, folded his voice into a deep bass and exclaimed: "Tom Corbett . . . Space Cadet!" Thomas chimed in, "Stand by to raise ship! Blast off minus five . . . four . . . three . . . two . . . one . . . zero," and Beck intoned, "As roaring rockets blast off to distant planets and far-flung stars, we take you to the age of conquest of space . . . with Tom Corbett . . . Space Cadet!"

"When I came to the show, they changed the concept," Thomas explains. "They already had Jan Merlin to play Roger and Al as the Venusian. But the original idea, based on Robert Heinlein's novel *Space Cadet,* was to have Tom play the slightly younger of the three. He was sort of Luke Skywalker with the other two boys being Hans Solo and Chewbacca. But then they decided to make Tom the oldest and most dominant character and turn us into a kind of Three Musketeers. At first the show was *Chris Colby, Space Cadet;* however, they thought that Chris Colby sounded a little too juvenile."

Thomas, already in his late twenties, played the teen-age fireplug with a mixture of naïve enthusiasm and mature determination. Corbett was a child of tomorrow, always wanting to reach for the sky. "I'm Tom Corbett," he said at the opening of a record merchandised during the

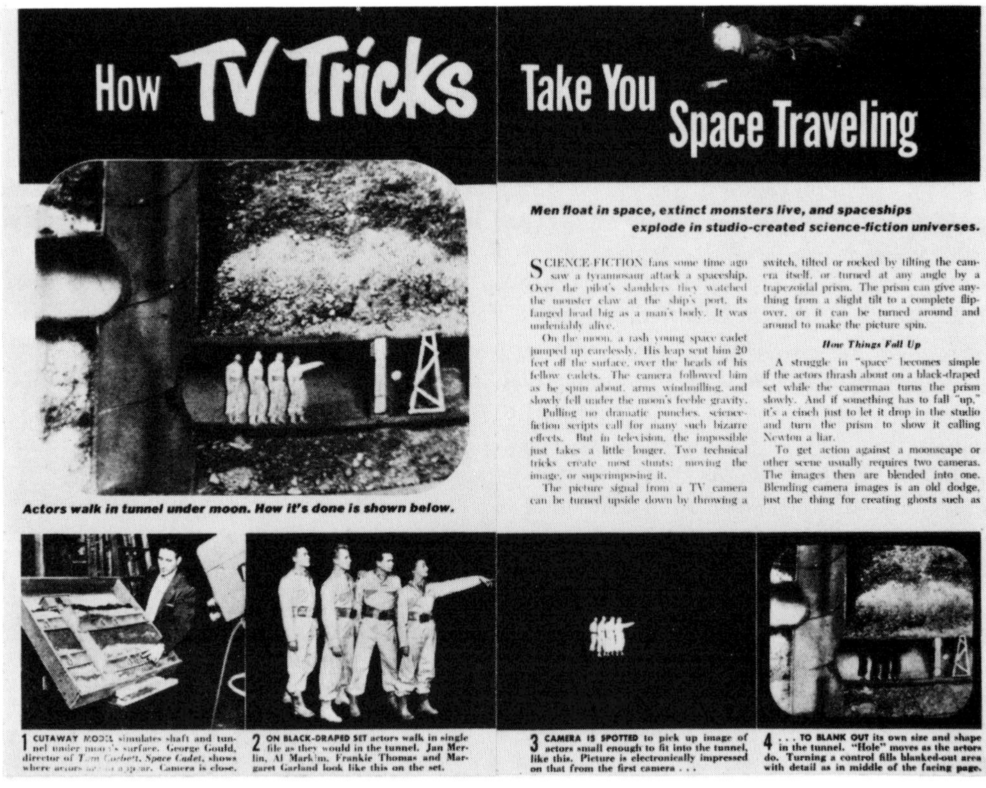

How TV Tricks Take You Space Traveling

Men float in space, extinct monsters live, and spaceships explode in studio-created science-fiction universes.

Actors walk in tunnel under moon. How it's done is shown below.

SCIENCE-FICTION fans some time ago saw a tyrannosaur attack a spaceship. Over the pilot's shoulders they watched the monster claw at the ship's port, its fanged head big as a man's body. It was undeniably alive.

On the moon, a rash young space cadet jumped up carelessly. His leap sent him 20 feet off the surface, over the heads of his fellow cadets. The camera followed him as he spun about, arms windmilling, and slowly fell under the moon's feeble gravity.

Pulling no dramatic punches, science-fiction scripts call for many such bizarre effects. But in television, the impossible just takes a little longer. Two technical tricks create most stunts: moving the image, or superimposing it.

The picture signal from a TV camera can be turned upside down by throwing a switch, tilted or rocked by tilting the camera itself, or turned at any angle by a trapezoidal prism. The prism can give anything from a slight tilt to a complete flip-over, or it can be turned around and around to make the picture spin.

How Things Fall Up

A struggle in "space" becomes simple if the actors thrash about on a black-draped set while the camerman turns the prism slowly. And if something has to fall "up," it's a cinch just to let it drop in the studio and turn the prism to show it calling Newton a liar.

To get action against a moonscape or other scene usually requires two cameras. The images then are blended into one. Blending camera images is an old dodge, just the thing for creating ghosts such as

1 **CUTAWAY MODEL** simulates shaft and tunnel under moon's surface. George Gould, director of *Tom Corbett, Space Cadet,* shows where actors are to appear. Camera is close.

2 **ON BLACK-DRAPED SET** actors walk in single file as they would in the tunnel. Jan Merlin, Al Markim, Frankie Thomas and Margaret Garland look like this on the set.

3 **CAMERA IS SPOTTED** to pick up image of actors small enough to fit into the tunnel, like this. Picture is electronically impressed on that from the first camera . . .

4 . . . **TO BLANK OUT** its own size and shape in the tunnel. "Hole" moves as the actors do. Turning a control fills blanked-out area with detail as in middle of the facing page.

Reprinted from Popular Science *with permission*

production years. "As a boy I dreamed of piloting space ships. When I was old enough, I took all the exams and was admitted to the best school in the universe—Space Academy."

There Corbett took the school oath:

I solemnly swear to safeguard the freedom of space, protect the liberties of the planets and defend the cause of peace throughout the universe.

"He was a symbol," Thomas continues. "He wasn't Superman, he was liable to the dangers and the faults of the human flesh that we are all susceptible to. But viewers always had the feeling that one way or another he'd succeed. So when Tom came on, you could sit there and indulge in the excitement of the moment and the suspense of what's going to happen next. And yet, at the same time, your fears were cushioned knowing this character had the inexorable ability to pull it off."

For years his television career was as successful as his outer-space exploits. "Corbett was the only show on two networks simultaneously," Thomas adds. "It was the only show on all four of them before we finished and one of the only programs that went from television to radio."

The program began as a fifteen-minute production, airing Monday, Wednesday, and Friday at 6:45 P.M. on twelve CBS stations. January 1, 1951, Corbett began a two-year run on ABC. Kinescopes of the three-day-per-week 6:30 P.M. broadcasts were edited and run on NBC at 7:00 P.M. Saturday during the summer of 1951. A year later the series was also carried by ABC radio on Tuesday and Thursday and moved to a 9:30 A.M. Saturday morning TV spot on NBC. A 1953 stint on DuMont ended in November 1954, when NBC outbid the fourth-place network for rights. Kraft, Tom Corbett's sponsor after Kellog's jettisoned the show, also opted for NBC because DuMont, struggling to stay alive, could not air the show in enough markets. Inadvertently, the peaceful Tom Corbett dealt a death blow to DuMont.

When necessary, the cadets would unlock the weapons closet and combat an alien. Primarily, however, the stories pitted the trainees against natural forces. Thomas believes the production would have been better if it had presented more human battles. "That's the problem with science fiction today," he says. "There are too many man-versus-nature clashes. We did it too, and I swear, an asteroid storm isn't quite as exciting as seeing a fight against space pirates!"

To young viewers, everything on *Tom Corbett* was exciting. Whether the hero was investigating a space outpost, Neptune's moon, or trying to recapture an escapee from an asteroid prison, the adventures were moved along by gadgetry, effects and jerryrigged devices unequaled even on shows with bigger budgets.

"Space programs are not cheap. And we held it down as much as we could," the star explains. "But we pulled every trick with superimpositions, and *Tom Corbett* really looked bigger than it was. We didn't have very much to go on, but our original producer had the foresight to go out and spend some money on basic sets. They amortized out eventually, but for a children's show at the dawn of television, the exterior of the *Polaris* fin with smoke pouring out of it and us climbing down the ladder looked remarkably similar to Neil Armstrong later taking the first step on the moon. That cost money. The control deck cost money and the radar installation cost money. But it paid off."

George Gould, the program's director, was the real magician. In 1951 he helped design a video

CREWMAN MAKING REPAIRS on space ship loses his hold and drifts up into space. Actually, prop hull is hung from ceiling, and man drops to floor as a prism turns scene upside down.

ANTIGRAVITY FLIGHT was shown by rolling black-draped dolly, with actor face up on it, under trees hung upside down from ceiling. A prism turned the picture over.

INSIDE AN ASTEROID, men are pinned to walls as it spins out of control. They simulate action while a motor-driven prism on camera spins the picture. The three stunts above were on CBS's *Out There.*

Scrooge in *A Christmas Carol.* You expect to see the furniture through him. But it would spoil the illusion of the flying cadet if the moonscape showed through him.

It doesn't, thanks to an electronic rig in the control room. Technically a discriminator amplifier, it is called the Gizmo by the studio staff that puts on *Tom Corbett, Space Cadet.* Their version was developed by George Gould, director, and David Fee and Rolf Drucker, ABC engineers.

Gizmo Makes Men Fly

The Gizmo can pick up the picture of an actor on a black-draped set from one camera, and insert it in a picture of a moonscape set with other actors, picked up by a second camera. The first actor jumps, the camera dips (making him go up), and the prism is turned to spin his image around while he flails his arms about. In the blended picture, he seems to take off before the astonished eyes of his friends.

When the script called for a jungle setting, one camera focused close up on a jungle photo that showed a clearing in the foreground. The actors worked on a black-draped set, and the Gizmo blended the images. Wherever the actors walked, the "jungle" behind was blocked out solidly.

Moving the camera in or out can create the illusion of size from small props. In a chase across boiling mud flats of a primeval world, the actors leaped on prop rocks on a black floor. A close-up of a panful of boiling breakfast cereal, blended in by the Gizmo, furnished the terrifying natural setting—with plenty of steam and action.

Tyrannosaurs Live on TV

Look over Tom Corbett's shoulder as he takes his spaceship in for a lunar landing. The moon grows larger and larger in the view port over the control panel, craters and fissures stand out clearly as the ship comes in, tilt as it banks on turns.

This could be a moving-picture film of the lunar landscape on a screen behind the port. But filming takes time and money. With the Gizmo, one camera can pan in on a model lunar landscape. The other, behind Tom Corbett, takes in the view port but sees only a black drape through it. The Gizmo blends the two. You see the moon through the open portions of the port.

Tyrannosaurus Rex, in the terrifying scene of the attack on the ship, was noth-

TV Tricks Take You Space Traveling

[*Continued from page 108*]

ing more than a baby alligator. With a crest of paper spines taped to its back, it was placed on a sloping sheet of glass. The camera shot a relatively big image. Blended with a picture from another camera shooting over the pilot's shoulder, this produced as neat a visual nightmare as any TV addict could ask.

We haven't invented a tractor beam yet, but some invaders from space used one in *Out There.* An invisible beam swept across earth like a controlled cyclone, sucking animals, trees, soil and houses into the air. Producer John Haggott had a miniature landscape built with a trench running through it. The bottom of the trench was covered with screening, and the trench filled with chopped cork. Miniature houses, trees, and animals were placed over this. When a CBS prop man moved an air jet under the trench, things flew skyward.

A Lobsterscope Is a Glockamora

Space ships in the same show were big cardboard Easter eggs, suitably painted and fitted with eyelets to slide down taut wires strung before a black backdrop. Inverted by a prism before the camera lens, the picture showed the ships shooting up. When attacked by Earth's defenders, they obligingly exploded. Flashlight powder and a tiny detonator in each did the trick.

The effect of light from rocket blasts, or of shimmering reflections from water, is produced by rotating a perforated disk in front of a spotlight. Called a lobsterscope in ABC studios, it's the glockamora to CBS.

But tell the kids that dinosaurs are only eight inches long, that boiling mud is the same stuff mother serves for breakfast, and they'll only nod before turning back to the show. Because in science-fiction TV, it's fun to be fooled.—*Harry Walton.*

switcher called The Gizmo, which allowed him to superimpose an actor from one set into another without the image washing out. Gould developed the apparatus for only $100 with the assistance of ABC engineers Ralph Drucker and David Fee.

The Gizmo was used to depict the cadets walking on the ocean bottom with fish swimming around them or across the spine of a prehistorical dinosaur. The electronic invention brought down production costs, since the special effects became quicker to set up and shoot. Kellogg's was also pleased with the Gizmo because it permitted them to make their cereal boxes pour themselves and fly through the air during the frequent commercial breaks.

Of course, not everything on *Tom Corbett* went according to the intended flight-plan. On the first live NBC Saturday show in 1953, *Variety* caught flubbed lines, missed cues, and forgotten musical backgrounds as the cast covered for an inadvertent flash of a Kellogg's logo when the weekend episode was actually sponsored by International Shoes.

"I remember that all too well," Thomas says. "It was our first half-hour program of the year for NBC and Ralph Ward's first show as director. He'd been our technical director at ABC, and he knew the show backward and forward. We opened as we had three hundred times with film of a Titan rocket blast-off. Then the Kellogg's identification came up as it had on the earlier shows. Somebody apparently forgot to splice it out.

"I had already been given the signal to walk out and deliver a pitch for a new formula or some such thing, but I suddenly got a wave-off," Thomas recalls. "We had to backtrack, get the right sponsor-identification on, and start over. Aside from that we were okay."

In live television, particularly programs involving special effects, mistakes had to be forgotten as quickly as they occurred. There was no time to worry; no time to brood. From the moment the *Tom Corbett, Space Cadet* announcer stepped up to the microphone and read the expository lines over the music, it was a race to the finish and a race to finish successfully.

Space Academy, U.S.A. in the world beyond tomorrow. Here, the Space Cadets train for duty on distant planets. In roaring rockets they blast through the millions of miles from Earth to far-flung stars and brave the dangers of cosmic frontiers, protecting the liberties of the planets, safeguarding the cause of universal peace in the age of the conquest of space.

The words were a cue to *go!* Thomas said that sometimes he felt he'd be more comfortable in running shoes than space boots.

"We'd do the equivalent of a hundred-yard dash to make an entrance or exit from one side of the studio to another. That was part and parcel of live television. Everything was moving. We didn't stand still very often."

Sets were rolled in and out in seconds. Wardrobe changes were accomplished between commercials when time permitted, but more likely between scenes.

"It was not unusual for us to be battling some space villain and in the midst of the big fight, I'd cross to my right, take a punch, and stagger against the wall. There, I'd get the cut-sign and start heading for the commercial set with Eddie Talliferro, our costume designer on one side, making any alterations."

Whenever the show's time needed mending, Thomas would also be flanked by associate producer Muriel Maron. The last scene was usually reserved for speeding up or padding. Thomas would be told by her what was necessary and he'd lead the cast through the end of the show.

"They made a practice of writing Corbett long because they knew we could do it," he remembers. "When Jan Merlin left for California we very fortunately got Jack Grimes, who has a clock inside his head. Sometimes he didn't know how far behind we really were. I'd get a speed-up sign through a porthole and I didn't even have to look at him. I'd start to turn and he somehow knew just how fast to pick up the pace.

"We always fixed the show in scenes in which the boys participated. When the time was against us, I wanted them in there with me. We'd usually know the situation by the middle commercial. Usually we were behind and I used to say to the producer, 'Can't you get some faster actors, because I'm doing the last act like I don't like the lines.' "

Tom Corbett's supporting cast might not have had the speediest delivery in early television, but since the 1950s many rolled into brilliant careers.

Besides Frank Sutton, who costarred on *Gomer*

Margaret Garland portrayed Tom Corbett's girl friend, Dr. Joan Dale, in the 1950 adventures on ABC. She is seen with Frank Thomas, wearing the uniform of twenty-fourth-century space cadets.

Pyle, U.S.M.C., Jack Lord, William Windom, Jack Klugman, Jack Warden, and Tom Poston received a good boost from the rocket show.

Thomas says that Corbett's orbit began to decay in 1953, though the show stayed on through the summer of 1955. "Tom Corbett had his golden time from 1950 to 1952 when we were sponsored by Kellogg's. After they left, we just didn't have all the stuff going for us that we did under their banner. For all intents and purposes, that was the beginning of the end."

When it came time for the last show, Frankie Thomas, a regular writer on the program, mulled over Tom Corbett's closing words. This time he realized no one could utter one of the phrases fans had picked up from the show such as "Blow your jets!" "So what happens now, space heroes!" "By the rings of Jupiter!" and "Spaceman's luck!" The last lines would have to be more thoughtful. "And so, knowing it was the end, I had one of the boys asking me, 'Where are we going, Tom?' 'Out boys,' " he answered, sounding like Captain Kirk at the conclusion of Gene Roddenberry's 1979 *Star Trek: The Motion Picture*. " 'Further than we've ever gone before!' "

With the Russian Sputnik launches in 1957 and the fledgling American space program in need of media support, there was talk of recalling the crew of Tom Corbett for another assignment in the Space Patrol.

"We might have come back then," Thomas says. "We thought about it. We had laid off for short periods before and come back, and for all we knew, we might. But I never really thought so."

Frank Thomas had to be content watching NASA imitate art on television.

"Over the years I saw many things that we dealt with as fantasy come true. I must say it affected me."

Thomas pointed to the space suits, the jargon, and, most of all, the actual 1969 moon landing. "I remember watching and feeling as if they were coming out of the *Polaris*. They landed the same way we had. They had a little more equipment on their backs, but I said aloud, 'Good Lord, that's our stuff.' It was kind of odd, and I half-expected Captain Strong to say something and Roger Manning to come in with a wisecrack. I felt like I had been there so many times before I could have pointed the way."

Ed Kemmer and Virginia Hewitt rehearse a scene from Space Patrol. *The pair portrayed Commander Buzz Corry and Carol Karlyle in what is presumed to be TV's first Saturday morning West Coast production broadcast live across the country.*

Seven hundred years after Tom Corbett had earned his wings at the Space Academy, Buzz Corry carried on the rocketeer's legacy aboard the thirtieth-century starcruiser *Terra.* Corry, the steel-jawed commander of *Space Patrol,* policed the galaxy for the United Planets, a peaceful fusion of interstellar governments that had not forgotten, when necessary, how to fight.

Space Patrol debuted as a daily local Los Angeles show, the creation of Mike Moser, a U.S. Navy Air Force veteran in charge of training hurricane-hunter squadrons in World War II. Moser said in a 1952 interview with *Time* that he conceived *Space Patrol* while flying across the Pacific. "It started me wondering and thinking about the universe." Moser said he wanted to design a program that would bring the future to children just as he had grown up with *Buck Rogers* and *Flash Gordon.*

In 1950, Moser brought that vision to Los Angeles station KECA-TV with a real-life air hero playing the fictional space jockey. Ed Kemmer was barely out of Pasadena Playhouse acting school when Moser signed him for *Space Patrol* duty. He was well qualified for the military role; his first acting experience was in a POW camp after being shot down over Germany on his forty-eighth mission.

"TV was new," Kemmer explains, "and Lyn Osborn, a friend of mine from the Playhouse, called and told me that a show he had been hired for was looking for a lead and would I be interested? I said, 'Sure.' "

Kemmer was handed the assignment, but only after another lead actor, cast as Commander Kit Corry, had come and gone. "I missed the first twenty-five or thirty daily shows. I didn't know what the devil TV was all about, but I thought it looked fascinating. I got an $8 paycheck per show then. We did the program on a shoestring, thinking, hoping, praying it would go network."

Osborn, a World War II radioman, received the same pay for portraying Corry's comic sidekick, Cadet Happy. By 1955, Osborn said the investment had paid off. He told *TV Guide* that he was earning approximately $45,000 a year.

Besides Kemmer and Osborn, *Space Patrol* employed Norman Jolley (Mr. Karlyle, Secretary General of the United Planets), Virginia Hewitt (Carol, the diplomat's daughter), Ken Mayer (Major Robertson), and Nina Bara (Miss Tonga, a reformed criminal.)[3]

Space Patrol chartered a network course along ABC, June 9, 1951. Each week the crew boarded the *Terra* for three live broadcasts, including a Saturday edition at 11:00 A.M. Eastern time. Because of the three-hour time difference, the weekend production rolled at 8:00 A.M. in California.

Space Patrol's Los Angeles mission-control center made it TV's first regular live West Coast to East Coast Saturday morning network program. It beamed east via a combination of cable and relay stations and mesmerized viewers from the moment announcer Jack Narz introduced the show:

> *Space Patrol! High adventure in the wild reaches of space . . . missions of daring in the name of interplanetary justice. Travel into the future with Buzz Corry . . . Commander-in-Chief of . . . the Space Patrol.*

Kemmer has fond recollections of the show and terrible memories about the debilitating schedule. At one point the show aired on radio and television, making the typewriters that turned out the 82,000 words per week smoke as much as the *Terra* on takeoff.

"We all worked our butts off on *Space Patrol,*" Kemmer says. "It was a struggle just to come up with a plot and learn the lines and get it on the air. We'd find out on the air that we were five minutes too long, so we'd jump on each other's lines and cut the show. It's a pressure we didn't need. You do those things, but you pay a price in production, lighting, and performance.

"Extras and guest actors who weren't used to the pressure could crumble and often did," Kemmer continues. It was the story of *Tom Corbett, Space Cadet, Captain Video,* and other live productions of the day. The walls were usually plastered with cue cards to help guest actors along when they forgot their dialogue. But sometimes even lines written in bold letters couldn't ease the tension. "There were occasions when I could look at their faces and I'd know they couldn't tell me their own names. When that happened we had to do some fast talking. Lyn would say, 'Well, what do you think, Commander?' And I had to say something. We prayed for the weekday show to go off, because it was just too much."

When *Space Patrol* was trimmed to one program a week, the budget skyrocketed to $25,000 to pay for seven prop men, five electricians, nine carpenters, two directors, a cast of five to fifteen actors, a full technical crew, and the crack special-effects team of Oscar, Paul, and Franz Dallons.

The trio of brothers had transported themselves from science to science fiction. They had originally worked in medical research but found television and motion pictures more profitable. In addition to *Space Patrol* the Dallonses worked on *Donovan's Brain, The Devil Commands,* and TV's *Captain Midnight.*

"They did special effects that were unbelievable," says Kemmer. Yet sometimes, under the pressure of the hour, the gimmicks backfired.

"We had some great things happen live that were belly busters," Kemmer admits. "I remember we went back in time and encountered a tribe of Amazons. I think they hired all the tall girls in Hollywood for the episode. They captured us, tied us to a tree, and aimed a crossbow at me.

3. Bara was released from *Space Patrol* in 1953. However after her dismissal, she sued the production on January 18, 1954, claiming $75,333 damages to cover the unauthorized use of any kinescopes in which she appeared. The case was settled out of court for an undisclosed sum.

"Usually I was very careful. I used to talk to the Dallonses and check everything out. This time they said, 'Don't worry, the string that throws the arrow is a very weak rubber band, so it won't go more than two feet.' Well, wouldn't you know that during the show an Amazon had her finger near the trigger and the arrow went sailing. It didn't hit my head. It landed about three feet directly below!

"I remember another time when we were supposed to be sleeping in a pup tent and another Amazon stalked up to our sleeping bags and aimed an arrow right at mine. Of course, I wasn't in it, but she supposedly didn't know that. She pulled the bow way back and somehow the arrow's feathers caught on the string and it just dangled there. We quickly faded to black, but it was already on the air. After the commercials when we came back, we ignored what had happened and showed the arrow sticking in the bag."

Such mishaps might lead to gales of laughter, but Kemmer says everyone was usually "too damned scared to break up." Only once did he recall losing his composure.

"For some reason, Major Robinson and I had unearthed some old Spanish armor. Unfortunately, the helmet and paraphernalia arrived in time for the show and not the rehearsal. Come airtime, we started putting on the helmet. By the time we got the breastplate on, I looked at Robby and he looked at me and we realized we looked hysterical and we both turned away from the camera and couldn't talk. We tried to swallow and avoid the lens while we pulled ourselves together. It took a good ten or fifteen seconds and I think it was a reaction to the pressure of the show."

Kemmer said that the most important qualification for live television was fast footwork and a clear head. There were days when he'd see a setpiece about to topple over, so he'd walk over on camera without the director knowing why, and lean against the fake wall to hold it up. There were other days when a light would burn out and he'd automatically stroll into a brighter area.

As if such quick thinking wasn't enough, live commercials added another element to the hazards of *Space Patrol.*

"You can't believe the sponsors," he says, talking of Ralston Purina, Wheat and Rice Chex, and Nestlé. "They wanted Lyn and me to eat their cereal and make Nestlé's Quik right after a fight scene. We could be up in the rafters of the studio catwalk and have to rush down, sometimes with real blood on our faces from a hit that connected. We'd be out of breath, totally exhausted, dirty from the fight, and we'd still have to calm down in seconds to do the commercial. There was really no time to catch your breath let alone clean up, but it was live and we just did it."

There were intentionally light moments on the show, usually due to the antics of Cadet Happy. The junior varsity player on the team was always providing comic relief. Sounding like Batman's pal Robin, Happy used to exclaim, "Smokin' rockets!" meaning "Holy Cow!" "Blast off!" meant "Scram!" And "He's lost his rockets" commonly translated to "He's lost his marbles."

Writing the lines were Norman Jolley, Lou Houston, and show creator Mike Moser. Directors for the harrowing production were Dick Darley, Lou Spence, and Helen and Mike Moser. The production team concocted outrageous plots in which Buzz traveled a thousand years in the past to locate a blood donor or visited exotic and erotic planets where mad scientists succumbed to the dark side of the force and tried to kill the intrepid patrollers. They fended off the Wild Men of Procyon, Captain Dagger, the diabolical Mr. Proteus (Marvin Miller on *The Millionaire*), an assortment of zombie-like robots, Mazna the invisible creature, Ahyo a villain who wanted to destroy the universe and the most dangerous *Space Patrol* nemesis Prince Baccar-

Science Fiction with Depth

by Jim Thompson

Those old enough to remember *Creature From the Black Lagoon* are probably also familiar with 3-D and the loose-fitting glasses which made the monster seem to leap toward the audience and off the screen. In 1953 technology attempted to transfer that same achievement to television, but TV was not ready to explore another ratti (played by associate producer Bela Kovacs).

Space Patrol's last trip to Saturday morning was February 26, 1955, after Nestlé and Ralston Purina both withdrew sponsorship. In 1958 there were rumblings regarding *Space Patrol,* but it was not the sound of the *Terra* taking off for new adventures. Comet Distribution Corporation merely expressed interest in airing the old kinescopes to capitalize on the satellite launches.

In 1962, Kemmer was recruited for more space travel. He appeared as an air force astronaut on the soap opera *The Clear Horizon* set at Cape Canaveral. Kemmer has since turned in his wings and settled down to Earth in roles on *The Edge of Night*, *The Doctors*, and *As the World Turns*.

Lyn Osborn died suddenly in the late 1950s, a victim of a brain tumor. Virginia Hewitt, Corry's love interest, Carole, married a crystal merchant and runs a chandelier manufacturing firm with him.

The success of Commander Corry and Cadet Corbett suggested that television's path to the future was bright and profitable. If such newcomers were mining the unchartered territory and striking it rich, then it seemed natural that Buck Rogers and Flash Gordon, two veteran space pilots, could zoom past them directly into the black.

Their TV vehicles, however, were not as well constructed as the Buster Crabbe science fiction serials of the 1930s. Both *Buck Rogers* (1950)

---

dimension. It was having enough difficulty with the first two.

Nonetheless, ABC was granted permission by the Federal Communications Commission to explore the feasibility of 3-D TV. And in May, the network ran a trial broadcast of the live series *Space Patrol* in Los Angeles at the National Association of Radio and Television Broadcaster's 31st annual gathering.

The ABC affiliate station, KECA-TV, aired the show but the viewers at home were treated to nothing more than a blur on their screens. News reporters at the convention suffered from a similar problem because the specially designed TV receiver needed to see the image was on the blink. Midway through the telecast the twin-tubed set reversed polarization and viewers had to turn their glasses upside down.

Some scientists still believed 3-D was feasible, but they recommended that developers wait until color was perfected. Dr. Thomas T. Goldsmith, Jr., of the DuMont Research Labs emphasized this point, saying the "realism of 3-D is so great it just cries out for color."

Three decades later color TV has been perfected and there's renewed talk of 3-D TV. Tokyo Movie Shinsha Co. Ltd. has one three-dimensional TV series in production and has plans for a second series. The programs, science fiction naturally, are aimed for the American market. The Japanese system still requires the use of glasses to obtain the 3-D illusion.

Jim Thompson is a free-lance writer from New England.

and *Flash Gordon* (1951) barely moved audiences.

In the *Buck Rogers* TV production, Kem Dibbs played the World War I air ace who lapsed into suspended animation for five hundred years after exploring an abandoned mineshaft. Awakened, the erstwhile dogfighter turns into a rocketeer, helping Wilma Deering (Lou Prentis) and Dr. Huer (Harry Sothern) shoot Black Barney (Harry Kingston) out of the sky. Dibbs remained in the twenty-fifth century only for six months after the 7:00 P.M., April 15, 1950, premiere. In September, Robert Pastene battled fantastic opponents in his place, but by 1951 he could not fight reality. The ratings, like the show, were deplorable. ABC cancelled *Buck Rogers* January 30, 1951.

In April 1954 a revised series of thirty-nine episodes was planned, but it wasn't until September 20, 1979, that a new prime time *Buck Rogers in the 25th Century* would be seen. This time Gil Gerard portrayed the time traveler, and in a gesture to the 1939 serial, Buster Crabbe made a cameo appearance in the second episode, playing a retired fighter pilot named Brigadier Gordon.

Flash Gordon, meanwhile, may have been able to disarm Ming the Merciless in the twenty-first century with either sword or blaster, but he was no match for *New York Times* TV critic Jack Gould.

Flash Gordon appeared on the DuMont network, 6:30 P.M., Saturday, February 10. Two weeks later he had lost a battle of words with the media writer. Gould damned the serialized adventure calling it "a macabre and sordid half hour," which in his mind had no other purpose than as "a stimulation of horror, fright and ghoulish suspense."

Gould observed with disdain as Flash (Steve Holland) arrived at Ming's Kingdom of Mongo only to be quickly thrown into a wire-enclosed arena to struggle for his life against an apeman. After escaping, the hero is shown falling into a pit. At the same time, heroine Dale Arden (Irene Champlin) undergoes "dehumanization," a process that removes her will so she can become Ming's slave bride. And Dr. Alexis Zarkov (Joe Nash) deals with a variety of monsters before being shunted to a Mongo laboratory.

Gould called the scenario "an utterly deplorable and irresponsible abuse of television's welcome in the home, one which would make any reasonable parent anxious to shake some sense in the heads of video broadcasters." He argued that the airing of the program just before bedtime was "an instance of reckless social behavior that is wholly inexcusable."

When viewers tuned in a week later for the continuing saga of *Flash Gordon,* they found a Western movie instead. Gould had won. The DuMont network executives, whom he described as, "men of sensibility and judgment" had acted with dispatch. They canceled the show.

The move prompted hundreds of viewers left on the edge of their seats seven days earlier—to call and complain. They were told, however, that Gordon was gone and the show that would flash on the screen from then on was the movie serial *Don Winslow.*

Gould's victory, celebrated at first, was not permanent. The critic had indeed managed to influence the network. But television was not a giant force in 1951. It was felt that adverse public opinion could affect program viewing and, more important, TV-set sales. DuMont, a manufacturer as well as a broadcaster, therefore wanted good press, positive reviews, and no controversy splashed across the pages of the nation's most influential newspaper.

Within two years, however, enough of the country had plugged into TV that the rantings of an angry critic mattered much less. *Flash Gordon* returned, not before bedtime at 6:30 P.M., and not merely on the incredible shrinking DuMont network. *Flash Gordon* was syndicated throughout the country and primarily aired on Saturday morning.

Young viewers, concerned more about the quality of the adventure than the terror of the moment, never made this TV version of *Flash Gordon* a hit, however. The production values and stories of the German-filmed show couldn't compare with America's homemade heroes. Everything about it looked like the rush job it had been, for as soon as the fifteen-year Universal rights to the character had lapsed in 1951, thirty-nine new episodes were hastily shot for television. The show was continually distributed in the 1950s but rarely talked about. Flash would reacquire youngsters' attention in 1979, when NBC presented Filmation's *The New Adventures of Flash Gordon* as a regular weekly Saturday morning production.

Steve Holland stepped into Buster Crabbe's space shoes to portray Flash Gordon in the 1953 series.

While Hollywood generated *Space Patrol* and New York turned out *Tom Corbett, Space Cadet,* San Francisco television produced a show in 1951 that went into syndication three years later.

Captain Z-Ro defined the expression low budget but earned the respect of television reviewers. Critics looked beyond the flimsy sets and the cheap effects and saw a weekly program that tried to be instructive as well as entertaining. Even without adequate production facilities, *Variety* once called it "easily the best local product" and predicted it had a "networthy future."

Captain Z-Ro was a close cousin of *You Are There* and a precursor of Jay Ward's Sherman and Peabody cartoons. Each week the intrepid time-traveler crossed decades and centuries, chasing villains and explaining history. Episodes were often linked to holidays and celebrations, giving added historical meaning to Thanksgiving, Easter, and the Fourth of July.

Roy Steffens wrote the show and portrayed the scientist-explorer who had all the time in the world. Bobby Trumbull played his young assistant, Jet. Because the budget was meager, no more than two or three other actors were usually allowed to appear in an episode.

In 1954, *Captain Z-Ro* expanded from fifteen to thirty minutes, switched from a local live production to a syndication and film, and was distributed for one year by Atlas TV Corporation.

Science fiction was a smokescreen for Cold War politics in the live 1953 NBC series, *Atom Squad.* Steve Elliot (Bob Hastings) and his assistants (Bob Courtleigh and Bram Nossem) manned the squad, a mythical Manhattan-based organization that protected the United States from foreign operatives who attempted to pilfer America's nuclear secrets (see Chapter XIV, "The Cold War Brigade").

CBS's *Rod Brown of the Rocket Rangers* also championed patriotic fervor and required living room members of Omega Base to take an oath to the United States Constitution and obey parents and teachers. The 1953 series, presented live at 11:30 A.M. Saturday mornings, replaced *Smilin' Ed's Gang* and starred Cliff Robertson, Jack Weston, and Bruce Hall. The production's

Cliff Robertson starred in Rod Brown of the Rocket Rangers, *a live 1953 Saturday morning science fiction show. Jack Weston* (upper left) *portrayed Wormsey Wormser, and John Boruff and Bruce Hall copiloted the "Beta" through a year of intergalactic adventures.*

first adventure came well before the April 18 premiere. The twenty-second century show raided behind-the-scenes staffers of *Tom Corbett, Space Cadet.* Captured by a CBS contract were Corbett's original director, George Gould; the first-string writing team; and, according to lawyers for Rockhill Productions, the Corbett format. Corbett star Frank Thomas also says that CBS made a bid for him.

Rockhill retaliated with a lawsuit. *Variety* watched the space battle from the sidelines and noted in a June 3, 1953, article, "A hot war in the realm of space rover boys and Martian rockets was touched off this week, but happily since it was just a legal battle claiming piracy of TV show gimmicks, not a soul has been wounded by blast-off guns."

Rockhill president Stanley Wolfe filed suit against CBS-TV, charging that *Rod Brown of the Rocket Rangers* (scheduled to air opposite Corbett) was a copy of the show. Like Corbett, Brown used three space cadets, Wolfe told *Variety.* The leader seemed shaped from the Tom Corbett mold: "hard, snide, sarcastic and overbearing." The "blast-off" and landing procedure terminology of the Rangers duplicated the Cadets' jargon. The Rangers' school was similar to the Space Cadets' Solar Guards; and finally, *Rod Brown of the Rocket Rangers* allegedly borrowed Corbett's references to "electronic blanking devices, free fall in space, spaceship walks and making repairs to the hull of the ship in space."

CBS countered that *Tom Corbett, Space Cadet* originated on CBS before transferring to ABC, and therefore the network retained certain rights to the property. Four months later the case was settled out of court. The terms were not disclosed.

Cliff Robertson portrayed the young pilot looking for star status. He would attain it as Ranger Brown and two years later in his film debut, *Picnic. Rod Brown of the Rocket Rangers,* he explains emphatically, was and will be his only regular TV series. He acted in the production while also attending the Actors Workshop and performing in the Broadway play *Late Love* with Elizabeth Montgomery.

"I really had my hands full," Robertson says. "I'd get up around 4:00 A.M. Saturdays and drive to the CBS studio uptown in New York. We would have a dress rehearsal and do the show live a few hours later at 11:30. After we finished, I'd go down to the theater for a matinee and then an evening show. By Saturday night at eleven, I was really stumbling around.

"I would say that with the blend of doing a Broadway show, studying at the studio, and appearing in a live TV program, I was sharpening three edges of the sword."

Robertson recalls being paid approximately $175 a week for his weekly sojourn to CBS, an amount he says "was hot stuff in those days."

"I didn't consider TV a comedown, then," he adds. "I saw it as a chance to put some bread on the table and practice my trade."

Robertson admired the acting of Jack Weston, his sidekick, Ranger Wilbur "Wormsey" Wormser, John Boruff (Commander Swift), Bruce Hall (Ranger Frank Boyle), and Shirley Standlee. "We also had guys like Don Knotts do guest shots and comedy relief, and we had one extra we often used that we just called 'the nut.' He had walk-on roles, but we felt he was kind of zany. During our rehearsals, or even when he wasn't on the air, he'd go behind a flat and the most amazing and weird sounds would come our way—all kinds of things like machine guns, bomb blasts, and everything imaginable." Robertson could have been describing only one comic—Jonathan Winters.

Talent abounded on *Rod Brown.* Years before John Frankenheimer directed *The Manchurian Candidate, Birdman of Alcatraz, Seven Days in May,* and *Grand Prix,* he was a floor manager on Robertson's weekly show. Bill Dozier produced *Rod Brown.* He would later return to science fiction and hire Robertson for an appearance in an episode of his *Batman* TV series called "Come Back, Shame."

Reviewers were split over the program. *Variety* said *Rod Brown* might be lifting off too late but still had a chance to succeed as a "rear guard entry into the universal sweepstakes." *TV Guide* argued that stories bordered too "closely to the line of violence" with "little or no attempt to be educational, informative or even entertaining." Thirty-five youngsters signed a letter of rebuttal to the magazine, insisting that "the program is not educational, but we go to school to be educated. . . . We consider the Rangers exciting and look forward to seeing it every week."

Rod Brown provided fodder for viewers' sci-

Rocky Jones (Richard Crane) inside the Orbit Jet with Verna Ray (Sally Mansfield), 1954

ence fiction tastes. One week he rocketed to Venus to explore the origin of a winged humanoid, other weeks he was busy preventing Planet H from flooding the earth, arresting a robot who robbed the First Martian Bank, finding a cure to a poisonous seed from the jungles of the planet Titan, traveling to Neptune on the trail of hidden treasure, and discovering a planet identical to Earth on the other side of the sun.

His exploits ended on May 29, 1954, when CBS replaced the show with *The Abbott and Costello Show*. Robertson says it was definitely time for him to walk the Earth for other roles, but he's not certain why the show was cancelled. "Blame it on the great sagacious pundits up at the executive level who make the decisions," he offers.

"While we were doing it, I had a ball," he says, his voice cracking in mild laughter. "It was amusing, and it was needed work."

No one stops Robertson on the street today and takes him for Rod Brown. And only occasionally will he meet another actor from the program and reminisce. Still, he takes time to think of the show himself. "We had a lot of fun on *Rod Brown*, and because I had work I was considered very fortunate."

As for acting full-time in another TV series, Robertson rejects the notion. "Life's far too short to do that."

At twenty-second century Rocket Ranger school, Rod Brown might have read of the hundred-year-old exploits of *Rocky Jones, Space Ranger*. This stoic starship commander traveled the vastness of space in the *Orbit Jet*, bringing middle-class values to far-off planets.

Rocky Jones, Space Ranger premiered on January 20, 1954. For years it has been incorrectly called a copy of *Rod Brown*, but the series, in fact, was cast November 1951. Production was under way by January 29, 1952, and a pilot screened by Roland Reed Productions on October 8, 1952.

Richard Crane played the heroic lead, conjuring up an image of a space-age scout leader in a T-shirt and baseball cap. Crane was an experienced warrior compared to young Corbett and Brown, who were still wet behind the ears. His ship was fast, his punch powerful, and his mind lightning-quick. Keeping up with Jones was

Bobby, a Ranger-in-training (Robert Lyden); Vena Ray, Rocky's ever-in-trouble Lois Lane (Sally Mansfield); and Professor Newton, the scientist with a knack for designing life-saving inventions (Maurice Cass).[4] Also appearing were Scott Beckett as Winky, Dian Fauntelle as Yarra, and Crystal Reeves, Ralph Brooks, and Robert S. Carson.

Only thirty-nine episodes of *Rocky Jones, Space Ranger* were shot. The adventures resembled movie serials and required three weeks to conclude. Besides airing on TV, the footage was reedited into a series of movies, released between 1953 and 1954. When the show's initial ABC run concluded in 1955, *Rocky Jones* zoomed into syndication, distributed by United Television and later MCA-TV.

4. Sally Mansfield was promoted as an up-and-coming superstar in 1954. She not only appeared on *Rocky Jones, Space Ranger* but was appointed "Miss Emmy" for the year's Academy of Television Arts and Science Awards. Maurice Cass may be familiar to viewers of *The Adventures of Superman* as Meldini, the scientist who bakes homemade kryptonite, the man of steel's Achilles' heel, in the 1953 episode "The Defeat of Superman."

One of the best-remembered shows of the 1950s was *Captain Midnight*, a combination Cold-War–science fiction series featuring a contemporary Lone Ranger figure who jockeyed in a jet plane dubbed the *Silver Dart* instead of on a horse named Silver.

Captain Midnight actually debuted on TV as the host of a daily 1950 fifteen-minute TV production that contained old movie serials. According to *The Great Television Heroes* by Donald F. Glut and Jim Harmon (Doubleday & Co., Inc., 1975), the program began with a film introduction in which the Captain said, "Hello, Secret Squadron members. We'll get right to our thrilling story in a moment, but first let me tell you how Ovaltine builds strength and health." When the commercial ended, viewers saw a chapter of a Republic Western serial.

The character had originated on radio in 1938, named for Captain Albright, a mythical World War I flier who survived a dangerous mission at midnight that turned the tide of the war to

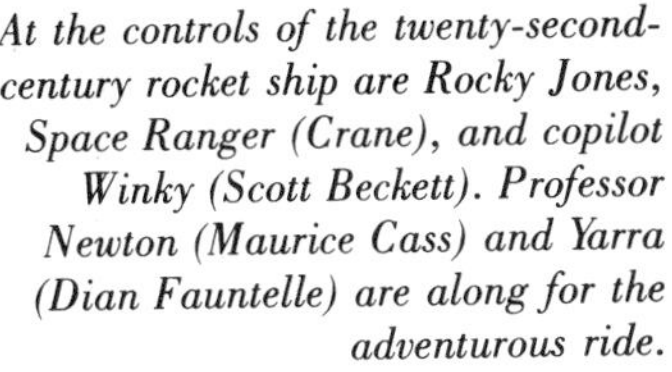

At the controls of the twenty-second-century rocket ship are Rocky Jones, Space Ranger (Crane), and copilot Winky (Scott Beckett). Professor Newton (Maurice Cass) and Yarra (Dian Fauntelle) are along for the adventurous ride.

© Screen Gems

Richard Webb proudly wore the emblem of the Secret Squadron as he starred as Saturday TV's most uprighteous hero, Captain Midnight. Sid Melton costarred as Ichabod Mudd.

the Allies. After the armistice, listeners were told he directed an undercover operation that sent democracy's best pilots into airborne espionage missions.

The mercenary headlined one motion picture serial, *Captain Midnight* (1942), with Dave O'Brien leading the Secret Squadron (SQ).

Richard Webb, a cool-eyed, fair-skinned actor with a linebacker's build, played Midnight during its network and syndicated television run. Webb, a World War II captain, seemed naturally suited to portray the noncommissioned freedom fighter. The graduate of Officer Candidate School and an expert in hand-to-hand combat, judo, and explosives says, "I had to go into the military to prepare for *Captain Midnight*." In addition to his distinguished military career, he acted in the powerful wartime stories *The Sands of Iwo Jima* and *O.S.S.* As Midnight he bravely fought the undeclared Cold War on TV, just as he had in the 1951 feature film *I was a Communist for the FBI.*

Midnight was leader of a crack squad of private citizens that was committed to routing Communist spies and apprehending domestic crooks. The Secret Squadron elite included Ichabod Mudd (Sid Melton), Tut (Olan Soule), and young viewers who communicated with one another and deciphered Midnight's televised messages via a decoder badge[5] (see Chapter VIII, "Batteries Not Included").

Captain Midnight premiered on Saturday morning in 1953, but attained such a strong adult following ABC moved it to Monday night at 8:00 P.M. in September to compete with CBS's *Burns and Allen* and NBC's *Name That Tune.*

During its first season *Captain Midnight* was thoroughly action-packed and prompted *TV Guide* to call it "a violent series with gallons of gore." When the show returned, the magazine observed that the gore had been "mopped up quite a bit."

The show's dabbling in science fiction never took Midnight beyond the stratosphere, but he

5. Melton, a crew-cut character with a big swing that usually missed its target, played Webb's aide. His comic capers were consistently a source of laughs. He was the perennial adolescent in a suit and tie whose TV counterparts included Cadet Happy, Wormsey Wormser, and Roger Manning. Melton, an accomplished radio and TV actor, is also known for his continuing role as Danny Thomas's manager, "Uncle Charley" Halper on *Make Room for Daddy* and guest appearances in *Superman, Dragnet, Twilight Zone, December Bride,* and *It's Always Jan.* Film performances still screened today are *Beau James, The Lemon Drop Kid,* and *Knock on Any Door.* Melton resides in Southern California and owns a videotape production company.

Captain Midnight Decoder Code

"Setting B6"

Q	1	Z	10	K	19
D	2	O	11	U	20
I	3	Y	12	J	21
C	4	N	13	T	22
H	5	X	14	S	23
B	6	M	15	F	24
G	7	W	16	R	25
A	8	L	17	E	26
P	9	V	18		

still supervised experimental robot-bombs and test-rockets and assisted others who were harnessing volcanic energy and constructing space stations.

Webb's pride in the series is as deeply rooted as that of any surviving veteran of a foreign war. While in his mid-thirties, he fought for the role when Screen Gems wanted a man years younger.

"I was out here on vacation from New York and Max Arnow, casting director at Columbia, called and said get over here, I want to talk to you. He sent me to Screen Gems, which was a new outfit on the other side of the Columbia fence and told me not to admit how old I was. 'Tell them you're no more than thirty because the people doing the show really don't want anyone older.' I went, and about an hour later, I walked off with the part."

Captain Midnight was filmed for roughly $21,000 per episode. Costs were minimized as the production relied on illusions rather than effects. Instead of building regular scenes around the Bell X-IA jet takeoffs, for example, a model was pulled by wires along an eighteen-foot platform and photographed at an angle to suggest greater size. Despite such shortcuts, Webb says "the shows hold up extremely well against stuff that is supposed to be adult today. They were beautifully produced and beautifully done for the money. The ideas might have been far out, but the people were always realistic. That carried the show. And according to the ratings we had six million kids watching and 10 million adults. In those days, that would be comparable to a rating of 60 today."

Captain Midnight was in production for only a year and a half. It aired for four seasons under Ovaltine sponsorship on both ABC and CBS and then continued in syndication as *Jet Jackson, Flying Commando* through the 1950s and early 1960s.

Other shows changed titles for their syndicated life, but only Webb's show devised an elaborate system that replaced all audio references to Captain Midnight with Jet Jackson.

"Screen Gems made a deal with the Ovaltine people that when they'd shoot a segment in which the name Captain Midnight was mentioned, they'd also record a 'wild line' of the same person saying 'Jet Jackson.' Then they'd spend a couple of thousand dollars to strike a print of their

Science wiz Tut (Olan Soule) gets an examination by Captain Midnight after enemy agents made a move against the Secret Squadron member.

own which could run as *Jet Jackson, Flying Commando,* in all the areas of the country where Midnight wasn't taken. When Midnight went off the air, they blanketed the country with the other version. It was one of the strangest production deals ever. Unfortunately, I believe Ovaltine destroyed all the negatives and film of *Captain Midnight,* so Screen Gems' *Jet Jackson* is the only thing that exists."

On the street, Webb says he'll answer to either name, but he adds that Jet Jackson never had the impact on viewers that Captain Midnight did. Recognizing the commercial difference between the two titles, the studio attempted to negotiate for rights to *Captain Midnight,* using Webb as their go-between.

"Screen Gems called me and in great secrecy asked me to talk to Ovaltine. They said, 'We authorize you to offer up to $1.5 million for the series, but don't let them know we're behind it. You offer this in your own name. If you're able to get it, then you'll become part of the production and get money.' So I went back and asked for the rights, but they told me no, and added that they pulled the series and put it in a vault. In four or five years they planned

Richard Webb is met by faithful fans in the 1950s. The crowds have not abandoned him today. He's asked for autographs and pictures wherever he travels.

Judd Holdren had an unsuccessful flight as Commando Cody in 1955.

to take it out and try it on the market again. They said that if they were successful, they'd get another Captain Midnight. The president of the company looked at me and said, 'A *younger* Captain Midnight!' "

Apparently Ovaltine primarily saw the program as a marketing tool. When their breakfast drink sold, they were happy. When it didn't, they yanked *Captain Midnight*.

"As I remember, the public just was not buying it," Webb states. "They were stealing the jars for the premiums, or buying it once. But they really weren't sold on the product."

The reaction to Ovaltine was never more powerfully demonstrated than during a mid-1950s Webb public appearance at Boston Garden. "I walked out onto the stage. There were thousands upon thousands of kids there and I said, 'Hi, boys and girls,' and there was a big hubbub. Then I shouted, 'I'm going to ask you one question and one question only. Are you ready?' And they screamed back, 'Yes,' 'All right then,' I said, 'what breakfast drink do you like the best?' And with one voice came the resounding reply—'Bosco!' "

Throughout his Midnight service, Webb presented the unblemished image of the American hero: efficient, brave, reverent, and patriotic. To this day Webb claims that Midnight's principles shape his life.

"I believe in Captain Midnight," he states, adding that the character's traits provided an important role model to youngsters in the 1950s and helped guide his own life during some troubled years.

Webb, author of *These Came Back* (Hawthorn Books, 1974), a book on reincarnation, an autobiography, two collections of ghost stories, and numerous screenplays, insists that he still enjoys being remembered for his thirty-year-old Captain Midnight role.

"Today I do a lot of traveling around the country and I usually carry fifty to a hundred pictures because I'm used to being recognized at airports and even on planes. For some people I meet, the same look comes into their eyes that I'm sure they had when they were nine or ten years old.

"On one 747 trip, the flight engineer was standing next to the stewardess checking people in," he recollects. "As I walked toward him he did a double take and said, 'Captain Midnight!'

When we got under way he announced over the PA system, 'We're very honored to have Captain Midnight on board today.' My God, I must have given away all my pictures."

Webb is also recognized for his 1959 starring performance in *Border Patrol,* but above and beyond anything else, Captain Midnight seems to have catapulted him into the legion of superheroes.

"I've written and copyrighted a new *Captain Midnight* series," he explains. "The script is currently in the hands of a syndicator. If we go into production, I'll find a new twenty-eight or thirty-year-old Captain and I'll make an appearance once in a while as Colonel Midnight. I wasn't going to write myself in it, but everybody said, 'Dick, you have to for the older audience.' "

Webb says the premise is quite similar to his old series with the exception of an updated science fiction twist. "I've been on another planet for a couple of years," he says. "And suddenly, a huge mother ship brings the Captain and the Colonel back down to Earth's atmosphere. We leave it in a flying saucer scout ship. A mountaintop opens up and we settle in at our new headquarters."

For true nostalgia impact he intends to have Sid Melton appear in his amended sidekick role as Professor Ichabod Mudd (still with two *d*'s).

Commando Cody was a bit more sluggish than his science fiction brethren. Maybe it was the cumbersome uniform.

Production rolled on January 15, 1952, but it was July 16, 1955, before *Commando Cody—Sky Marshal of the Universe*—finally reached the audience. Even then, not all of its thirty-nine half hours initially aired (episodes were released earlier to movie theaters). The program was only scheduled as a Saturday morning replacement until August 8.

Cody was supposed to be an invincible character who fought against the forces of tyranny.

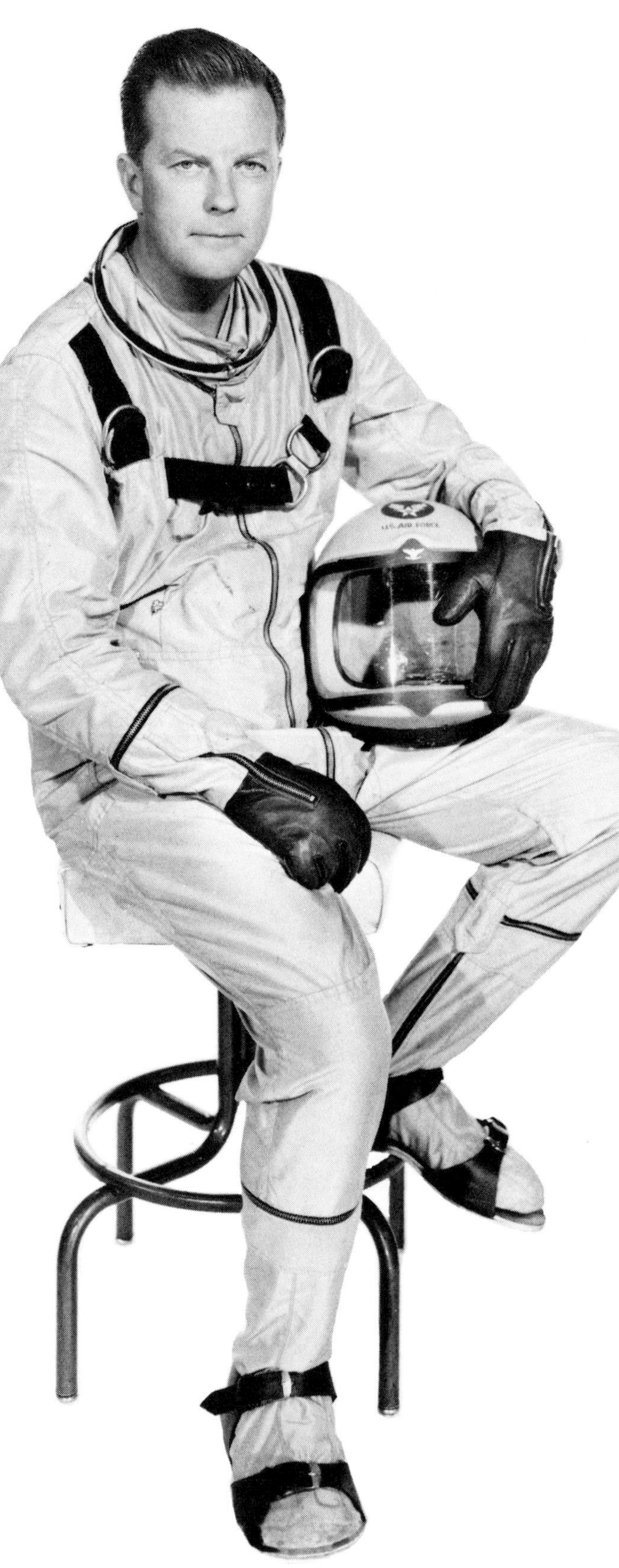

William Lundigan starred as Colonel Edward McCauley in TV's most realistic science fiction show of the 1950s, Men Into Space. *The CBS prime time series repeated on Saturday mornings in the 1960s.*

He wasn't that strong a fighter and certainly unable to hold an audience.

Republic Pictures, short on ideas and money during its last production years, recycled costumes just as it did stock footage. Commando Cody's rocket backpack and helmet uniform, which usually inspired more laughter from viewers than fright from villains, was right off the shelf. The studio had outfitted Tristram Coffin, George Marshall, and Judd Holdren in the same suit for their serials *King of the Rocket Men* (1949), *Radar Men From the Moon* (1952), and *Zombies of the Stratosphere* (1952).

Judd Holdren, film's *Captain Video,* also played the Commando on TV, exhibiting the gamut of emotions from A to B. His acting, however, was not as important as the fantastic plots. Actress Aline Towne (Joan Albright) and actor William Schallert (Ted Richards) learned the same lesson as they faced the machinations of Gregory Gay (Retik the Ruler), whose evil one week brought an epidemic to Earth and another week dislodged Earth from its axis. The stories borrowed freely from Republic's existing motion picture library. Cody's fight scenes, flying, and rescues came from the serials. Even Gay's scenes were intercut with shots of Roy Barcroft from *The Purple Monster Strikes* (1945) and *Zombies of the Stratosphere.* The studio's stock footage supply offered Republic an advantage over other independent television producers, but the procedure had an inherent disadvantage. The films were dated. Car chases with ten-year-old automobiles and clothing a decade or more behind the times destroyed any semblance of credibility. Commando Cody was supposed to be a modern hero, but he looked more like he was fighting crime inside a time capsule.

When Cody was finally seen darting across the horizon in 1955, declaring himself ready for action, the airwaves seemed overcrowded with flying avengers. The nation's young air controllers, tired of the traffic, downed the Sky Marshal by turning to the competition.

Science fiction shows—like the experimental Vanguard rocket—could hardly get off the ground at the dawn of the space age. Earlier in the decade there had been science fiction anthologies on the order of CBS's Sunday night series *Out There* (October 28, 1951, to January 13, 1952), the syndicated *Inner Sanctum,* the Friday night radio and TV series *Tales of Tomorrow* (1951–1953), and NBC's live 1953 Sunday summer series *Operation Neptune,* which investigated the disappearance of Navy ships.

By 1958, however, *Variety* announced that the science fiction era had ended. Of the 115 shows scheduled for the fall, only one—*Invisible Man*—was a science fiction entry. *The Twilight Zone* was in development, as was *One Step Beyond.* But most proposed series, like Eddie Fisher's *Galaxy,* would remain unproduced.

Saturday, previously a busy space-port, failed to house any new productions in the late 1950s. Occasionally, a few of the prime time science fiction shows such as CBS's *Men into Space* (1959) and NBC's *The Man and the Challenge* found renewed interest on the weekend, but only after their initial runs had ended.[6]

It would be years before Saturday's television producers would again venture into the realm of science fiction. Most were content with big cartoon profits and lowbrow plots. The cycle didn't begin to swing around again until 1974, when Filmation Studios produced *Shazam!*

The show, loosely based on the comic book superhero Captain Marvel, was shot totally on location and was geared to teach more than excite. Young Billy Batson (Michael Gray) had the wherewithal to transform himself into an older, wiser, stronger caped crusader by uttering the magic word "Shazam." Though he possessed and, indeed, exercised amazing powers, the scripts suggested that common sense, not brute strength, were life's true heroic qualities. Billy learned that as a normal teen-ager his entrances might not be as dramatic as his flying alter ego's, but his impact could ultimately be as powerful. Billy's companion in his cross-country journeys was Mentor (Les Tremayne), a man with implied but never seen super abilities.

Captain Marvel was not a superman. According to Filmation co-owner Norm Prescott, that

6. *The Man and the Challenge* was an earthbound show produced by Ivan Tors and starring George Nader as researcher Glenn Barton, who weekly pushed the limits of human endurance for the sake of scientific experimentation. Viewers were introduced to centrifugal force, G-forces, and jet planes reaching supersonic speeds. Barton never broke through Earth's gravity; however, Colonel Edward McCauley (William Lundigan) would in *Men Into Space,* a drama with prophetic proportions. Lundigan played a believable astronaut destined for the moon and intermediate stops. The series's penchant for realism guaranteed it an early demise.

was never the intention. "Every story had a moral," he says. "If you remember, Captain Marvel didn't usually come in until the last minute-and-a-half, and really only to add advice and air fâir warning."

Filmation Studios' next live-action production struck the same moral tone. "We really snuck in *The Secrets of Isis* in 1975 with little notice," Prescott says. "She was the first female superhero and a coup for us, because we did it about a year before the whole fad started with *Wonder Woman* and *The Bionic Woman*." (Prescott says that most of the show's mail came from adults. No wonder, considering the spell actress-model Joanna Cameron, not the magical Isis, put on the audience.)

According to the plot, Isis was high school teacher Andrea Thomas, who had discovered a long-lost Egyptian pendant that could transform her from a mortal into an indestructible being with the powers of the ancient Egyptian goddess of fertility. For a unique touch, when she summoned the strength of Isis, Thomas flew in a vertical position. The unorthodox style never seemed to hinder her ability. She always arrived in time to thwart a crime or disaster.

Isis and *Shazam!* were never violent. The only casualty of either show was excitement. Action was always stifled, predictable, and, by past standards, dull. Nonetheless, given the restraints of new TV standards governing children's shows, Filmation attempted to fill the void created when live-action Saturday heroes disappeared. The productions were expensive and the financial rewards were less than most cartoons would bring, but Prescott and partner Lou Scheimer believed that science fiction would again be bought by the networks, advertisers, and viewers.

In 1974, Sid and Marty Krofft wished on the same stars and produced their own live-action science fiction series for NBC called *Land of the Lost*. The series ran three years and, like *Shazam!*, contained a bold-faced moralistic theme. Stories centered on the Marshall family members, who fell over a waterfall while boating and inexplicably ended in a strange land where dinosaurs (animated by stop-motion photography) roamed the plains.

Spencer Milligan starred as Forest Ranger Rick Marshall. Wesley Eure and Kathy Coleman portrayed his son and daughter, Will and Holly.

The videotape program usually costarred an extinct creature each week. So important were monsters to the story that when *Land of the Lost* began its third season in 1976, the Kroffts devised an earthquake that loosened huge boulders and permitted new giants to stalk the Marshalls. It was in this last season that Rick disappeared and Uncle Jack Marshall fell through the time vortex and helped Will and Holly cope with two-headed, snake-faced, and fire-breathing monsters.

Among the prehistoric people befriended by the family were Chaka and Sa, a monkey boy and girl (Philip Paley and Sharon Baird) and Zarn, a creature lost in time but speaking with the familiar voice of TV's "Millionaire," Marvin Miller.

Filmation leaped centuries ahead of *Land of the Lost* and leagues beyond most other science fiction series when *Ark II* premiered on CBS in 1976. The production, set in 2476, was one of the most humanistic shows to appear on Saturday morning TV at any age. Combining the weekly moral of *Shazam!* with the space-age wizardry of *Tom Corbett* and the homespun sincerity of *Fury*, the teenage crew of *Ark II* set out in their Land-Rover to rebuild society after a devastating global holocaust. With great hope for the future they found that feudal tribes had sprung up where great nations once stood. Through cunning, technological razzle-dazzle, and a hand extended in friendship, they were able to rekindle the spark of civilization. The expedition was led by Jonah (Terry Lester). His dutiful crew included Ruth (Jean Marie Hon), Samuel (Jose Flores), and Adam, their trained chimpanzee.

The Kroffts added comedy to science fiction when they sent Jim Nabors and Ruth Buzzi adrift as two bumbling androids from an advanced planet in a regular segment of *The Krofft Supershow* called "The Lost Saucer." The ninety-minute ABC Saturday morning program also featured the comical adventures of "Wonderbug," a magical VW with three buzzing teenagers; "Dr. Shrinker," a farcical tale about four youngsters miniaturized by an egocentric villain; and "Electra Woman and Dyna Girl," a serialized story of two reporter-disguised superheroes.

A year later *The Krofft Supershow* returned with a new science fiction–oriented segment, "Magic Mongo," which concerned a male genie

Right: JoAnna Cameron leaped from TV commercials into Saturday morning airtime as the heroine of Isis, *a live-action Filmation series.*

Below: Philip Paley dressed in the ape costume in NBC's Land of the Lost. *Ron Harper, Kathy Coleman, and Wesley Eure wore contemporary clothes even though they were swept through a time vortex to another age.*

Below right: Filmation's Shazam! *featured two actors as Captain Marvel. John Davey is pictured here as the flying hero. Jackson Bostwich also suited up.*

Chuck McCann, Bob Denver, and an alien friend on Sid and Marty Kroffts' 1975 comedy for CBS, Far Out Space Nuts.

Electra Woman (Diedra Hall, right*) and Dyna Girl (Judy Strangis) strong-arm their way into a weekly segment of* The Krofft Supershow *on ABC (1976).*

whose plans usually went awry whenever he tried to help his three teen-age companions.

Sid and Marty Krofft also produced the 1975 CBS comedy *Far Out Space Nuts,* with Bob Denver and Chuck McCann as two reluctant astronauts who accidently launched into space from Cape Kennedy.

In 1977, Hanna-Barbera produced one serial in its hodgepodge program, *The Skatebirds.* Amid the cartoons and human-sized puppets was "Mystery Island," a live-action story about an airplane crew that crash-landed on an unchartered island. Stranded, they attempted to keep their computer-controlled robot, "P.O.P.S." out of the hands of Dr. Strange, and tried to find their way back to civilization.

The same year Filmation opened the doors to *Space Academy,* a futuristic astronaut school that paid homage, but no royalties, to *Tom Corbett, Space Cadet.*

The stories in the CBS series dealt with the teen-age rocket rangers who darted off from their asteroid school directly into old cliff-hanger action. Jonathan Harris, the nefarious Dr. Zachary Smith on *Lost in Space,* played a tough academician with a heart of gold.

Spinning off from *Space Academy* in 1978 was *Jason of Star Command,* a twenty-second century star trek in which the *Enterprise*'s engineer, James Doohan, even appeared as Jason's commander.

Jason of Star Command was a direct descendant of the 1950s space heroes. He was young, fearless, and spirited—as quick with his tongue as with his phaser. The Filmation production began in 1978 as a fifteen-minute serial contained in *Tarzan and the Super 7.* A year later he became popular enough to warrant his own noonday slot on CBS. John Russell of TV's *Lawman* replaced Doohan in the second season.

Though obviously pleased with Jason's success, Filmation's Norm Prescott predicted that the space-age production actually represented a dying era rather than the shape of things to come.

"We may have to stop doing live-action shows in the years to come, because the networks may not give us enough money," Prescott says. "And if they don't pay the money that's required, then we just can't produce them."

In animation, Prescott explains, residual costs are minimal. They're paid only to actors. Writ-

Above: Terry Lester starred as Jonah, leader of Ark II, *a CBS live-action science fiction show that followed a group of young people charged with reestablishing civilization after a global atomic war.*

Jason (Craig Littler), 1979

Below: Spinning off the Space Academy *orbit was* Jason of Star Command. *James Doohan, another fellow space traveler (Scotty on* Star Trek*), played Commander Canarvin in the 1978 premiere season. Craig Littler portrayed Jason. Farther down the chain of command were Susan O'Hanlin as Nicole Davidoff and Charles Dell as inventor E. J. Parsafoot. Sid Haig appeared as the villainous Dragos. Jason debuted as a segment on* Tarzan and the Super 7 *and won his own half hour in 1979.*

ers, directors, and animators do not collect on each broadcast. "In live action, the actors, writers and directors all get additional money through seven runs of a show in each new market. That's money that often must be allocated in the initial budget. And when the network looks at the economic differences between live action and animation, it's easy to see why live action is disappearing again. We were the first to come back to it in the 1970s and now we're the last to continue it.

"A half-hour animated show such as *Tarzan* might cost us a total of $165,000 today. A show like *Jason of Star Command* probably comes in for around $220,000." Videotape can reduce the cost somewhat, but for all its benefits, most producers still consider film more manageable, reliable for outdoor use, and better-looking on camera.

Prescott says there's another reason space shows have run their course. They may be futuristic, but they still become quickly dated by rapid changes in technology, jargon, and society.

TV's 1950 view of space age weaponry, women, clothing, and attitudes would never hold up today. Likewise, the science fiction of the 1960s and even the 1970s is not liberated from the calendar simply because the setting is a far-off time and place. Everytime social strides are taken, a TV show—particularly one that deals with tomorrow—must keep in step.

Cartoons, with androgynous talking animals, need not be concerned by small changes. They're swept along from decade to decade by fast cuts, noisy scenes, and frenetic plots. Live-action shows, by their basic nature, are slower. They rely more on dialogue than action, character shadings instead of overt stereotypes. "Most of our live-action shows do not have the fast-moving, fast-cutting, and short-scene action that a Bugs Bunny would have," the producer affirms. "And it's true, we lose a lot of preschool kids who get bored.

"Few studios are willing to do live-action fantasy anymore, and I don't blame them," Prescott concludes. "They can lose their shirts. In fact, I think *Jason of Star Command* may end up being the last of the live-action Saturday morning science fiction shows."

Right: Veteran space traveler Jonathan Harris disembarked from his Lost in Space *rocketship where he played Dr. Smith, and signed on as Professor Isaac Gampu in Filmation's entertaining* Space Academy.

Opposite: Jay Robinson portrayed the evil Dr. Shrinker, curator of a miniaturizing ray, in another serialized segment of The Kroffts Supershow.

6

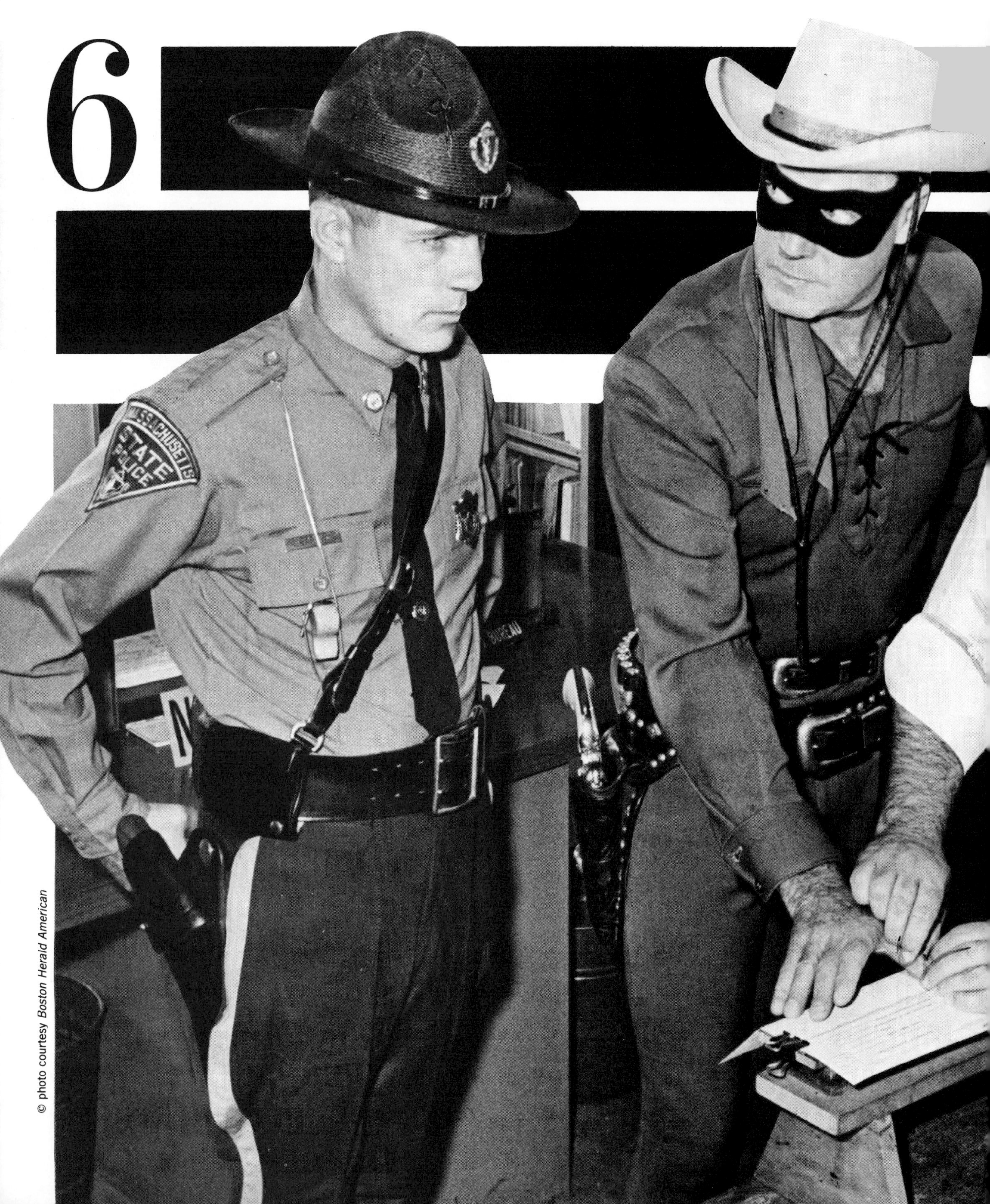

Stable Programming: The Westerns

The dusty Hollywood Western backlots look more like ghost towns than movie studios today. Tumbleweeds race back and forth across the empty streets, and the Santa Ana winds play tricks as they rustle strange sounds from the shutters of the livery stables and saloon windows.

The Western movie and TV boom has been dead for years, yet the outdoor sets remain standing like flimsy monuments to a once great and popular culture.

Visitors to these abandoned corners of Warner Brothers, Universal, CBS, Twentieth Century-Fox, and MGM sense that time has stopped amid the façades. For now, only rerun memories help recall the days when Roy Rogers would gallop into town or the Lone Ranger would ride off.

The devout Western fan can find quiet solitude in this tinsel Mecca. Yet while the studios themselves have turned from the past to the future, the Western TV stars of the 1950's hope aloud that they'll ride through the streets again.

The Lone Ranger gets fingerprinted by Massachusetts State Troopers for a permit to holster his six-guns during a 1964 personal appearance tour through New England.

In this age of space travel and warp-speed adventures, Clayton Moore, star of *The Lone Ranger*, says, "You can't kill American heritage. The pioneers settled the West. Their experience is the story of our country, and I don't think the space patrol will ever put the cowboy out of business."

Today, however, kids are more familiar with R2D2 than a sidekick like Tonto. And critics, in retrospect, equate Saturday Westerns with violence and good heroes with bad examples. It's not like the 1950s, when characters with names like Hoppy and Hickok appeared in thirty-minute stories that were generally taken for nothing more than what they were: cinematic recapitulations of Homer's *Odyssey*, of Christian and pagan fights to the finish, of the classic struggle between good and evil and of Perseus of the purple sage.

Most Western stars admit that their stories were action-packed. But as Guy Madison, TV's Wild Bill Hickok argues, "Few of us instilled violence for violence's sake." "*The Range Rider* was not violent," adds Jock Mahoney, star of the early 1950s show. "We had some wing-ding fights where I'd completely demolish some stores and cabinets, but good always won out. That was the message of the TV Western. And that's something that should be on TV again."

Clayton Moore insists that force was never made to look attractive or fun. It was just occasionally necessary on *The Lone Ranger*.

"We never killed anybody in any of our shows," said Cisco Kid Duncan Renaldo during a 1959 interview. "We shot in self-defense, we shot the guns out of bandit's hands, but we didn't kill."

Renaldo said adult Westerns gave the entire genre a bad name. The children's Western was victim of unfounded character assassination. "We had action and entertainment, but not murder or gore or vengeance."

The criticism was overblown, said Roy Rogers in a mid-1950s interview. "We were careful to make our villains very repulsive. Too often the villains are more attractive than the hero. We make certain that doesn't happen with our show."

While violence is linked, no matter how unfairly, with the Saturday morning Western, historians have a valid argument over the liberal interpretations the shows made with actual figures and events.

TV generally ignored Western reality and wrote its own history of the old West. What viewers saw was a popularized myth, fattened with falsehood and exaggeration. Heroes were sanitized, their acts embellished, and their historical as well as physical stature often stretched to great lengths. In real life Wyatt Earp was a tough businessman, less concerned about law and order than a fast financial killing. He reorganized the Dodge City red-light district and charged for protection.

Bat Masterson's only resemblance to the TV character was his cane. Rather than being the dapper gentleman hero as portrayed, he created his own myth as a reporter for *The New York Telegraph*. And Wild Bill Hickok was anything but the clean-shaven, clean-thinking, clean fighter shown in Guy Madison's escapades.

"He was nothing like the original Hickok," confesses Madison. "He was just a guy who could handle his guns, take care of bad situations, and know right from wrong."

Kids didn't tune in for originality or accuracy, however. According to Bill Williams, the actor who portrayed Kit Carson, "They wanted action and that's what they got."

Hollywood created an image of the Western hero that hardly existed and a characterization that most starring actors fought to uphold. "The minute we got out of line we were finished," explains Jock Mahoney. "The proof of the pudding was that those who were not hacking it on the outside were quickly shuffled off and lost in limbo."

When one TV Western hero bet he could outdraw anyone in Hollywood, a TV counterpart upped the ante to $2,500 and demanded live ammunition. The duel, like both actors' shows, was canceled in 1961.

"You couldn't be a successful cowboy star then and not live an exemplary life," says Mahoney. He feels he always tried to live up to his TV role and even told a skeptical Detroit father that he shouldn't worry if his son idolized the Range Rider. "As far as my deportment is concerned," he said, "I think he can follow me and everything will be all right."

Hoppy reportedly changed William Boyd. After riding Topper he stopped drinking except for an occasional glass of champagne to toast his success, and he gave up womanizing to settle down for good. Said *Time*, "as far as the public was concerned, he had virtually assumed a new identity, that of Hopalong Cassidy."

Clayton Moore subscribed to the Lone Ranger's credo even after he cornered his last villain. "I will not let my fans down," he still says. To this day he reports that, like the Lone Ranger, he will never smoke, use profanity, or drink in public. "I think playing the role made me a better person," he adds.

The TV cowboys worked hard to uphold their image. But in order to succeed they needed to be both a fast draw and a fast study. Clayton Moore's best recollection of *The Lone Ranger* is not a shoot-out but the nightly struggle to master lines for the next day. "It was constantly 'study, study, study, study, study.' There were a lot of lines and the main thing was to get the dialogue out."

The pace was fast. In the 1950s, crews worked six-day work weeks and long hours. Teams from low-budget Western movies excelled in television. "All of the knowledge that had been gained in the history of motion pictures was used on our TV shows," says *Fury* star Peter Graves. "We had to make our stories in a hurry for

Mount the rider from column I on the correct horse in column II.

I		**II**	
A	Hopalong Cassidy	**1**	Diablo
B	Dale Evans	**2**	Fury
C	Roy Rogers	**3**	Flicka
D	Gene Autry	**4**	Loco
E	Kit Carson	**5**	Topper
F	Lone Ranger	**6**	Rex
G	Tonto	**7**	Buckskin
H	Joey	**8**	King
I	Cisco Kid	**9**	Trigger
J	Pancho	**10**	Scout
K	Range Rider	**11**	Buttercup
L	Velvet Brown	**12**	Silver
M	Ken McLaughlin	**13**	Champion
N	Sergeant Preston	**14**	Buttermilk
O	Annie Oakley	**15**	Rawhide

answers:

A 5
B 14
C 9
D 13
E 7
F 12
G 10
H 2
I 1
J 4
K 15
L 8
M 3
N 6
O 11

Tris Coffin, one of 26 Men, *Arizona's roving rangers. The prime time series reran on Saturdays throughout the country in the late 1950s.*

Excerpts from the Lone Ranger TV Writer's Guide

- The Lone Ranger believes that our sacred American heritage provides that every individual has the right to worship God as he desires.
- The Lone Ranger never makes love on radio, television, in movies, or in cartoons.
- [He is] a man who can fight great odds, yet takes time to treat a bird with a broken wing.
- The Lone Ranger never smokes, never uses profanity, and never uses intoxicating beverages.
- The Lone Ranger at all times uses precise speech, without slang or dialect. His grammar must be pure. He must make proper uses of "who" and "whom," "shall," and "will," "I" and "me," etc.
- The Lone Ranger never shoots to kill. When he has to use guns, he aims to maim as painlessly as possible.
- The Lone Ranger keeps out of saloons. Scenes of gambling and drinking must be played down. When this cannot be avoided, writers must try to make the saloon a café, and deal with waiters and food instead of bartenders and liquor.

very little money, and we had the people to do it."

"We couldn't waste any time in TV," adds Guy Madison. "We made a half-hour show in two-and-a-half days. That included dialogue, action, and everything. At one point we knocked off seven films in seventeen days.

"We never had any problem on the set," Madison continues, "because we worked too damn hard. I'd lose ten to fifteen pounds every production season wearing the heavy leather pants, jacket, and guns. Sometimes we wouldn't get a chance to sit down. We were so busy that in the entire time we were in production I think I saw only three or four episodes."

"Time was literally money," explains Roy Rogers's manager, Art Rush. When Rogers picked up the bug, production was halted for two days. A setback like that on *The Roy Rogers Show*, one of TV's more expensive Westerns, could cost the production thousands of dollars, particularly since two scripts were usually shot simultaneously over the course of a sixty-six-hour work week.

When shows and staffs outnumbered existing facilities, new Western towns were built. Gene Autry constructed a studio on Sunset Boulevard, opposite Hollywood High School, to house his own show and his other Flying A Productions—*The Range Rider, Buffalo Bill, Jr., The Adventures of Champion,* and *Annie Oakley.* Warner Brothers built six acres of newer old towns on its Burbank lot in 1954 and suburban ranches—including Corriganville, Iverson's, and Columbia—operated at peak efficiency.

The Western gold of the 1840s was nothing compared to what television was mining in the 1950s. For example, thirty-nine episodes of *Steve Donovan, Western Marshal* were filmed by Jack Chertok in 1951, John Lupton and Michael Ansara mended the differences between the white man and the Indians as Tom Jeffords and Cochise on *Broken Arrow* (1956), and John Bromfield played *The Sheriff of Cochise,* the same year.

The Adventures of Jim Bowie cut into the schedule in 1956, *Pony Express* was delivered four seasons later. Meanwhile, viewers could travel west on *Wagon Train* and *Union Pacific.*

According to TV, the West was won with the help of John Payne's *Restless Gun,* Lash LaRue's whip, and Chuck Connors's rifle.

There were twentieth-century Westerns, such as *The Roy Rogers Show* and *Tales of the Texas Rangers,* in which horses and cars shared the road, and *Sky King,* in which the aviator swung a plane through the treacherous mountains, locating desperadoes from 12,000 feet.

In 1958 there were more than forty Westerns on the networks and in syndication.[1] The sets were brimming with colorful action, and the cowboys were earning healthy overtime checks.

Today, the Western streets are barren, the buildings have been baked by the sun to a pale gray and brown, and many of the actors are out of work.

"Hollywood just stopped making the rah-rah, shoot-'em-up, good-guys-wear-white-bad-guys-wear-black Westerns," explains Dick Jones, star of *Buffalo Bill, Jr.* "There were a whole bunch

On the set of When the West Was Fun: A Western Reunion—*Clayton Moore and Chuck Connors.*

1. Reycar TV Productions of San Antonio, Texas, even proposed a Western series acted entirely by children aged three to thirteen. *Texas Little Buckaroos,* patterned after Hal Roach's Our Gang twelve- to twenty-minute films, was intended as a takeoff of the existing Westerns, with all the visual and verbal clichés intact.

of psychological Westerns like *Gunsmoke* and *Maverick*, and people forgot about our Saturday morning shows."

"Everything goes in cycles," says Jock Mahoney. "In the old days, before the advent of TV, they made Westerns. When TV came around they continued because they sold. TV's bread and butter was the good cowboy shows. But I, too, have a feeling Westerns are coming back. They'll have to be more mature and more realistic, but I think we'll see them again."

"Youngsters need heroes today," states Clayton Moore. "Sports figures are not enough. The kind of contact and identification people got from *The Lone Ranger* is missing. I'm for any show that fights for what is right and good. But unfortunately, we don't have very many and we need them badly."

"All kids have now on Saturday morning are cartoons," adds Mahoney. "But they don't offer anything for kids to relate to. You can't relate to a cartoon—not in my book."

"Westerns will come back," Moore says resolutely. "They'll find their way back. You can't kill American heritage."

William Boyd knew more about corralling TV ratings than roping an angry steer. The man who played Hopalong Cassidy never branded a cow and never fixed a fence, yet the silver-haired Boyd successfully headed the first stampede of Westerns to television.

In 1948, Boyd released his old films to television, and a year later, under the auspices of William Boyd Productions, filmed new Hoppy stanzas with Edgar Buchanan as his sidekick. With TV sales in every market and merchandising tie-ins visible in every toy store display,

Remembering the TV Western Reunion

by Jim Thompson

Brad Marks, a California TV-producer, assembled most of film and television's best-remembered cowboy stars for a top-rated June 1979 network retrospective called *When the West Was Fun: A Western Reunion.* He shares his recollections on working with his childhood heroes:

The era of the Westerns provided a time of great fantasy. I was just lucky and old enough to watch a lot of Western movies, listen to the shows on the radio, then see the programs play out on television.

The Western form on TV was initially a very basic copy of the "B"-Western movie. It slowly went through an evolution where it expanded and improved. The first change occurred as TV went from showing old Hoppy movies to producing entirely fresh episodes for the new medium. Westerns grew along with TV.

In 1977, I was thinking about those days in one of my quiet idea times behind closed doors in my office. I put my thoughts down about the early years of television and the Western's impact on the media. Soon, I came up with a show outline for a cowboy reunion. Basically, I wanted to capture a piece of the past and put it into the present—if only for a moment.

I sent the proposal to the McCann Erickson advertising agency. They, in turn, showed it to Buick, and that was the beginning of the project. It took two years before the show aired, but that's the nature of our business.

When we finally got into the studio, it was a warm and wonderful experience. I especially loved the show opening because we were making a dream come true as the group pretty much reappeared as we had known them. They all paraded into the saloon: The Lone Ranger, Bart Maverick, the Rifleman, the Virginian, Buffalo Bill, Jr., the Lawman, and dozens of their colleagues. They were all there thanks to great help from Jock Mahoney.

The only frustrating thing about the production was the amount of material we had to cut. We just couldn't include all the things I wanted because we only had an hour's airtime from the network.

Probably the most touching moment of the production was when Glenn Ford, our host, told me the boys wanted to dedicate the show to John Wayne, who was then in the hospital. Of course, I agreed, and he simply said on the air, "This one's for you, Duke."

We taped until 3:30 in the morning and I've never seen a bunch of guys who were so willing and interested in helping.

Nobody smashed an image I had of them. And it was incredible seeing the human side of tough Western stars like Neville Brand, Slim Pickens, Bill Williams, and many others. Apparently everyone else working on the show felt the same way. A stagehand, for instance, said he'd been working in television for twenty-seven years and he'd never witnessed such excitement or had such a thrill as

William Boyd, a movie hero and a TV merchandising phenomenon. His Hopalong Cassidy movies appeared in 1948, and his television-produced show premiered a year later.

just being there with the cowboy characters.

Doug McClure felt something else. He said that it was "strange, spooky, and eerie" to be back with the old gang. He said it was like going back in time.

And I can't tell you how many of the other guys came up to me when we finally finished taping to say, "This is history, Brad. This will never happen again. This get-together is it."

Obviously our business sees many cycles. Westerns have come and gone, but I think they'll slowly come back. They're starting to sneak in already.

After When the West Was Fun: A Western Reunion, *I realized that one day I'd really love to do a Western myself and maybe even create a brand-new form for today's marketplace. It wouldn't be too difficult either, considering how much talent I saw around here. But most of all, whether I do it, or someone else does, it would be wonderful to have these fellas back at work.*

Boyd demonstrated that he might not have the quickest draw in Hollywood, but he certainly had the Midas touch.

William Boyd had not always had such fortune. The Ohio-born laborer's son went West in 1915 in search of romance, fame, and fun. He won and lost each of the spoils many times. Boyd had five marriages, went from a $30-a-week job with producer Cecil B. De Mille to $100,000 a year roles in such films as *The Volga Boatman*, *Two Arabian Knights*, and *Dress Parade*. His expenses and life-style exceeded his income. A Beverly Hills mansion, a Malibu beach house, a ranch in the coastal hills, the Internal Revenue Service, and his social life taxed him heavily.

But it was a case of mistaken identity, not his extravagances, that brought him down. In 1931 another actor named William Boyd was arrested by police during a noisy party and thrown in jail for having illegal gambling equipment and whiskey. When newspapers incorrectly ran the story with a picture of the Hoppy-to-be, RKO was said to have torn up his $3,000-a-week contract and told him to take a walk.

It took four years before Boyd secured another steady job. Harry Sherman, a proven "B" Western producer, signed the struggling actor for fifty-four Hopalong Cassidy pictures. The films had little in common with author Clarence Mulford's original pulp-paper stories about a ragged, whiskery, tobacco-chewing, limping cowboy. Boyd played a soft-spoken sagebrush sage who never kissed a girl and tried to apprehend villains instead of exterminate them. As for the disappearance of the limp, he told Hoppy fans that the wounded leg had healed.

In 1943, Sherman stopped filming, but Boyd continued on his own, making twelve other Hoppy movies. Four years later, Boyd was out of work again at age fifty-two because "no one in Hollywood thought of me as anything but Hopalong Cassidy." He converted his last $300,000 in assets to cash, bought the rights to his Westerns, and released them to television. Hoppy made a killing (see Chapter II, "Tested Patterns").

In 1948, when no more than one American in ten had seen television on the 325,000 TV sets in use, Hoppy syndicated his films. Within two years the actor was a bona fide national hero. Hopalong Cassidy was President Harry Truman's guest of honor for the 1950 "I Am an American Day." The same year an estimated 350,000 people circled twenty-five Manhattan blocks to see him. He drew the largest circus attendance ever at the Chicago stadium, headlined the Macy's Thanksgiving Day Parade, and greeted 85,000 people who rushed through a Brooklyn department store in four hours for a momentary glimpse of Hopalong Cassidy.

"Look at the way those crowds act," Boyd told a reporter for *Time*. "They all want to touch Hoppy. The women want to kiss him and the men want to hug him. They hold up their babies to him . . . their own flesh and blood. What do those babies know of Hoppy? Nothing . . . but the men and women want to see those kids. Crowds never pull at Hoppy or try to tear his clothes. If they start pushing, I just say, 'Now kids . . . be good kids.' I call them all kids—grownups and all—and they settle down."

"People are astonished at the percentage of my fans who are adults," he continued. "They're not new fans, they're merely my young fans of 15 years ago grown up a little bit."

Hoppy's fans were devoted, but they were not blind. His stories were simple yarns that were losing meaning in a more complicated age. By the mid-1950s, the thin plots wore through, and even years before his 1972 death the black-suited Cassidy would be passed in popularity by a man dressed in white.

Shortly after *The Lone Ranger* premiered on ABC-TV, September 15, 1949, *The New York Times* called it "just another Western, and not a notably good one at that." Critic Jack Gould couldn't have been more wrong in his October 22 assessment, for although the masked hero hid his face from the public, the show has been visible for thirty years.

Filming for the television version began June 21, 1949, a full sixteen years after the mysterious Lone Ranger first appeared on radio. The character was the creation of George W. Trendle, a prosperous Detroit businessman, who outlined in staff memos that he "intended to give the youngsters a great deal of action and excitement without arousing unwholesome desires and instincts." His figure, he said, would "teach patriotism, tolerance, fairness, and a sympathetic understanding of fellow men and their rights and privileges." Trendle added that he also "wanted a good, clean show to keep the Parent-Teacher Association off our neck."

On the plains, the Lone Ranger was unbeatable. In production meetings, he was securely under Trendle's thumb.

According to those who worked with Trendle, the creator kept tight reins on both Silver and the masked man. Said one friend, "The Lone Ranger doesn't cough or make a move without Trendle putting it in the script or okaying it."

Trendle had owned a chain of movie theaters in the 1920s, but he sold his interests and parlayed his money into Detroit radio station WXYZ. Since investment capital and broadcasting revenue were in short supply in the Depression, he decided to drop the radio outlet's network affiliation and build his own competitive programming. Believing that youngsters were more susceptible to advertising than their parents, he geared his ideas to children. His leading character was a synthesis of Robin Hood and Zorro.

The figure was given a complete history. Listeners were told he was the one Texas Ranger to survive an ambush staged by the murderous Butch Cavendish gang. As fortune would have it, the dying law man, John Reid, was discovered by an Indian brave, and in time, nursed back to health.

To avenge the deaths of his fellow lawmen and continue to battle against crime, Reid changed his name, donned a black face-mask, and roamed the West with his trusted friend, Tonto.

Through the 1930s, the war years, and much of the Cold War period, children tuned to the broadcasts of the Detroit station, carried over as many as 224 nationwide outlets. Three nights each week they spoke in unison with announcer Fred Foy:

With his faithful Indian companion Tonto, the daring and resourceful Masked Rider of the Plains led the fight for law and order in the early western United States. Nowhere in the pages of history can one find a greater champion of justice. Return with us now to those thrilling days of yesteryear. From out of the past come the thundering hoofbeats of the great horse Silver. The Lone Ranger rides again!

Beneath the narration and playing throughout the show were strains of Rossini's *William Tell Overture*, a composition that derived new meaning after *The Lone Ranger* premiered.[2]

In 1938 and 1939 Republic Pictures produced two contrived movie-serial adaptations of *The Lone Ranger*. The stories ignored the popular mythology and angered Trendle. However, the broadcaster had no legal recourse. He had foolishly assigned film rights to the studio without stipulating that the movie plots had to remain as faithful to the hero as Tonto.

The Lone Ranger (1938) dealt with five "men of mystery," anyone of which could be the actual ranger. After fifteen weeks of guessing, only one masked man remained alive—Allen King (Lee Powell).

In *The Lone Ranger Rides Again*, Gill Andrews (Robert Livingston) became the hero. Only under dire circumstances would he wear the mask, and then it was simply a black handkerchief. Chief Thunder-Cloud played Tonto in both productions.

The only saving grace of the serials was the sound track, according to David Rothel, author of *Who Was That Masked Man?* (A. S. Barnes, 1976). The score, composed by Alberto Colombo, was eventually incorporated in the radio and television series.

General Mills sponsored *The Lone Ranger* on radio. The cereal company similarly underwrote the video series. Production costs averaged $12,500 for each of the first fifty-two episodes.

The series filmed at locations in Utah and in California at Corriganville, Iverson's Ranch, Big Bear, and Sonora. *The Lone Ranger* pitched camp at the Hal Roach Studios, and later General Services Studios.

The first programs recounted the hero's background from Texas Ranger to Lone Ranger. The initial two installments contained what *Variety* called "dyed-in-the-wool" cliff-hanger endings and what *New York Times* critic Jack Gould considered manipulative. He accused ABC, General Mills, and Trendle of keeping children "emotionally hopped up" and trying to "capitalize on the normal anxiety and sensitiveness of young-

2. With the success of the ranger, Trendle introduced The Green Hornet. The character was a contemporary crime fighter named Britt Reid, who by day published *The Daily Sentinel* and at night made news fighting villains with his karate-swinging Japanese valet, Kato. Reid, according to Trendle's grand design, was the great-grandnephew of John Reid, the Lone Ranger. After Pearl Harbor, December 7, 1941, Kato became a Filipino.

sters" by presenting unresolved, continuing stories.

"Use of the old cliff-hanging technique should be abandoned promptly. . . . Everyone concerned with the TV version of *The Lone Ranger* should stop and think what they are doing," he wrote.

They had been. The idea had never been to broadcast the series as a serial. Only the introductory episodes were presented in chapters. To reassure the critic, however, ABC officials advised Gould on October 4, 1949, that the program would no longer end on a note of suspense.

Within a year the Thursday night, 7:30 P.M. show was in the top ten and a money-maker. Trendle received a percentage of each broadcast's profits, a figure inflated later when the show aired twice per week.

Jack Chertok, producer of the films *The Omaha Trail, Northern Pursuit, The Conspirator,* and *The Corn is Green*, headed the TV series. His TV director was George B. Seitz, Jr., son of the famed director of many Andy Hardy features and dozens of other silent and sound features.

In 1940 the elder Seitz directed the Western film *Kit Carson*, which featured twenty-six-year-old Clayton Moore in a small role. Moore was to work with Seitz's son when he was signed to star in *The Lone Ranger*.

Casting the TV show was entirely up to George W. Trendle. Brace Beemer, radio's ranger, reportedly wanted the part. His deep voice would have been a thrill to hear from behind the mask, but his stocky build prevented him from competing with the front runners. When word spread that Beemer would not appear in the TV series, Clayton Moore's agent forwarded a few of his client's Westerns to Chertok and Trendle, hoping that Moore's work and his voice would be a powerful calling card.

The casting office saw the films and sent for Moore. Jay Silverheels, a full-blooded Mohawk by birth, became Tonto.[3]

3. Silverheels was born in Ontario at Canada's Six Nations Indian Reservation. He became an accomplished lacrosse player in the 1930s and was encouraged by actor Joe E. Brown to consider a movie career. In 1938 he came to the United States and mixed the punches between Golden Gloves boxing and motion pictures. He qualified as a runner-up in the sport and a leading contender in his profession. His first film was *Captain From Castile* (1947). He later appeared in *Key Largo* (1948), *Yellow Sky* (1949), and *The Cowboy and the Indians* (1949). Concurrent with *The Lone Ranger* were roles in *Broken Arrow* (1950), *Red Mountain* (1952), *Saskatchewan* (1954), and *Walk the Proud Land* (1956). He had cameo appearances in a number of TV commercials with Moore. Silverheels died March 5, 1980.

Moore, a World War II Air Force veteran, started flying when he was eight. The early flights were as an acrobat, not a pilot, however. By the time he reached his early twenties, he had hit great heights with two circuses and the World's Fair. Moore claims he appeared in the youngest aerial act at the time, the first flying troupe to work on the high bars without a net, and the first to work over water. For a few years he stayed put on the ground, taking jobs as a model. In the spring of 1938 he made the decision to leave New York, where he was then working, and go to Hollywood and strike gold. There were the inevitable long periods of struggling as a stunt man and an extra before he would even find Silver. "I dug ditches, mixed cement, and poured foundations," he remembers. "Anything to keep me eating."

Gradually his luck changed and Moore became the last "King of the Serials," starring in *Perils of Nyoka* (1942), *Jesse James Rides Again* (1947), *The Adventures of Frank and Jesse James* (1948), *G-Men Never Forget* (1948), and *Ghost of Zorro* (1949).

Like most actors who turned to television when movie production slowed in the late 1940s, he received only a guaranteed weekly salary.

Moore couldn't afford to live a lavish Hollywood life on his income. His salary was quoted as less than $500 per show, roughly $25,000, discounting public appearance fees. After production ended in 1950, Moore reportedly threatened to quit unless he received a substantial raise. Trendle balked at his demands and hired John Hart to replace him, believing the audience would not realize a switch had been made under the mask.

Oddly, audiences quickly noticed this new actor was not their first Lone Ranger, but they hardly recognized Clayton Moore in what he did appear in: *Radar Men from the Moon* (1952), *Son of Geronimo* (1952), *Jungle Drums of Africa* (1953), *Gunfighters of the Northwest* (1954), and *Buffalo Bill in Tomahawk Territory* (1952). Moore was, without a doubt, better known as the Lone Ranger. His rich, deep voice was powerful, even mesmerizing.

Hart never looked more than adequate in the same garb. The star of Columbia's *Jack Armstrong* serial in 1947 did not have the endurance for *The Lone Ranger*. He appeared in only twenty-six episodes.

In 1954, Chertok auditioned actors again for the role. George Trendle visited California to pass judgment on the finalist, but it was wisely decided to sign Clayton Moore again.

After August 3, 1954, *The Lone Ranger* rode for a new boss. For $3 million, Trendle sold complete rights to the character, commercial tie-ins, radio scripts and shows, and TV episodes to oil man–industrialist Jack Wrather. Industry observers called it the biggest TV deal since NBC acquired an ownership stake in *Hopalong Cassidy*.

In 1956, Wrather Corporation filmed thirty-nine new installments in color. Wrather told the press that the show, costing approximately $25,000 per episode, would employ three "distinguished" novelists to assist the screenwriters "retain *The Lone Ranger* precepts and teachings." The owner was concerned, however, that his children's show hero might not stand up to the adult Western characters coming along. Consequently, there was talk of redesigning the Ranger to appeal to older viewers. General Mills's advertising agency, Dancer Fitzgerald Sample, approved the plan, stating "adults eat cereal too."

Trendle, not associated with the show after the multimillion-dollar transaction, retained at least a verbal interest in the production. He argued that the Lone Ranger should not change his posture.

"For years our rating indicated that half our listeners and viewers were adults and this, without blood and thunder of the 'adult westerns,' " he said. "The fights in today's shows seem more gruesome. If your scripts are good, you can have a hero who doesn't go around spitting tobacco juice. Nowadays, they don't glorify the leads—they're not enough inspiration for children. You don't need a lot of bloodshed to get fans—children or adults."

After consideration, the Lone Ranger stayed on his beaten TV path. His only detours from the familiar were two color motion pictures: *The Lone Ranger* (1956), starring Moore, Silverheels, and actress Bonita Granville (Jack Wrather's wife) and *The Lone Ranger and the Lost City of Gold* (1958).

Production for thirty-nine more color TV episodes were planned for 1959, but the cameras would not roll. Wrather stood with the 221 programs already in the can.

General Mills remained holstered to the show through its first full run. In 1958, it relinquished a portion of its commercial time, to alternate week-to-week with Cracker Jacks and Popsicle.

Through much of the 1950s, the series aired on both ABC and CBS. ABC carried the prime time broadcasts, CBS owned Saturday afternoon repeat rights. In 1960, NBC telecast *The Lone Ranger* on Saturday morning. The network telecasts ended September 23, 1961, and thereafter episodes have been syndicated to stations.

CBS presented a Saturday morning cartoon version of *The Lone Ranger* from 1966 to 1969, which troubled Trendle. David Rothel quoted him in *Who Was That Masked Man?* as having said that the cartoons were "downright ridiculous" (see Chapter XVI, "Insurance Policies: Cartoon Payoffs"). Actor Michael Rye dubbed the Lone Ranger's voice in the Filmation production.

George Washington Trendle died May 10, 1972, of a heart attack at the age of eighty-seven. Brace Bell Beemer, the last of radio's Lone Rangers, died March 1, 1965, at sixty-two.[4]

Even after Clayton Moore stopped his horseplay in front of the movie cameras, he continued to ride to personal appearances as the Lone Ranger. With syndication sales in nearly every market, he was a renewable attraction who never seemed to age behind the mask.

"I just never wanted to do anything else after I started *The Lone Ranger,*" he said after a 1977 Decatur, Georgia, appearance. "I fell in love with the character." Moore hasn't appeared as another character since *The Lone Ranger* ended production. He has, however, performed as the Lone Ranger in a Gino's pizza commercial and guest-starred on ABC's *Silver Anniversary Celebration* (1978) and in producer Brad Marks's prime time special *When the West Was Fun: A Western Reunion* (1979).

When Jack Wrather announced his intention in 1978 to produce a new Lone Ranger motion picture, Moore's name was not mentioned in the release. In fact, hearing the news, Moore said, with resignation cracking his firm voice, "They're going to do another without Silverheels or myself.

4. The first man to play the ranger on radio was George Seaton. Seaton left Detroit in 1939 after appearing as the masked man for about six months. He has remained active in Hollywood as a writer, producer, and director. Seaton co-authored the Marx Brothers' *A Day at the Races* and wrote and directed *Miracle on 34th Street*, and *Airport*.

Clayton Moore behind the Lone Ranger's mask in the 1950s and pictured in 1979, stripped of his disguise per court order.

Thank You, Masked Man

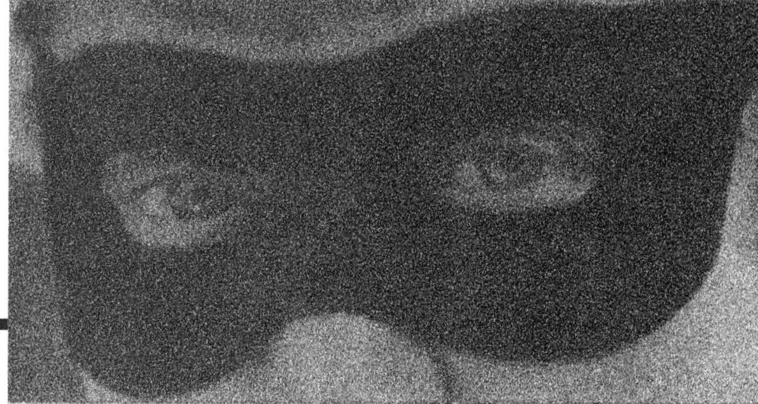

By Sam Donato

In 1955 five cents would buy a black paper mask at the corner store. To some the mask might symbolize a game of cops and robbers, but to me it was a chance to portray my hero: the daring and resourceful masked rider of the plains—the Lone Ranger! I could have pretended I was Roy Rogers or Gene Autry without having to spend five cents, but there was something about *HIM;* something mysterious, something noble. He never killed anyone and never waited to be thanked for whatever job he had done to make the West a safer place to live.

As the cynical years of adulthood snuck up on me, I slowly realized that the Man was just another actor and he probably took his money and went home. I soon learned differently.

In 1967 I began working as an actor at Pleasure Island Amusement Park in Wakefield, Massachusetts. It was a great job for the young at heart, because our duties required us to emcee stage shows and play Cowboys and Indians for the benefit of the people who came to the park. We also had to assist the many celebrities who came to make personal appearances.

One day the park announcer and I were called into the office of the general manager to be briefed on the requirements of our next celebrity—Clayton Moore.

Clayton Moore! The Lone Ranger!

We were then told that he would be arriving in two days and preparations had to be made. We went to work to make his stay as pleasant as possible.

The park announcer at that time was a good friend of mine, an Emerson College buddy, Dave Campanella. As we emerged from the manager's office he turned to me and said, "Where can we get a copy of the *William Tell Overture?*" That's where it started. Dave and I went to his office and wrote out the entire opening narration to the *Lone Ranger* television show. We located the music, planned the format for the outdoor show. Finally the day came for Mr. Moore's arrival.

"Hello, gentlemen, my name is Clayton Moore," he said upon our first meeting.

His voice may as well have been a thunderclap for the way it struck me. That was the Voice, the voice of the Lone Ranger.

He then gave us a rough format of what he was to do for the show. He would ride into the show bowl from the top of the hill on a large white horse. (Not the original Silver.) He would then do some tricks, dismount, and come up on to the stage to talk to the crowd. After his mini-lecture on the legend of the Lone Ranger, some backstage stories on the production of the television show and some gun- and rope-spinning tricks, he would then take questions from the audience, say his good-byes, and mount up and ride off into the sunset. As he described his format we could tell he'd done this many times before, but we could detect no sign of boredom in his words.

The next day the first show was scheduled at 2:00 P.M. It was Standing Room Only as parents and kids crowded into the bowl not quite sure what they were going to see. The intro music began with a kind of festive circus sound as Dave's voice rang out, "Ladies and Gentlemen, boys and girls, welcome to Pleasure Island's outdoor show bowl . . ." As the general introduction continued I scanned the hill waiting for the cue; then I heard it. The *William Tell Overture.*

In his best Fred Foy imitation, Dave started the introduction. I was enthralled. Then just as Dave got to the words, "Return with us now to those thrilling days of yesteryear—the Lone Ranger rides again," I looked to the hill again and there he was!

The crowd gasped! They had good reason to. There on the hill astride a snow-white horse was a man who looked ten feet tall. He reared the horse up, and his front hoofs pawed the air. The exhilaration charged the crowd.

From that point on, the show went just as he had planned it. He spoke of the high ideals the Ranger stood for and how in all the films, the Ranger never killed anyone. The audience listened and believed. They really believed he was the Lone Ranger. And I believed. I believed that this man took his responsibility to his young fans seriously. His smile, his warmth, and his voice couldn't be a put-on.

At the end of the show I approached a little girl with a microphone so that everyone in the audience could hear her ask the Lone Ranger her single question. "Are you married?" she asked.

The audience laughed. The Ranger paused and summed it up with a statement of more than one meaning.

"Honey, I'm the Lone Ranger."

Sam Donato is a musician and TV performer. He lives in Boston.

I suppose that's the way the old cookie crumbles."

But there was fight in Moore when he learned soon thereafter that Wrather sought to prevent him from making personal appearances as the character he had played for so many years. Wrather argued that Moore, in his mid-sixties, could no longer personify the youthful hero. Furthermore, the corporation insisted that Moore would confuse the public if dressed as the Lone Ranger when another actor would actually portray the figure in the motion picture. Moore went to court charging, in a $30 million suit, that Wrather had exploited him and "wrongfully deprived" him of his earnings for the use of his "likeness, voice and actual photographs and movie clips."

Wrather also asked for a restraining order against Moore.

In August 1979, Los Angeles Superior Court Judge Vernon Foster issued an injunction forbidding Moore from wearing "The Lone Ranger mask or any mask substantially similar in appearance."

The judge acted on behalf of a suit filed by Lone Ranger Television Inc., a Wrather Corporation subsidiary, which insisted that Moore is "no longer an appropriate physical representative of the trim, nineteenth century Western hero in his mid-30's that the Lone Ranger character represents."

"They say I'm too old and out of condition to be the Lone Ranger," Moore offered in a precourt interview. "However, my waist is thirty-four and I'm ten pounds lighter than I was when I played the Lone Ranger."

Nonetheless, a Wrather attorney told the judge, "If Mr. Moore wants to go out and earn a living as someone who portrayed the Lone Ranger, we have no objection, but when he puts on the mask, he becomes the Lone Ranger."

The decision followed a temporary restraining order issued by Superior Court Judge Jerry Pacht, banning Moore from billing himself as the Lone Ranger.

Moore is appealing the ruling. Should his case be heard by a jury, it might resemble the climax of *The Miracle of 34th Street.* Instead of the bearded Kris Kringle arguing that he is indeed Santa Claus, the masked Moore would steadfastly maintain that he is the Lone Ranger. Put any TV-wise youngster on the stand and ask him to point to the Lone Ranger, he would undoubtedly identify Clayton Moore.

Even without the mask, Moore's voice clearly gives him away today. Other actors may play the role in the movie, but as Trendle found out when John Hart donned the mask, no one can replace Clayton Moore.

"They can't take that away from him," says Moore's personal manager and advisor, Arthur Dorn. "To most people, George Reeves was Superman even after the new movie came out. Clayton will always be the Lone Ranger."

Since Moore has ceaselessly stood for the law, he obeys it. The actor does not wear a mask, but large sunglasses still shield his eyes. The cover-up may not make criminals fret, but it must concern the Wrather Corporation, for Clayton Moore is more active now than in years on the public appearance trail.

"The reaction in favor of Clayton has been tremendous," adds Dorn. "People can't understand why Clayton shouldn't be allowed to make personal appearances as the man he played."

It is a complete reversal from the early days when Moore's contract stipulated that he could not make a tour without the full regalia and mask.

The irony perplexes Moore, who today says he's simply trying to earn an honest living. "We were the very first Western TV show back in 1949," he adds. "The only other thing around were Hopalong Cassidy's shows, and at first they were movies cut down for television. We pioneered it, and I honestly think I have more coming."

The Singing Cowboy, Gene Autry.

Right behind *The Lone Ranger* was the singing cowboy Gene Autry. His half-hour TV series premiered July 23, 1950, and remained on CBS until August 7, 1956. *The Gene Autry Show* boiled down the elements of his full-length features into a thirty-minute program. Each week he would ride into town, assist a rancher, right a wrong, or expose a corrupt sheriff, then strum a few bars before jumping back in the saddle again.

Pat Buttram provided comic relief in most of the ninety-one episodes. Thirteen were filmed in color.

The program initially ran uninterrupted by commercials. Autry appeared preceding and following the story with on-camera appeals for Wrigley gum. Chewing up the rest of the time were stories that made critics into fans. *Billboard* called *The Gene Autry Show* "Slick and competent" and said the hero "should make Autry one of TV's big guns." *Variety* concurred, saying the dusty cowboy had "sterling qualities." The trade publication believed the show would help sell Wrigley to kids and outdoor film programs to the networks. They noted that the "good guys on the right side of the law are of the gum-chewing variety."

In his autobiography, *Back in the Saddle Again* (co-authored by Micky Herskowitz; Doubleday, 1978), Autry quotes Pat Buttram as saying, "Autry used to ride off into the sunset; now he owns it."

Autry argues that his former saddle pal exaggerates. Buttram, however, was not far from the truth. The star built an empire bigger than the Ponderosa. In 1950, Autry shot the series at Pioneer Town near Palm Springs, California. By 1951 he could afford his own Hollywood studio facilities. Autry eventually turned his winnings into investments and gave up six-gun duels for boardroom fights with executives of his TV and radio enterprises and his California Angels baseball team.

Roy Rogers sang "Happy Trails," but for a time the top Western star found life less than rewarding. In a matter of a few years Rogers lost his first wife in childbirth, a child to illness, and his livelihood in a prolonged lawsuit with Republic Pictures (see Chapter II, "Tested Patterns"). The studios considered him an untouchable, while fans still clamored for him. The obvious path back to stardom was television.

On Sunday night, December 30, 1951, NBC premiered *The Roy Rogers Show* and a half-hour variety program that also starred the famed film star. Monday morning he was the talk of the town. Tuesday, favorable ratings were reported, and Wednesday, *The New York Times* critic Jack Gould took a potshot at the cowboy. "Mr. Rogers is billed as 'the king of the cowboys'—but on the basis of the first film, he's got a piece to travel before catching up with his rivals—Bill Boyd and Gene Autry.

"Rogers," wrote Gould, "could easily carry greater forcefulness if he spoke his lines with greater enthusiasm and a more genuine sense of participation. As it is, his heroism leans to detached efficiency, which suggests that he is walking through rather than living his part."

Those were fighting words, and over two decades the king would prove he had the power to command audiences', if not critics', attention.

Rogers, born Leonard Slye in Cincinnati, Ohio, had initially risen to popularity as Republic's wartime replacement for Gene Autry. Once he was inside the low-budget studio, stardom came quickly. The journey there had taken years, however.

He arrived in California in 1931 at age nineteen and performed factory, farm, road construction, and truck-driving duties, not acting roles. His first show business job was singing in a Los Angeles theater for $1 a performance. Next came assorted radio spots and more days of manual labor.

Rogers got his break by literally sticking his foot in Republic's door after hearing that studio boss Herbert Yates was in the market for a new singing cowboy. Not having a studio pass, he argued with a guard to gain entrance. Republic executive Sol Siegel overheard the commotion, took one look at Roy, and gave him an audition.

By 1943, Rogers was the leading Western box office attraction. Some people say he couldn't have gotten there without Trigger. Rogers had paid $2,500 for the palomino in 1938. Doubtless mid-1940s insurance policies for his horse were costing many times more than the purchase price.

In 1947, he rode off with his leading lady,

Roy Rogers, King of the Cowboys, during a 1970s interview.

© photo courtesy *Boston Herald American*

Dale Evans, Queen of the Sagebrush, and her horse, Buttermilk, take a refreshing production break.

Dale Evans, and married her. Together, they made movies and millions. Within a few years of the TV premiere, merchandise bearing the Rogerses name reportedly earned manufacturers $33 million. A healthy portion went to the couple. Their bank account was fattened by rodeo receipts, television royalties, and personal appearances.

In the late 1950s, Rogers bought out the NBC-TV interest in his series and, with 100 percent ownership, turned his 104 episodes into a personal bonanza. He resold the show to CBS and later repackaged it again for syndication.

The Roy Rogers Show was set in twentieth-century Mineral City where telephones replaced the nineteenth-century telegraph and Pat Brady's temperamental horseless carriage, Nellybelle, could have, but never did outrace Trigger. The Sons of the Pioneers, Rogers's movie singing group, also appeared, and Trigger shared the animal crackers with Roy's German shepherd, Bullet.

The episodes were noted for heavy-duty fights, bloody noses, haggard looks, and not a sequin out of place on Roy's $250 shirts.[5] Both Roy and Dale generally chose to perform their own stunts.

5. "It's frightening to see five- and six-year-old tots sitting spellbound before TV sets soaking up this sadism," complained Chicago *Daily News* critic Jack Mabley, after seeing an episode of *The Roy Rogers Show.* The reporter noted that in a single episode, "two men beat an old man . . . the old man is permanently blinded by the attack. Two men beat a dog [Bullet] about the head with a pistol. . . . The men again attack the dog as he is leading the old man on a mountain trail. The old man cries for help, plunges over a cliff to his death. . . . A veterinarian who is a thief kills an injured companion with an injection of poison. . . . The dog is doped but attacks a man. Two men kidnap a girl, then beat her."

Less rigorous and less popular was *The Roy Rogers and Dale Evans Show,* a variety-musical program telecast for three months on ABC in 1962. In years since their last series the king and queen have graced other shows as guests and discarded TV violence for prayer. After repeated personal tragedy to family members, their joint careers have taken a sincere evangelical turn.

In 1976, Rogers made his first motion picture in three decades. Unfortunately, *Mackintosh and T. J.* failed to elevate Rogers to the box office prominence he had once known.

If the Lone Ranger and Tonto were television's most revered pair of lawmen, then Wild Bill Hickok and his sidekick, Jingles, must have been the TV Westerns' most unusual duo. The lean Guy Madison, who spoke in a quiet tenor voice, was teamed with the overweight, ever-giggling, raspy-sounding Andy Devine. Madison pulled his own weight on the show, and Devine's extra-stocky horse carried his partner.

The syndicated *Wild Bill Hickok* premiered in 1952. Children saw it as an enjoyable Western. Its creators saw the show as a valuable merchandising tool.

"The idea," says Madison, "was formed by people from a few department stores who said, 'Look at what Hopalong Cassidy is doing with his old pictures . . . he's showing them everywhere on television and he's merchandising the hell out of it. Why don't we do a TV show? We know how to merchandise and we'll make a mint.'

"Well, they knew selling," Madison continues, "but they didn't know the motion picture business. So when it came time for *Wild Bill Hickok* to happen, they couldn't find a producer who could do the show for $12,000 an episode.[6] That's when the package came through my agent's office."

Madison explains that his agent found a producer, William F. Broidy. "Naturally, since he was producing he wanted to own the show. And by the time he got all finished, Andy and I were under contract to Broidy. We each had

Sugar Pops' best salesmen: Wild Bill Hickok (Guy Madison) and Jingles (Andy Devine).

6. Eventually the production costs increased to $16,000 a show. When Screen Gems bought *Wild Bill Hickok,* the budget escalated to $25,000 per episode.

a percentage of the profit and we made pretty good money for the time."

Andy Devine explained the same story in a 1953 interview. "The producer said the money wasn't very good when he asked me to do the part for the *Wild Bill Hickok* pilot film—and it wasn't, only $250 a show. But I said I'd be happy to do it for a little percentage, say 10 percent? They agreed and it worked out fine."

Madison played James Butler (Wild Bill) Hickok, a U.S. marshal who reached for a fast gun, a hard punch, and a straight-line. "It had a very simple format; lots of action and comedy," says Madison. "We wanted to show a little bit of the West and with Andy, add some comedy."

Though the show has not been seen in most markets for years, and Madison has primarily performed in European films for the last two decades, he still wears the Western brand. "Even now adults come up to me and say, 'You know, Guy, you showed me the difference between right and wrong while I was watching.' It amazes the hell out of me, but people remember it as a clean show, and I think it would be excellent for kids today."

Madison believes *Wild Bill Hickok* is still a valuable property, particularly since it was shot in color. But his attempts to rerelease it with new introductions have not paid off. Syndicators and stations are leery of satisfying nostalgic curiosity, since they believe that 1950 Westerns might attract more than young audiences. They fear criticism from parents and special-interest groups and "no sales" from advertisers. The show remains locked in the Columbia vaults.

"When it first aired," Madison states, "it was one of the most popular Westerns on TV. The thing really took off."

Two years after the premiere, *Wild Bill Hickok* was so successful that one New York station was willing to run it a second time each week without charging sponsor Kellogg's for the airtime. WOR-TV officials reasoned that if they could slice out one minute from each episode, then fill the time with a new commercial, they'd still make a profit. The station did the same with the popular *Sky King*.

A year later other stations were reporting great sales and top ratings. It was seen on eighty ABC and independent stations in 1954 and pulling as much as 80 percent of the audience in its time period.

In addition to the 120 TV episodes, between 300 and 400 national radio productions were recorded at Los Angeles station KHJ.

In 1956, Madison made a move to expand the show to sixty minutes to compete with adult Westerns. He urged Kellogg's to invest in his plan, but neither the sponsor nor Screen Gems agreed. By 1959 Westerns were dying, and *Wild Bill Hickok* bit the dust.

"The year we went out, everyone started going for situation comedies," Madison recalls. "Only about one show in twenty continued to make it."

For the duration of the production the chemistry of Madison and Devine greatly contributed to the overall success of the show. They gambled and guffawed their way into situations and always rode off with Jingles tagging behind the marshal yelling, "Hey! Wild Bill, wait for me!"

Actually, Devine was ahead of Madison—years ahead. The actor, known for a gravel voice (owing to a teenage accident when he fell with a stick in his mouth) had been appearing in films before his TV costar was barely old enough to step into a horse's stirrup.

In the silent era, Universal planned to make him a romantic star. The notion was sound until 1927, when *The Jazz Singer* was heard by movie audiences. Devine's career seemed doomed, but a director wisely cast him in a comedy. Thereafter he appeared in hundreds of motion pictures including *We Americans* (1928), *The Spirit of Notre Dame* (1931), *Yellow Jack* (1938), *Stagecoach* (1939), *Torrid Zone* (1940), *Ali Baba and the Forty Thieves* (1944), and *Sudan* (1945). He also appeared as Roy Rogers's sidekick in a succession of mid-1940s Republic Westerns. In 1954, Devine starred as the heir apparent to *Smilin' Ed*, in NBC's *Andy's Gang*. One critic said he was so visible to TV viewers that "only the stations' test patterns are seen more often."

Guy Madison, 168 pounds, almost half Devine's weight, first caught the attention of Hollywood producers when he charmed bobby-soxers with an appearance in *Since You Went Away* (1944). Roles in *Till the End of Time* (1946), *Honeymoon* (1947), and *Massacre River* (1949) followed. During the years when he wore the buckskin suit on TV, Madison also appeared in *The Charge at Feather River*, *The Command*, *The Last Frontier*, and the science fiction drama *On the Threshold of Space*, among others. He was a candidate for the role of Charles Lindbergh in *The Spirit of St. Louis*, but lost to Jimmy Stewart.

While youngsters tracked his TV career, Madison was known by hunters for his bow-and-arrow proficiency. He took careful aim in both career and hobby, succeeding in each. Madison hit the bull's-eye with a six-picture deal with Columbia while he was still in his twenties. "I think I was the youngest actor to have a co-production deal with a major studio," he states.

Doubling for Madison on *Wild Bill Hickok* were some of the best stunt men in film. "I used doubles whenever there was a chance of breaking my leg or hurting myself," Madison volunteers. The top Hollywood stunt man, however, wasn't working on *Wild Bill Hickok*. He had his own show, *Range Rider*.

Clayton Moore describes Jock Mahoney as "fearless." Guy Madison says "He was the best jumper. We called him an antelope." Mahoney's costar on *Range Rider*, Dick Jones, agrees that there's no one better in the business. Even Jock Mahoney himself adds that there was once the saying in Hollywood, "If Jocko walked away from a stunt, no one else wanted a part of it."

Mahoney and Jones performed *all* their own stunt work. "We always had men on the set who got paid for whatever Dick and I did, but we did the transfers from horses to stagecoaches and wagons and all the fights. Everything you saw on *Range Rider* was our work," Mahoney says with pride.

Jock Mahoney started taking chances with his life and limb years before *Range Rider*, a Flying

The tables are turned on the Range Rider (Jock Mahoney) and Dick West (Dick Jones) by gun-toting youngsters from the Nickerson Home of the Massachusetts Society for the Prevention of Cruelty to Children during the pair's 1954 Boston rodeo appearance.

A Production, was filmed by Gene Autry's cameras in 1951. A decade earlier he was regularly doubling for Errol Flynn, Randolph Scott, Sonny Tufts, Willard Parker, Gregory Peck, and many other actors. In fact, during the trickiest fencing scenes in *Adventures of Don Juan*, Mahoney was in for Flynn. The six-foot-four-inch athlete had begun tumbling for fun years earlier. In 1938 he won an athletic scholarship to the University of Iowa, where he established swimming records. After moving to Los Angeles he taught swimming and riding, served as a pilot in World War II, and became a flight instructor. For much of his later aerial work, however, he didn't use an airplane.[7] As a stuntman, Mahoney would take forty-seven-foot dives into six-foot tanks of water, leap over a cattle fence, fall forty feet into a moat, and vault thirty feet from a rooftop into a net. "He'd jump twenty-five feet across buildings," adds Guy Madison. "He'd damn near break the Olympic record just doing that!"

Over the years every one of his ribs have been torn loose or fractured. He's suffered numerous broken noses and split kneecaps. A sword was run through his leg in a filmed duel, and he's been thrown headfirst through a leaded glass window so many times, he's lost count.

"I've always been able to control pain pretty good," he says modestly. "I even set my own broken nose and my left elbow after it broke in a 1954 personal appearance in the Providence, Rhode Island, arena."

A year earlier at a booking at the Boston Garden, he was kicked by his horse in the middle of a stunt. After struggling to get back on, he announced to the crowd of 10,000 that he was not hurt and rode off.

"It took six men to get me back off the horse because I couldn't move forward, backward, or sideways," he remembers. "Every move I made was a killer. After finally dismounting I saw the doctor. He took my shirt off and felt around and said, 'Yup, yup, yup, yup' a lot and told me I popped a bunch of ribs in my chest and ruined some cartilage. He then taped me up, but left an opening down the side to allow me to move. I said, 'Doc, that's all well and good, but I'm going to finish the act so patch me up completely.'

"The doctor did what I asked him to do," Mahoney adds. "I stood up and said, 'Man, that feels great,' and I passed out colder than white water."

The next day Mahoney was back at work.

"Even if I can't ride for a few days," he told a reporter on the scene, "I'll do the narration, making my appearance on foot instead of horseback." But Mahoney was not to be stopped. He performed everything but the leaps and fights—tricks that rodeo stars often told him that at peak health they "wouldn't do for all the tea in China." Still, Mahoney thought for the first time that maybe "It would help if I could do some singing like Autry and Rogers."

"I've never considered myself macho," explains the solid 200-pound actor. "I was born with damn near a perfectly coordinated body. And I've always kept in shape with ballet, gymnastics, fencing, tap dancing, and swimming. High bars and parallel bars were my good buddies in school. All my life I've just done what I wanted to do, and the man upstairs has always been a close friend of mine. I let him know whenever he was goofing, and he's taken care of me. He just gave me one warning. It was a bitch of a warning and I slowed down."

7. One of his children somewhat continued in his aerial tradition. Actress Sally Field took off as TV's *Flying Nun* in 1967.

Jock Mahoney as Range Rider (1951), Yancy Derringer (1958), Tarzan (1960), and on the set of Burt Reynolds's The End *(1978).*

Mahoney talked of a stroke he suffered while on the *Kung Fu* set in the early 1970s.

"It was 10:30 in the morning when it hit. I knew what had happened, I told my wife who happened to be visiting that day, and I swore her to secrecy." With just one stunt left to do after the lunch break, he wanted to stay. "It wasn't a macho trip," he states. "It's just that I've never held up a set in my whole life and I guess I just don't know when to quit."

At 1:30 P.M. the limp actor mounted his horse for what normally would have been a simple bit of business. He had to drop a loop around a man four feet away. The horse gave Mahoney the height advantage for the roping. His body would not cooperate, however.

"I hit that man in the face and everyway from Sunday. I hit him five times and I finally lost my temper, which I have never done before, and told the director, 'Goddamnit! Get somebody who can use a rope!' They all looked at me and were stunned, because that wasn't my way of doing things." The director patiently asked him to try a few more times. With encouragement he got it, then left for the emergency ward.

Surprisingly, it was Mahoney's first visit to a hospital bed after a stunt, and even then it was not directly related to a death-defying trick. "I was never checked in because of an injury during a personal appearance or a studio stunt. As a matter of fact, that's one reason why I've been able to continue to do all my own work. I've never put in for an insurance claim."

Although he's still recovering from the stroke, Mahoney continues to perform. He's been on TV stunt specials, made guest shots on shows like *B.J. and the Bear*, and appeared in Burt Reynolds's *The End* as an old man who topples over a hill in a wheelchair. Mahoney also advised Reynolds in *Hooper*, a film about a stunt man, which he admits is a semibiographical story, costarring Brian Keith as a character named Jocko.

Mahoney, born Jacques O'Mahoney in Davenport, Iowa, carries a line of French, Irish, and Cherokee blood. "Jacques, or even Jock or Jocko, wasn't American-sounding enough for Gene Autry, however," he says. "So for *Range Rider* he renamed me Jock Mahoney."

Autry similarly dubbed Mahoney's costar, Dick Jones, with the surname West and dispatched the two for seventy-nine half-hour episodes, which initially aired on CBS.

In order to sell the wanderings of the nearly lone ranger and his justice-seeking sidekick, New York station WCBS initiated an inspired plan. The outlet scheduled a week of daily 6:30 P.M. showings. WCBS's intention was to interest prospective sponsors in the series with actual screenings from March 26 to March 30, 1951. Mahoney flew cross-country to appear live each day to hype the show. It sold.

Range Rider's sponsors were obviously happy with the production. Table Talk pies, for example, kept his freezer packed. All but one of the flavors went down fine.

"At one time they had a chocolate cream pie that was absolutely marvelous, but they wanted me to push the lemon and instructed me to say in the commercials '. . . and save the lemon pie for Dad.' Well, more men stopped me on the street and in taxis and said, 'Please Jocko, anything but the lemon. My kids save all that for me and I'd rather have the chocolate that they get!'

"We were on everywhere," he continues. "But it was early in TV's development and the network couldn't believe they needed any more episodes. We had great ratings, yet CBS just didn't know

Duncan Renaldo riding in one of the 176 episodes of the international hit The Cisco Kid.

they could run for twenty years and have great rerun value, especially if they were shot in color, which we were not.

"It wasn't complete stupidity on their part," he explains. "They didn't know. Nobody knew anything about television in those days. Autry had simply walked into CBS and said, 'Okay, you put up the money and you get the first run.' The network did and then all the films reverted back to Autry. He got all the benefits and most of the commercial tie-ups. No one could now make a deal like that with a network for any amount of money."

As for his own financial or personal relationship with Gene Autry, Mahoney says he has no complaints. "I was learning my trade at that point," he responds. "TV was a marvelous school where I could try things and immediately see what the public reaction was. I really didn't deserve more than I got."

In 1958, Mahoney starred in the TV series *Yancy Derringer* and in 1962, at age forty-two, shed his Western garb and wore only a loincloth in *Tarzan Goes to India*.[8]

In recent years Mahoney has taken up hot-air ballooning and flown with the Blue Angels precision team. Now in his sixties, he would like to land a new TV Western. If anyone can start another professional life in the typical years of retirement, it's Jock Mahoney. He's got the lithe body of a cat and more lives than any critter around.

Mahoney may be the most enduring stunt man in Hollywood, but neither of his TV series had the broadcast strength of Duncan Renaldo's *The Cisco Kid*.

The syndicated program premiered in 1951 and was still riding the ratings until the early 1960s. In 1950, a year before it aired, three NBC-owned and operated stations in New York, Washington, and Cleveland paid ZIV-Television $1 million for five-year rights to the show. Within three years it was airing on seventy-five more

8. Mahoney says that by the time *Yancy Derringer*, his series about a riverboat gambler-turned-lawman and his Indian friend Pahoo (X Brands) aired, networks had become wiser, in fact greedier. "After our first year on the air, Johnson's Wax telegrammed they wanted thirty-four more episodes and CBS came to us and said they wanted a 25 percent cut. 'No way,' we answered. They weren't going to give us any more for that. They were just going to take a quarter of our show. When it came down to the nitty-gritty, we lost our time slot, and because our sponsor had no place to put the show, that was it for us."

stations and earning $44,000 per week profit. In 1956, the show was dubbed and distributed to twenty countries including France, Italy, Switzerland, Luxembourg, Belgium, Cuba, Puerto Rico, Argentina, and the Dominican Republic. And in 1959 it had grossed a total of $11 million in domestic sales.

The Cisco Kid proved triumphant partly because it was the first Western series to be filmed in color. Tinting especially paid off once technology caught up with foresight in the late 1950s.

Warner Baxter, Cesar Romero, and Gilbert Roland had portrayed Cisco in films stretching back to 1941, but best remembered in the black outfit was Duncan Renaldo. In 1943 the former stunt man mounted Diablo and charged onto the screen in the role. Within six years he was shooting his first fifty-two episodes near Palm Springs, California. They were released in 1951. By the time he dismounted for good he had made 176 episodes and broken some bones.

As Donald F. Glut and Jim Harmon wrote in *The Great Television Heroes* (Doubleday, 1975), Renaldo was instructed to dodge a sixty-five-pound papier-mâché boulder that was filled with bedsprings to give it bounce. Instead of rolling down a cliff in his general direction, the prop struck him directly in the head, breaking two neck vertebrae. Renaldo was paralyzed for 60 days.

Leo Carrillo was already in his seventies when he was fitted for Pancho's sombrero and signed as Renaldo's sidekick. Off screen, the two stars were not always comrades. In 1956 word leaked that Renaldo and Carrillo were not speaking to one another and that Carrillo was even intending to make a similar series starring Gilbert Roland. Such a version never went before the cameras, however. Carrillo aborted his plan for a TV showdown with his Western partner, and ZIV-Television continued to be the sole producer of *The Cisco Kid.*

Color film reeled through the cameras shooting Westerns other than *The Cisco Kid.* In September 1951 color production began on *Cowboy G-Men,* a series that had the plot but not the humor of *The Wild, Wild West.* The program concerned two undercover agents who investigated federal offenders in the 1880s.

Russell Hayden starred as Pat Gallagher—the stereotypical upright and handsome agent.[9] Jackie Coogan, Chaplin's *The Kid,* portrayed Stoney Crockett, his bumbling partner. The thirty-minute syndicated production sponsored by Taystee bread, debuted in 1952, well before the residual rules went into effect. Nonetheless, in 1956 the Screen Actors Guild filed suit, hoping to collect more than $20,000 in back pay reportedly owed the actors for repeat telecasts.

The action was directed against Harry B. Donovan's Telemount Pictures, Inc., Mutual TV Productions, and two other firms.

The simple and warranted introduction of residual payments boosted production costs and helped nudge live-action shows off the schedule. Part of the reason for residuals was the guild's

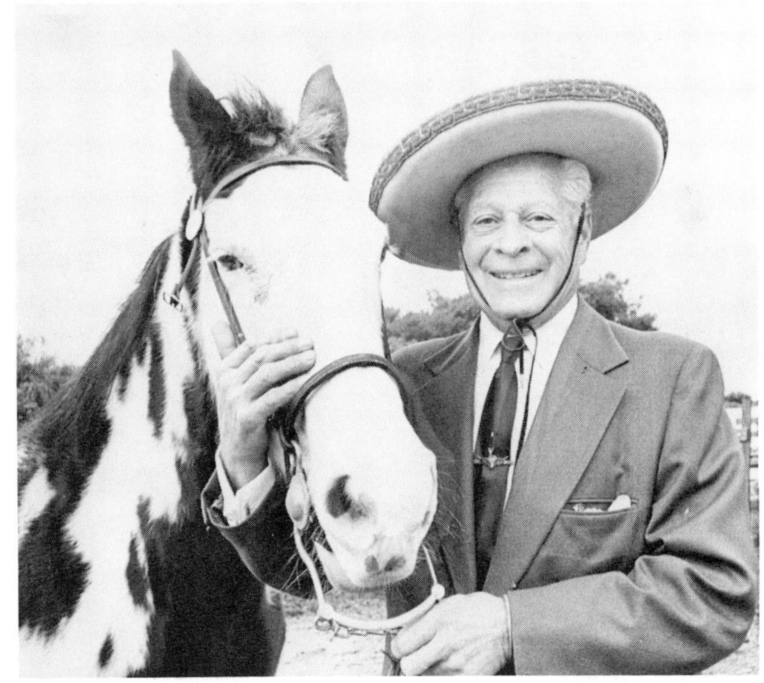
Renaldo in the 1970s

9. In 1958, Hayden gave up his horse for the studio limo and became producer of *26 Men.*

Estimated Production Costs Per Half-Hour Program

(Sources: *Variety* and *Billboard*)

1951:	
Hopalong Cassidy	$7,500
The Lone Ranger	$15,000
The Gene Autry Show	$17,000
Howdy Doody	$2,000
Big Top	$8,500
Small Fry Club	$4,500
Tom Corbett, Space Cadet	$4,500
Lucky Pup	$5,000
1952:	
The Lone Ranger	$17,000
Sky King	$16,000
Smilin' Ed's Gang	$12,000
Wild Bill Hickok	$15,000
Howdy Doody	$6,800
Super Circus	$6,800
The Paul Winchell-Jerry Mahoney Show	$18,500
Space Patrol	$5,000
1954:	
Howdy Doody	$4,170
Captain Midnight	$7,500
Lassie	$25,000
The Lone Ranger	$25,000
Space Patrol	$10,000
The Roy Rogers Show	$28,000

Opposite: Bill Williams, TV's Kit Carson, perched, waiting to get the drop on desperadoes.

realization and the industry's recognition that television was not a passing fad, as suspected by many. As the medium expanded and airtime became more valuable to broadcasters, producers, and sponsors, actors reasonably deserved more. Their requests, however, helped inflate budgets.

Whereas *The Lone Ranger* could be produced for $17,000 an episode in 1952, and $18,000 in 1954, it rose to $20,000 in 1955 and $27,000 a year later. *The Gene Autry Show* and *Wild Bill Hickok* experienced similar increases. And though the expense was low by today's standard half-hour price tag of $150,000 to $300,000 per show, the number of productions that could earn out their investment was narrowing as the costs rose.

One of the ways to keep the budget down was to work where there were crews experienced in bargain-basement technique. Nowhere was there a more qualified staff than at Republic Studios—the facility commonly known as "The King of the 'B's." One of many programs to shoot on the lot was *The Adventures of Kit Carson,* starring former swimmer Bill Williams, whose greatest stroke was luck. The MCA-TV Western began production in 1952 and was, according to *Variety,* reaching more children's homes than any other series in 1954. Three-and-a-half million households were estimated to be tuned in to the weekly exploits of scout Christopher "Kit" Carson and his Mexican sidekick, El Toro (Don Diamond).

Number two in the 1954 list of top kids' shows was *Annie Oakley.* Gail Davis starred as the girl who was fast at everything but love. She could outride, outdraw, and outfight any villain, but like her cowboy counterparts this cowgirl was more at home on the range than in the bedroom.

Annie Oakley wasn't Gail Davis's first claim to fame. She had been selected as the most beautiful baby in Arkansas when she was two and years later attracted Autry in a camp show when she was a student at a Texas university. Impressed with her good looks and acting ability, he told Davis that if she ever went to Hollywood, look him up. Within a year she took advantage of the offer. Autry signed her for fifteen feature films and thirty of his TV episodes. She began work on her own series, September 10, 1952, and continued through 1956.

Autry held up the airdate of *Annie Oakley,*

arranging for more money from sponsors and waiting for more stations to sign on. The show finally premiered in a hundred markets, January 1954. Canada Dry and T.V. Time Popcorn were the sponsors.

Helping Annie in her appointed tasks as sheriff of Diablo were Deputy Lofty Craig (Brad Johnson) and her brother Tagg (Jimmy Hawkins).

Filming across the lot was *Buffalo Bill, Jr.* This 1955 syndicated series starred Dick Jones (Range Rider's sidekick Dick West). The show ran easily for four years. Jones had a tougher time putting them on film, for as in his previous series he performed his own stunts and took quite a few bruises.

"Jock has always taught me to do the stunts realistically," he states. Sometimes he paid through the nose, sometimes the elbow, the leg, wrists, or chest.

Buffalo Bill, Jr. owed no allegiance to the legitimate character. Junior and his sister Calamity (Nancy Gilbert) were orphans adopted by Judge Ben Wiley (Harry Cheshire), founder of Wileyville, Texas.

"Compared to *The Range Rider, Buffalo Bill, Jr.* comes in second," says Jones. What was more entertaining for him than the show were the promotional tours. "There's nothing like a personal appearance," he says. "The most gratifying part of acting was seeing kids in the stands, giggling, laughing, and enjoying the performances."

It was no surprise that Jones enjoyed the rodeo road shows. He was born in Texas, and by age five was riding with Hoot Gibson. His first movie was *Wonder Bar* (1934) with Al Jolson and Dick Powell. In 1937 he appeared in King Vidor's *Stella Dallas* and signed for roles in *Renfrew of the Royal Mounted* (1937), *Destry Rides Again* (1939), *Heaven Can Wait* (1943), and many other

Right: Gail Davis brought $2 million of T.V. Time popcorn's advertising budget to Gene Autry's Flying A Productions in 1954 when Annie Oakley *debuted.*

Opposite: Dick Jones, Range Rider's partner, went solo in the 1955 Gene Autry production of Buffalo Bill, Jr. *He portrayed a lawman in a small Texas town.*

Below: Gail Davis, with her boss, friend, producer, and cowboy hero, Gene Autry, at a 1957 personal appearance. Annie Oakley *had been out of production for one year.*

features. "I did a lot of films for Gene Autry before the two series as well," he adds, saying that the legendary star was "warm and friendly." Sounding like a true cowboy with his staccato answers and a mellow voice, he politely adds, "It was a good outfit to work for . . . like one big family. And I still get Christmas cards from Mr. Autry."

As so often was the case, Jones was shut out of the wide-open TV industry after helping pioneer it. "I did very few films or shows afterwards because I got typecast," he admits. "I was under contract for Autry for so long that it was difficult to get back into work anywhere else. Anyway," he says, "TV had begun to change drastically and I just didn't enjoy it anymore."

In a departure from the typical cowboy series, Roy Rogers's Frontier Productions developed a series about a young Indian. In its 1955 prime time airing, *Brave Eagle* was defeated by *Coke Time with Eddie Fisher* and Walt Disney's *Disneyland.* The Cheyenne later settled into the Saturday morning schedule in some cities but was overrun by cartoons and cowboys. Keith Larsen starred as the peaceful young chief. Keena (Keena Nomkeena) was his foster son. Brave Eagle spent his serious moments with beautiful Morning Star (Kim Winona) and enjoyed lighter diversions with Smokey Joe (Bert Wheeler). Stories dealt with the encroachment of the white man into Indian land.

Tales of the Texas Rangers, also premiering in 1955, showed the Indians' struggle and the

Opposite: Clayton Moore unmasked, but undaunted, 1979

white man's dominance. The series was unique because its featured players—Ranger Jace Pearson (Willard Parker) and Ranger Clay Morgan (Harry Lauter)—covered 120 years of Western history and fiction.

Tales of the Texas Rangers had another dual life. It debuted on CBS, Saturday morning, September 3, 1955, sponsored by General Mills and Tootsie Roll. In October 1958 it moved to ABC for broadcast at 5:00 P.M. Thursdays, and a few months later to prime time, Mondays at 7:30 P.M.

Because Parker and Lauter were portraying "realistic" characters, they were not the familiar Western twosome with the hero-sidekick relationship. They played tough policemen, as accomplished at 90 mph on the highway as they were in a horse chase through the hills. Scripts consequently failed to fit the traditional moralistic mold. Contemporary episodes dealt with spies (see Chapter XIV, "The Cold War Brigade"), terrorism, gangsters, and oil tycoons; installments about days past covered bank robberies, Mexican bandits, and horse thieves.

Perhaps as well remembered as the double-barrel format were the advertisements that pushed General Mills's "Trix." Between scenes of the Rangers roping burglars, the Trix rabbit tried in vain to steal the children's cereal. The bunny was never successful, however, because as every viewer knew, "Trix" were for kids.

Throughout the 1950s, Western characters rode circles around most other personalities. On both Saturday morning and prime time, cowboys were viewers' favored choice. Ten of the fifteen top-rated shows in 1958 were Westerns. But within a few years there would be a gigantic roundup, fatal to nearly all with a ten-gallon hat. The TV heroes might have prevailed in the open spaces, but crowded onto the small screen they eventually became victims of overpopulation.

Harry Lauter (left) *and Willard Parker covered the Old West and contemporary villains on* Tales of the Texas Rangers. *Like their Texas colleague, the Lone Ranger, they gunned for bad guys, but they also aimed for more serious drama.*

©photo courtesy *Boston Herald American*

7

Cops, Captains, and Commanders

If nail-biting increased in the 1950s, then Saturday morning adventure shows might be to blame. Anxiety-producing programs appeared throughout the decade, and it's a wonder that precomputer-generation youngsters, keyed up over electrifying scenes, didn't gnaw their fingers to the bone.

Today, the networks red-pencil any prolonged action that would make so much as a palm sweat. In the past, however, nerves were touched, poked, proded, and wracked. Captain Gallant, so named for his heroic flair, wrestled Arabs. Robin Hood's arrows made the Sheriff of Nottingham quiver with fear. And Sky King's aerobatics caused viewers' hearts to stop and stomachs to flip-flop.

Children recognized that crime didn't pay, particularly on Saturday morning. Producers, meanwhile, knew that fear-inspiring programs usually did. Collecting from TV sales was simple until Hollywood found they had to please two factions: congressional committees, which were ready to pound a disapproving gavel if too much violence appeared, and young viewers, who were ready to turn off the program if there wasn't enough violence. As they waited for the sound of the boom or click, they heard the jingle of coins in the TV coffers.

Children's shows didn't come under prolonged heavy fire in the 1950s. Washington and the industry had called a temporary truce after rounds of juvenile delinquency hearings earlier in the decade. And although special interest groups argued that many of the shows were unhealthy, devoted young viewers got the last word, usually making the questioned programs like *Sergeant Preston* and *Highway Patrol* top hits.

There were rules governing violence, but they were negotiable. The networks said that criminals and crime couldn't be illuminated by any sympathetic light. Law had to be upheld and violators must be punished. Detailed descriptions of crimes were outlawed. Marriage and family had to be presented in a reverent manner. And anything detracting from a youngster's respect for good behavior, clean living, and adult authority had to be cleared anywhere from thirteen days to six weeks in advance.

Opposite: Buster Crabbe and his ten-year-old son Cuffy (Cullen), in a scene from Captain Gallant of the Foreign Legion. *The series was filmed on location in the Middle East before revolution made changes in the map and forced the withdrawal of the French.*

The criteria were vague, however, and for many years TV had an "anything goes" attitude in regard to Saturday programming.

Adventure show programming was the next step in a progression of Saturday morning's evolution. Storybook ladies and uncle hosts had been seen since the earliest years. Westerns and science fiction shows aired soon thereafter. It was time for yet another change. And the past and present began to merge in 1951, when *Sky King* debuted.

Kirby Grant, a Montana rancher turned actor and aviator, starred in the high-flying Western. Instead of merely heading horse-riding crooks off at the pass as other cowboys had done, Sky King took to the air from his private landing strip at the Flying Crown Ranch and red-dogged the villains to justice in his Cessna 310-B.

The twin-engine airplane, the *Songbird*,[1] conveniently spirited Sky King in and out of action and helped deliver him to viewers every week. The *Songbird* was so popular an attraction that children swarmed airfields whenever Grant flew in for a personal appearance tour. "I was amazed to find the number of kids who even knew the horsepower rating of its engines, its cruising speed, and its range," Grant says.

The kids never found the plane more interesting than its pilot, however. Sky King—a first-class hero—was the star of the show. He never acted less than honorably and never gave cause for a discouraging word. He took his performance seriously and totally believed that his role could be a model for young viewers.

"I'm not so naïve," he confessed in a 1958 newspaper interview, "to think that 'goody-goody' television programs are going to solve any world issue or even make a big dent in the problem of juvenile delinquency, but I sincerely feel that anything I can do to instill the idea of settling disputes peacefully in the minds of my young audience is of paramount importance. In my actions on the screen I try to crystallize that belief."

These days Grant reaffirms his three-decade-old view, assuring that he was beyond reproach both on and off air.

"There are people who don't pay any attention to their responsibility and go on their merry way not thinking about their public or the image they create. But I tried to remain responsive to this. I did enjoy a drink, but I never took one in front of kids. I never smoked near them and I watched my language. It all had a tendency of making a better person out of me. I tried to live up to the character that I portrayed."

Grant acknowledges that the show contained a certain degree of violence, but he called it "controlled." "We only used what violence was necessary to bring a culprit to justice." Even when in pursuit of villains, he never killed, he adds. "In fact, no heavy—regardless of how ruthless he was—was ever pistol-whipped or clubbed in any episodes." Sky King relied on the swift judo chop and kept his gun holstered or, more often than not, on the wall of his ranch house headquarters.

Grant was qualified for his unique role. Having been born and raised in Montana, he was a legitimate cowpoke. And having spent a World War II tour of duty as an Air Force flight instructor, he was amply prepared to fly the *Songbird*. His performing credits made him a cinch for the part.

Grant made his debut as a concert violinist at age twelve with a Seattle orchestra. Critics called him a prodigy and cheered him on. He

Excerpt from Section VIII of the 1949 Television Production Code:

All shows which essentially are not the proper material for viewing by children under 18 years of age shall be scheduled for telecast after 9 P.M., and before 5 A.M. local time.

1. The Cessna 310-B, with its wing tanks that provided fuel for more than a thousand miles at an average of 210 mph, was Sky King's second plane. In the first season, 1952, the Western hero flew over the mythical Grover City in a Cessna P-50.

heard other applause as well, for Grant played semipro baseball, acted at the University of Washington and Whitman College, and sang with a Chicago dance-band.

After performing with a midwest stock company in 1937, he entered the Gateway to Hollywood talent contest and won the first-place prize, a six-month RKO film contract. The RKO deal ended, but his acting career continued as he appeared in *Blondie Goes Latin* (1941), *Hello, Frisco, Hello* (1943), *Ghost Catchers* (1944), a string of Universal musicals, singing cowboy films, and Canadian Mounted Police features before piloting the *Songbird.*

"I tried out for *Sky King* just like anyone would audition for a screen test in a movie," Grant says. "I made the test opposite Barbara Whiting. Gloria Winters, the young woman who actually portrayed my niece Penny on the show, tested with someone else. They picked her, Ron

Pair the Sidekicks of Column I with their Partners in Column II.

I		**II**	
A	Red Connors	**1**	Circus Boy
B	Dick West	**2**	Davey
C	Pat Brady	**3**	Crusader Rabbit
D	Cadet Happy	**4**	Captain Midnight
E	Tagg	**5**	Captain Michael Gallant
F	Chim	**6**	Billy Batson
G	Patches	**7**	Buster Brown
H	Augie Dogie	**8**	Shari Lewis
I	Tamba	**9**	Range Rider
J	Bimbo	**10**	Jace Pearson
K	Pancho	**11**	Jungle Jim
L	Tonto	**12**	Buzz Corry
M	Ichabod Mudd	**13**	Joey
N	Wormsey Wormser	**14**	Stubby Kaye
O	Reddy	**15**	Annie Oakley
P	Lamb Chop	**16**	Kit Carson
Q	Clay Morgan	**17**	King Leonardo
R	Kenny Williams	**18**	Lone Ranger
S	Mentor	**19**	Hopalong Cassidy
T	Odie Colognie	**20**	Rod Brown
U	El Toro	**21**	Ruff
V	Rags the Tiger	**22**	Jimmy Weldon
W	Goliath	**23**	Roy Rogers
X	Fuzzy Knight	**24**	Sheena
Y	Webster Webfoot	**25**	Dogie Daddy
Z	Tige	**26**	Cisco Kid

Chief Dan Mathews ran the Highway Patrol *in the 1950s, but in 1977 the freeways belonged to* CHiPs *and young officers like Larry Wilcox and Erik Estrada* (right) *seen here ticketing speeder Crawford in a 1977 cameo appearance.*

A	19	N	20
B	9	O	21
C	23	P	8
D	12	Q	10
E	15	R	14
F	24	S	6
G	13	T	17
H	25	U	16
I	11	V	3
J	1	W	2
K	26	X	5
L	18	Y	22
M	4	Z	7

Haggerty for Clipper, and me for Sky King.[2] With nobody except the radio character to follow, I just played myself on the show."

The first *Sky King* episodes were made for Peter Pan peanut butter for a little less than $9,000 an episode. A falling out between the sponsor and the advertising agency led to the cancellation after the production ended in 1952.

"I went back to Chicago as a writer and director for Wilding Pictures," continues Grant. "A friend of mine working with the McCann Erickson advertising agency told me that Nabisco was interested in doing *Sky King* and they wanted to make a deal. So in 1955 I took a leave of absence from Wilding and filmed another season's episodes.

"We worked six days a week and it was hard to keep track of what we were doing," Grant remembers. "We'd shoot exteriors up at Apple Valley near Victorville in the high desert and in Arizona, then come back to the studio and shoot two and a half days of interiors. It was a daybreak-to-dark routine, and then at night we'd study lines for the next day."

Kirby Grant took to the air in 1952, and episodes of Sky King *stayed aloft for two decades.*

Sky King touched down on human interest, cops 'n' robbers, and ecologically minded territory. Grant says the best scripts covered a mixture of the three. The show was also often an advertisement for electronic gadgetry and modern science. "We used Geiger counters, tape recorders, dish antennas, and lots of things that are in common use now."

Grant believes most of the stories would hold up today. But the chance of seeing *Sky King* soaring again is slim.

"We made over 130 episodes. Unfortunately, they were all packed away in a New York film library. The 35 mm negatives, the masters, and the 16 mm release prints were all in one room and a fire broke out. We lost all but seventy-two films."

Grant took the loss personally because he had taken the show seriously. "I insisted that everything be as realistic as possible, even my character. Sky King might have been larger than life, but he made his mistakes and got his lumps, too."

Those lumps were felt by Kirby Grant.

2. Gloria Winters, a California neighbor of Grant's in the 1950s, played Babs to Jackie Gleason's Riley in the original *Life of Riley* TV series. She is retired from acting today. Ron Haggerty deplaned the *Songbird* after one season when he went into the military.

Gloria Winters as Sky King's niece Penny in a 1952 photograph.

"I used stunt men because they can make you look pretty good, but in some scenes I just had to appear," he adds. "In one episode I flew with an odd man in a twin Beechcraft. He had been sitting in the car with his mouth open and was sound asleep until we needed him to pilot a plane." With only a few grunts upon awakening he got behind the controls, lifted off the ground and headed straight for two poles that were thirty feet apart.

"I thought there was no way in the world that we would get through those lines, and I said to myself with a gulp, 'This will be interesting,' when suddenly he turned the airplane on its side and went right between the poles. He knew what he was doing, he just didn't tell me."

Even in such unpredictable and dangerous stunts the airborne Grant was usually at ease. The experienced pilot, however, could not stand heights when he wasn't in an airplane. "I let them know how I felt. I wouldn't climb oil rigs or anything high like that. It doesn't bother me when I'm in an airplane, but I have acrophobia if I'm high up but still attached to the ground," he admits.

Recently, Grant has given up the captain's chair for the passenger's seat. The Federal Aviation Administration suspended his license after he underwent open-heart surgery. His post–Sky King career, however, keeps him close to Earth. In the 1970s, Grant tirelessly operated The Sky King Youth Ranch of America for homeless teenagers. "My wife and I thought we should do something for someone else and that's what we intended to do," he says. His plans were to open facilities throughout the country, but tight money late in the decade forced Grant to postpone his schedule. In the meantime he has been handling publicity for Florida's Sea World. Grant is a resident of southern Florida.

Though he's put miles and years between his Hollywood term as Sky King and his private life today, Grant still finds he's walking in the shadow of the *Songbird*.

"I've met airplane pilots who have told me they're flying commercial jets because of the show. And I met a woman who said she married a returning GI in Germany, and when she came to America, *Sky King* was the first thing she watched. She didn't understand English then, but she said that everything was so clear from a visual standpoint that she knew what was going on.

"If I never do anything else in my life, at least I know I've accomplished something good with *Sky King*," Grant adds with great satisfaction.

In 1976, NBC premiered Muggsy, *a socially relevant drama with great potential and few viewers. Sarah MacDonnell starred with Ben Masters* (right) *and Paul Michael* (left).

Sky King was not the only TV aviator to be cleared on Saturday morning. Besides *Captain Midnight* (see Chapter V, "Star Treks and Time Travels"), the syndicated helicopter adventure series *The Whirlybirds* lifted off in 1957, and *Ripcord* was released in 1961. Most of the other programs presented sea-level or below-sea-level adventures.

Buster Crabbe (Clarence Linden Crabbe) was one man suited for both environs. The 1932 Olympic swimmer—the first champion to best the five-minute mark for the 400-meter course—traded in his bathing trunks for the Foreign Legionnaire's outfit, starring as NBC's Captain Gallant.

It was by no means Crabbe's first plunge into television. After playing Flash Gordon, Buck Rogers, and Tarzan and appearing in sixty other motion pictures, he became host of his own New York televison show, *The Buster Crabbe Show*, in 1951. A year later he starred on an exercise program, *Figure Fashioning*. *Captain Gallant of the Foreign Legion* properly took him out of local

Dramatic License

Dramas have been the cod-liver oil of the Saturday morning diet. Children haven't liked the taste, especially when they could choose far sweeter programming. And network administrators have hated force-feeding dramatic shows to youngsters, even though they occasionally hear from parents that it does kids some good.

Morality plays have succeeded in adventure shows like *Fury, The Adventures of Rin Tin Tin,* and *Shazam!* However, straight dramas, the kind that networks are even reluctant to air today in prime time against *Charlie's Angels* and *The Love Boat,* have usually come in small and unpopular helpings.

In 1951, a year before CBS checked *City Hospital* into the weekday schedule, the soap opera appeared in many cities around the country on Saturday morning. The same season ABC's *Betty Crocker Star Matinee* presented Saturday morning vignettes, and the nighttime series *Schlitz Playhouse of Stars* premiered as *Saturday Playhouse.*

NBC introduced *True Story* in 1957. The thirty-minute anthology series hosted by young Kathi Norris presented live dramas from New York, giving work to Dick Van Dyke, Lorne Greene, and many other actors who would soon move to their own programs.

In 1963, NBC attempted to revive quality programming with *NBC's Children's Theatre.* In its five years on the air it presented a variety of classics including *The Reluctant Dragon, The World of Stuart Little,* and *Little Women.*

A year later, Dr. Frank Baxter read Shakespeare on NBC, and in 1976, *Muggsy* brought classic drama up to date in a contemporary urban setting. Sarah MacDonnell played the title role of a freckle-faced thirteen-year-old who treats her ghetto like a castle.

ABC's *Afterschool Specials* telecast relevant stories on weekday time slots beginning in 1972. NBC did the same on Saturdays beginning in 1976 with a series of monthly programs called *Special Treat.* Editions of both earned the industry's top awards.

Buoyed by prestige and not public reaction, dramas continued to appear sporadically on all three commercial networks in the late 1970s. But the networks, which take children's ratings seriously and serious programming for children with a grain of salt, obviously have tried not to let quality dictate what gets on Saturday morning.

TV and gave the national hero back to the nation.

As Captain Gallant he portrayed a swashbuckling Foreign Legion officer. But the series had all the earmarks of a Western. Instead of wearing a ten-gallon hat and chasing down cattle rustlers, Crabbe searched for camel thieves. He worked for an unnamed "mother country," and policed feuding Arabs instead of warring Indians.

Like all good Western heroes he needed a comic sidekick. Cowboy veteran Fuzzy Knight fit the bill after having ridden with Johnny Mack Brown, Russell Hayden, and Tex Ritter. For human interest the show relied on a ten-year-old scene-stealer played by Crabbe's son, Cullen.[3] The first production season, legitimate French Foreign Legion officers played supporting roles.

In early 1954 the crew filmed at an outpost on the edge of the Sahara Desert, six hundred miles southeast of Casablanca. Other backgrounds during the premiere year included ancient French forts, Moroccan streets, Marrakech, Paris, and Athens.

The second year, producer Harry Saltzman (later coproducer of many James Bond motion pictures) filmed in Libya and Tripoli because war for independence had broken out in Algeria. Interiors were shot in Rome.

The series of sixty-five episodes, sponsored at various times by Heinz, General Mills, and Chunky chocolate, appeared on network TV until 1963 and thereafter was syndicated as *Foreign Legionnaire.*

Crabbe explains that the show was shot abroad not so much for realism, but to cut expenses. "It took us four days to shoot a half-hour episode overseas. That was a day more than a Hollywood crew working on the show if we had filmed in the Mojave Desert. It took longer, but it was cheaper abroad by six or seven thousand dollars per show," he says.

The total budget for each installment was approximately $21,500.

3. *The New York Times* published a humorous interview in 1955 with Cullen Crabbe after he returned to his Mamaroneck, New York, home after the first season of filming. "I rode a camel," he said with marked enthusiasm. "And once I was on a beautiful little black horse that almost ran away with me—but I stopped him in time." The younger Crabbe seemed a reluctant TV star, however. He was more interested in the Italian motor scooter his father bought him for his work than in the admiration he was receiving from peers. Today, the African desert and scooter far behind him, Cullen is a successful Arizona real estate broker.

Crabbe thought that the best way to wash the desert out of his pores after production concluded was a dunk into the water. He proposed a film series about frogmen in 1957 called *Davy Jones.* "We did a pilot, but nobody wanted to pick it up," he states. "It wasn't bad either, but since we couldn't get it sold, we forgot about it."

With water yet on his mind, Crabbe returned to upstate New York and took a job as resident swim instructor at a Catskill Mountain resort. He ran an Adirondack Mountain camp in the early 1970s and now lives in Scottsdale, Arizona, and occasionally hops a Hollywood-bound plane for a guest TV appearance. He says it's a more comfortable ride than a camel.

There were other military units that served Saturday morning television. In the late 1950s children saw syndicated reruns of *Tales of the 77th Bengal Lancers.* The series, only in production during the 1956–57 season, depicted the fictional exploits of Britain's nineteenth-century Indian division. Phil Carey and Warren Stevens starred.

Three able-bodied Royal Canadian Mounted Police were also enlisted in the foreign service. Each withstood facsimiles of freezing Klondike temperatures, but two died when audiences gave them the cold shoulder. *Renfrew of the Royal Mounted,* starring James Newill as Sergeant Douglas Renfrew, was syndicated in 1953. The episodes were based on the 1941 Monogram features and a Renfrew radio show. Corporal Jacques Gagnier (Gilles Pelletier) maintained peace in the 1960 syndication show *Royal Canadian Mounted Police.* Some people also knew the series as *R.C.M.P.*, but apparently not enough to keep it on the air.

The beat was never better patrolled than when *Sergeant Preston of the Yukon* was on the job. The Mountie and his dog, Yukon King, first scouted the Northwest in 1955. Their exploits made prime time viewing at 7:30 P.M. Thursdays on CBS until they wrapped up their last case in 1958. Thereafter, *Sergeant Preston* repeated on Saturday morning.

The program starred rugged six-footer Richard Simmons, who was cut from the very mold that turned out real Royal Northwest Mounted Police recruits. For work he had flown airplanes. For pleasure he swam, fenced, and broke wild horses. Though he had been athletic since childhood, he didn't muscle his way into acting.

"I never wanted to be an actor. I was happy being a pilot," he told *TV Guide* in 1956. But when Metro-Goldwyn-Mayer's Louis B. Mayer saw him tame an Arabian stallion on a dude ranch near Palm Springs, the impressed movie mogul immediately offered him a contract at twice his pilot's salary and guaranteed Simmons "outdoor roles."

"They put me in three pictures, then they gave me a screen test." When *Sergeant Preston* came along, he said, he was ready-made for the part. Simmons auditioned with two dozen actors and says he earned the role because of his own ability, the luck of the moment, and the help of a young, anonymous Newhall, California, ranchhand. When his turn came to wear the brilliant red coat and gallop off in front of the camera, he saw the teen-ager riding by on "the prettiest quarter horse you ever saw."

Everyone else was vying for the role on used studio animals—"four or five real dogs," Simmons said. "I asked to use the boy's horse in the test. He was tickled to death. Well, that little mare landed me my job, she was so full of spirit. I've always felt grateful to that kid, whoever he was."

Most weeks Sergeant Preston tracked gangsters bent on turning the Canadian Northwest into a crime capital. While the law officer talked to witnesses, victims, and officials, Preston's malamute sniffed the air for clues.

The villains were easy to deal with compared to some production problems. During filming of the very first episode in the California mountains, Simmons's horse threw him when a badger neared. The actor suffered a broken wrist but finished the scene and returned to complete the premiere story with a wrist-cast hidden by his glove.

Later in the production sixteen sled dogs arrived at the airport for a Hollywood studio sequence. The dogs were tired and nervous from the flight and ready to bite. No one would handle them, so Simmons left a dinner party to help.

Sergeant Preston of the Yukon was the property of George W. Trendle, the Detroit broadcaster who had owned and developed *The Lone Ranger* for radio and television. The first seventy-eight episodes were filmed in black and white; the

Sergeant Preston of the Yukon *(Richard Simmons) traveled across the Klondike on skis, snowshoes, and dogsled. He was only surpassed in his pursuit of north country criminals by his malamute, Yukon King.*

Richard Greene's The Adventures of Robin Hood *premiered in prime time in 1955, but the legendary bandit of Sherwood Forest found new recruits on Saturday reruns through the early 1960s.*

last twenty-six were color. Quaker Oats and Mother's Oats sponsored the series.

Sergeant Preston had taken clear aim for the children's audience, but *The Adventures of Robin Hood* had him beat by a long bow-and-arrow shot. The American-produced, English-filmed series debuted on Monday, September 26, 1955, and scored a quick bull's-eye. In all, 143 episodes were produced, each featuring prewar Hollywood heartthrob, Englishman Richard Greene.

Production began February 10, 1955. For authenticity the crew filmed 60 percent of the program in Sherwood Forest and Nottingham. The remainder was shot in Surrey, England.

At the show opening, *The Adventures of Robin Hood* catapulted viewers to the twelfth century with the speed of the arrow breezing through the air.

Robin Hood, Sir Robin of Locksley, was a bandit only because politics forced him to the woods. The evil Norman, Prince John (Donald Pleasence), declared him an outlaw when Robin objected to the heavy taxes the monarch levied on the Saxons while benevolent King Richard the Lion-Hearted (Ian Hunter) fought in the Holy Land Crusades. Rather than face the gallows, Robin escaped to Sherwood Forest, where he formed a band of freemen who challenged the prince's oppressive rule.

Chief among his merrymen were the jovial Friar Tuck (Alexander Gauge) and an incredible hulk named Little John (Archie Duncan), who turned lesser men green with envy. Robin's love interest and confidant was Maid Marian (Bernadette O'Farrell in 1955–57 and Patricia Driscoll, 1957–58). Meanwhile, Prince John's dirty work was carried out by the Sheriff of Nottingham (Alan Wheatley).

An estimated 32 million people tuned to Richard Greene's Monday night derring-do. The audience sat through Saturday morning repeats beginning in 1959.

Exceptional acting, believable swordplay, and action-filled stories usually made the Robin Hood TV show as exciting to watch as the 1938 Errol Flynn motion picture, *The Adventures of Robin Hood.*

In the same way many science fiction producers paid strict attention to possible futuristic invention, Robin Hood producer Hannah Weinstein made historical accuracy her business. She hired researchers to delve into background at the British Museum and told set designers to model castles on existing structures.

The show's five hundred costumes were checked for authenticity and weapons (longbows, crossbows, morning stars, swords, quarterstaffs, daggers) were designed from period sketches.

Reality was fudged for the candy bar generation, however. Trees, fireplaces, stone walls, and halls were built on wheels by a wartime camouflage expert so they could be quickly moved into place. And duels were thoroughly scripted with actors memorizing written directions as they would spoken lines. To Richard Greene, "POL" meant parry attack on left or ward off the enemy's sword on the left. "POR" told him to duck his head to the right, and "PVH" signified a vertical head-blow.

Above: Playwright, author, and actor, Robert Shaw appeared in the 1956 series The Buccaneers. *The program was set in seventeenth-century Nassau and premiered in the evening before moving to Saturdays.*

Left: Robin Hood had one of Cupid's arrows in his quiver. It hit Maid Marion (Bernadette O'Farrell).

Provide the missing information for the incomplete TV listings:

1. ________________ (science fiction) Prince Bacarratti, false pretender to the throne of Venus and a king among cutthroats returns to bring trouble to Buzz and Hap.

2. ________________ (adventure) Disguised as radio repairmen, the Captain and Ikky fly to Mexico to find the radio that has been sending messages to a foreign power.

3. ________________ (science fiction) The Captain and the Ranger smuggle themselves into Lyna after they discover that King Mergo is planning a universal war using the Federal Empire as his base.

4. ________________ (children) Monty Hall hosts old-time oaters and action-packed serial adventures.

5. ________________ (cartoon) T. C. is in need of some cash to pay a debt. He and his gang come up with the idea of a "wishing well." Voices: Arnold Stang, Allen Jenkins, Maurice Gosfield, Marvin Kaplan.

6. ________________ (variety) Gunga and Rama risk their lives in an effort to find wild honey for the ailing Maharajah. Also today, Froggy makes trouble for Midnight.

7. ________________ (adventure) Corky proves that camels run faster than horses. Mickey Braddock stars.

8. ________________ (Western) A masked man is pursued by a pair of fearless lawmen. Stars: Jock Mahoney, Dick Jones.

9. ________________ (variety) Paul Winchell and Jerry Mahoney introduce the cartoons. Animated characters include Goodie the Gremlin, Sheriff Saddle Head, and Scat Skit.

10. ________________ (adventure) Penny and her uncle tour an army special-projects plant, unaware that an enemy may make their return flight in the *Songbird* their last trip anywhere.

11. ________________ (cartoon) (1) Itchy and Biggy are defendants in "Trial of the Traitors." (2) The Hunter in "Statue of Liberty."

12. ________________ (Western) Bullet leads the way to "No Man's Land," a lawless stretch of desert.

13. ________________ (children) Nani Darnell and Rebo the clown assist in an escape from a clothes bag.

14. ________________ (adventure) Joey and Packy are engrossed in a book entitled *How to Be a Detective.* They put the book to use when burglars steal a new saddle. Joey: Bobby Diamond; Jim: Peter Graves.

15. ________________ (adventure) Dale and Dr. Zarkov chase an Earthman. Steve Holland.

16. ________________ (children) Mr. Moose is down in the mouth. Miss Worm and Bunny Rabbit try to cheer him up. Also Tom Terrific in "Instant Tantrums."

17. ________________ (comedy) Charlie Horse decides to become a good boy after everybody is so nice to him at his birthday party. It isn't long before Charlie learns how to keep his resolution. Hush Puppy and Charlie sing "I Like Everybody."

18. ________________ (quiz) Sonny Fox is host and quizmaster for this half-hour taped show in which children nine to thirteen, all of whom wish to pursue the same career, compete by answering questions about their choice. The winning prize helps the victor further his ambition. Today: children want to be astronauts.

19. ________________ (comedy) Judy thinks that a career is more glamorous than marriage until an unmarried career woman teaches her otherwise. Judy: Pat Crowley.

20. ________________ (adventure) Pat and Stoney travel to Rawhide to track down a murderer and recover the gold he has stolen. Jackie Coogan and Russell Hayden star.

21. ________________ (crime) Two men inspire a series of savage massacres by selling firearms to the Indians. Pearson and Morgan are sent to stop the killings.

22. ________________ (variety) When Mr. Leader loses the feather from his hat, he can't give the downbeat for the music in Pipertown. Jack Spear stars.

23. ________________ (puppet) Captain Steve Zodiac is assigned to destroy a ghost planet.

24. ________________ (variety/quiz) Children compete in various showbiz routines for a prize of a week's work at Hamid's Steel Pier in Atlantic City. Host: Gene Crane.

25. ________________ (educational) Eleven-year-old Richard Thomas visits Cape Canaveral with host Jack Lescoulie and learns what it's like to be an astronaut.

The dangerous morning star—a chain with attached iron ball—was constructed of rubber. Rather than wearing heavy army armor, knights and soldiers were clad in knits that were sprayed with silver paint. Miniature toy troops were made from scrap metal.

In the late 1950s, there was talk of filming *The Son of Robin Hood.* Ronald Howard, actor-son of Leslie Howard and star of the 1954 syndicated *Sherlock Holmes,* was rumored to take the title role. The adventure series never saw production.

A real-life countryman of Greene's and a legendary contemporary of Robin Hood appeared on TV when syndicators bought Roger Moore's 1957 British-made *Ivanhoe.* The series, based on the characters created by Sir Walter Scott, depicted the adventures of the young Saxon knight struggling against the same foes who troubled the bandit of Sherwood Forest.

Although the program was only seen in some U.S. markets, Screen Gems prepared an *Ivanhoe* study guide in 1960. In Chicago the Community Department Stores tied into the campaign by donating copies of the publication to six hundred public- and parochial-school instructors.

One other twelfth-century Englishman made it to twentieth-century Saturday morning reruns. In 1958 the previous year's ABC series *The Adventures of Sir Lancelot* was syndicated to local stations. William Russell played the brave knight who broke bread at King Arthur's Round Table until he caught Queen Guinevere's eye.

Saturday morning also became a rerun home for other adventure shows of the 1950s. Local stations bought *China Smith,* Dan Duryea's syndicated program about an American agent working the night shift in the Orient. Preston Foster chugged his tugboat into danger on *Waterfront.* Reed Hadley infiltrated the underworld and the children's lineup with *Racket Squad,* and young viewers received Broderick Crawford's "ten-four" loud and clear on *Highway Patrol.*

Twenty years before a killer shark got a taste of Robert Shaw in *Jaws,* TV audiences found him agreeable as Dan Tempest in *The Bucca-*

1. Space Patrol
2. Captain Midnight
3. Captain Video
4. Cowboy Theater
5. Top Cat
6. Smilin' Ed's Gang or Andy's Gang
7. Circus Boy
8. Range Rider
9. Cartoonsville or Cartoonies
10. Sky King
11. King Leonardo
12. Roy Rogers Show
13. The Magic Land of Allakazam
14. Fury
15. Flash Gordon
16. Captain Kangaroo
17. Shari Lewis
18. On Your Mark
19. A Date with Judy
20. Cowboy G-Men
21. Tales of Texas Rangers
22. Pip the Piper
23. Fireball XL-5
24. Grand Chance Roundup
25. 1, 2, 3—Go!

Inspector Rocky King (Roscoe Karns) mulls over a police report as Sgt. Lane (Earl Hammond) looks on in an episode of the popular 1950 cops 'n' robbers show Rocky King, Detective.

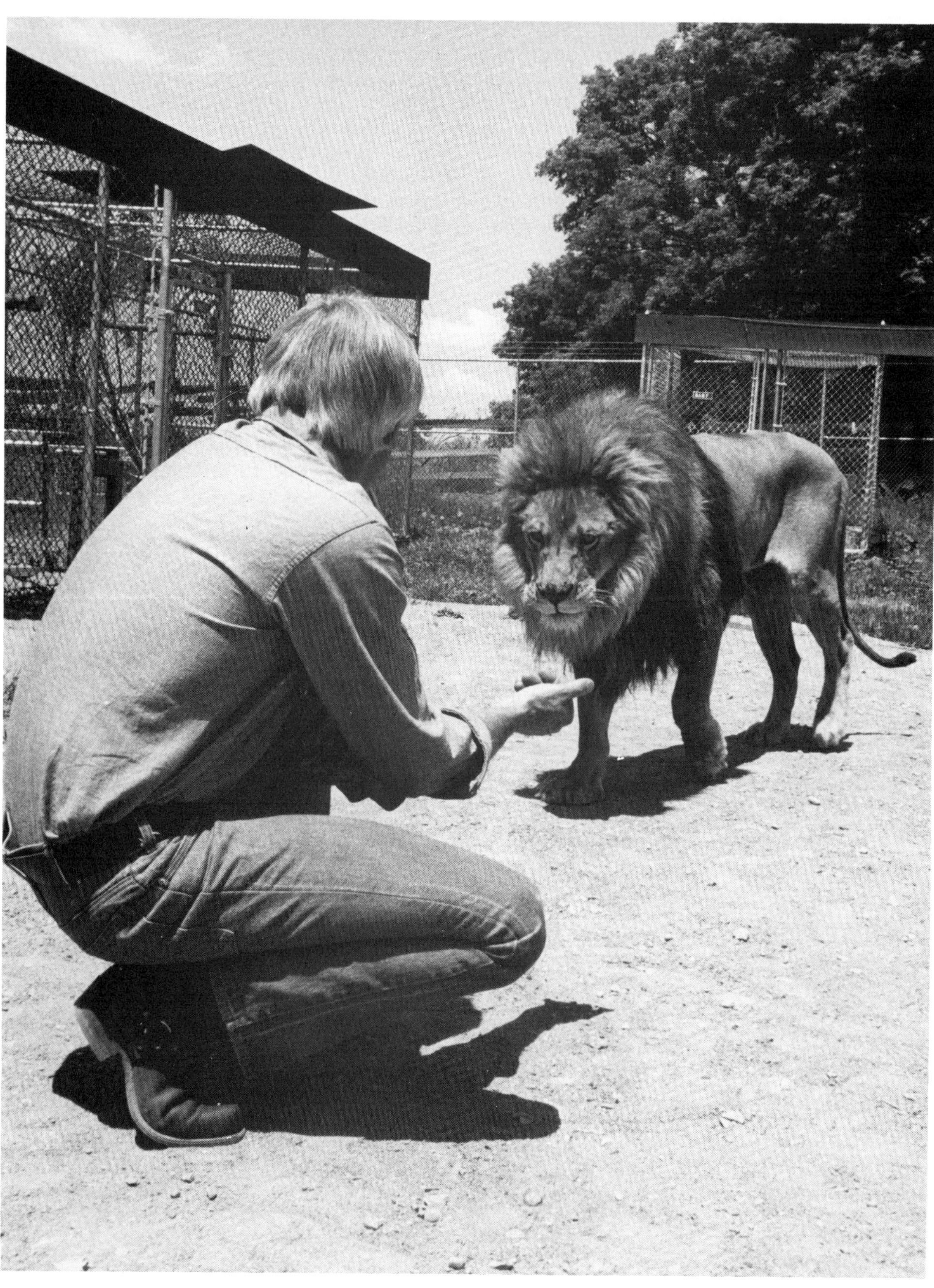

neers. The seventeenth-century sailor engaged Spanish foes in the Caribbean, while halfway around the world a peg-legged coot and a young adventurer named Jim Hawkins fought side by side in *Long John Silver.* Robert Newton portrayed the irascible Robert Louis Stevenson pirate.

Youngsters saw repeats of John Russell playing a spirited American mercenary in *Soldiers of Fortune* and Richard Webb surveying American soil in *U.S. Border Patrol. Dick Tracy* (starring Ralph Byrd) captured the same criminals on Saturday morning that he had when episodes aired originally on ABC in 1950 and 1951. Roscoe Karns also chased bad guys as plainclothesman *Rocky King, Detective* (originally called *Inside Detective*) when the series premiered on DuMont in 1950.

And *The Last of the Mohicans,* with John Hart and Lon Chaney, Jr., had its last shot at TV audiences on Saturday in many locales.

Opposite: Michael J. Reynolds portrayed a widower who cared for two teen-age children and wild animals in NBC's 1977 adventure series Search and Rescue: The Alpha Team.

The Red Hand Gang (clockwise, top left, *James Bond, Jolie Newman, J. R. Miller, and Matthew Laborteaux, with Boomer the dog), an NBC serialized 1977 urban adventure program.*

Casey Jones rolled onto the schedule in 1957. The non-network train series, set in the late 1800s, was as unsuccessful attracting people as Amtrak often is today.

"I thought Casey Jones was a nice character and the program was entertaining, but we didn't seem to click," says series lead Alan Hale, Jr. "We were betwixt and between whether we should make *Casey* for adults or for kids. Apparently it showed."

Appearing with Hale in the Screen Gems production were Bobby Clark as Casey, Jr. and Mary Lawrence as Casey's wife, Alice. Eddy Waller played conductor Red Rock, and Dub Taylor was fireman Willie Sims. The production checked out of the Columbia Pictures lot in Hollywood to shoot at fifty-two miles of track laid for a lumber company in central California. With some additional dressing, the makeshift backdrop became Jackson, Tennessee, circa 1880, and the program's steam engine passed for Illinois Central Railroad Number 382—the Cannonball Express.

The existing facilities required Hale to disregard an important railroad rule. The train yard was too crammed to position cameras and lights on the right side of the engine, so actors boarded and departed from the opposite side—the reverse of safe and standard procedure. The Brotherhood of Railroad Engineers pointed out to Hale that he worked the "dead man side of the track," and as a result they would not give him an honorary engineer's card.

In 1961 the program was televised in England, where the screen direction matched railroad regulations. "They had no problem with the setup there. For them, I got in and out on the correct side of the track," Hale says.

The studio shot twenty-six episodes of *Casey Jones.* Hale, who costarred in *Gilligan's Island* and today runs a West Hollywood restaurant called The Lobster Barrel, admits, "I've never seen any of them."

In the early 1960s, reruns of Lloyd Bridges' 1958–59 *Sea Hunt* series were released for Saturday morning along with *Sea Hawk,* an adventure show with John Howard as an ocean-bound detective. A decade after the aquanauts dried off, Joe and Ken Jones became kings of the sea as Captain Chet King and Kip King, stars of *Barrier Reef.* The NBC Saturday morning children's show premiered September 11, 1971, and lasted for one year. The program was set in Australia, where the marine biologists studied the shoal in their windjammer, the *Endeavor.*

In 1977, William D'Angelo, Ray Allen, and

Harvey Bullock delivered *The Red Hand Gang* into the palms of NBC programmers. The thirty-minute series chronicled the adventures of five city kids and halfheartedly revitalized the once popular cliff-hanger technique. Tales were extended over four or five episodes, during which time the gang would struggle and ultimately endure everything but the ratings.

The same season, NBC tried to win the audience's affection with animals. But even the Canadian import *Search and Rescue: The Alpha Team* could not best ABC's *Super Friends.* Michael J. Reynolds portrayed widower Bob Donell. Donann Cavin and Michael Tough played his daughter and son. The trio attempted to save endangered species from extinction, but the Alpha Team, could not even save itself. It was gone in 1978.

By the 1970s, the flesh and bones human heroes had lost to the celluloid cartoon figure. Animation had conquered the previously live-action medium. Occasionally a network would commission a producer to make a new live-action assault against the cartoon kingdom, but such attacks usually proved to be suicide missions. *Barrier Reef, The Red Hand Gang,* and *Search and Rescue: The Alpha Team* were three of the last kamikazes.

Industry rulings, parental concern, convincing lobbyists, and network fear had made the once invincible Saturday morning hero impotent. The weekend warriors became weak-kneed snivelers. Lone rangers were replaced by team players, and daring sky marshals were shot down. Where gallant captains, romantic swashbucklers, mounted police, and foot soldiers had once been in force, children's TV was invaded by friendly ghosts, fantastic foursomes, oversized puppets, and super presidents, men, women, and dogs.

The new Saturday morning heroes who would happen along had no old-fashioned moxie. They were designed to pass tough oversight standards but not to win any hand-to-hand combat. Only UHF and independent stations kept an active film-library card, but even they found that cartoon repeats were usually more competitive against the networks than dated live-action adventures.

FAIR RODEO

8 Batteries Not Included

Nostalgia merchants have placed a hefty price tag on popular culture. And millions of people, clutching for childhood memorabilia they had thrown in the garbage in the course of growing up, are now willing to pay top dollar for comparatively worthless items.

How strange it is that thirty-year-old comic books are often more valuable than rare first-edition books from the eighteenth century. Who would have expected that the brightly colored plastic products marketed with short-lived TV shows would exist long past the time the black-and-white kinescopes faded to soft grays.

And yet, Ovaltine's Captain Midnight decoder badges that once cost twenty-five cents currently sell for forty dollars. Free 1954 membership certificates to Rin Tin Tin can be bought for five dollars. NBC canceled *Howdy Doody* because the show couldn't make money, but today any merchandise with the character's name on it brings a small fortune. And hardware from *Rod*

Leo Carillo rides atop a specially designed 1952 Chrysler Town and Country convertible. On the front, The Cisco Kid's *costar's custom-made auto had a pair of Texas steer horns measuring seventy-four inches across. The cow's eyes blinked. The car's horn simulated the bellow of a steer. The upholstery was genuine cowhide. Sheet metal was painted gold. Also pictured are Joseph A. O'Malley, assistant general sales manager, at the wheel, and Chrysler president David A. Wallace, standing beside the vehicle.*

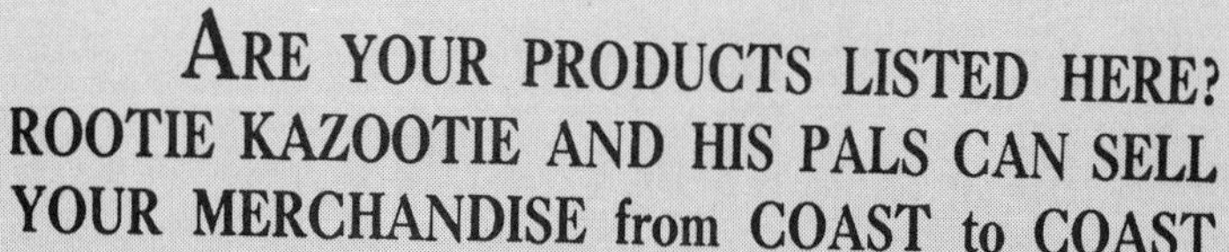

Every merchandise category is available for Rootie Kazootie licensing. Below is a sample listing.

Wearing Apparel and Accessories
Knitwear
Pajamas and Sleeping Garments
Hats and Caps
Piece Goods, Fabrics and Silks
Neckwear and Scarves
Rainwear and Umbrellas
Beach Clothes and Accessories
Play Clothes and Accessories
Athletic Clothes and Equipment

Plastic and Rubber Products
Furniture and Furnishings
School Supplies
Musical Instruments
Games, Novelties and Puzzles
Toys and Electrical Gadgets
Books, Comic Books, Paint Books
Phonographs, Radios and Records
Dolls
Leather Goods

Hand Bags and Muffs
Puppets and Marionettes
Gloves and Mittens
Costume Jewelry
Watches and Bands
Glassware, Dishes, Linens
Lighting Fixtures
Food Products
Toiletries
Motion Pictures

LICENSEES WILL HAVE AVAILABLE TO THEM THE SERVICES OF ONE OF THE NATION'S FOREMOST MERCHANDISING ORGANIZATIONS

ROOTIE KAZOOTIE Inc.
Bruno-New York Building

Kukla, Fran, Ollie and Beulah Witch return home after a day at the Fair.

Cut this out and mail with 10¢ to
Little Nipper Club
509 West 56th St.
New York 19, N. Y.
You then become a member of my club.
LITTLE NIPPER

(Insert Dime Here)

Mail to:
Little Nipper Club, 509 West 56th St., New York (19) N. Y.
I like your records, and I would like to join your "Little Nipper" Record Club. Enclosed is my ten cents for membership dues for one year. I am ______ years old. My birthday is ______
Please send me my Club Pin and Membership Card.

My Name is ______
I live at ______
City ______ Zone ______ State ______

Parents!
Little Nipper Club Members will receive
1 Membership card
2 Little Nipper Club Pin
3 Letters from "Little Nipper"
4 Mailings from record and entertainment celebrities
5 Periodic mailings of the "Little Nipper" News—containing stories, games, comics, news on music and entertainment of interest to children
There is no obligation, other than the ten cents "dues" which helps to cover cost of mailings!
Offer expires September 1, 195[illegible]

Brown of the Rocket Rangers and *Tom Corbett* is as cherished by collectors as moon rocks are by geologists.

Few children, however, were ever enterprising enough to know that cereal box freebees would be worth anything. And still fewer adults wanted to keep the toys after their youngsters discarded them, particularly in an increasingly mobile society. A 1950s-conscious public is now paying for their myopia.

Actually, premium peddlers never intended to make their wares more important than their TV shows. Only time has done that.

"When a program is on the air for more than one year, we stand the chance of selling merchandise," says Joseph Barbera, cofounder of the Hanna-Barbera cartoon studios. "If it doesn't stay on the air, and the networks don't renew it, then merchandisers just aren't interested."

Barbera explains that a program needs only to be on the air, not in full-time production, to cash in on commercial tie-ins and premium offers. "It started for us in the 1950s when we delivered a full series, then the next year half as many, and the following year a third again. It at least gave manufacturers a chance to do something with Yogi Bear and Huckleberry Hound. So very quickly we did very well in merchandising."

Today, more than 1,500 licensees produce some 4,500 different Hanna-Barbera products from Flintstone window shades to bubble bath and vitamin pills.[1] The animation company also has walk-around costumed versions of its major characters involved in the Ice Capades and other traveling shows, and in the Kings Island, Kings Dominion, and Marineland family parks.

The most convenient way to package TV paraphernalia has been in cereal boxes. Post, General Mills, and Kellogg's have for years wedged TV-related gifts in with their snappy Honeycombs, crackling Rice Krispies, and Sugar Pops. For the regular price of the cereal, kids have gotten a little, often very little, something extra.

Another reliable marketing tactic throughout the 1950s, one usually profitable for a middleman, encouraged kids to clip the box top, side

1. The Television Bureau of Advertising reported that in 1971, $4.7-million was spent advertising children's vitamins. Of that amount, $4-million went into children's shows. In 1972 three major drug companies agreed to end vitamin advertising on children's television in response to pressure from Action for Children's Television. The companies—Miles Laboratories, Bristol-Myers and Hoffmann-LaRoche separately agreed to discontinue airing the ads during kidvid hours. Hudson Drugs followed suit in 1976.

panel, product label, or other required manufacturer's logo and with ten cents or more, write for desired items. The cheap merchandise was then rushed—if four to six weeks can be considered rushed—at a quick profit to the "fulfillment house." This procedure was particularly favored by cereal manufacturers since the premiums usually didn't cost them anything and often resulted in higher sales.

"It's called a self-liquidating premium," says Buffalo Bob Smith. "We used them a great deal. For example, we'd tell kids to buy a box of Kellogg's Rice Krispies, then send in a box top with fifteen cents and we'd return a punch balloon."

The fee would cover the cost of mailing and the premium and still leave a few cents profit. "If they're making even one-and-a-half cents on each toy and they have five million replies, then they've made a tremendous deal," Smith explains.

"We used them all the time," Smith continues, adding that *Howdy Doody* still holds the all-time record for successful self-liquidating premiums. "We'd plug the hell out of them. We used the punch balloon throughout the show and then I'd say, 'And here's how you can get yours . . .' There'd be a flood of mail, all handled by the premium company."

Escalating postal rates have helped to usher the end of the low-cost premium. Consumer groups and government policymakers have wanted to see them eliminated at any cost.[2]

In 1974, a year in which more than half of all cereals involved some type of premium, Federal Trade Commission chairman Lewis Engman proposed a ban on the practice. He initiated hearings asking the fellow commissioners to prohibit all TV premium offers when the majority of viewers were under 12. A 1972 guideline had restricted premium pitches to 20 seconds within a one-minute commercial.

In calling for the hearings, Engman maintained that premiums were "unfair to children." Robert Thurston, senior vice-president of Quaker Oats disagreed slightly. He said they were unfair, but unfair to many advertisers. "It would

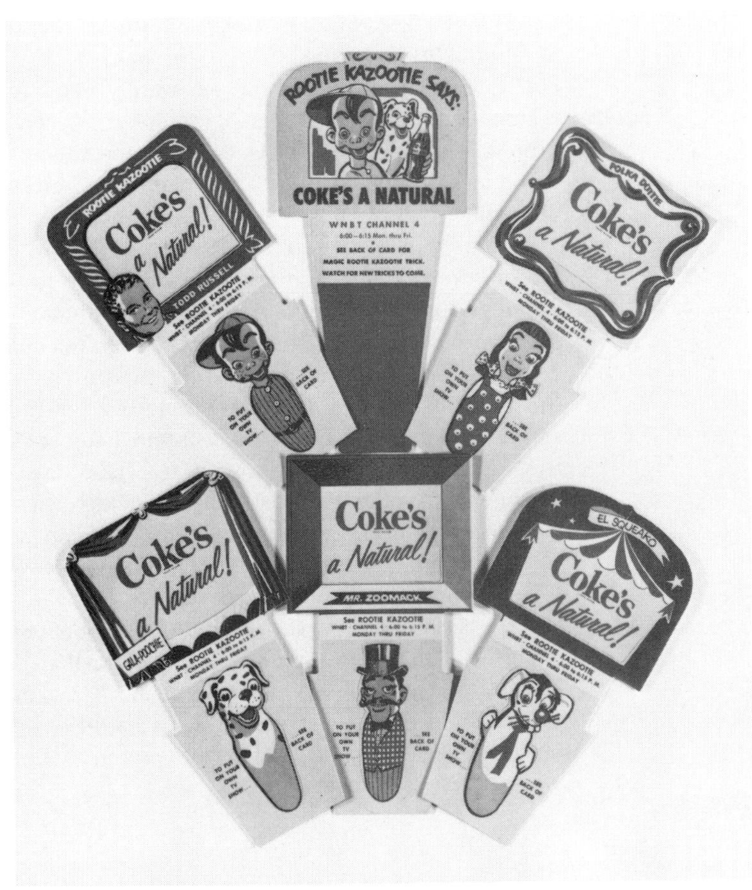

Coca-Cola premiums from NBC's 1950 puppet show Rootie Kazootie.

2. In 1969, ABC tried to revive the glory days of premium offers by introducing its own self-liquidating incentive. *Super Saturday Club* invited kids to send in fifty cents for a membership card, badge, pennant, poster with network cartoon characters, and a book of premium coupons. For a nominal fee and a coupon, ABC would send out another network-related tie-in each month.

be good for everyone if a way could be found to eliminate premiums. When we tried to discontinue them on our own, we were forced to resume premiums because of competitive conditions," he said. Quaker Oats attempted to market educational items, but the maneuver failed all commercial tests.

In the 1974 testimony before the FTC, Action for Children's Television also applauded the proposed ruling. ACT officials said that the inducements promote unfair competition. "Only a small group of manufacturers can afford to purchase the number of spots which are required for the saturation tactics typically used in television selling to children. The children's television premium is an effective instrument for diverting customers from smaller firms which can compete in quality and price, but cannot sustain the cost of a national advertising campaign."

The Premium Advertisers Association of America termed the proposal "drastic." Kellogg's argued that premiums were crucial. Cracker Jacks proposed a compromise. Kids could write for premiums without buying the product. The Premium Merchandise Club of New York insisted that "there is no rational justification for the cost of offering a premium if the purchase requirement is eliminated."

In 1976, Quaker Oats reversed its position, stating that premiums were not overly manipulative. And within a year the FTC concluded that there was insufficient evidence that TV advertisements that induced kids to buy cereals and other products by offering them toys or prizes as come-ons were "inherently or invariably unfair or deceptive."

Though the ban did not pass, self-liquidating premiums have generally self-liquidated. Part of the decline can be attributed to a 1972 National Association of Broadcasters' provision that prohibited children's show hosts or cartoon and puppet characters from participating in commercials during their own programs or typical kidvid hours.[3]

3. Despite the NAB ruling, in 1977 nationwide monitors of the Massachusetts-based Action for Children's Television found children's hosts still pitching merchandise, stores, and amusement parks in four cities.

Opposite: In 1949, DuMont's Small Fry Club *offered viewers a beany if they'd send in a Kolynos ™ toothpaste carton and a quarter. In four weeks the network received 20,000 requests. Besides beanies, Big Brother Bob Emery merchandised puppets and shirts.*

SMALL FRY CLUB
BIG BROTHER
Bob Emery
SMALL FRY CLUB
SMALL FRY CLUB
BIG BROTHER
SMALL FRY CLUB
SMALL FRY CLUB
SMALL FRY CLUB

Insofar as commercial tie-ins are concerned, size has never been a restriction. Merchandise too big to fit in cereal boxes or too expensive to send through the mail has been sold over the counter.

Perhaps the greatest American TV figure of all time to exercise his sales options was Howdy Doody.

Bob Smith first gauged the show's commercial impact in March 1948 when a toy buyer for Macy's contacted him. "He said he'd been having requests for Howdy Doody dolls. They had none, but he was interested in making some," Smith recalls. "Thereafter, licensees came pounding on our door. One later said that the Jordan Marsh department store in Boston had bought all the products and they thought they could sell a helluva order if we would make a personal appearance. I'll never forget what happened. We went up September 24, 1948, and I thought we'd be there a half an hour and see a couple of hundred kids. But my God! There had to have been six blocks of people. We had only been on the air for some nine months and it was unbelievable."

Smith, Clarabell, Howdy, and puppeteer Rhoda Mann stayed at the store for four hours and entertained thousands of youngsters. "I said that if it was this way in Boston, it had to be the same in Philadelphia, New York, and Wash-

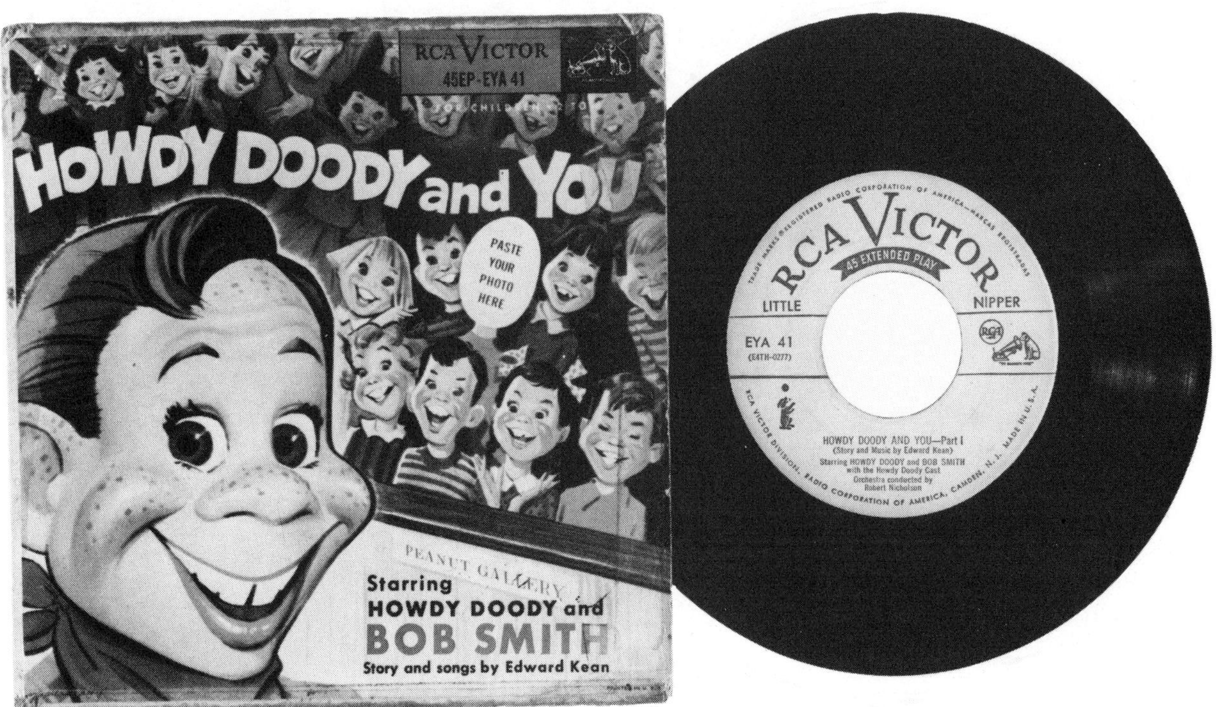

ington. I realized that this thing was dynamite."

Advertisers were finding *Howdy Doody* equally explosive. The NBC sales manager said the show was TV's "greatest success story—the most forceful demonstration to date of television's drawing power."

By the fall of 1948 clothing manufacturers had reported that they had tried Howdy on for size and felt the show was custom-made for tie-ins. Other companies flooded NBC. *Variety* predicted the puppet was sure to "become the Mickey Mouse of the TV era."

Howdy Doody, Inc. was formed to handle the volume of licensing requests. Already five clothing firms had been signed. With record and book deals close to completion, the puppet was about to become TV's most valuable salesman. In January 1949, *Howdy Doody* viewers were offered a humming lariat for two Mason Candy Company wrappers. The give-away was mentioned on five shows.

Meanwhile, Bob Smith was as well received in other cities as he had been in Boston. On February 26, 1949, he made a long-awaited appearance at Macy's in New York and was greeted with fans who had waited long in line. Anxious kids were bombarded with Howdy Doody merchandise as they stood for hours. Records played continuously in the background. Display after display of Doodyville salables filled the counters.

Soon Howdy's name was baked onto Ovaltine mugs and stitched into ninety-eight-cent bow ties, suspenders, and belts. Matching shirts and sweaters were sold for $3.49 to $4.98.

Poll-Parrot Shoes produced a Howdy Doody album that was given away with each purchase. As a result of a single announcement on the show, J. L. Hudson Company in Detroit phoned in an order for 1,000 additional records. The Philadelphia Gimbels' outlet reported selling 200 in one day, and youngsters were seen queued up in front of stores in New York.

"We also had a Howdy Doody beany," Smith remembers. "We'd have every kid in the Peanut Gallery wear one. The next day, stores would run out of them. And of course, I wore Howdy T-shirts when they came out," Smith adds. "We gave them out at the show, and the kids wore them too. You can guess what happened next."

Supervisory chores shifted from Howdy Doody Inc. to Kagran Corporation in January 1951. The newly formed company, co-owned by Bob Smith

eg R-1485-21-2

(Revised)

AUDIO	VIDEO
HOWDY: Why, it's ME........ But what am I doing up there?	HOWDY, FOLLOWING CLARABELL's GESTURING, SEES HIMSELF ON SCREEN, WALKS OVER TO IT
SMITH: Don't you see, Howdy? It's that swell big cut-out of you that Poll-Parrot has been giving the kids.	SMITH STANDING ON OPPOSITE SIDE OF CENTER SCREEN INDICATES IT AS HE TALKS ACROSS TO HOWDY
HOWDY: Well, so it is! Gee, it's almost like looking in a mirror!	LEANS OVER FROM END OF DESK, INSPECTING HIMSELF ON THE SCREEN
SMITH: Sure, it looks just like you! That's why so many of the boys and girls have been wanting this cut-out.	SMITH ON OPPOSITE SIDE OF CENTER SCREEN REPLIES TO HOWDY, FIRST TWO SENTENCES
And because there are so many who haven't been able to get it yet, Poll-Parrot has decided to extend this offer just two weeks more!	SMITH, STANDING IN FRONT OF HOWDY IMAGE ON SCREEN, ADDRESSES CAMERA ON SENTANCE BEGINNING "AND BECAUSE"
Yes, kids, here's your chance to get this swell cut-out of Howdy -- in full color, real as life! All you do is have your Mom or Daddy take you to the store where you get Poll-Parrot Shoes, and ask for YOUR Howdy Doody cut-out ! They'll be glad to give it to you!	CENTER CURTAIN CLOSES & LIGHTS COME UP FOR LINE BEGINNING "YES, KIDS"--SMITH WITH ACTUAL CUT-OUT IN HAND, HOLDS IT TOWARD CAMERA, POINTS AT IT SMITH PUTS CUT-OUT DOWN BY LIVE HOWDY AT END OF SPEECH

from the collection of Burt Dubrow

Left: A Poll-Parrot shoe commercial from a 1950 Howdy Doody *script* and Martin Stone, purchased all rights to the puppet. Stone, acting as general manager, cleared licensing activities. Smith served as agent and continued to host the show. The firm was backed on Wall Street. After Kagran signed a long-term contract with NBC, financial observers described the transaction as one of the major capital-gains deals of the year.

One if its first pacts involved the production of Howdy Doody Eggs by White Gold Enterprises of Lakewood, New Jersey. Cartons featured cut-outs of the puppets and actual pictures of Howdy were stamped on the eggs.

"At one time we had three of our Howdy Doody albums among the ten top records," Smith adds. "Of course, whenever we had one out, we'd play it on the air and act it out to help it sell."

By the end of 1957, total gross sales of *Howdy Doody*–licensed merchandise was estimated at $25 million.

Howdy Doody had a powerful impact on the American public, and Buffalo Bob Smith was a financial guru with all the attendant benefits. Children considered him a hero. Popular culture has termed Smith a legend. But Buffalo Bob Smith, self-effacing in retirement, acknowledges, "We were real hucksters. You might say we were real whores."

"The whole damn business is prostitution," says Jim Brown, star of *The Adventures of Rin Tin Tin*. "We marketed products all the time. Presumably we were cut in for a percentage of the producer's percentage, but I don't recall seeing a penny of it."

"We never did anything like that," says *Sky King* star, Kirby Grant. "We never did that unfortunately," he adds for emphasis. "Nabisco wouldn't allow it. I don't know why. I wanted to desperately. I submitted plan after plan for shirts, hats, guns, planes, and all the things that were great to sell and would have made so much money on the side. But they turned everything down."[4]

In the 1950s, deals were regularly negotiated without the TV stars pulling a share of the wealth card. "A merchandising corporation was set up on *Wild Bill Hickok* without our knowledge," says the series' lead, Guy Madison. "We really

SOUND

HOWDY DOODY (SINGS)

Brush your teeth with COLGATE'S (COLGATE DENTAL CREAM)

It cleans your breath (what a toothpaste!)

While it cleans your teeth

Cleans your breath

And it tastes so good!

BOB SMITH

Howdy and I both hope you'll brush your teeth with COLGATE'S every time right after eating--because that's a proved, effective way to help stop tooth decay before it starts.

HOWDY DOODY

That's right, kids! So for happy teeth, remember to use COLGATE DENTAL CREAM the way Mr. Smith told you! And don't forget COLGATE DENTAL CREAM, with its swell [illegible] flavor, comes in a red and white box...

(SINGS)

You know it's right

If it's red and white!

from the collection of Burt Dubrow

Above: A Howdy Doody *Colgate commercial from a 1950s script*

4. Sky King toys were in short supply in the Nabisco years, but earlier, Peter Pan peanut butter initiated a number of innovative children's safety campaigns with related premiums.

Burr Tillstrom:

We worked the commercials right into the plot. They just gave us the facts and said use it anyway you want to. Sometimes they were getting five-minute commercials, and that's why our shows couldn't be repeated.

Pinky Lee:

I don't think any sponsor ever got shortchanged on my show. If they bought a minute, they could rest assured they'd get a minute and a half.

Soupy Sales:

I certainly gave sponsors more than a minute's time. It's really an endorsement. But I turned down commercials if I didn't believe in a product.

Claude Kirchner:

Most of us got a piece of the action in those days. There were almost no restrictions. On the local cartoon programs, particularly, we really loaded the things with commercials. It was pretty shady stuff, and I don't suppose it showed much character on the part of the stations, but I don't think it did any harm. The broadcasters were just greedy.

LEARN TO DRAW

WITH

JON GNAGY

America's television art instructor

didn't have a damned thing to say. We were just told to do the commercials for the show—you know, the ones where we'd shoot off the guns—boom, boom—and the announcer would say 'Sugar Pops are Tops.' "

Peter Graves also remembers that marketing was downplayed on *Fury*. With the exception of the usual lunch boxes and shirts, he says, "we didn't do much at all. The show just wasn't marketed properly."

Other producers were more willing to cash the merchandising buck rather than pass it.

The most successful of all was *Hopalong Cassidy*. In the early 1950s, Hoppy products were said to be bringing in $70 million annually.

The lonesome cowboy used his maximum exposure to sell the heritage of the West and his Hollywood name. In 1950 alone he was seen on 63 TV stations, heard on 152 radio outlets, and read in 155 newspapers. Well over 100 manufacturers were turning out Hoppy merchandise including shirts and pants to wear during the day and Hoppy pajamas for night. Hopalong Cassidy wallpaper outsold all other designs, and Hoppy bicycles, with handlebars shaped like

steer horns and room for a six-shooter in the frame, were peddled fast by department stores.

Boyd refused to license bubble gum, but sold his name to candy bars, peanut butter, cookies, and pocket knives. Kids bought Hoppy watches, compasses, hair cream, toothpaste, records, guns, roller skates complete with spurs and jewel-studded ankle straps, hats, chaps, books, and belts.

Boyd claimed that he always insisted on good quality before making a deal, turned down nine out of ten offers, and awarded 56 percent of his contracts to American firms.

"We aren't going to overdo it," he promised a *Time* interviewer in 1950, a year that grossed him $800,000. "We'll just keep throwing wood on the fire. We don't think it's phenomenal. Years ago a fellow got an idea to build a bridge across San Francisco Bay. People told him he was nuts. One morning he looked up and traffic was going across. Hopalong Cassidy was merely an idea that took thirteen years to pay off."

Merchandisers found the price of acquiring Hoppy's name worth every plug nickel. Because of the rush for Hopalong Cassidy clothes, the supply of black dyes in the United States was badly strained. Fifteen million comic books taxed the paper industry, and the Los Angeles bakery that had struggled in seventh place for years with Barbara Ann bread galloped forward once it carried Hoppy.

Said Boyd after the first full year of *Hopalong Cassidy* marketing, "I don't think there's any limit to what can be done."[5]

Pulling in right behind Hopalong Cassidy in the sweepstakes was a beautiful horse named Silver and his fearless rider, the Lone Ranger. Sixty items were merchandised in the early 1950s, all helped by radio and TV airplay in every city and print coverage in 250 daily newspapers and 53 foreign publications. Additionally, the masked man appeared in a monthly comic book, a *Silver and Tonto* quarterly, and an annual ninety-eight-page *Lone Ranger Treasury*. Better Little Books and Cozy Corner Books published further exploits.

5. An advertising account executive explained the phenomenon of TV marketing this way: "If we had a product and felt it appealed to kids, we just put it on Saturday. We could make an industry overnight." Jon Hall, who portrayed Ramar of the Jungle, seemed to agree. "We were one of Bosco's first sponsors as I recall. They were a small operation and we actually helped make their company."

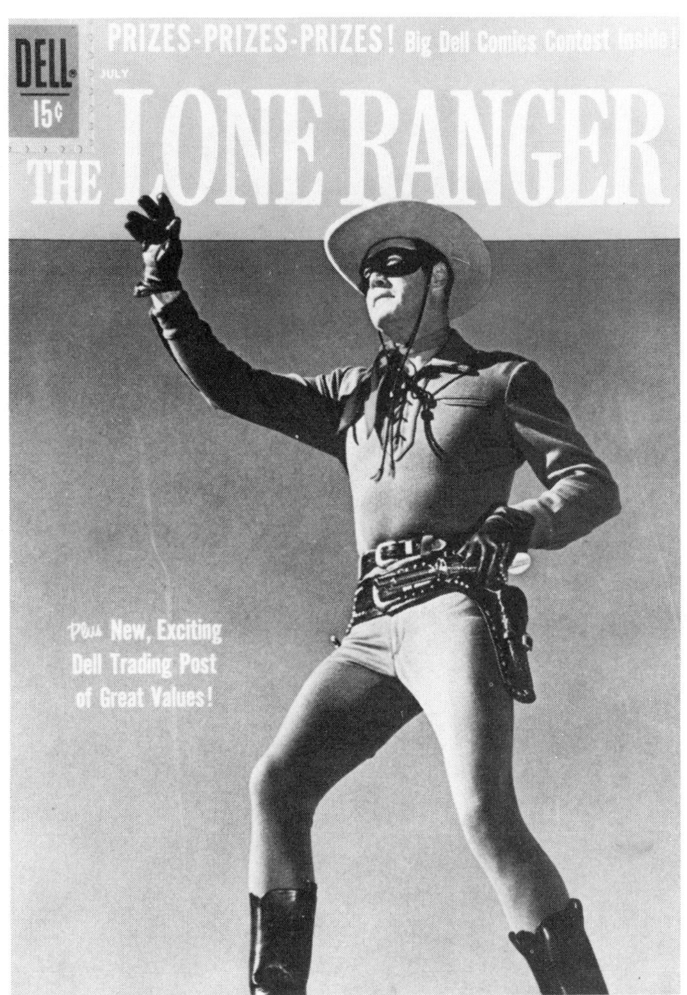

VARIETY, December 13, 1952:

It's argued by some sponsors that although kids are watching as much as ever, they can't attribute sales to their pitches for minors. Their reason, that in the early days of TV, mom was in the living room with the younger set. But today, she lets the receiver baby sit. Thus, it's argued the kiddie bank-roller is reaching only non-buyers. These sponsors add, however, that when a premium pitch is made, the small fry will badger parents into getting them box tops proving their ability to sell.

The Lone Ranger in two media: TV and Sunday comics

With the Lone Ranger stories visible or audible everywhere, the public was ripe for further exploitation.

The *Lone Ranger* was once described as a "corporation on horseback." A commercial stampede might be more to the point. Silver bullets were shot into the market. Kids bought records, guns, and hobbyhorses and sent for membership cards and pedometers, and viewers cut out cardboard pistols from Cheerios boxes.

Gene Autry had been merchandising his name seventeen years before his 1951 TV show signed on. But the new medium did wonders for the old hand, considering that in addition to his own series Autry also holstered rights to *The Range Rider*, *Buffalo Bill, Jr.* and *Annie Oakley*.

The price-span for Flying A Production wares varied from the ten-cent Gene Autry club cards to the $135 Range Rider coats in Saks Fifth Avenue and Nieman-Marcus. Besides the typical rings, guns, belt buckles, comics, and records, Autry licensed buckskin outfits that matched his character's garb, a singing cowboy harmonica, and an Annie Oakley sewing kit. Milky Way issued Buffalo Bill iron-on patterns, and T.V. Time popcorn gave away 1,500 Oakley dolls to lucky girls and stagecoaches to an equal number of boys who sent in the best drawings of their favorite toys.

Roy Rogers found gold in the Hollywood hills. By 1956 his merchandising corporation was grossing $50 million annually on the sale of one million pairs of jeans, two million lunch kits, and hundreds of thousands of pencil boxes; miniature cowboys, horses, and Double R Bar ranches; guns, shirts, and 350 other items. Of course, not all the money went to the bank. Roy Rogers Enterprises employed more than 2,000 people throughout the country and spent as much as $50,000 a year answering fan mail.

While the cowboys kept young buckeroos in clover with merchandise and premiums, TV's astronauts catered to the budding space cadets.

Tom Corbett settled into a commercial orbit in the early 1950s with an assortment of far-out tie-ins. "Kids began buying everything with the name Corbett on it," says the grown-up cadet, Frank Thomas. "In some respects that

Above: Roy Rogers reads his comic-strip exploits to his son Dusty (left) *and two youngsters (1950).*

A Post Cereal premium

provided a considerable help to the show's popularity, but I wasn't associated with them."

In all, there were 135 separate Corbett selections including lunch boxes, hardcover books, watches, and space goggles.

The space vehicle was fueled by Kellogg's. For the going rate of twenty-five cents, kids would receive a membership card, a badge with the Space Academy emblem, a patch, a certificate, and an autographed picture. For a time fellow cadets also received the Space Academy newspaper.

"If you have any of the things around today," Thomas advises, "hang on to them. They're worth quite a bit of money."

While Captain Video drifted in space between 1949 and 1957, commercial tie-ins kept him close to a hundred manufacturing plants. For a quarter and a cereal-box top, children could purchase the character's most desired self-liquidating premium, a Captain Video ring. Post sent a Captain Video helmet to video rangers who mailed in one dollar and a box top.

Not to be outdone, for a wrapper and twenty-five cents, the manufacturers of Power House™ candy bars offered a plastic ray gun that shot a beam of light and a "Lumo-Glo" card that directed a ray with secret symbols. Captain Video games also spun into stores along with dishes and bed spreads.

Tragically, though the *Captain Video* merchandise is valuable to collectors, the man who played the TV astronaut died in 1979, penniless and in obscurity. Al Hodge, radio's Green Hor-

Below: Space Patrol *merchandise*

Captain Midnight Premiums

1952—59
Television

1952
Captain Midnight Hot Ovaltine Mug

1953
Captain Midnight Hot Ovaltine Mug
Captain Midnight Shake-up Mug

1954
Cold Ovaltine Shake-Up Mugs
Captain Midnight Hot Mug

1955
Captain Midnight Shake-Up Mug
Secret Squadron Decoder Badge
Captain Midnight Photo

1956
Captain Midnight Shake-Up Mug
Secret Squadron Decoder Badge
Captain Midnight Photo
Flight Commander Certificates
Flight Commander Commission

1957
Captain Midnight Silver Dart Decoder Badge
Flight Commander Signet Ring
Shake-Up (Fifteenth Anniversary Offer)
Hot Ovaltine Mug (Fifteenth Anniversary Offer)

1959
Captain Midnight Hot Mug
Captain Midnight Shake-Up Mug
Flight Commander Ring

Above: The Captain Midnight Secret Squadron emblem

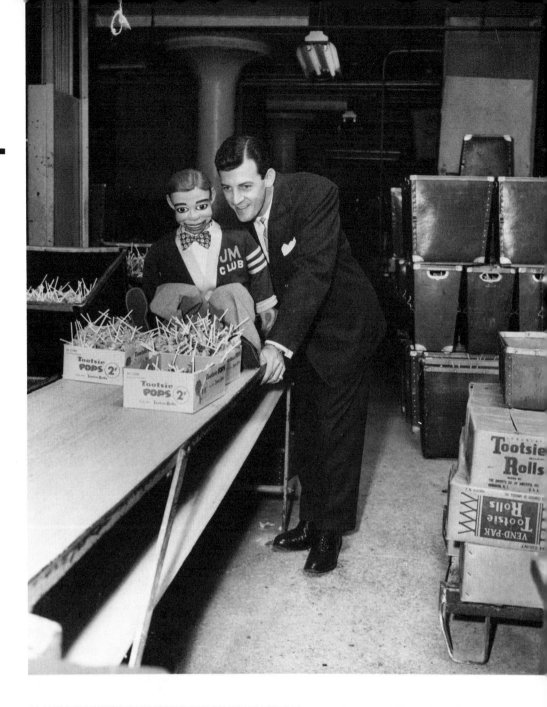

Above: Paul Winchell guides Jerry Mahoney down the conveyor belt with boxes of Tootsie Pops™ during a visit to his sponsor's factory.

Left: A familiar refrain . . .

net as well as Captain Video, had not acted in years. He had been typecast as the character, and while others became rich on his commercial pitches, the science fiction hero had no future.

Cliff Robertson's science fiction collectibles, on the other hand, were never as coveted as the *Captain Video* products, but the actor's career rebounded after he abandoned his rocket ship and space junk.

For twenty-five cents and a box top, Robertson's *Rod Brown* viewers could receive a certificate signifying admission to the Rocket Rangers Officer Corps, identification cards for friends, and the Junior Rocket Ranger Oath (see Chapter XIV, "The Cold War Brigade").

Sylvania, meanwhile, hoped to sell television sets when kids dragged their parents to the store for the Buck Rogers space ranger punch-out kits. Sets sold, but Rogers didn't.

Space Patrol gave the scientific age a boost and the cardboard industry a lift. For the proper cutouts from a Ralston Wheat or Rice Chex box and some silver, kids received a makeshift Space Patrol City that could transform any 1952 living room into a thirtieth-century rocket port. A mailing to Nestlé's, *Space Patrol*'s other sponsor, would bring a cardboard rocket cockpit certain to whisk away any youngster with a rich imagination.

Between battles with alien forces, Buzz Corry also pushed *Space Patrol* binoculars and periscopes. After Corry sent a flashlight signal to Cadet Happy in one episode, kids were offered a similar model. Following a trip to an aboriginal tract of Mars, cardboard totem heads were sold for stacking, saving, and swapping. And when the cadets wore hats merchandisers were quick to respond with a chapeau that bore the commander's insignia.

Space Patrol communicators were sold, though the same effect could be achieved for free with two empty juice cans and a taut string. When junior patrollers wanted to talk secretly they used their decoder attached to a buckle that glowed in the dark. And presumably for defense purposes, when danger neared, the Cosmic Smoke Gun fired clouds of smoke. After the explosion cleared up, however, there was baking soda to clean up. A superhero's work could indeed be messy business.

In July 1951, where Western wear once sold in Los Angeles's May Company department store, decorators and merchandisers pooled efforts to install a full-scale replica of the interplanetary battle cruiser *Terra*, stacked with Space Patrol helmets, shirts, and pajamas. By noon of the first day Earth-bound police were summoned to calm the throng of thirty-thousand kids who had jammed the store.

Space Patrol's most impressive excursion into marketing—in fact the biggest premium ever offered to TV audiences—was still to come. In 1953, Ralston-Purina toured the country with a thirty-five-foot-long promotional vehicle—a sleek mock-up of the rocketship *Terra*, roomy enough to sleep eight. The $30,000 model traveled on a truck-bed, promoting the show, its sponsor, and a contest to rename Planet X, home of evil Prince Baccarratti.

The *Terra* was ultimately awarded to a contest winner, Ricky Walker of Washington, Illinois, for his entry, "Cesaria." On January 14, 1954, the ship was delivered to Walker. The ceremony was highlighted by a parade and a grade school pageant. The mayor proclaimed January 16 "Ricky Walker Day" in honor of its local space son.

A few years after Walker won the ship, his parents sold it to a traveling carnival outfit for $1,000. Eventually two Quincy, Illinois, residents, Harry and Eleanor Nolin, acquired the rocket and outfitted the ship as a mobile NASA museum. As recently as 1980 the Nolins reported they constantly received calls from across the country and are even bombarded with purchase offers from film producers.

Rocky Jones, Space Ranger also explored varying commercial possibilities. Before the show signed on in 1952, twenty-three manufacturers were contracted to market clothing, toys, records, and novelties. Whitman Publishing agreed to print a comic book two years before the first airdate.

Ovaltine, a merchandising leader since the radio years, stirred up the TV market with Shake-Up Mugs on *Howdy Doody* and *Captain Midnight*. The *Captain Midnight*–Ovaltine relationship was initially successful, but the drink and the corporate orders did not always go down smoothly with star Richard Webb.

"I wouldn't drink it. They'd scream at me, because I'd pick up the cup and say, 'Kids, drink it like we do here at headquarters.' I'd move it toward my lips and the account executive would motion for me to sip. I'd grin and move it a little closer. I'd hear, 'Drink it!' It would go closer, but I wouldn't."

"I didn't care," Webb explains. "I wasn't going to because I had a running feud going with the Ovaltine people. Other guys who were doing cereal pitches were getting trips around the planet and their wives were getting fur coats. I only made one special request. I told the president of the company that there were a bunch of boys and girls out here in the San Fernando Valley schools that were broke. They couldn't afford Ovaltine. All I wanted was to get a few cases and give them the bottles so they could cut out the waxed paper disc and send it in and become a member. He said fine, took out a notepad, and wrote a message for me that said: 'To the manager of a local market: This will identify Mr. Webb who plays the role of Captain Midnight on TV. Please allow him to purchase all of the Ovaltine that he wants at cost.' " Webb was furious.

The waxed disc in each jar was the membership requirement for admittance to Captain Midnight's Secret Squadron. With the seal and a quarter, home members of the SQ received an arm patch embossed with Midnight's jet the *Silver Dart*, an identification card containing the motto, "Justice through Strength and Courage," a manual, a personal code number, and a decoder badge.

With a decoder, viewers could decipher a message given by Webb at the end of each show and know the subject of the next episode. The badge had various translation settings. Almost always, however, the dial was set on B6 when Captain Midnight read the numbers over the air.

Variety congratulated Ovaltine on the *Captain Midnight* promotion in 1955, stating "The bowout gimmick of a television message which only members can decode" is one of the most unique ways seen "to hypo the merchandising." The trade paper also considered Webb's personality a real boon to the show.

In 1955 the Toy Guidance Council, an industry megaphone, decided to spoonfeed the commercial appetite of the nation's youngsters. They cut out the delivery men like Hoppy, Roy, and Tom Corbett and presented a weekly Saturday TV show that had the sole intention of selling toys.

Opposite: Super Circus *star Mary Hartline endorsed a line of dolls dressed in her baton-twirler outfit in 1952. Mary Hartline Enterprises ™ also sold children's wear, toys, and food products.*

Below: A Super Circus *record*

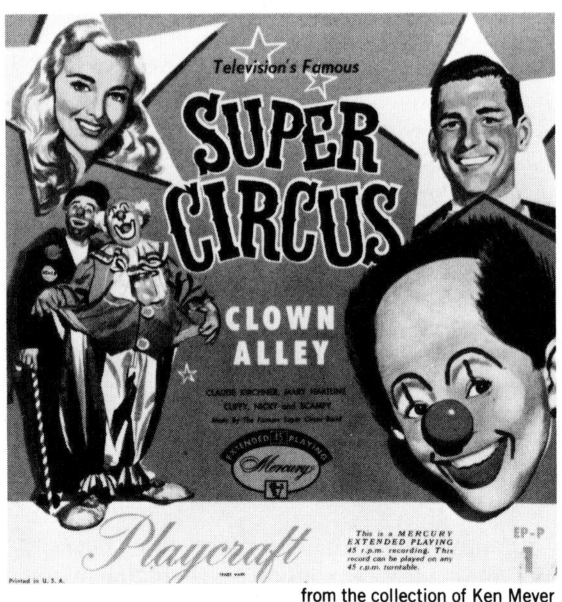

from the collection of Ken Meyer

A Conversation with Farfel

Q. YOU AND JIMMY ARE ONE OF TV'S FAVORITE TEAMS. DO YOU REALLY GET ALONG WELL, FARFEL?

Farfel: Frankly he takes me for granted. He doesn't have to work on material for me. He pulls a string, I open my mouth, and people laugh.

Q. YOU MUST HAVE A SWEET TOOTH, CONSIDERING ALL THOSE NESTLÉ'S COMMERCIALS YOU'VE MADE.

Farfel: Well, I love chocolate, if that's what you mean. And the nice thing about dogs is they don't get acne.

Q. THERE ARE A LOT OF PEOPLE WHO WOULD HAVE YOU REMAIN IN THE DOGHOUSE BECAUSE THEY DON'T THINK CHOCOLATE SHOULD BE ADVERTISED ON CHILDREN'S SHOWS. WOULD YOU BITE THEM IN THE LEGS?

Farfel: I've learned never to bite the legs that feed me. Anyway, I think that all of the sweet tooth things kids and I like should be taken in moderation.

Q. YOU MUST WATCH A GOOD DEAL OF TV. WHAT DO YOU LIKE?

Farfel: I've seen very little except the inside of a suitcase, so I'm really no authority. Jimmy only lets me out once a week to watch *Lassie.*

Q. HAVE YOU EVER THOUGHT ABOUT BREAKING AWAY AND STARTING AN ACT ON YOUR OWN?

Farfel: You want to know something, that's exactly what I'm doing now. I'm on new commercials for Nestlé's. They didn't want Nelson to appear, they just hired me. Folks don't even see him. He lies on the floor and pulls my strings, believe me, and that smarts.

Q. WHY DO YOU ALWAYS SOUND SO SAD EVEN WHEN YOU SAY CHOCOLATE?

Farfel: That's my nature. It's the way I look. I have that dog-eared expression or would you rather I say hangdog expression?

Toyland Express an unadulterated fifteen-minute commercial, premiered three months before Christmas and starred Paul Winchell and Jerry Mahoney. The duo were chosen for their popularity and commercial potential—appropriate casting, since more than 300,000 Jerry Mahoney dolls had been sold during the previous two years.

With Paul Winchell venting his energy directly on other products, the Toy Guidance Council felt they could peak fourth-quarter sales. *Toyland Express,* syndicated to fifty markets, simply showed Winchell and Mahoney playing with various toys and games that were available at any neighborhood department store. Figures proved the program warranted a second run, and in November 1956 the series returned for a 9:45 A.M. Saturday airing with Jimmy Nelson and Danny O'Day replacing Winchell and Mahoney.

David T. Marke, director of the council's educational activities rationalized the show's public-service value by saying that "a girl's layette set may help a young miss to adjust to a new member of the family or that guns give a child respect for law enforcement."

"We ran the show right until Christmas," recalls Jimmy Nelson. "And sure, it was done strictly to promote toys. It was a very loosely strung together commercial. It was hard sell that we tried to make soft by playing with the kids, picking up a toy, talking about it, and taking a little train farther along to do the same at another part of the set."

Considering TV merchandising had literally become a three-ring circus for merchandisers, advertisers, and broadcasters, it was only reasonable for *Big Top* and *Super Circus* to cash in on the concession. In the early 1950s, *Big Top*'s best mail-order premium offers were a two-piece atomic submarine milkshake container and a lazy susan designed by architect Raymond Loewy. The revolving tray could be filled with reusable plastic dishes in which Sealtest sold their cottage cheese.

"We viewed merchandising as an important responsibility," says an advertising executive assigned to the show. "We all felt that we could stimulate Sealtest sales with on-air promotion. It was part of the total package." *Super Circus,*

meanwhile, sold a line of Mary Hartline toys, dolls, and a set of records and books containing stories of fierce animals.

What beasts the circus shows didn't snare, *Ramar of the Jungle* caught for an African display set up in 1954 and 1955 in Philadelphia's Lit Brothers store and in New York's Macy's.

Children were charged twenty-five cents' admission to cover the cost of the $10,000 jungle. For the quarter they'd walk through the artificial surroundings in the converted toy department and eye the exhibits and displays. Children on the paid safari also saw rows of Ramar merchandise including shirts, pith helmets, stuffed animals, air rifles, spears, doctor kits, trousers, and jackets.[6]

Jon Hall, star of the show appeared for the November 1954 opening and was greeted by the mayor, a city zoo chimpanzee, and actress Grace Kelly.

The Philadelphia Zoological Gardens, in turn, received two new inmates compliments of *Ramar*'s candy sponsor, Good and Plenty.™ The adver-

6. Fearful that a bola, a jungle weapon with a lethal-sized rock tied to each end of a leather thong, would be a hazard to children, Hall ruled, "We're definitely not marketing THAT one."

Reflections off the Tube

By Nat Segaloff

No one can learn faster than a child while understanding less. The desire for gratification, coupled with the appeal of commercial products, is often an awesome stimulus aimed directly at youngsters. Yet the information, the spiels, and the images for dolls, cars, and sugar-coated cereals are stored for years even when they're not acted upon immediately.

Our home admitted television about the same time I started school, a coincidence I now view as a blessing—rather like not encountering VD until they had invented penicillin. I never suffered any confusion about which was the show and which was the commercial. That didn't stop me, however, from driving my mom nuts with slogans. Rote learning, I found, was about as easy to control as my bladder.

There's a near-physical satisfaction to the recitation of a rote-learned phrase. Think not? Spell *encyclopedia.* Both of us probably hear Jiminy Cricket singing it from *The Mickey Mouse Club.*

And how many file clerks alphabetize papers to the mental strains of the ABCs as memorized—by rote, of course—from that vaguely remembered children's record (78 rpm, yellow plastic), "Happy, happy, now we'll be/that we've learned our ABCs"?

The phenomenon wasn't limited to TV. Can't you recall, more in your throat than in your mind, the exact order of songs on the Beatles' "Sgt. Pepper" album?

Children whose vocabularies are limited can generate some pretty imaginative mental pictures when new contexts are tossed at them from the tube. Take, for example, the line in *Sky King* that told me the show was "brought to you by Nabisco." This meant, of course, that each week the *Songbird* landed on my lawn, supported by a huge Oreo cookie whose "luscious creme filling" was laced with film. And that Quaker Puffed Wheat and Puffed Rice were "shot from guns" was never disputed. But since I saw it demonstrated on *Super Circus* by the believable ringmaster-host, I reasoned that each bowl was fired separately from its own tiny cannon. And what's so dumb about that? If Uncle Ben's rice could individually steam-press "iron" and "vitamins" into each grain (as opposed to Brand X, which scraped them off), why not Claude Kirchner blowing cereal across the Big Top?

Repetition produces familiarity without comprehension; the only

After Kids and Company *and Dumont signed off, Johnny Olsen* (left) *appeared on ABC's 1956* Red Goose Kiddie Spectaculars *with Story Princess Alene Dalton and Ranger Andy (Andy Andrews).*

just causes may be the times tables and the alphabet. Thereafter, one's lobes become constipated with advertising jingles—some so ingrained that they can be recited a quarter of a century after the fact:

"Fresh-up Freddie sez, 'nothing does it like 7-Up.' "

"Brusha, brusha, brusha," implored Bucky Beaver for Ipana toothpaste, bouncing his way upside down along a circus guywire. (The acrobatics were to illustrate Ipana's large cap, which allowed the tube to stand on its head—to what end, no one ever knew.)

How could the old cartoon prospector who sang, "Kell-ogg's Sugar Corn Pops (bang bang) Sugar Pops are tops!" know that those two shots would set a rhythm that would cross three decades?

Wonder bread acknowledges their sloganeering by updating it. Twenty years ago it helped "build strong bodies eight ways" if one just looks "for the red, yellow and blue balloons on the wrapper." It still seems to taste and look the same today, but it "helps build bodies twelve ways." Inflation?

And as surely as Jon Gnagy could teach me to draw, I recall Markie's father's anguish at not being able to get his kid to eat his Maypo, even when the breakfast spoon became an airplane and the boy's mouth the hangar. "Loaded with delicious . . . Mmmmmmaple-flavored . . . Maypo™!" (sound of mouth closing) (sound of father's groan).

And then there's Farfel singing "N-E-S-T-L-É-S, Nestlé's makes the verrrrry best . . . Choc'late (clap)." Nowadays the dog sings "Co-coa."

And mine was one of the 1,250,000 Winky Dink vinyl screens sold in 1954 through which I watched Jack Barry assure, "Winky Dink and you, Winky Dink and me, always have a lot of fun together."

These nostalgic reminders of youth are shaken by one nightmare: If we remember this trivial stuff, what happened to the important things TV was supposed to be teaching us? More frighteningly, given the aim of broadcast advertising before it was policed, if we could glean such minutiae from a television industry then in its unsophisticated infancy, what sort of culture-crippling notions are our offspring absorbing from a medium now at the height of its manipulative powers?

Nat Segaloff, film critic and screenwriter, hones his chariness of television while working on Westinghouse TV's *Evening Magazine.*

tiser donated a pair of monkeys named, as expected, Good and Plenty.

Ramar of the Jungle overran the market with merchandise. Television Programs of America, the show's production company, inaugurated a comprehensive self-liquidating premium campaign that offered membership certificates, cards, comic books, and autographed photos of Jon Hall. Further sales were registered with a 25-cent Jungle Adventure Kit and a $1.49 game in which participants tried to find their way to the Temple of the Love Goddess along a board with snares and pitfalls.

The jungle explorer discovered that personal appearances could spruce Ramar sales. Wherever Hall appeared, children lunged to see him and walked away with Ramar products.

"We did a tremendous amount of business," Hall said in 1979. "In fact, we made almost as much on the tie-ins as we did off the show. Happily, I got a slice of everything."

When stars couldn't appear, there were other promotional alternatives, as evidenced by a 1956 Boston ploy for *Jungle Jim* in which a huntress and a gorilla drove around the city in a Corvette.

Throughout the decade there seemed no end to commercial TV tie-ins. Half a million Captain Gallant of the Foreign Legion caps were sold in 1955, and a year later, eighteen different manufacturers earned $6 million with Robin Hood shirts, books, gum cards, and other products.

Also in 1955, Little Rascal comic books and records grossed $2 million. For a few months railroad-engineer hats put *Casey Jones* on a commercial track, *Sergeant Preston of the Yukon* kept pace with Quaker Puffed Wheat and Puffed Rice pedometers, and *Captain Kangaroo* merchandising took a profitable jump after the Captain's 1955 premiere.

In 1959, a Mattel creation named for the daughter of owners Ruth and Elliot Handler, changed the entire Saturday morning TV advertising picture. Barbie came out with more fanfare than any debutante ever enjoyed. In short order she quickly proved that a toy without a TV show tie-in could still be a big hit with children.

Previously, the children's ghetto had been ruled by cereal manufacturers who hyped their own quarter premiums and half-dollar snacks.

Actor Ken Curtis, star of the syndicated Ripcord, *demonstrated a parachute toy introduced by Woolworth's in 1963. The store predicted the merchandise would have the impact of the Hula-Hoop.* Ripcord *was canceled shortly thereafter, and the toy failed to fly.*

But almost overnight Barbie demonstrated that the captured audience had been free all along to buy other toys. They only needed enough encouragement and the proper product.

Ideal and Marx watched with great surprise as Mattel's little girl conquered toy sales. By July they, too, were buying airtime in hopes of persuading the 54 million children under fourteen to ask Santa for their goods.

Ideal bought all advertising time on the broadcast of Macy's Thanksgiving Day Parade. Lionel Corporation purchased airtime in *Broken Arrow* and *The Lone Ranger*. Marx made a huge effort to bring the toy store to TV, buying time in *The Adventures of Rin Tin Tin, The Paul Winchell Show, Rocky and His Friends, Heckle and Jeckle*, and *Howdy Doody*.

Following Mattel's lesson the majority of the advertising budgets went to local TV, not to the network. In 1959, $3 million was spent on local spot sales compared to $600,000 for the three surviving networks. (By the next decade top marketers reversed the trend and put as much as $70 to $100 million into network ads, while covering themselves with local sales to UHF independents year around and network affiliates during the Christmas rush.)

Barbie ushered out the age of gentle persuasion and established the era of high-pressure, fast-paced, and quickly edited commercials. Crowded into sixty seconds were minishows with maximum psychological push.

Marx gave their speedy commercials a voice with an Indy 500 delivery. Claude Kirchner, host of *Super Circus*, earned a new living and a critical reputation as the base announcer who riveted the Marx ads into viewers' minds.

"When it comes to that kind of delivery, very few people can do it," Kirchner says. "It's very hard sell and very successful. As a matter of fact, it was disliked by the industry at first, particularly the agencies."

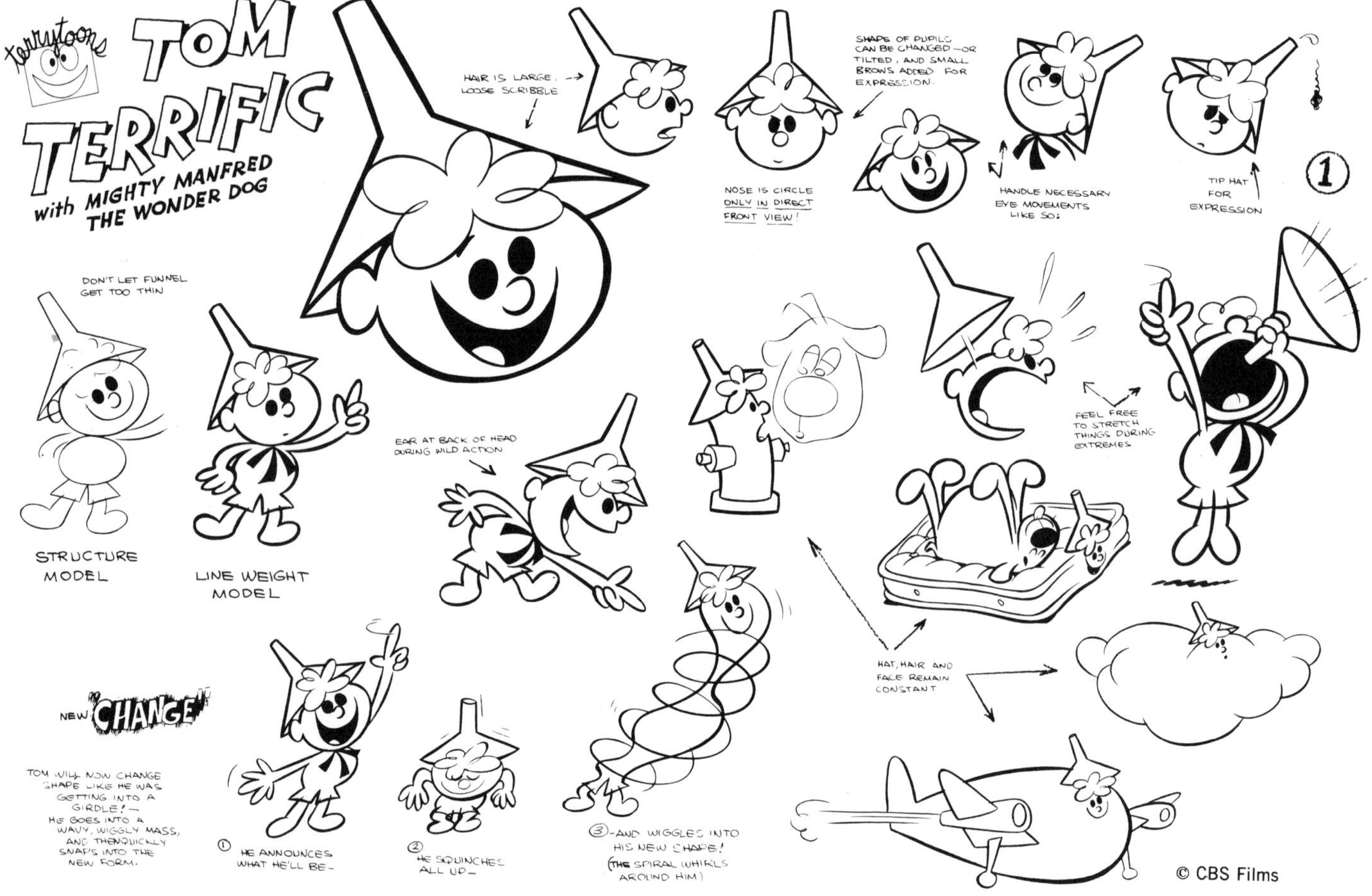

The anticommercial factions outside advertising answered the loud Marx ads and other speedy, noisy spots with a resounding argument of their own. The commercials, they said, were manipulative, dangerous, and often misleading. The attack broadened in the late 1960s when Action for Children's Television proposed the elimination of all advertising on children's shows. And in 1972, when the attack had intensified to include sweet cereals and candy and merchandise endorsements by TV hosts, ACT was winning its first battles.

"Today, I don't really believe in merchandising unless it has value in and of itself," Keeshan explains. "When someone comes to me and says he'd like to put my name on a doll, my first question is 'Why?' And if I'm told, 'It'll sell better,' and I find that it has no value on its own and it really needs my name to make it, I say no. If, however, it doesn't need my name to sell it, they usually don't come to me."

Keeshan says that now the only things readily merchandised are items that "quite naturally flow from the program, such as records and books."

Recently, Norm Prescott, co-owner of Filmation, has been equally sensitive about the haphazard approach previously taken to merchandising and the negative effects it has had on children.

"When we originally started *Fat Albert,* we did what every producer does," he says. "We licensed and merchandised all the so-called staple items: T-shirts, coloring books, games—the works. But when we saw *Fat Albert* suddenly emerge as a meaningful character who carried a lot of weight with the kids and grownups and became a symbol for good things, we never renewed any of those contracts. We said the hell with it, we're not interested in just making money

Opposite: Terrytoons sent manufacturers this character guide to help guarantee that Tom Terrific merchandise would look like the TV cartoon figure seen on Captain Kangaroo.

1980 Prohibitions on TV Advertising Outlined in the NAB TV Code

No language directing children to ask their parents to buy a toy

No scenes portraying fantasy

No use of animation

No product endorsements by living authority figures or celebrities

No puffery or language exaggeration

No over-glamorization of product benefits

No frightening situations or portrayals of violent or dangerous behavior

No fast-cut editing, slow motion or fast motion

No competitive, comparative or superlative claims

No augmented volume

No real-life counterparts involving the advertised toy (such as athletes and products bearing their names)

No auditory or visual attention-getting devices or irritating techniques

No special lighting

No unusual prop or props that are not a part of the product

No costumes on children or showing costumes that are not provided with the toy

No special camera lenses or trick camera shots

No heroic shots depicting unsubstantiated product benefits

No stock-film footage involving the advertised toy

No super-imposition of words or numbers except to disclose battery requirements

No camera distortion or dazzling visual effects

Procommercial commercials produced by the NAB in the 1970s

FROM TELEVISION INFORMATION OFFICE

of the National Association of Broadcasters / 745 Fifth Avenue, New York 10022

USE COMMERCIALS TO HELP YOUR CHILDREN - NON-FOOD PRODUCTS
30 Seconds - Color
AV 51

VIDEO	AUDIO
TV SET WITH OPEN SCREEN; SKATE, TRUCK, DOLL AND CHECKERS BOX IN FRONT OF IT. DOG PUSHES THE TRUCK.	DOG PUPPET: If you're a parent, this is a message for you about TV commercials. Now, your children see lots of them. And with your guidance they can learn a lot from them. Commercials can help you do your job when it comes to teaching your children a sense of values... what is and isn't important -- and why. Commercials can help you teach them the value of a dollar -- how to decide what's worth the
DOG PUTS COIN IN PIGGY BANK	money and what saving is all about. Why not use TV commercials to help your children? Hmm?
CARD DESCENDS ON SCREEN. "A PUBLIC SERVICE MESSAGE FROM THE TELEVISION INFORMATION OFFICE AND THIS STATION."	

May 1979

and jeopardizing what this character has become.

"He was our Mickey Mouse," Prescott adds, "and we wanted to protect that image, so we began to license him very selectively in three key areas. One was with McGraw-Hill. We okayed him for a visual reading and teaching program which is being used in elementary and grammar schools across America. The second transaction was with Dell Publishing Company. They agreed to novelize the show; not with picture or coloring books but making novels out of our scripts. The third project is our Fat Albert cookies, which on the surface sounds like crass commercialism. But they have no preservatives, only wholesome ingredients like honey with a low, very low, sugar content. We hope it will spark a line of Fat Albert health foods."

Prescott says that only one determining factor governs *Fat Albert* marketing today. "If he can't be associated with something good, then we're not interested in licensing him."

This new concern is a far cry from the naïve 1956 statements by the Toy Guidance Council that make-believe guns teach children respect for law enforcement or Jon Hall's belief that a bola was dangerous but Ramar air rifles were safe, and Hoppy's insistence on turning down bubble-gum endorsements but selling his name to other tooth-decaying foods.

The education of broadcasters, however, has come only after the adults themselves recognized that deceptive advertising on children's shows was squeezing their pocketbooks. Disgruntled parents organized into groups with the intent to expose unfair ad practices and tricky public relations tactics. They did their job so well that, for a time in 1979, the Federal Trade Commission scheduled controversial hearings to determine whether all commercials should be eliminated from children's television.

The FTC was labeled a "national nanny" by children's advertisers for even considering the requests of private citizens over big business. Similarly, the arguments of Action for Children's Television and other consumer groups have been met by bitter counter arguments from companies producing sugar-coated products. Yet, for all broadcasting's protestations over ACT's unsuccessful attempts to close the door on commercials, the organization and its allies have at least opened some broadcasters' minds to overcommercialization.

FROM TELEVISION INFORMATION OFFICE

of the National Association of Broadcasters / 745 Fifth Avenue, New York 10022

USE COMMERCIALS TO HELP YOUR CHILDREN - NUTRITION

30 Seconds - Color

AV 52

VIDEO	AUDIO
TV SET WITH OPEN SCREEN. MAN PUPPET STRAIGHTENS HIS TIE.	This message is for parents. It's about the commercials your children see for all kinds
SHOWS SNACK AND SODA POP CAN.	of things to eat and drink. These commercials give you a chance to talk to them about good nutrition. When they ask about those food
SHOWS CEREAL BOX.	products they see on TV, talk with them about what you approve of and what you don't. Not just what to eat and when, but what to do after
HOLDS UP TOOTHBRUSH AND TOOTHPASTE TUBE.	they eat, like brushing and flossing. TV commercials, why not use them to help your children?
MOTIONS FOR CARD TO DESCEND CARD READS: "A PUBLIC SERVICE MESSAGE FROM THE TELEVISION INFORMATION OFFICE AND THIS STATION."	

May 1979

9

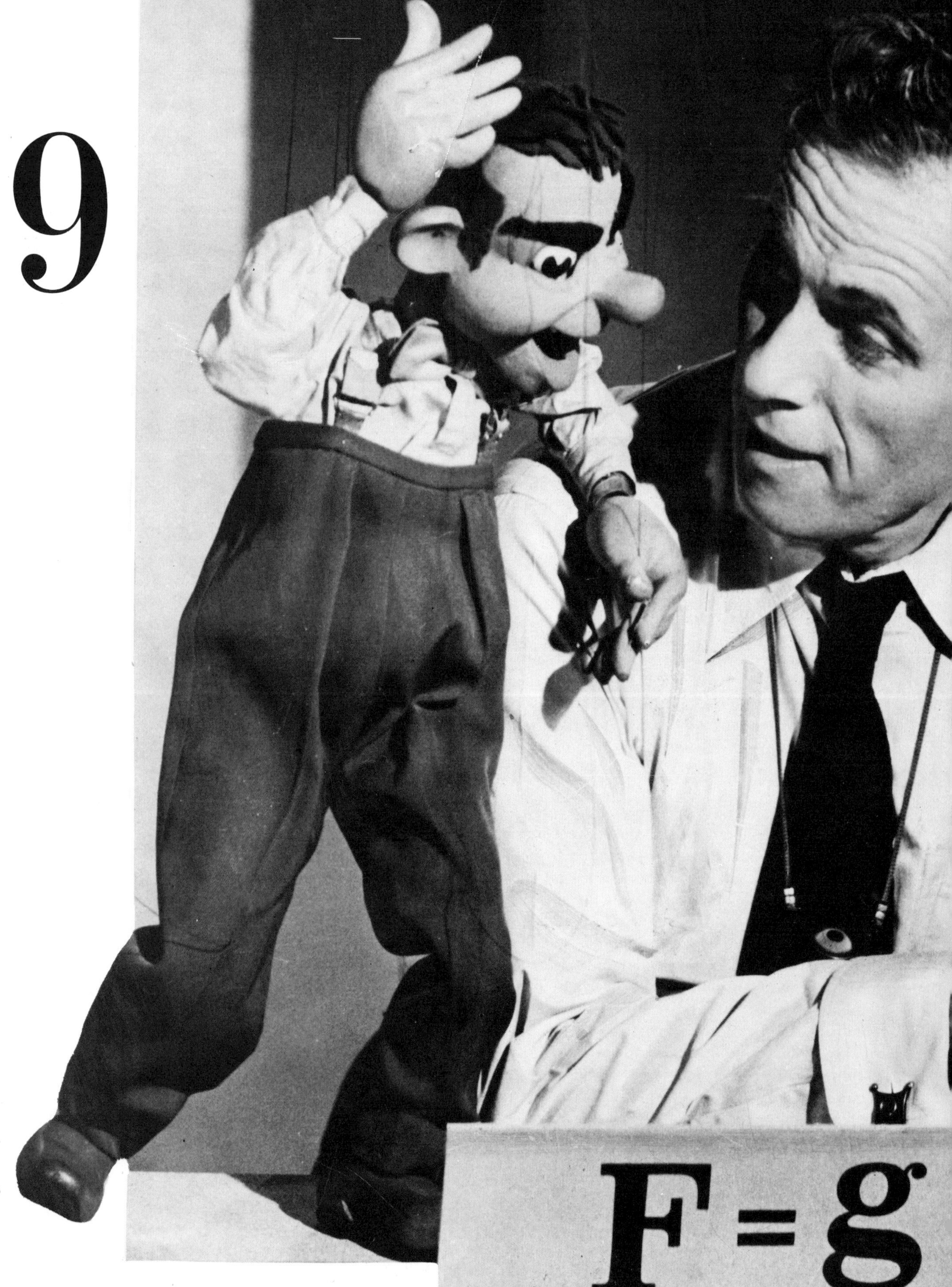

Plugged-in Pupils

Saturday has never been a particularly good school day. Kids, preferring to check their books in the lockers on Fridays, have favored cartoons and adventure shows on their days off. Networks and local station sales departments, more interested in measuring the audience's spending potential than their IQ's, have usually told programmers that educational entries would fail.

Still, what many of TV's educational shows have lacked in viewership, they've made up in prestige. Put on a good informational series, broadcasters learned early, and parents would actually encourage their youngsters to get into the television habit. Follow it with a cartoon, and kids, hooked on TV, might stay tuned. Indeed, the science series *Watch Mr. Wizard* helped build Saturday morning and sell TV sets in those early years just as *Howdy Doody* had done.

The first airing of *Mr. Wizard* originated from Chicago on Saturday afternoon, March 3, 1951. Twelve NBC stations carried the broadcast. By 1953, 54 affiliates were on the line, 4,400 Mr. Wizard science clubs were thriving across the country, and 200 schools had made the program required homework. NBC was pleased. In 1953 the Peabody Awards committee proclaimed *Watch Mr. Wizard* to be "a captivating example

$\frac{M_1 \times M_2}{r^2}$

Puppeteer Bil Baird simplifying math on Adventures in Numbers and Space *(1957)*

of how education can be made progressive without the loss of fundamentals." Four years later, during the International Geophysical Year, an estimated 850,000 viewers tuned to the weekly experiments of video alchemist Don Herbert, who turned younger viewers into network gold. And within five years the show had garnered seventeen additional national honors, including four prestigious Ohio State Awards and the coveted Thomas Alva Edison Foundation Award for the "Best Science TV Program for Youth." The program remained on NBC until 1965, then returned on September 11, 1971, for a year.

Today, Don Herbert resides in southern California, where he is still as much Mr. Wizard as ever. There he busily writes science texts, scripts for new TV segments, and proposals requesting government support for more Mr. Wizard films. He's written four books: *Mr. Wizard's Science Secrets*, *Mr. Wizard's Experiments for Young Scientists*, *Beginning Science with Mr. Wizard*, and *Mr. Wizard's Supermarket Science.* Additionally, he performs experiments on CBS's monthly daytime children's magazine program *Razzmatazz* and appears in the *Mr. Wizard Close-Ups*, syndicated science reports carried on many local news broadcasts.

Surrounded by three walls of science books in his study and seven filing cabinets containing thirty years of research, Herbert says that in many ways he's the stereotypical high school science teacher. With pipe in hand he explains he had studied science at La Crosse, Wisconsin, Teachers College. After graduation, he moved to Manhattan, where he intended to try out for Broadway but instead became interested in radio and television while working as a Rockefeller Center guide.

Career plans were postponed by the war. Herbert served as a B-24 pilot and flew fifty-six missions over Italy. In the late 1940s he settled in Chicago and became a freelance radio writer and actor, regularly featured on *Tom Mix*, *Jack Armstrong*, and *Captain Midnight*, plus his own radio documentary health series, *It's Your Life.* Television was the natural next step, and in early 1951 he appeared with zookeeper Marlin Perkins, on *Curiosity Shop* on WNBZ in Chicago. Mr. Wizard developed soon thereafter.

"When I first put the idea for Wizard together, I couldn't come up with a good title. All that I could think of was 'Your Fascinating World,' or some dumb thing like that. I was very unhappy with it. Before we went on the air, however, we had one opportunity to do a dress rehearsal for an advertising agency that was interested in it for a client. Just as we were getting ready to roll, one of the guys said, 'I don't like your title.' " Herbert nodded in agreement but shrugged his shoulders. "Why don't you call it *Wizard*," Herbert recalls the ad executive suggesting. "I told him I didn't like it because it had a devilish quality to it. It really didn't give the essence of the show."

With some toning down, however, Herbert arrived at the perfect compromise—*Watch Mr. Wizard.*

As conceived, the program was a forum for scientific exploration geared for the postwar generation. Youngsters growing up with atomic age vocabulary, rocket ships, and satellites were generally inquisitive about their world. They asked how and why, and they expected answers. What parents couldn't explain, Don Herbert could. And during the course of his show's long run, Herbert presented more than ten thousand experiments that fed the viewers' awakening curiosity.

"In its quiet way," observed *Variety* upon tuning to *Watch Mr. Wizard*, "this cleverly contrived TV tour into the world of science probably adds as much to NBC's prestige as some of the networks more highly touted educational ventures."

The immense interest in the show was measured not only in enthusiastic reviews but in letters and phone calls that are still catching up with Herbert. "Even today," the host says, "I meet people who tell me that they're scientists or electronics experts or whatnot simply because they watched the program. When you realize the effect our weekly half hour had over the years, you can begin to realize the impact of the medium on society."

Throughout the educational program's tenure, Herbert claims, he never received a letter of complaint. There were, of course, the inevitable notes from perturbed parents who grew tired cleaning up a leftover mess. And there was one parent who objected to the names of the Mr. Wizard's science clubs. "The organizations," Herbert recalls, "sprang up nationwide wherever five youngsters banded together and wrote in for a charter. Each local club was supplied with a monthly mimeographed newsletter and an ex-

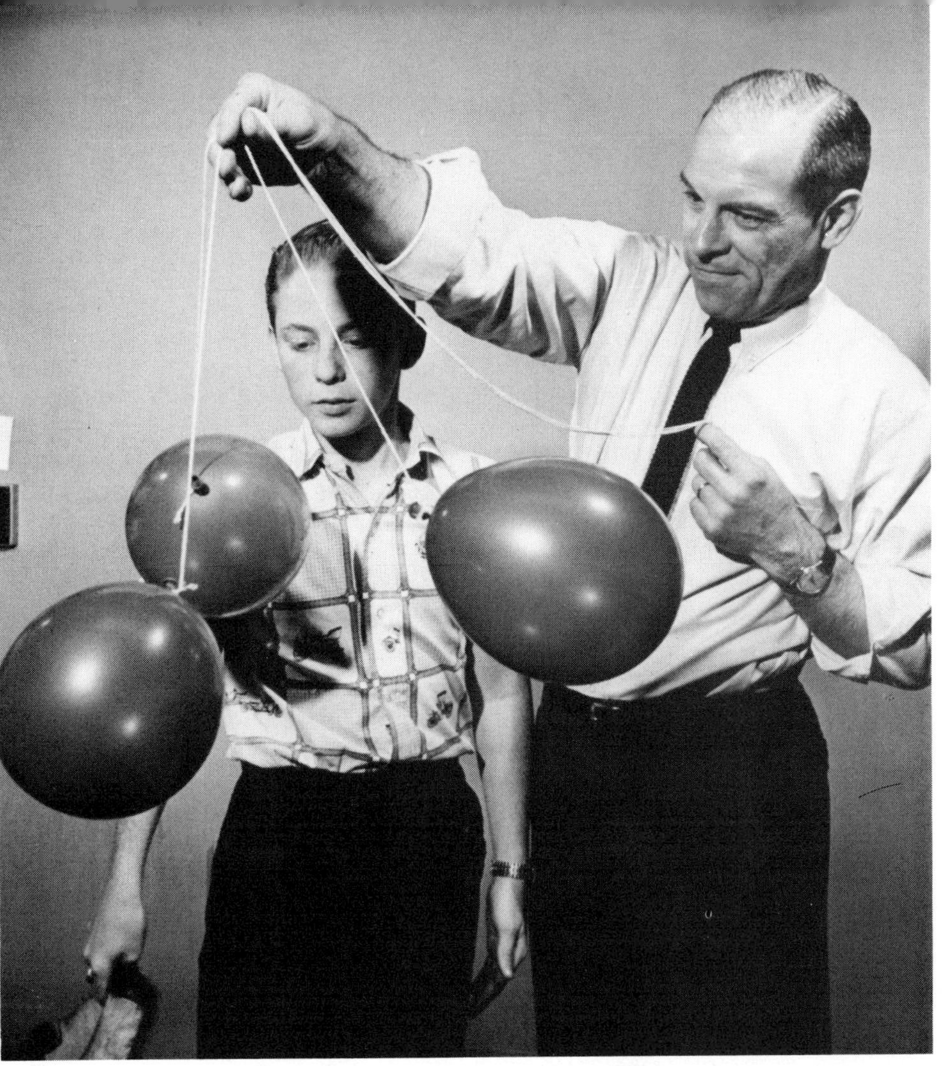

Philip Fox assists Mr. Wizard in an experiment on Don Herbert's long-running NBC series.

periment." For a time Herbert gave each group a name chosen from the chemical elements on the periodic tables. However, a concerned mother, apparently unaware of the science her child had grasped, demanded a change. "She didn't want her son belonging to anything called arsenic," Herbert says with a good-natured laugh.

Luckily, Herbert's chemicals didn't explode on the set. Experiments, however, often backfired.

"We developed a hot-air balloon out of a plastic clothing bag, taped it at the top, put a soda straw at the bottom and wire across that held a cup of canned heat on a piece of aluminum foil," Herbert explains. "The youngster with me held it up while I lit the canned heat. Soon the bag filled with hot air and it floated up." About three weeks later, Herbert says, a UFO scare was reported in the newspaper. "Based on what I read of the account, I'm convinced some kids had made the very thing I had shown."

He had trouble with another experiment in 1955. Though the LaCrosse Teachers College graduate knew his science, when the live TV cameras were pointed at him the elements didn't always cooperate. Herbert poured two colorless solutions into one glass. They were to remain clear only for a few seconds. "I was to start counting," he remembers, "and the solution was supposed to turn black suddenly."

To play it safe, Herbert announced that the change would take place before he reached the count of nine. By four or five, nothing had happened.

"I got up to twenty and decided I'd better stop. I explained that apparently other factors like temperature and acidity had interfered with the experiment." Just as he concluded his excuse, the liquid changed color. "It was embarrassing, certainly, but I discovered the answer. We hadn't used a fresh solution, so the reaction was slower than expected."

"The fact that we had to do things live," Herbert told a *New York Journal-American* reporter in 1961, "means we're not sure they'll work every time." He explained himself further, recalling the day he tried to demonstrate the manner in which rockets were launched from Cape Canaveral. It was early in the space race, he said, and like the United States government's Vanguard rocket, Herbert's model had difficulty leaving his tabletop launching pad. "We had the same trouble they were having. But on the fourth successive show, we got it."

The original concept of the program was elementary. As Herbert describes it, he'd play "a guy with a bunch of junk in his back room." Teen-agers would visit, learn something useful, interesting, or sometimes magical about science, and leave until next week, when Mr. Wizard would again busily explain another phenomenon. The subject of his work ranged from web-spinning spiders to space-walking astronauts, circulating blood to static electricity.

"We made the programs for fun," Herbert recalls. "Our experiments were always entertaining as well as instructive."

What worked for the kids, reasoned the Chicago-based Leo Burnett advertising agency, should also have commercial applications for adults. The ad company thus signed Herbert in 1952 to discuss proper auto care for forty-five seconds in a spot that was tagged with pitches for oil products.

The key to Herbert's success, whether in commercials or on *Mr. Wizard*, was his simplicity. "I never used a flask if a milk bottle or glass would do. It seemed natural that we should reach for household items. We weren't a scientific laboratory. I was really sort of a professional amateur. We didn't have much money to do the show, so we never bought a lot of equipment."

Surprisingly, the unsophisticated trappings and Herbert's deft manner made science less forbidding than it often seemed in school.

"We purposely avoided all of that stuff because in the early days one of our biggest jobs was to prevent people from assuming we were teaching them something. It was all fun and games, tricks and magic.

"If I showed a white liquid in a beaker," Herbert explains, "people would have thought it was a chemical, and therefore a science lesson, even if it had been milk. We purposely avoided the scientific trappings." He says his most functional item was the common soda straw, a device that has helped explain hundreds of experiments from pressure to propulsion.

The format was the same week in, week out, year after year. "We always opened on a tight close-up of an experiment. As soon as the show titles disappeared, the camera would pull back and a youngster would be at the door or window. I'd say, 'Hi, come on in.' The audience, like the child, would feel involved with the problem I posed."

Herbert hired young actors to play the inquisitive neighborhood kids. Bruce Lindgren, today a San Francisco advertising executive, was Willy, the program's first student. Other youngsters who worked in the lab included Rita McLaughlin, currently a daytime soap-opera actress, and Alan Howard, now a Los Angeles actor, according to Herbert.

Others to make the grade with Herbert were Tommy (Hugh Dunne), Susan (Pamela Fitzmaurice), Jimmy (Stanley Crochowski), Mike (Ralph Robertson), Buzz (Bruce Podewell), and Betsy (Susan Levin).

"Why actors?" Herbert rhetorically offers. "When we cast the show we looked for kids with acting ability, those who had the ability to ask an informed question and appear poised on the set." Herbert never used cue cards, however. "What I did was take five-by-six file cards and write the sequences on them, then scatter the notes around the floor. They'd have one-word reminders. But once we got on the air, we had a very ad-libbed attitude, and I rarely needed them."

Initially, the program aired live on the East Coast. West Coast viewers saw a kinescope of the show a week late. When tape was introduced, the show followed the technology. It was prerecorded and telecast nationwide the same day.

Watch Mr. Wizard was fed to the stations by the Cereal Institute.

The matching of *Wizard* and the amalgamation of cereal manufacturers developed for economic reasons. Despite the fact that the number of people eating cereal had remained the same over the years, the population rise accounted for a net loss. Through Mr. Wizard the cereal companies felt they could get their message across with subtlety and aplomb.

During the course of a show Herbert would find convenient ways to remind viewers to have a balanced breakfast that included cereal. "Eat a good breakfast of fruit and cereal, one with bread and butter or other foods and for variety, eggs or breakfast meats," he would say. Herbert never pushed any one cereal; however, he would often quote from a University of Iowa study on nutrition as the director switched to a shot of a bowl of cereal or the Cereal Institute logo.

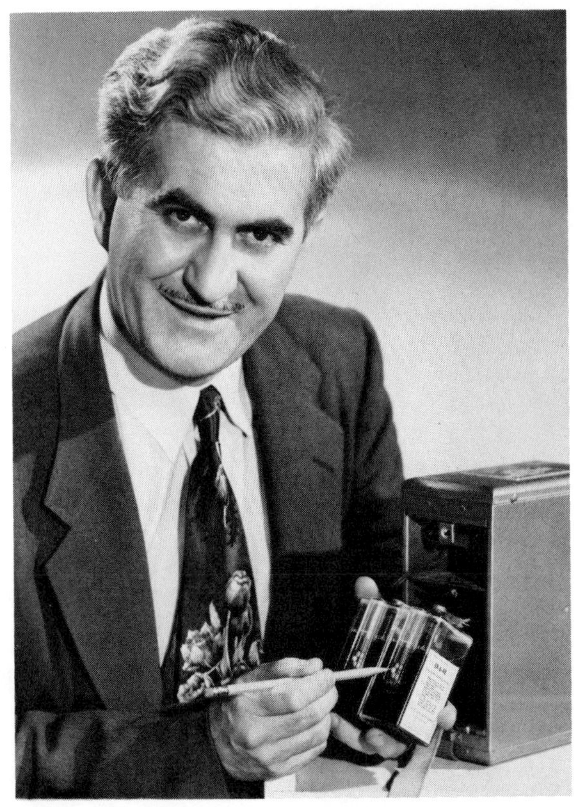

Dr. Roy K. Marshall describing the operation of a storage battery in a November 1951 edition of NBC's The Nature of Things.

Although *Watch Mr. Wizard* has been off American TV for years, Herbert says that NBC still syndicates the program worldwide, and he consequently receives mail from foreign viewers that often triggers his memory and amazes his friends. "We had a parrot-naming contest in a 1953 or 1954 program," Herbert says. "Not too long ago I received a letter from Australia with a suggestion for a name."

Asked why *Watch Mr. Wizard* isn't on these days, he quietly explains that TV has changed.

"You must remember, we began in the very early days of television. The medium has

Herbert in 1979, still TV's scientific wizard, here working on CBS's monthly daytime children's series, Razzmatazz.

changed considerably over the years. Initially, there was no competition for time. But as sets sold, more people tuned in, and airtime became more valuable. Competition became stiffer and educational programs such as ours fell by the wayside."

Herbert adds that *Watch Mr. Wizard* just ran out of steam. "The program had been on for so damn long. I went through six NBC presidents and finally one called me and said our time had passed."

On further pressing he says the show was a victim of upwardly mobile network egos. "When a program stays on the air for a certain length of time, executives automatically feel it must go. Change is important to them. It gives their administration a feeling of vibrancy. In the case of our show, they failed to see that the audience was changing all the time. We always had a new tide coming in. Adults might have been bored to death, but we constantly had new groups to broadcast to. But the programming executives just got tired of it."

Mr. Wizard lasted only a season when he was reintroduced in 1971. He came back again in the mid-1970s via fifty thirty-second science fillers—a matter of network convenience more than dedication. NBC gave Herbert the limited airtime after the Federal Communications Commission ordered a cutback in the number of commercial minutes allowed per Saturday-morning hour.

The wizardry of Don Herbert has never been equaled by any other TV performer on Saturday television. He has spanned thirty years of broadcast history, waging an unceasing campaign on behalf of science, and contributing more than his fair share to the space race, oil exploration, and cancer research by introducing many American youngsters to their ultimate careers.

The familiar TV host's primary objection to being out of the full-time TV picture is that no one else in the medium is really whetting the scientific interest of today's young viewers. TV isn't providing the service it had in years past, he says. Children are taking science for granted. They have digital games and radio-controlled toys. The printed circuit-boards and miniature chips have made do-it-yourself kits and home chemistry sets all but obsolete. It seems that technology is killing the seed of science. Mr. Wizard says that is not the legacy he wanted to leave.

W*atch Mr. Wizard* wasn't the only Saturday video science class in television's first period. In the early 1950s viewers also tuned to *John Kieran's Kaleidoscope, The Nature of Things* with Dr. Roy K. Marshall, and *Junior Science*, hosted by Gerald Wendt.

Kieran's show, also known as *The Johns Hopkins Science Review*, was produced by the Baltimore university and ran first on CBS in 1948 before switching to DuMont for a few years beginning in 1950.

Dr. Marshall set up residency at NBC during his 1948 to 1954 TV tenure. His series originated on weeknights, then transferred to Saturdays in 1951 and was often broadcast from Philadelphia's Fels Planetarium.

Dr. Gerald Wendt's *Junior Science*, a series of thirteen quarter-hour syndicated films, appeared in various markets in 1953 and was geared for eight- to fifteen-year-olds.

John Kieran, host of The Johns Hopkins Science Review, *first run on CBS in 1948, then DuMont. He's seen here on an early NBC radio stint.*

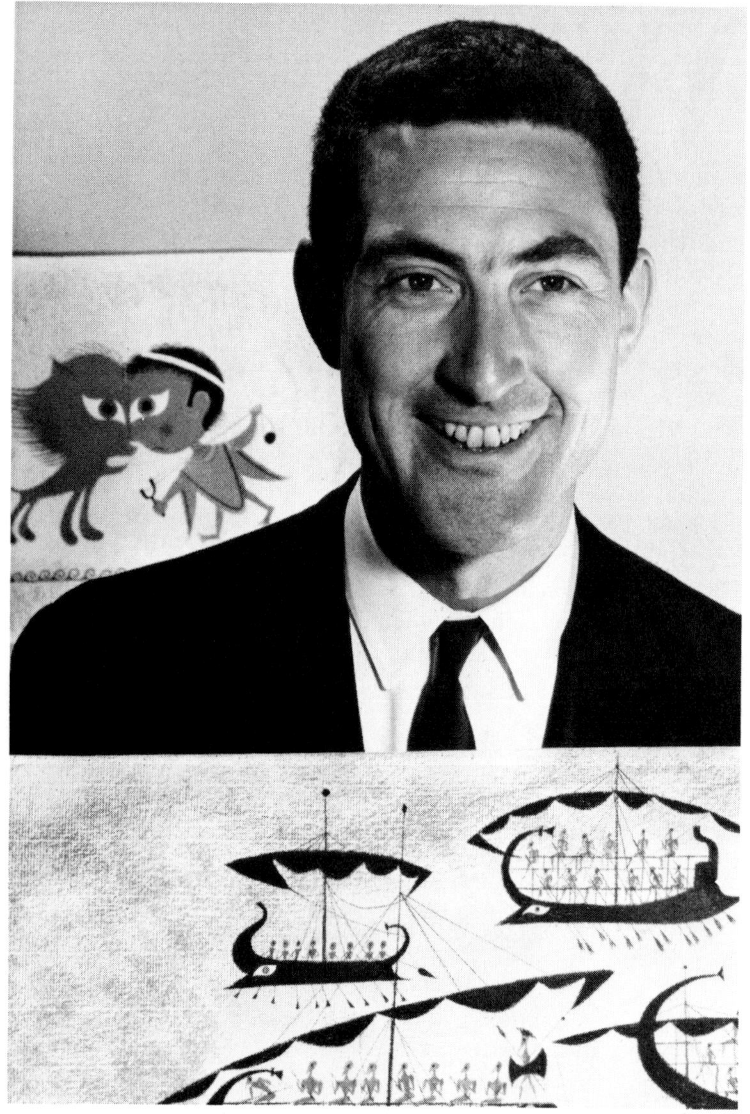

Dr. Albert Hibbs was discovered by the nation's youngsters in 1962 when he hosted NBC's Saturday educational series, Exploring.

Science also figured in *Personally Yours*, an hour-long series that NBC aired in 1961. The show, taking over *Watch Mr. Wizard*'s 12:30 P.M. time slot, was produced by Craig Fisher, former *Today Show* associate producer. The program tried to attract two audiences. The first half hour was aimed at youngsters between five and seven and focused on reading, music, and mathematics. The second section reached for the eight- to eleven-year-olds and covered geography, history, and science. The program encountered problems, and the problems were easily diagnosed. The preschoolers usually watched only early-morning Saturday shows. Later in the day older kids took over control of the set. It was impossible for *Personally Yours* to reverse a fundamental demographic reality of television.

Exploring, which premiered on NBC October 13, 1962, gave *Mr. Wizard* graduates something else of value in a Saturday full of cartoons. In its first year *Exploring* was judged the best TV children's program by the George Foster Peabody Award Committee, given the Ohio State Award, and the Thomas Alva Edison Award, and voted one of the three most inventive TV concepts by the nation's TV critics. The show combined history, pop culture, and science in a most unusual package. Segments varied from an animated version of "Casey at the Bat," a baseball ballet, and an explanation of curve balls to a biography of Johnny Appleseed, a discourse on how seeds germinate, and an examination of Frank Lloyd Wright's architecture. Dr. Albert Hibbs, a senior staffer at the California Institute of Technology Jet Propulsion Laboratory and an arms control and missile expert, hosted the series. Hibbs was assisted by the Ritts Puppets and the Gus Soloman Dancers.

In 1965, NBC presented a noon science series called *The First Look*. The programs, based on a series of books by Jeanne Bendick, included explanations of time, the human senses, prehistoric animals, weather, and machines.

The Smithsonian, a weekly NBC series that utilized the resources of the Smithsonian Institution in Washington, premiered in October 1966. The program translated the facility's research to TV via remotes from the Washington, D.C., museum, the Astrophysical Observatory in Cambridge, Massachusetts, a tropical research center in Panama, an archaeological dig in Missouri, and other Smithsonian project locations.

In 1969, NBC focused on science and geography and backed two-year passage to Africa for *Jambo*. The live-action Saturday morning series presented a travelogue of the African continent from elephants to tortoises, lions to chimpanzees. Marshall Thompson, star of *Daktari*, hosted and narrated *Jambo*. Ivan Tors, producer of *Flipper* and *Daktari*, created the series.

In 1972, Westinghouse Broadcasting produced a twenty-six-part science series, *Earth Lab*. The syndicated production, hosted by Rex Trailer and a studio-sized talking computer named Philo, was a throwback to *Watch Mr. Wizard* but aired during an age when children primarily looked forward to cartoons.

Fifteen years earlier President Dwight Eisenhower had called for emergency educational programs. In October 1957 the Russian satellite-launches blasted contemporary life into the realm of science fiction. But by the mid-1960s, fiction had again overtaken science.

It's sad to report that even when man was walking on the moon in 1969, children's TV ignored how. When the Three Mile Island nuclear power plant accident occurred ten years later, most Saturday morning TV programming ignored why.

In the mid-to-late 1970s it seemed that only ABC's *Science Rock* attempted to keep the science flame on the front burner. The featurettes, two-minute cartoons telescoping science themes to youngsters, were designed more to keep viewers mesmerized by music and fast cuts than quietly teach them any useful lessons. One of the productions, for example, "The Body Machine," depicted the human body as a hungry machine that devoured fuel to function. A song accompanied the cartoon and children saw food—the body's fuel—travel through the digestive system. Another two-minute report, "Them Not-So-Dry-Bones," explained the skeleton.

While science was a generally accepted early programming form, particularly on NBC, audiences could rarely count on a math show appearing on the schedule. Few aired over the years, and those that did had difficulty adding up viewers.

In 1957, Bil Baird attempted to reach viewers via a denominator common to most children. Using his puppets, Sparky and Gargle, he traced the history of man and simple arithmetic processes on a nine-part Westinghouse Broadcasting Company series, *Adventures in Numbers and Space*. Baird and his characters explained basic numerals, then moved on to a description of computers and binary systems, carrying off the subject matter with anecdotes, jokes, and music. Producer Richard Pack told *Time* the program was not meant to be a "course" in math, but "a kind of mathematical hors d'oeuvres, an appetizer, or stimulant." The show was hosted, narrated, and coscripted by Bil Baird.

Infinity Factory, a production of the Education Development Center, Inc. (EDC) of Newton, Massachusetts, similarly attempted to find the balance between numbers and entertainment. The eighty-two-part series, broadcast on PBS stations in the 1970s and now in syndication, sought to take the mystery out of math and demonstrate the role the exact science played in everyday life. *Infinity Factory* exercised a keen interest in appealing to minority viewers, using an upbeat magazine format that relied on animation, song, dance, and blackouts.

Generally, however, math didn't figure into the TV schedule. Reading didn't fare much better. Certainly early TV was full of local storybook ladies, like Ireene Wicker, who told heart warming tales. And there were such programs as CBS's *The Reading Room* (1962), in which authors discussed their books with children.[1] But unfortunately, TV had about as much regard for the library as it had for the math class.

Other more traditional educational shows—called anything from *Creative Cookery* to *Complicated Calculus*, took the form of sign-on seminars. The programs have survived at many stations but only air in the earliest of time slots and are produced on the scantiest of budgets. Often ponderous, usually conveying information to the smallest audience, unimaginative, and nearly always geared to older viewers, such shows are, by many station executives' own admission, throwaway public-service productions intended foremost to satisfy federal regulations.

Religious programs have been seen in a similar light. *Davey and Goliath*, two clay figures that first moved through their fifteen-minute theological allegories in 1963, have received the

1. *The Reading Room* was the first Saturday morning program produced by the CBS public affairs division. Ned Hoopes hosted the production during its single season.

most notice. Other religious shows, however, have appeared more like immovable rocks, fastened to precartoon time slots, forming the foundations for irreverent programs to follow.

For years now, hours before cowboys have loaded their guns and spacemen have shot into the unknown, networks and local stations have felt they've made their contribution by airing early-bird religious programs. At the flick of the dial there have been Bar Mitzvah services and Catholic masses, religious talk shows (*The Christophers*), and prayers from the video dais (*Thought for Today*).

Dutiful followers, or just those who couldn't sleep, have been able to tune to parochial dramas (*This is the Life*, *Insight*) and secular discussions *Lamp Unto My Feet*). But until recently, when stations owned by religious organizations began to blanket the country with *the word* later in the day, television had never been regarded as an obedient servant.

In the 1950s, when nighttime TV depicted children as suit-and-dress-clad young adults who spoke in grammatically correct sentences, kids' shows similarly showed them acting like grownups, interviewing famous newsmakers. *American Youth Forum*, for example, placed teenagers on opposite sides of the table from Senator Estes Kefauver during a break in the Congressman's 1951 juvenile delinquency hearings. In *Youth Wants to Know*, guests including author James Michener answered teens' questions. In CBS's weekly production *Youth Takes a Stand*, a panel of four high school students quizzed newsmen on world politics.

In 1954, CBS even weighed the possibility of airing a small-fry version of *Person to Person*. *Personality* was intended for broadcast beginning October 1954, but the show never appeared on the schedule.

In 1961, NBC followed a five-year-old programmatic route traveled by Sonny Fox's *Let's Take a Trip*. *1, 2, 3—Go!* visited places that intrigued children. However, where *Let's Take a Trip* usually confined its junkets to the radius of the New York subway, NBC sent its team globe-trotting to a walrus hunt in Alaska, Attorney General Robert Kennedy's Virginia home, and a Cape Canaveral rocket site. Ten-year-old actor Richard Thomas, who later achieved fame on *The Waltons* as John Boy, was the lucky lad to accompany host Jack Lescoulie on the weekly jaunts.

In 1969, NBC took a different turn with the Saturday educational block. Producers tested seven one-hour specials to determine which one had the staying power to make it as a regular series.

Hot Dog, the winner, was a mixture of Rowan and Martin's *Laugh-In* and *Exploring*—comedy and education, verbal gags, and visual lessons. The production, perhaps more precisely described by one youthful participant as "a program about stuff," affected shows to come, including *Hot Hero Sandwich*, and paid homage to the tried-and-true productions like *Watch Mr. Wizard*.

Hot Dog premiered as a regular series in 1970 and built a brilliant but short-lived career on the curious. The show's cameras journeyed everywhere to explore the various corners of a child's life. A typical episode could explain anything from a snore to how baseball bats are made. Hosts for these unpredictable excursions were equally unpredictable—Woody Allen, Jo Anne Worley, and Jonathan Winters.

Hot Dog, a coproduction of Lee Mendelson (who was also busily developing the Peanuts series) and Frank Buxton, immediately met with critical praise and deplorable ratings. Failing to attract enough children country-wide, the show was quickly deemed a glorious experiment but

Miss Frances's Class

Network television failed *Ding Dong School.*

The daily NBC-TV series signed on November 24, 1952, and cost only $6,400 a week to produce. Advertising brought in approximately $20,000 weekly, for an annual profit of better than half a million dollars, excluding merchandising tie-ins. However, network salesmen wanted to bargain on bigger returns. They pushed on *The Price Is Right*, December 28, 1956.

Ding Dong School had taught *Romper Room* the elements of children's television. Dr. Frances Horwich, former chairman of Roosevelt College of Education (now known as Roosevelt University) and a specialist in child education with teaching credits from eleven universities, said as she approached her first broadcast, "This is a novel venture. It'll be interesting if sponsors rise to the bait."

Sponsors, critics, and ratings all rose when Dr. Horwich first sang "I'm your schoolbell, sing dong ding/Boys and girls all hear me ring." The *New York Post* called it "The first network TV program really conceived to meet the preschool child's needs . . . a simple but truly great program." Within four months the show had escaped its initial basement ratings and even topped Arthur Godfrey.

Ding Dong School was creatively and practically aimed for two-to-five-year-olds. From a child's-eye view, three feet off the floor, the cameras focused on Dr. Horwich, seated on a hassock, explaining what would be done during each half-hour broadcast. She used a minimum of props, explaining to reporters, "I merely help children discover what is around them."

During the show she occasionally shared the stage with other performers: two dolls, Susie and Raggedy Andy; a rabbit puppet named Lucky; a monkey puppet named Jocko; and three live goldfish, Wynken, Blynken, and Nod.

Miss Frances, as she was called on the air, always punctuated her ad-libbed patter with questions ("What do you think of that? Wasn't that fun? Where have we seen that animal before?") and always waited for unseen and unheard answers from her home audience.

A television screen separated children from their nursery school teacher, but Dr. Horwich managed to convey the feeling that she was speaking personally to each moppet. She would reach millions, but her demonstrations of finger painting, clay modeling, and paper cutting; her songs; her readings; and her guest interviews seemed conducted right at home.

At the end of each edition Miss Frances instructed her students to summon their mothers to tell them what materials would be needed for the next day's lesson plan.

NBC began color-telecasting *Ding Dong School* on March 8, 1954, and appointed Dr. Horwich supervisor of all network children's programs.

In 1956, however, the network began to seek a more lucrative airtime investment than this limited-audience enterprise, and dissatisfied sponsors began to drop out. Horwich started the year with seven. Between April and September she lost five, and in October the last withdrew sponsorship. NBC decided not to air the show strictly as a money-losing public service, and Dr. Horwich was outraged: "With the lack of teachers and shortage of schools, many boys and girls are attending classes on a half-day basis. *Ding Dong School* filled a need." She believed that NBC did not show support for her, and she resigned from her executive post, effective the day of her last broadcast.

Horwich retained rights to the show and immediately canvased the syndication market for broadcast outlets. It took three years to find a new broadcast time, however. In 1959, *Ding Dong School* transferred to Los Angeles, where a new series of daily and Saturday shows were produced on film and tape. Nearly eighty stations began the morning with Horwich's school bell. Production concluded after 130 episodes, and thereafter *Ding Dong School* youngsters had to graduate to other programs.

a Saturday morning failure. "The day we got a Peabody Award we were canceled," says Mendleson. "It had a terrible time slot. On the West Coast it was rarely seen during baseball season because major league games regularly preempted the broadcast."

ABC was committed to a show with a similar theme, but aired in a significantly better time slot.

Curiosity Shop bowed in 1971, lasted for two seasons, and aired from 11:00 A.M. to noon. The program was created by Chuck Jones, ABC vice-president of children's programming and Academy Award–winning animator of Bugs Bunny, Porky Pig, Daffy Duck, and Road Runner.

Each week three youngsters—two boys and a girl—entered the shop, just as teen-agers had visited Mr. Wizard. Once there they would question, explore, and challenge the show's premise, which could vary from science to fantasy. The visitors were met by a gang of offbeat characters who lived in the shop. There was Gittel the Bumbling Witch; Oogle, a huge creature who used sign language; Baron Balthazar, who had the ability to talk to animals; and Monsieur Cou-Cou, a birdlike creature who constantly engaged in intellectual sparring matches with S. I. Trivia, a bookworm who inhabited a dictionary.

An added feature of the shop was a wall that housed animals, a computer, and an elevator that could transport the youngsters anywhere in the world.

Viewers also saw Dennis the Menace, Big George, Miss Peach, and B.C. cartoons.

The same year, NBC telecast *Take a Giant Step*, Saturdays at 10:30 A.M. NBC vice-president George Heinemann said his show's goal was "to help children make their own value judgments, to build oral vocabularies, and to enrich a generation of children who are already information-rich, but experience poor." Three teen hosts, supervised by Scholastic Magazines and NBC, anchored the assortment of fun and facts, entertainment and education, that Action for Children's Television commended in 1971 and *Time* called "more confused than spontaneous."

In 1973, NBC added *Go* to the schedule. The program, one of the first network children's shows to utilize the mobile videotape technology, was fashioned after the popular CBS Sunday show of the 1950s, *Let's Take a Trip. Go* trailed a New York City police team in action, ocean-going fire-fighters, recording artists at the microphone, a Boeing 747 pilot at touchdown, hot-air ballooning, and an actual birth. The program, aimed at six- to fourteen-year-olds, lasted two seasons.

Big Blue Marble, an independent production of I.T.T., was syndicated in 1974 and won an Emmy by 1975 as the outstanding children's series of the year. The title was derived from a space-view of earth, and, as expected, the show focused on close-ups of youngsters throughout the world, showing how they lived, what they ate, where they worked, and how they played.

In the mid-1970s, ABC introduced *Kidsworld* to their Saturday routine. The show used a trio of teen-age hosts who similarly traveled across the country to interview skateboarding youngsters, movie and TV personalities, and assorted

Cartoonist and producer Chuck Jones stepped before the camera to host ABC's Curiosity Shop *in 1971.*

everyday people. Film clips were punctuated by a fast pace, but the ABC hosts rarely appeared comfortable on camera. The show, camouflaged in fascinating visuals, was flat because the youngsters appeared more like adults-in-training than typical kids. The effect produced something less than a "kidsworld" and looked more like an adult's image of teen life.[2]

Probably the most popular of children-hosted programs was *ZOOM*. The Public Broadcasting Service show premiered in 1972 and took the old *Mickey Mouse Club* format and gave it a good twist toward reality. Sans ears but wearing brightly colored rugby shirts, the Zoomers sang, albeit off-key; danced, but hardly in step; and conducted games, read letters, and profiled contemporaries in film segments. Rivaling *Sesame Street* for popularity, *ZOOM* set the tone for numerous local commercial station spinoffs that never seemed to have the same momentum. By the end of the decade the show, produced at WGBH in Boston, had received more than 2.5 million letters.

NBC attempted to put all the elements of *ZOOM*, *Hot Dog*, *Curiosity Shop*, and *Let's Take a Trip* together in a 1979 series, *Hot Hero Sandwich*. Produced by Howard Malley and created and executive produced by Bruce and Carole Hart (*Sesame Street*, *Free to Be You and Me*, and *Sooner or Later*), *Hot Hero Sandwich* aired Saturdays at noon and presented such popular heroes as Bruce Jenner, Leonard Nimoy, Erik Estrada, Kareem Abdul-Jabbar, and Beverly Sills talking about their adolescent years. A repertory company of seven young actors aged sixteen to nineteen performed comedy sketches.

Key to the segments in the hour-long production, explained Carole Hart, were the "variety of themes, including: physical changes common to adolescence; the emotional and psychological hang-ups common at that time in life; the new awareness of sex; relationships with the family; new friendships; secret terrors; coping at school; and out-of-class activities."

by Joseph
have you ever tried to do a flip on bed I tried it once I got lot of headachs but no flips

TRAIL BALANCE
Dear Zoom,
I have a game to play,
Lie on your back on the floor with a cup of ten soft green cubes on your forehead without spilling any of the cubes.
good luck

Dear ZOOM,

I'd like to know more about in dangered animals. Can we do any thing to help them? My favorite animal is dogs and bears. I Like lions and tigers. Can we help to get rid of polution?

Sincerely,
Melissa

Zoom letters reprinted with permission from WGBH-TV, Boston

2. Don Herbert says shows using kid-hosts very often have trouble holding their audience. The danger, he says, is setting age limitations for viewers. "If you use a ten-year-old, then twelve-year-olds will look at it and say the show is kids' stuff. And then there's a credibility and performance factor. You don't want a performing child. When he speaks you want to feel he's got a little experience, but you don't want him to appear too professional. Adults usually like to see kids host their own shows because they think it's cute, but we're not programming to adults. I think it's best to give youngsters adult models. You don't always have to do a *ZOOM* treatment."

Public Education

Public television has done the best job of presenting educational programs. Yet before *Sesame Street* premiered in 1969, PBS or the then children's National Educational Television shows hadn't gone beyond the first grade. Production was often shoddy, shows were slow. Dull hosts generally conveyed material in a manner so boring that most viewers might have felt they were being punished rather than stimulated. The schedules were full of educational programs, but the viewers' minds were vacant.

Sesame Street changed that and the Public Broadcasting System's image. The show combined commercial TV's pace and educational television's lesson plan. Puppets were added, cartoons bridged segments, and handsome hosts sang catchy songs. It was *Howdy Doody* gone honest. Where children's TV had successfully sold cupcakes and candies, *Sesame Street* similarly sold numbers and letters.

Sesame Street became an institution with the lasting power and international acceptance that no previous kidvid show had received. A merchandising industry followed; so did criticism.

Sesame Street, it was argued, created a generation of speed freaks, marching to a drummer so fast that viewers lost their patience. "The formula is so fast-paced," said psychologists Jerome

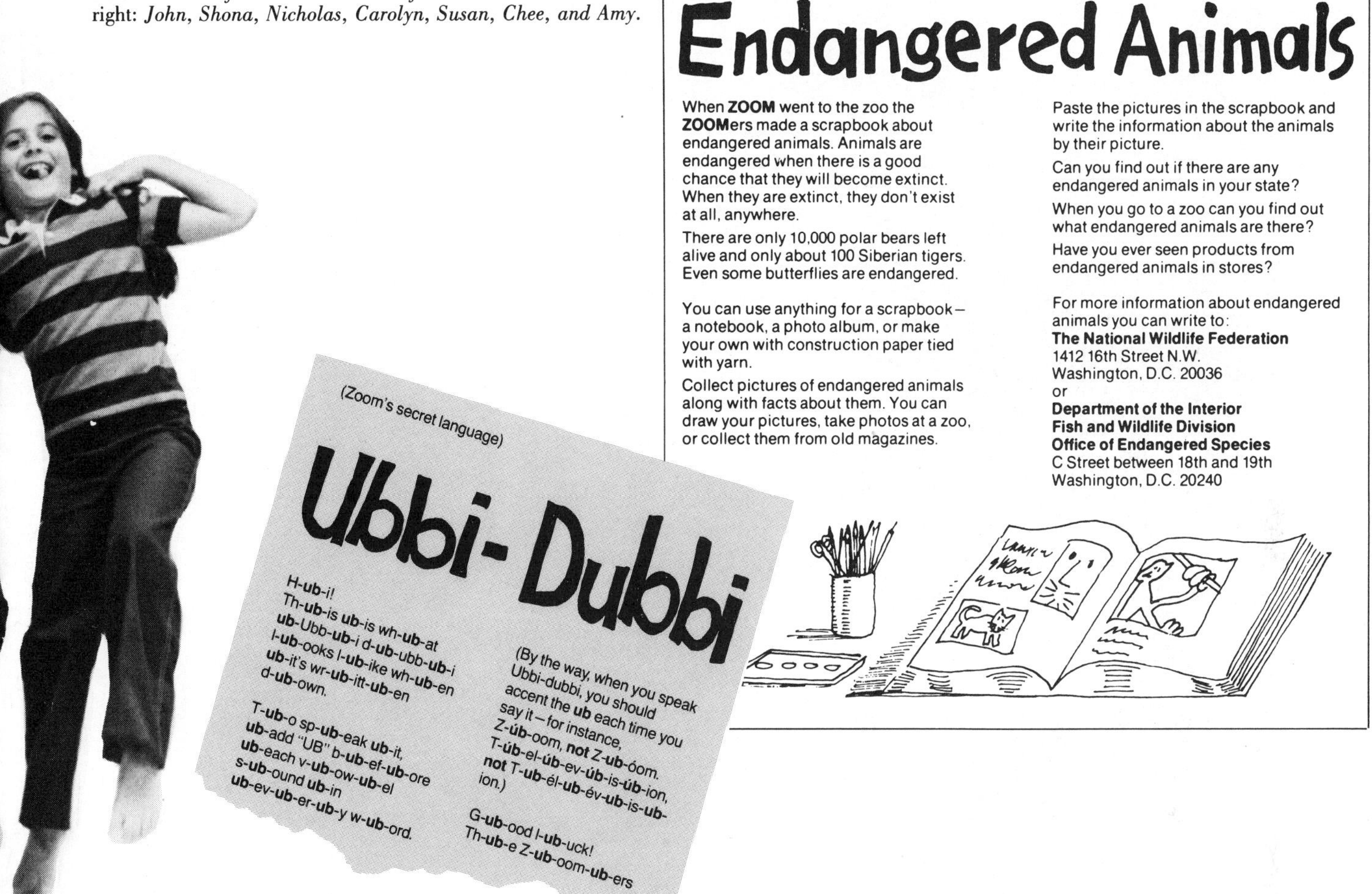

Endangered Animals
When ZOOM went to the zoo the ZOOMers made a scrapbook about endangered animals. Animals are endangered when there is a good chance that they will become extinct. When they are extinct, they don't exist at all, anywhere.
There are only 10,000 polar bears left alive and only about 100 Siberian tigers. Even some butterflies are endangered.
You can use anything for a scrapbook—a notebook, a photo album, or make your own with construction paper tied with yarn.
Collect pictures of endangered animals along with facts about them. You can draw your pictures, take photos at a zoo, or collect them from old magazines.
Paste the pictures in the scrapbook and write the information about the animals by their picture.
Can you find out if there are any endangered animals in your state?
When you go to a zoo can you find out what endangered animals are there?
Have you ever seen products from endangered animals in stores?
For more information about endangered animals you can write to:
The National Wildlife Federation
1412 16th Street N.W.
Washington, D.C. 20036
or
Department of the Interior
Fish and Wildlife Division
Office of Endangered Species
C Street between 18th and 19th
Washington, D.C. 20240
(Zoom's secret language)
Ubbi-Dubbi
H-ub-i!
Th-ub-is ub-is wh-ub-at
ub-Ubb-ub-i d-ub-ubb-ub-i
l-ub-ooks l-ub-ike wh-ub-en
ub-it's wr-ub-itt-ub-en
d-ub-own.
T-ub-o sp-ub-eak ub-it,
ub-add "UB" b-ub-ef-ub-ore
ub-each v-ub-ow-ub-el
s-ub-ound ub-in
ub-ev-ub-er-ub-y w-ub-ord.
(By the way, when you speak Ubbi-dubbi, you should accent the ub each time you say it—for instance, Z-úb-oom, not Z-ub-óom. T-úb-el-úb-ev-úb-is-úb-ion, not T-ub-él-ub-év-ub-is-ub-ion.)
G-ub-ood l-ub-uck!
Th-ub-e Z-ub-oom-ub-ers

PBS's Zoomers for the sixth season of the series. From left to right: *John, Shona, Nicholas, Carolyn, Susan, Chee, and Amy.*

L. Singer and Dorothy Singer, co-directors of Yale University's Family Television Research and Consultation Center, "that as soon as a child starts to understand one sequence, he must digest another completely different sequence. That holds his attention for a short time and just as he starts trying to understand that, along comes one more."

The Electric Company switched on PBS in 1971 as a natural program for post–*Sesame Street* viewers. The series added higher numbers together, made words of letters, and sentences of phrases. In every sense it was as important and as well-produced as *Sesame Street,* but without the muppets, *The Electric Company* never burned as brightly.

Sensing that *Sesame Street* might not be TV's educational panacea, other PBS shows set the metronome slower. *ZOOM,* first produced in 1972 at Boston's PBS station WGBH, was a magazine kids' show with blackouts, comedy bits, profiles, games, and songs.

Other PBS fare to air or repeat on Saturdays, depending upon the whim of the local PBS outlet, were *Rebop,* a series profiling children across the country; *Vegetable Soup,* a puppet and live-action kids' show; *Hodgepodge Lodge,* which housed programs on nature; *Villa Alegre,* a bilingual program for youngsters; *Infinity Factory,* where math was reduced to easy factors; *Mundo Real,* another bilingual program focusing on a Puerto Rican family living in the States; and *Que Pasa, U.S.A.,* which focused on three generations of a Cuban-American family in Miami.

The shows do relatively poorly against commercial TV's cartoons. Baba Louie and Yogi Bear still seem to speak to more Latinos today than the PBS characters do. Nevertheless, PBS has graduated from its early schooldays. Today's shows are slick and speedy; and, chances are, more children know what's on their local PBS affiliate than their parents.

10

Opposite: Sesame Street *on its tenth-anniversary celebration, November 27, 1979.*

Right: Oscar, at long last achieving his life-long ambition—a ride in a New York sanitation truck. Sesame Street *regular Bob McGrath and friends congratulate him.*

If there are two constants relative to children, it's that they enjoy watching cartoons and movies, and they enjoy seeing other youngsters in them. Taking full advantage of these facts, CBS initiated its one-hour *Children's Film Festival* in 1967. The program presented child-oriented films from around the world. But the real charm for some youngsters and a great many adults was the opportunity to once again see Kukla, Fran, and Ollie.

"It was the idea of Freddie Silverman," explained puppeteer Burr Tillstrom. "He was in charge of daytime programming at CBS then, and he thought of airing a film program for children."

The show was primarily a showcase for foreign films, but it also provided a new forum for Tillstrom's friendly trio.

"We went in without a script, as we always had done," continues Tillstrom. "In some cases we looked at show synopses. Other times we viewed the films. Fran and I would then sit down and ad-lib with a tape recorder until we had an intro and a commentary. A day or so later CBS would have it typed up for us. We had to do the show that way because it required tighter and shorter segments than our old shows."

After-hours in the basement of the L. Dullo Computer Company, Marlo tinkers, toys, and talks with his magic movie machine. The syndicated show pays homage to the adult-hosted programs abandoned by the cartoon-prone networks.

In addition to *The CBS Children's Film Festival,* the network paid its cultural dues by switching its long-running series *The Seven Lively Arts* to Saturday. The semiregular program featured interviews with dancers, actors, and artists and emphasized artistic careers for talented children.

The Corporation for Entertainment and Learning put films and history together with creative results in *Marlo and the Magic Movie Machine.* The syndicated series premiered in 1977 and proved that a high-quality and effective educational show could be produced on a shoestring budget.

The program, produced by Sandford Fisher, did miracles with comparatively little money. But then, Fisher had long recognized that worthwhile children's television shows did not always need inflated budgets. He learned the lesson while growing up, for he had known, worked with, and lived near Buffalo Bob Smith. In 1956, Fisher held cue cards for his neighbor when a heart attack forced Smith to appear on *Howdy Doody* from his New Rochelle, New York, basement.

He saw that a host in front of a simple set could at times attract and hold attention better than a team of fast-moving kids.

Appropriately, he set *Marlo and the Magic Movie Machine* in the basement of the L. Dullo Computer Company in New York City and put Marlo Higgins (Laurie Faso) to the task Buffalo Bob had done twenty years earlier.

Marlo visited the subterranean haunts every week to chat with his talking computer and view the machines' newsreels and video tapes. The existence of the friendly apparatus was unknown to the unseen Dullo colleagues but known to millions of weekly viewers. After working long, boring hours upstairs, Marlo entered his world of make-believe and ushered youngsters in to watch historical films.

From the beginning, production values were limited, but the show was quickly applauded for its content, not its hardware or effects. In each episode Marlo and his machine talked nuts and bolts about holidays, relevant occurrences, and the trivial. Features, usually edited to two and a half minutes or less, were visualized by library footage that hadn't been seen for years.

During the show's 1979–80 season, Marlo visited present-day Australia, Japan, France, Germany, and Thailand and continued his educational journeys into the past.

Mert Hoplin was the voice of the computer.

Perhaps one of the best blendings of information and entertainment came in 1972 when CBS introduced the fictional exploits of Bill Cosby—*Fat Albert and the Cosby Kids.*

"The beautiful thing about *Fat Albert,*" says Norm Prescott, co-owner of Filmmation and producer of the program, "is that it was a groundbreaking show which demonstrated that we could succeed with an educational show on commercial TV."

Credit for the characters and creation goes to Cosby, notes Prescott. "We simply realized the potential value of those characters. They're modern Dead End Kids. We called Bill on the phone, arranged a lunch, and after talking with us he agreed to do the show."

Cosby, a regular on PBS's *The Electric Company,* also starred in *Fat Albert.* Prescott says the back-up team was as important as the up-

Animated education—Fat Albert

front star. "*Fat Albert* utilized a procedure that's become almost standard in the business now. We brought in ten educators from UCLA. The group of philosophers and psychologists worked with our writers in the selection of story material, character development, and character relationships."

Prescott says a similar board advised Filmation's other educational-oriented shows including *Shazam!* and *Isis*. The purpose, he stated: "to try to give the kids positive social values, things that they can learn, that are realistic, that they can adopt, and that can help them grow up and deal with people and life's problems."

For their efforts, Filmation and Cosby received the Ohio State Award, congratulations from Action for Children's Television, and an Emmy. "It's the first animated series ever to receive those kinds of laurels," Prescott boasts.

The same year *Fat Albert and the Cosby Kids* premiered, ABC had a variation on the same theme. *Kid Power* presented the ramblings of a multicultural gang who dealt with environmental issues, racial prejudice, and personal growth. The production, based on the syndicated comic strip, "Wee Pals," lasted for two seasons.

Other producers and networks began instilling similar pro-social themes into their Saturday morning programs.

"At ABC, they're always looking for socially conscious values," says David DePatie, co-producer of *The Pink Panther*. "We see it all the time now with our *Spider-Woman* cartoons. We have to be very careful with the handling of issues."

Educational messages also managed to transform the picnic basket stealing Yogi Bear from treachery to ecology. In the 1970s, *Yogi's Gang* presented Yogi, Huckleberry Hound, Snagglepuss, Top Cat, Magilla Gorilla, and Boo Boo in a fight against the enemies of nature. Yogi's nemesis was no longer the park ranger of Jellystone Park but the enemies of everyone—The Envy Brothers, Mr. Dirt, Mr. Pollution, Mr. Bigot, Mr. Waste, and Gussie Gossip.

Yogi's facelift came after the networks were

ABC's Kid Power *(1972), based on the nationally syndicated comic strip "Wee Pals" by Morrie Turner, depicted the lives of a multicultural group of adolescents.*

pressured to cut violence, imitative behavior, and sexual stereotyping. Some executives saw the changes as simple cosmetic surgery. Others considered it a required operation if the networks were to continue to program Saturday morning cartoons.

"Children's attitudes are influenced by television, and we have to keep that in mind when we develop a children's schedule," explains Sonny Fox, former host of *Let's Take a Trip* and one-time NBC vice-president for children's programming.

In 1977, Fox redesigned the NBC Saturday morning lineup explaining to reporters that "As often as possible, we have people saying humane things to one another. And without calling any special attention to it in the stories, we've made a number of the characters in shows members of ethnic minorities."

Fox explained that he had two objectives. "First I wanted us to be number one. When I proved I could be a commercial success and tops, then I would swing my weight around. I wanted to do more live action and inserts as ABC had started. At that time we were the only network not doing anything of that sort and I fought very hard to get money to do that."

One project, a series of hourly inserts called *Junior Hall of Fame*, profiled youngsters who performed extraordinary feats. Fox intended to add more educational programs to the NBC lineup, including a sports journal, a kids' quiz show, and a Saturday morning dramatic series. He also proposed that the network cluster commercials into separate time periods rather than interrupt the shows and eventually turn the profits of children's programs back into the production pipeline, thus providing capital for still better shows.

Sonny Fox was out of work by the following

Early in his career Yogi tried to steal picnic baskets. Recently he's gone clean and tried to make sure the same holds true for the environment in the value-laden Yogi's Gang.

POWER

Rocky Diz Connie Sybil
Wellington

year. Now a successful Hollywood producer, he argues that children's programming has eroded considerably since the educational, informational departures of the mid-1970s.

"Today's programming shows a total abdication of responsibility and I know why," Fox reports. "It's strictly a matter of dollars and cents. And unless the networks or the stations believe that they have government pressure or they'll lose their licenses, it isn't going to improve."

Socially minded comic-strip characters and issue-oriented magazine shows were difficult to get on the air. News programs, meanwhile, were almost impossible to schedule. For years, most broadcasters saw news as a financial drain on their loaded Saturday morning pocketbooks. They'd never beat cartoons, so there seemed no logical reason to telecast them—no reason, of course, until executives were reminded of their responsibilities.

Fortunately, some local stations boldly preempted the more lucrative cartoon fare for a half-hour news broadcast, while other programs, such as Bill Hart's 1959 *Shorty's Cartoon Theater* in Philadelphia, integrated news updates with cartoons. Still, in most markets news was and probably always will be considered a Saturday morning turnoff.

Where local outlets have failed, however, networks, particularly CBS, have taken an interest in cultivating the news habit. The concern is both lofty and practical. News departments want to inform. They also want to train viewers early. And youngsters who tune to CBS news on Saturday are potential candidates for the network's evening news as they grow older. In 1959, CBS presented a half-hour update at 1:00 P.M. anchored by Robert Trout. Today's kids, however, get their news in much shorter snippets. The news briefs are just long enough to convey a story, just short enough to maintain the audience interest. The first of these abridged reports was CBS's two-and-a-half-minute production in 1969 called *In the Know*, which featured Hanna-Barbera's characters Josie and the Pussycats describing such varied topics as glassblowing and iron-ore mining. "We were approaching this very timidly," recalls CBS producer Joel Heller, "because we didn't know how kids would respond to news in that time. We tried to hold over

Sonny Fox won the affection of children as host of CBS's Sunday series Let's Take a Trip *(1955), ABC's Saturday morning program* On Your Mark *(1961), and the long-running local weekend production on New York station WNEW,* Wonderama. *Before becoming an independent Hollywood producer he also served as NBC's vice-president of children's programming in 1977. He's seen here at his network office surrounded by NBC children's show cartoon storyboards and the competitive lineup.*

the idea that their cartoon friends were taking them through the break."

Heller credits Fred Silverman, then CBS programming president, with introducing the concept. "For a long time, informational children's programming had disappeared," he continued. "Silverman had made CBS number one on Saturday by saying, 'Look, we don't have to buy the cartoons off the shelf. We can get involved in the storyboards right from the beginning and have them tailor-made.' " After turning CBS from a ratings has-been to a viewing favorite, Silverman snapped the news department to attention. "He came to us and said, 'Can you guys do five two-and-a-half-minute features a week?' "

The answer, of course, was a resounding Yes. And to CBS's great surprise, youngsters didn't desert the network once *In the Know* came on.

The following year, CBS and Mattel toys ® agreed to drop the cartoon narrations in *In the Know* and switch completely to news.

In the News debuted September 1970, and again the ratings held. "We were in a hammock," Heller explains. "We were only as good as what preceded us and what followed us. We learned that we wouldn't attract on our own. We were just carried along. But that seemed good enough to us.

"One of our aims of *In the News*," explains the executive producer, "is to help young people know and understand what is going on in the world. School-age children today have an appetite for hard news, but adult news-programs presuppose a great deal of knowledge about world events. We feel these short reports fulfill a great need."

Newsman Christopher Glenn narrates the mini-reports and usually succeeds in reducing complicated global events to popular jargon.

"We do twelve original news stories each week," Glenn says. "Seven or eight are hard news, three or four are what we call 'bank' pieces, which are general nondated features."

Glenn states that no topic is disallowed from coming into view of the *In the News* cameras. "The only rule we have about stories is that we try not to show dead people or actual acts of violence. With something like an airplane crash or the Jonestown disaster, however, there's not much we can do to avoid it, so we'll just talk about the death and the cause of the tragedy."

Since CBS was the pioneer of the truncated news stories for Saturday morning, it was only natural for the network to experiment again with longer forms. One attempt, *What's It All About,* met with popular acclaim but too few viewers. The semiregular series devoted thirty minutes to stories that required more than the mini-treatment on *In the News.*

CBS had greater hope, however, for *You Are There,* a series resurrected from the 1950s. Executives reasoned that while *In the News* could educate younger viewers about contemporary events, CBS would also demonstrate that it was interested in teaching kids something of yesteryear not contained in old *Lone Ranger* reruns.

Particularly with the Bicentennial celebration coming up, the network dusted off the format that for years had worked so well on radio, then television. *You Are There* returned September 1971 after a fourteen-year absence, and once again newsman Walter Cronkite was tagged to host the reenactments of historical events. Reporting from a Salem witch trial, Amelia Earhart's flight, the United States' entry into World War I, or the site of Lincoln's Gettysburg Address, Cronkite or his news team darted around like veritable time travelers, interviewing the now famous and now dead.

"What kind of day was it?" Cronkite intoned on the show. "A day like all days, filled with those unexpected events which alter our lives—and you were there."

Cronkite's staid appearance on Saturday morning struck a sharp contrast with George Jetson, Bugs Bunny, and Fred Flintstone. It was clear, however, he didn't belong. The series was canceled by the following fall.

"Our problem was the commercial interruptions. It seemed like we had to break into the broadcast every three or four minutes," says Cronkite. "We just couldn't do serious drama that way."

As for any renewed appearance on Saturday, the revered newsman begs the question. "I think it's a very important area of TV, but I don't think I'll be involved in it again until I'm through with the evening news."

The failure of *You Are There* did not dissuade CBS from taking another plunge into informational programming. It just made executives more aware what the market would bear.

"Let's face it," says CBS producer Heller, "there's no question about it. Children have the same terrible tastes as their parents. They are not bestowed with any great degree of insight or judgment. They are children. When you put on simple, easy-to-understand cartoon programming, it has universal appeal and they watch it. They don't want to be informed."

The creative challenge, therefore, is developing the mix of entertainment that also informs, information that also entertains. CBS News's *60 Minutes* discovered the formula for adults. It was natural that the network would pare down the concept for the children's audience and see if the same ratings magic could work.

"Jerry Golab, former vice-president of children's programming, came to us in the late 1970s and simply said, 'Can you do a program called *30 Minutes* for kids.' That was all he said," remembers Heller. "I asked what kind of program he was talking about. 'I don't know,' he told me. '*60 Minutes* is a big success—why can't you do the same thing on Saturday for the kids?' "

30 Minutes premiered in 1978.

The first season CBS provided a budget of roughly $70,000 per episode. Considering the show was repeated only once compared to the average $140,000 cartoon show, which repeated six or more times, *30 Minutes* was expensive by Saturday standards.

Critics raved. Parents cheered. But, as with *In the News,* little else happened. "We didn't lose our audience and sometimes we did slightly better than the *Children's Film Festival,* which had been in our time slot before," Heller acknowledges. "In that way we considered the show a ratings success—not a success compared to Bugs Bunny, but it was respectable."

Christopher Glenn added *30 Minutes* to his *In the News* chores. He was joined by cohost Betsy Aaron. Joel Heller supervised the production.

The irony of *30 Minutes* is that it tackled topics considered off-bounds in prime time. In-

CBS News correspondent Walter Cronkite began looking at historical events in the 1953 educational series You Are There. *The program was revived for one season in 1971.*

CBS-TELEVISIO
1
2

cluded in the first two seasons were reports on teen-age marriages, the confessions of an adolescent sentenced to a maximum-security prison, the life of a New York model, teen-age runaways, drug addiction, abortion, homosexuality, and suicide. Furthermore, tacked onto the tail end of each *30 Minutes* edition was a feature called "Who's Right," with Patricia McGuire, associate director of the National Street Law Institute of Washington, D.C. McGuire discussed legal topics pertaining to children, such as whether a school principal has the right to open lockers or censor school plays and newspapers.

"We feel we can do anything in the format as long as it's understandable and topical," Heller states.

"We don't claim to teach," explains cohost Glenn. "We just intend to pass along information. We take it for granted that the audience will understand. *30 Minutes* really zeroes in on high school students. We think they have the mental capacity to take in the news."

Pressure was mounting in the early 1970s for more responsive programming. Yet the networks' number one Saturday morning revenue-makers were the cartoons. Not wanting to give up valuable airtime for the sake of education, they designed alternate ways of covering themselves.

The networks devised informational inserts on the order of CBS's *In the News*. It was hoped that the introduction of such service items would quiet critics, entertain children, and maybe even do a little good.

Multiplication Rock premiered on ABC in 1972 with *Sesame Street*–type lessons on multiplication tables and numbers. Among the first of the three-minute mini-lessons were "Zero My Hero" and "Little Twelve Toes."

Michael Eisner, then ABC vice-president of daytime programming, explained to *The New York Times*, "Through music and animation, we will teach six- and seven-year-olds how to multiply; we'll teach them about civics." He stated that each segment would be repeated on a rotating basis, and as children memorized the lyrics of the songs they'd learn the multiplication tables.

Schoolhouse Rock followed in 1973 with a grammar curriculum. In 1974 the mini-lessons presented musical looks at the preamble to the United States Constitution and the legislative route of a bill. And in 1976, Bicentennial features were added under the aegis of *American Rock*.

Squire Rushnell, ABC's vice-president of children's programming, termed *Schoolhouse Rock* and its various spin-offs "teaching with entertainment." Widely accepted and highly praised, they were based on an idea by David B. McCall, president of the New York advertising agency McCaffrey and McCall, and produced by Scholastic Rock, Inc.

By 1978, ABC had added *Body Rock* health and nutritional spots to the stock of educational fillers. The series, animated like the rest, included reports on proper brushing ("Your Mouth"), a healthful breakfast that takes just sixty seconds to prepare ("Quickfast"), alternate foods ("The Munchies"), and protein pick-me-ups ("Nutty Gritty").

The same year ABC introduced *Body Rock*, NBC enrolled viewers in their own two-minute mini-course called *Metric Marvels*. Their short takes utilized a quartet of superheroes who fought to eliminate American ignorance of the metric system. Meter Man explained distances in the unfamiliar metric terms. Liter Leader measured space. Wonder Gram demonstrated metric weights, while Super Celsius masqueraded as a TV weatherman to describe how Fahrenheit translates to centigrade.

In 1979, NBC programmed a series of thirty-second public service announcements (PSAs) featuring ventriloquist Shari Lewis and her puppets discussing good eating habits. The network also produced another series of seventy-five-second spots called *Time Out*, which promoted physical fitness, health, and nutrition. And a year later, ABC added first aid tips titled *H.E.L.P.!! (Dr. Henry's Emergency Lessons for People)*.

In ABC-commissioned research, Stanford University professor Dr. Donald Roberts argued that such public service spots have had a positive effect on children. In a 1979 report to the network he asserted that children who watch the fast-paced PSAs learn from them. "We feel confident stating that public service announcements of the type evaluated in this study are well within the comprehension of the bulk of children who are likely to view Saturday morning television."

Although the networks accumulated data that supported the effectiveness of their advertised spot announcements, their overall benefits are still in doubt, for the fillers are just that—fillers.

They deserve praise for their basic attempts, but compared to many thirty-minute programs of the past, the contributions have primarily helped broadcasters, not viewers. When weighed against *30 Minutes, You Are There, Hot Dog,* or *Watch Mr. Wizard,* the shorts are fast, difficult to assimilate, and loud.

Defenders would link them to *Sesame Street*'s breezy lessons. Yet the analysis is invalid. They are not to be confused with the highly instructive vignettes in the PBS program. Certainly *Sesame Street* moves with the beat of the 1970s and 1980s, as do the commercial TV segments, but *Sesame Street* deals with one concept per animated film, then reinforces that lesson a dozen or more ways through each hour-long show. The frenetic messages on *Schoolhouse Rock* and its imitators deal with issues as complicated as women's suffrage so quickly that even Susan B. Anthony would be hard pressed to absorb the video accounts of her exploits.

The educational fillers, more precisely, program fragments, appease some critics of children's programming but ultimately do little to inform children. They capture nice awards, but they are primarily designed to hold viewers' attention. They rush through explanations with the pace of the Saturday morning cartoon. They are hypnotic, as are most children's shows, and they are merely more capsules of video speed taken by youngsters in the course of their weekly overdose.

30 Minutes *premiered in 1978. The CBS news-magazine show tackled hitherto unreported issues for Saturday children's audiences. Christopher Glenn and Betsy Aaron* (seated) *cohosted. Attorney Patricia McGuire* (standing) *was signed as the show's legal expert and anchor of a segment called "Who's Right?"*

10

Rock-ettes, Quiz Kids, and Contestants

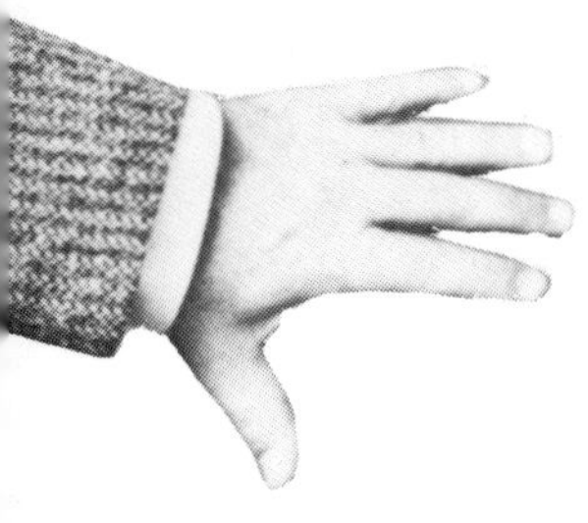

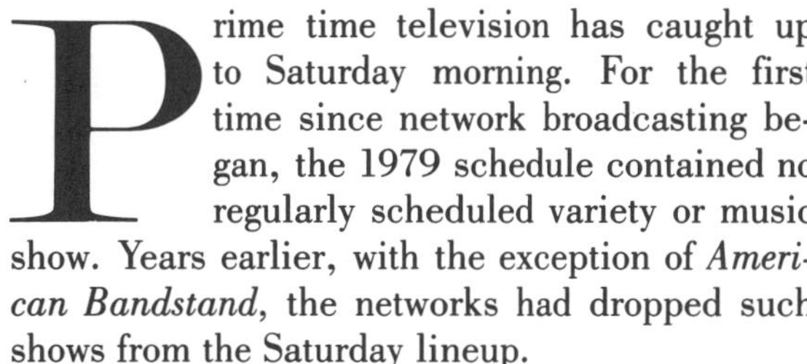

Prime time television has caught up to Saturday morning. For the first time since network broadcasting began, the 1979 schedule contained no regularly scheduled variety or music show. Years earlier, with the exception of *American Bandstand*, the networks had dropped such shows from the Saturday lineup.

In the 1950s, however, variety programs constituted a healthy portion of the audience's television diet and contributed to the broadcasters' bread and butter. Just as Milton Berle was a favorite of adults Tuesday nights, children tuned to Johnny Olsen, Paul Whiteman, Merv Griffin, and Jack Spear on Saturdays.

The upbeat kiddie variety show, however, like its prime time parent, was beaten down and kicked off by economics. Studio programs have always been expensive to produce. When they fall into second or third place, behind fast-paced action series or cartoons, they are quickly dumped. Excess baggage, no matter what's inside, usually isn't allowed to travel long on the airwaves. However, before animation drove non-cartoon shows out of existence, children had real variety on Saturday.

One of the earliest productions to swing onto the schedule was *Paul Whiteman's Teen Club*. The ABC talent contest aired in various night-time slots during its five-year Saturday life and starred the famous orchestra leader who had discovered Bing Crosby. Whiteman's daughter, Margo, shared hosting duties when *Teen Club* premiered on April 2, 1949.

Actor Stubby Kaye anchored ABC's Shenanigans *in 1964. The live program featured children vying for gifts by competing on a studio-sized game board.*

In New York City, *Market Melodies* debuted the same year. The local two-hour 10:00 A.M. Saturday show threw cooking tips into the same pot with music, fashions, sewing, and decorating tips. Anne Russell hosted the female-oriented show. Walter Herlihy assisted.

A durable Western star had a short stay on TV in 1950. For six Saturday evenings between July 15 and August 19, Ray "Crash" Corrigan hosted country and Western performers on his variety show *Corrigan's Ranch.* ABC held the mortgage.

Music, entertainment, and girl talk filled *The Kay Westfall Show* at 11:00 A.M. Saturdays in 1951. The live ABC Chicago production, also known as *Oh, Kay!*, premiered February 24.

Two months later, ABC booked *S.S. Tele-Cruise* on its stations from 9:00 to 10:45 A.M. Philadelphia was the home port for the program from its maiden voyage on April 28 until the last broadcast, June 2. Cap'n Jack (Jack Steck) steered for different musical and variety acts each week.

Johnny Olsen—the man who beckons contestants to "Come 'on down!" on *The Price Is Right* and who's hosted or announced dozens of other TV and radio shows—teamed with cartoonist Ham Fisher, on September 1, 1951, for DuMont's *Kids and Company.* The 11:00 A.M. talent program featured eight-year-old Leslie Uggams. Besides offering music each week, the show devoted a few moments to profiles of deserving children honored by the National Junior Chamber of Commerce.

The second year, *Kids and Company* awarded prizes to youngsters who had overcome handicaps or performed amazing feats. Winners of "Johnny Olsen's Youngsters' Hall of Fame" included a Pennsylvania girl who collected $500 for muscular dystrophy; a Michigan boy who seized the wheel of a school bus when the driver fainted; a New Hyde Park, Long Island, youth who saved a friend when model-airplane glue he was using caught fire; and an Elizabeth, New Jersey, lad who had been hospitalized for four years after being set afire by a gang of hoods.[1]

Johnny Olsen in an exchange with a youngster in a 1952 edition of Kids and Company, *Saturday mornings on the DuMont television network.*

1. NBC presented similar awards to young achievers in 1977. Winners of The NBC Junior Hall of Fame had to distinguish themselves in one of various ways: volunteer work, bravery, overcoming a handicap, achievement in the arts, science, or sports. Candidates selected for the honor role were profiled in ninety-second films inserted throughout the Saturday morning schedule. Alan Landsburg, producer of *In Search Of . . .*, prepared the NBC public affairs reports.

Paul Whiteman conducted interviews and his band on his ABC program Teen Club. *Five-year-old Andrea McLaughlin, a program regular, played along.*

The show was sponsored by "Red Goose" shoes™ and initially aired on a nine-city hookup. Olsen and the sponsor were reunited in 1956 when he was signed to appear in a series of their ABC *Red Goose Kiddie Spectaculars.*

The ninety-minute Saturday morning specials were broadcast at 11:00 A.M. to 12:30 P.M. August 24, October 6, and December 12 and presented zoo acts, storybook fantasies, and musical acts.

Paul Tripp returned to TV in 1954, two years after his *Mr. I. Magination* locomotive was derailed, for CBS's *On the Carousel,* and DuMont's Big Brother, Bob Emery, was back hosting talented youngsters on *Jacks and Jills.*

Associated Artists syndicated thirty-nine episodes of *The Kiddie Show* in 1955 with puppet Johnny Jupiter stringing together old movies and studio acts.

In 1957, the nation's teenagers strolled up to the TV set to watch ABC's *American Bandstand.* The dance party had been bouncing since 1952, but only for local Philadelphia viewers. Local deejay Bob Horn initially spun the records, but it was baby-faced Dick Clark who would put many rock 'n' roll artists and the show on the national charts.

Over the years *American Bandstand* had a weekday, a prime time, and an early Saturday afternoon time slot. The dancers became famous and Clark became a star. At the height of the show's popularity in the 1960s, he appeared in three movies—*The Young Doctors, Because They're Young,* and *Killers Three.* In the years since, he's cut back his *American Bandstand* schedule and his company has expanded into every corner of the entertainment industry. Clark has produced TV movies on Elvis and the Beatles, scheduled concert tours for the Supremes, Dionne Warwick, the Monkees, the Jackson Five, and dozens of other performers, and dubbed himself as heir apparent to Ed Sullivan in the ill-fated nighttime variety program *Dick Clark's Live Wednesday.*

Clark had worked his way up to the top of the Hollywood entertainment kingdom with small, sure steps. He had been a Fuller brush salesman; a summer replacement radio announcer in Utica, New York; a staff announcer at a Syracuse station; a rising talent at WFIL in Philadelphia; then TV host and producer. His only setback of note in his music-oriented career occurred more than twenty years ago when he was implicated in the record payola scandals.

Well over nine thousand singers have performed on *American Bandstand* from the 1950s to the 1980s. Most have long since left the business, but Dick Clark remains—strong, testy, and untiring.

In 1968, Clark introduced *Happening '68,* a

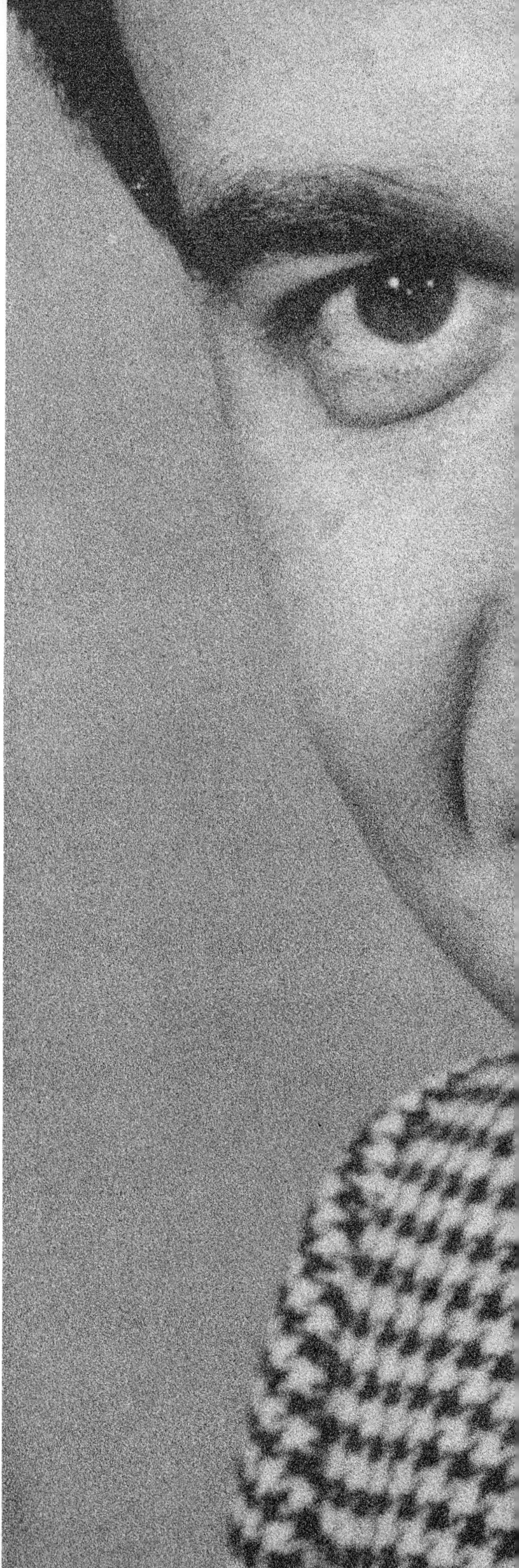

Dick Clark holds TV's best record. He's hosted the longest-running national kids' show—American Bandstand.

musical-variety program hosted by Paul Revere and Mark Lindsay. The 1:30 P.M. Saturday program featured guest performers, light interviews, fashion shows, and amateur band contests. The program lasted for two seasons on ABC and didn't hit any controversial chords. But then Dick Clark's dance card has never contained many slow, sad songs.

Merv Griffin chaperoned *Saturday Prom* starting on October 15, 1960. Unlike *American Bandstand*, the program featured live bands. But apparently they weren't playing the right songs for either the studio dancers or the home viewers. The party was over eight months later—April 1, 1961.

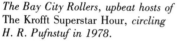

The Bay City Rollers, upbeat hosts of The Krofft Superstar Hour, *circling H. R. Pufnstuf in 1978.*

Saturday morning variety shows declined and nearly died in the 1960s as the networks placed cartoons in nearly every available time block. By 1966, Hanna-Barbera and Filmation were working overtime to fill television orders, while the live studios were all but empty.

There was a slight resurgence of musical variety shows in the mid-1970s after antiviolence forces chopped away at the animated characters and before the networks adapted by developing musical cartoons and nonviolent adventures.

In 1974 and 1975, CBS matched a team of goliaths with a pint-sized Davy and sent them forth to slay the Saturday morning competition. *The Harlem Globetrotters Popcorn Machine* costarred the Globetrotters and Rodney Allen Rippy in comedy sketches, songs, and studio games. The basketball players scored with safety rules and social messages while the diminutive Rippy, known for his Jack In The Box taco commercials, bossed around the athletes twice his height. Comedian Avery Schreiber put aside his Fritos long enough to appear as Mr. Evil.

On the heels of the basketball stars, at 11:30 A.M., was CBS's *The Hudson Brothers Razzle Dazzle Show*. The three brothers mimicked the Marx Brothers while also loading their skits with value-related messages of fair play, honesty, and love. The CBS affair was not long-lasting, however. The series aired in 1974, was off the next year, and returned for a season of Sunday broadcasts in 1976.

The Bay City Rollers appeared as hosts of NBC's *The Krofft Superstar Hour* in 1978. The sixty-minute show presented the five Scotsmen doing what they do best—singing, and what they do less well—comedy.

A year later, there were no musical shows outside old Josie and the Pussycat cartoons, reruns of such hellzapoppin' productions as *The Banana Splits* and *The Bugaloos* and, of course, *American Bandstand.* Dick Clark, an ABC favorite son, had a contract written in stone with the clearest printing guaranteeing that *Bandstand* would perpetually rock on.

Other producers, however, were told that the network philosophy was no longer *Name That Tune.* If they wanted a time slot in the 1980s, they'd have to agree to Stop the Music.

Mark Lindsay (left) *and Paul Revere of Paul Revere and the Raiders starred in Dick Clark's lively 1968 ABC Saturday afternoon music show,* Happening '68.

There were only a few hundred sets between New York City and Philadelphia when we brought *Juvenile Jury* to television in 1947. It was live, and I knew it wouldn't be seen by many people except executives at the advertising agency and engineers at the two-station NBC network. But it was an experiment and we hoped it would lead to something in the future."

For the child of the TV generation, it's hard at times to believe that television is so new. Frankly, Jack Barry's recollections of metropolitan Manhattan roofs without TV antennas seem centuries, not decades, old. Yet, it wasn't that long ago when uncertain video pioneers, such as Barry, nervously walked beneath the hot studio lights, faced the clumsy cameras, and were—for better or worse—married with the new medium.

"When we went on the air for our sixteen-week July to April run in 1947, NBC just wanted to see what the response would be to *television,*" says the quiz show emcee. "It was as simple as that. I was on radio with *Juvenile Jury* and our sponsor, General Foods,™ said, 'Let's try it. It's for kids. It doesn't cost much, and who cares.' " *Juvenile Jury* consequently became one of the first sponsored network shows in America, and the prototype of children's quiz formats.

Juvenile Jury, seen live in some markets at prime time and kinescoped in other markets in nonpeak and Saturday hours, was judged a favorite throughout its regular 1951 to 1954 term.[2] The show was the brainchild of Barry and partner Dan Enright and had premiered on CBS radio,

2. *Juvenile Jury* was revived by Jack Barry in 1971 for syndication. However, the series did not have a successful second life.

May 20, 1946. Each week a panel of five children, aged three to twelve, doled out advice to questions sent in by viewers or presented in person and tried to out-Groucho one another. There were no scripts and no rehearsals; only the red on-air light and the floorman's cue to "go."

Typical of the problems mulled over by the interracial panelists was the frustration of one youngster, who wrote, "My parents say I shouldn't let my dog kiss me. But when I don't want to kiss my relatives, they say I should because that's different. I don't think it's fair. My dog's in the family, too."

The *Juvenile Jury* rendered their opinion. Said jurist David Gordon, "Well, maybe the boy just thinks more of his dog than the mother and father do, and that's why he likes to kiss him. But then, maybe the dog just isn't his parents' type."

Elberta Fiderer offered, "I don't see why the parents should mind if the dog kisses the boy. At least he doesn't try to hug him." And Richard Goodall added, "There are some dogs I'd rather not kiss and I guess there are a couple of people I feel that way about, too."

When a mother wrote in to complain that her incorrigible daughter insisted on waking up early, disturbing the household, then arriving at school long before the doors opened, Richard stated, "There's one good thing about her getting up so early—the rest of the family won't have to get in line for the bathroom." Mai-Lan Rogoff recommended, "Instead of keeping everyone else awake, why doesn't she go out and walk around the block a few thousand times?" And David commented, "Maybe she gets ready fast and early now—but wait until she gets older. Wait until she starts putting on lipstick and wearing a girdle."

Considering the potential for disaster, Jack Barry says that week after week the show aired without a hitch. "Nothing ever went wrong. We never ever had to put up a sign that said 'please stand by.' I don't know why. It seems impossible, but we had no catastrophes."

Maybe there were no bloopers, but Jack Barry was fair game for the unpredictable panelists, and one six-year-old once put him in his sights. After Barry testified to the advantages of a mouthwash and demonstrated the product during a commercial break, he approached the youngster for the next question. The child caught a whiff of the sponsor's gargle, looked at Barry suspiciously, and joked, "Have you been drinking?"

The tot talk-show naturally evolved into teen tests. Network programmers put on their thinking caps and introduced *Quiz Kids* in 1949, while local stations eventually invited high school students to attend *Little Red Schoolhouse* or *It's Academic.*

Quiz Kids originated on Chicago radio station WNBQ-TV in January 1949 before graduating to prime time television in March of the same year and Saturday morning in January 1953. A panel of five children, chosen after surviving a round of pretests and outfitted in caps and gowns, competed by answering questions in their chosen categories—astronomy, arithmetic, literature, music, and so on.

CBS attempted to crib from the quiz kids, but missed the mark with *Do You Know.* The series paired children with authors and experts in a modified game-show format. It was broadcast at 12:30 P.M. Saturday only between October 12, 1963, and April 25, 1964.

Children quizzed celebrities and politicians in the 1972 syndicated *Kid Talk.* However, this time there were no prizes for correct answers. Bill Adler emceed to the panel of four children and two guests.

Quizzes and contests helped to fill out time on most local children's studio shows and to please both kids and sponsors. Youngsters loved competing, and, win or lose, they usually received a prize. Advertisers enjoyed on-air participation because their products had constant promotion during the show, often only for the price of the prize. Like adult premium shows, most children's quiz programs became thirty-minute commercials, buoyed by the toy industry, soft-drink manufacturers, and executives from candy land.

The most unorthodox of all TV kid contests was also one of the first. From ringside in Philadelphia came CBS's 1951 Saturday entry *Kid Gloves.* The half-hour show, as the title implied, was a boxing match with two punches. Contestants would engage in three thirty-second bouts refereed by Frank Goodman. Host Bill Sears could be heard giving the play-by-play

Happy Felton's Spotlight Gang, *a 1954 NBC potpourri of vaudeville acts, music, and contests, starred the rotund radio and stage veteran.*

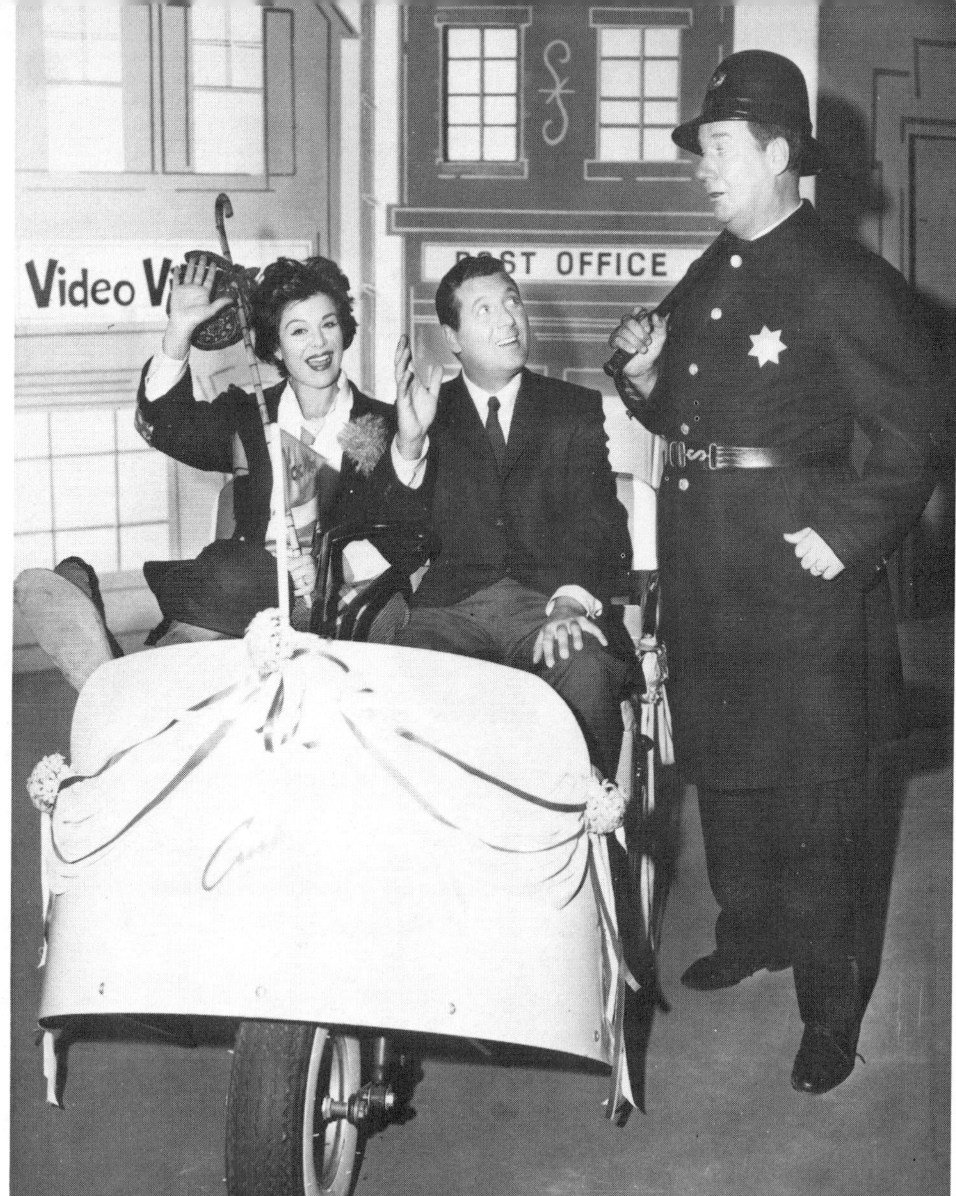

Ellen Parton and Monty Hall are pulled over by Video Village, Jr. *officer Kenny Williams in 1961. The Saturday morning game show was a spin-off of a weekday adult version.*

commentary. Between rounds, *Kid Gloves* delivered the second punch—audience question-and-answer sessions with John Da Groza, the Pennsylvania boxing commissioner.

The program originated in 1950 but became a twelve-station contender a year later. Participants aged three to ten qualified for the flea-, pebble-, or paperweight divisions and used soft gloves. They submitted to medical examinations before sparring, and all belonged to training clubs.

Sportsmanship and fellowship were stressed as much as self-defense, and often a loser might win the grand prize—a bicycle—because he had done his best.

The last bell on *Kid Gloves* rang twenty-six weeks after its February 24, 1951, premiere. The show failed to attract a sponsor.

Fleer's Dubble Bubble Gum(TM) chewed up commercial time in 1952 as sponsor of *Pud's Prize Party* (ABC, 11:30 to 11:45 A.M., Saturdays). The show, broadcast from the Philadelphia Town Hall, was basically an extended ad for Fleer with the company's jovial character in his horizontally striped shirt giving away both money and gum while host Todd Russell emceed the festivities.

Variety burst Fleer's bubble in a review of the show, noting that the sponsor's product was mentioned twenty-four times in the fifteen-minute show. The trade paper also reported that participants appeared "as much entranced with the penny product as with the program," a phenomenon taken full advantage of by Russell, who "gives half a dozen reasons to like Dubble Bubble and takes time out to do unadulterated commercials surrounded by packages of gum."

Pud's Prize Party could not air today. Recent industry regulations have condemned outright exploitation and prevented children's show hosts from selling products directly to youngsters on their own shows or in adjacent time slots. But for years Russell's program was typical of Saturday morning television.

A year before Pud gave away a small piece of gum, children were competing for the big time on Gene Crane's *Grand Chance Roundup.* Winners of this 1951 CBS talent competition broadcast were awarded a week's work at Hamid's Steel Pier in Atlantic City, New Jersey. The resort owner got only six months' worth of talent from the Philadelphia show, however. *Grand Chance Roundup* premiered Saturday, January 27, 1951, at 11:30 A.M. It was replaced August 4 by *Smilin' Ed's Gang.*

In 1953, twenty years before Bill Wendell became the off-camera voice on *Saturday Night Live,* he hosted DuMont's weekday children's quizzer, *The Silver Horseshoe.*

A year later NBC's *Happy Felton's Spotlight Gang,* a live Saturday morning show, presented dated film clips of European vaudeville acts from the network library and a quiz at the conclusion of the show. Felton was known for always ending the show with the phrase "Tell five," meaning viewers should tell five others to watch next week.

The same year, ventriloquist Jimmy Weldon and his dummy, Webster Webfoot, hosted NBC's Saturday kids' quiz *Funny Boners.* The series resembled *Truth or Consequences,* for players who could not answer a question correctly had to perform a stunt.

DuMont producers tried to tickle the funny bone as well on weekdays in 1954 with *The Funny Bunny.* Dick Noel dressed in a rabbit costume to host the show and introduce the cartoon adventures of Crusader Rabbit. A reviewer for *Broadcasting* termed the production "something out of a bad dream." The magazine warned, "If the kids want monsters on camera, here it is."

Jackie Robinson, the first black athlete to break major league baseball's color barrier, was similarly one of the first minorities to appear on television. The Brooklyn Dodger star guest-hosted a local 1955 New York Saturday kids' quiz, but his comments, like his play, were heard around the country. *Junior Champions* was telecast over WRCA-TV (WNBC) and was designed to interest youngsters in sports. He believed that TV was a perfect medium to bring together children and sports figures, but realized the medium had an aversion to blacks.

"The networks just can't sell a Negro nationally," he told *The New York Times.* "It's a very bad situation today when other people are looking to see what is happening in this country. A lot of Negro talent is not being used. Something should be done about it."

In 1956, Robinson was still starring at home plate if not on television, while perennial TV favorite Bert Parks gave away toys, model trains, microscopes, and Harvard scholarships to youngsters competing on NBC's prime time series, *Giant Step.* Abbott and Costello proposed, but did not produce, a children's quiz show for ABC called *Penny for Your Thoughts.* And on Saturdays, youthful Gene Rayburn, more successful than the aging comedians, stood center stage as participating teams raced one another to winner's circle prizes on *Choose Up Sides.*

"We had two different teams every week called the Space Pilots and the Bronco Busters," remembers Rayburn. "Since the NBC production was done in New York at the Hudson Theater, where I was also doing *The Tonight Show,* we picked kids from neighborhoods in Long Island, Manhattan, and New Jersey. The winning team got the lion's share of the prizes.[3] (The show had premiered locally in 1953 on WCBS-TV, hosted by Dean Miller.)

Rayburn's high-voltage personality drove the show during its three-month network stint. For children's game-show hosts, such kinetic energy had to be in abundant supply. Every on-air moment counted. Every word was intended to heighten the excitement. And the best in the business could speed through thirty minutes with hardly a hint of exhaustion.

Happy Felton pushed the limit for three and a half months from June 1 to September 21, 1957, with the Saturday morning game show, *It's a Hit.* Monty Hall did so on *Video Village, Junior* from 1960 to 1962. Stubby Kaye managed to turn his fat into fuel as he raced through *Shenanigans* in 1964 and Paul Winchell kept up with kids on NBC's *Runaround* in 1972.

Actually, CBS inaccurately titled *It's a Hit.* It wasn't. Felton dressed in umpire's blacks and officiated two teams of seven- to fourteen-year-

3. Sonny Fox's local New York production *Just for Fun* also built a show on the competition between two teams, as did local game shows in markets throughout the country. Where networks could stockpile prizes from national advertisers, hometown stations usually offered smaller items and free admission to movies and amusement parks, board games, and windup toys. Small as these prizes might have been, they were still desired by both youngsters and station employees and were, out of necessity, usually padlocked in secure off-limits rooms.

olds who were managed by legitimate sports figures. But like most umpires, this TV referee was booed, and the show quickly left the air.

Video Village, Junior was a Saturday version of an elaborate CBS daytime game show in which contestants moved along a studio-sized board as if they were pawns on a dining room table game. Two players competed by rolling huge dice, then advancing on the squares. The first to reach the finish line won the prizes, for kids—toys and bicycles. Kenny Williams joined Hall on the show as the Video Village town crier.

Williams also served as announcer on Kaye's ABC show, *Shenanigans*, a program similar in format to *Video Village*. Each week two children competed for play money by advancing to the goal on a three-dimensional game board. Along the way they rolled dice, obeyed the instructions in the square and either answered a question or performed a stunt. The winner exchanged his receipts for merchandise.

Williams stepped behind the microphone again in 1968 and 1969 for NBC's spin-off of *Hollywood Squares*, called *The Storybook Squares*. The busy announcer introduced celebrities dressed as nursery rhyme characters. Two children contestants were asked to agree or disagree with the star's answers to questions posed by host Peter Marshall. The tic-tac-toe format was successful against all comers on weekdays, but any hope that the slow-paced *Storybook Squares* would beat cartoons was strictly fantasy.

In 1972, Kenny Williams's voice once again stirred the already excited children to a feverish pitch as Paul Winchell bounded onto the stage of *Runaround*. This 11:30 A.M. Saturday morning production had an apt title. Nine children vied for gifts by running to any one of three lanes that they believed contained the correct answers to problems asked by the ventriloquist. Winners were given points, losers sat out time in a penalty box. At the show's end the players with the highest accumulations cashed in their points for prizes.

Everyone ran or walked away with something. Lesser prizes included two weeks at camp, a stereo set, a five-speed bicycle, a puppy, or pet food. Grand-prize winners were usually awarded a cross-country trip. Nobody won Dubble Bubble gum.

The game show scandals that began to rock the broadcast industry in 1958 had hardly caused a ripple in the Saturday morning schedule. The fix was in at night. On many prime time shows adults had been coached, told general areas to study and specific answers to questions. Youngsters appearing on Saturday morning quizzes, however, were still young enough to remember the Golden Rule. Besides, the shows themselves placed greater emphasis on fun than games and offered small prizes rather than big bucks. Even though the investigations did not touch Saturday morning contests, broadcasters were learning by the mid-1970s that devising the successful children's quiz show for that decade was no game. The information gap that separated what three-year-olds knew from the knowledge and experience of their older brothers or sisters was usually too great to cover in a single quiz show. Hard questions wouldn't appeal to tots, and baby games were a turnoff to teens. The solution was, of course, active not passive formats. Athletic or physical competition, as on *Choose Up Sides*, could, if done better, appeal to all young-age groups. Rather than advance or be penalized on the basis of a textbook question, a participant's fate would be a matter of a dial spin or a fifty-yard dash. They'd usually win or lose on luck, not ability.

In 1976, CBS entered the field with a competition called *Way Out Games*. Contestants, aged twelve to fifteen, were chosen from schools across the country with the aid of the American Alliance for Health, Physical Education and Recreation and appeared in two half-hour ath-

Jerry Mahoney had a new hairdo, Paul Winchell sported a mustache, and Knucklehead Smiff still had a painted headpiece when the trio hosted NBC's Runaround *in 1972.*

Paul Whiteman and Gerard Fremy in the Paul Whiteman TV Teen Club, *1952*

letic games. Players tried to clinch a berth in an hour-long championship special.

Way Out Games emphasized humor, just as ABC's *Junior Almost Anything Goes* did the same year.[4] The latter program, emceed by Soupy Sales, was a copy of the short-lived nighttime junk sports program, *Almost Anything Goes.* The Saturday morning clash pitted everyday youngsters against one another in zany encounters, all for the love of competition, prizes, and the national TV cameras.

"It was a marvelous show," boasts Sales. "It gave kids a chance; kids who never got to participate in rugged school sports. And it didn't make fun of them."

Sales has pride in the show despite the dismal ratings it averaged. "The show was a hit in Chicago, in New York, and in Los Angeles," he continues. "I think we might have been the first show to beat *Fat Albert* in some areas. But we weren't on enough markets. Cities like Pittsburgh, Columbus, Boston, and Detroit didn't keep us on, and Houston played the show early in the morning. So by the time the national results came around, we finished low. They took us off, but to me the show was better than any of the cartoons. At least it looked live, and real people were participating."

Odds seemed just as much against the athletic competitions as they were against studio quiz shows. A three-year-old could tell any mature TV executive why. Cartoons remained the safest bet to attract audiences. And especially after the National Association of Broadcasters red-flagged hosts from delivering ads in 1972, commercial programmers everywhere agreed that cartoons would bring easier revenue, fewer headaches, and higher ratings.

The dice were sent back to Las Vegas, and the quiz questions were given to *Family Feud.*

4. Both shows seemed patterned after a combination of party games and third-period gym class—a mixture previously seen on ABC's *Hail the Champ* in 1953. Herb Allen and Howard Roberts appeared as hosts on the early production, which presented six studio children in physical stunts and athletic contests.

"Junior Almost Anything Goes *was better than any of the cartoons," says show host Soupy Sales. ABC didn't share the crusty comedian's sentiments. The program didn't last beyond its premiere 1976 season.*

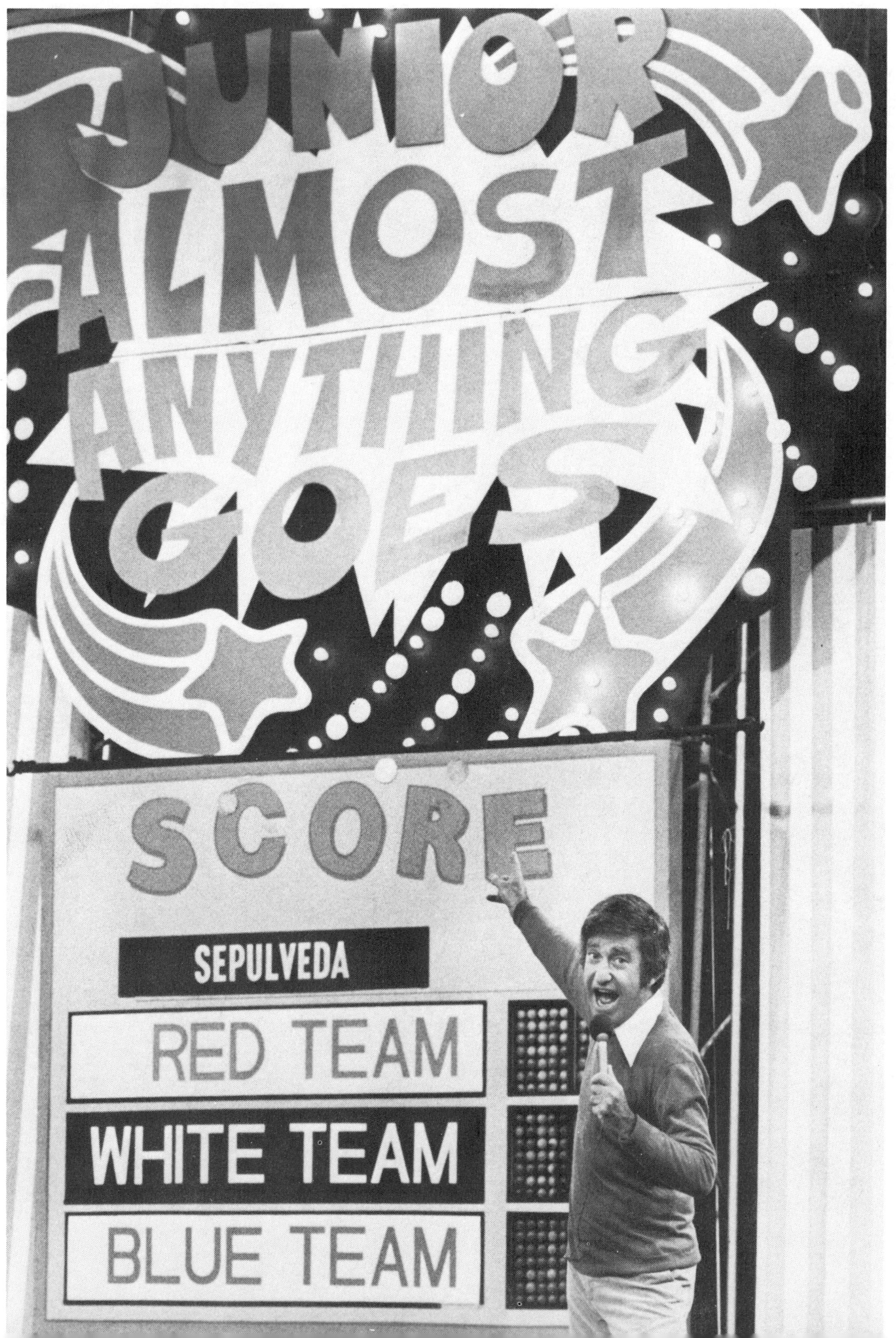

11 Sawdust

and White Rabbits

Television was quite serious about clowning around. For years circus shows were the center of attraction for many advertisers. They were fast and furious, full of action, animals, and adventure and a certain invitation to young viewers and advertiser interests.

During the first decade of commercial TV, sponsors competed for admission to network circus programs. The gate was expensive, but the shows were usually worth the cost. Sealtest, for example, dropped the ever-lovable *Kukla, Fran and Ollie* in 1950 to concentrate on CBS's *Big Top*. Kellogg's convinced children they were the greatest name in cereals during its four-year association with *Super Circus*. M & M™ candies, according to the William Esty advertising agency, became the "number one seller of all bagged candy" after eighteen months of commercial play on the show. Hartz Mountain put Dog Yummies on the tips of everybody's tongues in 1958 when they advertised on Paul Winchell and Jerry Mahoney's *Circus Time*. And Tootsie Roll rolled into the plus column in 1953 with ABC's *Tootsie Hippodrome*.

TV's most renowned ringleader was *Super Circus's* Claude Kirchner. The deep-voiced announcer, as familiar for his off-camera delivery on the Marx toy commercials as for his center-stage performances, actually earned a living in the 1930s as a carnival barker. In 1936 he left the circus and took a job with a Dallas radio station. Kirchner announced his way across the

Opposite: Super Circus *ringmaster Claude Kirchner*

The Super Circus *headliners—Cliffy, Nicky, Claude Kirchner, Mary Hartline, and Scampy*

Southwest and wound up at Chicago's WIND and ABC's *Super Circus* radio show. When the television lights clicked on, Kirchner was there.

"Television came into the city in a big way back in the late 1940s, and we were all just casting around for ideas. We'd been doing *Super Circus* on radio as a contest program for kids. It was built around circus stunts, but the client who had commissioned it went out of business and we were about to sell it to General Mills when we realized that it probably would make a pretty good TV show."

The series debuted Sunday, January 16, 1949, and remained in Chicago until late 1955, when *Super Circus* began a limited New York engagement.[1] Claude Kirchner also left for Manhattan, but not to wear the ringmaster's duds. ABC changed the cast and he starred instead on WOR-TV's *Terrytoon Circus*. Jerry Colonna took over as emcee of *Super Circus,* and Sandy Wirth (Miss Florida) appeared as the female costar. Through much of its intitial run the show had been TV's highest-rated children's program. In September 1952 it was the only daytime network show among the twenty-five top-rated national shows. With its new cast, however, it lost its audience and subsequently its airtime. *Super Circus* signed off June 3, 1956.

"When *we* did the show, it was pure television," explains Kirchner. "We had a marvelous production. Everything meshed, but it wasn't really a circus show. What we did was pure television. Real circus clowns performed their own routines, and that's what they do every day. Nothing changes. We had to do something different each week. And that meant our clowns were integrated into stunts and commercials. It wasn't a circus. It was a live show with a circus format."

Kirchner aptly handled the megaphone, but it was baton twirler Mary Hartline who held the key to both the show's success and the audience's heart. The beautiful bandleader added color to television, years before technicians supplied the appropriate hardware. Her dazzling pale-gold locks burned an indelible image into viewers' minds, and her smile lit up the screen. Mary Hartline was without a doubt one of early TV's glittering prizes and the object of conversation from coast to coast.

1. In the early 1950s, *Super Circus* was seen via kinescope—delayed broadcasts in many markets at 9:30 A.M., Saturdays.

*Fairy godmother, sex symbol, and the girl next door rolled into one—*Super Circus*'s Mary Hartline*

"She was a symbol for everybody," Kirchner says fondly. "For the kids she was like a fairy godmother. She was a sex symbol for men, and the women hated her because they knew what men thought. And then again, grandparents saw her as someone very, very sweet. She was wonderful, brassy, outgoing, and superb. She was a phenomenon!"[2]

Mary Hartline provided vision for the dreams of voyeurs, but her appearance alone could not sustain a show. *Super Circus* was built on teamwork, and Mary was only one player.

"We had an outstanding writer, a great producer, and terrific stagehands," says Kirchner. "Others could work a thousand years and they'd never get a group like we had. They'd also never find three clowns as fabulous as Cliffy, Nicky, and little Scampy."

Cliffy (Cliff Sobier) was the lead clown. Nicky Francis, a clown by trade, portrayed the musical Nicky. And Bardy Patton, son of producer Phil Patton, was Scampy, the youngest of the trio. When he outgrew the role, Sandy Dobritch, son of the series' booking agent, stepped into Scampy's shoes.

Every conceivable circus act was signed for the show. Jugglers shared the stage at the Kemper Insurance Building with cyclists, trampolinists, high divers, and singers. Youngsters even had the chance to participate on camera. In a contest segment each week a few children were chosen from the audience to dig into a jar of coins and keep whatever silver they could find amid the hundreds of copper pennies.

The focus of the circus show, but clearly not the focal point considering Mary Hartline's presence, were the animal acts. Kirchner says the cast and crew endured the occasional moments

2. Mary Hartline remained in Chicago when *Super Circus* picked up stakes for New York. She starred in a local children's program called *Princess Mary's Castle*. Between February 12 and June 15, 1951, she also costarred with piano player Chet Roble on a daily fifteen-minute ABC network show at 5 P.M., *The Mary Hartline Show*. The program originated at station WENR-TV in 1950.

of terror when the semidomesticated animals forgot themselves and the inevitable moments of embarrassment when the nonhousebroken creatures forgot where they were.

"We never knew what was going to happen," says Kirchner. "Lots of surprises occurred, but we became very adept at covering up or adlibbing any problem. It became quite natural."

During one show, quick thinking saved Mary from an attack by chimpanzees. Another week, cool heads helped quiet a troupe of nervous elephants. Kirchner explains that the huge beasts were afraid to walk from their trailer to the building for fear they would fall into a temporary streetside trench.

"We had to bring them in along the sidewalk, but they were scared of that damn pit. We got them in after our stage hands went next door to the Chicago Civic Opera House and borrowed some plush scenery from a Wagnerian opera. They leaned the flats against some columns and effectively hid the trench. Sure enough, the elephants walked in."

The incident didn't make the six-foot-five Kirchner any fonder of animals than he already was, however, "I don't like elephants," he confessed. "I don't like any of them, and I always tried to stay as far from them as I could."

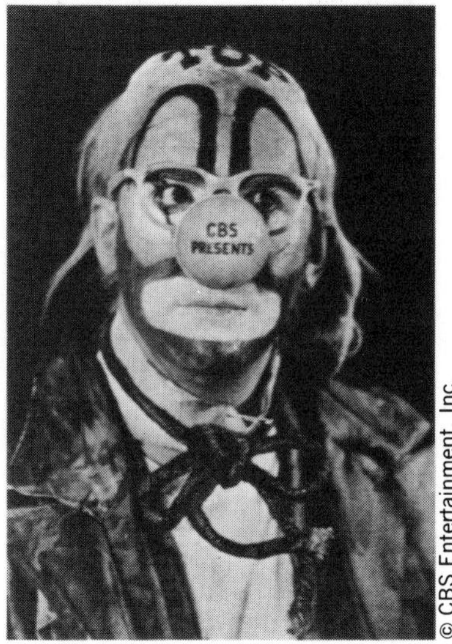

Years before he painted the town as Johnny Carson's announcer on The Tonight Show, *Ed McMahon painted his face and served as head clown on* The Big Top.

Memories of angry animals also bring a worried warble to Ed McMahon's usually sedate voice. McMahon, now familiar as Johnny Carson's sidekick, spent years disguised as a clown on CBS's successful circus program *The Big Top*. McMahon was the head clown on the show and star of thirteen other weekly TV shows at the WCAU-TV studios in Philadelphia. For the Saturday morning network production he wrote comedy sketches, some of which ended up being more frightful than funny.

"I used to have to deliver a clown act every week for several years. Right after the show I'd drive home and try to think what the hell we would do next week. One time I decided to base a gag on the cereal and snack promotions that offered a prize in every box. I wish I hadn't," McMahon says demurely.

"I planned to have a hot cereal that would be really hot because it was on fire. We'd have a cold cereal which was made to look freezing with dry ice. And the last thing was to be the world's biggest cereal box. Inside we'd have a horse and rider. The hot and cold boxes were supposed to build up to the finale, but what I didn't know was that the hot cereal we used could ignite and explode once it was ground into a fine form."

Here McMahon shivers with recollection. The set caught fire, he remembers, and the horse became extremely frightened. It was all seen by TV audiences across the country. The show was live.

"I'm telling you that was one of the scariest experiences of my life. When the explosion happened I told the other clowns to go right to the finish and get the horse out safely. It all worked out, but for a moment not only did I think my career was ended, I thought my life was over!"

The first *Big Top* audience filed into the Camden, New Jersey, Convention Hall and turned on their home TV sets Saturday morning, July 1, 1950. The show attracted throngs of circus fans until September 21, 1957.

The Big Top's *master of ceremonies, Jack Sterling, introducing an act to a youngster at the Camden, New Jersey, Convention Hall.*

Jack Sterling stepped into the ringmaster's spotlight. McMahon brought his own illumination—a red light bulb attached to his nose that blinked "CBS Presents." After lighting up, McMahon tilted his head down to bring into view the name of the show, painted on his headpiece.

Sterling, like Kirchner, had actual barker experience. The credentials paid off handsomely when mishaps occurred, and the show needed a voice that assured viewers that the unexpected event was "part of the act."

Sharing the stage with Sterling and McMahon were Chris Keegan, another clown, and Dan Lurie, the show's resident strongman. Behind the scenes were more than three hundred persons, making *The Big Top*, TV's largest regular live production in the mid-1950s.

"We treated it as though we were doing a nightime television," McMahon says. "We didn't subjugate it because it was on Saturday morning. We did it as well as it could be done."

Television invited every household with a television set to the circus. Some shows were switched off after a short excursion, but even those helped sell as many living room TV sets as real circuses were selling boxes of popcorn.

From 1949 to 1954 viewers clicked on to *The Magic Clown*. This NBC production starred Zovella the clown performing magic and comedy acts for fifteen minutes each week. *The Magic Clown* appeared on both Saturday and Sunday before it was canceled.

Acrobat Ranch stampeded onto ABC stations at 11:30 A.M., August 19, 1950. The cowboy/circus show, starring Jack Stillwell, was produced in Chicago for a skimpy $2,000 per week and sponsored by the General Shoe Corporation.

Hollywood Junior Circus played in four rings: CBS, NBC, ABC, and court. The circus-novelty show, sponsored by Hollywood Candy Company, makers of the "candy that makes you dandy," was intended for CBS starting January 27, 1951. But the network did not televise the program on its thirty-eight-station hookup, and the sponsor filed a $1 million suit that presumably caused CBS lawyers to choke on their candy bars.

The situation sweetened for Hollywood Candy when NBC aired the show from March to September, opposite ABC's *Super Circus*. On September 8, 1951, the show ended up on ABC, Saturday morning at 10:30 A.M.

Art Jacobson was emcee of *Hollywood Junior Circus*, on NBC. He was assisted by clown Carl Marx. At ABC the show starred ringmaster Paul Barnes and Buffo the Clown. Midget Max Bronstein was seen in both casts plugging the company's products.

ABC cameras zoomed into New York Stage A at 10:00 A.M., Sunday, February 3, 1952, for a live East Coast circus/variety show with Western acts. John Reed King emceed *Tootsie Hippodrome*, a delectable program laced with the taste of Tootsie Roll candies, telephone quizzes, comedy bits, and the usual circus attractions. The series moved to Saturdays on August 29, 1953.

The M&M Candy Carnival, a 1952 Sunday circus/talent show that promised prizes of $25 savings bonds and bookings at Atlantic City's Steel Pier, sank into oblivion after a short run. Barry Cossell and Gene Crane both appeared as the show's hosts. George Hamid, owner of the resort night spot, judged the contestants. He was assisted by two TV newspaper columnists who each week phoned in comments from around the country.

The offer of a personal appearance at Hamid's Steel Pier was also guaranteed the winner of *Contest Carnival*, a 1954 CBS Sunday afternoon show that presented a competition with aspiring young circus performers. Gene Crane was the barker on this WCAU, Philadelphia, production. Phil Sheridan and Harry Levin filled in as Kernel and Carny the clowns during the show's January 3, 1954, to December 18, 1955, life.

Lions and tigers ate into nighttime schedule when Paul Winchell brought ABC's *Circus Time* to 8:00 P.M. Thursdays for a nine-month stint beginning October 1956.

Circus shows have been top attractions, but making magic shows work on TV is the real trick. The problem exists because television itself is illusionary, and children, groomed on special effects, have understandably been skeptical of the magician in his oversized coat.

For more than thirty years technicians have been able to dig into an electronic and optical bag of tricks and make foot-high dinosaurs appear gigantic and average people look like Tom

Flamboyant magician Mark Wilson at work with wife Nani Darnell on The Magic Land of Allakazam

Thumb. Anybody who has watched Saturday morning long enough has seen Sky King hang from an airplane wing tip, Tom Corbett walk in outer space, Fury hurtle huge earthquake-formed crevices, or Jason defend "Star Command" with light-shooting energy rods.

Next to such video chicanery, few magicians have had a chance. Kids have seen it all. Television has had at hand precisely what magicians claim hasn't been up their sleeves. Try as they may, even the best magicians in the business haven't been able to outdo the acts performed by the TV engineers.

One of the first to make an attempt, however, was twenty-three-year-old Norman Jensen, host of the 1950 ABC series *Mr. Magic and J.J.* Jensen worked with a rabbit named J.J. that couldn't jump out of a hat simply because he was a hand puppet. The fifteen-minute show debuted on WPIX in 1949 and joined the network for weekday and Saturday telecast on April 12, 1950.

The same year, Geraldine Larsen appeared as *The Magic Lady*, host of a low-budget fifteen-minute film series that employed camera tricks as often as sleight of hand. She was assisted by Jerry Maren, a midget dressed as an elf.

From July 31 to September 4, 1955, CBS

Above: Claude Kirchner with Marx Magic Midway's *Bonnie Lee*

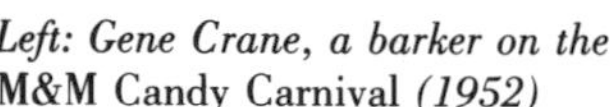

Left: Gene Crane, a barker on the M&M Candy Carnival *(1952)*

telecast *It's Magic* three days each week, with Paul Tripp as host.

Illusionist Mark Wilson pulled better ratings than his colleagues when *Magic Circus* premiered in 1959. He refined his act for *The Magic Land of Allakazam,* a 1960 CBS series that disappeared from the network in 1962, only to rematerialize on ABC for another two years.

Wilson, a slick magician with a voice as deep as his bag of tricks, was assisted by his wife, Nani Darnell, and son, Mike. The Saturday morning show was set in the mythical kingdom of Allakazam, where the Wilson clan and the King (Bob Towner), Rebo the Mixed-up Clown (Bev Bergerson), and Perriwinkle (Chuck Barnes) battled evil and nonbelievers and merged fantasy with the fantastic. Besides the usual and unusual array of magic acts, Wilson would talk to the show's resident puppets, Basil the Babbling Bunny, Doris the Dove, and Bernard the Rabbit, and introduce Huckleberry Hound, Pixie and Dixie, and Mr. Jinks cartoons.

ABC also offered a competing magic show before they managed to make the right numbers appear on Wilson's paycheck. For three months in 1961 the network presented *The Magic Ranch,* a thirty-minute videotaped show from Chicago with prestidigitator Don Alan and guest artists who would pop in from week to week.

Claude Kirchner returned to the network TV on September 22, 1962, to emcee *Magic Midway.* Even Kirchner's magical aura couldn't save this midway from folding. The show, produced by *Captain Kangaroo* co-creator Jack Miller, ended March 16, 1963.

"*Magic Midway* wasn't much of a show," confides Kirchner. "It was badly done. They did everything wrong and it just didn't work out."

Kirchner doesn't blame the cast for its failure. But he says that even the talents of baton twirling champion Bonnie Lee and the show's regular Bill "Boom Boom" Bailey (also seen on *The M & M Candy Carnival*), Phil "Coo Coo" Kiley, and Douglas "Mr. Pocus" Anderson couldn't stand up to the image of the original *Super Circus* team or Mark Wilson's magic.

The TV veteran, who remained with Marx for years as the toy company's commercial voice, says technology affected the show's chances.

"*Super Circus* was a live program. We could have given away ten thousand tickets every Sunday. The audience loved the show and they knew it was live. *Marx Magic Midway* was taped. We recorded them quite a few weeks before we were ever on the air. And we had to bring in audiences from schools and orphanages. The kids would sit there and they really didn't know what they were seeing."

Ed McMahon argues that videotape has helped, not hurt, circus and magic shows. The programs are enhanced by postproduction editing, he says, and had more sophisticated equipment existed in the 1950s, shows like *Big Top* and *Super Circus* might have lasted longer. Unfortunately, he adds, "TV as an art form didn't catch up fast enough to what we were doing. We put on a helluva show. It was like going to the circus every week. But what happened was that the art form, the technique, was archaic compared to now. We couldn't photograph the show as well and because of that people lost interest. The visual side was not strong enough to hold our eye."

McMahon draws an analogy to TV sports coverage. "It's like watching *Wide World of Sports.* You couldn't have done that show in 1952. It wouldn't have meant anything because it wouldn't have had that slick quality.

"I recently did a circus show in London," McMahon adds, "and we covered it with cameras from all directions. It didn't go on the air until we brought it back and put the technical touches on it. That's what has to be done these days."

In Ed McMahon's recent circus times he's dressed more like Claude Kirchner than a clown. The old uniform isn't around even if he wanted to wear it for nostalgia's sake. "I'd love to have it. I'd send it to a museum, but it's gone."

Kirchner, on the other hand, still has his TV tux. It's in the front of his closet because, he says, there's been recent talk of reviving *Super Circus* for network airing.

Greeting the crowds again would make Kirchner happy. Happy, but not proud, as one might expect. Kirchner has worked hard in radio and televison. He's seen hosts come and go, program content fall to commercialism, and broadcasters reap huge profits off children's television. He'd do the show again, but despite what Ed McMahon says about programming, Kirchner believes the glory days for him and television are over.

12 The Straw Hut Circuit

American viewers were taken for a ride in the 1950s when they thought they were going on a safari. Hollywood repeatedly presented a Tarzan-view of Africa and said it was real. For a decade television programs depicted natives as restless people who roamed through the jungle from one ancient ruin to another. Their faces were colorfully painted, as if they were on their way to a Halloween party, but the characters we saw never trick-or-treated for UNICEF. They had missionaries for dinner and lizard gizzards for dessert. The tribesmen spoke in grunts, traded beads, worshiped false idols, and fought with real vengeance. They looked Mexican or Caucasian and were almost never black.

These were the African travelogues audiences tuned to week after week. Years later the TV-educated public was unprepared to learn that the true barrier inhibiting Africa's emergence was our own ignorance, not thick jungle vines. The West had been whitewashed by thousands of scenes in which Ramar debunked voodoo

Johnny Weissmuller, overdressed for his Tarzan years but properly outfitted as Jungle Jim. With him in this scene from 1955 are Helene Marshall and Paul J. Guilfoyle. If they look concerned, it's because they're menaced by prehistoric lizards in the episode "The Land of Terror."

myths, Jungle Jim delivered civilization to bushmen, and Sheena cavorted with lions and chimps that appeared more intelligent than the natives.

How could the audience have expected Africa to be full of twentieth-century communities when most of the warriors spoke in the jumble of mumbo jumbo that was typified in one exchange on *Ramar of the Jungle:*

"Gun make no boom-boom," a chieftain told Ramar in an episode.

"You mean it makes no sound?" the American character replied.

"No boom-boom," the chief repeated.

"The gun must have been equipped with a silencer," the technocrat realized.

Jon Hall, the actor who played the physician know as Ramar, maintained in a 1953 *TV Guide* interview that the picture of Africans on his show was not doctored. He stated that he insisted on both historical and geographical accuracy and said, "Even our African dialects are genuine."

Educators who looked at the jungle shows disagreed. For example, *The National Parent-Teacher* Magazine argued in 1960 that it would "take an expert social studies teacher to counteract the false impressions."

In January 1954, Jon Hall announced that in order to capture the true flavor for the show he would travel with cast, equipment, and technicians to Africa and film twenty-six episodes of *Ramar*. Hall and company got no farther than the Florida Everglades, the makeshift Corriganville jungle in the San Fernando Valley, and the Eagle Lion Studios.

Jungle Jim similarly walked across town to the Columbia Ranch in Burbank where 5,000 square feet of transplanted African fauna choked in the California smog. And Sheena swung a little farther away, shooting principal photography in Cuernavaca, Mexico, where natives moved into the lean-to sets after the crew cleared out.

On an average $9,000 to $13,000 budget per episode, there was little else to do but explore Africa through the stock library files.

In 1955, when the jungle shows (known in the trade as the "straw hut circuit") had their densest TV coverage, African stock was bringing $2.50 to $15.00 per foot of film. Some scenes were very dated. More recent shots were filmed by big game hunters who defrayed the cost of their expeditions by taking along movie cameras.

The greatest demand for canned footage came when shows required shots of wild animals. According to Independent Producers Film Exchange, the most popular single item in the mid-1950s was a one-minute sequence of a panther stalking a man, then pouncing on him. The scene was used in at least fifteen shows by 1955, and was hardly ever recognized by viewers because the cat sometimes leaped from the left, sometimes from the right. It depended on which way the film was flipped.

Jon Hall first considered exploring the possibility of an African adventure in 1951 while working on a Columbia movie. The star of *The Hurricane* and *Ali Baba and the Forty Thieves* reasoned that cowboys had been overdone and enough space shows were already aloft. But since circus programs were popular, he thought, an action-adventure series with wild animals could snare winning ratings.

"Rudy Flotow and I were sitting around the dressing room kicking the idea around, and we finally settled on the notion of a doctor in Africa. Rudy became the producer and I starred as Dr. Tom Reynolds," Hall recalled in an interview shortly before his death in 1979.

Reynolds was dubbed "Ramar" (Great White Doctor) by the natives. In spite of his calling he seemed to reach more for his gun than his stethoscope and wrestled more with dangerous animals than with deadly viruses. The approach often put him in real peril.

"It takes courage and foolhardiness to fight with lions and tigers," he said. "They're tame. We'd get to know them and they'd snuggle up. But they still had their claws, and I occasionally got some of my clothes ripped."

Hall was thankful he was not in the show's hairiest scene. "We were doing an episode in which a gorilla and a lion have a fight. The trainer was in the gorilla outfit and the lion damned near killed the guy. I think he ended up with 140 stitches."

Irish McCalla, TV's most swinging female of 1955—Sheena, Queen of the Jungle

Born Free. . . More or Less

Wild animals have occasionally nibbled away at the weekend TV schedule and the gentle hands that have fed them.

Zoologist Marlin Perkins was once attacked by a deadly timber rattlesnake on his pet program, *Zoo Parade.* While he spent time recovering in the hospital, his replacement was knocked across the studio by an elephant. And in 1963, Perkins was again the brunt of an attack—this time from a charging bull seal during filming of a *Wild Kingdom* episode.

Usually, however, the animals making guest appearances on wildlife shows have been as tame as Lassie and as friendly as Flicka.

TV has been taking trips to the zoo and excursions to the African plains for thirty years.

ABC checked children into *Animal Clinic* in 1950. Dr. Wesley A. Young was the Saturday morning show's host. Later in the day the same network invited youngsters to *Saturday at the Zoo.* The production, emceed by William Bridges, shared the 1950 Peabody for best children's TV show of the year with *Zoo Parade.*

DuMont opened *Pet Shop* in Chicago for 7:30 P.M. Saturday airing over the entire network in December 1951. Gail and Gay Compton, a father and daughter team, operated the establishment and hosted the show. Meanwhile, Sheldon Gross visited the Philadelphia Zoo in *Let's Have Fun at the Zoo* and Billy Barty appeared on the Ralston Purina–sponsored ABC show *Your Pet Parade,* Sundays from 4:30 to 5:00 P.M. in early 1951. Barty, a midget actor, portrayed Billy Bitesize, a clown who could tear a telephone book in half after eating some of the sponsor's breakfast foods.

At 1:00 P.M. Saturdays from January 10 to May 30, 1953, Jack Whitaker, Freeman Shelly, and Roger Conant encouraged children to *Meet Me at the Zoo.* At 2:30 P.M., New York children tuned to *Animals Are Fun* on WPIX-TV, and in September 1953, CBS scheduled *Afternoon at the Zoo,* weekdays at 4:00 P.M.

Other syndicated animal shows that locked into the 1950s schedule included *Animal Fun and Mischief, Children Love Animals, Chummy's Animal Theatre,* and *Animal Adventures for Children.*

In 1966, Dr. Loren C. Eiseley, an internationally known anthropologist, explored the habitats of exotic and familiar creatures on NBC's Saturday afternoon series *Animal Secrets.* Jim Stewart guided the syndicated *Safariland* to Africa in 1963, and Bill Burrud narrated *Animal Kingdom* on NBC in 1968, *Animal World* for CBS in 1969, and the syndicated *Safari to Adventure* in 1971.

Arthur Jones described the capture of animals for zoos in the 1963 syndicated series *Wild Cargo* and *Call of the Wild* in 1970, and Bob Dale conducted tours of the San Diego Zoo in *Zoorama* (1968).

William Conrad first lent his narrative skills to *Wild, Wild World of Animals* in 1973, Lorne Greene presented *Last of the Wild* in 1974, and Hal Linden explored the animal world in art, history, music, and literature in ABC's *Animals, Animals, Animals.* The show premiered in 1976 and remained in production through early 1980.

Philip Carey took viewers to NBC's *The Untamed World* in 1969, and in 1972, John Forsythe discussed the nature of the beasts in the nonnetwork program *The World of Survival.*

Each show has been interesting and informative. But even the cagiest producers in television haven't been able to unseat Marlin Perkins as TV's resident zoologist.

Perkins, gray-haired for as long as he's been on television, began his broadcasting career in Chicago in 1946, when there were only a thousand TV sets in service. As curator of the Lincoln Park Zoo he had access to every animal on the premises. He proposed a weekly series, but the city fathers turned him down. Undaunted, he persuaded Buelah Zachary, producer of *Kukla, Fran and Ollie,* to help him. In 1947 he telecast more than two dozen unscheduled and unauthorized programs on WBKB,

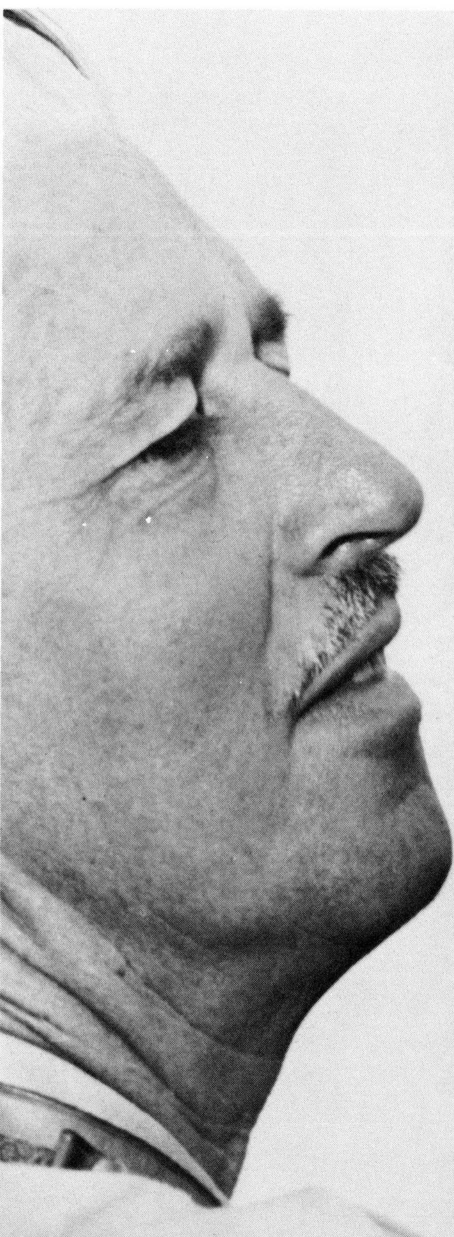

each featuring small animals he surreptitiously bundled into blankets and drove to the studio. By October 1950 he had his own regular NBC show, replacing the Hopalong Cassidy movies.

During its seven-year run *Zoo Parade* consistently attracted nearly half of the Sunday afternoon TV audience. The show was not a favorite of many animals, however. The guests were often uncooperative.

A jerboa, a tiny jumping mouse, for example, curled up under the heat of the studio lights and refused to budge. A "rope-walking" snake began his act, and just as Perkins boasted "they never fall," the snake slipped. And another week, a parakeet refused to perch on his fingers until the show was over.

In 1955, Perkins packed for Africa and shot nine episodes of the program. Two years later he signed off *Zoo Parade* and decided to point the cameras full time at animals running free rather than ones parading before spectators at the zoo.

His second show, *Wild Kingdom,* premiered on NBC in 1963, also settling into a Sunday afternoon slot. In 1968 the show moved to Sunday evening, where it remained until 1970, when *Wild Kingdom,* still in production, went into syndication.

Marlin Perkins holding a three-toed sloth in an episode of Wild Kingdom *(1963)*

Ramar of the Jungle never appeared on a network. Hall stated, "We went into syndication because we couldn't get the money from the networks that we wanted. Instead, we just went out and marketed it and put nearly everyone out of business in our time slots."

Nine months after its 1952 premiere the show was in the black. By December 1953 *Ramar of the Jungle* was airing in a hundred markets, reportedly earning a total annual gross of $1 million and rating among the top of all children's shows. And in November 1954, Hall reached the crest of commercial TV acceptance. He led Macy's Thanksgiving Day Parade.

The same year, the New York Supreme Court heard a suit regarding an alleged violation of stock-footage rights on *Ramar of the Jungle.* The brief, filed by Explorer Pictures, asked the court to confiscate all Ramar prints. They claimed that a number of episodes contained unauthorized clips of a feature called *Congorilla.* Explorer argued that the film's licensor, Cornell Films, had given Ramar the clips without legal permission to do so.

It wasn't a legal suit that ended Ramar's African work permit, however. Jon Hall, who at one time professed willingness to shoot 260 episodes of the series, left after just 52 programs.

"I got fed up and tired of it," he stated forthrightly.

Hall contended that the rigorous work schedule—three episodes every week for two years—and a near endless volley of criticism, wore him down.

Antiviolence factions assailed *Ramar* for its brutality. After the first year of production, Television Programs of America, agreed to red pencil violent scenes and "lay more stress on animal stories." Groups objecting to racist depictions asked for similar self-policing of invalid African stereotypes. The show ended production and, despite continuing negative reaction, enjoyed a healthy syndicated afterlife.

In 1957, Hall shot three episodes of another series, *Malolo of the Seven Seas,* but he indicated that he again disliked the grind. The programs were reedited into a feature, and Hall thereafter limited his acting to a few *Perry Mason* episodes ("The Case of the Festive Falcon," "The Case of the Feather Clock") before completely retiring from acting in the mid-1960's.

"When I quit, I quit," he said. "I did it with great aplomb. I really got tired and bored with it. I always wanted to do other things that were more meaningful to me."

Hall went directly into the airplane business, then became a restaurant owner, a Florida grapefruit farmer, and a resort entrepreneur. Until recently he owned a Los Angeles anamorphic lens company that marketed equipment to NASA and developed a panoramic camera.

Irish McCalla also doffed her jungle wardrobe and spear in favor of contemporary garb and a painter's brush. The attractive actress portrayed Sheena, Queen of the Jungle, a character who had lived amid the beasts ever since surviving a plane crash as a child.

Today, she paints new canvases at her Malibu, California, home and looks back fondly at the old TV pictures. "I loved the part of Sheena," she explained in an interview on *Dick Clark's Live Wednesday* in 1978, "because it was like when I was playing as a kid. You didn't have to be a very good actress to do the part," she said. Strength and agility were the primary requirements.

At nearly six-feet-tall, McCalla dominated most would-be assailants, be they two- or four-legged. She began her African affair after Anita Ekberg failed to show up for the title role in 1955.

TV Guide called her a "joy to watch . . . no wonder the rating services have discovered the show has more viewers among the adult males than among youngsters." New York *World-Telegram* reviewer Harriet Van Horne said "Sheena brings fresh air to TV." And while the willowy performer fluttered the hearts of many adolescent viewers, she got an unexpected rise from *New York Times* TV critic Jack Gould. "*Sheena,*" he wrote, "is so bad, it is completely fascinating." He added that the heroine and chimpanzee companion "run a traveler's aid booth in the jungle, helping an endless stream of outlaws and tribal chieftains to make the right turn at the many forks that abound in the Afro-Hollywood underbrush."

"The dialogue of *Sheena,*" he continued, "was basic Tarzan, and the acting elementary Ramar." He stated that McCalla was a bland derivative of Jane Russell who daintily stepped barefoot in the scenes. Gould added that the chimp played himself, and "at every available opportunity he ran into the jungle to be alone, which was thoroughly understandable."

Newsweek acknowledged that Sheena was not only queen of the jungle, she was also queen of the film quickies. The shows, the magazine said, were "thrown together ostensibly for juvenile audiences" and were as bad as they were "because they are so cheaply made."

Assisting McCalla in her battles to separate jungle rights from wrongs was Christian Drake, who played a white trader. Primarily, however, *Sheena* was a one-woman show that combined all the workable Hollywood cliff-hanger clichés with stock footage and sheer animal attraction.

Irish McCalla and Jungle Jon never bumped into *Jungle Jim.* This other pseudo-African syndicated series starred ex-vine-swinger Johnny Weissmuller.

Screen Gems acquired the rights to the Alex Raymond comic-strip character in October 1954 and quickly signed Weissmuller. Prebroadcast anticipation was so high for *Jungle Jim* that by September 7, 1955, the first week it was available for syndication, it earned $250,000. The program remained a money-maker for years to come.

Traipsing across the tropical set with the cunning African explorer were Jim's son Skipper (Martin Huston); his Hindu servant Kaseem (Norman Frederick); Skipper's dog, Trader; and Jim's chimpanzee, Tamba.

Weissmuller was quite familiar with the territory. He had portrayed the hero in a 1949 Columbia feature and, of course, the jungle had been his home even earlier. From 1932 to 1948 he swung from film to film as Tarzan.

Actually, *Tarzan* was intended for TV debut in 1955, too, but Weissmuller, already fifty-one years old, was not considered for the role. Producer Sol Lesser, associated with the ape man since 1933, planned on bringing Gordon Scott, the current movie Tarzan, to television. But the character would not make a successful leap to TV until 1966, when Ron Ely would walk and talk with animals.

The delay occurred because lawyers in three-piece business suits haggled over the man in a loincloth.

Commodore Productions and Artists, Inc. filed a $10,000 breach of contract suit against Edgar Rice Burroughs, Inc. over TV rights to *Tarzan.*

The complaint said an agreement was reached among the parties in 1950 that allegedly gave Commodore first refusal if and when the Tarzan character was offered to television. A proposal was submitted in 1955, but according to Commodore it wasn't made in good faith and it was designed to elicit a refusal.

Commodore testified that the offer contained demands, including the promise to employ actor Gordon Scott for $1,500 per episode for a minimum of thirty-nine stories, that film producer Lesser be paid $500,000 to keep his *Tarzan* features off TV for eighteen months, and that 20 percent of the TV profits go to Lesser. Two Gordon Scott test films were completed in March 1955, but litigation forestalled any TV adaptations for a decade.

A direct descendant of the Tarzan movies, *The Adventures of a Jungle Boy,* was syndicated in 1957. Michael Carr Hartley portrayed Boy, a youngster, like Sheena, orphaned after a plane crash. The series was filmed in Kenya, as was *The African Patrol,* which featured the investigations of a specially trained crime unit headed by Inspector Derek (John Bently).

The 1966 prime time African exploration series *Daktari* was rediscovered in Saturday reruns in the early 1970s. Marshall Thompson starred as Dr. ("Daktari" in Swahili) Marsh Tracy, protector of the continent's endangered species.[1] The show was filmed at Africa, U.S.A., a Los Angeles area park reserve.

The African show dramatically fell out of favor in July 1960, when the evening news presented reports of the Belgian Congo revolution and pictures of Patrice Lumumba and Joseph Kasavubu tangling with modern weapons instead of spears. As even more light was shed on the previously Dark Continent, it became obvious that an era of misrepresentation had ended. Hollywood had long been in love with the fantasy it created and suddenly producers cared very little for the reality exposed by newsfilm.

1. Six-year-old Erin Moran appeared on the show as Jenny Jones, Marsh's young admirer. Moran later was seen as Joanie Cunningham, Richie's sister on *Happy Days.*

From Chimps to Monkees

Years before Mickey Dolenz sang with the *Monkees,* he played with chimpanzees. Dolenz, son of George Dolenz (TV's Count of Monte Cristo), starred on *Circus Boy.*

Up until the time the credits rolled on the first show in 1956, the young actor went by his own name, collected stray cats, read comic books, and enjoyed his leisure time. Once he signed on with *Circus Boy* he became Mickey Braddock; his fondness for cats was devoured by lions; he read scripts instead of comics and worked long hours.

Braddock portrayed Corky, an orphaned teen-ager adopted by Robert Lowery and Noah Beery, Jr.

Braddock reportedly won his five-year Screen Gems contract after his father's agent, Mitch Hamilburg, urged Mickey to try out for the uncast series. Within a week he was ready to ride Bimbo the baby elephant in the first of three *Circus Boy* pilot films.

The series debuted on NBC, switched to ABC for prime time airing in 1957, and returned to NBC for Saturday morning telecasts in 1958. The show followed a *Fury*-gone-circus story line as Corky encountered adolescent problems while helping his adult friends satisfy their nagging creditors. New circumstances, faces, and loves appeared during each weekly stop of the circus train.

The circus lost network booking in 1958, but Braddock, nee Dolenz, found "The Last Train to Clarksville" and other Monkees hits another smooth ride to success eight years later.

Opposite: Mickey Braddock (Mickey Dolenz) riding Sinbad in an episode of Circus Boy *entitled "The Amazing Mr. Sinbad." In the 1956 edition, Mickey tried to prove that camels can run faster than horses.*

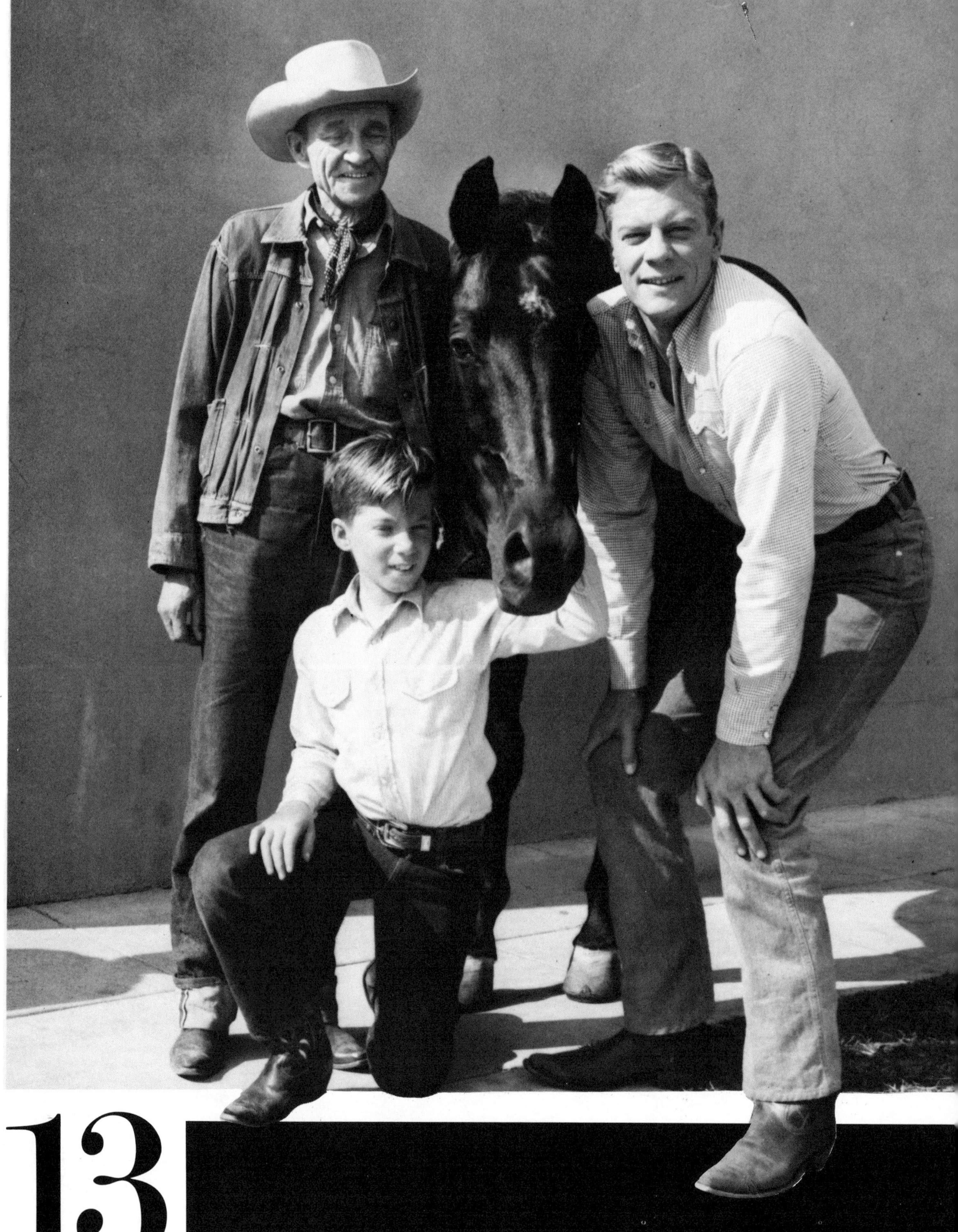

13

Animal Farms

For a time TV turned into the wild kingdom, and even zookeeper Marlin Perkins couldn't be blamed.

In the mid-1950s to the early 1960s, more than forty shows aired every week that starred or costarred animals. Two-legged actors took lower billing to creatures twice as endowed and often earned less money than their nonspeaking colleagues. During years when the average children's show actor was earning $300 to $500 a week, Fury rode off with a weekly $1,500, Rin Tin Tin raced for $2,300, Gene Autry's Champion cantered into an even higher bracket with a weekly income of $2,500, and Lassie ate fairly well on an average $4,000 per week.

Money was not the only allurement. Fury had four doubles. Trigger traveled in a $25,000 luxury van, Rinty relaxed in an air-conditioned doghouse, and Champion's stable echoed with piped-in music.

"It was tough playing second banana to a horse," recalls Peter Graves, ranch owner Jim Newton on *Fury*. James Brown, Rin Tin Tin's commanding officer, Lt. Rip Masters, agrees that it took time to get used to an animal costar. But he was consoled with the realization that even though Rinty sniffed out huge attention, "He couldn't sign his autograph worth a damn." And Jan Clayton, Lassie's housemother, added that without a doubt the collie was the top attraction. "And the minute the dog stops dominating the thing," she confided in a magazine interview, "we'll be canceled."

The Broken Wheel Ranch family—William Fawcett, Bobby Diamond, Fury, and Peter Graves (1955)

© Wrather Corp.

©photo courtesy *Boston Herald American*

Tommy Rettig—1954 and 1979

The *Lassie* TV shows, based on Eric Knight's 1940 novel, *Lassie Come Home* and the seven MGM movies filmed between 1943 and 1950, became TV's top-dog animal show. The series, in various formats, was continuously in production from 1954 until 1971 and remains in syndication today.

In the first version, containing 103 episodes, Lassie boarded with Jeff Miller (Tommy Rettig), Mrs. Miller (Jan Clayton), and Gramps (George Cleveland).[1]

In 1953, Tommy Rettig tested with a dozen other young actors for the role of Lassie's young master. "It was narrowed down to three of us," he remembered during a 1979 newspaper interview. "Each spent a week at Lassie's house. Whoever got along best with the dog got the part. It was Lassie's choice."

Prior to the TV audition Rettig had appeared in movies including *Panic in the Streets* (1950), *The 5,000 Fingers of Dr. T.* (1953), and *The Egyptian* (1954). He had been acting since age five, when he appeared in a 1946 road-show version of *Annie Get Your Gun.*

At first he found Lassie an agreeable companion. "I had fun working," he continued. "But after four years of the show it became the same old dialogue and the same old scripts. Either I saved Lassie, Lassie saved me, or we both saved somebody else."

By 1957, Rettig's opinion was a moot issue. The producers believed that he had outgrown the part, or, as *Time* described the situation, "Hair on the chest is permissible for a collie, but not a collie's young pal." A runaway orphan named Timmy (Jonathan Provost) was consequently written into the show. The following season, viewers watched Jeff depart for college.

However, even after Rettig left Stage A at Hollywood station KTTV, *Lassie* followed him. "All of the acceptance, the acclaim I'd had as a child was gone. I was capable of playing the parts as I was before, but nobody would give me roles because of the Lassie image." In time Rettig was cast in a few roles on *Wagon Train, Peter Gunn, Cheyenne,* and *The Fugitive,* but he remained unable to find steady acting assignments. To make ends meet he took jobs as

1. In 1956, Maxwell had proposed another series called *Waldo,* which would have featured the misadventures of a chimpanzee. The banana-eating character had little network appeal, however.

a salesman, a disc jockey, and a singer. In 1966 he returned to TV for nine months to costar with *Leave It to Beaver*'s Tony Dow on the ABC soap opera *Never Too Young*. Shortly thereafter his career stalled and he turned to farming, writing, and photography. Only recently has he decided to act again.

"As far as being a star," he admitted, "if it happens, it happens. If it doesn't, it doesn't. If somebody offered me a series, I'd probably jump at it." One steadfast rule guides his future plans, however. No dogs are allowed.

Jon Provost, Rettig's successor, appeared on the show until 1964. From the beginning he had a new family, for George Cleveland died soon after the start of the season, and Jan Clayton resigned, telling reporters she had wearied of wearing the same shabby dress. The first season of the new version, John Shepodd and Cloris Leachman were cast as Timmy's foster parents, Paul and Ruth Martin. Hugh Reilly and June Lockhart assumed the roles in 1958. Provost's episodes were syndicated under the title *Lassie and Timmy* (and alternately *Timmy and Lassie*).

George Cleveland's death provided a production problem. He was written out of the show, but not without some difficulty. Producer Robert Maxwell (coproducer of *The Adventures of Superman* in 1951) consulted a child psychologist and decided to develop a script around Gramps's heart attack. The notion was reported to have turned the nervous stomachs of Campbell's soups account executives, who argued against a TV death based on Cleveland's passing. Compromise followed debate, and Maxwell promised to remove specific references to death and opt for such sponsor-selected eulogies as "Gramps's gone," "Everybody loved him," and "He was a grand old man."

Timmy was allowed to kneel and beg God to "take care of Gramps in heaven," while Lassie whimpered at his side.

In 1964, when it was reasoned that Provost was getting too old, Lassie lost her second TV family. To make the transition to the third format, the Martins sold their farm and moved to Australia. Lassie, barred by quarantine restrictions, was left to Cully Wilson, an elderly friend played by silent film star Andy Clyde. When Clyde fell ill in an episode, Lassie ran for help, befriending forest ranger Corey Stuart (Robert Bray). Wilson, too sick to care for Lassie, en-

Lassie with Jon Provost

Yo-o Rinty!

Rin Tin Tin VII

Rin Tin Tin comes from Hollywood's oldest acting family. The dog seen in the opening and closing wraparounds in the 1976 broadcasts of *The Adventures of Rin Tin Tin* is the seventh-generation offspring of the pooch that debuted in silent films in 1924.

Rinty's heroic history goes even beyond his film exploits, however. On September 13, 1918, in an abandoned German infantry trench in Fleury, France, six pups were born to a near-starving German shepherd. Noncommissioned Air Corps pilot Lee Duncan heard a whimper from the territory he was patrolling. He located the shepherd and her six cold, damp, and dying puppies.

Duncan kept a male he named Rin Tin Tin and a female called Nanette. He chose the names in honor of the small knitted lucky charms that represented two legendary lovers who took refuge in a railway station during a German bombing attack. The station was demolished, and everyone but the two lovers was killed.

Unfortunately, Duncan's female puppy died of pneumonia three days after reaching the United States. Rin Tin Tin survived and eventually appeared in twenty-two movies, received as many as a million letters a year, and starred in hundreds of vaudeville dates before dying on August 10, 1932.

United Press noted his passing in a dispatch forwarded to the nation's newspapers: "Rin Tin Tin, greatest of animal motion picture actors, pursued a ghostly villain in a canine happy hunting ground today."

In 1947, Rin Tin Tin III followed in his grandfather's paw steps, starring in a new motion picture, *The Return of Rin Tin Tin.* His son raced into television in 1954, in the series produced by Herbert B. Leonard.

Today, Rinty VII enjoys a comfortable kennel complete with air conditioning, recorded music, and silver feeding dishes. He's currently retired, but no doubt there's more talent coming in the Tin family.

trusted the fire fighter with the dog. The two trudged off from Lassie's home town of Calverton for new exploits throughout the country, together biting off more trouble than Lassie alone would have eschewed.

Four years after Lassie first barked up the forest ranger's tree, Corey was seriously hurt fighting a fire and two new rangers, Scott Turner (Jed Allen) and Bob Erickson (Jack De Mave) became Lassie's newest partners. But even they could not keep up with the collie. By 1970, Lassie was performing a solo dog act, wandering independently for adventure and affection.

In 1971, Lassie was unleashed by CBS. The Federal Communications Commission's prime time access rule forced the networks to surrender a half hour of nightly airtime (7:30 to 8:00 P.M.) to local stations. Since it was Lassie's long-time home, Campbell initiated plans to resyndicate the pooch on non-network stations. It offered outlets a year's programs free. Campbell retained two minutes of commercial time, and the local stations sold four more minutes themselves. Two hundred stations signed for the first year.

Below and overleaf:
Lee Aaker—1955 and 1978

©photo courtesy *Boston Herald American*

Outpacing *Lassie* in action and adventure was *The Adventures of Rin Tin Tin*. The series, produced for prime time from 1954 to 1959, starred the great-grandson of the original 1922 silent-movie Rinty.

Herbert B. Leonard brought the famed film hero's relative to television after determining that Rinty had a ready-made audience. "He conducted a man-on-the-street survey, stopping people and asking them if they knew who Rin Tin Tin was," says James Brown, the show's adult human star. "Well over 60 percent of them knew the dog." *The Adventures of Rin Tin Tin* was presold based on news of the production. Telecasting began within sixty days of shooting. "Our popularity was reinforced by the mail we immediately received," continues Brown. "The majority of letters came from grownups, who wrote that they enjoyed watching the show with their children and explained to them, 'This is the dog I used to see as a kid.' "

The production schedule called for a show every three days, a six-day work week, and thirty-nine episodes a year. "It was frantic. When you're working with a boy and a dog it's especially tough. Lee could only be on the set four hours a day because of school, and the trainer needed time to work with the dogs."

There were three, sometimes four dogs posing as the bona fide Rinty. "J. R., or Junior, was the brilliant one," Brown explains. "But he wasn't comfortable with horses. He was friendly with them, but once he got kicked while licking one in the face. Hey You appeared in fights, but he couldn't take a good close-up because one eye was clouded over. And another dog did the long shots and the runs with horses.

"Sometimes we had a heck of a time shooting, but Frank Barnes, the trainer, always handled them with firmness and kindness. He ended up teaching his theories to Benji's trainer, Frank Inn."

The German shepherd, owned by Billy Duncan, was counter to type. Rather than living up to the often vicious, unpredictable image of the breed, he was friendly and gentle with children. "Everyone wanted to touch J.R. when we were out on the road. We visited children's hospitals everywhere, and although some youngsters needed guidance petting him, there was never any trouble," Brown says.

CBS was originally slated to carry the production, but when the show premiered on October 15, 1954, audiences had to tune to their local ABC stations at 7:30 P.M.[2] The wonder dog finally became a faithful four-year friend to CBS via reruns beginning in September 1962.

Rin Tin Tin was also devoted to Rusty, an orphan played by ten-year-old Lee Aaker. Rusty and Rinty, according to the plot, survived a brutal Indian attack that left everyone else on their wagon train dead. Upon being discovered by the U.S. Cavalry, the boy and dog were made honorary soldiers of U.S. Fort Apache in Arizona and assigned to Lt. Rip Masters's care.

Variety said the series was "pure formula, but it's the right formula and skillfully done." *TV Guide* noted that the show was "crammed with action, gun-play and chase scenes—fine viewing for kids."

Besides the predictable episodes in which Rinty had to struggle across the desert, brave a mountain lion's attack, and escape from locked boxcars, the show was often just a simple fable. One story paralleled the boy who cried wolf, with Rusty complaining one too many times that the fort was under attack. In another tale Rusty learned that government officials could be corrupt. And in yet another he discovered that former criminals can become honest citizens.

Although Indians were responsible for the death of Rusty's parents, the show didn't take the usual potshots at Indian stereotypes. A tenuous peace existed between the Apaches and the cavalry. And war was averted many weeks through the courageous acts of Rinty, Rusty, Masters, and the calm restraint of former warriors.

"We tried to preach without preaching," says James Brown. "Our stories simply taught that right was right and wrong was wrong. You don't get those kinds of values on television anymore."

Brown, hired over 150 competing candidates, had been seen in *Air Force* (1943), *Going My Way* (1944), *Objective Burma!* (1945), *Sands of Iwo Jima* (1949), *Chain Lightning* (1950), *The Pride of St. Louis* (1952), and forty other motion pictures. He filled out the new role and the cavalry uniform perfectly.

"I liked the story line and the chemistry between Lee Aaker [Rusty] and me," he says. Brown, a former tennis star as well as actor, played a stern but compassionate father figure. The military garb was a convenient costume for authority. The actor would have conveyed the same feeling in Bermuda shorts, however. He provided the voice of reason and experience, the very role model, as Brown suggests, that children tuned to Saturday morning television have not had in years.

Brown, oblivious of his impact because of the exhausting production routine, says he learned of his influence in a touching way. "Lee and I were out on tour in Chicago, and I had to cut a TV talk show appearance short because of an interview elsewhere. When I said goodbye, Lee came on. Since I still had some time before the next appointment, however, I watched from the control room. Lee was asked if he had any heroes. He didn't think I was there and he thought for a moment and said, 'Yes, Jim.' I just melted."

"No one knew what financial value Rin Tin Tin and other TV shows would have then," Brown continues. "But the program just took off."

A two-part episode was released in Europe and Mexico as a feature film after additional

2. In September 1959 the series aired twice each week on ABC—late Monday and Wednesday afternoons.

DONT TREAD ON ME

footage was shot, and tons of Rin Tin Tin merchandise was loaded on store shelves coast to coast. During the production breaks the cast toured in a rodeo show and Brown issued six records of his own for MGM, the biggest of which, "The Legend of the White Buffalo," was the subject of an entire show.

With such success in the 1950s it seemed natural to Stan Moger, executive vice-president of SFM Media Service Corporation of New York, that Rin Tin Tin could stand another run. In 1976, after he had spearheaded *The Mickey Mouse Club* revival, Moger repackaged the twenty-year-old show for the 1970s audience.

James Brown returned to the camera as host of the 164 episodes. With Rin Tin Tin VII at his feet, he introduced each story. The episodes, previously shot in black and white, were tinted sepia in an effort to convey historical flavor.

Following in *Lassie's* paw prints, Rinty was offered on a barter basis free of charge to stations as long as they would air the Crayola, Child Guidance toys, and Hunt-Wesson Snak-Pak commercials.

Rinty didn't find a warm welcome, however. The broadcasters, not the audiences, were to blame. "In Los Angeles, for example, it was put on at the ungodly hour of 8:30 in the morning," complains Brown. "Little toddlers wouldn't understand it. Then it was moved to 3:30 in the afternoon, which was just as bad. In cities like Tampa, Florida, where it aired on Saturday, the ratings were good, but most cities scheduled it completely wrong."

Brown has continued acting, though, like Tommy Rettig, he found more doors closed than opened since he completed his kids' show. "Back then I didn't worry about being overexposed, but it hurts nowadays. I'll go to a casting office and be greeted by a girl or guy young enough to wear braces and hear, 'Mr. Brown, you were my hero.' I think, 'great, I'm in.' But they usually won't have anything for me, because all they see is the cavalry uniform. Lee Aaker is smart; he's out of the business, making an honest living as a carpenter."

Brown still occasionally appears in guest roles and talks about working in another dog series for Herbert Leonard, perhaps with one of the remaining relatives of Rinty. The networks, however, haven't found the idea fetching.

Bobby Diamond rides film veteran Fury (Beauty) to TV. The horse had previously appeared in Giant, Lone Star, *and* Johnny Guitar.

Gene Autry tried to corral young viewers in 1955 with *The Adventures of Champion.* The Wonder Horse didn't have the creative legs to last in the ratings race, however. The series, starring the cowboy's horse, twelve-year-old Ricky North (Barry Curtis), and his dog, Rebel, aired only from September 30, 1955, to February 3, 1956. It was later repeated on Saturday mornings.

The real champion in 1955 was a horse named Fury. The program of the same name premiered on Saturday, October 15, and continued airing for twelve consecutive seasons, though only five years of episodes were shot.[3]

Fury was a contemporary Western, saddled with issues that were identifiable to young audiences. The show centered on a tough orphan, Joey (Bobby Diamond), who crossed the other side of the tracks to the Broken Wheel Ranch, where he was loved and adopted by widower Jim Newton (Peter Graves).

Each episode was a simple homily—a primer on civil defense, bicycle safety, wildlife preservation, freedom of the press, family responsibility, or fire prevention. The horse show received citations from the National Education Association, the Junior Achievement program, the U.S. Civil Defense agency, the United Fund, the Red Cross, the Boy Scouts, and the ASPCA. The National Parent-Teacher Association (PTA) favored the show because in it "courage is linked with compassion, strength with strategy, and respect for the law with respect for human beings."

"*Fury* had a lot to offer a whole generation of young people," stated Peter Graves. "Every story was sort of a moral tale without attendant violence. We taught them something about animals, life, parental authority, growing up, getting an education—basic values that we sometimes lose sight of in this country."

Irving Cummings, Jr., the program's producer, explained in 1958 that *Fury* wasn't really trying to "preach or write down to kids." *Fury,* he insisted, was not out to "win any wars." He basically wanted to entertain children "and still

3. *Fury* was retitled *Brave Stallion* when it was distributed for non-network syndication beginning in 1959. It had little difficulty selling, since the production had earned an average 17.8 rating over the first four seasons on NBC. The figure meant that an estimated 17.8 percent of the nation's TV sets were tuned to *Fury* on Saturday mornings, giving it a better rating than many prime time shows, and placing the horse in the winner's circle for Post™ cereals.

not contribute to their intellectual impoverishment."

"I think it was an all around excellent show for kids and for families, and today I look back on it very proudly," Graves adds.

However, the actor was ready to buck the horse when he learned that the pilot he had done was picked up for Saturday morning, not prime time.

"When I made the pilot, I thought it was going to be a good evening show. And I think everybody involved in it felt the same way at the time," Graves explains. "At some point after we finished, NBC made the decision to go for Saturday. That was the beginning of a serious network push for Saturday morning televison programming. NBC knew they had an enormous market for kids. But I was still disappointed at first, because I wanted it to be in prime time. I believed the show was a cut above just a children's program. But it was not my decision. And I had made a commitment to stay with it, so I went ahead and fulfilled the contract."

Graves, who rode *Fury* to national prominence and eventually dismounted for *Mission Impossible*, was actually advised by friends in 1955 that TV would ruin his career. "You have to remember, we came along fairly early. Episodic television was still new, and the question among other actors around town was whether exposure on the new medium would kill their film prospects."

Peter Graves (left) *grew up to star in* Fury *in 1955. The same year, his older brother, James Arness, debuted in* Gunsmoke.

photo courtesy Peter Graves

Both Graves and his brother, James Arness, decided to seek the answer themselves. Graves premiered in *Fury*, October 15, 1955; Arness portrayed Marshal Matt Dillon on *Gunsmoke* beginning September 10 the same year.

Graves signed with some trepidation. The money, or the promise of money, was good. And that alone was something more than what films were offering in the mid-1950s.

"The picture business was in a mess then. Few movies were being made. Studio contracts, the thing every young player had hoped for, were really dead. The thought of steady work and the chance of earning a weekly salary was pretty attractive. Like others, I had been working and jobbing a lot, but not into any significant amount of money. So when I started to add up what I could get for thirty or more shows a year, that suddenly became an important consideration.

"In retrospect," Graves adds, "even though I might have had some unhappy times with *Fury* when I felt I wasn't achieving some of my career goals, I feel very fond of that show and look back now and realize what an important little production it was."[4]

Fury's success belongs to Fury. The beautiful coal-black stallion, fifteen hands high, commanded great attention. Presumably, Joey was the only one who could ride the horse. Every budding equestrian watching the show must have been jealous.

Fury, whose real name was Beauty, had appeared in a number of movies before he jumped the hurdle to television. The stallion carried Elizabeth Taylor in *Giant* (1956), Clark Gable in *Lone Star* (1952), and Joan Crawford in *Johnny Guitar* (1954).

"Fury was a magnificent animal, and I grew very fond of him," Graves says. "But Ralph McCutcheon, his trainer, deserves special attention, too. He was extraordinary with him. He was one of those few people who could talk to animals."

Just as other Hollywood figures were pampered, Fury, too, received the royal treatment. In 1958, when the horse caught a cold, he was shipped to Palm Springs to recover. And Graves says that Fury, like everyone on the production team, occasionally showed up without any desire to work. Whenever that happened, McCutcheon would ask for a break and "by guile, wile, and sheer love of the animal, coax him."

When the horse wasn't mastering tricks, he was often gallivanting with the crew. On one occasion the employees were playing baseball and were in need of a center fielder. Fury joined in and saved a run by trapping a ball on one bounce between his teeth. Said one extra, "Those horses are all alike; good fielding, but no hits."

"He was marvelous to watch," Graves adds, "and the boy, Bobby Diamond, got very close to the horse."

Diamond, a pro since the age of two when he appeared on the cover of a magazine, hopped on Fury at age eleven. He had hopes that once he got off the horse he would walk into other roles.

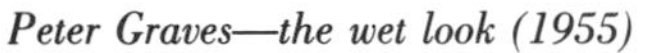
Peter Graves—the wet look (1955)

Peter Graves—the dry look (1979)

"When I grew up I still wanted to be an actor," he said in 1957. "I like acting. It's hard work, but it's fun."

Before *Fury*, he had been seen on *The Loretta Young Show* and *Cavalcade of America*. His movie credits included *The Glass Slipper* (1955), *Untamed* (1955), *The Greatest Show on Earth* (1952), and *To Hell and Back* (1955). In his post-*Fury* years Diamond found few acting jobs. He retired from the profession and is an attorney in southern California today.

Costarring with Diamond and Graves were William Fawcett as Pete, the ranch foreman, and Roger Mobley and Jimmy Baird as Joey's pals, Packey and Pee Wee. The production was filmed at the Iverson Ranch facilities in Chatsworth, California.

Fury was budgeted at approximately $25,000 per show, $5,000 to $10,000 more than most live-action Saturday morning shows. The money didn't go into lavish equipment, however; it just paid the ever-rising bills for the 114 episodes.

Graves makes the point understood when he describes a typical shooting day in which the crew tried to squeeze a few extra minutes of production time into the already full session. "We normally didn't travel with any lights. We just had reflectors on location. And even after the sun was almost set, I remember evenings standing in a close-up shot with the spotlight

4. In December 1956, Graves considered abandoning Joey and the ranch for a prime time series in which he would have played a New Orleans lawyer. The project never materialized, however, and Graves remained a Saturday morning father figure.

of a car shining on. We used what was available. In those days the guys knew all the tricks for shooting a picture and getting it done on time and on budget."

Despite production shortcuts, Graves said, everyone realized they were involved in a lasting production. "It was sometime during the first year that our line producer Leon Fromkess said to me, 'Peter, do you know that as long as black and white half-hour series play anywhere on television, *Fury* will be seen. It's a classic. It's timeless.' He's certainly been born out. It's still telecast all over the world."

Bolting from the starting gate five months after *Fury* was a horse named Flicka. Actors Anita Louise, Gene Evans, and Johnny Washbrook counted on a winner, but the Thoroughbred couldn't catch Fury's lead.

My Friend Flicka, based on the Mary O'Hara book and a 1943 movie, essentially told the story of a boy and his horse. A turn-of-the-century Montana setting allowed for sudsy soap opera scripts to wash with some Western action. Thus, when ten-year-old Ken McLaughlin (Washbrook) and his brown colt weren't hearing sweet advice, they were getting into sour pickles. Ken's parents, meanwhile, tilled the soil and cultivated their relationships with unruly neighbors.

Twentieth Century-Fox shot the program in color but initially released the episodes in black and white. The studio bet that the horse would become an equine Lassie, and more valuable considering the color investment. But Flicka rode off into the sunset instead of the foreground in 1958.

The flip side of *My Friend Flicka* and *Fury* was *National Velvet*. The girl/horse story had been filmed in 1944 with Elizabeth Taylor playing pretty Velvet Brown. The TV-version starred Lori Martin as the twelve-year-old with the dream of riding King in the Grand National steeple-

Right: Lori Martin, the star of National Velvet

Opposite: My Friend Flicka *didn't win any ratings races in 1956, but it ran well during Saturday morning repeats for years. Gene Evans, Johnny Washbrook, Flicka, and Anita Louise starred.*

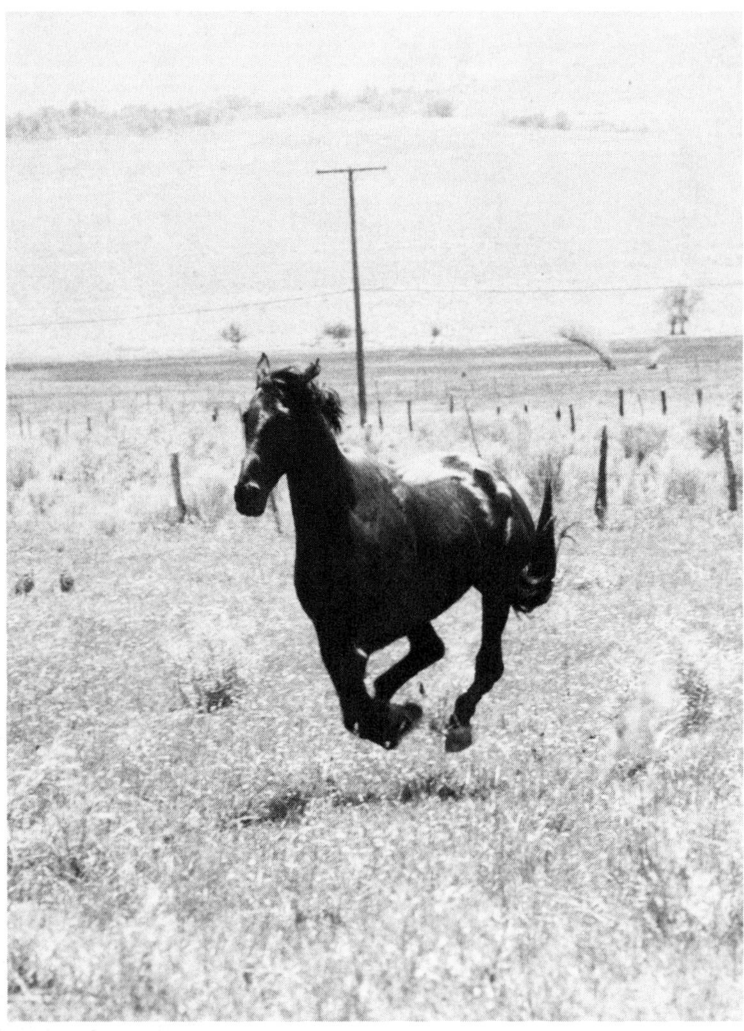

Flying over the fields is Thunder, a semiwild black stallion befriended by two young children. The 1977 series was developed by Fury's *original writer and producer.*

chase. Arthur Space and Ann Doran costarred as the youngster's encouraging dairy-farmer parents.

The program was as saccharin as King's treats and failed to be a long-distance runner. It aired from September 1960 to September 1962 before being put to rerun pasture.

In 1974, NBC gave a show to a German shepherd with a David Janssen complex. *Run, Joe, Run* attempted to combine Janssen's *The Fugitive* with *The Adventures of Rin Tin Tin.* Joe, whose off-camera name was Heinrich of Midvale, played an army guard dog, unjustly accused of attacking his master. Rather than facing prosecution and possible destruction, the innocent dog flees with both his revenge-seeking accusers and his sympathetic army trainer, Sergeant Cory (Arch Whiting), in pursuit. Episodes involved Joe's odyssey. However, the adventure series, like Joe, was a dog, and not pedigree as Rinty had been.

Run, Joe, Run was run off the air after the second season, but not before producers gave the show a new look. In September 1975, Cory was ordered back to his base and Joe adopted mountainman Josh McCoy (Chad States). The two then traveled across the country in search of adventure. They found only network cancellation.

Fury's original writer/producers, Irving Cummings and Charles Marion, attempted to saunter down the familiar bridle path in 1977 but found that the Saturday morning audience and horse stories no longer made a happy marriage. Their effort, *Thunder*, was a half-hour action-adventure series about a stallion that befriended eight-year-old Cindy Prescott (Melora Hardin), her young neighbor Willie (Justin Randi), and his stubborn mule, Cupcake.

The series was produced for NBC and, in keeping with the 1970s consciousness, dealt with educational themes such as C.P.R. (Cardiovascular Pulmonary Resuscitation) training.

In addition to the few new animal series to premiere in the 1970s, *Flipper* surfaced via reruns in the Saturday morning time slots where twenty years earlier Yukon King had helped *Sergeant Preston of the Yukon* strike gold and Bullet and Trigger had kept Roy Rogers company.

Other animals were not to make a home in the children's ghetto. Saturday morning had at last been zoned by the cartoon producers.

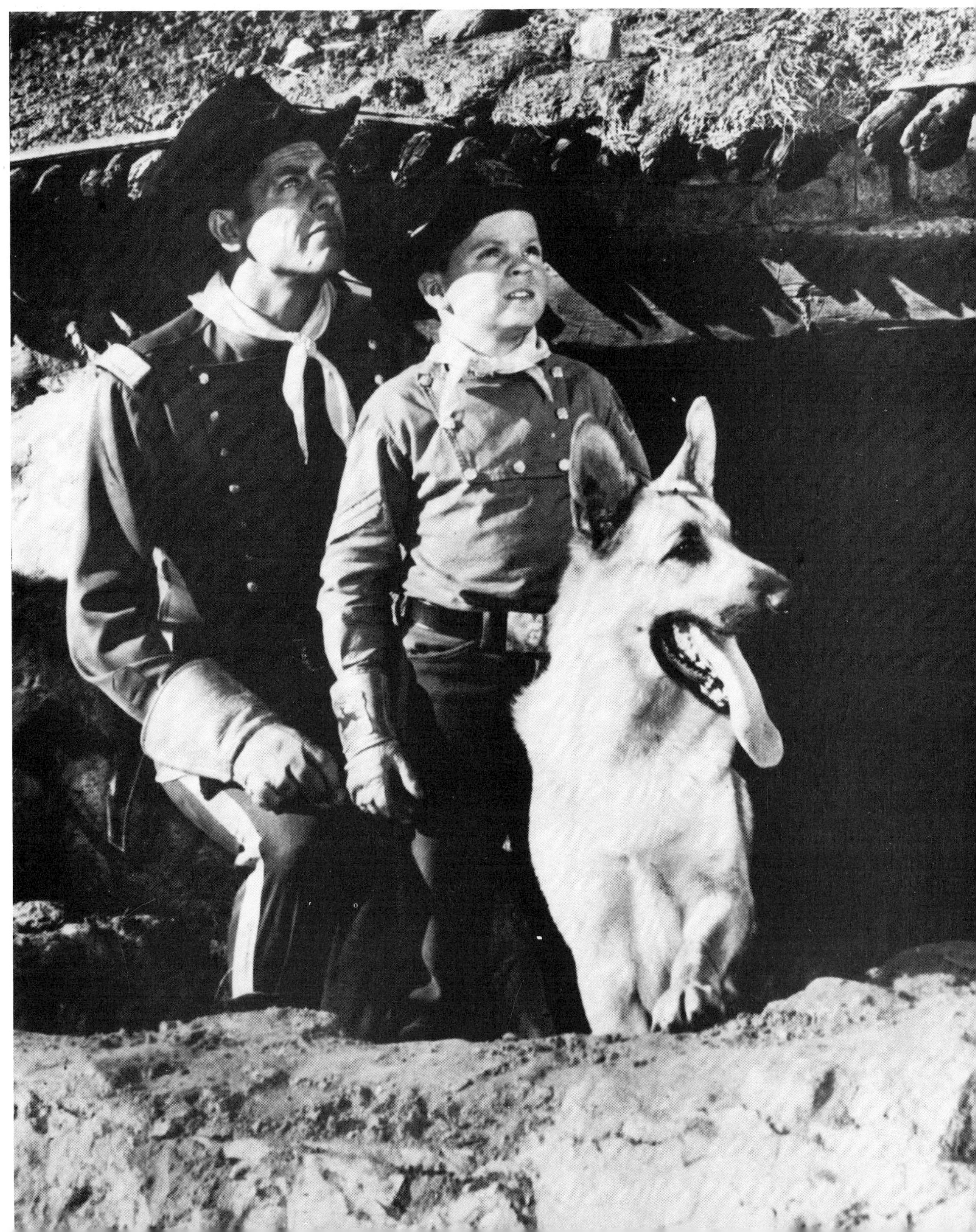

14

The Cold War Brigade

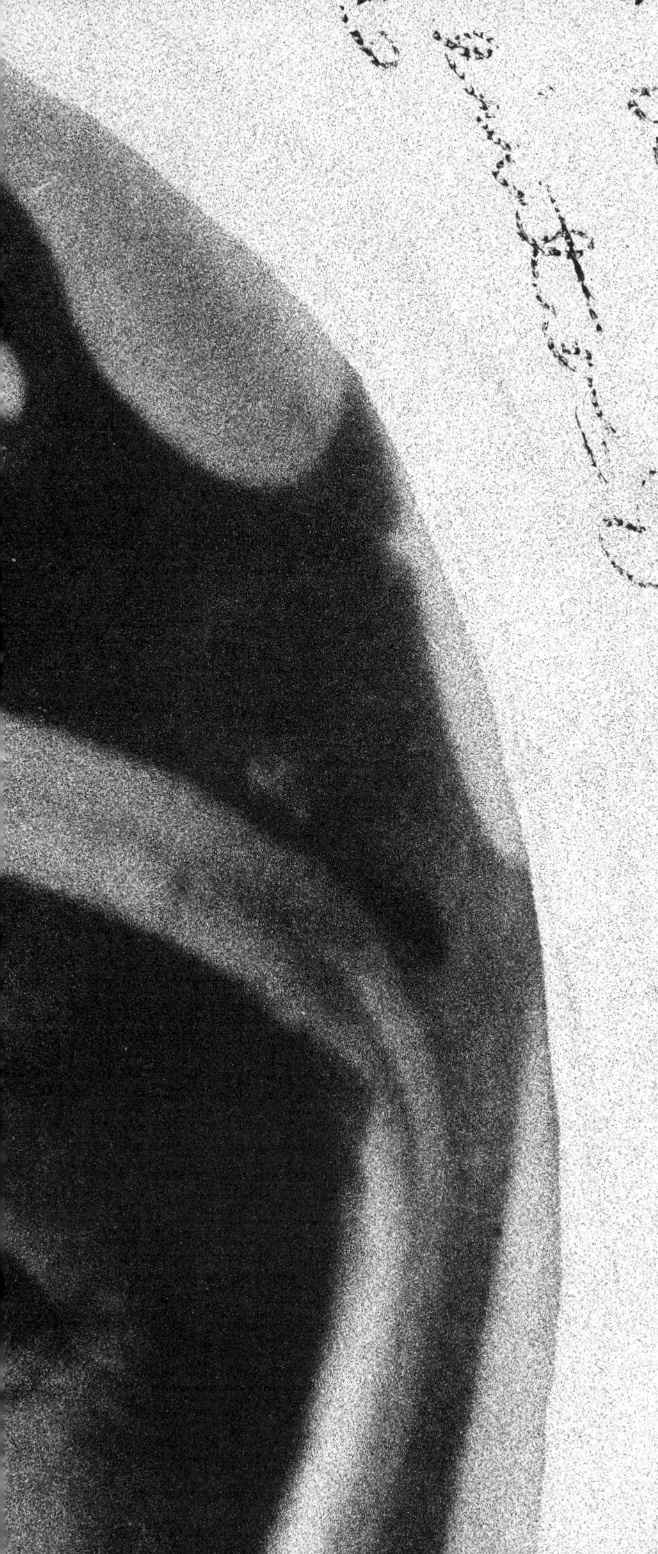

On August 6, 1945, the early morning sky over Hiroshima burned with the intensity of the sun. Three days later Nagasaki smoldered under the same fury. A hot war ended with the two fiery blasts; another—the Cold War—immediately began.

The Soviet Union was the enemy in this undeclared conflict. There were no direct engagements with the opposition army, no victories, and no heroes. Secret agents fought small battles while generals waited. Disguises, midnight rendezvous, cyanide tablets, and silencer-equipped handguns were substituted for uniforms, liberation forces, airlifts, and bloody beachheads. It was a difficult war to fight and a difficult war to film.

Hollywood tried and generally failed. Movies such as *The Girl in the Kremlin* (1957), *Big Jim McLain* (1952), *My Son John* (1952), *The Beginning or the End* (1947), and *I was a Communist for the FBI* (1951) were laughable, undistinguished motion pictures that traded on theories of conspiracy rather than bravery on the battlefield.

Television provided a much more successful channel for the Cold War propagandists. And children received a full dose of the message on Saturday morning. In the earliest years stations were looking for programs to televise. The Pentagon, sensing that both the needs of broadcasters and their own requirements could be satisfied through documentaries, geared for patriotic production. Soon black and white adventure shows and science fiction serials also showed the tinge of red, white, and blue. Viewers saw state-of-the-art jets swooping across the screen to the strains of "The Star-Spangled Banner" in government-produced station sign-on films, and watched as Saturday morning characters challenged representations of Eastern-bloc agents. Families tuned to short tips on preparing for air raids that never happened and televised advice on how to construct a bomb shelter to protect ourselves from a Communist leader who would one day request permission to visit Disneyland.

There were puppet programs in the early 1950s like *Barnyardville Varieties,* in which characters sang praise to the virtues of democracy, and there were ever-present Conelrad tests designed to remind us of the Soviet threat.

Industrial strength was held on a par with military might in a series of mini-documentaries that debuted October 1950. *Industry on Parade*, a long-running Saturday morning fixture on many local stations, maintained that America's global supremacy was due to its devoted working class.

NBC-TV initially filmed the series of thirteen-minute episodes. The National Association of Manufacturers bankrolled the rousing films, which showed such varied scenes as a Milwaukee dry cleaning plant, the electric-toaster industry, noncombustible vinyl, the manufacturing of horseshoes, and Ozark-mountain souvenir workshops. By 1954, 234 stations in the United States and ten countries abroad carried the featurettes.

Joining *Industry on Parade* in the pro-American labor-related documentary market was NBC's 1956 educational series *Progress* and *Agriculture on Parade* in 1964.

The Big Picture waved the flag higher and longer than any other production. J. Fred MacDonald observed in *The Journal of Popular Film and Television* ("The Cold War as Entertainment in 'Fifties Television," Bowling Green University Press, Vol. VII, No. 1) that although the show was distributed without orders on when it should air, because of "its breadth of distribution and length of availablility, it was probably the most widely viewed series in television history."

The U.S. Army–produced program began as an obscure local show on Washington station WTOP-TV in 1951. It was the first TV production of the Pentagon and initially offered government-focused newsfilm at an age when networks didn't have their own reports from the front. With its opening words *The Big Picture* commanded staunch patriotism:

> *All over the world the United States Army is on the alert to defend our country—you, the American people—against aggression. This is* The Big Picture, *an official television report to the nation from the United States Army.*

In 1952, CBS carried *The Big Picture* at 2:00 P.M. Sundays, and *The New York Times* heralded it as "absorbing and helpful in acquainting a stateside audience with the realities, hazards and unusual hardships that have marked the Far Eastern struggle."

By November 1952 ninety-six networks and independent stations carried the program, three in New York City alone.

No TV show found the Reds more menacing than *The Big Picture*. Captain Carl Zimmerman and commentator Bill Downs narrated brutal scenes of psychological warfare in Korea and Russian brutality in East Berlin.[1]

A 1954 edition that reviewed Communist horrors in Korea was actually withheld from broadcast for a month. Defense and State Department officials claimed they were concerned that spies operating in the United States might identify anti-Communist North Koreans depicted in the documentary. However, reporters learned that the film was tabled for fear that emphasizing Communist atrocities could hinder U.S.-Sino talks in Berlin.

Congressman Charles E. Potter (R-Michigan) said that it was "absolutely ridiculous" to withhold the film. He proposed an investigation. Stations had already received prints of the episode, but "Atrocities in Korea" did not air until two weeks after the Berlin Conference began. When

1. In later years Army Sergeant Stuart Queen was assigned narration duty. Additionally, *The Big Picture* featured guest announcers, including Edward R. Murrow, Alexander Scourby, Walter Cronkite, Lowell Thomas, and Ronald Reagan.

viewers finally saw it, the army's concern became clear. The narration warned that the documentary would prove "shocking," and as scenes of GI graves rolled by, the audience was told, "You are looking at the face of Communism. Never forget it."

The Big Picture was as impressive as it was heavy-handed. The noncommercial series, distributed free to stations, contained dramatic footage of the nations's military strength: film that made America seem unconquerable; film viewed by children who would grow old enough to fight and die in Vietnam.

The Big Picture was not the only program that kept a low flame under the Cold War. NBC's acclaimed 1952 historical series, *Victory at Sea* culled through 60 million feet of film to depict the U.S. and Allied naval operations during World War II, while CBS recounted aviation's effort in the 1956 to 1958 production *Air Power.*

Dramatic shows also bore the closing credit "Produced in Cooperation With . . ."

Treasury Men in Action recounted true cases found in the U.S. Treasury Department files. The series premiered as a live show on ABC in September 1950, costing Chrysler $10,000 per week to produce. Beginning in April 1954 the dramatizations were shot on film, and repeats regularly ended up on Saturday morning.

In 1955, CBS's *Navy Log* presented stories based on actual Navy records.[2] The series moved to ABC for a two-year hitch in 1956 and, like other military-oriented shows, was mustered off prime time only to have a renewed TV career on Saturday.

It was no secret when *O.S.S.*, ABC's adventure program about the U.S. World War II superspy agency, switched to Saturday after its initial 1957–58 airing. The submarine series *The Silent Service* also cast off as a weekend children's show, and stations enlisted youngsters' interest in repeats of *The West Point Story*, *The Blue Angels*, and *Men of Annapolis* in the late 1950s.

The Air Force also supplied previously unreleased footage of scientific equipment, ICBM lift-offs, and X-15 test flights to *Steve Canyon* in 1958 and advised the comic book hero on how to nose his F-102 into a realistic trajectory. One episode, for example, put a renewed chill on the Cold War. In "Operation Intercept," a window of a B-47 blows out at 46,000 feet and the pilot and copilot are frozen in midair. Canyon (Dean Fredericks) pursues the derelict plane and shoots the B-47 down with rockets rather than letting the winds carry it to Russia.

The Pentagon has cooperated with commercial broadcasters on such shows and scripts in order to help producers achieve authenticity and to help shape the public's perception of the armed forces. But the Pentagon has had another vested interest. In the 1950s and early 1960s the deluge of military stories helped maintain recruitment levels.

The relationship has helped producers as much as the government. Whenever the Pentagon approves a movie or TV script and determines a project is "in the national interest," materials, services, technical advice, and personnel are supplied for free or at a minimal cost.

The relationship between Hollywood and Washington began in 1923, when D. W. Griffith used more than a thousand enlisted men to film *America.* In the years to follow, director King Vidor managed to secure troops, combat footage, and trucks for *The Big Parade,* and William Wellman called in the small 1927 Army Air Corps for *Wings.*

Stringent Pentagon rules have meant that films like *Seven Days in May* (1964), *Dr. Strangelove* (1964), *Fail Safe* (1964), *Catch-22* (1970), and *Apocalypse Now* (1979) received no assistance because they were considered "inaccurate or inappropriate depictions of military activity." Meanwhile, recent TV shows including *The Six Million Dollar Man* and *The Bionic Woman* had the blessing of the U.S. authorities.

Many Saturday morning shows carried on the fight for American idealism without the help from the Pentagon. Production requirements might have been small on *Captain Midnight*, *Sky King*, and *Ramar of the Jungle*, but their patriotic intentions were as obvious as the rockets' red glare.

Captain Midnight followed the exploits of a secret operative who globe-hopped in his sleek jet plane to champion democracy in the most tyrannical corners of the Earth. In "Top Secret Weapon" he rescued a teen-age refugee from

2. An October 1957 episode recounted the sinking of John F. Kennedy's PT 109 by a Japanese destroyer while on patrol in the Southwest Pacific. Kennedy, a senator from Massachusetts, appeared on the show for a few moments. Another installment, "The Bishop of the Bayfield," turned from World War II to the Cold War. It concerned the evacuation of Vietnamese Christians from Haiphong harbor in North Vietnam as Communists pushed south to claim the rice fields and kill defenseless farmers.

Red agents. Communist spies were busy again fostering prison riots until Captain Midnight (Richard Webb) infiltrated in "Trapped Behind Bars." Midnight learned of secret and desired plans for a U.S. space station from a dying scientist in "The Lost Moon." In "The Frozen Man," the hero tracked down a missing nuclear scientist, and during "Operation Failure," he flew behind the Iron Curtain to free a man the Russians held prisoner.

Captain Midnight proudly wore the uniform of the Secret Squadron and collared many enemy spies. But Midnight was not the only weekend hero to disrupt the Communist timetable for world domination.

Ramar discovered "atomic poison gas" that agents wanted to test on an unsuspecting jungle tribal village in "Dark Venture," and Sky King zoomed out of the blue to defuse an enemy plot to blow up a secret desert research-center and break up a spy ring that had smuggled military secrets to the Kremlin.

"We didn't have that many episodes dealing with international spies," recalls *Sky King* star, Kirby Grant. "Most concerned smugglers, robbers, and everyday criminals." When Sky did fight for the country, however, he landed hard on enemy agents in "Boomerang" and "Operation Urgent," in which he turned the tables on lesser foes, and "Crystal Trap," in which he recovered a U.S. Government map of uranium deposits.

Uranium mines, nuclear secrets, and atomic bombs were also safeguarded in 1953 by *The Atom Squad*. The NBC-commissioned team was led by Steve Elliot (Bob Hastings) and his assistants, played by Rob Courtleigh and Bram Nossem.[3] The trio worked out of a camouflaged New York City headquarters and investigated destructive plans of Red spies Monday through Friday at 5:00 P.M.

The Atom Squad had their work cut out. They battled "The Scheme to Flood America," "The Bomb That Wouldn't Stand Still," and "The Merchants of Death." In a July 1953 serial, "The Five Steps to the Kremlin," Elliot and company sneaked inside Russia to search for the only man who could stop the use of a deadly weapon. After disarming the bomb they were assigned to apprehend an American traitor who built a super undersea magnet with Russian support in "The Ships That Sailed to Nowhere."

Other weeks the Atom Squad foiled a Russian attack on the Pentagon, another on Fort Knox, and a grandiose plan to destroy Washington, D.C.

Three years later the Cold War was being fought in the West. But rocket saboteurs again found they were no match for contemporary cowboys in *Tales of Texas Rangers*' episode "Return of the Rough Riders."

Flash Gordon and Tom Corbett might have been fighting futuristic villains, but youngsters recognized that the Space Academy was an American institution and the United Planets and Solar Alliance were futuristic projections of their own forty-eight states.

While the Reds were pushing farther into Korea and suppressing freedom in Hungary, *Commando Cody—Sky Marshal of the Universe* prevented Saturn from falling to similiar rule and Buzz Corry carried the fight against Communist-like totalitarianism into episodes of the *Space Patrol*. In "Terra, the Doomed Planet," Corry learned the limits to which a dictator named Io would go to defeat democratic system. When the fanatical leader could not make the free world join his collective order where "all beings are . . . beyond the plane of individual thinking," he attempted to annihilate them. Corry intervened, saved the world, and explained to Io that men must meet like diplomats, not warlords.

While Commander Corry espoused armchair political philosophy, Captain Video and Rod Brown actively recruited loyal followers for their cause. The Captain's living room rangers pledged allegiance to their stellar cause by reciting a TV version of the American loyalty oath:

Captain Midnight carried the flag to the stratosphere in the 1950s. With the Cold War beginning to chill the world again in the 1980s, his reruns or a proposed new series would fit right in.

3. Bob Hastings, brother of Captain Video's copilot, Video Ranger (Don Hastings), later portrayed Lt. Carpenter on *McHale's Navy*. Bram Nossem had himself appeared on *Captain Video*

We as Official Video Rangers, hereby promise to abide by the Ranger Code and to support forever the cause of Freedom, Truth, and Justice throughout the Universe.

Rod Brown's Junior Rocket Rangers were charged not only with upholding justice but with obeying America's greatest ideals:

On My Honor as a Rocket Ranger I pledge that:

1. I shall always chart my course according to the Constitution of the United States of America.

2. I shall never cross orbits with the Rights and Beliefs of others.

3. I shall blast at full space-speed to protect the Weak and Innocent.

4. I shall stay out of collision orbit with the laws of my State and Community.

5. I shall cruise in parallel orbit with my Parents and Teachers.

6. I shall not roar my rockets unwisely, and shall be Courteous at all times.

7. I shall keep my gyros steady and reactors burning by being Industrious and Thrifty.

8. I shall keep my scanner tuned to Learning and remain coupled to my Studies.

9. I shall keep my mind out of free-fall by being mentally alert.

10. I shall blast the meteors from the paths of other people by being Kind and Considerate.

Dutiful and paid-up members of these semi-secret societies would receive official membership cards, certificates, decoder rings, and Cold War paraphernalia including Atomic Cannons and Rocket Guns.

In 1953, when Senator Joseph McCarthy was making $1,500 for lecture appearances, Cliff Robertson pushed for his *Rod Brown of the Rocket Rangers* producers to hire out-of-work, blacklisted actors. "I used whatever influence I could to hire the poor actors who couldn't get work," he offers. England's Sherwood Forest also became a refuge for casualties of the political purge at home as *The Adventures of Robin Hood* gave blacklisted writers assignments.

No blacklisted talent would find a job on *I Led Three Lives.* The 1953 syndicated series, based on Herbert Philbrick's anti-communist undercover activity, raised Red-hunting to twenty-one-inch proportions. Richard Carlson starred as the U.S. agent working within the American

U. S. SAVINGS BOND PEACE PATROL
TREASURY DEPARTMENT
TREASURY DEPARTMENT
MEMBER
ADDRESS
AGE
SCHOOL
The Lone Ranger
LONE RANGER
NATIONAL DIRECTOR.
U. S. SAVINGS BOND DIVISION
OFFICIAL
ALBUM
25¢

Communist Party. *TV Guide* discovered that many sponsors bought airtime on the show figuring that patrons of their products would appreciate their presumed patriotism. "Oil and steel companies, banks and utility companies and other such concerns, many of whom have never before used television as an advertising medium, have picked up the series," wrote the magazine.

Opposite: Clayton Moore with Postmaster General Arthur E. Summerfield (1958)

Turning Silver into Gold

The Treasury Department put its stamp on the Lone Ranger in 1958. The masked man was thoroughly obliging.

The Wrather Corporation agreed to lend its character to the U.S. Government Savings Stamps campaign. More than 20,000 post offices and 80,000 schools distributed 8 million Lone Ranger Peace Patrol brochures and membership cards.

The promotion was kicked off in June 1958 with a Washington, D.C., personal appearance by goodwill ambassador for the U.S. Treasury, Clayton Moore.

Moore and Postmaster General Arthur E. Summerfield displayed an enlarged version of the Lone Ranger Peace Patrol membership card and told youngsters to invest in America's future—and their own—by buying the twenty-five-cent Savings Stamps, just as their parents bought larger bonds. Promotional TV spots were slotted in the show's regular broadcasts, and Moore also hyped the campaign during cross-country visits.

According to unofficial estimates, Savings Stamp sales doubled in three months. Upward of three million members joined by the end of the first school month.

Enthusiasm toward anti-Soviet shows was visible until such support was no longer fashionable or politically expedient. The turning point was the fall of Senator Joseph McCarthy in the last days of the 1954 televised Army-McCarthy hearings.

Television continued to promote American fundamentals through the 1950s, but Red-baiting hadn't brought any catch since the days of Julius and Ethel Rosenberg and Alger Hiss. Furthermore, audiences were being given dual messages, and they were beginning to get confused.

While adults tuned to such realistic dramas as the *Medic* episode about the blinding effects of an atomic bomb blast, children's eyes opened in wonder as Superman handily squashed a nuclear explosion as if it were play dough and rescued Jimmy Olsen and Lois Lane, who had been standing at ground zero during an explosion.

The fear of Russian subversion or invasion still lingered in many scripts after McCarthy's fall. But producers found that they walked a political tightrope whenever they attacked a Cold War story.

Producers of *Steve Canyon* found themselves dangling there in 1958 when the State Department asked NBC to "hold off" telecasting one Saturday episode that contained factual footage of a nuclear explosion. The Air Force had assisted in the production but worried that the broadcast would unwittingly sabotage East-West peace talks in Geneva. Spokesmen for the producers, Mike Meshekoff and David Haft, were told that the State Department felt that the story might be viewed as bad public relations considering the powwow aimed at halting H-bomb blasts. The film was eventually shown, but not without Hollywood recognizing that the newest danger connected with the Cold War was strictly economical. A production company could lose money by shooting and then not airing an espionage-oriented show.

Sensing the changing times, Brian Keith's 1955 *Crusader* modified its original anti-Red thrust and favored a nonpolitical approach. As originally conceived, the Friday night CBS show followed freelance writer Matt Anders (Keith) through harrowing rescues of victims from Communist regimes. The network and producers stated that they were not directed by "political wind or winds from Geneva," but by airtime they believed that the program would fare better if they discarded the heavy-handed international plots.

Even the Army's firm public-relations voice—*The Big Picture*—was whispering by 1958. The Signal Corps had dropped the heavily propagandistic tone and opted for documentaries on the aerospace programs, new weapons, the National Guard, and developments in the training program since the end of the Korean War.

Change was also noted the same year as quiz show producers Mark Goodson and Bill Todman offered Russian TV rights to *What's My Line?* And even more dramatically, ZIV-TV, five years earlier producers of *I Led Three Lives*, sent a representative to the Soviet Union to attempt to sell some of its syndication shows, including *Sea Hunt* and *Highway Patrol.*

A year later Soviet Premier Nikita Khrushchev's visit to the United States preempted the normal televison lineup. Prime time and the Saturday morning hours which in past years had carried anti-Communist plots were suddenly filled with the rotund body of the supreme Soviet leader. Khrushchev made news on talk shows and was talked about on news shows. The enemy had become a star.

Television rediscovered the Cold War after the October 1962 Cuban missile crisis. President John F. Kennedy appeared on prime time TV to announce the discovery of atomic warheads in Cuba and the consequential blockade of the island by U.S. ships. Within a few weeks NBC-TV had an hour Saturday special called *Who Goes There?* aimed at reeducating youngsters on the meaning and evils of Communism. In time, secret agent shows came back into vogue. Most parodied the manner James Bond zipped and unzipped his way around the world. Most had a great flair for comic-book action and no feeling for novel intrigue. Most failed in their televison assignments.

Occasionally a Saturday morning cartoon would rekindle a Cold War image. But besides Boris and Natasha's appearances on *Rocky and His Friends* and an episode about a professor smuggled from behind the Iron Curtain in *Fantastic Voyage*, most animated shows skirted political themes and simply depicted the exploits of inch-high detectives and super sleuths. Times were indeed changing. The Unfriendly Witnesses were back at work in the early 1970s. Alger Hiss started a new life. *The Big Picture* was brushed aside in 1972. Network news reporters discarded their well-worn Pentagon blinders and began to see Southeast Asia for real. And Saturday morning ceased being used for political indoctrinations and returned to what it knew best—selling cereal.

West meets East. Roy Rogers demonstrates how to twirl a revolver. His most interested student: the then 12-year-old son of Indonesia's President Sukarno, Gunter. Before coming to California in 1956, the boy had expressed a desire to meet the King of the Cowboys and his horse, Trigger.

15 Out of the Inkwell, onto the Tube

History's major cartoon characters can be counted on two hands," argues Joseph Barbera, co-owner of Hanna-Barbera, history's number-one television cartoon factory. "That's how slim the list is. And that's over years and years. Creating lasting characters is not as easy as a lot of people think."

Barbera knows all too well. As partner with William Hanna in TV's most prosperous animation studio, he's seen more characters fail than succeed. Producing for the much maligned, often profitable Saturday morning market is perhaps TV's most risky crap shoot. "We create over ninety shows a year," explains Barbera. "What one network loves, the other ones might not touch. It's that simple. NBC might be looking for adventure; CBS, comedy; and ABC, something with meaning. We have to supply each with what they want."

In a given time slot, Hanna-Barbera might compete against a show from Filmation or De-

King Leonardo and one of his short subjects, Odie Colognie

Patie-Freleng, two other major suppliers. Or worse, they might just as easily face one of their own shows on another network.

"We have no voice in the scheduling," Norm Prescott, president of Filmation Studios adds. "When we deliver a show, the networks have the right to air it anywhere they want. We pray they won't put our shows opposite one another." The prayers aren't always answered.

"It's a gamble, and every year there's agony for everyone in the business," complains Barbera. "It's a frightening existence."

Barbera, like his competitors, has become rich conquering both fear and the market. In 1979, for example, of the combined twelve hours of Saturday morning programming for the three commercial networks between 8:00 A.M. and noon, all but thirty minutes of airtime contained cartoons. It was no better in 1980. The networks may hold the cards in the expensive gamble, but the deck looks stacked.

Saturday morning, however, has not always been a profit center for cartoon producers. For years it was a refuge for old theatrical cartoons, not a haven for new ones.

In the earliest days of television, cartoons were purchased from motion picture overstocks. *Krazy Kat* clawed her way to TV. Distributors of *Farmer Alfalfa* found the TV schedule fertile ground. And Bugs Bunny successfully hopped to the new medium.

Out of the Inkwell drew audiences. Koko the Clown invited laughter. Pinky Doogie, Bobby Bump, Molly Moo Cow, Willy Whooper and Flip the Frog were early favorites. Puddy the Pup, Scrappy, Kiko the Kangaroo, Oswald the Rabbit, and Casper, the Friendly Ghost all appeared on TV by 1953.

In 1956, 234 Popeye cartoons, 168 of them in color, were sold to TV. The World War II–era Superman cartoons were on the airwaves a few years earlier, and CBS bought all of Paul Terry's 1,100 Terrytoon cartoons in 1955.

Stations stacked the cartoon supply as high as they could. Network cartoons opened the morning viewing after the test pattern, they filled in when movies ran short, and they appeared in hundreds of shows hosted by a virtual army of sea captains, space commanders, Western sodbusters, and neighborhood policemen.

Officer Joe Bolton introduced Popeye in New York. Fledgling comedian Dick Van Dyke hosted

Above: Heckle and Jeckle

Left: Kiko the Kangaroo

Right: Father and son—Chuck Jones and Bugs Bunny

Far left: Jack Mercer, the voice of Popeye since the 1930s, piped up for the character again in The All-New Popeye Hour *(1978).*

© Warner Brothers, Inc.

Right: Elmer Fudd, Bugs Bunny, and Daffy Duck returned to TV in 1979.

The CBS Cartoon Theatre and talked to Terrytoon characters in a three-month-long 1956 network run. Ringmaster Claude Kirchner emceed *Terrytoon Circus* for 10 years and in 1963 ABC assigned Paul Winchell for *Cartoonies* (initially called *Cartoonsville*).

Show titles invariably reached for inviting ways to inform kids that their cartoons were the funniest, the best, and the newest. WGRB in Schenectady ran *Kartoon Karnival*. Philadelphia's WFIL had *Funny Flickers*. Other outlets headlined their cartoons *Film Funnies*, *Lunch 'n' Laughs*, and *Terry Tell Time*.

With television quickly eating up previously produced movie cartoons, and color TV making black and white cartoons obsolete, it soon became necessary for the industry to set up its own animation stand and produce stories to fill the increasingly popular Saturday morning slots.

Prior to TV the cartoon industry had been rich with technique, budgets, and time. TV could afford no such luxuries. The theatrical cartoons were fully animated stories, containing as many as sixty drawings per foot of film. TV would have to settle for less, much less.

"Full animation," states Norm Prescott, "was very, very expensive, but the major distributors in those days got their money back before television sales. People of all ages went to the movies because it was the major form of entertainment. The cartoons were an important part of the program, and the costs could be amortized, then usually recovered within a year."

Below: CBS offered youngsters What's New, Mr. Magoo? *in 1977. As with the original UPA cartoons, Jim Backus provided the voice of the near-sighted character.*

Prescott says that when the American public turned on TV, they effectively turned off the theatrical animation business. "People began to care less about going to the movies. As a consequence it could take four or five years for studios to recoup their cartoon costs. In time the studios went out of the cartoon business.

"Television, in turn, couldn't support full animation," Prescott states. "The economics just wouldn't jive unless somebody could come up with a way of doing animation with fewer drawings."

"UPA, the studio that produced *Gerald McBoing-Boing* and *Mr. Magoo*," recalls cartoon producer Bill Scott, "proved that cartoonists could use fewer drawings and still do an excellent job telling their story. Success depended on just two hitches. The process would work providing: (a) they had a story to tell; and (b) they used a variety of angles, cuts, and camera moves to imply motion."

To the surprise of the entire industry, the system won approval. As testament to their work, UPA won an Oscar in 1950 for their likable little ragamuffin, Gerald.

Similar production methods were translated to TV in 1950 by a wily critter named Crusader Rabbit. Crusader, television's first cartoon character produced expressly for the new medium, was the brainchild of a young San Francisco animator who would eventually turn his garage work into an animation business. Well before Jay Ward teamed Rocky with Bullwinkle, he was busily burning the midnight oil with Alexander Anderson, sending Crusader Rabbit sketches to Hollywood film producer Jerry Fairbanks.

"When Jay did Crusader Rabbit," reports Bill Scott, Ward's partner on *Rocky and His Friends*, "it was still axiomatic that no one could produce a cartoon series for television. Jay refused to believe that."

With Ward drawing Crusader in San Francisco, and Fairbanks adding the sound track in Hollywood, each of the 19.5-minute cartoons came in for approximately $2,500. The cost was precisely what made *Crusader Rabbit* attractive for television sales.[1]

1. In 1957 a series of 260 new *Crusader Rabbit* episodes went into production. The color cartoons, costing $3,500 each or $900,000 for the total package, were animated by a producer who purchased the first set and rights to the characters and merchandise from Anderson and Ward.

"At the rock-bottom prices the networks or stations were able to pay for programming then, we had to develop shortcuts," says Fairbanks. "*Crusader Rabbit* was very limited. They often contained fewer than four cells per foot compared to ten times or more the amount for full animation. We would simply plan a story line so we could reuse some of the animation with a different background.

"Crusader and his companion Rags the Tiger were do-gooders," Fairbanks continues. "They were always doing positive things to influence kids, like teaching children not to cross the street in the wrong direction." The simplistic story seemed to have universal appeal. Stations lined up for broadcast rights.

Limited animation, however, was not to get its biggest boost from UPA or Jay Ward but from Bill Hanna and Joseph Barbera, the MGM

Right: Crusader Rabbit and Rags the Tiger—the first made-for-television cartoons (1950)

Below: "I taut I taw a puddy tat . . ."

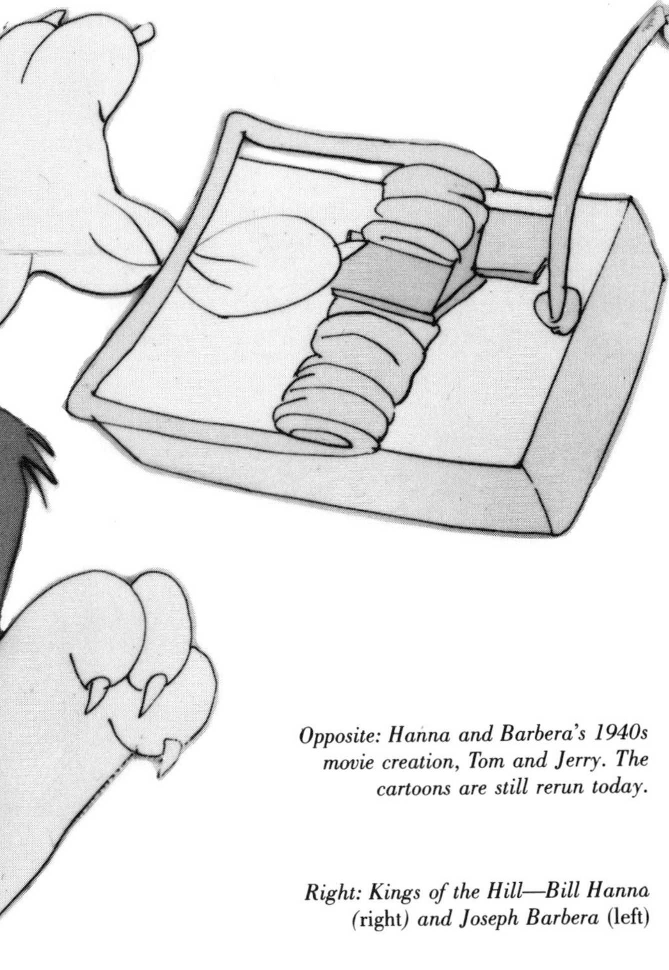

pair that had created and won seven Oscars for *Tom and Jerry*.

"When we went into televison with *Ruff and Reddy* in 1957," Barbera remembers, "there was practically no original animation produced for the medium. We had to help test new methods of animating for TV. Television didn't have the money; it also didn't have the time."

Barbera explains that in MGM's heyday he and Hanna produced five or six full-scale $40,000 theatrical *Tom and Jerry* cartoons every year. In the 1950's TV paid only a fraction of the price, and each five-minute cartoon had to be produced in two weeks. "We received about $2,700 instead of $40,000, and that was after great negotiating and pleading."

It was a buyer's market. With the movie cartoon market dead, producers like Hanna and Barbera had the choice of either producing cheap cartoons or closing their shops. They chose to stay alive, but in doing so, popularized what has been a severely criticized, streamlined form.

Hanna-Barbera discovered what other hungry animators would also find out—the timeworn, professional tenets of old weren't part of the new

Opposite: Hanna and Barbera's 1940s movie creation, Tom and Jerry. The cartoons are still rerun today.

Right: Kings of the Hill—Bill Hanna (right) *and Joseph Barbera* (left)

Below: Hanna-Barbera's premiere TV characters—Ruff (right) *and Reddy*

TV vocabulary. Speed was the most important rule, and the networks were shouting it with every telephone call.

Where movies had relied on endless tests that drove up budgets and postponed completion dates, Hanna-Barbera trimmed most schedule-delaying procedures, eliminated many preliminary sketches, and recorded sound tracks in one sitting.

"When we first started the limited animation," admitted William Hanna in a 1969 *New York Times* article, "it disturbed me. Then when I saw some of the old cartoons on TV, I saw that actually, limited animation came off better on the dimly lit television screen than the old fully animated things."

Pat Sullivan, producer of a new litter of 260 four-minute *Felix the Cat* cartoons, similarly insisted in 1959 that most people couldn't tell the difference between the latest product and the old standards.

Walter Lantz, the brilliant animator who carved out a comfortable career with Woody Woodpecker, viewed TV's cartoons somewhat more clearly. In 1957 he admitted that he was only working in the medium because "cartoons for theaters would soon be extinct." "Forced into TV," he said he would produce what the market would bear. Lantz integrated his existing cartoons with new footage, giving ABC's *Woody Woodpecker* TV show an updated look that satisfied both advertisers and himself. He encouraged colleagues, disgruntled, but busy with work, to likewise remember that animation was an art. The only way to make their cartoons respected was "to put some money into them," he said.

"Limited animation worked for the medium," Norm Prescott adds. "It worked for the economics and that's why it became the basis for all animation. Television is a close-up medium. Jack Webb on *Dragnet* demonstrated that we could successfully cut from close-up to close-up and maintain tremendous interest because people liked the intimacy of seeing an entire face tight on the screen. Applying the same rule to animation, we found that close-ups worked and that we could eliminate a great deal of action."

Though agreeing that such a technique is cost efficient, Bullwinkle creator Bill Scott argues that it's boring. "It drives us crazy—those long close-up dialogue scenes where two characters talk to each other and are edited head-to-head-to-head. We call it 'Hanna-Barbera palsy.' "

Talking heads, however, are inarguably quicker to make, easier to animate, and cheaper to shoot than full animation. Quality, previously the singular directive guiding animators, has receded, to be replaced by television's more economical philsophy—quantity.

TV's requirement for the slapdash product has consequently turned creators into mass produc-

1941

1950

ers, detailed animators into virtual house painters.

Still, Barbera says, critics should blame the networks, not the producers. "We have a terrible time problem. The networks usually don't close a September delivery deal until late spring."

"From the first of March or April to the first of November, we'll be required to turn out eighteen half hours of network TV shows," explains David DePatie, who with Friz Freleng created The Pink Panther. "Under that kind of pressure there's just no way to develop quality," DePatie complains sourly.

The pace has begun to drive Saturday morning producers to prime time, where higher budgets combined with additional production time have resulted in more fully animated productions. DePatie-Freleng, for example, enjoyed taking nearly a year to produce a Pink Panther or a Dr. Seuss special. And Hanna-Barbera has also broken the prime time barrier, using time and money to make a better product.

Woody Woodpecker's features over the years

Above: Mumbly, a snickering, unkempt gumshoe pooch in The Tom and Jerry/Grape Ape/Mumbly Show *(ABC, 1*

Right: Dynomutt, a robot dog, shared billing with Scooby-Doo in the 1976 Scooby-Doo/Dynomutt Hour *on ABC.*

Below: Scooby-Doo

Tattling Tailed Characters

Television has given animals what even Dr. Dolittle couldn't manage—the ability to speak English. From Crusader Rabbit's first words in 1950 to the Shmoo in 1980, TV's two-pawed, four-footed, web-footed, or otherwise mobile creatures have provided an endless stream of Saturday morning chatter.

The noisiest of all have been TV's dogs, which have often been caught barking up the wrong tree as bumbling crime busters.

Deputy Dawg was representative of the breed that roamed Saturday morning. Though dim-witted, he managed to corner the wiliest villains, surprising even his human sheriff.

Scooby-Doo was TV's greatest Dane and the medium's longest running character created exclusively for Saturday morning. "Scooby-Doo was a sidekick in 1969 who suddenly became a star," says Hanna-Barbera executive Joseph Barbera. "He was nothing short of a phenomenon."

Scooby-Doo's first starring role was in *Scooby-Doo, Where Are You?,* in which he was cast as a detective sniffing out clues. In the 1970s he headlined *The Scooby-*

Deputy Dawg, a canine cop who never strayed from his duty.

© CBS Films, Inc.

Doo/Dynomutt Hour, Scooby's All-Stars, and *Scooby's All-Star Laff-a-Lympics.*

Fangface appeared in 1978, the first joint effort of animators Joe Ruby and Ken Spears. The lead character was a lame-brain human who nightly transformed into a werewolf. Fangface, however, was more like a faithful mutt than the feared gothic killer.

Of course, Huckleberry Hound shuffled in and out of trouble, trying out various occupations, narrowly averting disaster with each new career. Daws Butler provided the familiar Southern drawl that marked the lazy hound's speech. The series debuted in 1958.

And a year earlier, Saturday morning villains had little chance whenever Hanna-Barbera's spunky pooch named Reddy and his sure-footed feline partner, Ruff, were around. The pair were the studio's first TV effort.

Ruff may have been a trusted companion, but she was by no means TV's most famous talking cat. Top Cat takes top honors in that category. The alley cat premiered in prime time but warmed up to youngsters on Saturday morning in 1963. Arnold Stang was the voice of the critter who was always conning Officer Dibble (Allen Jenkins) and making the thirteenth precinct's finest look like Manhattan's worst.

Though Tom never spoke a word in MGM's *Tom and Jerry* cartoons, the movie refugees certainly made a racket when CBS bought the old Hanna and Barbera cartoons in 1965.

Equally clamorous was Bob Clampett's klutzy Sylvester, always hungering for Tweety during cartoon segments on *The Bugs Bunny Show* (1960). And *The Houndcats,* a band of cat and dog secret agents, squeaked into the Saturday morning lineup in 1972.

Jerry was not the only mouse scampering for airtime on Saturday. There were the melodic *Mighty Mouse* (1955) and fast talking *Motor Mice* (1970).

One of TV's most lovable creatures was a squirrel who could not only talk, he could fly. Jay Ward, who had developed TV's premiere cartoon, *Crusader Rabbit,* returned to the animation stand in 1959 for the first of many successful seasons of *Rocky and His Friends.*

Chief among those buddies was an irascible moose named Bullwinkle. Together they battled the evil Natasha Fataley, Boris Badenov, and a little squirt known as Mr. Big. Bullwinkle, perhaps the world's only moose to stand upright, starred in his own spin-off show in 1961.

The characters had originated years earlier for a never-produced series called *The Frostbite Falls Follies,* proposed by animator Ward after he finished *Crusader Rabbit.*

"It didn't get off the ground and Jay retired to real estate," says Ward's partner, Bill Scott, who also created UPA's *Gerald McBoing-Boing* and recorded the voice of Bullwinkle J. Moose. Scott explains that the dumb moose and the smart squirrel of Frostbite Falls were given another chance.

"The Bullwinkle character and plots were almost always a parody of the old-fashioned films and melodramas," Scott says. "They contained all the things I remembered from my Saturday morning

Fangface, a teen-ager with a complexion problem that flared up whenever he faced a full moon or even a picture of one, appeared on ABC in 1978.

moviegoing. And I think there was also a good deal of the Hope and Crosby road pictures with Rocky and Bullwinkle stepping out of character and making remarks about being characters in a film. That's the kind of humor I grew up with, and that's what I thought was funny."

The success of these two talking animals over the rest of the video menagerie is owed primarily to the double- and triple-tiered humor. "Kids are inclined to watch things more than once. The second time around they really should see more than what they picked up the first time," Scott adds. "I think that's one of the things our show could do—kids could watch it and enjoy it on their level and come back a year later and see an entirely different kind of comedy. And when they get even older, they'd understand more of the in-jokes."

Rocky and Bullwinkle may have been the reigning monarchs of TV cartoon comedy, but frequently the king of the jungle also bit into the schedule.

In 1960, *King Leonardo and His Short Subjects* debuted on NBC. The setting was the mythical African duchy Bongoland where Leonardo's despotic rule was challenged by a treacherous rodent named Biggy Rat who plotted to put his Majesty's beatnik brother, Itchy, on the throne. Countering Biggy Rat's plans was the king's devoted skunk, Odie Colognie.

Other lions also ruled the airwaves including the trouble-prone Snagglepuss on *Quick Draw McGraw* (1959), *Lippy the Lion* (1962), *Linus the Lionhearted* (1964), and *Kimba, the White Lion* (1966).

Other African animals battled for survival in the Saturday morning jungle. There was Hanna-Barbera's *Wally Gator* (1962), *Peter Potamus* (1964), and the mischievous *Magilla Gorilla* (1964).

TV rounded up talking animals from other areas, as well. A happy-go-lucky penguin named Tennessee Tuxedo came from Antarctica in 1963 and Misterjaws, a shark, chewed up airtime on NBC's *Pink Panther Show* in 1977.

Crusader Rabbit was certainly not TV's only bunny to hop along. Hippity Hop bounced on the scene in 1958. Bugs Bunny popped up weeknights in 1960, then Saturdays in 1962, as did Hoppity Hooper.

Soaring high above these furry earthbound cartoon creatures was Walter Lantz's Woody Woodpecker, star of an ABC program as early as 1957. He was later syndicated in 1958 and 1964, then rereleased as an NBC entry in 1970 and again in 1976.

Woody, a roguish bird that pecked out a handsome profit in the theaters, originated on TV as a weekday series. Sponsor Kellogg's even tested the bird's wings on prime time in 1958, hoping to attract a flock of viewers.

Also flying high were the two irrepressible Terrytoon magpies named Heckle and Jeckle. The pair were first airborne via a syndicated show in 1955, then joined CBS for a run starting in 1956. The birds swooped onto NBC in 1969. Joining them in their misadventures were other Terrytoon characters—Little Roquefort, Gandy Goose, Dinky Duck, and the Terry Bears.

The character to prove that cartoons were the bare essentials of successful kids' programming was a fellow named Yogi. The program was released for syndication in 1961, and Yogi's picnic-lunch thievery made him a favorite almost immediately and the enemy of parents who considered his lessons inappropriate for youngsters. Most of all, however, the series put Hanna-Barbera's cartoon studio firmly on the Hollywood tourist maps. Neither Yogi nor Hanna-Barbera have been out of sight since.

Yogi lived in Jellystone Park. Meanwhile, three Hanna-Barbera cousins were caged in at Cave Block Number Nine at Wonderland Zoo. The Hair Bear clan, stars of the 1971 CBS series *Help! It's the Hair Bear Bunch,* tried to escape from their habitat every week. At the end of each episode they returned, realizing that nowhere is the grass greener than in their luxury dwelling.

Somewhat freer were the C. B. Bears, a group of bears whose technological and environmental base was a rubbish truck equipped with a 1977 citizens-band radio unit.

TV's talking horses also stampeded onto the schedule. Leading the team was Hanna-Barbera's avenging steed, Quick Draw McGraw. The series was first available through syndication in 1959, but Quick Draw and his Mexican burro assistant, Baba Louie, also found sure footing on network episodes.

Jay Ward's Rocky, Bullwinkle, Natasha, and Boris—direct relatives of the Crusader Rabbit cartoons animated by Ward earlier in his career

The irony of the Saturday morning TV picture is that after producers like Hanna-Barbera demonstrated that America's cartoonphiles could be mesmerized by limited animation, the networks went for even cheaper work from abroad.

"The Japanese material [*Speed Racer, Gigantor, Prince Planet, Astro Boy, Johnny Sokko and His Flying Robot*] that came in during the early and mid-1960s was abysmal," Bill Scott charges. "But we had to compete with it. I'd have to say that was the greatest decline in prestige, because all that the networks really wanted was 'x' number of yards of film. They'd show it on Saturday morning and they didn't care much about the quality or what it was going to do to the medium."

"The networks simply bought film by the pound," argues Norm Prescott. "They could care less what it was. Saturday morning televison became a garbage pile. There were no executives directly assigned to it; nobody wanted to be in charge of it. Saturday was considered worse than the mailroom job."

The situation looked bleak until 1965, when a mild-mannered CBS executive with a predilection for winning riches in the Saturday morning ghetto arrived on the scene. Almost singlehandedly Fred Silverman revolutionized children's television.

"He had grown up with all the cartoons in movies," explains Prescott. "He was very sentimental then, and when he saw the networks literally programming film by the pound, he decided to make Saturday morning more important and treat it as though it was as competitive as nighttime."

Silverman overhauled the CBS schedule in short order, introducing *The New Adventures of Superman*. The maneuver immediately catapulted CBS from third place right into first.

Silverman's move to generate original cartoon production, supervise scripts, and oversee storyboards, caught more than just the kids' eyes. Silverman touched the advertisers' pocketbooks, and that, of course, appealed to ABC and NBC as well. The competition soon revised their schedules.

"Saturday morning became an intricate and very, very important part of the network structure," states Prescott. "And Freddie was the guy who opened the door."

Silverman's successful new wave of cartoons,

still short on animation, were in no way short on action. Cartoon action, however, often exploited violence, and violence, particularly after the shocking assassinations of civil rights leader Dr. Martin Luther King and of Senator Robert Kennedy, was viewed by some with disdain.

The surveys began pouring in. *The Christian Science Monitor* recorded 162 threats or acts of violence on Saturday morning, the majority of which occurred between 7:30 and 9:00 A.M., when an estimated 26.7 million children from two to seventeen were watching.

In 1968, the highly publicized National Commission on the Causes and Prevention of Violence (Kerner Commission) report would second such findings. Children's TV, the study charged, was a profitable business and a dangerous babysitter.

By fall 1968, less than six months after the tragic assassinations, the Saturday morning schedule began to show the effect of public outrage. Many of the cartoon characters replaced their clubs with verbal assaults, ambushes with fast getaways, and cliff-hanging heroes with rock musicians.

NBC executives exhibited great sense when they decided to remove their most objectionable Saturday morning figures at a reported cost of $750,000. Don Durgin, then president of NBC's TV division, ordered corporate lawyers to buy up the contracts of two shows considered beyond apology. Dropped were Hanna-Barbera's *Birdman* and DePatie-Freleng's *Super President.* In their place NBC inserted *Untamed World* and *The Storybook Squares,* a children's version of the daytime quiz *Hollywood Squares.*

CBS followed suit replacing two of their action-adventure cartoon series with comedy cartoon shows that deemphasized violence. ABC, initially slow to react, finally revised their schedule.

Fred Silverman told a McCall's interviewer that the antiviolence shift was actually a hit. "*Archie,*" he said, " had been so successful that we're dropping all our noncomedy shows like *The Herculoids* and *Moby Dick and the Mighty Mighton* to go into character comedy for five out of six hours on Saturday."

By the fall of 1970 CBS had withdrawn four more violent shows; NBC had bumped three; and ABC had canceled five.

Additionally, each network appointed officers to oversee children's TV. For ABC it was cartoonist and producer Chuck Jones as executive director of children's programming. CBS appointed veteran radio producer Allen Ducovny as supervisor, and NBC, the first of the networks to name a children's TV official, elevated George Heinemann, creator of *Ding Dong School* (1952), to the post.

Under the rule of these network officers, TV's cartoon characters laid down their weapons.

"All of the networks are aware of the climate of the country, what's happening in Washington, and the statements about violence; and I would be less than truthful if I said that our fall programming does not reflect that atmosphere," said an ABC executive.

"What we're dealing with," added NBC daytime programming chief Larry White in the *McCall's* interview, "is fantasy and imagination rather than action-adventure. We're trying to get the kids working with us to create their own reality and stay away from super characters, strong conflicts, and all kinds of action."

The networks felt they had put their best foot forward. Said Marshall Kemp, ABC's vice-president of daytime TV in 1970, the new aim of children's programming was "to entertain, stimulate, and educate."

Thus, the children of the 1970s and 1980s have been treated to more serious "educational" themes in their cartoons.

Characters have since fought ecological ills rather than tough mobsters. They've used stun guns instead of deadly six-shooters, spoken in newsworthy buzz words, and crusaded for commendable causes.

Unfortunately, the lion's share of these cartoons have been indistinguishable from one another. The shows, in turn, are often similar to the animated commercials; and the commercials are regularly mistaken for educational fillers.

Today's cartoon characters travel to the ends of space, transform from humans to werewolves, and turn from reporters to supermen. Though they exhibit many of the wondrous and familiar abilities of old, they lack the strength of their ancestors. These new figures fly, walk, sing, and dance. But according to most producers working the grind, they have no life.

"I think the greatest change is because of the ladies in Boston—Action for Children's Televison (ACT)," says David DePatie. "I think

The Cartoon Invasion: A Bloodless Coup

Cartoon characters never drew blood. Heckle and Jeckle would fly into walls, Felix the Cat would be blown up, and Bluto would be foiled by Popeye, but gangsters, good guys, and comic characters alike would always survive to face another day.

Violence is nothing new in cartoons. Fighting it is. Animation obviously engages the suspension of belief. Cartoons are unreal; the action in them, unrealistic and exaggerated. But critics argue that children can not differentiate between make-believe and reality. They say that cartoon violence on the same medium in which Big Bird says to eat properly and clean your room confuses youngsters. Eliminate the false signals and TV, like children, will become much healthier.

Some critics claim there was reason to view Saturday morning TV with alarm. Violence was rampant on prime time TV, but evening's depiction was often kids' stuff compared to what was occurring on weekends.

Initially, TV bought the old and admittedly violent cartoons that parents had seen in theaters. In time, TV began producing its own cheaper versions. In 1966, Hanna-Barbera's *Space Ghost* premiered. The series focused on the title character, an interplanetary crime fighter who fought extraterrestrial villains that routinely ordered their accomplices to kill.

Violent cartoons need not be science fiction, however. In fact, more often they were strictly adventure tales, such as Hanna-Barbera's 1967 *Samson and Goliath.* This series featured a boy named Sam and his dog Goliath. The pair possessed incredible powers and could turn into a strong man and a lion, respectively. The show suggested to youngsters that brawn was more powerful than brain: that as Samson, the child could accomplish more than the mortal Sam.

The bellwether marking the slow death of heavily violent fare was the reaction to the assassinations of Dr. Martin Luther King and Senator Robert Kennedy, and the subsequent release of the Kerner Commission report on violence. The handwriting on the wall directly affected the drawing on the animation stand. Consequently, the science fiction and adventure cartoons began to give way to comedy-adventure as evidenced by the 1969 premiere of Hanna-Barbera's *The Perils of Penelope Pitstop.* Drawn with the specter of the cliff-hanger queen Pearl White in sight, Penelope was a young, beautiful heroine who was constantly in the clutches of money-hungry Sylvester Sneekly. Sneekly plotted unsuccessfully to kill Penelope, inherit her fortune, and steal away in her car, the Compact Pussycat.

Gary Owens, the announcer from *Laugh-In,* narrated the series. Paul Winchell and Don Messick provided the voices of the Ant Hill Mob. Janet Waldo dubbed Penelope, Paul Lynde was the villain, and the versatile Mel Blanc filled in as various other characters.

The same theme was exploited on CBS's *Dastardly and Muttley in Their Flying Machines.* This 1969 series, again utilizing the voices of Winchell and Messick, followed the trials of Dick Dastardly, an enemy World War I flier from the Vulture Squadron. His duty was to intercept messages carried by the brave, fearless Yankee Doodle Pigeon. Ever unlucky, he and his equally hapless canine companion, Muttley, returned for more losing battles until 1971. The series, produced by Hanna-Barbera, also featured a two-and-a-half-minute segment starring the snickering Muttley in Walter Mitty flights of fancy.

The same year, ABC countered with *Sky Hawks,* a cartoon adventure about a daredevil family in which Grampa Wilson, his son, and his grandchild attempt seemingly impossible tasks from sea rescues to dangerous airlifts.

Violence might have become taboo, but the adventures of heroes and villains still provided good vibrations between the networks and their youthful audience. Quickly pulling into the available programming slots were cartoon competitions modeled after the motion picture *The Great Race* (1965) and one of TV's most objectionable syndicated cartoons, *Speed Racer* (1967).

With comedic elements borrowed from the movie, and the pace of the Japanese-dubbed cartoon, *Speed Racer*, *Wacky Races* zoomed along in 1968. This Hanna-Barbera-Heatter-Quigley CBS series featured a weekly cross-country rally with a pair of stone-age drivers in their Bouldermobile; a haunted house on wheels called the Creepy Coupe; a parlor car, the Compact Pussycat; and many others.

ABC rolled along with *Hot Wheels* in 1969. The series sported an educational element, warning children to drive safely, but concluded each episode with a fast-paced race.

By 1974, with cartoon racing themes beginning to run out of gas, Hanna-Barbera still charged forward with *Wheelie and the Chopper Bunch,* an adventure about a near-human Volkswagon named Wheelie and his similarly hydraulic girlfriend Rota Lee. And in 1973, CBS aired *Speed Buggy,* which chugged along with Mel Blanc recording the car's voice until it ran out of ratings fuel the following season.

The theme was practically exhausted in 1978 when NBC introduced *Yogi's Space Race.* The series featured Hanna-Barbera regulars, including Yogi and Huckleberry Hound trying to outwit and outrace Phantom Phink and Sinister Sludge at warp speed.

they've exerted a great influence. Obviously, the type of show we make today, as opposed to ten years ago, is entirely different."

Joseph Barbera agrees that TV is indeed different in the 1980s than the productions of the 1960s or 1970s, but he sees this change as detrimental to the trade, and he blames such groups as ACT for the medium's decline.

"I feel very sorry for the generations of kids that are not allowed to participate in slapstick humor, comedic humor, and clown humor," Barbera argues.

The new regulations guiding cartoon action, of course, were not made law by consumer organizations alone. In fact, ACT and other watchdog organizations have maintained that the networks have misinterpreted concern for alarm and have stifled creativity rather than subdued violence.

Nonetheless, in response to the fiercely negative reaction against violent cartoons, each network developed a bible of rules and demanded that producers follow their edicts religiously. A network censor thus sits in on script meetings, approves storyboards, and vetoes subject matter right up to airtime.

In CBS's *Josie and the Pussycats*, for instance, a feline critter was supposed to escape from a monster and hide in a dish of spaghetti. The network called for a rewrite, fearful that youngsters would likewise dunk their cats in spaghetti.

Peggy Charren, president, Action for Children's Television

ACT's Grinder

Years ago, many broadcasters considered children's programming an inconvenience. It fulfilled their required public-service time, but it didn't bring in much money. In the mid-1950s, a make-believe teen named Barbie made the real-life industry think again. This ten-inch beauty doll and her optional and expensive wardrobe captured the hearts of America's little girls and the pocketbooks of the nation's advertisers.

There were big bucks in those Saturday mornings when the parents were asleep. And so Barbie was followed by an army of imitators. Within ten years, Chatty Cathy, GI Joe, Ken, Midge, and Tiny Tears invaded the market. Together these figures irreversibly changed children's television.

"As the network and advertising coffers began to overflow with sales receipts the program quality dissolved," remembers a Newton, Massachusetts, mother of two, who seemed more than typically concerned about children's viewing habits in 1968. "Saturday morning," says Peggy Charren, "became a haven for poorly animated monster cartoons, candy commercials, and all of Barbie's friends. Television hit rock bottom."

Charren decided to do something about the situation. She invited thirty neighbors and associates to her home to discuss whether the medium could be improved. A year earlier she was running the Newton Creative Arts Council. She worked toward bringing arts programs to the community's school system. But her work in the schools made Charren concerned that the Council's efforts were lost once children left for home and the inimitable television set.

Charren and the others assembled at her house were alarmed that television was feeding youngsters sexist, violent, and passive lessons between commercials.

Eventually, Peggy Charren's living room conclave grew to national proportions. Action for Children's Television emerged, with the express goal of eliminating commercials from children's viewing hours and cleaning up the program content.

Still short of achieving complete success, Charren, president of ACT, is pleased at her organization's profound accomplishments. Charren talks about those victories, surrounded by ACT's trophies: letters of commendation, posters from victorious campaigns, an adding machine to tabulate the membership dues from the 8,000-plus in the fold, and a videotape machine ready to record the evidence on which ACT has based TV challenges before the Federal Communications Commission and the Federal Trade Commission.

"Those first days were shaky," Charren admits, exhibiting the same flair and dynamism that have kept ACT alive through its formative years. "We had to kick in our own money to finance the initial expenditures while we waited for the federal and private grants to arrive. . . . Since we began, we've seen the weekend TV advertising time reduced from sixteen minutes per hour to nine-and-a-half minutes per hour. That's a good start," Charren concedes. "But consider what's still being sold to children during those minutes. TV tells youngsters to eat sticky-sweet candies between meals, cereals that often contain up to 60 percent sugar, and until recently, vitamins as if they were Life Savers."

Since ACT recognizes that Congress cannot force parents to watch television with their youngsters and thereby help children make decisions about program content and advertising ploys, Charren believes that the networks should be made responsible for their programming and commercials. Up to now, she says, they haven't been. Charren freely quotes studies that indicate that preschoolers spend more time in front of the TV than they will in a college classroom getting a bachelor's degree. And she cites medical and psychological testimony that warns about the harmful effects of television-watching without parental supervision. However, her most important point is that children demand special attention. "TV watching," she says with a passion, "is a problem, precisely because children spend so much time doing it!"

Charren's view of TV is not completely that of an outsider. In 1949, when the only places that TV sets could be found were bars, appliance store windows, and a few homes, Charren was working at WPIX-TV in New York.

"That was when the industry was simply trying to encourage people to buy their first TV set," she muses. "It wasn't until well after the majority of the country was plugged in that media insiders realized they could then sell the audience to the advertisers for a profit."

Charren is against neither commercial television nor television commercials in principle. She merely has no patience for the medium's propensity for turning children into naggers and beggers for the sake of Madison Avenue's growth.

Charren's work has taken ACT through Congressional hearings on the Family Viewing Hour, debates on television violence, and legal challenges against commercial content and programming practices. Yet, even though she is the guiding force behind ACT, Charren is by no means running the show alone.

Charren, a vivacious woman, keeps her staff of a dozen in virtual perpetual motion with continuous charges of her infectious energy. ACT never specifically lobbies to have a program removed from television, she tells all new interns facing a semester of work in the Newton office. "We just want to see less violence, less sexism, and the end to deceptive advertising."

She makes the point a little more dramatically when she's speaking into a row of microphones in a Capitol Hill caucus room.

"In 1977, most studies agreed that while violence was down on late night programs, it had increased on Saturday morning. Incredible!" she fumes. But if violence gets her upset, just listen to what she says about deliberate sexism. She points out that in the late 1970s advertisers promoted a macho Six Million Dollar Man doll that used a flashy repair station, but sold a similar Bionic Woman toy that was accompanied with the traditional beauty parlor. "That kind of blatant sexism is, among other things, precisely what we're fighting against."

Perhaps Charren's greatest battle with the broadcasters and the government, however, is the issue of deceptive advertising. "The Federal Communications Commission has regulations against false and misleading commercials for adults, but they don't seem to apply the same standards to children's ads," Charren argues.

She claimed a partial victory in the matter, when in 1978 the Federal Trade Commission finally granted a year-long study of the needs and effects of sugar-products advertising on Saturday morning. Charren braced for a monumental counteroffensive from the cereal industry. It came.

The cereal and candy companies naturally stated that the First Amendment guaranteed them the right to advertise at any hour, in any manner. However, Action for Children's Television disagreed. For her stand, Charren took real heat. She went from the cereal bowl directly into the hot soup.

Advertisers and broadcasters attempted to blame Action for Children's Television for the diminishing quality of Saturday TV. Charren responds that "people criticize ACT for the lack of creativity today. We never asked for that. They don't remember what it was like before we were around. There was no *Sesame Street* or *Electric Company.* It was never our idea to sanitize the superheroes and reduce the art of animation to its present standards. The broadcasters are responsible for what's on the air today, not Action for Children's Television. We're trying to see that the product is improved, not worsened."

ACT's battle plan is supported by approximately $300,000 yearly in public, private, and federal funds. That may sound like a great deal of money, but it barely approximates the amount the networks average for each one-minute commercial in the Super Bowl, and it wouldn't pay for a single episode of most hour-long prime time TV shows.

Charren acknowledges that the bankroll spreads pretty thinly over the salaries for an attorney, assistant director, publicity coordinator, and the remaining employees. Publication costs, consultants, legal fees, transportation, and correspondence drain the budget further. And since they've moved out of Peggy Charren's home and into an office that is cluttered with handouts and other business paraphernalia, there's little cash left except for nickels for Newton parking.

However, Charren insists that the ACT money is well spent. "ACT is clearly demonstrating that a nonprofit citizen's action organization can do more than simply wave placards and march in circles." Indeed, ACT's telephone calls to ad agencies get returned these days. Their letters to the networks are promptly answered. ACT is taken seriously in the industry now, and there's reason.

- In response to ACT pressure, broadcasters reduced their per-hour weekend advertising time.

- ACT lobbied the FCC to issue a decision that bans station and network children's TV hosts from pitching products on their own programs or during the other regular kidvid hours.

- After a five-year struggle, ACT convinced the Federal Trade Commission to restrict advertising of candy-coated vitamins to children.

- ACT pressure encouraged the FCC to issue a policy statement that children must be treated as "special members of the viewing audience."

Charren explains that today the networks look to ACT for approval as much as they expect to hear the organization's criticism. "They want to win our support now," she says. "They want to win our yearly ACT awards for programming excellence. It's kind of an endorsement. No matter what else they're doing to exploit kids between 8:00 A.M. and noon, they can at least say, 'But ACT likes what we're doing at 12:00 P.M.' "

In 1968, Peggy Charren and her associates didn't think that Action for Children's Television would remain a permanent operation. They figured they'd clean up television in short order. "We believed that when we finished, we'd move on to something else. But as we learned that we could only slowly alter the climate of decision-making at the networks and the government, we stopped talking about closing shop."

Charren characterizes herself as a TV-watcher dedicated to making the medium better, proving that the average citizen does have the power to change things.

But while she may have been an average woman in the late 1960s, she is clearly not so now. Peggy Charren commands a low-budget operation that has affected a multimillion-dollar industry. Not everyone in the country has that kind of power, and Charren knows it.

ABC ruled that if a building was damaged or destroyed during a story, it must be completely repaired by the cartoon's finale. And on the occasion when one studio announced its intention to insert a message critical of dictators at the conclusion of a tale, ABC reportedly allowed mention of Caesar and Napoleon, but disallowed reference to Hitler, presumably because the Nazi leader was associated with fanaticism and violence.

"The program-practices departments outlined four major don'ts," explains Norm Prescott. "No physical violence, no guns, no jeopardy, and no threats."

"Hyperbole is also out, which seems strange to me because animation is itself a hyperbolic medium," adds Bill Scott.

"They've legislated television," continues Joseph Barbera. "It's just as if they had legislated football and said you couldn't tackle anymore. I can guarantee that we could still have a product that would have kids screaming their heads off with laughter, but we'll never be allowed to do it again on Saturday morning."

"They've taken cartoons out of the hands of the creators," says Daws Butler, voice of Yogi Bear and hundreds of other characters. "Today, the networks and the agencies are really calling all the shots: what color the characters can be, what they should say, and how they can say it. They're going through the dialogue and approving all the scripts. But I think that they should leave it up to the people who know, the people who have the expertise."

Butler argues that work just isn't the fun it used to be. "It's gotten to the point where everything is rated on how cheap it is rather than how good it is. It's a shame. Nowadays, the lines aren't funny, they're silly. Back in what I call the 'Golden Days'—the 1950s—the writing was the leader, the road map. There were great and brilliant lines, and the networks didn't hassle the production companies. We had a ball. I still feel that all those original Yogis, Hucks, Snagglepusses, Fractured Fairytales, and Quick Draws had some very, very funny lines and non sequiturs. It was just butter to read. The characters would touch one another and they would love."

Butler, still active in the business as well as director of his own voice school, makes his point by describing the relationships between Yogi and Boo Boo. "There was a loving something between them. The same with Quick Draw and Baba Louie. Baba Louie knew that Quick Draw was a big jerk, but he loved him. The same bond existed between Augie Doggie and Doggie Daddy. You don't see that anymore. The shows aren't in the hands of the creators, they're network driven. If they have to make a cut in the script, they'll cut the funny line and keep the continuity. It's intimidated the whole industry. And I just don't think it's funny anymore."

"Each network has a different set of criteria governing Saturday morning cartoons," explains DePatie. "NBC is probably the most lenient, CBS has been midway, and ABC is by far the toughest of the three."

Bill Scott, who with Jay Ward has turned to producing animated commercials for such companies as Quaker Oats rather than dealing directly with the networks, must still obey the network commandments even when selling Captain Crunch™ cereal.

"We've had to remove the captain's sword. He can't even brandish it anymore. And we're forced to use boxing gloves on the ends of sticks for comic fights," Scott says.

The very worst, Scott emphasizes, is the elimination of "jeopardy," a decision he terms "ridiculous." "Captain Crunch is a sea captain, an adventurer who encounters strange beasts, animals, wild looking natives, pirates, and typhoons. Each cartoon gets us right up to the brink of the abyss as far as the program-practices people—the censors—are concerned, because it envisages peril, violence, jeopardy, and all those wonderful things with a dreadful name which make cartoons.

"There's no stomping or running. We can't show the flexibility that animated characters are known for," Scott concludes. "Once we lock ourselves like that, we might as well be doing live-action programs."

"I can't even have a character throw a pie in somebody's face anymore," complains Joe Barbera. "The reason is very simple. It's imitable, and the networks say we can't do anything bad that a child might imitate. It's gone that far. That's the name of the game."

"Obviously the rules have made it tougher for us," says Norm Prescott. "For a time we wondered how we could create action and adventure and sustain interest when we had to

A Conversation with Yogi Bear and Daws Butler*

Yogi: Heh-heh—It's Yogi Bear.

Q. HELLO YOGI, HAVE YOU BEEN WORKING WITH DAWS FOR VERY LONG?

Yogi: Heh-heh, he works for me. If it weren't for me, he'd be driving a truck.

Q. IN THE EARLY DAYS YOU USED TO BE A REAL CUT-UP, STEALING ALL THOSE PICNIC BASKETS, BUT NOW YOU'RE VERY DIFFERENT. . . . WHY?

Yogi: I think the writers are putting me on a diet.

Butler: Excuse me, Yogi, but I might add that what's really happened is that they've taken cartoons out of the hands of the creators. Today the networks and the agencies are really calling all the shots: what color the characters can be; what they can say; how they can say it. They're going through the dialogue and okaying scripts. But I think they should leave it up to the people who know—the experts.

Yogi: I have to be philosophical, heh-heh. Some producers like Jay Ward are sticklers for artistic control, but for most, it isn't economically feasible any more. They can't do the cartoons for what the market will, ah . . . bear.

Q. SO THE BUSINESS HAS COMPLETELY CHANGED OVER THE LAST TWENTY YEARS?

Butler: Work isn't the fun it used to be . . . it's getting to the point where everything is not how good it is, but how cheap it is. It's a shame today. The lines aren't funny, they're silly. Back in what I call "The Golden Days" when we started on TV, the writing was the leader; the road map. There were great and brilliant lines and the networks didn't interfere.

Q. ARE YOU HANNA-BARBERA'S OLDEST CONTINUING TV CHARACTER, YOGI?

Yogi: There was Ruff and Reddy and then Huckleberry Hound. I was just kind of doing a walk-on during his show, but everyone said, heh-heh, here's the real star of the program. I'm buffing my fingernails as I say that, but I won't tell Huck that, I don't want to hurt his feelings, he's a terrific guy.

Q. GO ON, YOU'RE ROLLING, YOGI.

Yogi: So, I came on his show and that's how it started. Then came Quick Draw McGraw and then Snagglepuss. Our early residuals have run out, so we all bump into one another at the unemployment office now.

*Interviewer: Sam Donato

Hair Bear · Quisp · The Sun · Funky Phantom · Capt. Skyhook · Bumble · Lambsy
Chilly Willy · Cap'n Crunch · Loopy-de-Loop · Baba Looey · Quick-Draw McGraw
Mr. Jinks · Snagglepuss · Dixie · Yogi Bear · Fibber Fox · Augie Doggie
Henry Orbit · Huckleberry Hound · Hokey Wolf · Blabber Mouse · Super Snooper
Lippy the Lion · Elroy · Cogswell · Wally Gator · Peter Potamus

take away the basic psychological means for creating that. But we learned to get around it. It's like the nighttime guys. Car chases have replaced gunfights and other forms of violence, while still giving viewers a form of action and adventure. We do the same thing with our superheroes by constantly flying them places and getting them involved in situations with exotic characters, animals, and villains," Prescott adds. "They may not be as tough and as rough and as crazy as they used to be, but we have to make up for it in every way we can. It takes a lot of imagination. It's tough, but we manage to do it."

The producers do manage. They must, if they want the next network sale. But their complaints echo throughout the Hollywood Hills.

"If Charlie Chaplin, Buster Keaton, or Harold Lloyd had to work with NBC, CBS, or ABC today, they'd throw up their hands in disgust and walk away," snaps Joseph Barbera.

The network influence is so pervasive, reports David DePatie, that executives oversee, if not regulate, ideas as soon as they leave the typewriter. "It's my experience that it goes all the way back to the original story outlines." DePatie explains that there are three basic creative stages to cartoons. First comes the four- or five-page story outline; second, the actual script; and third, the preliminary storyboard drawings.

"I'd say that the control begins as early as the story outline. And if we're creating a new series, it'll go back even further. You can be

Above: Joseph Barbera studies a cel from the 1979 NBC series The New Fred and Barney Show. *The original* Flintstones *program, perhaps TV's most successful animated show, remains in syndication.*

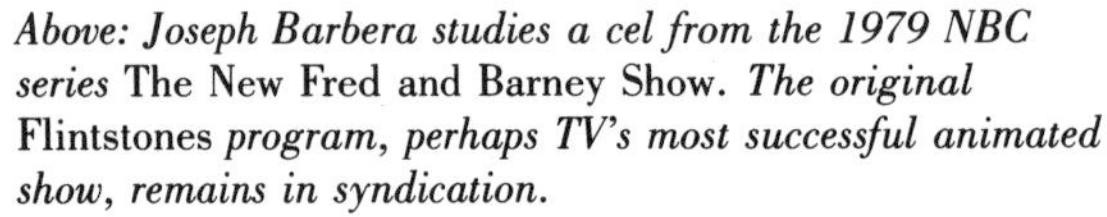

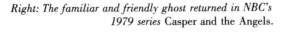

Right: The familiar and friendly ghost returned in NBC's 1979 series Casper and the Angels.

damned sure they'll be involved right from the beginning."

There's one glaring and disturbing Catch-22, however. What isn't allowed on the network Saturday morning—the older, violent cartons—airs on independent and UHF stations throughout the day. The contradiction hasn't gone unnoticed in Hollywood.

"If you turn on some stations, you'll see both the cartoons made forty years ago plus many of the 1960s Japanese cartoons." Because the total schedule reflects a heavy slant toward violence, Barbera feels undue blame is still directed at his studio.

"That's the mistake the watchdog groups have made. They'll handcuff the new productions, but nowhere do they really seem to affect the running of the old productions," Barbera states.

One thing has become obvious to discontented producers, consumer organizations, and network officials alike. Youngsters will watch any Saturday morning cartoons, whether the offerings are violent or lighthearted. Put a TV in a house, and barring a blackout, children are tuned in summer or winter.

The reality has meant good business despite the protestations. Animation studios have consequently overflowed with work, so much so that, to the displeasure of the American unions, the operations have parceled out work to some overseas cartoonists.

Hanna-Barbera set up shop in Australia, arguing that Hollywood didn't have the creative force to deal with the work load. DePatie-Freleng opened up a Korean office, Jay Ward shipped orders to Mexico, while others opted for studios in Taiwan and Spain.

"The union goes bananas over the foreign productions," explains DePatie, "but when we called them and say, 'Hey, we needed five animators,' they often say 'sorry.'"

The animators' union called a ten-day strike in 1979 to protest the foreign jobbing practices. The job action, coming in late summer, delayed the delivery dates of many fall shows, and ended only when the local extracted a promise that producers would ask for union permission before farming out work.

"No one is out of work in our business when we're in production," explains Joseph Barbera. The problem and impetus for the strike, however, was the limited production season: six months on, six months off; feast or famine. The prospect of being well paid for half a year and unemployed for the remainder discouraged younger talent from entering the field and encouraged producers, in a crush for employees, to look for more and cheaper labor overseas.

Mel Blanc and his many personalities

The best alternative to foreign work, and one sought by both unions and production houses, has been a training period and a year-around work routine filled with Saturday morning assignments, prime time specials, and theatrical cartoons. The industry seems to be moving exactly in this direction.

Still, while there are more cartoons produced today than ever before, and more producers and artists working to keep the Saturday morning hole plugged with programs, one problem persists: The content is terrible. Joseph Barbera probably speaks for most animators when he says, "We're not doing what I instinctively think would be funny or what the kids really want. We're not doing it, because we can't."

To the Rescue

When *live*-action characters were killed by the networks, it was the superhero cartoons that delivered the death blow.

Superman scouted the territory first. Max Fleischer's impressive and expensive World War II–era Superman cartoons were early TV favorites. Much of their colorful brilliance was lost in black and white broadcasts, but the animation still dazzled viewers and encouraged other animators to try their hands at creating new superheroes.

Bud Collyer, later the host of *Beat the Clock* and *To Tell the Truth,* read the Man of Steel's lines. When Filmation produced a new version of *Superman* in 1966, Collyer returned to the microphone.

The program, Filmation's first TV series, included two Superman adventures and one Superboy exploit. The show was an easy ratings-winner and a difficult production to produce.

"Most people don't know that humanoids, superhero characters, are very hard to animate," explains Filmation's codirector, Norman Prescott. "It's easy to animate animals because they're so exaggerated, but with human beings, it's tough."

Rotoscoping, a process developed by Disney, was the program-saving answer. "To rotoscope, first we shoot the action with live actors in black and white, directing them to run, swim, walk, jump, or whatever it is that we need," Prescott explains. "Next we blow up those little 35 mm frames. Then we trace them, taking just the perimeter line of the action, and draw into those lines the animated character's face and features. Finally, we ink, paint, and photograph those scenes and they really look fully animated" (see Chapter II, "Tested Patterns").

Although the Superman cartoons of the 1960s were susceptible to criticism from fans who remembered the handsomely animated and rotoscoped work of Fleischer, the new series took off. Prescott says the production was a milestone in Saturday morning. *Superman* pulled animation out of the barnyard and gave viewers far-out plots."

In producing a hit, however, Prescott created a monster. Filmation was typecast as Hollywood's home for superheroes. Prescott didn't care to turn his California studio into Superman's Fortress of Solitude, but for years he had little choice in the matter. "Superheroes kept flying our way," he states. "The networks kept saying, 'Gee, get Filmation to do it, they're terrific with action-adventure humanoid characters.' In those days they would never say that we were good at comedy. Hanna-Barbera was known as the comedy-animal studio. And we were known for our superheroes. We were typecast. We've kind of cross-pollenated since then, and now we're known for both."

As time and Superman flew by, Clark Kent became less important to the cartoon. Perhaps the producers and the network feared that TV audiences, bitten by the action bug, would grow restless when Superman wore his worldly disguise and led his boring life. By the mid-1970s, Clark was out of the picture. Hanna-Barbera artists were drawing the Kryptonian then, and Superman was simply fighting side by side with Batman, Robin, Wonder Woman, and Aquaman.

Superman's closest cousin was a little rodent who first streaked across the airwaves in 1955.

What distinguished Mighty Mouse from TV's other caped crusaders was not his agility at flying or his ability to talk. It was his operatic flair. The Terrytoon cartoon character, at one

Able to spring any mousetrap and sing any opera—Terrytoon's Mighty Mouse

Another incarnation of Yogi Bear was Yogi's Space Race, *a ninety-minute intergalactic frolic telecast on NBC in 1978. Scare Bear is the ship's copilot.*

Hanna-Barbera's Super Friends—*comic book heroes and TV money-makers for ABC in 1973*

time directed by now famous animator Ralph Bakshi, sang his way through his exploits, saving assorted animal friends from wicked plotters.

His enemies, however, were more than mere cartoon figures. In 1959, for example, the National Congress of Parents and Teachers tried to ground Mighty Mouse. Though unsuccessful, the group charged in its magazine, *The National Parent-Teacher,* that the superhero was "not only cynical but corny." They said the show should merely be "Recommended for mice."

In his heyday, however, Mighty Mouse was so popular that the United Nations Children's Fund (UNICEF) named him their official ambassador for their 1961 and 1962 "Trick or Treat" fund-raising drive. And now Mighty Mouse is back with twice the punch. His old stories are in syndication, and his new Filmation adventures premiered on CBS in 1979. Filmation made one obvious change for *The New Adventures of Mighty Mouse and Heckle and Jeckle,* however. The studio boss cut Mighty Mouse from the glee club. "No more opera, I don't think that a singing superhero mouse would fly with contemporary audiences," Prescott says.

Saturday morning has been a happy home for super mice and men. But the schedule has also had room for other spectacular crime fighters.

In 1963, a year after Hanna-Barbera developed *The Jetsons,* the cartoon producers aired *Jonny Quest,* a series about a boy who helps in his father's scientific experiments, fights crime with chemistry, and battles the elements.

The same year that Quest premiered, NBC bought the American rights to Japan's successful *Astro Boy.* The program was based on a popular Japanese comic strip about a doctor whose wife and son died in an automobile accident. Grieving, the scientist creates an android to uphold the law. *Astro Boy* was produced by Mushi Productions, which also sold *Eighth Man, Jet Boy, Speed Racer, Prince Planet,* and *Johnny Sokko and his Flying Robot* to American TV.

Space Angel followed in 1964. The TV Comic Strips Inc. series was noted for its use of "syncro-vox," a technical process that inserted human lips on animated mouths. "Syncro-vox" was also used in *Clutch Cargo.* The procedure might have cut costs, but the animation was static. Lips moved, but characters' hands and bodies seemed frozen in frame. The "syncro-vox system" wasn't synchronized with audience taste, and *Space Angel* was never the hit that *Underdog* was in 1964.

Character actor Wally Cox dubbed the voice for this superpup version of Mr. Peepers. Like Mighty Mouse and Superman, Underdog spent most of his air time saving an innocent young female, Sweet Polly Purebred, from the clutches of gangster Simon Bar Sinister.

A year later, *Secret Squirrel* debuted. This Hanna-Barbera series featured a secret agent squirrel who traveled the world with his sidekick Morocco Mole to defeat the Goldfinger-like gangster, Yellow Pinky. *Atom Ant,* another Hanna-Barbera creation, also flew along in 1965.

Space Kidettes rocketed onto NBC in 1966 with adventures that by then were anything but alien. The show featured a band of youngsters who operated out of their extraterrestrial clubhouse and roamed through the galaxy.

Even more successful was *Space Ghost* (1966), a Hanna-Barbera creation that chronicled the account of a crime fighter who could become invisible.

In 1966, NBC presented *The Super Six,* a cartoon featuring

superheroes for hire. Available for the Super Service, Inc. agency were Elevator Man, Super Stretch, Magneto Man, and Granite Man.

Birdman, yet another Hanna-Barbera superhero, aired in 1967. The series featured a flying crime fighter who vows to "battle evil and spread the light of justice into the darkest recesses of the human soul." Birdman was actually a police investigator who received his powers from an ancient Egyptian sun spirit.

The same year, Hanna-Barbera's *The Herculoids* was set on an idyllic world where a band of superheroes guarded their Shangri-La from would-be invaders. And when a brother and a sister discovered a magic ring in the 1967 Hanna-Barbera program *Shazzan!* they were instantly transported back to the days of the Arabian nights, where they met a friendly genie who tried to help them return to their own era.

Packed with laughs as well as action was *Roger Ramjet,* a 1960s syndicated cartoon that featured such guest characters as a gumshoe named Armlock Hertz. Said Roger in one cartoon, "Come on, Hertz, let Ramjet put you in the pilot's seat."

Undoubtedly, one of TV's worst superhero series was *Super President.* The 1967 DePatie-Freleng cartoon program featured the adventures of James Norcross, President of the United States, who could draw on any imaginable power to ward off the enemies of freedom.

The program transcended the fantastic. It ventured into the absurd. *Super President* gave American children a national leader who was invincible. Coming only four years after President Kennedy was assassinated, it was a particularly odious, unfair, inaccurate, and irresponsible notion. The show was erased from the network schedule in 1968, and even *Super President* producer David DePatie says he was glad.

"I think it was really the worst thing we've ever made. It was a real turkey. We tried to put our comedy people on it," DePatie admits, "but it really looked terrible."

In 1973, Hanna-Barbera had high hopes for *Inch High, Private Eye.* Inch High was a crime fighter who could shrink to the height of an inch upon taking a swig of a secret formula. The only problem with the beverage was that its lasting power was not reliable, and without notice the detective could spring back to normal size.

TV continued to beam science fiction superheroes to audiences through the 1970s and into the 1980s, but in recent years the themes on the network shows have become rooted in earthbound ecology rather than black holes in deep space.

Heroes like Filmation's *The Space Sentinels* (1977), a trio of superhero teenagers, protected the environment more than some metropolis's streets. And DePatie-Freleng's Spider-Woman fought for women's rights in 1979 with the same zeal that her predecessors would have mustered to down a dastardly criminal.

Some syndicated series still didn't appear to obey the stringent rules governing violence. *Battle of the Planets* (1978), for example, with its *Star Wars* influence evident in an R2D2 look-alike robot named 7-Zark-7, seemed more violent than most of the competition. The series relied on action-filled ship-to-ship battles in which a team of five orphans always triumphed over the aliens.

Most of the superheroes, however, obeyed the dictates of a force more powerful than extraterrestrials. They flew a straight and narrow course outlined by the networks.

The Young Sentinels, *retitled* The Space Sentinels

16

The networks have held up a distorted mirror to other mediums. Cartoon offspring of old movie characters, comic-strip figures, or singing groups haven't always been faithful reflections.

Translated to a Saturday morning cartoon, for example, Charlie Chaplin became a cat; the Three Stooges, robots; King Kong, a lovable chimp with an overactive thyroid condition; and Godzilla, an obedient, puppy-like monster. Rather than being enhanced once freed from the confines of live-action film, the animated versions very often appeared so lifeless and so dull that there was little reason, except perhaps the obvious commercial tie-in, even to adapt them for kids.

Nonetheless, these distorted images greatly contributed to the TV product pipeline in the late 1960s and 1970s. They are, as Filmation Studios executive Norm Prescott offers, "insurance policies"; reliable proposals, likely to receive network approval.

"We go to bat every year with all kinds of original characters," explains Prescott. "But in all honesty, we sell fewer original characters than we do established characters. The networks will buy an original creation only occasionally, and then usually only if we surround it with well-known figures."

Prescott argues that most producers believe new characters could be favorably received by young viewers if the networks gambled more. But gambling reduces the networks' chances of succeeding, and conservative TV executives are not inclined to push their luck. "The problem" he says, "is that the networks are in a very commercial and competitive ratings business. They feel that if they start out with something that has a preacceptance, that's universally recognized, that has a history of success in the comics, films, or books—then their chances of

Opposite: The Addams Family *Saturday morning cartoon lurched onto the NBC lineup in 1973.*

Insurance Policies:

Cartoon Payoffs

Tarzan landed on Saturday morning with Filmation's 1978 ninety-minute CBS-aired production Tarzan and the Super 7.

coming up with winners are far better. When they start out with the 'insurance policies,' they feel they're ahead of the game. So they dictate what shows they'll buy, and that in turn tells us which shows we have to make."

The networks have ordered adaptations of every sort. From existing motion-picture stock NBC bought DePatie-Freleng's sincere but hazy Chaplin reflection called *Baggy Pants.* This 1977–78 feline version of the Tramp never spoke. And with the exception of music and sound effects, the cartoon itself was silent. Producers David DePatie and Friz Freleng borrowed freely from Charlie's films. They managed to convey some of Chaplin's humor but little of his humanity. Like most other Saturday morning productions, colorful action became more important than subtle character-shadings. *Baggy Pants* was a salute to Chaplin, but without his pathos it fell short of tribute.

Faring far worse were *Laurel and Hardy* (1966), *The Robonic Stooges* (1977), and Hanna-Barbera's syndicated *The Abbott and Costello Show* (1966), which was only distinguished by Bud Abbott's voice.

A cartoon version of the Marx Brothers was also planned in the early 1960s. And in 1979, Robert King, owner and distributor of *The Little Rascals,* produced the first of a series of thirty-minute cartoon specials featuring the likenesses of Spanky, Alfalfa, Porky, Stymie, and the blackeyed pooch Petey. Animation for the NBC-aired productions was supplied by Murakami-Wolf.

In addition to motion picture comedians, Hollywood's most gruesome creatures have been shrunk to fit into the TV cartoon. Moby Dick, the famed whale of Herman Melville's classic novel became a frolicsome, oversized guppy when Hanna-Barbera caught him in 1967. The former terror of the North Atlantic romped through the world's oceans with his pal, a seal named Scooby. When the opportunity surfaced he also protected two shipwrecked youngsters from dangers by expanding or contracting his "elastic" body. So much for Ahab.

The same studio transformed Mary Shelley's classic horror novel, *Frankenstein,* into a frightless cartoon in 1966. Naturally, Hanna-Barbera couldn't draw an accurate picture of the confused and lumbering monster. He would have scared kids to another network, and network executives to another job. The result, therefore, was a flying robot who teamed with rock 'n' roll detectives for *Frankenstein Jr. and the Impossibles.*

As if enough damage had not yet been caused, ABC's 1966 series *King Kong* was, according to the network's own press releases, "a lovable ape" who could be counted on "to perform awesome, sometimes earth-shaking deeds to bring evildoers to justice."

Hanna-Barbera similarly turned *Godzilla* from a rampaging killer to a benevolent reptilian; gave him the voice of actor Ted Cassidy (Lurch on *The Addams Family*); awarded him custody of Godzooky, a winged, fun-loving nephew; and ordered him to do battle with the competition on *The Godzilla Power Hour* in 1978.

In 1968, ABC presented the *Adventures of Gulliver,* an animated series with all the familiar faces but only a hint of Jonathan Swift's underlying political criticism.

NBC prescribed more comedy than whimsy in its 1970 cartoon version of Hugh Lofting's

Above: Filmation borrowed Isis *from its own studio for* The Freedom Force in the Super 7.

Left: DePatie Freleng's cartoon adaptation of Charlie Chaplin—Baggy Pants, featured character in the 1977 series Baggy Pants and the Nitwits

CALICO

Dr. Dolittle. DePatie-Freleng produced the program, titled it *The Further Adventures of Dr. Dolittle,* and sent the good doctor sailing on his ship, the *Flounder,* with Mooncat, a lunar kitten added to the nineteenth-century story for space-age viewers.

In 1975, NBC turned Walter Mitty into *Walter Kitty* and also aired *Return to the Planet of the Apes,* loosely drawn on the movie original.

Most noticeably airing in an altered state was Oriental movie-sleuth Charlie Chan in the 1972 Hanna-Barbera-produced CBS series *The Amazing Chan and the Chan Clan.* The ill-conceived format revolved around gumshoe Chan and his ten musical children who solved a case or two, then played contemporary tunes with an Oriental flavor.

Tarzan was much more faithful to the original story when it swung onto Saturday morning. The Lord of the Jungle was the lead attraction in CBS's ninety-minute series, *Tarzan and the Super 7* (1978). Between Tarzan's adventures, Filmation producers Norman Prescott and Lou Scheimer inserted animated segments that included "Web Woman" (A NASA scientist who could communicate with insects), "Super Stretch and Micro Woman" (a pair who could, as their names suggested, change shape), and the "Freedom Force" (cartoon versions of Filmation's *Isis* program).

Filmation also adapted the successful H. G. Wells story *Journey to the Center of the Earth* for a 1967 cartoon series. The program, like the book and movie before it, recounted the harrowing escapades of an archaeological team trying to find its way back to the surface of the earth after being sealed inside the planet's deepest caverns. Ted Knight (Mary Tyler Moore's Ted Baxter) and Pat Harrington, Jr. (Schneider on *One Day at a Time*) recorded the major voices.

Later, Filmation also produced a spin-off of the science fiction adventure film *Fantastic Voyage.* Each week members of the Combined Minature Defense Force (C.M.D.F.) combated deadly diseases by traveling through a patient's blood system in their micro submarine. And in 1979, Filmation clinched a $2-million deal—TV's most expensive to date—for a series of Saturday morning *Flash Gordons* featuring the popular hero.

One cartoon figure liberated from the movies

Hanna-Barbera gave Godzilla, once the terror of Japan, a soft touch and a happy-go-lucky nephew named Godzooky in The Godzilla Power Hour *(NBC, 1978).*

*Filmation's insurance policy for 1979 and 1980—*Flash Gordon. *On either side of the legendary comic-strip and movie hero are Dr. Zarkov and Dale Arden.*

actually found TV a compatible medium beginning in 1969. Feeding on all three commercial networks over ten years, The Pink Panther won a generation of fans too young to follow him in the theater and adults usually too old to watch Saturday morning television.

"He actually started back in 1963," remembers David DePatie. "We had just formed our company and movie producer Blake Edwards called and said he was going to make a picture called *The Pink Panther* that was just crying for some sort of animation in the opening credits."

One hundred sketches later, on a Sunday morning in Edwards's living room, the Pink Panther was born.

At one point during his NBC tenure, *The Pink Panther Show* used a live host. Comedian Lenny Schultz was hired to introduce cartoons and perform short sketches.

"It was awful," testifies DePatie. "It was just terrible. Next NBC decided to have riddles. We did the animation for those, but under protest."

The Pink Panther towered over most of his Saturday morning company. Not because he was taller, but strictly thanks to DePatie-Freleng's animation. The company doubled the number of drawings normally used per foot in the typical weekend cartoon. The animation was still limited compared to 1940s standards, but his body appeared more lifelike and more flowing than many of TV's other cartoon characters. "He needed movement," DePatie claims. "He's not the easiest guy in the world to work with."

At one point, there was talk of giving the Panther vocal cords. "In fact, years ago we even experimented with a Cary Grant and a David Niven type voice," the producer states. "It just didn't work, however. He completely lost his personality. A lot of it has to do with that long

Left: DePatie-Freleng brought the Pink Panther cartoons to TV in 1969. The jungle cat romped through the medium for more than a decade.

Below: From the comics came Archie, and from The Archie Show *came a new character named Sabrina. The two teamed in 1977 for* The New Archies/Sabrina Hour.

Alley Oop and the Captain and the Kids leaped out of the Sunday comics for NBC's The Fabulous Funnies *in 1978.*

extended nose of his. It doesn't lend itself to talking.

In 1979 the Panther migrated from Saturday morning to greener, more lucrative prime time pastures.

In 1961, UPA distributed *The Dick Tracy Show*. The series of five-minute cartoons cut animation techniques to the quick, repeating stock footage and showing characters from the rear to save the expense of animating their mouths.

The syndicated cartoons were obviously drawn with an eye focused more toward the Keystone Kops than Chester Gould's cartoon strip or the violent movies, serials, and live action TV adaptations. Each story invariably began with Tracy barking orders to his goony squad, Hemlock Holmes, the Retouchables, Joe Jitsu, Speedy Gonzolez, and Heap O'Calorie. Their objective would always be the same: Capture villains Sketch Paree, the Mole, Itchy, Prune Face, Flatop, or Mumbles. Everett Sloane provided Tracy's voice while the versatile Mel Blanc and deep-voiced Paul Frees played many of the other characters. Dick Tracy later reappeared in *Archie's TV Funnies* (1971).

Archie debuted in 1968 as a half-hour CBS

© Filmation Studios

Right: The Groovie Goolies *mixed musings with music in 1976.*

© Hanna-Barbera Productions

Left: The Harlem Globetrotters bounced around on TV in the 1970s in various series. A 1979 production presented the super players as superheroes.

series featuring the bumbling comic book teenagers of Riverdale High—Jughead, Reggie, Betty, Veronica, and the all-American freckled fellow himself. To help the ratings along, the quintet formed a rock band and performed one tune each show.

The Filmation program quickly produced three hit songs: "Sugar Sugar," "Jingle Jangle," and "Who's My Baby." More importantly, Archie demonstrated that the highly rated superhero cartoon shows were vulnerable. They could be beaten in the ratings with kindness and innocence. Certainly no character was ever more qualified on those two counts than Archie.

"The beautiful part about Archie," says one of his TV parents, Norm Prescott, "is that he and his friends are like real kids—contemporary teen-agers living in a contemporary society, having the kinds of problems and interests that most youngsters can identify with."

Prescott says Archie succeeded for another reason. "I think he represents the awakening of the relationship between the sexes. Just as Archie, Veronica, and Betty have been discovering for thirty-five years of comic-book adolescence, today's TV teen-agers learn that the

The Beatles *Saturday morning style (1965)*

opposite sex is never as bad as childhood made them seem."

The hit series was expanded to sixty minutes in 1969, changed titles to *The Archie Comedy Hour*, and added a new character, Sabrina, the teen-age witch. (The young sorceress won her own hour-long CBS show in 1970, *Sabrina and the Groovie Goolies,* in which she toured with a rock group starring Frankenstein, Dracula, and the Wolfman. The second season, the show lasted a half hour and was retitled *Sabrina, the Teen-age Witch.*) In 1970, Archie evolved again into *Archie's Fun House Featuring the Giant Juke Box.*

A year later, the show signed on with yet another format, thirty minutes less airtime and the name *Archie's TV Funnies.* In this outing Archie was treated as a "real" character and host of a TV show from Riverdale. It was his responsibility to introduce the cartoon adventures of "Emmy Lou," "Nancy and Sluggo," "Broom Hilda," "The Captain and the Kids" and "Dick Tracy." These characters then spun off into their own series in late 1978, *The Fabulous Funnies.*

In 1973, Archie became a musical comedy series called *Everything's Archie,* and in 1974, *The U.S. of Archie* reviewed historical events associated with the Bicentennial celebration.

The fact that Archie appeared in so many forms was not accidental. Filmation realized Archie could be a winner only as long as it stayed ahead of any imitators. "We tried to give the show continuing life and longevity," Prescott admits. "That's the game. We always have to look for other ways to utilize the characters in new forms to regenerate interest. Sometimes we succeed. Sometimes we fail."

Saturday cartoons also imitated life, adapting real-life characters to make-believe exploits. *The Beatles* premiered in 1965 with a mixture of music and mirth. Basketball's *Harlem Globetrotters* rebounded onto TV in Hanna-Barbera's 1970 CBS series. Filmation transferred Muhammad Ali from the ring to acetate in 1977, for his cartoon series *I Am the Greatest: The Adventures of Muhammad Ali,* and *Smokey the Bear* came out of the forest in 1969 only to discover that youngsters had no burning desire to see him.

Recording artists also won their own cartoon series. The first of note was David Seville's *The Alvin Show* (1961). The program was based on the multimillion seller *The Chipmunk Song,* writ-

The Fantastic Four

Al Capp's Shmoo, an odd character from "Li'l Abner," warmed up to audiences in NBC's The New Shmoo *and* Fred and Barney Meet the Shmoo *in 1979.*

ten and performed in 1958 by Ross Bagdasarian (Seville) and repeated on NBC and CBS for nearly twenty years.

The Jackson Five got into the Saturday morning TV groove in 1971, and *The Osmonds* spun onto the schedule the following year. Undoubtedly the best source of cartoon material was neither the movies, classic books, top-selling records, nor real life. The Saturday morning machine viewed prime time as its most important proving ground. Should an evening series attract kids, it was a likely candidate for an animated adaptation.

"We've always tried to maintain the flavor and feeling of the original nighttime show when we bring them to Saturday," explains Filmation's Prescott. "People know the characters. They can easily detect flaws and the differences. A good translator will try to keep the Saturday animated series as close to the original as possible."

Often, unfortunately, the Saturday offspring turns out more of a mutant than a true clone. Some characters and premises, though humorous, appear so changed that the only similarity between the bona fide TV show and the cartoon copy may be the laugh track. Thus, *The Honeymooners* begot a prehistoric version of family feuders called *The Flintstones*. Instead of Ralph and Alice Kramden, the Hanna-Barbera cartoon series offered Fred and Wilma Flintstone. Ed and Trixie Norton became Barney and Betty Rubble. The program premiered in 1960 and has been on the networks or in syndication via one form or another ever since.

The Flintstones hardly qualified as a kids' show in its initial airing. The stone-age comedy reached for primitve but adult laughs. Gags about marital squabbles and family rivalry sailed over the heads of youngsters. In time, however, the program evolved into a kids' show, with the Flintstone and Rubble children becoming popular enough to eventually earn their own 1971

I Am the Greatest: The Adventures of Muhammad Ali *premiered in 1977. The NBC comedy-adventure series presented fictionalized but morally sound exploits of the champ.*

Opposite: Alvin and the Chipmunks *were brought to TV for a show in 1961. Reruns continued until the end of the next decade.*

CBS series (and cereal), *Pebbles and Bamm Bamm.*

In 1961, Hanna-Barbera released *Top Cat,* an entertaining version of Sergeant Bilko from *The Phil Silvers Show.* Rather than Silvers barking orders, TC (voice of Arnold Stang) scratched and clawed his way out of the alleys of New York and onto Broadway. Maurice Gosfield (Private Doberman on the *Silvers Show*) even appeared as Benny the Ball, one of Top Cat's gang. The show debuted in prime time on ABC and later moved to Saturday morning.

Calvin and the Colonel, an *Amos 'n' Andy* look-alike featuring the voices of the original radio team (Freeman Gosden and Charles Correll), appeared in 1961.

In 1966, NBC presented a *Get Smart* takeoff called *Cool McCool.* The series concerned a super agent whose pratfalls and contrivances approximated Maxwell Smart.

My Favorite Martians landed on the schedule

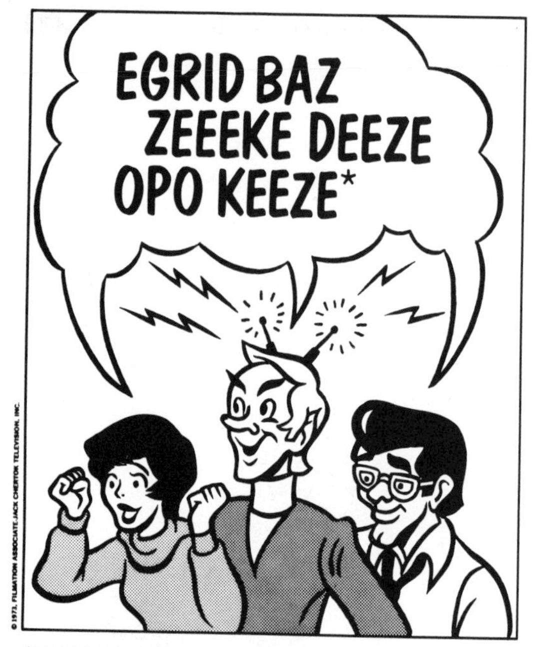

*EARTH TRANSLATION: WATCH "MY FAVORITE MARTIANS" EVERY SATURDAY MORNING. A NEW ANIMATED CHILDREN'S SHOW BASED ON THE ORIGINAL COMEDY SERIES. "EEEEKEBUT" (KIDS WILL LOVE IT).

MY FAVORITE MARTIANS

Lassie, coming home again to TV in 1973

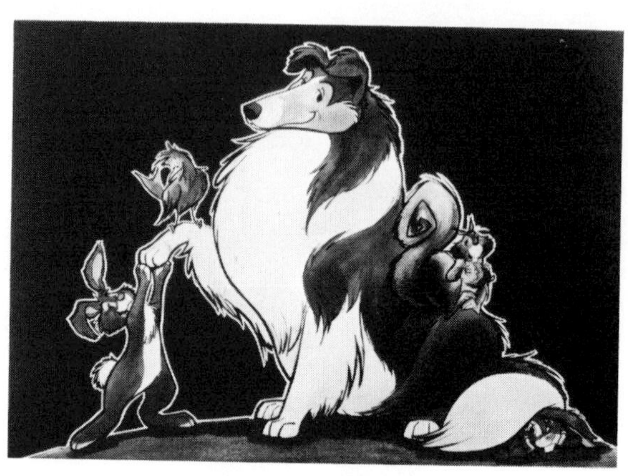

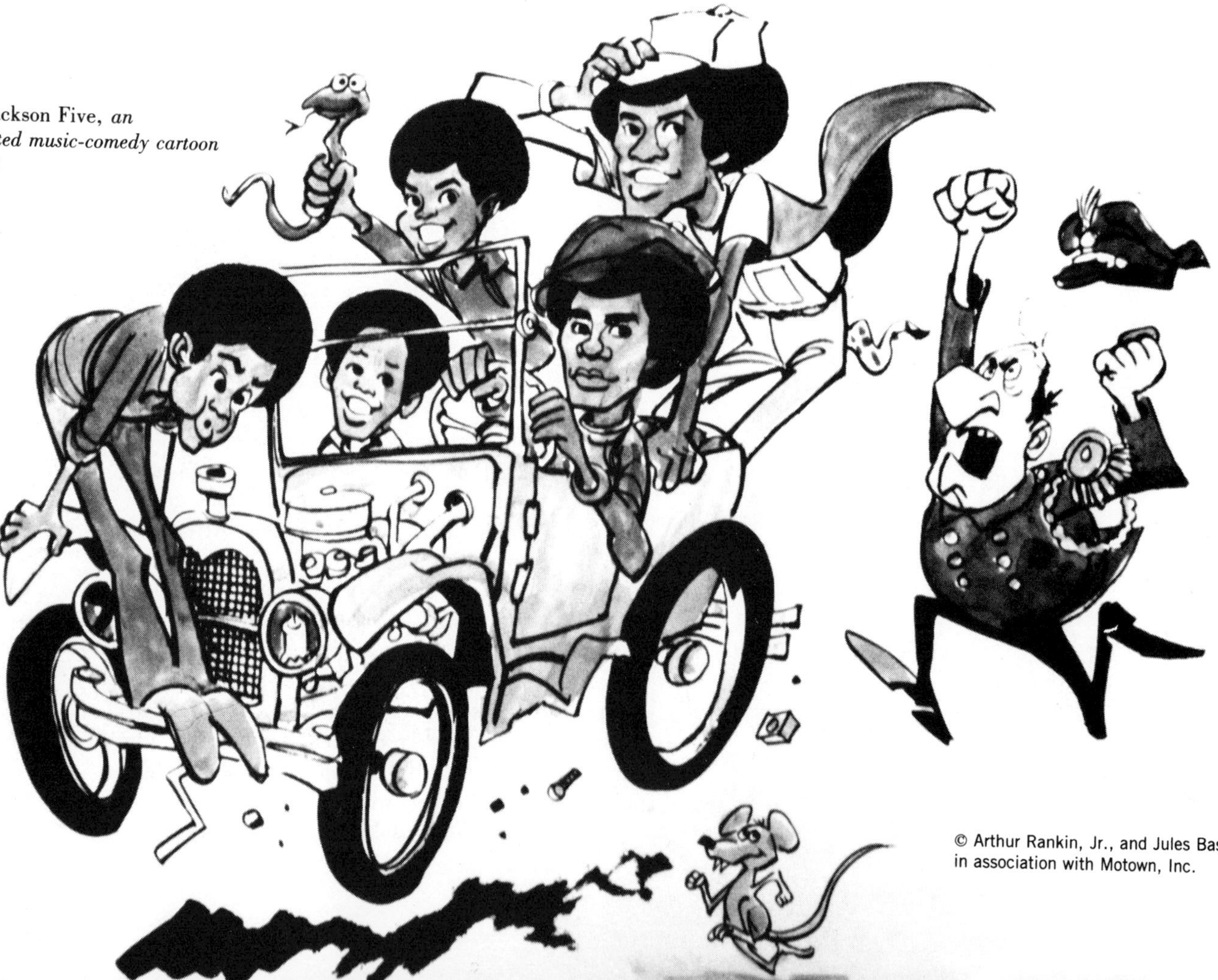

The Jackson Five, *an animated music-comedy cartoon (1971)*

© Arthur Rankin, Jr., and Jules Bass in association with Motown, Inc.

The Brady Kids *were less animated in their 1972 cartoon series than in their prime time show.*

ABC's Saturday Superstar Movie *animated TV shows, novels, movies, and fairy tales. One edition reprised the 1965 series* Lost in Space.

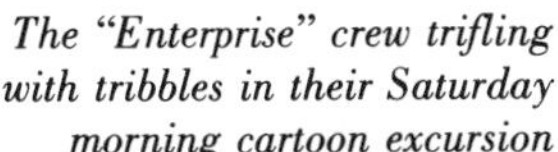

The "Enterprise" crew trifling with tribbles in their Saturday morning cartoon excursion

in 1973. In addition to prime time holdovers (Uncle Martin, Tim, and Mrs. Brown), the cartoon series introduced an alien named Andy; his dog, Oakie Doakie; and a young girl named Katy. *Jeannie*, based on *I Dream of Jeannie*, likewise appeared in 1973, as did a futuristic adaptation of *The Partridge Family* called *The Partridge Family: 2200 A.D.* The kids remained the same, but the science fiction slant gave the show a boost that didn't exist in the earthbound original.

The characters from *The Brady Bunch* moved from their suburban home to a treehouse and discarded their sibling differences to harmonize in a rock group when they turned up on Saturday morning as ABC's *The Brady Kids* (1972). Likewise, Lassie left Timmy and Jeff back at the farm and ran off to the Saturday morning schedule on *Lassie's Rescue Rangers*, also 1973.

The *Gilligan's Island* stick figures were colored in for the ABC cartoon program *The New Adventures of Gilligan* in 1974. ABC's *The Hardy Boys*, once just detectives who pressed criminals to sing on the witness stand, became guitar-strumming rock sleuths on a world-wide concert tour in 1969. And in 1973 *The Addams Family* sold their gothic house, hitched their car to a haunted trailer, and drove on to NBC. The same year, NBC gave *Butch Cassidy and the Sundance Kids* a recording contract, and then added four youngsters to the Los Angeles paramedics staff and premiered the cartoon series *Emergency Plus Four.*

Thoroughly departing from convention was *The Lone Ranger* cartoon series of 1966. None of the original TV voices were used in this CBS version, which depicted the masked rider of the plains more as a space-age hero. Instead of gunning for Butch Cavendish, the Ranger's super-Western adventures pitted him against such unfamiliar villains as Frogman, Dr. Destructo, and the Puppetmaster.

Equally lamentable was NBC's 1972 attempt to cast the *All in the Family* characters as squabbling pooches on *The Barkleys*, and pass off the *Mission Impossible* crack team as bumbling dogs and cats on *The Houndcats.*

The Oddball Couple was a poor distant relative of Neil Simon's *The Odd Couple* with a sloppy dog and a compulsively neat cat subbing for the original characters. *The C. B. Bears* paralleled *Charlie's Angels* right down to the three

De Patie-Freleng borrowed Gladys and Tyrone from Laugh-In *and called them the Nitwits in 1977. Arte Johnson and Ruth Buzzi recorded the voices for the characters they had portrayed on the nighttime series.*

characters receiving their orders via a CB radio from an unseen, sultry-voiced female named Charlie. And time and legend lost all meaning in the syndicated series, *Rocket Robin Hood.*

Of all prime time excusions to Saturday morning, only *Star Trek* stayed on the course set by the original series. Story editor Dorothy C. Fontana, a veteran from the evening production, steered the *Enterprise* through the Filmation Studios. William Shatner, Leonard Nimoy, DeForest Kelly, James Doohan, Nichelle Nichols, Walter Koenig, George Takei, and Majel Barrett reprised their roles when the animated production beamed across NBC from 1973 to 1975.[1] *Star Trek* creator and executive producer Gene Roddenberry consulted on the series. The show's regular writing team handled many of the scripts.

"When we did *Star Trek,*" Prescott affirms, "we made a decision." Prescott realized that in order to remain faithful to the live-action program, the dialogue and the plots would have to be sophisticated, perhaps too sophisticated for the typical Saturday morning audience. The first thing we told the network was that we probably weren't going to appeal to preschool kids, and therefore the show should be scheduled at a time when the older kids are watching.

"As a result of that decision, we sacrificed up to 50 percent of our audience," Prescott says. "We expected a good portion of them would switch to another show, yet oddly enough *Star Trek* performed very well. It was not a major, major hit, but it wasn't a failure because it did get the older kids and also a lot of adults who rarely watch Saturday morning cartoons."

With a few exceptions, Prescott's "insurance policies" came to term as the 1970s ended. With costs for rights rising as quickly as the costs for producing cartoons, the networks have slowly returned to older recognizable properties like Mighty Mouse and Casper. Indeed, such timeless creations may be a safer bet than TV adaptations whose residual future often depends on audience memory. But children's TV is as cyclical as nighttime programming. Concepts come, concepts go, and concepts return. The Saturday morning spin-offs have only temporarily spun out.

1. Prescott says that the actors didn't always assemble together for their recording sessions. Often he had to track the trekkers down with his tape machine, cornering them in offices, backstage, and even men's rooms. "That's the beauty of doing a cartoon adaptation of a prime time show," Prescott explains. "I can record the actors separately anywhere in the world and then cut the tracks together."

Appendix A

A Compilation of Network and Nationally Syndicated Television Programs Primarily Produced for the Saturday Children's Schedule or Rebroadcast on Saturdays Between 1947 and 1980.

compiled and edited by
Timothy C. Rupp and Gary Grossman

The following alphabetized list includes specific program information and premiere or initial broadcast dates. Animated cartoons that have appeared as segments on local or national shows are not listed as independent programs. The appendix is limited primarily to Saturday programming. Additional information on weekday or Sunday children's shows can be found in the text.

A

ABC CHILDREN'S NOVELS FOR TELEVISION

see *ABC Weekend Specials*

THE ABC SATURDAY SUPERSTAR MOVIE

premiere broadcast: 9/9/72, ABC

60-minute animated comedy, adventure, and science fiction films, including such titles as *Gidget, Lost in Space, Oliver Twist, The Mini Munsters, Yogi's Ark Lark* (with Yogi Bear and friends), and *Say Hey, Kid,* a biography of Willie Mays that utilized his voice.

ABC SHORT STORY SPECIALS

see *ABC Weekend Specials*

ABC WEEKEND SPECIALS

premiere broadcast: 9/10/77, ABC

A series of 30-minute multipart, live-action, and animated telecasts of short stories, *ABC Short Story Specials*, and novels adapted for TV, *ABC Children's Novels for Television*, plus repeats of *The ABC Afterschool Specials*. Prior to its incorporation into *ABC Weekend Specials, ABC Short Story Specials* had aired as an independent series premiering Saturday 1/29/77. *ABC Afterschool Specials* premiered Wednesday 10/4/72. *ABC Children's Novels for Television* premiered 9/10/77. For the 1979–80 season, *ABC Weekend Specials* expanded to a full 52-week year, with Michael Young as host.

ACROBAT RANCH

broadcast dates: 8/19/50–5/12/51, ABC

Jack Stillwell hosted circus-show acts in a Western setting. The Chicago-based show was 30 minutes initially, reduced to 15 minutes in 1951.

THE ABBOTT AND COSTELLO SHOW

syndicated: 1966

Hanna-Barbera cartoon series based on the vaudeville, radio, movie, and TV comedians. Bud Abbott recorded the voice of his own TV-animated representation.

THE ADDAMS FAMILY

initial broadcast dates: 9/8/73–8/30/75, NBC

Hanna-Barbera cartoon version of the live-action television comedy *The Addams Family*, created by Charles Addams. Jackie Coogan and Ted Cassidy reprised their prime time TV roles of Fester and Lurch. Jody Foster recorded the voice of Pugsley. 30 minutes.

THE ADVENTURES OF BLACK BEAUTY

syndicated: 1972

30-minute live-action British-produced series about a sleek horse named Beauty and her teen-age companion, Victoria Gordon (Judi Bowker).

THE ADVENTURES OF BLINKEY

syndicated: 1952

15-minute marionette film production featuring Blinkey, a male counterpart to *The Wizard of Oz*'s Dorothy, who wandered through a puppet land. Actor Michael Mann transformed into a puppet upon entering the enchanted territory. Directed by "Rootie Kazootie" puppeteer Paul Ashley, produced by Murray King, and created by child psychologist Lucille Emerick.

THE ADVENTURES OF CAPTAIN HARTZ

syndicated: 1954

15-minute live-action film series depicting the tales of sea captain Hartz (Philip Lord), as told to young Bruce Lindgren. Sponsored by Hartz Mountain Products.

THE ADVENTURES OF CHAMPION

prime time broadcast dates: 9/30/55–2/3/56, CBS, thereafter syndicated

30-minute live-action Western produced by Gene Autry's Flying A Productions. Barry Curtis played 12-year-old Ricky North, and Jim Bannon starred as his uncle, Sandy. The series featured Autry's "Wonder Horse" and Rebel, the German shepherd dog.

THE ADVENTURES OF CYCLONE MALONE

syndicated: 1950; originally aired in 1949

as a local Los Angeles show on KNBH-TV
Puppet series with a Western setting, available in either 15-minute or 30-minute versions. The voice of Cyclone Malone—Ross Jones. Produced by Carl Hittleman and directed by John Gaunt.

THE ADVENTURES OF GULLIVER

initial broadcast dates: 9/14/68–9/5/70, ABC
Hanna-Barbera cartoon series adapted from Jonathan Swift's novel *Gulliver's Travels*. 30 minutes.

ADVENTURES IN NUMBERS AND SPACE

syndicated: 1957
30-minute nine-part educational series on mathematics hosted, narrated, and coscripted by puppeteer Bil Baird and with Dr. Howard F. Fehr. Produced by Richard Peck for Westinghouse Broadcasting Company.

THE ADVENTURES OF JIM BOWIE

prime time broadcast dates: 9/7/56–8/29/58, ABC, thereafter syndicated
Live-action, 30-minute adventure series set in New Orleans after the Louisiana Purchase. Scott Forbes starred as the knife-throwing Bowie. Louis F. Edelman and Lewis Foster produced the program.

THE ADVENTURES OF KIT CARSON

syndicated: 1956
Live-action Western with Christopher "Kit" Carson (Bill Williams) and sidekick El Toro (Don Diamond). Kit rode his horse in a total of 104 episodes. 30 minutes.

THE ADVENTURES OF A JUNGLE BOY

syndicated: 1957
Live-action adventure program set in Nairobi, Kenya, about "Boy" (Michael Carr Hartley), a young, orphaned airplane-crash survivor, and Dr. Laurence (Ronald Adam), his scientist friend. 30 minutes.

THE ADVENTURES OF LONG JOHN SILVER

syndicated: 1956
Actor Robert Newton as the legendary pirate. 30 minutes.

THE ADVENTURES OF POW WOW

syndicated: 1957
Five-minute moralistic cartoons of Pow Wow the Indian Boy, produced by Tempi-Toon Company. The twenty-six adventures were telecast on *Captain Kangaroo* and syndicated by Screen Gems to eleven Western states not then receiving the CBS children's program.

THE ADVENTURES OF RIN TIN TIN

prime time broadcast dates: 10/15/54–8/28/59, ABC, thereafter rebroadcast on Saturday morning over ABC and CBS
Live-action series set at Fort Apache in the 1880s, starring James Brown, Lee Aaker, Joe Sawyer, Rand Brooks, and John Hoyt. Produced by Herbert B. Leonard for Screen Gems. Episodes were repackaged and syndicated with new color openings in 1976. 30 minutes.

THE ADVENTURES OF ROBIN HOOD

initial prime time dates: 9/26/55–9/22/58, CBS
Saturday premiere broadcast: 10/4/58, CBS
Richard Greene as the English hero who used the cover of the forest to fight the evil rule of Prince John (Donald Pleasence). Also appearing: Alexander Gauge, Archie Duncan, Bernadette O'Farrell, Patricia Driscoll, and Alan Wheatley. 30 minutes. Syndicated title: *Sherwood Forest.*

THE ADVENTURES OF SIR LANCELOT

prime time broadcast dates: 9/24/56–6/24/57, NBC, thereafter syndicated
Adventure series following Sir Lancelot's quests in twelfth-century England, starring William Russell. 30 minutes.

THE ADVENTURES OF SUPERMAN

syndicated: 1953–present
The Man of Steel in 104 live-action adventures filmed 1951–57. George Reeves, Phyllis Coates, Noel Neill, Jack Larson, and John Hamilton starred. 30 minutes. See also *Superman* and *The New Adventures of Superman*.

THE ADVENTURES OF THE SEA HAWK

syndicated: 1958
The live-action tales of the crew manning an electronics-equipped schooner in the Caribbean. 30 minutes.

AFRICAN PATROL

syndicated: 1957
Live-action 30-minute series depicting the African Police Patrol. John Bently starred as Inspector Derek, head of the specialized crime unit.

THE ALDRICH FAMILY

prime time dates: 10/2/49–5/29/58, NBC, thereafter syndicated
30-minute reruns of the 1949 NBC sitcom about the bumbling middle-class family based on the characters created by Clifford Goldsmith.

ALL ABOARD

initial Sunday broadcast dates: 10/19/52–1/11/53, CBS, with rebroadcasts Saturdays in some markets
15-minute comedy series hosted by ventriloquist "Skeets" Minton and his dummy Jimmy Morton. Teen-age singer Junie Keegan was also featured, along with guests from the entertainment world. The show originated in New York and was sponsored by the Lionel Corporation.

THE ALL-NEW PINK PANTHER SHOW

see *The Pink Panther Show*

THE ALL-NEW POPEYE HOUR

see *Popeye*

THE ALL-NEW SUPER FRIENDS HOUR

see *Super Friends*

ALVIN AND THE CHIPMUNKS

see *The Alvin Show*

THE ALVIN SHOW

prime time broadcast dates: 10/4/61–9/5/62, CBS initial Saturday morning broadcast dates: 6/23/62–9/18/65, CBS return: 3/10/79–9/1/79, NBC, as Alvin and the Chipmunks

30-minute cartoon series about Ross Bagdasarian's "Chipmunks" (Alvin, Theodore, and Simon, plus David Seville). The show also included stories about a hapless inventor entitled "The Adventures of Clyde Crashcup," with Shepard Menken as the voice of Clyde.

THE AMAZING CHAN AND THE CHAN CLAN

initial broadcast dates: 9/9/72–9/22/74, CBS

Hanna-Barbera's animated production based on the famed movie sleuth. Keye Luke, Number Two son in the films, finally played the Oriental detective. 30 minutes.

THE AMAZING TALES OF HANS CHRISTIAN ANDERSEN

syndicated: 1954

30-minute color series filmed in Copenhagen, Denmark, and based on the stories of Hans Christian Andersen. George and Gene Sheldon, pantomimes, were included in the cast.

THE AMAZING THREE

syndicated: 1967

30-minute cartoon series set in the twenty-first century, in which three aliens come to earth disguised as a horse, a dog, and a duck and befriend a young boy as they combat evil.

AMERICAN BANDSTAND

weekday broadcast dates: 8/5/57–8/30/63, ABC
prime time broadcast dates: 10/7/57–12/30/57, ABC
Saturday premiere broadcast: 9/7/63, ABC

Dick Clark's record-making, record-breaking, three-decade-long dance party from Philadelphia and later, Los Angeles. The program originated in 1952 as *Bandstand*, a local show on ABC affiliate WFIL-TV, Philadelphia, hosted by Bob Horn and Lee Stewart. Clark became host in 1956.

AMOS 'N' ANDY

prime time broadcast dates: 6/28/51–6/11/53, CBS, thereafter syndicated

TV's version of the long-running radio sitcom with Alvin Childress and Spencer Williams as Amos and Andy. The original radio voices of Freeman Gosden and Charles Correll were heard in the 1961–62 cartoon adaptation, *Calvin and the Colonel*. 30 minutes.

ANDY'S GANG

premiere broadcast: 8/20/55, NBC, and also syndicated in markets not served by the NBC network

The replacement production to *Smilin' Ed's Gang* with all the characters intact and starring Andy Devine. 30 minutes. See also *Smilin' Ed's Gang*.

ANIMAL CLINIC

broadcast dates: 8/19/50–1/13/51, ABC

30 minutes. Chicago-based broadcast with Dr. Wesley Young.

ANIMAL FAIR

see *Your Pet Parade*

ANIMAL SECRETS

broadcast dates: 10/15/66–4/8/67, NBC

Color educational series produced by the Graphic Curriculum in association with NBC Public Affairs, featuring studies of how various forms of animal life adjust to their environments. Narrated by renowned anthropologist Dr. Loren C. Eiseley of the University of Pennsylvania. 30 minutes.

ANNIE OAKLEY

syndicated: 1954

Gail Davis starred as Annie Oakley, Western heroine, in this Flying A Production. Jimmy Hawkins and Brad Johnson costarred as brother Tagg Oakley and deputy Lofty Craig. 30 minutes.

AQUAMAN

syndicated: 1970

Rebroadcast cartoon adventures about an aquatic hero born to an Atlantean mother and a human father. The animated tales were originally broadcast on CBS in 1967 as part of "The Superman-Aquaman Hour," produced by Filmation Studios.

THE ARCHIE SHOW

initial broadcast dates: 9/14/68–9/6/69, CBS

Filmation's 30-minute cartoon series based on Bob Montana's comic-strip characters: Archie, Jughead, Betty, Veronica, Reggie, et al. Each week a special song and dance segment featured music by the Archies, a rock group. The second season of Archie cartoons introduced Sabrina, the Teen-Age Witch, who used her exceptional powers to help her friends at Riverdale High School. Included also was a segment of features, sketches, and music called "Archie's Fun House." This series was broadcast 9/13/69–9/5/70, CBS, as *The Archie Comedy Hour*, 60 minutes. The third season, a comedy and variety hour was broadcast 9/12/70–9/4/71, CBS, as *Archie's Fun House Featuring the Giant Juke Box*, 60 minutes. The fourth version featured Archie and the gang operating a TV station that televised cartoons of Dick Tracy, Broom Hilda, Emmy Lou, Moon Mullins, Here Come the Dropouts, Smokey Stover, Nancy and Sluggo, and The Captain and the Kids. It was broadcast 9/11/71–9/1/73, CBS, as *Archie's TV Funnies*, 30 minutes. The fifth incarnation of Archie was broadcast 9/8/73–1/26/74, CBS, as *Everything's Archie*, 30 minutes. For the Bicentennial period, Archie and his cartoon friends retold the exploits of great Americans in a series broadcast 9/7/74–1/11/75 (Saturday) and 1/19/75–9/5/76 (Sunday), CBS, as *The U.S. of Archie*, 30 minutes. The seventh version of Archie was broadcast 9/10/77–11/5/77, NBC, as *The New Archies/Sabrina Hour*, 60 minutes. It was succeeded by *The Bang-Shang Lalapalooza Show*, 11/12/77–1/28/78, NBC, 30 minutes.

ARCHIE'S FUN HOUSE FEATURING THE GIANT JUKE BOX

see *The Archie Show*

ARCHIE'S TV FUNNIES

see *The Archie Show*

THE ARCHIE COMEDY HOUR

see *The Archie Show*

ARK II

initial broadcast dates: 9/11/76–9/1/79, CBS

Filmation's 30-minute live-action series set in the year 2476, with three young scientists and a chimp named Adam traversing the pollution-ravaged and anarchic earth in an attempt to help rebuild civilization.

AROUND THE WORLD IN 80 DAYS

initial broadcast dates: 9/9/72–9/1/73, NBC

30-minute Australian-produced cartoon series based on the Jules Verne book and movie of the same name.

ASK NBC NEWS

premiere broadcast: 9/8/79, NBC

75-second inserts with reports of current events for children, broadcast three times each Saturday morning. Contributing correspondents include Edwin Newman, Tom Brokaw, John Chancellor, Jane Pauley, and Garrick Utley. Emmy Award, 1979–80.

ASTRO BOY

syndicated: 1963

30-minute Japanese-made science fiction cartoon set in the year 2000, featuring the adventures of a scientist and his superpowered robot, Astro Boy. The series was based on a Japanese comic strip and produced by Mushi Productions, a company that also delivered *Eighth Man*, *Johnny Sokko and His Flying Robot*, *Gigantor*, *Speed Racer*, *Jet Boy*, and *Prince Planet*.

ATOM ANT

initial broadcast dates: 10/2/65–9/2/67, NBC; also a segment on The Atom Ant/Secret Squirrel Show *9/9/67–9/7/68, NBC*

30-minute Hanna-Barbera cartoon series about a superhero insect. Both Howard Morris and Don Messick recorded the voice of the mighty mite.

THE ATOM ANT/SECRET SQUIRREL SHOW

broadcast dates: 9/9/67–9/7/68, NBC

30-minute Hanna-Barbera cartoon series combining episodes of Atom Ant and Secret Squirrel, both of which were telecast previously as independent series. See also *Atom Ant* and *Secret Squirrel*.

B

BAGGY PANTS AND THE NITWITS

initial broadcast dates: 9/10/77–10/28/78, NBC

DePatie-Freleng's 30-minute animated comedy about a tramp cat. The stories were loose representations of Charlie Chaplin's silent films. Also in each episode was a cartoon called "The Nitwits"—an animated version of Tyrone and Gladys from *Laugh-In*, with Arte Johnson and Ruth Buzzi recording the voices of their original characters.

BAILEY'S COMETS

initial broadcast dates: 9/8/73–1/26/74, CBS

Cartoon contest in which Roller Derby teams covered a course to compete for a $1-million prize. Clues to the whereabouts of the finish line were presented in rhymes. 30 minutes.

THE BANANA SPLITS ADVENTURE HOUR

see *Kellogg's Presents the Banana Splits Adventure Hour*

THE BANANA SPLITS AND FRIENDS SHOW

syndicated: 1971

Hanna-Barbera's repackaged segments from the Banana Splits, including cartoons of Atom Ant, Secret Squirrel, Precious Pupp, Hillbilly Bears, Winsome (Winnie) Witch, Squiddly Diddly, and the combined live action and animation of Huck Finn. 30 minutes.

THE BANG-SHANG LALAPALOOZA SHOW

see *The Archie Show*

THE BARKLEYS

initial broadcast dates: 9/9/72–9/1/73, NBC

30-minute cartoon takeoff of *All in the Family*, with a dog family imitating the Bunkers.

BARNYARD VARIETIES

see *Barnyardville Varieties*

BARNYARDVILLE VARIETIES

syndicated: 1951

15-minute puppet series featuring a hen, a bull, a monkey, and a sexy blond pig named Shirley Swine (also dubbed Penny Pig). Marionettes by Sue Hastings and produced by Puppet Plays, Inc.

BARRIER REEF

initial broadcast dates: 9/11/71–9/2/72, NBC

Australian 30-minute live-action series about marine biologists who study the Great Barrier Reef from aboard their 220-ton windjammer, *Endeavor.*

BATMAN

prime time broadcast dates: 1/12/66–3/14/68, ABC, thereafter syndicated

The Dynamic Duo doing dynamic work in Gotham City. Adam West and Burt Ward starred in the 30-minute production.

THE BATMAN/SUPERMAN HOUR OF ADVENTURE

broadcast: 9/14/68–9/6/69, CBS

Filmation's combination of Batman and Superman cartoon exploits in separate segments. A more serious Batman and Robin made their cartoon debut, and Superboy joined Superman.

THE BATMAN/TARZAN ADVENTURE HOUR

initial broadcast dates: 9/10/77–9/2/78, CBS

Filmation's combination of Batman and Tarzan cartoon exploits in separate segments.

THE NEW ADVENTURES OF BATMAN

broadcast dates: 2/12/77–9/3/77, CBS

Filmation's 30-minute cartoon series featuring Adam West and Burt Ward as voices of characters they had previously portrayed in the *Batman* live-action series. Featured also were the voices of Melendy Britt as Batgirl and Lennie Weinrib as Batmite, a mouse.

BATTLE OF THE PLANETS

syndicated: 1978

30-minute cartoon series about the exploits of the "G-Force," a group of young defenders of Earth. Series of seventy-eight episodes set in the year 2020.

THE BAY CITY ROLLERS

initial broadcast dates: 11/4/78–1/27/79, NBC

Sid and Marty Krofft's live-action, musical/variety comedy series with the Bay City Rollers singing group. Originally a segment on the *Krofft Superstar Variety Hour* (premiere 9/9/78), NBC.

THE BEAGLES

initial broadcast dates: 9/10/66–9/2/67, CBS

30-minute cartoon adventures of two rock 'n' roll singing pups, Stringer and Tubby. Thirty-six episodes produced. 30 minutes.

BEANY AND CECIL

syndicated: 1950

15-minute puppet series produced by Bob Clampett and featuring the voices of Stan Freberg, Daws Butler, Jerry Colonna, Jerry Lewis, Spike Jones, Liberace, and Will Rogers, Jr. Written by Bill Scott and Charlie Shos. Episodes concerned the global adventures of a small boy (Beany) aboard his boat, *The Leakin' Lena*, and his pet sea serpent. Cecil. The show was originally titled *Time for Beany* and premiered on KTLA-TV, Los Angeles, February 1949. Series syndicated through Paramount TV Productions and became KTLA-TV's first show to be viewed in the New York City market via kinescope. *Time For Beany*, created by Clampett (former writer and director of *Bugs Bunny*), won Emmys in 1949, 1950, and 1952. A cartoon version, *Matty's Funnies with Beany and Cecil*, premiered on ABC, Saturday evening, January 6, 1962. The title was shortened to *Beany and Cecil* in April and began color broadcast on September 29, 1962. Saturday morning broadcasts ran from January 1963 to December 19, 1964.

THE BEATLES

initial broadcast dates: 9/25/65–9/7/68

30-minute cartoon adventure series featuring likenesses of the Beatles, and their music.

BETSY AND THE MAGIC KEY

syndicated: 1952

Sue Hastings Marionettes in 260 15-minute episodes produced by Dynamic Films, Inc., New York, and released through CBS Syndication Sales, Children's Television Films, and Texas Film Enterprises.

THE BETTY CROCKER STAR MATINEE

broadcast dates: 11/3/51–4/26/52, ABC

30-minute talk-drama show hosted by Adelaide Hawley. Conversation and demonstrations were complemented by dramatic scenes performed by such actors as Thomas Mitchell, Brian Aherne, Dane Clark, Melvyn Douglas, Audrey Hepburn, Celeste Holm, Diana Lynn, Raymond Massey, David Niven, Pat O'Brien, William Prince, Robert Sterling, Teresa Wright, Hume Cronyn, and Jessica Tandy. The series was also listed as *Betty Crocker Time.*

BEWITCHED

prime time broadcast dates: 9/17/64–7/1/72, ABC, thereafter syndicated
Saturday morning premiere broadcast: 9/11/71, ABC

30-minute situation comedy starring Elizabeth Montgomery as the beautiful witch Samantha, who attempted to maintain some semblance of a normal marriage with her husband, Darrin (Dick York, later Dick Sargent), who worked for an advertising agency in New York City. Agnes Moorehead portrayed Samantha's mother, Endora.

BIG BLUE MARBLE

syndicated: 1974

30-minute "magazine" series aimed at children eight to twelve and focusing on the social and cultural life of children around the world. Emmy Awards 1975–76 and 1977–78. Henry Fownes, creator and producer for I.T.T. Corporation.

BIG FOOT AND WILDBOY

initial broadcast dates: 6/2/79–8/19/79, ABC

30-minute live-action adventures of the

legendary Big Foot (Ray Young) and two teen-agers as they roam the Pacific Northwest. Originally premiered as a segment on *The Kroft Supershow '77*, 9/10/77, ABC.

BIG JOHN, LITTLE JOHN

premiere broadcast: 9/11/76, NBC

30-minute situation comedy with Herb Edelman as forty-five-year-old school teacher who, after drinking from a fountain of youth, transforms back and forth between himself and a twelve-year-old played by Robbie Rist.

THE BIG PICTURE

syndicated: 1951

30-minute U.S. Army–produced documentaries supplied free to local stations. Narrated by Captain Carl Zimmerman and focusing at first on American action in Korea and later, army preparedness.

BIG RASCALS

syndicated: 1959

Leon Errol comedies repackaged for 15-minute broadcast.

THE BIG TOP

broadcast dates: 7/1/50–9/21/57, CBS aired from 7/1/50 to 1/51 at 6:30 to 7:30 P.M. ET and thereafter Saturday noon ET, with kinescopes shown at various times in some markets.

Live (except when on kinescope) circus show that originated over CBS affiliate WCAU-TV, Philadelphia. Jack Sterling was the show's ringmaster. Ed McMahon and Chris Keegan were clowns. Sponsored by Sealtest. 60 minutes.

BIRDMAN

initial broadcast dates: 9/9/67–9/14/68, NBC

Hanna-Barbera cartoon about a crime fighter who receives amazing superpowers from the Egyptian Sun God. 30 minutes.

BIRTHDAY HOUSE

syndicated: 1963

Birthday celebrations with three in-studio children and their friends. Hosted by Paul Tripp (formerly Mr. I. Magination). 60 minutes.

BLONDIE

prime time premiere broadcast: 1/4/57, NBC
initial Saturday broadcast dates: 7/5/58–10/4/58, NBC

30-minute sitcom featuring the Bumstead family, based on the comic strip by Chick Young. Dagwood—Arthur Lake; Blondie—Pamela Britton.

THE BLUE ANGELS

syndicated: 1960

Fictionalized adventure series based on the lives of the U.S. Navy precision-flying team, the Blue Angels. 30 minutes.

BOBO THE HOBO AND HIS TRAVELING TROUPE

syndicated: 1955

Puppet production featuring the voice of Brett Morrison (radio's The Shadow) as Bobo. 15 minutes.

THE BOING-BOING SHOW

initial Sunday broadcast dates: 12/16/56–3/24/57, CBS, thereafter syndicated

UPA's avant-garde animated cartoon series that featured Gerald McBoing-Boing, a little boy that spoke only in sound effects. Except for segments of UPA theatrical cartoons (minus Mr. Magoo), the show contained original TV segments: Dusty of the Circus; The Twirliger Twins, with songs and dances; a series on contemporary artists such as Chagall, Miro, and Dufy; humorous stories about American inventors such as Edison and Fulton; and Musical Vignettes, abstract animation with jazz backgrounds. The series was telecast in both color and black and white, and contained more than thirty original songs composed for the show. Bill Goodwin was the narrator, and Gerald McBoing-Boing was the host.

BONKERS

syndicated: 1978

The Hudson Brothers in a 30-minute musical/comedy series produced in England. Initially aired in most markets in prime time access (7:30 P.M. EST) and then appeared on Saturdays in some areas.

BOZO THE CLOWN

local and syndicated: 1951–1980

30-minute series featuring games, contests, variety acts, and cartoons hosted through the years by either a locally franchised Bozo or a central Bozo syndicated nationally. In 1962, WHDH-TV, Boston, produced 130 color programs for national syndication with Frank Avruch in the starring role. In 1976, a new syndicated version titled *Bozo's Big Top* was produced by Larry Harmon. The 130 programs were listed for syndication with the alternate title of *The All-New Bozo Show*.

THE BRADY KIDS

initial broadcast dates: 9/16/72–8/31/74, ABC

Filmation's 30-minute cartoon version of the prime time sitcom *The Brady Bunch*. The rock 'n' rollers were based in their treetop clubhouse, and the series dealt with their school life, romances, and adventures.

BRAVE EAGLE

prime time broadcast dates: 9/28/55–6/6/56, CBS, thereafter syndicated

30-minute live-action Western series starring Keith Larsen as Brave Eagle, a young Cheyenne chief.

BRAVE STALLION

see *Fury*

BROKEN ARROW

prime time broadcast dates: 9/25/56–9/18/60, ABC, thereafter syndicated

30-minute live-action Western series set in the Arizona territory, where white settlers and Apache Indians maintained a tenuous peace. Michael Ansara starred as Cochise, with John Lupton as Tom Jeffords.

BUCK ROGERS IN THE 25TH CENTURY

initial broadcast dates: 4/15/50–1/30/51, ABC

Live-action science fiction adventure series with Kem Dibbs and Robert Pastene portraying the World War I flier who awoke in the future after spending 400 years in suspended animation. Program premiered Saturday, 7:00 P.M., EST, and moved to Tuesday at 8:30 P.M. EST before its cancellation. Lou Prentis costarred as Lt. Wilma Deering and Harry Sothern played Dr. Huer. 30 minutes. Series remade by Universal Studios for NBC prime time in 1979.

BUCKAROO 500

syndicated: 1963

Variety series with host Buck Weaver introducing acts in a Western setting. 30 minutes.

THE BUCCANEERS

prime time broadcast dates: 9/22/56–9/14/57, CBS, thereafter syndicated

30-minute live-action adventure with Robert Shaw portraying Captain Dan Tempest, an ex-pirate who joined the British to fight pirates and the Spanish.

BUFFALO BILL, JR.

syndicated: 1955

Flying A Productions show with Dick Jones as Buffalo Bill, Jr., and Nancy Gilbert as Calamity taming the West. Produced by Gene Autry. 30 minutes.

BUFORD AND THE GALLOPING GHOST

initial broadcast dates: 2/3/79–9/1/79, NBC

30-minute Hanna-Barbera cartoon series combining two segments that had originally premiered on *Yogi's Space Race*, 9/9/78, NBC. *The Buford Files* featured a Confederate bloodhound named Buford (voice of Jim Nabors) and a Southern sheriff and his dim-witted deputy. *The Galloping Ghost* featured Nugget Nose, a 150-year-old ghost who haunted a dude ranch and harassed its owner and two hostess–social directors. See also *Yogi's Space Race*.

THE BUGALOOS

initial broadcast dates: 9/12/70–9/2/72, NBC

Live-action series with oversized puppets cavorting with a swarm of friendly bees, known as the Bugaloos, and the evil witch Benita Bizarre (Martha Raye). Produced by Sid and Marty Krofft. 30 minutes.

THE BUGS BUNNY SHOW

initial prime time broadcast dates: 10/11/60–9/25/62, ABC, 30 minutes
Saturday premiere broadcast: 4/7/62, ABC, 30 minutes
revised: 9/14/68–9/4/71, CBS, as The Bugs Bunny/Road Runner Hour, *60 minutes*
return: 9/11/71–9/1/73, CBS, and 9/8/73–8/30/75, ABC, as The Bugs Bunny Show, *30 minutes*
return: 9/6/75–9/2/78, CBS, as The Bugs Bunny/Road Runner Hour, *60 minutes*
prime time return: 4/27/76–6/1/78, CBS, as The Bugs Bunny/Road Runner Show, *30 minutes*
revised: 9/9/78, CBS as The Bugs Bunny/ Road Runner Show, *90 minutes*

Warner Brothers cartoon adventures of the "silly wabbit" in various program lengths, on both ABC and CBS. Included also in the large cast of characters were the Road Runner and Wile E. Coyote, Elmer Fudd, Porky Pig, Sylvester and Tweety, Daffy Duck, Speedy Gonzales, Pepe Le Pew, Foghorn the Leghorn, and Yosemite Sam. Voices: Mel Blanc. See also *The Road Runner Show.*

THE BULLWINKLE SHOW

initial Sunday broadcast dates: 9/24/61–9/15/63, NBC
initial Saturday broadcast dates: 9/21/63–9/5/64, NBC
Sunday return: 9/20/64–9/2/73, ABC, thereafter syndicated

Spin-off cartoon series from Jay Ward's *Rocky and His Friends* that featured Bullwinkle the moose and Rocky the flying squirrel. See *Rocky and His Friends.*

BUTCH CASSIDY AND THE SUNDANCE KIDS

initial broadcast dates: 9/8/73–8/31/74, NBC

Hanna-Barbera 30-minute cartoon series with teen-age undercover agents posing as a world-touring rock group. Among the voices heard on the series was former *Monkees* singer Mickey Dolenz.

BWANA MICHAEL OF AFRICA

syndicated: 1966

30-minute documentaries of African culture and customs hosted by explorer George Michael.

C

THE C. B. BEARS

initial broadcast dates: 9/10/77–9/2/78, NBC

Hanna-Barbera cartoon series in 60- and 30-minute versions, featuring three bears (Hustle, Bump, and Boggie) whose curiosity involves them in a variety of comic adventures. They operate from a rubbish truck that contains communications equipment and a telescreen by which they receive their assignments from an unseen female—a takeoff on *Charlie's Angels.* Other segments included Undercover Elephant, a private eye; Shake, Rattle, and Roll, three ghosts who run an inn; Hey, It's The King, a city cat; Blastoff Buzzard and Crazy Legs, a snake; and Posse Impossible, three bumbling cowboys.

THE CBS CHILDREN'S FILM FESTIVAL

Sunday premiere broadcast: 2/5/67, CBS
Saturday premiere broadcast: 9/11/71, CBS

Originally broadcast as a series of hour-long specials Sunday afternoons until 1971, hosted by Kukla, Fran, and Ollie and featuring film packages about children throughout the world. The series received an ACT Commendation, 1971–72, and the Peabody Award, 1967. Alternate title: *The CBS Saturday Film Festival.* 60 minutes and 30 minutes.

THE CBS LIBRARY

Sunday premiere broadcast: 10/21/79, CBS

Three hour-long dramas broadcast throughout the schedule with Saturday repeats. Productions are based largely on contemporary young people's literature with the goal of encouraging children twelve and younger to read. Premiere broadcast (repeated Saturday 2/16/80) was titled "Once Upon a Midnight Dreary," hosted by Vincent Price.

CALL IT MACARONI

syndicated: 1975

Westinghouse Broadcasting Company (Group W) filmed series in which ten- to twelve-year-olds were selected from various parts of the country for adventures in new environments. 30 minutes.

CALVIN AND THE COLONEL

prime time broadcast dates: 10/3/61–9/22/62, ABC, thereafter syndicated

30-minute cartoon takeoff of *Amos 'n' Andy* with Charles Correll and Freeman Gosden reprising their original radio roles as the voices of Calvin and the Colonel respectively.

CAPTAIN CAVEMAN AND THE TEEN ANGELS

premiere broadcast date: 3/8/80, ABC

30-minute Hanna-Barbera cartoon series that originally premiered as a segment on *Scooby's All-Star Laff-A-Lympics,* 9/10/77, ABC. Billed as "the world's first superhero," Captain Caveman was discovered frozen in glacial ice by three teen-age girls, Brenda, Dee Dee, and Taffy. The comedic and accident-prone "Cavey" would come to the assistance of his female friends by reaching into his hollow club of tricks or, if necessary, by exclaiming, "Captain Caveman," and transforming into the superhero.

CAPTAIN GALLANT OF THE FOREIGN LEGION

Sunday afternoon premiere: 2/13/55, NBC, and also syndicated in markets not served by the NBC network; thereafter on ABC, NBC, and syndicated

30-minute adventure film series set in North Africa and starring Buster Crabbe as the commander of a Foreign Legion troop. Crabbe's son Cullen "Cuffy" Crabbe also appeared in the series, which was syndicated as *Foreign Legionnaire.*

CAPTAIN KANGAROO

weekday morning premiere: 10/3/55, CBS
Saturday morning broadcast dates: 10/8/55–9/19/64, CBS
Saturday return: 10/65–9/7/68, CBS

Bob Keeshan, once Clarabell on *Howdy Doody,* hosting and performing his long-running 60-minute award-winning educational series. Set in the Treasure House, the Captain is joined by Mr. Greenjeans (Hugh "Lumpy" Brannum) and a variety of human and puppet characters, including Dancing Bear, Grandfather Clock, Mr. Moose, Bunny Rabbit, Miss Frog, Silly Billy, and Mr. Bainter the Painter. Between Saturday morning telecasts Keeshan appeared in another series titled *Mister Mayor* on CBS. See also *Mister Mayor.*

CAPTAIN MIDNIGHT

syndicated: 1952
Saturday morning network premiere broadcast: 9/4/54, CBS

Richard Webb starred as Captain Midnight, a contemporary aviator hero who battled enemy agents and American gangsters. The 30-minute series was sponsored by Ovaltine and resyndicated without Ovaltine's label as *Jet Jackson, Flying Commando.* Costarring were Sid Melton and Olan Soule. The thirty-nine episodes were produced and distributed by Screen Gems.

CAPTAIN SAFARI OF THE JUNGLE PATROL

initial broadcast dates: 5/21/55–8/13/55, CBS

Live-action fantasy series featuring explorer Captain Safari (Randy Kraft) and his sidekick, Zippy the chimp, who tuned into jungle adventures via a TV screen. 60 minutes.

CAPTAIN SCARLET AND THE MYSTERONS

syndicated: 1967

Sylvia and Gerry Anderson's "Supermarionation" science fiction puppet series set on twenty-first-century Mars, where American agent Scarlet battles the Mysterons, beings able to re-create any person or object after it has been killed or destroyed. 30-minute series filmed in England.

CAPTAIN VIDEO AND HIS VIDEO RANGERS

weekday broadcast dates: 6/27/49–8/16/57, DuMont network and WABD-TV, New York
Saturday broadcast dates: 1/28/50–11/25/50

TV's vanguard science fiction series with Richard Coogan and Al Hodge in the title role, and Don Hastings as the Video Ranger. It was telecast in both 15- and 30-minute episodes. A revised 30-minute version titled *The Secret Files of Captain Video* premiered on Saturday morning 9/5/53 (alternating with *Tom Corbett, Space Cadet*), with Hodge still in the title role. Both series were telecast in various time slots Monday through Saturday.

CAPTAIN Z-RO

syndicated: 1954
30-minute filmed science fiction series that originated as a 15-minute local, live on KRON-TV, San Francisco, in 1951. Roy Steffens starred as a time traveler and doubled off-screen as the show's writer. Bobby Trumbull played his young assistant named Jet.

CARRASCOLENDAS

premier broadcast: 1972, PBS
Bilingual Spanish/English educational series produced by KLRN-TV, San Antonio–Austin, Texas. Aimed at ages four to nine. 30 minutes.

CARTOONIES

broadcast dates: 4/13/63–9/28/63, ABC
Paul Winchell and Jerry Mahoney hosted Gremlin, Sheriff Saddle Head, and Scat Skit cartoons. Original title for the 30-minute premiere telecast (4/6/63): *Cartoonsville*.

CARTOONSVILLE

see *Cartoonies*

CASEY JONES

syndicated: 1957
30-minute live-action series about the legendary train engineer (played by Alan Hale, Jr.) and his late-1880s run along the Illinois Central Railroad line. Also starring Mary Lawrence, Bobby Clark, and Eddy Waller.

CASPER, THE FRIENDLY GHOST

syndicated: 1953
Television packaging of Casper motion picture cartoons. Rebroadcast 10/5/63–9/5/67 as *The New Casper Cartoon Show*, ABC, 30 minutes.

CASPER AND THE ANGELS

premiere broadcast: 9/22/79, NBC
Casper the Ghost depicted in 30-minute space-age cartoons as a guardian angel to two female intergalactic patrol officers, Maxie and Minnie.

THE CATTANOOGA CATS

initial broadcast dates: 9/6/69–9/5/70, ABC
Sunday broadcast dates: 9/13/70–9/5/71, ABC
Hanna-Barbera cartoon series about five rock 'n' roll singing cats. The show was 60 minutes on Saturdays, 30 minutes on Sundays. See also *Motor Mouse*.

CHALLENGE OF THE SUPER FRIENDS

see *Super Friends*

CHARLIE CHAPLIN

syndicated: early 1950s
Silent film shorts of comedian Charlie Chaplin released in 30-minute length and supplemented in some instances with narration.

CHESTER THE PUP

initial broadcast dates: 10/7/50–1/13/51, ABC
Sundays: 1/21/51–9/30/51, ABC
15-minute cartoon adventures of Chester, drawn on-camera by artist Sid Stone. Narrated by Art Whitfield; created by George O'Halloran. Broadcast from Chicago.

THE CHILDREN'S CORNER

broadcast dates: 8/20/55–9/10/55, 12/24/55–4/28/56, NBC
Musical and variety series created by Josie Carey and Fred Rogers for WQED-TV, Pittsburgh. Carey hosted and sang (the only human on camera), and collaborated with Rogers on the scripts and music. Rogers manipulated and voiced his puppets, many of which appeared later on *Mister Rogers' Neighborhood*.

THE CHILDREN'S HOUR

syndicated: 1951
60-minute films made for TV by Hal Roach Studios, and hosted by Maureen O'Sullivan. Titles available in this series included "Crummy the Clown," "Stray Lamb," "Hal Roach Rascals," "The Little People," "The Children's Story," "Impie and Angie," and "The Bible Story." This series should not be confused with the show of the same title (in abbreviated form) that had a long run on radio before its appearance in 1948 as a local Sunday morning TV show in Philadelphia, and later New York. Ed Herlihy hosted the series, which had a full title of *The Horn and Hardart Children's Hour*.

CHOOSE UP SIDES

broadcast dates: 1/7/56–3/31/56, NBC
30-minute Goodson-Todman audience participation show hosted by Gene Rayburn. Premiered 11/2/53 as local weekday show on WCBS-TV, New York, with Dean Miller as emcee followed by Rayburn.

CIRCUS BOY

prime time broadcast dates:
9/23/56–9/8/57, NBC
9/19/57–9/11/58, ABC
Saturday syndication: 10/58
30-minute episodes regarding the life and adventures of Corky, an orphaned boy (Mickey Braddock) and his adult friends, including Big Tim Champion (Robert Lowery), Joey the Clown (Noah Beery, Jr.), Pete (Guin Williams), and Circus Jack (Andy Clyde). Braddock later went on to costar in *The Monkees* under his real name, Mickey Dolenz. Forty-nine episodes filmed.

THE CISCO KID

syndicated: 1950
30-minute Western series first shot in 1949 for ZIV-TV Films. The production starred Duncan Renaldo and Leo Carillo and was set in New Mexico during the 1880s. *The Cisco Kid* characters were based on figures created by author O.Henry.

CITY HOSPITAL

Saturday broadcast dates:
11/3/51–4/19/52, alternate weeks, ABC
30-minute soap opera about Dr. Barton Crane (Melville Ruick) and his associates and patients at a New York City hospital. Moved to prime time 3/25/52–10/1/53, CBS, alternate weeks.

THE CLIFFWOOD AVENUE KIDS

syndicated: 1977
30-minute live-action comedy about preteen members of the crime-solving Cliffwood Avenue Club who speak their own special language (adaga) among themselves. Poindexter (Randy Yothers, Jr.) starred as Poiny, the leader of the gang.

THE CLUE CLUB

initial broadcast dates: 8/14/76–9/3/77, CBS
30-minute Hanna-Barbera cartoon series about four teen-age investigators and their two talking dogs, Woofer and Wimper. Voices included Paul Winchell and *Atom Squad* costar Bob Hastings.

COLONEL BLEEP

syndicated: 1957
30-minute cartoon science fiction series set in the future with Colonel Bleep of the Pheutora Police Department battling the evil Dr. Destructo.

COMMANDO CODY—SKY MARSHAL OF THE UNIVERSE

initial broadcast dates: 7/16/55–10/8/55, NBC
A thirteen-episode series of 30-minute live-action science fiction adventures produced by Republic Pictures for theatrical release in 1954. Judd Holdren starred as the Sky Marshal of the Universe. Aline Towne, William Schallert, Peter Brocco, Craig Kelly, and Gregory Gay costarred.

COOL MCCOOL

broadcast dates: 9/10/66–8/31/68, NBC
return dates: 5/17/69–8/30/69, NBC
Satirical 30-minute cartoon version of James Bond, created by Bob Kane, the creator of Batman. Executive producer: Al Brodax.

COWBOY G-MEN

syndicated: 1952
Live-action Western adventure set in the 1880s where two secret agents (played by

Russell Hayden and Jackie Coogan) maintained law and order. 30 minutes.

COWBOY THEATRE

initial broadcast dates: 9/15/56–3/9/57
Saturday return: 6/9/57–9/15/57, NBC
Western motion pictures hosted by Monty Hall. 60 minutes.

CRUSADER RABBIT

syndicated: 1949
The first made-for-TV cartoon series (195 films), produced by Jay Ward and Alexander Anderson for Jerry Fairbanks Productions. A second series of 260 4-minute color episodes was produced by Shull Bonsall in the late 1950s for release in 15-minute and 30-minute programs. Featured were Crusader and his pal, Rags the Tiger.

CURIOSITY SHOP

initial broadcast dates: 9/11/71–9/2/72, ABC
Sunday return: 9/9/72–9/9/73, ABC
30-minute educational series aimed at the six-to-eleven age group, with live-action segments, music, films, animation, and sketches built around familiar objects and subjects. ACT Commendation, 1971–72. Hosted by creator and producer Chuck Jones.

CYBORG BIG "X"

syndicated: 1965
Japanese-produced 30-minute cartoon series featuring a robot crime-fighter. 59 episodes.

D

THE DAFFY DUCK SHOW

premiere broadcast: 11/4/78, NBC
Theatrical Daffy Duck cartoons in a 30-minute TV package released by Warner Brothers Television.

DANNY THE DRAGON

syndicated: 1970
Live-action science fiction series about an alien visitor and the trio of youngsters who befriend him. Episodes starred Jack Wild, Peter Butterworth, Christopher Cooper, and Sally Thomsett. 17 minutes. Ten episodes.

DASTARDLY AND MUTTLEY IN THEIR FLYING MACHINES

initial broadcast dates: 9/13/69–9/4/71, CBS
Hanna-Barbera 30-minute cartoon adventures of World War I enemy pilot Dick Dastardly and his muttering dog Muttley as they aim for the patriotic American, Yankee Doodle Pigeon.

A DATE WITH JUDY

initial broadcast dates: 6/2/51–2/23/52, ABC
A radio sitcom with Pat Crowley starring as a boy-crazy teen-ager. Also appearing was Jimmy Sommer as her boyfriend Oogie Pringle. In 1952, much of the original cast was replaced and the series moved to prime time: 7/10/52–9/30/53, ABC

DAVEY AND GOLIATH

syndicated: 1961
15-minute religious puppet series produced by the Lutheran Church in America that utilized stop-motion animation. Title characters were a ten-year-old boy and his talking dog. Sixty-five episodes were supplemented with ten half-hour specials timed to seasons of the year.

DEAR ALEX AND ANNIE

premiere broadcast season: 1978–79, ABC
A 5-minute musical advice column of the air that responds to personal problems submitted by young viewers. Letters are answered by child psychologist Eda LeShan, whose responses become the basis for original contemporary music written by Lynn Ahrens, author of many of ABC's *Schoolhouse Rock* segments. The songs are sung by Alex and Annie, two teen-agers played by Bing Bingham and Donna Drake. The segments combine live action and animation. After airing originally as a segment on ABC's *Kids Are People Too* in 1978–79, the series was broadcast throughout the children's weekend programming schedule beginning with the 1979–80 season. *Dear Alex and Annie* is produced by Dahlia Productions.

DENNIS THE MENACE

prime time broadcast dates: 10/4/59–9/22/63, CBS
Saturday morning reruns: premiere broadcast: 10/5/63, NBC, thereafter syndicated
30-minute situation comedy based on the Hank Ketcham comic strip and starring Jay North as the menacing Dennis.

DEPUTY DAWG

syndicated: 1960
30-minute Terrytoon cartoon series about a hapless pooch sheriff who bumbled his cases along to a successful close.

DETECTIVE'S DIARY

broadcast dates: 3/16/57–9/9/61, NBC
30-minute filmed series that was the syndicated version of various Mark Saber detective shows previously broadcast under alternate titles.

DEVLIN

initial broadcast dates: 9/7/74–2/15/76, ABC
30-minute Hanna-Barbera cartoon series about three orphaned siblings (Ernie, Todd, and Sandy) as they earn money on a motorcycle stunt circuit and attempt to remain together as a family. Voices included Michael Bell, Mickey Dolenz, Michele Robinson, and Bob Hastings.

DICK TRACY

prime time broadcast dates: 9/11/50–2/12/51, ABC
initial Saturday broadcast dates: 2/17/51–3/31/51, ABC, thereafter syndicated
Live-action 30-minute made-for-TV film series starring Ralph Byrd, who had previously played title role in RKO features and Republic serials. Production of twenty-six episodes began November 1949.
Cast included Angela Greene as Tess, his wife, and Joe Devlin as Sam Catchem, his assistant. UPA Pictures syndicated an animated cartoon version in 1961 featuring Everett Sloane as the voice of Tracy. Filmation presented additional exploits as a segment of *Archie's TV Funnies* premiering 9/11/71, CBS.

DING DONG SCHOOL

initial weekday broadcast dates: 11/24/52–12/28/56, NBC
weekday mornings return syndication: 9/59
Dr. Frances Horwich hosted a relaxed educational series aimed at preschoolers. Horwich, a former academician and later an NBC executive, owned rights to the show and took the concept to syndication after NBC canceled the long-running and popular but commercially failing series. Series also ran as local show in Chicago between network and syndication broadcasts.

DO YOU KNOW?

broadcast dates: 10/12/63–4/25/64, CBS
Bob Maxwell hosted 30-minute educational and quiz show that featured reading and discussion of books on a variety of topics.

DR. WHO

syndicated: 1975
BBC live-action science fiction serial adventures distributed in the U.S. by Time-Life Films. Various actors portrayed Dr. Who in the American-screened versions, including Jon Pertwee and Tom Baker. The multipart episodes had aired in England since 1963.

DODO—THE KID FROM OUTER SPACE

initial broadcast dates: 9/10/66–8/30/69, NBC
30-minute cartoon series chronicling the exploits of Dodo, a being from another planet who, with his pet, Compy, assisted Earthling scientist Professor Fingers.

DON Q., DICK AND ALADDIN

syndicated: 1953
15-minute filmed marionette series drawing on the tales of the Arabian Nights. Written and directed by Palmer Martin.

DRAW WITH ME

see *Jon Gnagy*

THE DUDLEY DO-RIGHT SHOW

initial Sunday broadcast dates: 4/27/69–9/6/70, ABC, thereafter syndicated
Bill Scott and Jay Ward 30-minute cartoon production featuring reluctant Canadian Mountie (voice of Bill Scott) as he pursued villains in the Northwest and saved his girl friend Nell Fenwick (June Foray) from the machinations of Snively Whiplash (Hans Conried). Paul Frees narrated and doubled as Inspector Fenwick, Nell's father. Originally a segment on both *Rocky and His Friends* and *The Bullwinkle Show* as "The Adventures of Dudley Do-Right."

DUSTY'S TREEHOUSE

syndicated: 1971
Stu Rosen as Dusty, host of a 30-minute series featuring the Tony Urbano and Company puppets. Characters included Maxine the Crow, Stanley Spider, and Scooter Squirrel.

DYNOMUTT

initial broadcast dates: 6/3/78–9/2/78, ABC
30-minute Hanna-Barbera cartoon series featuring a robot dog wonder that was faithful companion to the Blue Falcon, champion of law and order. Originally a segment on *The Scooby-Doo/Dynomutt Hour*, 9/11/76, ABC.

E

EARTH LAB

syndicated: 1971
Westinghouse Broadcasting Company's series of twenty-six hour-long science shows hosted by Rex Trailer and a studio-sized computer named Philo. Geared for eight- to fourteen-year-olds. ACT Commendation, 1971–72.

THE EIGHTH MAN

syndicated: 1965
Japanese 30-minute science fiction cartoon series about a twenty-first-century police force where Tobor the Eighth Man, a human-turned-robot, combats crime and Metro City's Saucer Lip. Producer: Mushi Productions.

THE ELECTRIC COMPANY

premiere broadcast: 10/25/71, PBS
30-minute education shows aimed at *Sesame Street* graduates. Programs taught and reinforced grammatical and mathematical skills through musical and comedy sketches, cartoons, and demonstrations. Regulars included Rita Moreno, Bill Cosby, Skip Hinnant, Judy Graubart, Jimmy Boyd, Morgan Freeman, and Lee Chamberlain. Produced by The Children's Television Workshop. Emmy Award, 1972–73.

EMERGENCY PLUS FOUR

initial broadcast dates: 9/8/73–9/4/76, NBC
Cartoon clone of the prime time NBC series *Emergency*, with four children aiding the paramedics of the Los Angeles County Fire Department Rescue Division. Produced by Fred Calvert and Universal Television. Voices by Kevin Tighe and Randolph Mantooth. 30 minutes.

ESPER

syndicated: 1968
30-minute science fiction cartoon depicting the exploits of a young boy combating evil throughout the universe.

EVERYTHING'S ARCHIE

see *The Archie Show*

EXPLORING

broadcast dates: 10/13/62–4/10/65, 10/16/65–4/19/66, NBC
60- and 30-minute educational series teaching social studies, science, music, and art with explanations, songs, and demonstrations by Dr. Albert R. Hibbs, the Ritts Puppets, and the Gus Soloman Dancers. Peabody Award winner, 1962. Created and produced by Craig Fisher.

F

THE FABULOUS FUNNIES

initial broadcast dates: 9/9/78–9/8/79, NBC
30-minute prosocial cartoon adventures of comic-strip characters, including Alley Oop, The Captain and the Kids, Broom Hilda, and Nancy and Sluggo.

THE FAITH BALDWIN THEATRE OF ROMANCE

initial broadcast dates: 1/20/51–10/20/51, ABC, alternating weekly with films and later, The Kay Westfall Show *and* I Cover Times Square.
30-minute dramatic anthology series featuring writer/narrator Faith Baldwin. The show was sponsored by Maidenform Brassieres ™. The premiere telecast, "My Beloved Wife," starred Walter Abel and Sylvia Field. Subsequent programs featured Nina Foch, Betsy Von Furstenberg, and other stars of stage and screen.

THE FAMOUS ADVENTURES OF MR. MAGOO

prime time broadcast dates: 9/19/64–8/21/65, NBC
30-minute cartoon series featuring the UPA animated character Quincy Magoo, a nearsighted comedic figure speaking with the voice of Jim Backus. Magoo served as host, narrator, and star in these tales from history and literature, including William Tell, Ulysses, and Captain Ahab. A new series titled *What's New, Mister Magoo*? premiered Saturday morning 9/10/77, CBS, 30 minutes, with Magoo, his dog McBarker, and his teen-age nephew. Produced by DePatie-Freleng.

FANGFACE

initial broadcast dates: 9/9/78–9/1/79, ABC
30-minute cartoon series about a teen-age boy who turned into an amiable werewolf whenever he saw a full moon or a picture of it. It was revised in 1979 into "Fangface and Fangpuss" as a segment on *The Plasticman Comedy Adventure Show.*

THE FANTASTIC FOUR

initial broadcast dates: 9/9/67–8/30/70, NBC
Saturday return premiere: 9/9/78, NBC
Sunday return: 9/7/69–3/15/70, NBC
30-minute Hanna-Barbera cartoon series based on Stan Lee's Marvel comic-book characters: Mr. Fantastic, Invisible Girl, Human Torch, and The Thing. In 1978 Herbie the Robot (aka Charlie the Computer) was turned on and the Human Torch was extinguished in a new version produced by DePatie-Freleng.

FANTASTIC VOYAGE

initial broadcast dates: 9/14/68–9/5/70, ABC
30-minute Filmation science fiction cartoon series based on the motion picture of the same name. United States government scientist-agents were reduced to microscopic size for travel within the human circulatory system. Voices included Marvin Miller, Jane Webb, and Ted Knight.

FAR OUT SPACE NUTS

premiere broadcast: 9/6/75, CBS
30-minute live-action comedy series with Bob Denver and Chuck McCann playing two NASA food loaders who inadvertently launch themselves into space aboard a rocket ship that they were servicing. Along their intergalactic travels they adopted a space creature named Honk (Patty Maloney) and met Lantana (Eve Bruce) and Crakor the Robot (Stan Jenson).

FAT ALBERT AND THE COSBY KIDS

premiere broadcast: 9/9/72, CBS
30-minute Filmation cartoon series hosted, created, and primarily voiced by Bill Cosby. The Cosby characters were presented in adventures intended to provide insight into real-life experiences and problems. Series retitled as *The New Fat Albert Show* and premiered 9/8/79, ABC.

FEDERAL MEN

see *Treasury Men in Action*

FEELING FREE

broadcast: 1978, PBS
30-minute educational series designed to ease "mainstreaming" of handicapped children into normal school systems and life. Series utilized a *zoom* magazine format with show regulars performing, playing, and talking in studio and on location.

FEELINGS

premiere broadcast: 10/13/79, PBS
Thirteen-part 30-minute series hosted by child psychologist Dr. Lee Salk, featuring discussions and sketches on the concerns of eight- to fourteen-year-olds.

FELIX THE CAT

syndicated: 1960
260 episodes of Felix, the talking cat with a bag of tricks. Cartoons released in 6-minute and 30-minute program formats. Motion picture cartoon character created by Pat Sullivan.

FESTIVAL OF FAMILY CLASSICS

syndicated: 1972
30-minute cartoon adaptations of classic fairy tales including *20,000 Leagues Under the Sea, Snow White and the Seven Dwarfs,* and *Around the World in 80 Days.*

FIREBALL XL-5

initial broadcast dates: 10/5/63–9/25/65, NBC, thereafter syndicated
Sylvia and Gerry Anderson's 30-minute science fiction "Supermarionation" series featuring space-age exploits of Captain Steve Zodiac. Thirty-nine episodes produced in England.

THE FIRST LOOK: WONDERS OF THE WORLD

initial broadcast dates: 10/16/65–4/9/66, NBC
30-minute live-action education series focusing on cultures, history, and people around the globe.

FIVE STAR COMEDY

see *Popsicle Five Star Comedy*

FLASH GORDON

syndicated: 1951, DuMont, thereafter further syndicated
30-minute science fiction series set in the twenty-first century and starring Steve Holland as Flash Gordon, Joseph Nash as Dr. Alexis Zarkov, and Irene Champlin as Dale Arden. This series produced in West Germany should not be confused with the classic Buster Crabbe serials produced from 1936 to 1940 for theatrical release and later syndicated for TV broadcast. A 30-minute cartoon version produced by Filmation and King Features 9/8/79–1/5/80, NBC, titled *The New Adventures of Flash Gordon.* All of the above productions were based on Alex Raymond's comic strip.

THE FLINTSTONES

prime time broadcast dates: 9/30/60–9/2/66, ABC, 30 minutes
color premiere telecast: 9/28/62
Saturday morning premiere: 1/7/67, NBC
network revision: 9/9/72, CBS, as The Flintstones Comedy Hour
syndicated return: 1977, as Fred Flintstone and Friends, *30 minutes*
network return: 2/3/79–9/15/79, NBC, as The New Fred and Barney Show *with seventeen new 30-minute episodes*
network revision: 9/22/79–12/1/79, NBC, as Fred and Barney Meet the Thing, *60 minutes*
network revision: 12/8/79, NBC, as Fred and Barney Meet the Shmoo, *90 minutes*
Prime time's longest-running animated cartoon series with an even longer run on Saturday mornings. The Flintstones and the Rubbles, reminiscent of the characters in *The Honeymooners,* were two families living a seemingly modern existence in the prehistoric suburb of Bedrock. Fred Flintstone's voice was recorded by Alan Reed, and Barney Rubble's by Mel Blanc. A 1971 spin-off series titled *Pebbles and Bamm Bamm* featured the Flintstones' daughter and the Rubbles' son. *The Flintstones Comedy Hour* included variety and music, featuring a newly created rock group, the Bedrock Rockers, plus Fred and Barney and Pebbles and Bamm Bamm.

FLYING TIGERS

initial broadcast dates: 4/14/51–5/26/51, DuMont
Sunday return: 7/29/51–3/2/52, DuMont
Low-budget live-action serial about two members of the famed World War II aviation unit. Eric Fleming played the role of Major Del Conway in the first Saturday series, succeeded by Ed Peck in the Sunday series. Bern Hoffman played his sidekick Caribou in both versions.

FOODINI THE GREAT

broadcast dates: 8/25/51–12/29/51, ABC
30-minute film series produced by puppeteers Hope and Morey Bunin that was a revision/spin-off of their former show titled *Lucky Pup.* Ellen Parker and Lou Prentis hosted the puppet escapades of the villainous but inept magician Foodini and his stooge assistant Pinhead. See also *Lucky Pup.*

THE FOREST RANGERS

syndicated: 1962
Canadian-made live-action adventure series set in the North Woods, where Junior Rangers and their adult counterparts faced danger, excitement, and the unknown. 30 minutes. 104 episodes.

FRANKENSTEIN JR. AND THE IMPOSSIBLES

initial broadcast dates: 9/10/66–9/7/68, CBS
30-minute Hanna-Barbera comedy cartoon series about a thirty-foot-tall robot character who dwarfed his teen-ager friends but still needed their assistance.

FUN FAIR

broadcast dates: 12/30/50–3/10/51, ABC
30-minute production of KECA-TV, Los Angeles, in which host Jay Stewart presented interviews and contests with young studio participants.

THE FUNKY PHANTOM

initial broadcast dates: 9/11/71–9/2/72, ABC
30-minute Hanna-Barbera mystery/comedy about a trio of teen-agers (two boys, one girl), their pet dog, and a friendly ghost from the Revolutionary War.

FUNNY BONERS

broadcast dates: 11/20/54–7/9/55, NBC
Quiz and stunt/variety show with ventriloquist Jimmy Weldon and his duck dummy Webster Webfoot. As a local Fresno, California, program it was titled *The Webster Webfoot Show.*

THE FURTHER ADVENTURES OF DR. DOLITTLE

initial broadcast dates: 9/12/70–9/4/71, NBC
30-minute cartoon series based loosely on the famous character of children's literature.

FURY

initial broadcast dates: 10/15/55–9/3/66, NBC
30-minute live-action contemporary Western series produced by Television Programs of America. 114 episodes. The adventures of a young boy named Joey (Bobby Diamond), his horse Fury, his foster father, Jim Newton (Peter Graves), and Broken Wheel ranchhand Pete (William Fawcett). Program presented morality plays and stressed proper health, good citizenship, and fair play in an action setting. Syndicated title: *Brave Stallion.*

G

GALAXY GOOF-UPS

initial broadcast dates: 11/4/78–1/27/79, NBC
30-minute Hanna-Barbera cartoon series set at a zany outer space army post. Premiered as segment on *Yogi's Space Race,* 9/9/78, NBC.

THE GENE AUTRY SHOW

prime time broadcast dates: 7/23/50–8/7/56, CBS, thereafter syndicated
Cowboy hero Gene Autry in 30-minute Western adventures produced by his own Flying A Productions company. Costarring Pat Buttram and Champion, the world's Wonder Horse. In 1955, fifty-six of Autry's Republic feature films were also syndicated in 60-minute form by MCA-TV Film Syndication.

THE GEORGE HAMILTON IV SHOW

initial broadcast dates: 9/6/58–9/27/58, CBS
60-minute musical variety series hosted by George Hamilton IV and featuring such

vocalists as Danny Costello, Peggy King, Snooky Lanson, Denise Lor, Lu Ann Simms, and folksinger John Dee Laudermilk. After his brief Saturday series Hamilton returned for a 30-minute weekday show on ABC in spring 1959.

GEORGE OF THE JUNGLE

initial broadcast dates: 9/9/67–9/6/70, ABC

30-minute Jay Ward and Bill Scott cartoon series set in Africa, where a tree-swinging klutz named George was seen looking like Johnny Weissmuller's outtakes. Additional comedy segments: Super Chicken, the world's richest chicken, and Tom Slick, Racer, who will race anything, anywhere.

GERALD MCBOING-BOING

see *The Boing-Boing Show*

GET IT TOGETHER

broadcast dates: 1/3/70–9/5/70, ABC

Rock music and variety show hosted by Sam Riddle. 30 minutes.

GETTIN' OVER

premiere broadcast: 1975, PBS

Fifty-two 30-minute episode series of consumer and health care information for minority teens, produced by the Northern Virginia Educational Television Association. Producer: Art Cromwell.

THE GHOST BUSTERS

initial broadcast dates: 9/6/75–9/4/76, CBS

30-minute live-action series reuniting *F Troop* stars Larry Storch and Forrest Tucker in a situation comedy as a pair of investigators who tracked down ghosts of famous criminals. Filmation.

GIGANTOR

syndicated: 1966

Japanese science fiction cartoon set in A.D. 2000, where "the world's mightiest robot" is controlled by a twelve-year-old boy named Jimmy Sparks. 30 minutes, produced by Mushi Productions.

GIGI AND JOCK

syndicated: 1955

30-minute puppet series produced by the Tee Vee Company and syndicated by Sterling Television Company.

GILLIGAN'S ISLAND

prime time broadcast dates: 9/26/64–9/3/67, CBS, thereafter syndicated

30-minute live-action comedy series about seven castaways marooned on an unknown island in the South Pacific. Bob Denver and Alan Hale, Jr., starred as the zany Gilligan and The Skipper, respectively. Filmation's cartoon version aired 9/7/74–9/4/76, CBS, as *The New Adventures of Gilligan*. The 30-minute show featured five of the voices from the live-action show (Denver, Hale, Jim Backus, Natalie Schaefer, and Russell Johnson), plus Jane Webb and Jane Edwards.

GO

premiere broadcast: 9/8/73, NBC

30-minute live-action educational series in which a videotape camera crew recorded people at work and play throughout the country and world. Narrator: Gregg Morris. Programs moved to Sunday 9/8/74. Third season titled *Go—U.S.A.* for the Bicentennial and returned to Saturdays 9/6/75–9/4/76.

GO GO GLOBETROTTERS

see *The Harlem Globetrotters*

THE GO GO GOPHERS

initial broadcast dates: 9/14/68–9/6/69, CBS

30-minute cartoon series set in the West during the nineteenth century and featuring the adventures of two gopherlike Indians, the double-talking Ruffled Feather, and his sidekick and interpreter, Running Board. Their constant adversaries were Colonel Kit Coyote and Hokey Loma, his blundering assistant, who unsuccessfully sought to eradicate the gopher population.

GO—U.S.A.

see *Go*

GODZILLA

see *The Godzilla Power Hour*

THE GODZILLA POWER HOUR

initial broadcast dates: 9/9/78–10/28/78, NBC, 60 minutes
return broadcast: 11/4/78, NBC, as Godzilla Super 90, *90 minutes*
return dates: 9/8/79–12/1/79, NBC, as Godzilla, *30 minutes*
12/8/79–4/5/80, NBC, as The Godzilla/Globetrotters Adventure Hour, *60 minutes*
4/12/80, NBC, as Godzilla, *30 minutes*

Watered-down adventures borrowing from the Japanese science fiction monster character Godzilla. Cartoon representation was pictured as a lovable creature with a nephew Godzooky. The pair helped oceangoing friends in trouble. As *The Godzilla Power Hour* the Hanna-Barbera production contained episodes of Jana of the Jungle, a female Tarzan-type character. *Godzilla Super 90* included episodes of Jonny Quest and Jana of the Jungle. *The Godzilla/Globetrotters Adventure Hour* combined the monster with comic cartoon tales of the Harlem Globetrotters. See *Jonny Quest*.

THE GODZILLA/GLOBETROTTERS ADVENTURE HOUR

see *The Godzilla Power Hour*

THE GODZILLA SUPER 90

see *The Godzilla Power Hour*

GOOBER AND THE GHOST CHASERS

initial broadcast dates: 9/8/73–8/31/74, ABC
Sunday return: 9/8/74–8/31/75, ABC

Hanna-Barbera 30-minute cartoon series about a lovable dog (Goober) who becomes, in times of stress, invincible. Series contained guest appearances by the Partidge Kids. Principle voice: Paul Winchell (Goober).

GRAND CHANCE ROUNDUP

broadcast dates: 1/27/51–8/4/51, CBS

Live 30-minute contest program from CBS Philadelphia affiliate WCAU-TV. Contestants competed in show-business routines for the chance of a week's work at Hamid's Steel Pier in Atlantic City, New Jersey. Hosted by Gene Crane. The series was replaced by *Smilin' Ed's Gang*.

THE GREAT GRAPE APE SHOW

Sunday initial broadcast dates: 9/11/77–9/3/78, ABC

Hanna-Barbera 30-minute cartoon adventures about a thirty- to forty-foot-tall purple gorilla and his fast-talking dog friend Beegle Beagle. The ape was originally a segment on *The New Tom and Jerry/Grape Ape Show*, 9/6/75, and *The Tom and Jerry/Grape Ape/Mumbly Show*, 9/11/76, ABC.

THE GROOVIE GOOLIES

initial broadcast dates: 9/12/71–9/3/72, CBS

30-minute Filmation cartoon series about practical-joke-playing creatures based on movie monsters. Seen each week: TV versions of Frankenstein, Dracula, the Werewolf, and the Mummy. See also *Sabrina and the Groovie Goolies*.

THE GUMBY SHOW

initial broadcast dates: 3/16/57–11/16/57, NBC

Bobby Nicholson (TV's second Clarabell on *Howdy Doody*) and later Pinky Lee hosting 30-minute episodes of an animated clay figure named Gumby. Program utilized stop-motion animation.

H

H.E.L.P.!!

premiere broadcast season: 1979–80, ABC

Brief animated fillers that spelled out Dr. Henry's Emergency Lessons for People—first-aid tips between the network's Saturday morning programs. Emmy Award, 1979–80.

HAIL THE CHAMP

Saturday prime time broadcast dates: 9/22/51–6/14/52, ABC
Saturday morning return: 12/27/52–6/13/53, ABC, alternating weekly with Sky King

30-minute Chicago-based game show featuring children from the studio audience competing in athletic stunts. The initial version was hosted and produced by Herb Allen. Howard Roberts was head coach for the second series, assisted by co-emcee Angel Casey.

HAL IN HOLLYWOOD

initial broadcast dates: 4/7/51–5/26/51, ABC

30-minute variety/interview series hosted by Hal Sawyer and featuring screen stars as guests. The show was listed also as *Sawyer Views Hollywood.*

HALF-PINT PARTY

weekday premiere: 2/12/51, ABC, with rebroadcasts Saturdays in some markets
Saturday broadcast dates: 3/8/52–5/10/52, WCBS-TV, New York

15-minute live children's musical series hosted by pianist Al Gannaway. The show was expanded to 45 minutes in the local version.

HAPPENING '68

broadcast dates: 1/6/68–9/20/69, ABC

Mark Lindsay and Paul Revere cohosted this 30-minute musical series produced by Dick Clark. The variety production included performances by guest stars, weekly amateur band contests, comedy sketches, teen reports from throughout the country, films produced by high school and college students, fashion shows, and tunes by Lindsay and Revere's group, Paul Revere and the Raiders.

HAPPY FELTON'S SPOTLIGHT GANG

broadcast dates: 11/20/54–2/26/55, NBC

30-minute live show combining clips of European vaudeville acts with quizzes and studio segments. Featuring Happy Felton as host.

HAPPY PATCHES PARTY

syndicated: 1962

Birthday celebrations with taped educational segments from historic sites. Produced by American Artists Association Corporation for Telecast Visuals, Inc. 2 hours.

HAPPY'S PARTY

broadcast dates: 9/6/52–5/9/53, DuMont

30-minute studio show hosted by Ida Mae Maher and her hand puppet.

THE HARDY BOYS

initial broadcast dates: 9/6/69–9/4/71, ABC

30-minute cartoon adaptation of the Hardy Boys mysteries with an updated twist: The teen-age investigators doubled as rock 'n' roll stars on a world concert tour.

THE HARLEM GLOBETROTTERS

initial broadcast dates: 9/12/70–9/2/72, CBS
Sunday return: 9/10/72–5/20/73, CBS

30-minute Hanna-Barbera cartoon comedy series presenting fictionalized adventures of the famed basketball players. They were reincarnated in a two-hour cartoon show titled *Go Go Globetrotters*, broadcast 2/4/78–9/2/78, NBC.

THE HARLEM GLOBETROTTERS POPCORN MACHINE

initial broadcast dates: 9/7/74–8/30/75, CBS
Sunday return: 9/7/75–9/5/76, CBS

Live-action, prosocial production featuring the actual Harlem Globetrotters and Rodney Allen Rippy and Avery Schreiber. Produced by Funhouse Productions, Inc. and Viacom. 30 minutes.

THE HECKLE AND JECKLE CARTOON SHOW

initial Sunday broadcast dates: 10/14/56–9/8/57, CBS, 30 minutes
initial Saturday broadcast dates: 1/25/58–9/24/60, CBS, 30 minutes, thereafter syndicated
return: 9/25/65–9/3/66, CBS, 30 minutes; 9/6/69–9/4/71, NBC, 60 minutes and 30 minutes
revised: 9/8/79, CBS, as The New Adventures of Mighty Mouse and Heckle and Jeckle, *60 minutes*

Terrytoon's theatrical cartoon about two irascible magpies, plus Dinky Duck, Gandy Goose, Little Roquefort the mouse, Percy the cat, and the Terry Bears, mischievous twin bruins. The Terrytoon characters, including Heckle and Jeckle, originally premiered on the prime time *CBS Cartoon Theatre*, 6/13/56–9/5/56. For their Sunday afternoon debut, new material making Heckle and Jeckle emcees for the series was added to the older cartoon segments. *The New Adventures of Mighty Mouse and Heckle and Jeckle* presented new Filmation cartoon segments of the magpies. Alternate title: *The Heckle and Jeckle Show.*

THE HECTOR HEATHCOTE SHOW

initial broadcast dates: 10/5/63–9/26/64, NBC

30-minute comedy cartoon series about a time-traveling scientist and his misadventures through history.

HELP! IT'S THE HAIR BEAR BUNCH

initial broadcast dates: 9/11/71–9/2/72, CBS

30-minute Hanna-Barbera cartoon series featuring three zany bears who weekly escape from their zoo cage, always to return at show's end.

THE HERCULOIDS

initial broadcast dates: 9/9/67–9/6/69, CBS

Science fiction cartoon series about a group of futuristic animals who protect inhabitants of a peaceful utopian planet. 30 minutes.

HERE COME THE DOUBLEDECKERS

initial broadcast dates: 9/12/70–9/4/71, ABC
Sunday return: 9/12/71–9/3/72, ABC

British-produced live-action series set on a London bus/clubhouse where seven children meet, play, and experience life. 30 minutes.

HERE COMES THE GRUMP

initial broadcast dates: 9/6/69–9/4/71, NBC

30-minute DePatie-Freleng cartoon fantasy about a fantasy land ruled by an evil creature, the Grump, and populated by Princess Dawn, her dog Bip, and visitor Terry Dexter.

HIGHWAY PATROL

syndicated: 1956

Broderick Crawford as Highway Patrol Chief Dan Mathews in the 30-minute live-action adventure series produced by ZIV.

THE HILARIOUS HOUSE OF FRIGHTENSTEIN

syndicated: 1975

30-minute live-action comedy/musical series with Billy Van as Count Frightenstein and Rais Fishka as Igor. Created, written, produced, and directed by Rife Markowitz.

HIPPODROME

see *Tootsie Hippodrome*

HODGEPODGE LODGE

premiere broadcast: 1970, PBS

Educational series with emphasis on the natural world, produced by the Maryland Center for Public Broadcasting. Producer Jean Worthley ("Miss Jean"), two children as guests, plus "Aurora" the parrot, participated in each show, joined frequently by adult guests with specialized knowledge or skills. 30 minutes.

HOLD 'ER NEWT

initial weekday broadcast dates: 9/11/50–10/13/50, ABC
Saturday morning dates: 1/26/52–2/23/52, ABC, alternating weekly with Hollywood Junior Circus.

Don Tennant served as writer, producer, puppeteer, as well as providing the voices, in series about Newton Figg, proprietor of a small-town general store in Figg Center. The 15-minute puppet show originated in Chicago, where it began as a local program on WENR-TV in 1950.

HOLLYWOOD JUNIOR CIRCUS

initial Sunday broadcast dates: 3/11/51–7/1/51, NBC
Saturday broadcast dates: 9/8/51–3/1/52, ABC

Circus/novelty show sponsored by Hollywood Brands ™ Candy Company that originated in Chicago. 30-minute series had two casts: Art Jacobson and clown Carl Marx; Paul Barnes and Buffo the Clown. Max

Bronstein as "Zero" did commercials with both casts.

HONG KONG PHOOEY

initial broadcast dates: 9/7/74–9/4/76, ABC
return: 2/4/78–9/2/78, NBC

30-minute Hanna-Barbera cartoon series about Penrod Pooch, a janitor in a police department who battles crime disguised as Hong Kong Phooey. Scatman Crothers recorded the voice of the lead character. Joe E. Ross, Richard Dawson, and Don Messick were also heard.

HOPALONG CASSIDY

feature films telecast in New York: 1945
syndicated edited films: 1948
syndicated TV series: 1949, NBC

TV films—30-minute adventures of Hoppy, his sidekick (played by Edgar Buchanan), and Hoppy's horse Topper.

HOPPITY HOOPER

syndicated: 1962

30-minute cartoon comedy with Chris Allen dubbing the voice of Hooper, a talking frog. Other characters on the series included Uncle Waldo the fox (Hans Conried) and Fillmore the bear (Bill Scott). Narrator: Paul Frees. Also titled: *Uncle Waldo*.

HOT DOG

broadcast dates: 9/12/70–9/4/71, NBC

Award-winning educational series canceled because of low ratings. The program utilized a magazine format with material narrated and hosted by Woody Allen, Jo Anne Worley, and Jonathan Winters. Lee Mendelson and Frank Buxton produced the series.

HOT FUDGE

syndicated: 1976

Prosocial 30-minute live-action and puppet series with Patty and Bob Elnicky, puppeteers.

HOT HERO SANDWICH

initial broadcast dates: 11/3/79–4/5/80, NBC

60-minute musical/comedy/variety show geared for adolescents and distinguished by its interviews with adult personalities about their teen years. Besides conversation with such stars as Leonard Nimoy, Donna Pescow, Kareem Abdul-Jabbar, Beverly Sills, Erik Estrada, Henry Fonda, and many others, the series offered skits on friendship, family, grades, growth, and sex. Bruce and Carole Hart were the show's executive producers, while Howard Malley produced the eleven upbeat educational programs. Emmy Award, 1979–80.

HOT WHEELS

initial broadcast dates: 9/6/69–9/4/71, ABC

30-minute cartoon series featuring a group of young drivers that have formed an auto club. At the end of each weekly adventure with their driving activities, the Hot Wheelers offered a safe driving tip to viewers.

THE HOUNDCATS

initial broadcast dates: 9/9/72–9/1/73, NBC

30-minute cartoon series featuring cat and dog secret agents. Voices by Daws Butler, Aldo Ray, Arte Johnson, Joe Besser, and Stu Gilliam.

HOWDY DOODY

original production broadcast dates: 12/27/47–9/24/60, NBC, variously titled Puppet Playhouse *and* Puppet Television Theatre *during the first few months of telecasting*
return syndication: 1976, as The New Howdy Doody Show, *30 minutes*

Buffalo Bob Smith hosted TV's best-remembered and most popular children's series, which featured both live action and marionettes. Show premiered Saturdays, moved to weekdays and eventually to Saturday mornings exclusively on 6/16/56. Series centered on a small boy character (Howdy), his surrogate father (Smith), and their escapades in Doodyville. Two distinctly designed Howdy puppets appeared: one prior to June 1948, another from that date through the syndicated production. *Howdy Doody* also featured three actors in the role of Clarabell: Bob Keeshan, Bobby Nicholson, and Lew Anderson. It was TV's first show to complete a thousand broadcasts and the first to utilize a split screen on a cross-country telecast. Production was ended by NBC after 2,343 shows. *The New Howdy Doody Show*, a syndicated version videotaped in Miami, Florida, appeared September 1976 but failed to return Howdy Doody to the forefront of children's television.

H. R. PUFNSTUF

initial broadcast dates: 9/6/69–9/4/71, NBC
return: 9/9/73, ABC

Live-action fantasy series starring Jack Wild (the Artful Dodger of the 1968 *Oliver* motion picture) as Jimmy, a youngster with a magic flute stranded on an island governed by Pufnstuf and threatened by the evil Witchipoo (Billie Hayes). Produced by Sid and Marty Krofft. 30 minutes.

HUCKLEBERRY HOUND

syndicated: 1958

30-minute Hanna-Barbera cartoon series about a dim-witted but hardworking dog who tried different occupations each episode. Also appearing in this series were Pixie and Dixie, the mice; Jinks, the cat; Hokey, the wolf; and Yogi Bear, with the latter becoming the first featured cartoon character to graduate to stardom and earn his own series. Daws Butler provided the voices of Huckleberry and Yogi. Emmy award, 1959–60.

THE HUDSON BROTHERS RAZZLE DAZZLE COMEDY SHOW

broadcast dates: 9/7/74–4/17/77, CBS

The Hudson Brothers, a musical group, hosting and performing in a 30-minute variety series. Also featured were Stephanie Edwards, Gary Owens, Katie McClune, and Ronny Graham.

I

I AM THE GREATEST: THE ADVENTURES OF MUHAMMAD ALI

initial broadcast dates: 9/10/77–9/2/78, NBC

30-minute fictionalized cartoon adventures featuring the voice and likeness of Muhammad Ali.

I COVER TIMES SQUARE

prime time broadcast dates: 10/5/50–1/11/51, ABC
Saturday broadcasts: 1/20/51–10/27/51, ABC

30-minute adventure/mystery series with Harold Huber portraying a Broadway newspaper columnist who covered show business, but whose investigations regularly crossed over to underworld activities.

I DREAM OF JEANNIE

see *Jeannie*

I MARRIED JOAN

prime time broadcast dates: 10/15/52–4/6/55, NBC
initial Saturday broadcast dates: 5/5/56–3/9/57, NBC

30-minute situation comedy starring Joan Davis as Joan Stevens, wife of Judge Bradley Stevens (Jim Backus). In 1956, reruns of the series were telecast Monday through Saturday, replacing Pinky Lee's weekday show.

IN THE KNOW

premiere broadcast: 9/12/70, CBS

2½-minute news briefs aired five times each Saturday, produced by CBS News. The reports were succeeded in 1971 by *In the News*.

IN THE NEWS

premiere broadcast: 9/11/71, CBS

Series of 2½-minute news segments aired initially eight times each Saturday from 8:56 A.M. to 12:26 P.M. at half-hour intervals, later increasing to twelve weekend telecasts. Produced by CBS News and narrated by Christopher Glenn. ACT Commendation, 1971–72; Emmy Award, 1979–1980.

INCH HIGH, PRIVATE EYE

initial broadcast dates: 9/8/73–8/31/74, NBC

30-minute cartoon comedy featuring the investigations of a presumably world-famous but diminutive detective employed by the Finkerton Organization. Voices included Ted Knight, Lennie Weinrib as Inch, Jamie Farr, Don Messick, Kathy Gori, Bob Luttell, and John Stephenson as Finkerton.

THE INCREDIBLE HULK

syndicated: 1966
30-minute cartoon adventures based on the Marvel comic character who transformed from doctor to green monster when enraged. Not to be confused with the 1978 prime time series starring Bill Bixby.

INSIDE DETECTIVE

see *Rocky King, Inside Detective*

INSIDE/OUT

premiere broadcast: 1973, ETV (Educational TV)
15-minute educational series produced by the National Instructional Television Center, Bloomington, Indiana. Designed for fourth- to sixth-grade classes. Shows provided dramatic segments on family problems and growing up to encourage follow-up classroom discussion. Emmy Award, 1973–74.

ISIS

see *Secrets of Isis*

IT'S A HIT

broadcast dates: 6/1/57–9/21/57, CBS
Happy Felton as host of a sports quiz show. Felton dressed as a baseball umpire to officiate the 30-minute contests.

IVANHOE

syndicated: 1957
30-minute live-action series produced in England with Roger Moore as the twelfth-century Saxon knight. Based on the literary character created by Sir Walter Scott.

J

JABBERJAW

initial broadcast dates: 9/11/76–9/3/77, ABC
Sunday return: 9/11/77–9/3/78, ABC
30-minute Hanna-Barbera cartoon series about a futuristic underwater civilization in which a sad sack shark, Jabberjaw, is the pet of four teen-agers and their rock band, The Neptunes.

JABBERWOCKY

syndicated: 1974
Prosocial series produced by WCVB-TV, Boston, with live action and puppetry in 30-minute programs. Syndicated in seventy cities.

THE JACKSON FIVE

initial broadcast dates: 9/11/71–9/1/73, ABC
30-minute cartoon series about the fictionalized adventures of a pop singing group. Produced by Arthur Rankin and Jules Bass in association with Motown Records, for whom the human group recorded. ACT Commendation, 1971–72.

JAMBO

initial broadcast dates: 9/6/69–9/4/71, NBC
30-minute live-action adventure series co-hosted by Marshall Thompson and his pet chimp Judy, in which they presented films about animals in the wild.

JASON OF STAR COMMAND

initial broadcast dates: 9/8/79–12/29/79, CBS; originally premiered as segment on Tarzan and the Super 7, *9/9/78, CBS*
Filmation's 30-minute live-action episodic science fiction series starring Craig Littler in the title role and James Doohan (Scotty on *Star Trek*) as Commander Canarvin.

JEANNIE

initial broadcast dates: 9/8/73–8/30/75, CBS
Hanna-Barbera 30-minute cartoon series based loosely on the prime time series *I Dream of Jeannie*. Stories depicted a teen-age surfer who found a bottle containing a genie who protects her new master from other high school suitors. Voices included Mark Hamill, Bob Hastings, Sherry Jackson, Don Messick, and Judy Strangis.

JEFF'S COLLIE

see *Lassie*

JERRY LEWIS

see *Will the Real Jerry Lewis Please Sit Down?*

JET JACKSON, FLYING COMMANDO

see *Captain Midnight*

THE JETSONS

Sunday prime time broadcast dates: 9/23/62–9/8/63, ABC
Saturday morning premiere: 9/21/63, ABC (reruns)
30-minute Hanna-Barbera cartoon comedy series about the twenty-first century George and Jane Jetson family and their teen-age children Judy and Elroy. Voices included Penny Singleton, George O'Hanlon, Janet Waldo, Daws Butler, and Mel Blanc. The series premiere 9/23/62 also marked the debut of color television on ABC. The cartoons eventually ran on ABC, CBS, NBC, and in syndication into the 1980s.

JIM AND JUDY IN TELELAND

syndicated: 1953
5-minute cartoons in serials made for TV, with voices by Honey McKenzie and Merrill Jolls.

THE JIMMY DEAN SHOW

Saturday prime time broadcast dates: 6/22/57–9/7/57, CBS
Saturday noon broadcast dates: 9/28/57–8/30/58, CBS
60-minute live musical show from Washington, D.C., featuring country-music singer Jimmy Dean. Series premiered as 45-minute weekday morning show 4/8/57 before moving to Saturday slots. Dean replaced *The Big Top* in the Saturday noon slot and was himself replaced by *The George Hamilton IV Show*.

JOE 90

syndicated: 1968
Sylvia and Gerry Anderson's 30-minute "Supermarionation" science fiction puppet series about a nine-year-old secret agent.

THE JOE PALOOKA STORY

syndicated: 1952
30-minute live-action series coproduced by its star, Joe Kirkwood, and based on the Ham Fisher comic strip. Also appearing were Cathy Downs as Anne Howe/Mrs. Joe Palooka; Sid Tomack as Knobby Walsh, his manager; and Maxie Rosenbloom as Clyde, his trainer.

JOHNNY JUPITER

initial broadcast dates: 3/21/53–6/13/53, DuMont
syndicated version: 9/5/53–5/29/54
30-minute puppet satire on modern society produced in two versions. The first starred Vaughn Taylor as Ernest P. Duckweather, janitor of a TV station who contacted an inhabitant of the planet Jupiter. The second starred Wright King as Duckweather, a general store clerk. Both series were produced by Martin Stone's Kagran Productions (Stone headed merchandising for *Howdy Doody*). Carl Harms was puppeteer.

JOHNNY SOKKO AND HIS FLYING ROBOT

syndicated: 1968
30-minute science fiction cartoon series produced by Japan's Mushi Productions.

JOKER! JOKER!! JOKER!!!

syndicated: 1979
30-minute children's version of *The Joker's Wild*, with game-show host Jack Barry emceeing young participants' attempts to win prizes on giant slot machines. Barry had previously hosted the Saturday morning program *Winky Dink and You*.

JON GNAGY

syndicated: 1950s
15-minute filmed art demonstrations conducted by self-taught artist Jon Gnagy. Special drawing kits were merchandised to encourage viewer participation as well as imitation of his methods and style. Gnagy appeared originally on local shows in New York City and on NBC and CBS in both prime time and daytime series from late 1946 into the early 1950s. Titles for his various shows included *You Are an Artist, Draw with Me*, and *Learn to Draw*.

JONNY QUEST

initial prime time broadcast dates: 9/18/64–9/9/65, ABC
initial Saturday broadcast dates: 9/9/67–9/5/70, CBS

Sunday return: 9/13/70–9/5/71, ABC
Saturday return: 9/11/71–9/2/72, ABC; 9/8/79–11/3/79, NBC; 4/12/80, NBC
30-minute Hanna-Barbera cartoon series about scientist Dr. Benton Quest and his twelve-year-old son on their global adventures. They were accompanied on their expeditions by Roger "Race" Bannon, pilot and bodyguard; Hadji, an Indian boy and Jonny's companion; and Bandit, their pet dog. Voices included John Stephenson, Tim Matthieson, Mike Road, Danny Bravo, and Don Messick.

JOSIE AND THE PUSSYCATS

initial broadcast dates: 9/12/70–9/2/72, CBS
return broadcast dates: 9/6/75–9/4/76, CBS
30-minute Hanna-Barbera cartoon series about an all-girl singing group. Voices of the trio were Janet Waldo (Josie), Jackie Joseph (Melody), and Barbara Pariot (Valerie). Cheryl Ladd (as Cherie Moore) added her singing voice to the Pussycats long before her entry into *Charlie's Angels*. The series was revised 9/9/72 on CBS with a space-age setting and retitled *Josie and the Pussycats in Outer Space.*

JOSIE AND THE PUSSYCATS IN OUTER SPACE

see *Josie and the Pussycats*

JOURNEY TO THE CENTER OF THE EARTH

premiere broadcast: 9/9/67, ABC
Filmation cartoon series based on the Jules Verne science fiction adventure novel. 30 minutes.

JUDO BOY

syndicated: 1969
30-minute Japanese cartoon about a boy who uses the martial arts to fight evil.

JUMP JUMP OF HOLIDAY HOUSE

syndicated: 1951
15-minute marionette musical series about an elfin figure, his puppet friends, and a young woman. Produced by Consolidated TV Productions and featuring the work of Mary and Harry Hickox.

JUNGLE BOY

see *The Adventures of a Jungle Boy*

JUNGLE JIM

syndicated: 1955
30-minute Johnny Weissmuller African adventure series. Produced and distributed by Screen Gems. Martin Huston played Skipper, his 10-year-old son.

JUNIOR ALMOST ANYTHING GOES

initial broadcast dates: 9/11/76–1/22/77, ABC
Sunday return: 1/23/77–9/4/77, ABC
Saturday spin-off of ABC's prime time series *Almost Anything Goes*, with Soupy Sales hosting three teams that competed outdoors along obstacle courses and in humorous setups. Eddie Alexander was commentator for the 30-minute show.

JUNIOR CROSSROADS

syndicated: 1952
15-minute films for children on topics ranging from fairy tales and nature lore to music and science.

JUNIOR JAMBOREE

see *Kukla, Fran and Ollie*

JUNIOR RODEO

broadcast dates: 11/15/52–12/13/52, ABC (alternated with Sky King *on 11/22, 12/6, and 12/20; replaced by* Hail the Champ *on 12/27/52)*
Cowboy singer Bob Atcher hosted 30-minute show featuring contests, games, and music. Valerie Alberts was a cast regular. Atcher had appeared on puppet show titled *Meadowgold Ranch*, telecast locally on WBKB-TV, Chicago, in 1951.

JUNIOR SCIENCE

syndicated: 1953
15-minute TV film series hosted by Dr. Gerald Wendt, chief of science education for UNESCO. Series of thirty-nine episodes explored different facets of science and was aimed at eight- to fifteen-year-olds.

JUVENILE JURY

premiere prime time broadcast: 4/3/47, NBC. Kinescopes repeated on Saturdays in various markets.
Host Jack Barry with adolescent panelists waxing philosophically and humorously. 30 minutes. Series broadcast off and on through 1955.

K

THE KAY WESTFALL SHOW

see *Oh, Kay!*

KELLOGGS' PRESENTS THE BANANA SPLITS ADVENTURE HOUR

initial broadcast dates: 9/7/68–9/5/70, NBC
60-minute live-action comedy series featuring rock musician characters in animal costumes who introduced variety acts, serialized adventures, and cartoons. Cartoon segments included *The Arabian Knights, The Hillbilly Knights, The Hillbilly Bears,* and *The Three Musketeers*. Also titled *Kelloggs' of Battle Creek Presents the Banana Splits Adventure Hour.*

KID GLOVES

prime time broadcast dates: 2/24/51–8/4/51, CBS
Children's boxing competition that began as a local show in 1950 on WCAU-TV, Philadelphia. Frank Goodman was referee, Bill Sears added commentary, and Barry Cassel was ring announcer. Pennsylvania boxing commissioner John "Ox" Da Grosa also appeared as guest. Network telecast ended after twenty-six weeks when the series failed to attract a sponsor.

KID MAGIC

syndicated: 1955
15-minute series with Frank Scannel, produced by Aladdin TV Productions, Inc.

KID POWER

initial broadcast dates: 9/9/72–9/1/73, ABC
30-minute series based on the "Wee Pals" cartoon strip by Morrie Turner presenting comedy adventures of multiethnic neighborhood kids.

KIDDY KITCHEN

syndicated: 1955
30-minute filmed series produced by Edwin James and syndicated by Dagger Productions.

KIDS AND COMPANY

broadcast: 9/1/51–5/31/52, 8/9/52–5/2/53, DuMont
Johnny Olsen hosting a variety/talent series sponsored by Red Goose shoes. Young performers (e.g., eight-year-old Leslie Uggams) appeared with older professionals. A special feature, called Johnny Olsen's Youngsters' Hall of Fame, profiled deserving children.

KIDS ARE PEOPLE TOO

Sunday premiere broadcast: 9/10/78, ABC, 90 minutes. Also occasionally telecast Saturday.
Host Bob McAllister in studio interviews with sports figures, performers, celebrities, and experts who appealed to youngsters. In 1979, Michael Young (former host of Warner Qube's *America Goes Bananaz!*) replaced McAllister. Additional segments besides pop music included "Dear Alex and Annie." Emmy Award, 1978–79. See also *Dear Alex and Annie.*

THE KIDS FROM C.A.P.E.R.

initial broadcast dates: 9/11/76–11/20/76, NBC
return: 4/16/77–9/3/77, NBC
30-minute live-action comedy about a gang of youngsters who formed a special unit of the local 927th police district called the Citizens Authority for the Protection of Everyone Regardless (C.A.P.E.R.). The series was set in the mythical town of Northeastsouthwestern and starred "kids" Steve Bonimo, Cosie Costa, Biff Warren, and John Lansing. Also appearing: Robert Emhardt and Robert Lussier.

KIERAN'S KALEIDOSCOPE

syndicated: 1952
15-minute series with an emphasis on science and nature as it examined interest-

ing aspects of our world. John Kieran was host for this educational and entertaining program, 104 episodes of which were distributed as a package by ABC Film Syndication, Inc.

KIMBA, THE WHITE LION

syndicated: 1966

30-minute cartoon series, produced by Japan's Mushi Productions, featured the exploits of a rare white lion who guarded his home country from evil predators.

THE KING AND ODIE

see *King Leonardo and His Short Subjects*

KING FEATURES TRILOGY

syndicated: 1963

Cartoon adventures of King Features comic strip characters Barney Google, Krazy Kat, and Beetle Bailey.

KING KONG

initial broadcast dates: 9/10/66–8/31/69, ABC

Seventy-eight episodes of the 30-minute cartoon adventure series based on the motion picture beast. In cartoon form, however, King Kong was depicted as a sympathetic creature who helped the citizens of New York.

KING LEONARDO AND HIS SHORT SUBJECTS

initial broadcast dates: 10/15/60–9/28/63, NBC

30-minute cartoon series about an African kingdom ruled by a benevolent lion, King Leonardo, and his assistant, Odie Colognie, a skunk. Show focused on their struggles against villains Biggy Rat and Itchy Brother. Jackson Beck was the voice of both Leonardo and Biggy Rat. Odie and Itchy were voiced by Allen Surft. Segments of "The Hunter" and "Tooter Turtle" alternated weekly. Syndicated as *The King and Odie*.

KIT CARSON

see *The Adventures of Kit Carson*

KORG: 70,000 B.C.

initial broadcast dates: 9/7/74–8/31/75, ABC

30-minute live-action adventure series narrated by Burgess Meredith and featuring tales of a Neanderthal family. Produced by Hanna-Barbera.

THE KROFFT SUPERSHOW

initial broadcast dates: 9/11/76–9/2/78, ABC
season premiere: 9/10/77, ABC, as The Krofft Supershow '77

60-minute live-action adventure/musical variety series produced by Sid and Marty Krofft. Kaptain Kool and the Kongs, a rock group, hosted the science fiction and adventure segments: Dr. Shrinker, Electra Woman and Dyna Girl, The Lost Saucer, and Wonderbug. For the second season Kaptain Kool and the Kongs were joined by segments of Wonderbug, Big Foot and Wildboy, and Magic Mongo.

THE KROFFT SUPERSTAR VARIETY HOUR

broadcast dates: 9/9/78–10/28/78, NBC

60-minute live-action series that utilized recycled segments from previous Krofft Supershows of 1976 and 1977 and was hosted by the Bay City Rollers. Segments included Electra Woman and Dyna Girl, Kaptain Kool and the Kongs, Dr. Shrinker, and H. R. Pufnstuf, which previously was telecast as an independent show.

KROFFT SUPER STARS

syndicated: 1978

30-minute live-action adventure/comedy series with recycled episodes from previous Krofft programs. Included are The Bugaloos, Electra Woman and Dyna Girl, The Far Out Space Nuts, H. R. Pufnstuf, Sigmund and the Sea Monsters, Land of the Lost, The Lost Saucer, Dr. Shrinker, and Wonderbug.

KUKLA, FRAN AND OLLIE

premiere weekday broadcast: 10/13/47, as Junior Jamboree, *60-minute local show on WBKB-TV, Chicago; title changed to* Kukla, Fran and Ollie *early 1948*
Midwest weekday network premiere: 11/29/48, NBC, from affiliate WNBQ-TV, Chicago, 30 minutes
East Coast weekday network premiere: 1/12/49, NBC, 30 minutes; kinescopes rebroadcast on Saturdays in some markets
network production change: 11/26/51, NBC, show cut to 15 minutes
network production change: 8/24/52, NBC, show moved to Sunday afternoon, 30 minutes; closed 6/13/54, NBC
return weekday network broadcast dates: 9/6/54–8/30/57, ABC, 15 minutes
return weekday network broadcast: 9/25/61, NBC, videotape, 5 minutes
return weekly network broadcast: 9/75, NBC- owned and -operated stations, produced in Los Angeles, 30 minutes
return syndication: 1976, by Burr Tillstrom and Martin Tahse

Outstanding long-running series for children and adults created by puppeteer Burr Tillstrom and starring Fran Allison on camera. The Kuklapolitan players included Kukla, Ollie (Oliver J. Dragon), Beulah the Witch, Fletcher Rabbit, Madam Ophelia Ooglepuss, Colonel Cracky, Cecil Bill the sailor, Clara Coo Coo, Mercedes, and various and sundry members of the Dragon family. *Kukla, Fran and Ollie* also appeared regularly on *The CBS Children's Film Festival* as hosts beginning 2/5/67. They have appeared as guests on numerous programs and specials through four decades of TV broadcasting. Emmy Award, 1953.

L

LANCELOT LINK, SECRET CHIMP

initial broadcast dates: 9/12/70–9/4/71, ABC, 60 minutes
9/11/71–9/2/72, ABC, 30 minutes

Live-action satire in which chimpanzees emulated humans. Episodes concerned the exploits of APE (Agency for Prevention of Evil) members as they battle the machinations of CHUMP (Criminal Headquarters for Underworld Master Plan). Eighteen chimps participated in the production, all trained by Hubert Wells, who himself appeared as a robot character. Cartoon segments featuring Daffy Duck and Pepe Le Pew, plus music by the chimp rock group, Evolution Revolution.

LAND OF THE GIANTS

prime time broadcast dates: 9/22/68–9/6/70, ABC, thereafter syndicated

60-minute live-action series set in 1983 about a group of Earthlings marooned in a parallel world inhabited by giants living in a repressive society. Series produced by Irwin Allen with cast including Gary Conway, Deanna Lund, Stefan Arngrim, Kurt Kasznar, Don Matheson, Don Marshall, and Heather Young.

LAND OF THE LOST

initial broadcast dates: 9/7/74–9/4/76, NBC
return: 9/11/76–9/9/78, NBC

30-minute live-action series produced by Sid and Marty Krofft and set in a prehistoric world where modern time travelers had been unwillingly transported. UCLA linguistics department chairwoman Victoria Fromkin created a 200-word "Paku" language for the show. Story editor David Gerrold was also the author of the *Star Trek* episode entitled "The Trouble with Tribbles."

LASH OF THE WEST

syndicated: early 1950s

15-minute Western series with cowboy film star Lash LaRue and his sidekick Al (Fuzzy) St. John.

LASSIE

prime time Sunday broadcast dates: 9/12/54–9/12/71, CBS; syndicated during and after prime time network telecast

30-minute live-action morality plays focusing at first on the famed dog linked to young boys and their families and, later, forest rangers. Tommy Rettig (Jeff) and Jon Provost (Timmy) starred as boy pals to the collie. Other leading actors included Jan Clayton, Cloris Leachman, June Lockhart, George Cleveland, Jon Sheppodd, George Chandler, Hugh Riley, Andy Clyde, Robert Bray, Jed Allen, and Jack DeMave. Series went through numerous format and cast alterations and was syndicated under titles *Jeff's Collie*, *Lassie and Timmy*, and *Timmy and Lassie*. Emmy Award, 1954.

LASSIE AND TIMMY

see *Lassie*

LASSIE'S RESCUE RANGERS

initial broadcast dates: 9/8/73–8/31/74, ABC
Sunday return: 9/8/74–8/30/75, ABC
Filmation's 30-minute cartoon series featuring Lassie as the leader of a rescue team comprising other animals called the Forest Force. Voices included Ted Knight's.

LAST OF THE WILD

syndicated: 1974
30-minute nature films hosted and narrated by Lorne Greene. Alternate title: *Lorne Greene's Last of the Wild.*

LAUREL AND HARDY

syndicated: 1948
Comedy shorts of the famed team edited in varying lengths for television release. In 1966, 156 5-minute Hanna-Barbera color cartoons made for TV were syndicated.

LEARN TO DRAW

see *Jon Gnagy*

LEAVE IT TO BEAVER

prime time premiere: 10/4/57–9/12/63, CBS (ABC after 10/58), later syndicated
30-minute live-action comedy about the Cleaver family and its two boys, Beaver (Jerry Mathers) and Wally (Tony Dow). Also starring Hugh Beaumont and Barbara Billingsley.

LEON ERROL COMEDY THEATER

syndicated: 1957
RKO film shorts starring Leon Errol in comedies available in 15-, 30-, and 60-minute formats.

LIDSVILLE

initial broadcast dates: 9/11/71–9/1/73, ABC
return: 9/8/73–8/31/74, NBC
Sid and Marty Krofft live-action production about a young boy lost in a world inhabited by various hat characters, costumed figures, and puppets.

THE LIFE OF RILEY

prime time premiere first version: 10/4/49, NBC
prime time premiere second version: 1/2/53, NBC, thereafter syndicated
30-minute sitcom about a hapless, harrassed, and harried airplane mechanic and his trials and tribulations with family and friends. Based on the radio series, format one starred Jackie Gleason and format two starred William Bendix.

LIFE WITH UNCLE JOHNNY COONS

broadcast dates: 9/4/54–12/3/55, CBS
additional broadcast dates: 3/3/56–12/1/56, NBC
30-minute live-action series from Chicago where it had originated as a local show. Ventriloquist John David Coons starred with his dummy George and performed in stories as well as introduced sketches. Producer: James Green. Announcer: Bruce Roberts. Also titled *Uncle Johnny Coons.*

LINUS THE LIONHEARTED

initial broadcast dates: 9/26/64–9/3/66, CBS, later ABC
Sunday return: 9/25/66–8/31/69, ABC
30-minute cartoon series about a gentle-hearted lion who ruled his fellow animals. Voices included Carl Reiner, Sheldon Leonard (Linus), and Sterling Holloway.

THE LITTLE RASCALS

syndicated: 1954
30-minute television releases of the Hal Roach Our Gang comedies, initially syndicated by Interstate Television Corporation (a division of Allied Artists) and Onyx Pictures. The films are currently syndicated by King World Productions. A prime time cartoon version of the Our Gang kids aired in December 1979.

THE LONE RANGER

prime time premiere: 9/15/49, ABC
Saturday premiere broadcast: 6/13/53, CBS
Saturday network cancellation: 9/23/61, NBC, thereafter syndicated
From out of the East came the mighty radio character, The Lone Ranger, with his great horse, Silver, and his faithful Indian companion, Tonto. Transformed to TV, *The Lone Ranger* has been the longest-running Western series, continuously airing (first run and syndication) since 1949. Clayton Moore portrayed the masked man in 195 episodes produced between 1949 and 1956. John Hart played the Ranger in 26 episodes filmed in 1952. Jay Silverheels appeared as Tonto in all 221 adventures. Created by Detroit broadcaster George W. Trendle (station WXYZ) in 1933 and sold to Jack Wrather, August 1954. Color production commenced in 1956. Thirty-nine shot in color. Two movie versions of *The Lone Ranger* were produced, in 1956 and 1958. A 30-minute Filmation cartoon series based on the further exploits of the George W. Trendle character who, as a Texas Ranger, was the lone ranger to survive a brutal attack and thus decided to wear a mask and forever fight injustice was broadcast 9/10/66–9/6/69, CBS.

LOONEY TUNES

syndicated: 1954
191 theatrical cartoons featuring Porky Pig, Daffy Duck, and other Warner Brothers animated characters. The cartoons were initially syndicated by Guild Films Co., Inc. of New York, and appeared on many local productions in the 1950s, including *Cartoon Carnival* (KTLA-TV, Los Angeles), *Willie and Carney* (WCAU-TV, Philadelphia), and *Cartoon Club* (KSD-TV, St. Louis). Though some are dated, the cartoons still air in the 1980s.

LOST IN SPACE

see *The ABC Saturday Superstar Movie*

THE LOST SAUCER

initial broadcast dates: 9/6/75–9/4/76, ABC
30-minute live-action comedy series set in the twenty-fifth century. The Sid and Marty Krofft production featured two androids, Fum (Jim Nabors) and Fi (Ruth Buzzi), and their nontalking dog-horse animal mascot called the Dorse. Later became a segment on *The Krofft Supershow,* 9/11/76, ABC.

LUCKY PUP

broadcast dates: 8/23/48–6/23/51, CBS
Saturday broadcast dates: 1/49–6/51, CBS
30-minute puppet adventure series hosted by Doris Brown and featuring the puppet characters of Hope and Morey Bunin. The tales concerned Lucky, a playboy dog with a $5-million inheritance, and the evil magician Foodini and his stooge, Pinhead, who plotted to steal the money.

LUNCH WITH SOUPY SALES

see *The Soupy Sales Show*

M

McDUFF, THE TALKING DOG

broadcast dates: 9/11/76–11/20/76, NBC
30-minute live-action comedy about a veterinarian and the century-old English sheep dog that haunts his office and talks to him. McDuff's voice: Jack Lester. Dr. Calvin Campbell: Walter Willson. Executive producers: William D'Angelo, Ray Allen, and Harvey Bullock.

THE MAGIC CLOWN

initial Sunday broadcast dates: 9/11/49–6/27/54, NBC, with rebroadcasts Saturdays in some markets
15-minute circus-oriented production starring Zovella, the Magic Clown. Children participated in the show by singing commercials for Bonomo's Turkish Taffy™, eating the candy on camera, wearing Turkish fezzes, and assisting Zovella with tricks. Richard DuBois assumed the starring role in 1952.

THE MAGIC LADY

syndicated: 1951
15-minute filmed magic series produced by Telemount Pictures, Inc., with Geraldine Larsen as the Magic Lady or Magic Queen, and midget Jerry Maren as Boko the elfin assistant.

THE MAGIC LAND OF ALLAKAZAM

initial broadcast dates: 10/1/60–9/22/62, CBS
return broadcast dates: 9/29/62–12/28/63, 4/25/64–12/12/64, ABC

30-minute magic/variety/cartoon series hosted by magician Mark Wilson. The back-up cast included his wife, Nani Darnell, son Mike, Rebo the Mixed-Up Clown (Bev Bergerson), and the King (Bob Towner). Action was set in the magic land of Allakazam, where the Wilsons performed and introduced cartoons. In 1977, eighty-five 5-minute segments were syndicated as *The Magic World of Mark Wilson* and aired in 30-minute programs.

MAGIC MIDWAY

broadcast dates: 9/22/62–3/16/63, NBC

Claude Kirchner as ringmaster of a short-lived 30-minute circus/magic show. Cast included baton twirler Bonnie Lee. Also known as *Marx Magic Midway*.

THE MAGIC RANCH

broadcast dates: 9/30/61–12/23/61, ABC

30-minute Chicago-based production with magician Don Alan and guest magicians.

THE MAGILLA GORILLA SHOW

syndicated: 1964

30-minute Hanna-Barbera cartoon about a zany gorilla and his pet-store owner, Mr. Peebles. Voices by Allan Melvin, Mel Blanc, Howard Morris, and Don Messick.

MAKE A FACE

broadcast dates: 9/29/62–12/22/62, ABC

30-minute game show based on a fall 1961–spring 1962 prime time production in which contestants attempted to identify celebrities' faces formed by three revolving wheels. Host: Bob Clayton.

MANDRAKE THE MAGICIAN

syndicated: 1954

30-minute live-action adventure based on the Lee Falk comic strip. Coe Norton starred as Mandrake and Woody Strode played Lothar. In 1978 a prime time *Mandrake the Magician* TV movie also aired.

MARINE BOY

syndicated: 1966

30-minute Japanese cartoon adventure series set on twenty-first century Earth where Marine Boy, an underwater, undercover agent, represented the Ocean Patrol. Twenty-six color episodes.

MARLO AND THE MAGIC MOVIE MACHINE

Sunday premiere broadcast: 4/3/77, CBS-owned and -operated stations, and syndicated in other markets on Saturday
Saturday return: 1978 and 1979, NBC, and syndicated

60-minute educational series representative of early TV productions with an adult host introducing informative segments, here vis-à-vis a talking computer simply called "Machine." Laurie Faso played the only human character, Marlo Higgins, a computer operator of L. Dullo Computer Company who developed the talking friend in the basement of the New York company. Episodes utilized old film clips, historical tie-ins, and one-line jokes. Voice of the machine: Mert Hoplin.

MARX MAGIC MIDWAY

see *Magic Midway*

MATTY'S FUNDAY FUNNIES

premiere Sunday broadcast: 10/11/59, ABC
Saturday evening broadcasts: 10/14/61–12/30/61, ABC

30-minute series of Harvey Films theatrical cartoons, including Casper, the Friendly Ghost; Katnip, a cat, and Herman, a mouse; Baby Huey, an overgrown baby duck; Little Audrey, a mischievous little girl; Buzzy, a crow; and Tommy, a tortoise. The cartoons were hosted by Matty and Sister Belle, two animated characters. The series was sponsored by Mattel ®, and was replaced by *Matty's Funnies with Beany and Cecil*, 1/6/62. See also *Beany and Cecil*.

MATTY'S FUNNIES WITH BEANY AND CECIL

see *Beany and Cecil*

MEET ME AT THE ZOO

broadcast dates: 1/10/53–5/30/53, CBS

30-minute series telecast live from the Philadelphia Zoo by CBS affiliate station WCAU-TV, with Freeman Shelly, Roger Conant, and Jack Whitaker, and different animals each week.

MEN INTO SPACE

prime time broadcast dates: 9/30/59–9/7/60, CBS, thereafter syndicated

30-minute realistic science fiction adventure series about NASA astronaut Col. Edward McCauley (William Lundigan) and his moon-base operations.

THE METRIC MARVELS

premiere broadcast dates: 1978–79, NBC

2½-minute educational inserts using specially created animated superheroes to teach children the metric system.

THE MICKEY MOUSE CLUB

network weekday broadcast dates: 10/3/55–9/25/59, ABC
syndicated: 1962–65

Walt Disney's four-year-long series of music, cartoons, mini-dramas, and skits starring Jimmie Dodd and such "Mousketeers" as Annette Funicello, Cubby O'Brien, Karen Pendleton, Bobby Burgess, and Darlene Gillespie. A 30-minute revival of *The Mickey Mouse Club*, strongly reminiscent of its parent production, was produced in 1975. *The New Mickey Mouse Club* was videotaped and syndicated in fifty-four markets.

THE MIGHTY MOUSE PLAYHOUSE

initial broadcast dates: 12/10/55–9/2/67, CBS, thereafter syndicated

30-minute Terrytoon cartoon series featuring 150 episodes of the opera-singing Mighty Mouse, Pearl Pureheart, and villain Oilcan Harry. Tom Morrison was both voice of the hero and narrator. The final network season included a segment of the Mighty Heroes, a flying but bumbling quintet of cartoon supermen. The title became *Mighty Mouse and the Mighty Heroes.* Revised as *The New Adventures of Mighty Mouse and Heckle and Jeckle*, 9/8/79, CBS. The 60-minute Filmation cartoon series featured new versions of the old Terrytoon characters (no longer singing), plus the magpies Heckle and Jeckle. Safety tips for young viewers were included between cartoon segments.

MILTON THE MONSTER

initial broadcast dates: 10/9/65–9/2/67, ABC

30-minute cartoon series produced by Hal Seeger in which a lovable monster cavorted with other unusual creatures at Horrible Hill, Transylvania.

MISSION MAGIC

initial broadcast dates: 9/8/73–8/31/74, ABC

30-minute Filmation cartoon series about six students and their teacher who were transported to other times and places through their magical blackboard.

MISTER MAYOR

broadcast dates: 9/26/64–9/18/65, CBS

Bob Keeshan's one-year-long educational series that replaced his Saturday morning version of *Captain Kangaroo.* Keeshan played the surrogate mayor of a small town who talked with characters living in the community. Live and puppet characters included Aunt Maud, Dudley, Miss Melissa, and Rollo the Hippopotamus. This 60-minute show was replaced in turn by *Captain Kangaroo* on Saturday mornings.

MISTER ROGERS' NEIGHBORHOOD

initial weekday broadcasts: 1967, NET (on a limited number of ETV stations) 1970, PBS (on more than 200 stations)
currently syndicated to PBS stations with repeats Saturday mornings in some markets

30-minute educational and fantasy series aimed primarily at younger children. Produced at WQED-TV, Pittsburgh, under clergyman/educator/puppeteer Fred Rogers, who was involved previously with NBC's *The Children's Corner* in 1955 and 1956. This show appeared originally for 15 minutes on CBC, Toronto, in 1963 before its debut on NET. Rogers has served as creator, writer, producer, and executive producer, in addition to hosting, performing, and manipulating and voicing puppets. John Costa is music director, and the human cast includes Betty Aberlin as Lady Aberlin, Joe Negri as Handyman Negri, Don Brockett as Chef Brockett, David Newell as Mr. McFeely, Bob Trow as Robert Troll and Bob Dog, and Francois Clemmons as Officer Clemmons. Puppets voiced by Rogers include King Friday XIII, Queen Sara Saturday, Lady Elaine Fairchilde, Henrietta Pussycat, Daniel S. Tiger, X the Owl, Cornflake S. Pecially (Corny), Donkey Hodie, and Henri Frederic de Tigre (Grandpère). William P. Barker, a fellow Presbyterian clergyman, voices Dr. William Duckbill Bagpipe Platypus IV (Dr. Bill), his wife Elsie Jean, and Dr. Tadpole Frog (an M.D.). Bob Trow is the voice of Harriet Elizabeth Cow and has done also Donkey Hodie. Visitors to the Neighborhood have included Van Cliburn, Marcel Marceau, Julia Child, and Margaret Hamilton (as Princess Margaret H. Witch). Fred Rogers has produced numerous PBS prime time and weekend specials aimed at children and/or parents.

MOBY DICK AND THE MIGHTY MIGHTOR

initial broadcast dates: 9/9/67–9/6/69, CBS

30-minute Hanna-Barbera cartoon loosely based on the Herman Melville sea story. In this TV version, however, Moby Dick was a friendly, not dangerous, whale that protected two children. Also featured on the series were tales of a teen-age prehistoric lad, Tor, who could transform himself into a superhero (Mighty Mightor) when danger threatened. Voices included Bobby Diamond, Don Messick, and Paul Stewart.

THE MONKEES

initial prime time broadcast dates: 9/12/66–8/19/68, NBC
prime time return: 9/13/69–9/2/72, CBS
initial Saturday return: 9/9/72–9/1/73, ABC

30-minute situation comedy fashioned after The Beatles' movies *A Hard Day's Night* and *Help!* but featuring the American singing group The Monkees, expressly created for the TV series. The four singer/comedians were Davy Jones, Peter Tork, Mike Nesmith, and Mickey Dolenz.

THE MONSTER SQUAD

initial broadcast dates: 9/11/76–9/3/77, NBC

30-minute situation comedy where wax-museum monsters were activated by a young criminology student working his way through college as a night watchman. Frankenstein (Michael Lane), Bruce Wolfman (Buck Katalian), and Dracula (Henry Polic, II).

MOTOR MOUSE

initial broadcast dates: 9/12/70–9/4/71, ABC

30-minute Hanna-Barbera cartoon spin-off of *The Cattanooga Cats* Saturday morning series, with road-racing stories pitting Motor Mouse (voice of Dick Curtis) and Auto Cat (Marty Ingels). Also included were episodes of "It's the Wolf," with Paul Lynde dubbing the voice of Mildew Wolf and Marty Ingels as Lambsy.

THE MOUSE FACTORY

syndicated: 1972

30-minute series of seventeen episodes drawn primarily from existing Walt Disney productions. Featured: Annette Funicello, Wally Cox, Pat Buttram, and cartoon characters.

MOVIETONE CHILDREN'S NEWSREEL

syndicated: 1952

15-minute educational news series produced and distributed by Twentieth Century-Fox's Movietone News. Commentator: Frank Luther. Writer: Don Doherty.

MR. I. MAGINATION

Sunday premiere: 4/24/49, WCBS-TV, New York show
initial Sunday network broadcast dates: 5/29/49–6/17/51, CBS
Sunday return: 1/13/52–4/13/52, CBS
Saturday broadcast dates: 4/19/52–6/28/52, CBS

Live 30-minute production with Paul Tripp (author of *Tubby the Tuba*) as Mr. I. Magination, a tour guide who led children along his train to lands of make-believe where heroes of history or fiction were visited. Regulars: Tripp's wife, Ruth Enders; Ted Tiller; and Richard Boone; plus a rotating troupe of children. Produced by Worthington Miner.

MR. MAGIC AND J.J.

network premiere broadcast: 4/12/50, ABC (Wednesday, Thursday, Friday, and Saturday); originally aired on WPIX-TV, New York, in 1949

Twenty-three-year-old magician Norman Jensen hosted this 15-minute series with assistance from J.J., a hand-puppet rabbit. Produced by Chuck Vincent and Gerry Law.

MR. MAGOO

see *The Famous Adventures of Mr. Magoo*

MR. WIZARD

see *Watch Mr. Wizard*

MUGGSY

initial broadcast dates: 9/11/76– 4/2/77, NBC

30-minute prosocial live-action series geared to eight- to fourteen-year-olds. Sarah MacDonnell starred as a thirteen-year-old white ghetto child with hope for revitalizing her community. She was assisted by her half-brother Nick (Ben Masters) and a garage owner named Gus (Paul Michael).

MY FAVORITE MARTIANS

initial broadcast dates: 9/8/73–8/30/75, CBS

30-minute Filmation series adapted loosely from the 1963–66 prime time show *My Favorite Martian.* Two aliens and their dog are protected by a reporter and his niece while they attempt to repair their damaged spacecraft. Voices by Jonathan Harris, Jane Webb, Lane Scheimer, and Howard Morris.

MY FRIEND FLICKA

initial prime time broadcast dates: 2/10/56–5/18/58, production premiered in black and white on CBS and moved to NBC for color telecast of reruns 9/57. Thereafter thirty-nine episodes rerun on ABC, CBS, NBC, and again CBS.

30-minute heartwarming, live-action film series about young Ken McLaughlin (Johnny Washbrook) and his horse. The series, set at the turn of the century, was based on the book by Mary O'Hara and costarred Gene Evans, Anita Louise, and Frank Ferguson.

MY LITTLE MARGIE

prime time broadcast dates: 6/16/52–8/24/55, CBS, thereafter syndicated, NBC

30-minute sitcom with Gale Storm playing Margie Albright, a love-struck, adventurous twenty-one-year-old, and her conservative, trouble-prone, widower father Vern (Charles Farrell). Produced by Hal Roach, Jr., and Roland Reed.

N

NBC CHILDREN'S THEATRE

Sunday premiere broadcast: 11/3/63, NBC

60-minute production with varied themes, including puppetry by Paul and Mary Ritts, comedy with Jonathan Winters, and discussion featuring Jack Parr. Dramatic specials have included Kukla, Fran, and Ollie in "The Reluctant Dragon" and a new ballet version for TV of "Little Women."

NBC JUNIOR HALL OF FAME

premiere broadcast: 9/10/77, NBC

1½-minute profiles broadcast three times each Saturday during the 1977–78 season that honored outstanding youngsters, aged fourteen or less, who had gained recognition through volunteer work, bravery, arts, sciences, sports, or by overcoming a handicap. Produced by Alan Landsburg Productions.

NATIONAL VELVET

initial prime time broadcast dates: 9/18/60–9/10/62, NBC

30-minute live-action series based on the book and motion picture about young Velvet Brown (Lori Martin) and her attempts to ride her horse King in the Grand National steeplechase.

THE NEW ADVENTURES OF BATMAN

see *Batman*

THE NEW ADVENTURES OF FLASH GORDON

see *Flash Gordon*

THE NEW ADVENTURES OF GILLIGAN

see *Gilligan's Island*

THE NEW ADVENTURES OF MIGHTY MOUSE AND HECKLE AND JECKLE

see *The Mighty Mouse Playhouse*

THE NEW ADVENTURES OF SUPERMAN

initial broadcast dates: 9/10/66–9/2/67, CBS
return: 9/13/69–9/5/70, CBS

Filmation's 30-minute cartoon series featuring the Man of Steel. Bud Collyer recorded Superman's voice, reprising his role in both the Fleischer-Paramount cartoons and the radio broadcasts.

THE NEW ARCHIES/SABRINA HOUR

see *The Archie Show*

THE NEW CASPER CARTOON SHOW

see *Casper, the Friendly Ghost*

THE NEW FAT ALBERT SHOW

see *Fat Albert and the Cosby Kids*

THE NEW HOWDY DOODY SHOW

see *Howdy Doody*

THE NEW MICKEY MOUSE CLUB

see *The Mickey Mouse Club*

THE NEW SCOOBY-DOO MOVIES

see *Scooby-Doo, Where Are You?*

THE NEW SHMOO

initial broadcast dates: 9/22/79–12/1/79, NBC

30-minute cartoon series in which the character derived from Al Capp's "Li'l Abner" comic strip becomes an assistant to three teen-age investigators of the paranormal. The series was revised into *Fred and Barney Meet the Shmoo*, 12/8/79, NBC.

THE NEW TOM AND JERRY/GRAPE APE SHOW

see *Tom and Jerry*

THE NEW ZOO REVUE

syndicated: 1972

30-minute series with live-action and costumed characters dressed in animal outfits designed by Sid and Marty Krofft. Produced and created by Barbara Atlas and Douglas Momary, featuring Momary as Doug, Emily Peden as Emmy Jo, Yanco Inone as Freddie the Frog, Larri Thomas as Henrietta Hippo, and Sharon Baird as Charlie the Owl. Production geared for young children with a strong educational angle in songs, dances, and jokes.

NORTHWEST PASSAGE

prime time broadcast dates: 9/14/58–8/8/59, NBC, thereafter syndicated

30-minute action/adventure film series set in the 1750s during the French and Indian War. Keith Larsen starred as Major Robert Rogers, the famed explorer who searched for the Northwest Passage, a water route thought to link the Eastern and Western portions of North America. Buddy Ebsen co-starred as Sergeant Hunk Mariner.

O

THE ODDBALL COUPLE

initial broadcast dates: 9/6/75–9/4/76, ABC

30-minute cartoon adaption of *The Odd Couple*. This Saturday morning version featured Fleabag the dog (voice of Paul Winchell) and Spiffy the cat (voice of Frank Nelson) as a pair of reporters for a magazine. Produced by DePatie-Freleng.

OH, KAY!

broadcast dates: 2/24/51–10/13/51, ABC

30-minute musical/conversation/variety series hosted by Kay Westfall and produced in Chicago. Guests on premiere show: Florence Bourke Ellis and lecturer Burton Holmes. Regulars: David LeWinter, Jim Dimitri, and Mary Ellen White. Also titled *The Kay Westfall Show*.

ON THE CAROUSEL

broadcast dates: 12/19/53–10/3/59, WCBS-TV, New York

60-minute and 30-minute educational/variety production with Paul Tripp (formerly Mr. I. Magination) and his wife, Ruth Enders. Allen Ludden guest hosted 4/3/54 and 4/10/54.

ON YOUR MARK

initial broadcast dates: 9/23/61–12/30/61, ABC

30-minute studio quiz show hosted by Irwin "Sonny" Fox. Nine- to thirteen-year-old contestants answered questions about their career choices. In New York, the show was televised on independent station WNEW-TV, not the network affiliate WABC-TV, because Fox was under exclusive contract to WNEW-TV, which prohibited him from appearing on another station in the market. *On Your Mark* was ABC's first Saturday morning children's program since the discontinuance of Saturday morning service to affiliates in the early 1950s.

ONCE UPON A CLASSIC

premiere broadcast: 1978, PBS

60-minute multipart children's novels remade for television. Host Bill Bixby introduced and narrated each episode. Titles included *Pinocchio* and *The Last of the Mohicans*.

1, 2, 3—GO!

Sunday broadcast dates: 10/8/61–5/27/62, NBC
Saturday rebroadcasts in some markets

30-minute tape and film series with host Jack Lescoulie and eleven-year-old Richard Thomas exploring occupations and talking with noted personalities. The premiere show featured mountain climbing with Supreme Court Justice William O. Douglas; other shows visited the home of Attorney General Robert F. Kennedy and traveled to various locales in the United States.

THE OSMONDS

initial broadcast dates: 9/9/72–9/1/74, ABC

30-minute cartoon adventure/fantasy about the Osmond Brothers rock group. Voices were recorded by the Osmonds themselves, with Paul Frees voicing their dog Fugi. A Rankin/Bass production.

P

THE PARTRIDGE FAMILY: 2200 A.D.

initial broadcast dates: 9/7/74–3/1/75, CBS

30-minute Hanna-Barbera cartoon based on the prime time series but set in the future. Susan Dey, Brian Foster, Dave Madden, Danny Bonaduce, and Suzanne Crough all reprised their roles from the original production and recorded their characters' voices.

PAUL WHITEMAN'S TV TEEN CLUB

broadcast dates: 4/2/49–3/28/54, ABC
Saturday rebroadcasts in some markets

30-minute early-evening talent show hosted by conductor Paul Whiteman in which young singers, dancers, and musicians competed for the prize of professional coaching. Whiteman's daughter Margo was the show's first cohost. Other young regulars included Nancy Lewis, Stan Klet, Junie Keegan, and four-year-old Andrea McLaughlin.

THE PAUL WINCHELL AND JERRY MAHONEY SHOW

Saturday morning premiere broadcast: 11/20/54, NBC

30-minute children's show with ventriloquist Winchell and his dummies Jerry Mahoney and Knucklehead Smiff. The variety/music/comedy series was set in Mahoney's clubhouse, with a live studio audience à la *Howdy Doody*. Winchell also hosted other prime time and Saturday morning shows. See also *Cartoonies, Toyland Express*, and *Runaround*.

PEBBLES AND BAMM BAMM

initial broadcast dates: 9/11/71–9/2/72, CBS
return broadcast dates: 3/8/75–9/4/76, CBS

30-minute animated spin-off of *The Flintstones* with the two Hanna-Barbera prehistoric teen-agers. Voices: Pebbles, Sally Struthers; Bamm Bamm, Jay North.

THE PERILS OF PENELOPE PITSTOP

initial broadcast dates: 9/13/69–9/5/70, CBS

Mack Sennett–type cartoon series complete with title cards and piano accompaniment. The 30-minute comedy/adventures concerned young racer Penelope (voice of Janet Waldo) and her nemesis Sylvester Sneekly (Paul Lynde). Additional voices on the Hanna-Barbera series were provided by Mel Blanc, Paul Winchell, and Don Messick.

PERSONAL APPEARANCE THEATRE

broadcast dates: 1/5/52–4/19/52, ABC
30-minute dramatic series featuring such actors as Hugh Beaumont, Robert Clarke, Reginald Denny, Steve Dunne, Leif Erickson, Glenda Farrell, Marjorie Lord, Joseph Schildkraut, and Arthur Shields.

PET SHOP

initial broadcast dates: 12/1/51–3/14/53, DuMont
30-minute pet show originating from WGN-TV in Chicago, where it had been previously broadcast as a local production. Gail and Gay Compton appeared as a father and daughter proprietor of the program's shop.

THE PETER POTAMUS SHOW

syndicated: 1964
30-minute Hanna-Barbera color cartoon series about a purple hippopotamus (voice of Daws Butler) and his cohort, So So monkey (Don Messick). Ricochet Rabbit was another segment.

PETS AND PALS ANIMAL FAIR

see *Your Pet Parade*

THE PINK PANTHER AND FRIENDS

see *The Pink Panther*

THE PINK PANTHER LAUGH AND A HALF HOUR AND A HALF

see *The Pink Panther*

THE PINK PANTHER MEETS THE ANT AND THE AARDVARK

see *The Pink Panther*

THE PINK PANTHER SHOW

premiere broadcast: 9/6/69, NBC, 30 minutes
revised: 9/12/70, 9/11/71, NBC, as The Pink Panther Meets the Ant and the Aardvark, *30 minutes; 9/11/76, NBC, as* The Pink Panther and Friends, *90 minutes; 9/10/77, NBC, as* The Pink Panther Show, *30 minutes; 9/9/78, NBC, as* The All-New Pink Panther Show, *30 minutes*
Various TV incarnations of the Blake Edwards character developed for the credits of the Pink Panther motion pictures, and produced by DePatie-Freleng, with music by Henry Mancini. Segments included in the shows were Inspector Clouseau, Texas Toads, The Ant and the Aardvark, Misterjaws, and Crazylegs. The Paul and Mary Ritts Puppets were hosts for the fourth season. The prebroadcast title for *The Pink Panther and Friends* in 1976 was listed as *The Pink Panther Laugh and a Half Hour and a Half.*

THE PINKY LEE SHOW

prime time broadcast dates of first series: 4/19/50–11/9/50, NBC
Saturday evening broadcast dates: 9/50–10/50, NBC
30-minute variety show starring vaudevillian Pinky Lee in an adult production.

THE PINKY LEE SHOW

weekday broadcast dates: 1/4/54–5/11/56, NBC
Saturday morning broadcast dates: 3/5/55–6/9/56, NBC
30-minute comedy series broadcast six days a week through much of its programming life. Betty Jane Howarth joined the comedy/variety format in her role of Lily Chrysanthemum. Lee, noted for his fast-paced style and slapstick humor, collapsed on his show from exhaustion and a sinus condition 9/20/55 during a telecast from NBC's Burbank, California, studios. He returned only to face new pressures from the competing *Mickey Mouse Club.* His shows were replaced on weekdays by reruns of *I Married Joan*, and on Saturday morning by *Howdy Doody.*

PIP THE PIPER

Sunday broadcast dates: 12/25/60–5/28/61, ABC
Saturday color return: 6/24/61–9/22/62, NBC
30-minute live-action fantasy series set in Pipertown, a wonderland in the clouds where Pip (Jack Spear), Miss Merrynote (Phyllis Spear), and Mr. Leader (Lucian Kaminsky) met varying adventures spiced with magic and music.

PLANET PATROL

syndicated: 1963
30-minute marionette series set on twenty-first-century earth, where agents of Galasphere Patrol protected member planets of the solar system.

THE PLASTICMAN COMEDY ADVENTURE SHOW

premiere broadcast: 9/8/79, ABC, 60 minutes; expanded to two hours, 9/22/79; reduced to 90 minutes, 12/29/79
Superhero Plasticman hosted cartoon series featuring segments of his own adventures, plus Fangface and Fangpuss (two cousins who become werewolves after looking at the moon, and back to normal by looking at the sun), Rickety Rocket (four black teen-agers aboard a junky spaceship), Mightyman and Yukk (the world's smallest superhero in the form of Brandan Brewster/Mighty Man, plus his partner Yukk, the world's ugliest dog, who wears his house on his head), and 30-second consumer tips. Produced by Ruby and Spears. See *Fangface.*

PLAYTIME

initial weekday broadcast dates: 11/26/47–2/18/48, NBC, Wednesday
Saturday evening return: 11/13/48, NBC
Children's show originating in Washington, D.C., replaced on Wednesday 2/25/48 by *Howdy Doody.*

POPEYE

syndicated: 1956
network premiere broadcast: 9/9/78, CBS, as The All-New Popeye Hour
Max Fleischer's original 200 theatrical cartoons produced from the 1930s to the 1950s, plus a new package of made-for-TV cartoons released by King Features in the early 1960s. Episodes ranged from 6 to 10 minutes in length. The Thimble Theater cast returned in *The All-New Popeye Hour*, comprised of new Hanna-Barbera cartoons devoid of the violence that was typical of the two older series. In addition, health and nutritional tips were offered. Popeye the Sailor Man was joined once again by Olive Oyl, Bluto, and Wimpy. Jack Mercer has recorded the voice of the spinach-eating sailor for more than four decades.

POPSICLE FIVE STAR COMEDY

broadcast dates: 5/18/57–6/15/57, ABC
Paul Winchell and his dummies acted as one of five hosts on this short-lived musical/variety late-afternoon show. The other hosts were Jerry Colonna, Ben Blue, Olsen and Johnson, and Senor Wences. Announcer: Bill Brophy. Cast: Bob Bean and Anne Marstin. 30 minutes.

PORKY PIG AND HIS FRIENDS

see *The Porky Pig Show*

THE PORKY PIG SHOW

syndicated: 1964, ABC; returned in syndication
Warner Brothers Looney Tunes character and other studio cartoons in a 30-minute program. Also known as *Porky Pig and His Friends.* Voices by Mel Blanc. Directed by Chuck Jones.

PRINCE PLANET

syndicated: 1966
Fifty-two-episode, 30-minute Japanese cartoon about twenty-first-century Earth city New Metropolis where Prince Planet battles on behalf of the democratic order. Producer: Mushi Productions.

PUD'S PRIZE PARTY

broadcast dates: 6/21/52–12/13/52, ABC
15-minute variety show with Fleer's Dubble Bubble Gum ® messages and products evident throughout the show. Host of the entertainment/competition program was Todd Russell, who also hosted *Rootie Kazootie.* Telecast by ABC affiliate WFIL-TV, from Town Hall, Philadelphia.

PUPPET PLAYHOUSE

see *Howdy Doody*

PUPPET TELEVISION THEATRE

see *Howdy Doody*

Q

Q. T. HUSH

syndicated: 1960

30-minute cartoon series about Q.T., a private eye, his dog Shamus, and his shadow, Quincy, who could operate independently.

QUE PASA, U.S.A.?

premiere broadcast: 1975, PBS

30-minute bilingual situation comedy series aimed at Anglo and Hispanic teen-agers and their families. The twenty-eight episodes depict the lives and endeavors of three generations of a Cuban-American family, with the expressed goal of encouraging mutual understanding and appreciation between both ethnic groups. The title translates into English as *What's Happening, America?*

QUICK DRAW McGRAW

syndicated: 1959

30-minute Hanna-Barbera cartoon series about a lazy marshal horse and his sidekick, Babalouie. Program introduced Yogi Bear and Boo Boo. Principal voices by Daws Butler.

QUIZ KIDS

prime time broadcast dates: 3/1/49–9/27/56, NBC, CBS; also telecast in various daytime slots
syndicated 1980

30-minute adaptation of old radio series in which a panel of children knowledgeable in specific subject-areas competed. The TV show was hosted by radio quizmaster Joe Kelly and, finally, Clifton Fadiman. A new syndicated version went into production March 1, 1980, at WNAC-TV, Boston. This 1980s *Quiz Kids*, a joint venture of RKO General and Columbia Pictures Television, also presented five youngsters tackling difficult questions. Network TV game-show host Jim McKrell emceed the revamped 30-minute program.

R

RAMAR OF THE JUNGLE

syndicated: 1952

30-minute live-action jungle adventure series with Jon Hall as Dr. Thomas Reynolds, a physician known to the natives as Ramar, or white witch doctor. Episodes were set in Nairobi, Kenya, but shot in Hollywood.

THE RANGE RIDER

syndicated: 1951

30-minute live-action Western series produced by Gene Autry's Flying A Productions. Series starred Jock Mahoney (credited as Jack Mahoney) as a rough-and-tumble lawman with his teen-age partner Dick West (played by Dick Jones).

RAZZMATAZZ

premiere broadcast: 4/16/77, CBS, 60 minutes
season premiere broadcast: 11/5/77, 30 minutes

Variety/feature-oriented show produced in cooperation with Scholastic Magazines, Inc. and CBS News. By 2/1/79—its third season—the production aired the first Thursday of each month at 4:00 P.M., EST. Among the regulars was Don Herbert (Mr. Wizard). Host for the pilot was Barry Bostwick, with Brian Tochi hosting in 1979. Emmy award, 1978–79.

THE READING ROOM

premiere broadcast: 9/22/62, CBS

Ned Hoopes as host of this educational show designed to stimulate reading. A panel of youngsters talked with authors and celebrities about their work and lives. The 30-minute show was the first Saturday children's production of CBS News's Public Affairs Department.

REBOP

premiere broadcast: 10/9/76, PBS, thereafter syndicated

30-minute filmed profiles of youngsters throughout the country produced by Boston Public Broadcasting Service station WGBH-TV. Project director and series producer: Jesus Henrique Maldonado. 52 programs.

THE RED HAND GANG

initial broadcast dates: 9/10/77–1/21/78, NBC

30-minute live-action adventure series concerning five inner-city kids involved in a variety of shenanigans from investigating crimes to exploring haunted houses. Cast: Matthew Laborteaux, J. R. Miller, Jolie Newman, Johnny Brogna, and James Bond III. Executive producers: William P. D'Angelo, Ray Allen, and Harvey Bullock.

RED RYDER

syndicated: 1956

30-minute Western series about lawman Red Ryder (Rocky Lane) and his Indian companion, Little Beaver (Louis Letteri).

THE RELUCTANT DRAGON AND MR. TOAD

initial broadcast dates: 9/12/70–9/4/71, ABC
Sunday return: 9/12/71–9/3/72, ABC

Rankin-Bass cartoon series based on Kenneth Grahame's *The Wind in the Willows*. The 30-minute program was set in Willowmarsh Village, England, where Sir Malcolm protected Tobias, a well-intentioned 400-year-old fire-breathing dragon, from the justifiably perturbed.

RENFREW OF THE ROYAL MOUNTED

syndicated: 1952

30-minute live-action adventure series based on stories by Laurie York Erskine with James Newill as Canadian Mounted officer Douglas Renfrew. The filmed series set in the Yukon also featured Dave O'Brien as Constable Kelly and Louise Stanley as Carol Girard, Renfrew's love interest.

RETURN TO THE PLANET OF THE APES

broadcast dates: 9/6/75–9/4/76, NBC

30-minute DePatie-Freleng adventure cartoon spin-off of the motion picture *Planet of the Apes*, set 2000 years into the future. In this animated version, astronauts Bill, Judy, and Jeff travel through time into an era when talking apes ruled the Earth and humans were considered the lower species.

RICHARD THE LION HEARTED

syndicated: 1963

30-minute adventure series on the life of England's King Richard I, with Dermot Walsh playing the Crusader monarch.

RIN TIN TIN

see *The Adventures of Rin Tin Tin*

RIPCORD

syndicated: 1961

30-minute live-action series about two skydivers who face aerial adventures and down-to-earth danger. Ken Curtis played parachutist Jim Buckley and Larry Pennell costarred as his partner, Ted McKeever.

THE ROAD RUNNER SHOW

premiere broadcast: 9/10/66, CBS
return: 9/14/68–9/4/71, CBS, as a segment on The Bugs Bunny/Road Runner Hour*, 60 minutes*
return: 9/11/71–9/2/72, ABC, thereafter telecast as a segment on The Bugs Bunny/Road Runner Hour *and* The Bugs Bunny/Road Runner Show

Warner Brothers 30-minute cartoon series about the forever unsuccessful attempts of Wile E. Coyote to catch and eat the spirited bird, the Road Runner. Voice effects by Mel Blanc. See also *The Bugs Bunny Show*.

ROBIN HOOD

see *The Adventures of Robin Hood*

THE ROBONIC STOOGES

initial broadcast dates: 2/4/78–9/2/78, CBS

30-minute cartoon show, loosely based on The Three Stooges film comedies, that originally ran as a segment of *The Skatebirds* (premiere 9/10/77, CBS).

ROCKET ROBIN HOOD

syndicated: 1969

30-minute science fiction cartoon series set in the year 3000, with space age descendant of Robin Hood who rocketed from New Sherwood Forest Asteroid to battle the evil Prince John and his henchman, the Sheriff of Nott. Produced by Trillium Productions, Ltd., Canada.

ROCKY AND HIS FRIENDS

initial broadcast dates: 9/29/59–9/3/61, ABC

Jay Ward and Bill Scott cartoon comedy about a high-flying squirrel (Rocky) and his oafish moose friend, Bullwinkle. The sharply written, quick-paced, humorous episodes were punctuated by satire and narrated by William Conrad. Voices: Rocky (June Foray), Bullwinkle (Bill Scott), Boris Badenov (Paul Frees), Natasha Fatale (June Foray). In the "Aesop's Fables" segment, Paul Frees narrated and Charlie Ruggles played Aesop. "Peabody's Improbable History" featured Walter Tetley as Sherman and Bill Scott as Peabody. "Fractured Fairy Tales" was narrated by Edward Everett Horton. See also *The Dudley Do-Right Show* for cast of that segment and *The Bullwinkle Show*.

ROCKY JONES, SPACE RANGER

syndicated: 1953

30-minute science fiction cliff-hanger series filmed by Roland Reed Productions at Hal Roach Studios. Episodes were set on twenty-first-century Earth, where Rocky (Richard Crane), chief of the Space Rangers, led a fight against those who threatened the peace within the United Solar System. Cast: Winky (Scott Beckett), Vena Ray (Sally Mansfield), Bobby (Robert Lyden), Professor Newton (Maurice Cass), and Yarra (Dian Fauntelle). Rocky's ship: the *Orbit Jet*.

ROCKY KING, INSIDE DETECTIVE

prime time broadcast dates: 1/14/50–12/26/54, DuMont; thereafter kinescopes were syndicated

30-minute live dramatic series with Roscoe Karns as New York plainclothesman Rocky King and his son, Todd Karns, as Detective Hart. Mabel King was portrayed off-camera by Grace Carney.

ROD BROWN OF THE ROCKET RANGERS

broadcast dates: 4/18/53–5/29/54, CBS

30-minute live-action science fiction series set on Omega Base in the twenty-second century, where Rod Brown (Cliff Robertson) piloted his rocket ship, the *Beta*, to adventures with fellow rangers Frank Boyle (Bruce Hall), Commander Swift (John Boruff), and Wilbur "Wormsey" Wormser (Jack Weston).

ROMAN HOLIDAYS

initial broadcast dates: 9/9/72–9/1/73, NBC

30-minute Hanna-Barbera cartoon series about life with the Holiday family in first-century Rome. Voices included Daws Butler, Dom DeLuise, Hal Peary, Judy Strangis, and Janet Waldo.

ROMPER ROOM

syndicated: 1953

Long-running 60-minute and 30-minute children's show geared to preschoolers with locally produced versions and a nationally syndicated edition. The national show, produced in Baltimore like the local productions, included musical, instructional, patriotic, and entertainment segments and, for years, commercial pitches for Romper Room toys.

ROOTIE KAZOOTIE

initial Saturday broadcast dates: 10/14/50–7/7/51, local show on WNBT-TV, New York, 30 minutes, under original title, The Rootie-Tootie Club, *until title changed to* Rootie Kazootie *12/26/50*
initial Monday–Friday broadcast: 7/2/51–11/21/52, NBC, 15 minutes
Saturday return broadcast dates: 10/13/51–5/17/52, NBC, 30 minutes, color
Monday–Friday return: 12/22/52, local show on WJZ-TV, New York, 15 minutes
Saturday return broadcast: 1/3/53, ABC, 30 minutes

Puppet show featuring songs, quizzes, games, and conversation, hosted by Todd Russell (the Chief Rooter). The series was written and produced by Steve Carlin, with the puppetry handled by Paul Ashley, Frank Milano, and Michael King. The cast included Rootie Tootie/Kazootie, a little boy sports fan (Naomi Lewis); Little Nipper/Gala-Poochie Pup, his dog (Frank Milano); El Squeeko Mouse, the Catador who spoke rapidly with a Latin American accent (Naomi Lewis); and Poison Zoomack, the villain who tried to steal Rootie's "majic kazootie" (Frank Milano). Mr. Deetle Dootle, a mute human policeman, was played by John Schoepperle and, later, John Vee.

THE ROUGH RIDERS

prime time broadcast dates: 10/2/58–9/24/59, ABC

30-minute Western adventure series set in the post–Civil War period and featuring the adventures of two Union soldiers, Captain Jim Flagg (Kent Taylor) and Sergeant Buck Sinclair (Peter Whitney), and one Confederate, Lt. Kirby (Jan Merlin), as they moved westward.

THE ROY ROGERS SHOW

Sunday broadcast dates: 12/30/51–6/23/57, NBC
Saturday return: 1/7/61–9/19/64, CBS

30-minute Western series starring the King of the Cowboys and his wife, Dale Evans. Rogers portrayed a rough-and-tumble sheriff of Mineral City who, with his bumbling sidekick, Pat Brady; his horse, Trigger; and his dog, Bullet, rode herd on contemporary villains. Initial broadcast replaced *Hopalong Cassidy* on NBC. In 1955, sixty-seven of Rogers's Republic feature films were syndicated in 60-minute form by MCA-TV Film Syndication.

ROYAL CANADIAN MOUNTED POLICE

syndicated: 1960

30-minute adventure series about the famed Canadian police protecting the Northwest. Gilles Pelletier portrayed the lead character, Corporal Jacques Gagnier, with John Perkins (Constable Scott) and Don Francks (Constable Mitchell).

RUFF AND REDDY

initial broadcast dates: 12/14/57–9/26/64, NBC, thereafter syndicated

Hanna-Barbera's first TV cartoon series, produced with Screen Gems, and hosted by Jimmy Blaine and later Captain Bob Cottle. 30-minute comedy featured a cat (Ruff) and a dog (Reddy).

RUN, JOE, RUN!

broadcast dates: 9/7/74–9/4/76, NBC

30-minute live-action series about a German shepherd that ran away from an army base after being unfairly accused of attacking his master, Sergeant William Cory (Arch Whiting). A second version of the show premiered in 9/6/75 in which Joe befriended backpacker Josh McCoy (Chad States) and encountered new adventures. Both seasons were produced by William P. D'Angelo.

RUNAROUND

broadcast dates: 9/9/72–9/1/73, NBC

30-minute quiz show hosted by Paul Winchell and his dummies, Jerry Mahoney and Knucklehead Smiff. Participants raced in elimination contests, trying to determine the correct answers to questions in order to win weekly grand prizes. Announcer: Kenny Williams.

S

S.S. TELE-CRUISE

broadcast dates: 4/28/51–6/2/51, ABC

A one-hour, 45-minute musical/variety series with Jack Steck as "Cap'n Jack," an emcee on an imaginary ship that visited different ports each week. The series had an initial test run on ABC affiliate WFIL-TV, Philadelphia, in early 1951, prior to moving to WJZ-TV, New York, for the network premiere.

SABRINA AND THE GROOVIE GOOLIES

initial broadcast dates: 9/12/70–9/4/71, CBS, 60 minutes; title changed to Sabrina, the Teen-age Witch *for telecasting 9/1/71–9/1/73, 30 minutes*

Spin-off from Filmation's "Archies" cartoon series featuring a friendly teen-age witch who also appeared on CBS's news inserts *In the Know* (1970–71).

SAFARI TO ADVENTURE

syndicated: 1971

Documentaries on the animal kingdom narrated by Bill Burrud. 30 minutes.

SAMSON AND GOLIATH

broadcast dates: 9/9/67–8/31/68, NBC

30-minute Hanna-Barbera cartoon series about a young boy who could transform himself into a superhero using his magic wristlets, and whose dog Goliath transformed into a mighty lion. Voice of Samson: Tim Matthieson. A segment featuring The Space Kidettes was included each week.

SATELLITE POLICE

see *Space Patrol*

SATURDAY AT THE ZOO

premiere local broadcast: 9/23/50, WJZ-TV, New York
network broadcast dates: 10/7/50–12/23/50, ABC

30-minute zoo program hosted by William Bridges. The series was a cowinner (with *Zoo Parade*) of the 1950 Peabody Award for best children's show. It was canceled before receiving the honor, probably the first example in television of an award-winning show enjoying only a short broadcast period.

SATURDAY PLAYHOUSE

broadcast dates: 9/28/57–6/28/58, CBS

Saturday morning reruns of dramas originally aired on *Schlitz Playhouse*. Premiere telecast featured Eddie Albert in a Western drama titled "Too Many Nelsons." 30 minutes.

SATURDAY PROM

broadcast dates: 10/15/60–4/1/61, NBC

Late-afternoon dance party hosted by Merv Griffin and featuring the music of Si Zentner and his orchestra. Premiere telecast presented guests Anita Bryant, Conway Twitty, and Johnny and the Hurricanes. 30 minutes.

SATURDAY SUPERSTAR MOVIE

see *The ABC Saturday Superstar Movie*

SCHOOLHOUSE ROCK

premiere broadcast season: 1972–73, ABC

Schoolhouse Rock is the umbrella title for the informational series telecast in various slots on a rotating basis throughout the weekend children's programming schedule on ABC. *Multiplication Rock* (prebroadcast title was *Multiplication Is*) initiated the first season with 3-minute films that taught multiplication tables and the characteristics of numbers by using segments titled "Zero My Hero," "Three Is a Magic Number," "Figure Eight," "Naughty Number Nine," and "Little Twelve Toes." *Grammar Rock* premiered 9/8/73 with three ½-minute films designed to teach graphically the parts of speech; segments included "Conjunction Junction" and "Verbs—That's Where the Action Is." *American Rock* premiered 9/7/74 with five new 3-minute segments related to history and government, including a musical look at the preamble to the United States Constitution and an animated look at how a bill proceeds through the Congress. *Schoolhouse Rock* was aired four times on Saturdays and twice on Sundays, for a total of more than 350 times during the 1974–75 season. In 1975–76 and 1976–77 the three elements of the series were expanded to twenty-eight programs, with special emphasis on *American Rock* and its bicentennial orientation. In 1977–78 the series expanded again to thirty-one programs with the addition of *Science Rock* and its segments on science, health, and the environment. It was telecast more than 300 times during the year. In 1978–79 the series was expanded to thirty-four programs with the addition of *Body Rock*, and was telecast four times on Saturdays and once on Sundays, for a total of more than 300 airings during the year. For 1979–80 three more segments of *Science Rock* were added dealing with gravity, outer space, and energy and its conservation. *Body Machine* (formerly *Body Rock*) examined systems of the human body. The series was telecast three times on Saturdays, once on Sundays during the year. *Schoolhouse Rock* was produced by Scholastic Rock, Inc., a division of McCaffrey and McCall, Inc. Emmy Awards, 1975–76, and 1979–80.

SCOOBY'S ALL-STAR LAFF-A-LYMPICS

see *Scooby-Doo, Where Are You?*

SCOOBY'S ALL-STARS

see *Scooby-Doo, Where Are You?*

SCOOBY AND SCRAPPY-DOO

see *Scooby-Doo, Where Are You?*

THE SCOOBY-DOO/DYNOMUTT HOUR

see *Scooby-Doo, Where Are You?*

SCOOBY-DOO, WHERE ARE YOU?

premiere broadcast: 9/13/69, CBS, 30 minutes
revised: 9/9/72, CBS, as The New Scooby-Doo Movies, *60 minutes*
revised: 9/11/76, ABC, as The Scooby-Doo/Dynomutt Hour, *60 minutes*
revised: 9/10/77, ABC, as Scooby's All-Star Laff-A-Lympics, *two hours*
revised: 9/9/78, ABC, as Scooby's All-Stars, *90 minutes*
revised: 9/22/79, ABC, as Scooby and Scrappy-Doo, *30 minutes*

Hanna-Barbera cartoon productions featuring the many adventures of a reluctant Great Dane named Scooby who became involved in activities of four southern California high school students as they delved into mysterious situations. Don Messick provided the voice of the chickenhearted Scooby-Doo. Dynomutt segments in 1976 featured tales of a robot dog wonder. *Scooby's All-Star Laff-A-Lympics* was the first two-hour Saturday morning network cartoon series and presented forty-five Hanna-Barbera characters. A brave nephew named Scrappy-Doo was introduced in 1979.

SEA HUNT

syndicated: 1958

30-minute live-action series with Lloyd Bridges as former Navy frogman Mike Nelson, who was available for hire to explore the oceans for treasures and adventures.

SEALAB 2020

initial broadcast dates: 9/9/72–9/1/73, NBC

30-minute Hanna-Barbera cartoon series about an ocean laboratory where 250 men, women, and children lived and worked. Voice of Dr. Paul Williams: Ross Martin.

SEARCH AND RESCUE: THE ALPHA TEAM

premiere broadcast: 9/10/77, NBC

30-minute live-action adventure series about widower Bob Donell (Michael J. Reynolds) and his two teen-age children Jim (Michael Tough) and Katy (Donann Cavin). Together the trio rescued endangered species and trained wild animals such as Simba, a circus lion.

THE SECRET FILES OF CAPTAIN VIDEO

see *Captain Video and His Video Rangers*

THE SECRET LIVES OF WALDO KITTY

broadcast dates: 9/6/75–9/4/76, NBC

30-minute cartoon and live-action series about a cat and a bully bulldog. Waldo's voice: Howard Morris, Tyrone the bulldog: Allan Melvin.

SECRET SQUIRREL

initial broadcast dates: 10/2/65–9/2/67, NBC; also a segment on The Atom Ant/Secret Squirrel Show *9/9/67–9/7/68, NBC.*

30-minute Hanna-Barbera cartoon adventure program with Secret Squirrel as agent 000 and Morocco Mole playing a Peter Lorre–type sidekick. See also *The Atom Ant/Secret Squirrel Show.*

THE SECRETS OF ISIS

premiere broadcast: 9/17/77, CBS; initially aired as a regular segment on The Shazam!/Isis Hour *(premiere 9/6/75), also CBS*

30-minute live-action series produced by Filmation in which top-flight commercial performer JoAnna Cameron played high school teacher Andrea Thomas, a mortal imbued with the powers of the ancient Egyptian goddess Isis. Costarring Brian Cutler as Rick and Cindy Lee as Joanna. Andrea's pet crow was named Tut. See *The Shazam!/Isis Hour.*

SERGEANT PRESTON OF THE YUKON

prime time broadcast dates: 9/29/55–9/25/58, CBS; seventy-eight black and white shows were syndicated 10/58; twenty-six new shows filmed in color starting 11/15/58 also syndicated

30-minute live-action series with Richard Simmons starring as William Preston, a Canadian Mountie sergeant who patrolled the rugged Northwest to search for his father's murderer and later other criminals. Preston's horse: Rex. His malamute dog: Yukon King.

SESAME STREET

premiere weekday broadcast: 11/10/69, NET, PBS, repeated Saturdays in many markets

60-minute award-winning educational series produced by The Children's Television Workshop and featuring live actors, cartoons, Jim Henson's Muppet characters, and costumed figures. Episodes have taught basic reading, comprehension, language and math skills, and introduced segments on learning disabilities and Spanish. The cast has included: Bob McGrath (Bob), Roscoe Orman (Gordon), Loretta Long (Susan), Willie Lee (Mr. Hooper), Northern J. Calloway (David), Emilio Delgado (Luis), and Sonia Manzano (Maria).

THE SHARI LEWIS SHOW

broadcast dates: 10/1/60–9/28/63, NBC

30-minute series featuring the multitalented Shari Lewis and her puppet characters, including Lamb Chop, Hush Puppy, and Charlie Horse. Ronald Radd was Mr. Goodfellow, and Jackie Warner was Jump Pup, the Saint Bernard. This production replaced *Howdy Doody* on NBC. Ventriloquist Lewis had appeared previously on *Captain Kangaroo* and her own local shows in New York, including *Shari and Her Friends, Hi Mom*, and *Shariland*.

THE SHARI SHOW

prime time premiere broadcast: 10/7/75, NBC's five owned and operated stations; rebroadcast on Saturdays in 1977

A series of 30-minute telecasts in which Shari and her puppets worked for the BBS (Bearly Broadcasting Studios). More than twenty puppets, including Captain Person and Lamb Chop, were seen in this series produced at WMAQ-TV, Chicago, by Penthouse Productions, Inc., and Tarcher Productions.

SHAZAM!

premiere broadcast: 9/7/74, CBS
season premiere: 9/6/75, CBS,as a segment on The Shazam!/Isis Hour, *60 minutes*
return: 1/5/80, CBS

Filmation's 30-minute live-action series derived from the comic-book character Billy Batson, who transforms himself into superhero Captain Marvel by saying the word "Shazam!" In this moralistic series, Batson (Michael Gray) is depicted as a young radio broadcaster who has been chosen by the five immortal elders (Solomon, Mercury, Zeus, Achilles, and Atlas) to be the world's mightiest mortal. Teen-ager Batson is advised and accompanied by Mentor, an adult portrayed by Les Tremayne. His super alter ego was portrayed by two actors: Jackson Bostwick for the first season, followed by John Davey. The elders are portrayed as animated characters when they communicate with Batson and Mentor. See also *The Secrets of Isis*.

THE SHAZAM!/ISIS HOUR

broadcast dates: 9/6/75–9/3/77, CBS

Filmation's 60-minute live-action adventure series that combined one 30-minute segment each of both *Shazam!* and *Isis*, with each continuing in rebroadcasts after the close of this program. See also *Shazam!* and *The Secrets of Isis*.

SHAZZAN!

initial broadcast dates: 9/9/67–9/6/69, CBS

30-minute cartoon series about a pair of siblings (Chuck and Nancy) who are transported back into the Arabian Nights by a sixty-foot-tall powerful genie named Shazzan.

SHEENA, QUEEN OF THE JUNGLE

syndicated: 1955

30-minute adventure series featuring Irish McCalla as an airplane-crash survivor who grows up in the jungle and successfully defends her territory, friends, and natives with only a spear. The production was filmed in Mexico.

SHENANIGANS

broadcast dates: 9/26/64–12/18/65, ABC

30-minute game show hosted by Stubby Kaye. Two children competed on a three-dimensional game board with advancement contingent upon the successful completion of a stunt or response to a question. The production originated as a local weekday show on WPIX-TV, New York, in 1952, hosted by Bob Quigley. Kenny Williams was the announcer.

SIGMUND AND THE SEA MONSTERS

initial broadcast dates: 9/8/73–10/18/75, NBC

Live-action Sid and Marty Krofft production about an unhappy but friendly sea monster named Sigmund who befriended two California youngsters after his sea monster clan disowned him because he couldn't scare humans. Cast: Sigmund Ooz (Billy Barty); Johnny Stuart (Johnny Whitaker), Scott Stuart (Scott Kolden), Zelda Marshall (Mary Wickes), Sheldon, a sea genie (Rip Taylor), and Miss Eddels (Margaret Hamilton). 30 minutes.

SING A DOODLE

syndicated: 1953

15-minute filmed series with seventeen-year-old Joan Lee doing line drawings that illustrated songs. Also appearing were Lazy Bill Huggins and children from the studio audience.

THE SKATEBIRDS

premiere broadcast: 9/10/77, CBS

60-minute Hanna-Barbera live-action and cartoon series hosted by three large costumed characters—a woodpecker, a pelican, and a penguin—constantly pursued by Scat Cat. Additional segments included cartoon antics of the space-age Robonic Stooges, Wonder Wheels, Woofer and Wimper, and a live-action science fiction cliff-hanger called "Mystery Island."

SKY KING

initial Sunday broadcasts: 9/6/51–10/12/52, NBC
Saturday morning return: 11/8/52–9/12/53, ABC, alternating weekly with Junior Rodeo, Hail the Champ, *and other shows, thereafter syndicated*

30-minute contemporary adventure series starring Kirby Grant as aviator Sky King and Gloria Winters as his niece, Penny. For the first season only Ron Haggerty joined King in the copilot seat of the *Songbird* as his nephew Clipper. Action for the 130 episodes was set in, around, and above the Flying Crown Ranch in California, owned by the flier-lawman.

THE SKYHAWKS

initial broadcast dates: 9/6/69–9/4/71, ABC

30-minute cartoon series about the Wilsons, a daredevil globe-trotting family in the business, as Skyhawks, Inc., of rescuing people. Music for this series was composed by *Kukla, Fran and Ollie* musical director Jack Fascinato.

SMILIN' ED'S GANG

Saturday evening premiere: 8/26/50, NBC, alternating weekly with Say It with Acting
initial Saturday morning broadcast dates: 8/11/51–4/11/53, CBS (replaced by Rod Brown of the Rocket Rangers)
return broadcast dates: 8/22/53–4/16/55, ABC
revised: 8/20/55, NBC, as Andy's Gang

30-minute TV version of the old Buster Brown radio show that featured the storytelling of Smilin' Ed McConnell. Smilin' Ed conversed in the studio with Froggy the Gremlin, Midnight the Cat, and Squeeky the Mouse, as well as introducing the filmed adventures that were a segment of each show. The series was sponsored on both radio and TV by Buster Brown shoes. Filmed adventures featured Nino Marcel as both Little Fox and Gunga Ram, an American Indian and an Asian Indian, respectively. Vito Scotti played Gunga's companion, Rama, in the tales from India. Voices included McConnell as Froggy, June Foray as Midnight, Jerry Maren as Buster Brown (Maren also played Boko on *The Magic Lady*), and Bud Tollefson as Tige. In 1955, Andy Devine became host of the show, with little change in format but with the title changed to *Andy's Gang*. McConnell died in 1954. See *Andy's Gang*.

THE SMITHSONIAN

initial broadcast dates: 10/15/66–4/8/67, NBC
Sunday evening reruns: 6/25/67–8/27/67, NBC

30-minute educational series that focused on the resources and research of the Smithsonian Institution based in Washington, D.C. The program was hosted by Bill Ryan, and created, produced, and written by Craig Fisher, the creator and producer of *Exploring*.

THE SMOKEY BEAR SHOW

initial broadcast dates: 9/9/69–9/5/70, ABC
Sunday return: 9/13/70–9/12/71, ABC

30-minute cartoon series about Smokey's efforts to fight forest fires and protect the inhabitants of the woods.

SNIPETS

syndicated 1975

Seventy 60-second instructional inserts produced successively by Kaiser Broadcasting and Field Communications. Peabody Award, 1975.

THE SOUPY SALES SHOW

initial weekday broadcast dates: 7/4/55–8/26/55, ABC; 15-minute summer replacement series for Kukla, Fran and Ollie *from WXYZ-TV, Detroit*
initial Saturday broadcast dates: 10/3/59–6/25/60, 8/27/60–4/1/61, ABC, as Lunch With Soupy Sales
syndicated: 1966–68, produced at WNEW-TV, New York, where it aired as a local show 1964–1966;
1979, produced in Los Angeles

30-minute live (later taped) comedy series hosted by the pie-throwing comedian and assisted by his puppets White Fang and Black Tooth (seen only by their paws), and Pookie and Marilyn Monwolf. Clyde Adler assisted both on and off camera.

SPACE ACADEMY

initial broadcast dates: 9/10/77–9/1/79, CBS

30-minute science fiction series produced by Filmation. Jonathan Harris starred as Commander Isaac Gampu, who supervised the training of space cadets in the year 3732. Cast included Rick Carrott as Captain Chris Gentry, Pamelyn Ferdin as Cadet Laura Gentry, Brian Tochi as Tee Gar Sume, and Eric Greene as Loki. Peepo was the small, mobile robot that appeared later on Filmation's *Jason of Star Command.*

SPACE GHOST

initial broadcast dates: 9/10/66–9/7/68, CBS

30-minute Hanna-Barbera cartoon series about an invisible outer-space crime fighter (voice of Gary Owens). Included also were segments about Dino Boy, and the series was syndicated under the title *Space Ghost and Dino Boy.*

SPACE GHOST AND DINO BOY

see *Space Ghost*

SPACE KIDETTES

initial broadcast dates: 9/10/66–9/2/67, NBC

30-minute Hanna-Barbera cartoon series about a group of children fighting evil in outer space. Voices include Daws Butler, Don Messick, and Janet Waldo.

SPACE PATROL

weekday network premiere: 9/11/50, ABC;
Sunday broadcast dates: 1/21/51–6/3/51, 9/9/51–6/1/52, ABC
initial Saturday broadcast dates: 6/9/51–9/1/51, ABC
return broadcast dates: 6/7/52–7/3/54, 9/4/54–2/26/55, ABC

15-minute live daily show and 30-minute Saturday production starring Ed Kemmer as Commander Buzz Corry and Lyn Osborn as Cadet Happy. The science fiction series set in the twenty-first century originated as a local show on KECA-TV, Los Angeles. It is claimed to be the first West Coast TV show to have a national airing on Saturday morning. Cast also included Virginia Hewitt as Carol Karlyle, Nina Bara as Tonga, Bela Kovacs as Prince Baccarratti, and Jack Narz as the announcer. Mike Mosser was the producer. The series was also syndicated in some markets as *Satellite Police.*

THE SPACE SENTINELS

initial broadcast dates: 9/10/77–9/28/78, NBC

30-minute cartoon series about Mercury, Hercules, and Astraed, three teen-age superheroes who returned to earth with fantastic powers to serve as guardians of the human race and the environment. Original title: *The Young Sentinels.*

SPEED BUGGY

initial broadcast dates: 9/8/73–8/31/74, CBS
reruns: 9/6/75–9/4/76, ABC; 2/4/78–9/2/78, CBS

30-minute Hanna-Barbera cartoon series about three teen-agers traveling around the country in their remote-controlled car (voice of Mel Blanc).

SPEED RACER

syndicated: 1967

30-minute action cartoon produced by Mushi Productions of Japan. Speed Racer, the main character, drove his "Special Formula Five" to violent adventures with his girl friend, Trixie; his brother, Spridal; and his monkey, Chim Chim, in the passenger seats.

SPIDER-MAN

initial broadcast dates: 9/9/67–8/30/69, ABC
Sunday return: 3/22/70–9/6/70, ABC

30-minute cartoon series based on the web-slinging Marvel comic-book character, Peter Parker, who, after being bitten by a radioactive spider, assumes extraordinary powers. In 1978 a limited prime time series starred Nicholas Hammond on CBS, with Ellen Bry added to the cast for the 1978–79 season as Parker's girl friend.

SPIDER-WOMAN

initial broadcast dates: 9/22/79–3/1/80, ABC

30-minute cartoon/adventure series produced by DePatie-Freleng. Episodes concerned the exploits of a female named Jessica who could transform herself into a superhero. Exeuctive producer was Marvel Comics kingpin Stan Lee.

STAR TREK

initial broadcast dates: 9/8/73– 8/30/75, NBC

30-minute animated cartoon version of Gene Roddenberry's prime time science fiction series. This Filmation spin-off featured the voices of *Star Trek*'s original cast (William Shatner, Leonard Nimoy, DeForest Kelly, James Doohan, George Takei, Majel Barrett, Walter Koenig, and Nichelle Nichols) reproduced in their cartoon versions. Emmy Award, 1974–1975.

STEVE DONOVAN, WESTERN RANGER

syndicated: 1951

30-minute action-adventure series with Douglas Kennedy portraying a Texas Ranger and Eddy Waller as his sidekick, Ranger Rusty. Produced by Jack Chertok. Thirty-nine episodes. In 1955, the series was resyndicated as *Steve Donovan, Western Marshal.*

STINGRAY

syndicated: 1965

Gerry and Sylvia Anderson's "Supermarionation" puppet series about Troy Tempest, pilot of an undersea transport, and his twenty-first-century assignments with the World Aquanaut Security Patrol. 30 minutes.

THE STORYBOOK SQUARES

broadcast dates: 1/4/69–8/20/69, NBC

Saturday morning and weekday children's version of *Hollywood Squares.* In this spin-off series, Peter Marshall hosted regular guests who dressed as nursery-rhyme characters. For example, Paul Lynde portrayed Georgie Porgie, Rose Marie was Little Bo Peep, Marty Allen was Humpty Dumpty, and Joan Rivers played Little Red Riding Hood. The program had weekday runs, two weeks yearly, in the *Hollywood Squares* time slot.

THE STU ERWIN SHOW: THE TROUBLE WITH FATHER

prime time premiere: 10/21/50, ABC
Saturday premiere: 10/13/51, ABC

30-minute situation comedy set in the small town of Hamilton where high school principal Stu coped with the many trials and tribulations of his school and family. Also featured: Jan (June Collyer), Joyce (Ann Todd), Jackie (Sheila James), Marty Clark (Martin Milner), and Willie (Willie Best). Also titled *Life with the Erwins, The New Stu Erwin Show,* and *The Trouble with Father.*

SUPER CIRCUS

Sunday premiere broadcast: 1/16/49 on the ABC East Coast network, shown in other markets on Saturdays via kinescopes
revised: 12/25/55–6/3/56, ABC, with new cast

60-minute live (except kinescoped) circus show that had originated as a Chicago radio program. Claude Kirchner was the ringmaster and baton twirler/band leader Mary Hartline was the show's heartthrob. Appearing as clowns were Cliff Soubier, Nick Francis, and Bardy Patton. A New York–based production replaced the Chicago edition in 1955, with Jerry Colonna and Sandra Wirth cast as the headliners. Jerry Bergen and the Baron Twins appeared as clowns.

SUPER FRIENDS

initial broadcast dates: 9/8/73–8/30/75
return: 2/21/76–9/4/76, ABC
revised: 9/10/77–9/2/78, 9/9/78–9/8/79, and 9/15/79, ABC

60-minute Hanna-Barbera cartoon series featuring the adventures of National Periodical Publications comic-book characters including Superman, Batman and Robin, Wonderwoman, Aquaman, and two teen-age characters, Wendy and Marvin. The story advisor was Dr. Haim Ginott, author of *Between Parent and Child* (New York: Macmillan, 1965). Production was revised 9/10/77 as *The All-New Super Friends Hour* with added emphasis of prosocial messages, and on 9/9/78 as *Challenge of the Super Friends*, adding health and safety tips. It was expanded to 90 minutes 11/4/78, ABC.

THE SUPER GLOBETROTTERS

initial broadcast dates: 9/22/79–12/1/79, NBC

30-minute Hanna-Barbera cartoon series with the famed basketball team cast as comedic superheroes. The series was revised 12/8/79–4/5/80, 60 minutes, as *The Godzilla/Globetrotters Adventure Hour*. See also *The Harlem Globetrotters*.

SUPER PRESIDENT

broadcast dates: 9/16/67–9/14/68, NBC

30-minute DePatie-Freleng cartoon series about U.S. President James Norcross who, because of a cosmic storm, possessed amazing superpowers.

THE SUPER SIX

initial broadcast dates: 9/10/66–9/6/69, NBC

30-minute DePatie-Freleng and Mirlsch-Rich cartoon adventures of Super Service, Inc., a superhero force available for hire. Also included were segments of Super Bwoing, a guitar-strumming superhero.

SUPER WITCH

initial broadcast dates: 11/12/77–1/28/78, NBC

30-minute Filmation cartoon comedy adventures about Sabrina, the Teen-age Witch, who had previously appeared in the "Archies" and various spin-off shows. Jane Webb dubbed the voice of Sabrina. Also appearing were Archie, Betty, Jughead, Veronica, and The Groovie Goolies. See *Archie* listings.

SUPERMAN

syndicated: 1950s

Seventeen fully animated cartoons produced between 1941 and 1943 by Paramount Pictures and Fleischer Studios. Titles: "The Mad Scientist," "The Mechanical Monsters," "Billion Dollar Limited," "Destruction, Inc.," "Electronic Earthquake," "Showdown," "Terror on the Midway," "Arctic Giant," "The Bulleteers," "The Eleventh Hour," "The Japoteurs," "The Magnetic Telescope," "Volcano," "Jungle Drums," "Secret Agent," "The Mummy Strikes," and "Underground World." Voices of Superman and Clark Kent: Bud Collyer. See also *The Adventures of Superman* and *The New Adventures of Superman*.

THE SUPERMAN-AQUAMAN HOUR OF ADVENTURE

initial broadcast dates: 9/9/67–9/7/68, CBS

Filmation's repackaging of both Superman and Aquaman episodes into a 60-minute show. Other comic book heroes that appeared on a rotating basis were the Flash, the Green Lantern, Hawkman, the Teen Titans, the Atom, and characters from the Justice League. See also *The Batman-Superman Hour of Adventure*.

SUSAN'S SHOW

broadcast dates: 5/4/57–1/18/58, CBS

30-minute fantasy series with twelve-year-old Susan Heinkel and her terrier Rusty taking weekly trips to various wonderlands. The series had originated as a local WBBM-TV Chicago show in 1956 called *Susie's Show*. Also included were songs, stories, and Popeye cartoons. Produced by Paul Frumkin and Frank Atlass.

SYLVESTER AND TWEETY

initial broadcast dates: 9/11/76–9/3/77, CBS

A 30-minute potpourri of Warner Brothers theatrical cartoons featuring the ever-hungry cat Sylvester and his ever-agile prey, Tweety the canary. Also included were cartoon episodes of Porky Pig and Elmer Fudd.

T

TAKE A GIANT STEP

broadcast dates: 9/11/71–8/26/72, NBC

60-minute discussion of pressing personal, philosophical, political, and social issues with teen-agers and so-called "giants" from specific fields. See also *Talking with a Giant*.

TALES OF THE 77TH BENGAL LANCERS

prime time broadcast dates: 10/21/56–6/2/57, NBC; thereafter syndicated

30-minute live-action adventure about the British forces occupying India. Philip Carey and Warren Stevens starred as Lieutenants Rhodes and Storm.

TALES OF THE TEXAS RANGERS

Saturday morning premiere: 9/3/55, CBS
prime time broadcast dates: 10/58–5/59, ABC

Western adventures set in contemporary Texas and the 1880s. Versions alternated and both starred Willard Parker and Harry Lauter as rangers Jace Pearson and Clay Morgan. 30 minutes.

TALKING WITH A GIANT

broadcast dates: 9/9/72–9/1/73, NBC

30-minute successor program to *Take a Giant Step*, in which teen-agers talked with experts in various fields of interest.

TARZAN, LORD OF THE JUNGLE

premiere broadcast: 9/11/76, CBS

30-minute Filmation cartoon version of Edgar Rice Burroughs's novels about the ape man, with emphasis placed on ecological themes for this production. This series became a segment of *The Batman-Tarzan Adventure Hour* in 1977 and of *Tarzan and the Super 7* in 1978.

TARZAN AND THE SUPER 7

premiere broadcast: 9/9/78, CBS

90-minute (1978) and 60-minute (1979) Filmation productions combining both cartoon and live-action segments. Animated portions of the show included Tarzan, Batman and Robin, Web Woman, Super Stretch and Micro Woman, Manta and Moray, and the Freedom Force. "Jason of Star Command" was introduced as a live-action segment and in 1979 became an independent series. See also *Jason of Star Command*.

TENNESSEE TUXEDO AND HIS TALES

initial broadcast dates: 9/28/63–9/3/66, CBS

30-minute cartoon series about a sarcastic penguin (Tennessee Tuxedo) and his friends. Also featured were reruns of episodes from *King Leonardo and His Short Subjects*.

TERRY AND THE PIRATES

syndicated: 1952

30-minute live-action series based on the Milton Caniff comic strip about a U.S. Air Force colonel's adventures in the Orient. John Baer starred, with William Tracy as Hotshot Charlie, Jack Kruschen as Chopstick Joe, Gloria Saunders as The Dragon Lady, and both Mari Blanchard and Sandra Spence in the role of Burma. DuMont's flagship station, WABD-TV, New York, telecast the series in prime time 11/25/52–6/23/53, alternating weekly with *Death Valley Days*.

TERRYTOONS

syndicated: 1956

156 Terrytoon black-and-white theatrical cartoons syndicated by CBS-TV Film Sales, featuring Farmer Al Falfa, Puddy the Pup, and Kiko the Kangaroo. Other Terrytoon animated cartoons were telecast on *The Mighty Mouse Playhouse* from its premiere date in 1955.

THESE ARE THE DAYS

initial broadcast dates: 9/7/74–8/30/75, ABC
Sunday return: 9/7/75–9/5/76, ABC

30-minute dramatic cartoon series about a turn-of-the-century rural American family dealing with their own growing pains and the changing world. Voices included June

Lockhart, Mickey Dolenz, June Foray, Don Messick, Vic Perrin, William Schallert, Janet Waldo, and Paul Winchell.

THE THINK PINK PANTHER SHOW

see *The Pink Panther Show*

30 MINUTES

premiere broadcast: 9/16/78, CBS

30-minute news-magazine show, like its parent program *60 Minutes* but aimed at teen-agers. The CBS News–produced series, anchored by Christopher Glenn and Betsy Aaron, was designed to present controversial issues (abortion, unwed parenting, suicide, juvenile delinquency) as well as features and profiles. Legal advice provided by Patricia McGuire. Executive producer: Joel Heller. Emmy Award, 1979–80.

THE THREE STOOGES

syndicated: 1950s

Recycled live-action motion-picture-comedy shorts starring the slapstick trio (Moe Howard, Larry Fine, and at various times Shemp Howard, Curly Howard, Joe DeRita, Joe Besser). In the 1950s the films generally were introduced on local broadcasts by live hosts. Later, episodes usually aired without wraparounds. Cartoon spin-off: *The Robonic Stooges.*

3-2-1 CONTACT

premiere weekday broadcast: 1/14/80, PBS, with rebroadcasts Saturdays in some markets

30-minute science series aimed at eight- to twelve-year-olds and designed to stimulate an awareness of and an interest in the world around us. The sixty-five programs offered the first season were produced by the Children's Television Workshop, the creators of *Sesame Street* and *The Electric Company.* Utilizing a general theme each program, the series presented documentary films, location footage, live action, animation, and electronic special effects to investigate some aspect of science and technology. "The Bloodhound Gang" was a special segment based on the adventures of three children who work for a detective agency and track down the answers to scientific questions.

THUNDER

initial broadcast dates: 9/10/77–9/2/78, NBC

30-minute live-action series about a feisty black stallion tamed by an eight-year-old girl and the boy next door. Produced by *Fury*'s producer and original writer, Irving Cummings, and Charles Marion.

THUNDERBIRDS

syndicated: 1966

A "Supermarionation" science fiction puppet series created and produced by Gerry and Sylvia Anderson. The 60-minute production concerned the exploits of the Tracy family, members of the International Rescue, a worldwide rescue team.

TIM McCOY

syndicated: 1955

Thirty-nine 15-minute made-for-TV Western tales produced by MPTV Syndication Corporation. The episodes featured McCoy appearing in a short stand-up before each film. The series had originated as a live KTLA-TV program in Los Angeles, February 17, 1950.

TIME FOR BEANY

see *Beany and Cecil*

TIME OUT

premiere broadcast season: 1979, NBC

75-second spots on physical fitness, health, and nutrition, produced by NBC Sports. Three telecasts were scheduled for each Saturday morning. Some segments were hosted by Shari Lewis and her hand puppets.

TIMMY AND LASSIE

see *Lassie*

TOM AND JERRY

initial broadcast dates: 9/25/65–9/3/66, CBS, thereafter syndicated

Hanna-Barbera's fast-paced, action-packed theatrical cartoons produced at MGM during the 1940s. Episodes were also syndicated, and new adventures were filmed for telecast on ABC's *The New Tom and Jerry/Grape Ape Show* (60 minutes, premiere 9/6/75) and *The Tom and Jerry/Grape Ape/Mumbly Show* (60 minutes, premiere 9/11/76. Mumbly, a detective character in the latter production, was a snickering dog who sniffed out villains. The Grape Ape, meanwhile, was a giant purple gorilla described variously as thirty to forty feet tall. See also *The Great Grape Ape Show.*

THE TOM AND JERRY/GRAPE APE/MUMBLY SHOW

see *Tom and Jerry*

TOM CORBETT, SPACE CADET

premiere M/W/F broadcast: 10/2/50, CBS, 15 minutes
return M/W/F broadcast dates: 1/1/51–9/26/52, ABC, 15 minutes
Saturday evening broadcast dates: 7/7/51–9/1/51, NBC (two kinescopes of ABC 15-minute weekday serial were combined and edited into 30-minute edition)
initial Saturday morning broadcast dates: 9/12/53–5/22/54, DuMont, alternating weekly with The Secret Files of Captain Video
return: 12/11/54–6/25/55, NBC

Live-action science fiction series performed live in New York on both TV and radio, with Frank Thomas playing the twenty-fourth-century space cadet. Costars included Michael Harvey (Captain Strong), Jan Merlin (Cadet Roger Manning), Margaret Garland (Dr. Joan Dale), Jack Grimes (Commander T. J. Fissell), Al Markhim (Astro), plus guest appearances by Jack Lord, Jack Klugman, Tom Poston, and Jack Weston. Series technical advisor was Dr. Willy Ley. Corbett's rocket ship was the *Polaris.*

THE TOMFOOLERY SHOW

initial broadcast dates: 9/12/70–9/4/71, NBC

30-minute cartoon series based on the work of Lewis Carroll and Edward Lear, with such characters as the Worrying Whizzing Wasp and the Ornamental Ostrich. The content included stories, riddles, limericks, songs, and jokes.

TONY THE PONY

syndicated: 1979

30-minute live-action fantasy series combining young actors with oversized puppets. Randy Yothers, Jr. (also billed as Poindexter) portrayed Jonathan, a youngster who, with his magical pony, experienced various relevant lessons. Premore Productions, Inc. produced the series.

TOOTSIE HIPPODROME

initial Sunday broadcast dates: 2/3/52–6/28/53, ABC
Saturday morning return: 8/29/53–1/30/54, ABC

Variety show featuring an assortment of circus, animal, and Western acts, plus telephone quizzes, games, and commercial pitches for Tootsie Roll candies. John Reed King, Whitey Carson, and Boyd Heath all hosted the first series, with Carson returning to emcee the Saturday version. Characters appearing on the show included Captain Tootsie, the Sheriff, Big Jim, Cactus Pete, and cowgirl Tootsie Candy. Sunday telecasts were originally fifteen minutes, expanding to thirty minutes 2/1/53. The Saturday series was thirty minutes throughout its run.

TOP CAT

prime time broadcast dates: 9/27/61–9/26/62, ABC
initial Saturday broadcast dates: 10/6/62–3/30/63, ABC
return: 4/3/65–12/31/66, NBC, thereafter syndicated

30-minute Hanna-Barbera cartoon adaptation of the Sgt. Bilko series, with Arnold Stang as the voice of T. C. and Bilko regular Maurice Gosfield as the voice of sidekick Benny the Ball. Also featured were the voices of Marvin Kaplan (Choo Choo) and Allen Jenkins (Officer Dibble).

TOYLAND EXPRESS

syndicated: 11/55–12/55, 11/56–12/56

15-minute weekday and Saturday film production hyping items available for Christmastime. The series was produced by the Toy Guidance Council and was hosted by Paul Winchell (1955) and Jimmy Nelson (1956). Both emcees also utilized their dummies. Sixty stations telecast the thirteen programs in the 1955 series.

TREASURY MEN IN ACTION

prime time broadcast dates: 9/11/50–9/30/55, ABC, NBC, thereafter syndicated

30-minute live-action dramatic anthology based on U.S. Treasury Department files. Kinescopes were syndicated as *T-Men in Action* and *Federal Men*. Walter Greaza starred as The Chief.

THE TROUBLE WITH FATHER

see *The Stu Erwin Show*

TRUE STORY

broadcast dates: 3/23/57–9/9/61, ABC

30-minute dramatic anthology series hosted by teen-ager Kathi Norris. Weekly stories were presented live from New York and featured such actors as Lois Nettleton, Philip Abbott, and Lorne Greene.

26 MEN

syndicated: 1958

Western adventure series set in Arizona Territory at the turn of the century. Episodes presumably were based on the actual files of the twenty-six lawmen who constituted the Arizona Rangers. Series star: Tris Coffin.

TWO GIRLS NAMED SMITH

broadcast dates: 1/20/51–10/13/51, ABC

30-minute situation comedy about two country girls who tried for fame, fortune, and love in New York as models. Babs Smith was portrayed by Peggy Ann Garner and later, Marcia Henderson, and Peggy Smith by Peggy French.

U

UFO

syndicated: 1972

60-minute live-action science fiction series produced in England by Gerry and Sylvia Anderson. Contemporary adventures depicted the work of a superscientific agency called S.H.A.D.O. as it maintained a secretive war against the vanguard of an Earth-invading alien force.

ULTRAMAN

syndicated: 1967

Japanese live-action series set on twenty-first-century Earth when a grateful alien, saved by an earthling, gives his friend the ability to transform himself into Ultraman by taking a special capsule. 30 minutes.

THE UNCLE AL SHOW

broadcast dates: 10/18/58–9/19/59, ABC

Music, variety, and storytelling program with Al Lewis as the friendly uncle-host, Wanda Lewis as Captain Windy, and Janet Greene as Cinderella. The 60-minute series also featured Larry Smith and his hand puppets.

UNCLE CROC'S BLOCK

broadcast dates: 9/6/75–2/14/76, ABC

Live-action and cartoon spoof of children's TV show hosts with Charles Nelson Reilly as the irreverent Uncle Croc. Jonathan Harris costarred as Mr. Bitterbottom, and Alfie Wise appeared as Rabbit Ears. In addition to the costumed characters, editions featured cartoon adventures including Fraidy Cat, Wacky and Packy, and M*U*S*H. Produced by Filmation in 60-minute and, from 10/25/75, 30-minute programs.

UNCLE JOHNNY COONS

see *Life With Uncle Johnny Coons*

UNCLE MISTLETOE

syndicated: 1952

15-minute puppet film series produced for television and distributed by Kling Studios. The twenty-six episodes were telecast on WGN-TV, Chicago, for Marshall Field department stores, in addition to being syndicated in other markets. Marshall Field sponsored the series when it originated as a local show on WENR-TV, Chicago, for the 1948 Christmas-merchandising season. The series was renewed locally in Chicago, expanding from the annual Christmas-season broadcasts to longer cycles through much of the year. Johnny Coons supplied the puppet voices, and both Jennifer Holt and Doris Larson starred, in turn, as the show's hostess and only human member. In the syndicated version, Corny Peeples and Elmira Roessler provided voices for the hand puppets of Pat Percy and Helen York.

UNDERDOG

initial broadcast dates: 10/3/64–9/3/66, NBC
return: 9/10/66–9/2/67, CBS; 9/7/68–9/1/73, NBC

125 episodes about a Washington, D.C., dog named Shoeshine Boy who (in the guise of Underdog) kept vigil over the city and his TV-reporter girl friend, Sweet Polly Purebred. His major nemesis: Simon Bar Sinister. Wally Cox provided the voice of the super canine. Also included were episodes of "The Hunter." 30 minutes.

THE UNTAMED WORLD

broadcast dates: 1/4/69–8/30/69, NBC, thereafter syndicated

30-minute documentary films about people and animals of relatively unseen areas. Narrator: Philip Carey.

UPDATE

broadcast dates: 9/16/61–1/27/62, NBC

30-minute news program telecast live from New York and anchored by newsman Robert Abernethy. The series was aimed primarily at junior and senior high school students, and featured segments on the past week's news, in-depth analyses of important stories, and interviews with prominent newsmakers by student reporters. The format also included filmed features.

THE U.S. OF ARCHIE

see *The Archie Show*

V

VALLEY OF THE DINOSAURS

initial broadcast dates: 9/7/74–9/4/76, CBS

30-minute Hanna-Barbera cartoon adventure series about the Butler family, a clan transported back to the Stone Age.

VEGETABLE SOUP

premiere weekday broadcast: 9/15/75, PBS, thereafter syndicated, with rebroadcasts Saturdays in some markets

Seventy-eight half-hour educational episodes produced by the New York State Department of Education to further racial understanding in elementary-school–age children. Executive producer of the magazine-format show: Yanna Kroyt Brandt. The first series was telecast as thirty-nine half-hour or seventy-eight quarter-hour programs.

VIDEO VILLAGE, JUNIOR (VIDEO VILLAGE, JR. EDITION)

broadcast dates: 9/30/61–6/16/62, CBS

Children's game-show version of the weekday Heatter-Quigley production *Video Village*, which utilized a studio-sized game board. Monty Hall hosted the 30-minute program as the village mayor. Also appearing were Eileen Barton as the assistant mayor and Kenny Williams as the town crier.

VILLA ALEGRE

premiere weekday broadcast: 9/23/74, PBS, syndicated, with rebroadcasts Saturdays in some markets

30-minute bilingual series primarily geared for four- to eight-year-old Latin American immigrants. The 159 programs attempted to give children the opportunity to learn new language skills, ease assimilation into a new country, and provide important data on food, nutrition, and the environment. The series was set in the mythical Happy Village and utilized live-action, animation, and puppetry.

W

WACKO

premiere broadcast: 9/10/77, CBS

30-minute live-action comedy featuring Julie McWhirter, Charles Fleischer, and Bo Kaprall in slapstick, Hellzapoppin-type routines, all less than two minutes long.

WACKY RACES

initial broadcast dates: 9/14/68–9/5/70, CBS

30-minute Hanna-Barbera and Heatter-Quigley animated series featuring crazy cars and crazier drivers on the order of *The Great Race*. At the head of the pack were Dick Dastardly and his dog Muttley in their Mean Machine (#00). Also on the road was femme fatale Penelope Pitstop in her Compact Pussy Cat, a mobile beauty parlor.

WAIT TIL YOUR FATHER GETS HOME

syndicated: 1972

Cartoon series with Tom Bosley lending his voice to the title character, Harry Boyle, a traditional father who was out of step with his contemporary youngsters, Alice and Chet.

WATCH MR. WIZARD

initial broadcast dates: 3/3/51–9/5/64, NBC return: 9/11/71–9/2/72, NBC; series host Don Herbert also syndicated 5-minute Mr. Wizard Close-Ups *in the 1970s and appeared on CBS's monthly news magazine show* Razzmatazz *in 1978 and 1979*

Don Herbert's straightforward explanations of scientific processes, phenomena, and theories, always with a youngster who assisted and asked questions. The 30-minute program was ad-libbed and helped to encourage children throughout the world to consider careers in varied fields of science. Originally titled *Mr. Wizard* in the 1950s, the series was produced in Chicago and New York by Jules Pewowar. ACT Commendation, 1971–72; Peabody Award, 1953.

WAY OUT GAMES

broadcast dates: 9/11/76–4/2/77, CBS

30-minute game show that pitted two teams, each with three boys and three girls, against one another in athletic round-robin competition culminating in a special championship program.

WESTWIND

broadcast dates: 9/6/75–9/4/76, NBC

Live-action adventure series about an oceanographic photographer and his family. Produced by William P. D'Angelo and starring Van Williams as Steve Andrews.

WHAT'S IT ALL ABOUT?

premiere broadcast: 7/8/72, CBS

Series of specials that explored political conventions, the presidency, Communism, cities, inflation, the Senate, the Middle East, the Supreme Court, the CIA, the Loch Ness monster, and the Apollo-Soyuz mission. Reporters for the CBS News productions included Walter Cronkite, Roger Mudd, Daniel Schorr, Christopher Glenn, Nelson Benton, Dan Rather, Bruce Morton, Richard Roth, and Fred Graham.

WHAT'S NEW, MISTER MAGOO?

see *The Famous Adventures of Mr. Magoo*

WHEELIE AND THE CHOPPER BUNCH

initial broadcast dates: 9/7/74–8/30/75, NBC

30-minute Hanna-Barbera cartoon series about a pair of friendly talking Volkswagens, Wheelie and Rota Lee, and the evil motorcycles that plot to overrun them. Voices by Frank Welker, Don Messick, Paul Winchell, Len Weinrib, and Judy Strangis.

THE WHIRLYBIRDS

syndicated: 1957

Adventure series about two pilots working for a helicopter charter service. The 30-minute production starred Ken Tobey and Craig Hill as aviators Chuck Miller and P. T. Moore. Alternate title: *Copter Patrol.*

THE WHISTLING WIZARD

premiere weekday broadcast: 10/15/51, CBS, 15 minutes, in incompatible color Saturday morning broadcast dates: 11/3/51–9/20/52, CBS, 30 minutes, black and white

An imaginative marionette comedy/fantasy series created by puppeteers Bil and Cora Baird. The two central characters, a boy named J. P. and his horse Heathcliffe, were carryovers from an earlier Baird Show, *The Life of Snarky Parker.* Also included among a charming cast of characters were Dooley, a leprechaun who was the show's title figure; Spider Lady, a villainess; Kohlrabi, her assistant; Ting-a-Ling, a firefly; plus Zoltan Pepper, Davy Jones, J. Fiddler Crab, Flannel Mouse, and dozens more.

WILD BILL HICKOK

syndicated: 1951

30-minute live Western series set in the post–Civil War era with U.S. Marshal James Butler Hickok keeping order. Guy Madison starred as Hickok and Andy Devine was his partner, Jingles.

WILD KINGDOM

broadcast dates: 1/6/63–9/5/73, NBC, thereafter syndicated

Marlin Perkins's long-running 30-minute series focusing on wildlife of all kinds in habitats and zoos around the world. Also listed as *Mutual of Omaha's Wild Kingdom.*

WILD, WILD WORLD OF ANIMALS

syndicated: 1973

30-minute documentary films that examine a wide range of animal life in their native environments. Series is narrated by William Conrad.

WILL THE REAL JERRY LEWIS PLEASE SIT DOWN?

broadcast dates: 9/12/70–9/2/72, ABC

30-minute cartoon adventures based on the characters from Jerry Lewis's motion pictures, including *The Nutty Professor, The Bellboy,* and *The Errand Boy.* The series was created by Lewis and produced by Filmation.

WILLIE WONDERFUL

syndicated: 1952

195 episodes of a 5-minute puppet cliffhanger adventure series featuring a young boy, his fairy godfather (Phineas Q. Throckmorton, a W. C. Fields takeoff), Eleanor the elephant, and Girard the giraffe. The series was offered in both 15- and 30-minute programs.

WINKY DINK AND YOU

initial broadcast dates: 10/10/53–4/27/57, CBS

A unique 30-minute show in which host Jack Barry conversed with cartoon characters Winky Dink and his dog Woofer, with home viewers participating in the program by drawing on a transparent screen attached to their TV set. Winky Dink drawing kits were sold for fifty cents, but young viewers also improvised with cellophane and crayon to assist the animated characters upon instructions from Barry. A syndicated cartoon version was released in 1969.

WONDERAMA

local Sunday New York premiere: 9/25/55, WABD-TV, six hours; continued on the same station after the call letters changed to WNEW-TV; and aired in a 2½-hour form on other Metromedia stations throughout the country

Studio participation program hosted throughout its long broadcast life by Sandy Becker, then Herb Sheldon, Sonny Fox, and ultimately Bob McAllister. Besides games and interviews, *Wonderama* also included remotes, civic dicussions, geography lessons, and (at various times) drawing sessions with Jon Gnagy, routines with Al (Captain Video) Hodge, weather forecasts, variety acts, cartoons, and performances.

THE WOODY WOODPECKER SHOW

premiere weekly afternoon broadcast: 10/3/57, ABC, thereafter syndicated Saturday morning return: 9/12/70–9/2/72, NBC; 9/11/76, NBC

30-minute animated escapades of the world-famous woodpecker and other Walter Lantz characters, including Andy Panda and Chilly Willy. Host-producer Lantz integrated new footage with his theatrical cartoons and appeared with informative looks at the animation process. The 1976 show featured cartoons from 1940 to 1965, all the products of full animation that created the appearance of natural movement. Other characters featured were Buzz Buzzard, Gabby Gator, Wally Walrus, Smedley, and Knothead and Splinter. Voices were Grace Stafford (Mrs. Walter Lantz) as Woody, and Daws Butler, Walter Tetley, Dal McKennol, June Foray, and Paul Frees.

THE WORLD OF SURVIVAL

syndicated: 1971

30-minute nature films hosted and narrated by John Forsythe. This series examined wild creatures in relation to their struggles for survival in the face of man's encroachments upon their environments.

YANCY DERRINGER

prime time broadcast dates: 10/2/58–9/24/59, CBS, thereafter syndicated

30-minute adventure series set in New Orleans in the post–Civil War period with a riverboat gambler and his Indian companion who attempted to clean up the city in cooperation with public officials. Jock Mahoney starred as Derringer, X. Brands as Pahoo, Kevin Hagen as city official John Colton, Frances Bergen as Madame Francine, and Julie Adams as Amanda Eaton.

YOGI BEAR

syndicated: 1961

30-minute Hanna-Barbera cartoon spin-off series from *Huckleberry Hound* about a bear inhabitant of Jellystone National Park who plotted constantly to steal visitors' picnic baskets. Daws Butler was the voice of Yogi, and Don Messick recorded the voices of both Yogi's companion Boo Boo and nemesis Ranger John Smith. Also included in the long-running, oft-repeated series were segments about a lion named Snagglepuss (Daws Butler) and Yakky Doodle Duck (Jimmy Weldon, a ventriloquist who had used his duck voice previously for Webster Webfoot on his NBC series *Funny Boners* in 1954–55).

YOGI BEAR AND FRIENDS

see *Yogi's Gang*

YOGI'S GANG

initial broadcast dates: 9/8/73–8/30/75, ABC

30-minute revision and spin-off of the original "Yogi Bear" series but focused on such prosocial concerns as environmental issues, bigotry, and cheating. The villains included Mr. Dirt and Mr. Pollution. Also appearing were other stock Hanna-Barbera characters, including Huckleberry Hound, Top Cat, Boo Boo, Doggie Daddy, and Ranger Smith. Syndicated title: *Yogi Bear and Friends.*

YOGI'S SPACE RACE

initial broadcast dates: 9/9/78–3/3/79, NBC

Hanna-Barbera cartoon productions featuring such characters as Yogi Bear, Huckleberry Hound, Scare Bear, and Quack Up as they attempt to outwit villains Phantom Phink and Sinister Sludge in races through outer space. Additional segments included "The Buford Files," "The Galaxy Goofups," and "The Galloping Ghost." The series was reduced from its original 90 minutes to 60 minutes 11/4/78, with "The Galaxy Goofups" becoming an independent show. It was reduced to 30 minutes 2/3/79, with both "The Buford Files" and "The Galloping Ghost" combining into another independent show. See also *Buford and the Galloping Ghost* and *The Galaxy Goofups.*

YOU ARE THERE

prime time Sunday broadcast dates: 2/1/53–10/13/57, CBS
Saturday return broadcast dates: 9/11/71–9/2/72, CBS

30-minute CBS News dramatic production with Walter Cronkite presenting on-the-spot interviews with historical figures such as Amelia Earhart, Woodrow Wilson, and Paul Revere. The fanciful series recreated events of the past, and in its 1971–72 run, received an ACT Commendation.

THE YOUNG SENTINELS

see *The Space Sentinels*

YOUR PET PARADE

Sunday broadcast dates: 3/11/51–9/2/51, ABC, with rebroadcasts Saturdays in some markets

30-minute New York–based show in which each week three children brought on their trained pets to be judged by an animal trainer. The cast included Bob Russell and Jack Gregson as successive hosts; Billy Barty as "Billy Bitesize," who assisted with commercials for Ralston Purina cereals; and Barney the Pony. Alternate titles: *Animal Fair* and *Pets and Pals Animal Fair.*

Z

ZEE COOKING SCHOOL

premiere broadcast: 10/1/74, PBS

30-minute cooking show for eight- to sixteen-year-olds, conducted by Colette Ross and produced by the South Carolina Educational Television Network.

ZOOM

premiere weekday broadcast: 1/9/72, PBS, with rebroadcasts Saturdays in some markets

30-minute award-winning educational series hosted and performed by a troupe of preteens, and featuring songs, games, dances, quizzes, jokes, stories, and tips, many of which were submitted by the young viewing audience. The cast of "Zoomers" changed for each production season. PBS affiliate WGBH-TV, Boston, produced the series. Emmy Award, 1973–74.

Appendix B

Emmy Awards for Children's Television Shows

Each year since 1948, members of the broadcasting community's National Academy of Television Arts and Sciences have bestowed awards for excellence in television production and performance. The following list indicates the "Emmys" given to network or nationally syndicated children's shows or performers.

* denotes programs produced specifically for Saturday morning or Saturday afternoon telecast

1948

none

1949

Time for Beany (KTLA-TV, Los Angeles; syndicated series)

1950

Time for Beany (KTLA-TV, Los Angeles; syndicated series)

1951

none

1952

Time for Beany (KTLA-TV, Los Angeles; syndicated series)

1953

Kukla, Fran and Ollie (NBC series)

1954

Lassie (CBS series)

Disneyland (for single episode, "Operation Undersea," of ABC series)

1955

Lassie (CBS series)

Disneyland (ABC series)

1956

none

1957

none

1958–59

none

1959–60

Huckleberry Hound (syndicated series)*

1960–61

Aaron Copland's Birthday Party, New York Philharmonic Young People's Concert (CBS special)

1961–62

New York Philharmonic Young People's Concert (CBS special)

1962–63

Walt Disney's Wonderful World of Color (NBC series)

1963–64

Discovery '63 and *Discovery '64* (ABC series)

1964–65

New York Philharmonic Young People's Concert (CBS special)

1965–66

A Charlie Brown Christmas (CBS special)

1966–67

Jack and the Beanstalk (NBC special)

1967–68

none

1968–69

none

1969–70

Sesame Street (PBS series)

1970–71

Sesame Street (PBS series)

Burr Tillstrom and Kukla, Fran, and Ollie for their performance on *The CBS Saturday Film Festival* (CBS series)*

1971–72

Sesame Street (PBS series)

1972–73

Sesame Street (PBS series)

the writers of *The Electric Company* (PBS series)

performance of Shari Lewis in "A Picture of Us," an *NBC Children's Theatre* presentation (NBC series)

producers Hanna-Barbera for "Last of the Curlews," an *ABC Afterschool Special* (ABC)

1973–74

Marlo Thomas and Friends in Free to Be You and Me (ABC special)

Charles M. Schulz, writer, *A Charlie Brown Thanksgiving* (CBS special)

ZOOM (PBS series)

The Rookie of the Year, a presentation of *The ABC Afterschool Special* (ABC)

Make A Wish (ABC series)

The Runaways (ABC special)

Inside/Out (syndicated series)

performance of The Muppets on *Sesame Street* (PBS series)

the writers of *Sesame Street*, 11/19/73 (PBS series)

1974–75

Star Trek (NBC animated series)*

"Harlequin," a presentation of *The CBS Festival of Lively Arts for Young People* (CBS special)

Yes, Virginia, There Is a Santa Claus (ABC special)

Elinor Bunin, umbrella title animation for weekend morning programming (ABC)

1975–76

Big Blue Marble (syndicated series)*

"Danny Kaye's Look-In at the Metropolitan Opera," a presentation of *The CBS Festival of Lively Arts for Young People* (CBS special)

Go (NBC Series)*

Happy Anniversary, Charlie Brown (CBS special)

Grammar Rock (ABC inserts)*

performance of The Muppets on *Sesame Street* (PBS series)

You're a Good Sport, Charlie Brown (CBS special)

Huckleberry Finn (ABC special)

1976–77

"Ballet Shoes" (parts one and two on *Piccadilly Circus*) (PBS special)

videoanimation on "Peter Pan," a presentation of *The Hallmark Hall of Fame* (NBC special)

costume design and tape editing on *Pinocchio* (CBS special)

1977–78

Animals Animals Animals (ABC series)

"Very Good Friends," a presentation of *The ABC Afterschool Special* (ABC special)

Schoolhouse Rock (ABC inserts)*

performance of Tom Aldredge as Shakespeare in "Henry Winkler Meets William Shakespeare," a presentation of *The CBS Festival of Lively Arts for Young People* (CBS special)

"Hewitt's Just Different," a presentation of *The ABC Afterschool Special* (ABC special); individual award also given to writer Jan Hartman

writer David Wolf for "The Magic Hat," a presentation of *Unicorn Tales* (syndicated series)

Halloween Is Grinch Night (ABC special)

1978–79

Christmas Eve on Sesame Street (PBS special)

Kids Are People Too (ABC series)

The Tap Dance Kid (NBC special)

Big Blue Marble (syndicated series)

Razzmatazz (CBS special)

The Lion, The Witch and the Wardrobe (CBS animated special)

1979–80

Ask NBC News (NBC inserts)

H.E.L.P. (ABC inserts)

In the News (CBS inserts)

Schoolhouse Rock (ABC inserts)

Sesame Street (PBS series)

30 Minutes (CBS series)

"Why a Conductor," New York Philharmonic Young People's Concert, *CBS Festival of the Lively Arts for Young People* (CBS special)

"The Late Great Me: The Story of a Teen-Age Alcoholic," a presentation of *The ABC Afterschool Special* (ABC special); individual awards also given to writer Jan Hartman, actress Maia Danziger, and director Anthony Lover

Hot Hero Sandwich (NBC series)

Fred Rogers for "Mister Rogers Goes to School" (PBS special)

Melissa Sue Anderson for "Which Mother Is Mine?" (ABC special)

Butterfly McQueen for "The Seven Wishes of a Rich Kid" (ABC special)

Arthur Allan Seidelman for "Which Mother Is Mine?" (ABC special)

Appendix C

Peabody Awards for Children's Television Shows

In 1940, the University of Georgia initiated the George Foster Peabody Broadcasting Awards for excellence in news, entertainment, education, public service, and children's programming. The following list indicates network or nationally syndicated children's television shows to receive the prestigious "Peabodys."

* denotes programs produced specifically for Saturday morning or Saturday afternoon telecast

1948

Howdy Doody (NBC series)

1949

Kukla, Fran and Ollie (NBC series)

1950

Zoo Parade (NBC series)

Saturday at the Zoo (ABC series)*

1951

none

1952

Ding Dong School (NBC series)

1953

Watch Mr. Wizard (NBC series)*

1954

Disneyland (ABC series)

Adventure (CBS series)

1955

Lassie (CBS series)

1956

Youth Wants to Know (NBC series)

1957

Captain Kangaroo (CBS series)*

1958

College News Conference (ABC series)

1959

none

1960

The Shari Lewis Show (NBC series)*

G-E College Bowl (CBS series)

1961

Expedition (ABC series)

1962

Exploring (NBC series)*

Walt Disney (NBC series)

1963

none

1964

award to Burr Tillstrom, creator of *Kukla, Fran and Ollie*

1965

A Charlie Brown Christmas (CBS special)

1966

The World of Stuart Little (NBC special)

1967

The CBS Children's Film Festival (CBS series)

1968

Mister Rogers' Neighborhood (NET series)

1969

Sesame Street (PBS series)

1970

Hot Dog (NBC series)*

the "Dr. Seuss" programs (CBS specials)

1971

Make a Wish (NBC series)

1972

ABC Afterschool Specials (ABC specials)

Captain Kangaroo (CBS series)

1973

"The Borrowers," a presentation of *The Hallmark Hall of Fame* (NBC special)

"Street of the Flower Boxes," a presentation of *The NBC Children's Theatre* (NBC series)

1974

Marlo Thomas and Friends in Free to Be You and Me (ABC special)

Go (NBC series)*

1975

Call It Macaroni (syndicated series)

The ABC Afterschool Specials (ABC specials)

Snipets (syndicated series)

Big Blue Marble (syndicated series)

1976

Animals Animals Animals (ABC series)

In the News (CBS inserts)*

1977

The Hobbit (NBC special)

1978

The Muppets (syndicated series)

awarded to Bob Keeshan (Captain Kangaroo)

30 Minutes (CBS series)*

Index

A

B

C

D

E

F

G

H

I

N

O

P

Q

R

S